TERRORISM

From Robespierre to Arafat

TERRORISM

From Robespierre to Arafat

BY ALBERT PARRY

The Vanguard Press, Inc. New York, N.Y.

Copyright © 1976 by Albert Parry.
Published simultaneously in Canada by Gage Publishing Co., Agincourt, Ontario.
All rights reserved.
No part of this publication may be reproduced or transmitted in any form or by any means,
electronic or mechanical, including photocopy, recording, or any information or retrieval
system, or otherwise, without the written permission of the publisher, except by a
reviewer who may wish to quote brief passages in connection with a review for a news-
paper, magazine, radio, or television.
Library of Congress Catalogue Card Number: 76-12006
ISBN: 0-8149-0746-6
Designer: Ernst Reichl
Manufactured in the United States of America.

Revolutionaries who take the law into their own hands are terrifying, not as villains, but as mechanisms out of control, as runaway machines.

Boris Pasternak, *Doctor Zhivago*

Contents

Introduction   xi

Part I: The Nature of Terrorism

1 Violence: Genesis of Terror   3
2 Terror: An Overall View   12
3 Terror as Aberration   21

Part II: History

4 Robespierre's Bloody Virtue   39
5 The Guillotine Athirst   55
6 In the Name of Marx   67
7 Anarchists: Philosophers with Bombs   78
8 America's Pie   92
9 Hunting the Tsar   107
10 Azef: Terror Chief as Double Agent   120
11 Lenin: High Priest of Terror   131
12 Now Is the Time   146
13 Thought Waves of Hatred   161
14 Trotsky: Target of Boomerang   171
15 Stalin's Archipelago   187
16 Hitler's Holocaust   203
17 The Final Solution   211

Part III: Modern Times

18 Mao's Muzzle   223
19 Three Innovations   234
20 Wanton Romantics: Guevara, Debray, Marighella   244
21 The Morbid Tango   261

22 Heirs to Tupac-Amaru   274
23 *Siempre la Violencia!*   286
24 Fanon and the Black Panthers   301
25 The Weatherman   322
26 The Days of Rage and After   330
27 The Symbionese and Patty Hearst   342
28 Canada's White Niggers   365
29 Crimson in the Irish Green and Orange   376
30 New Europe's Old Hatreds   395
31 Vietnam and Other Jungles, Other Pyres   417
32 Red Samurai and Turkey's Nihilists   433
33 Arafat and Other Sacrificers   449
34 Fire in the African Bush   469
35 Right-wing Terror   488

Part IV: Terror with a Difference

36 Genghis Khan with the Telephone   509
37 The New Robin Hoods, the Media, and the Police   516
38 Terrorists Then and Now   525
39 The New International   537
40 Five Minutes to Midnight   545

Appendix: The Lethal Record   563
Bibliography   577
Notes   581
Index   607

Illustrations

The illustrations follow page 210

Robespierre gets his own medicine
Tsar Alexander II is attacked and killed by Narodniki bombs
The Haymarket Riot, Chicago
Four anarchists, blamed for Haymarket Riot, are hanged
Grand Duke Sergei is assassinated
Terror in the Russian Civil War: captured Bolsheviks are ordered to
    disrobe
In a museum in the Soviet Union (*cartoon*)
In a Stalinist concentration camp
A Nazi shoots a mother and child
A Jew awaits death on the edge of a corpse-filled pit, Poland
A Jewish victim is stripped before execution, Poland
Maoist terror: Beheading in Red China
Mainland Chinese washed ashore at Hong Kong
Chinese prisoners on display in a public square
Ché Guevara at United Nations
The Castrojet (*cartoon*)
Argentina: Marxist guerrilla is rushed to morgue
A royal portrait: Huey Newton
Weathermen's explosion: The house on Eleventh Street,
    New York City
Symbionese pyre: the house of the last stand, Los Angeles
LaGuardia Airport aftermath: the temporary morgue
IRA Provisionals proclaim their historical tradition (*poster*)
A street in Belfast, 1974
Member of German Meinhof-Baader Gang dying in hunger strike

Lone survivor of terrorist attack on West German embassy in Stockholm is searched by Swedish police
Maalot, Israel, May 1974
Yasir Arafat addresses the United Nations, November 1974
Captured Arab guerrillas, Golan Heights
Israeli trooper returns to Tel Aviv after rescue operation at Entebbe

Introduction

Terror: a junkie mugs an old woman to get money for a fix; a young girl is raped in the park; a lonely man's shabby quarters are ransacked for no apparent reason—these are a few of the manifestations of the world we live in. But it is not of this kind of terror, or its perpetrators, of which we speak in this book.

This book is about another kind of terror—a terror more insidious, more virulent than those crimes for petty profit or of gross passion or senselessness that so often darken the newspaper headlines. This terror strikes at the body politic, involving not random individuals, but whole masses of society—entire nations and continents, entire economic and political structures, an entire body of mores and morals.

Such terror is double-edged. It is the terror used to achieve the overthrow of the existing government. It is also the terror employed when these very same terrorists, having tasted victory and seized the state, wield their new-found power to victimize their opponents, both real and imagined.

In both categories, the weapons are intimidation, systematic violence, continual bloodshed.

The aim of the game is "revolution." Its slogan: "In the name of humanity and justice." And while the method of these terrorists of both categories appears to be revolutionary, the substance of their activities is reactionary. For they—particularly when they come to power—throw mankind back thousands of years, by their mass-scale killings, by their overwhelming negation of humane values.

We tend to think of political terrorism as a modern development, and indeed its latter-day story as a distinct phenomenon begins with the late eighteenth century. But the terrorizing of humans by fellow humans on political or political-ethnic grounds goes much further back, in many different forms. As a white missionary in Burundi sadly said about the massacre of 100,000 Hutu tribesmen by the ruling Tutsi in 1972 (the toll grew to 200,000 by 1974): "This has been going on for centuries and it will happen again." Nevertheless, political terrorism today is quite different from what had gone on before. Our kind of terrorism starts with Robespierre and his Great Terror (also known as the Grand Terror) of nearly two centuries ago.

The nature of modern terrorism is dimmed by misconception. For instance, it is common for sociologists, socio-psychologists, and other well-meaning intellectuals to suggest that terrorism would abate and finally disappear if an end were put to deep-rooted and widespread socio-economic oppression and political corruption. But not all terrorism is caused by socio-economic and political misery. History is our witness that revolutions and their violence come not only on empty stomachs but often on half-full or even full ones. When people are subjected to starvation and conditions of fear for long stretches of time, they become incapacitated; and in their struggle for sheer survival, they have neither the energy nor the time for revolt.

And what of the idea that far-reaching reforms would thwart or even abolish terror? Often well-meant efforts have yielded unexpected, counterproductive results. Ugly surprises nullify the would-be glorious societies envisaged and fought for by violent revolutionaries. The revolution of November 1917, as led by Lenin, ushered in the opposite of what had been promised. It laid the foundation for the Soviet state that, first under Lenin and certainly later under his heir Stalin, degenerated into horrors of systematic mass terror. Reforms are needed, but they do not safeguard us from terrorism. Even less so do revolutions.

Still, there are pundits who tell us we are unduly exercised about recent terrorism. For terrorists, it is claimed, if given a chance to come to power, to exercise power without interference from the outside world, will inevitably settle down and become reasonable and respectable rulers. We will see what such beliefs ignore when we come to know the terror of Lenin, Trotsky, Stalin, Hitler, and Mao.

As history and common sense allow us to understand, terrorists feed on problems without solving them. They exacerbate injustice. Even when they overthrow the existing Establishment and form a new Establishment, they do not bring the promised reign of happiness and harmony.

Before his early death, Frantz Fanon, the black proselytizer of terror, said that he would regard his fight for Algeria's freedom from the French colonialists as lost if, on prevailing, the Algerian rebels would simply replace the foreign masters by native lords, if the victory of the rebels would mean merely that their chiefs had moved into the villas and offices of the ousted French rulers, if little or nothing was done to alleviate the plight of the masses. Alas, what he hoped would not come to be was precisely what happened after Algeria's independence.

Few terrorists ever recognize the unjustifiable horror or the long-range futility of their bloody ways. Far from repenting, they continue with their gory business in the firm belief that the path to their ultimate righteousness lies only through their own evil. They seem not to know or appreciate the truth of Condorcet's maxim: "From force to injustice there is only one step."

This writer is not at all sanguine that terror will abate or disappear: not so long as there are—all around us—individuals, groups, and governments who believe with Mikhail Bakunin that change for a better society is impossible without violence, or, as a Red Chinese delegate once proclaimed at a United Nations session, that unrest and disorders are to be hailed as positive phenomena because "the world advances amid turbulence."[1]

But this does not make turbulence and violence either desirable or necessary, even if, ostensibly, it is used to bring about a change for the better. Not every radical change is beneficial: Lenin's violence was no improvement upon Kerensky's inefficiency, nor Hitler's madness upon the mildness of the Weimar Republic it succeeded. Positive change can be brought about through peaceful action—via evolution and not revolutionary terror. The long-term gradualism in England is proof enough. The bloody price does not have to be paid.

Although quite inclusive, this book does not aim to be encyclopedic. For reasons of space, certain episodes of terrorism are not given chapters of their own but are merely mentioned. In such curtailment I have tried to be evenhanded. Thus, while the Arab guerrillas of Algeria of the immediate post-World War II period are discussed only in passing, as it were, so the violent activities of the Jewish Irgun and Stern Gang in Palestine of the same time are referred to equally briefly.

It was impossible, not to say dangerous, for me to seek any interviews with terrorists anywhere, since they generally knew my negative attitude toward them. My only direct contact with them was the occasional presence, as uninvited but most curious visitors, of certain Weathermen in my classes on the history of Russian revolutionary movements and terrorist organizations that I held at Case Western Reserve University in Cleveland in the latter 1960s. But my interviews with terror's victims were numerous and worldwide, as detailed in my book.

I wish I could express my personal thanks to those experts who have helped me in my researches in various countries, particularly in

Ulster, England, and Israel. For obvious reasons, however, they must remain unnamed.

To Bernice Woll, I am greatly indebted for her early and late interest in this book—her close and helpful reading of the manuscript, her thoughtful and valuable suggestions in the process of my work, her many editorial contributions to my ideas and material. Similarly, I am thankful to Dana Randt for his perceptive editorial assistance in the molding of these pages and to Miriam Shrifte for her meticulous care with the proofs. Yet, while deeply appreciative of their help, I do not hold them in the least responsible for the main thesis and particular judgments in this volume, which are solely mine.

Albert Parry

Greenwich, Connecticut

PART I

The Nature of Terrorism

"Liberty is not Anarchy"

(Cartoon by Thomas Nast—Public Affairs Press)

1

Violence: Genesis of Terror

Not every violence is political terror, but every political terror is violence. Be it caused by Robespierre or Bakunin or the old West European anarchists or Lenin, Trotsky, Stalin, Hitler, or today's urban guerrillas the world over, terror is essentially a ferocious violence of humans against humans.

As the inhumanity of man to man, violence has woven its fearsome thread from caveman to technological man. *"Homo homini lupus est"* (Man to man is wolf), declared Titus Maccius Plautus, the Roman playwright (c. 254-184 B.C.) in his comedy *Asinaria* (The Asses). Violence seethes in many a person, family, clan, tribe, nation, state—even though, according to Thomas Hobbes, writing in *The Leviathan* (1651), the state was evolved by man to check his savageness.

For thousands of years in the West, where Robespierre, Marx, and Hitler would be born and where modern terrorism would have its beginnings, torture as a form of violence was part of the legal codes of many states, sometimes as a technique used in forcing confessions, sometimes as sheer punishment. Ancient Greek law and notably Roman law prescribed torture in detail, stipulating when, how, and on whom it was to be used. The very word "torture" comes from the Latin *torquere*, to twist. Since, in later centuries, Roman law was the source of the codes of so many European nations, the legal framework of those nations included torture as both logical and necessary. But even those national codes that did not owe much, if any, historical debt to Roman law had their own indigenous practices of torture and harsh death. Certainly neither the English phrase, "rack and ruin," nor the Russian word *pytka*—interrogation by torture—came from Rome.

In Western lands, torture for God's greater glory was widespread and lasted for centuries under the Inquisition. In 1252, Pope Innocent IV, by his bull *Ad extirpanda*, authorized torture of the accused to obtain the victims' confessions and the names of additional heretics.

Unable to bear the horrible pain, many shrieked their confessions, and—guilty or innocent—were executed publicly. Many were burned at the stake, among them John Huss in 1415 and Joan of Arc in 1431. In the late fifteenth century, under Grand Inquisitor Tomás de Torquemada, brutalities were ingenious and numerous—some 2,000 humans were put to the torch. In later times, as both state and Church mitigated certain forms of violence, torture was officially limited and at last nominally abolished.

But in fact, officially or not, torture persisted. The alleged enlightenment of the eighteenth century did not stop the West European, American, and Arab traders and owners of African slaves from inflicting pain and injury on their human property. Ostensibly it was a required form of discipline, usually involving whipping and starving, or a function of necessity, involving suffocation in dungeons or in the holds of ships or drowning at sea—in storms captains would lighten their vessels by casting their slaves overboard. But actually the blacks were often the victims of sheer sadism. In Latin America the Spanish grandees and soldiers intimidated reluctant Indians into submission by pulling their rebel leaders apart: their limbs were tied to two horses that were then prodded in different directions.

The progressive nineteenth century saw the King of the Belgians introduce Western culture into the Congo with the aid of unspeakable atrocities visited upon the natives. Our own twentieth century has brought two significant changes in the methods of torture: the use of electrical and other technological advances, and the development of various forms of psychological torment—devised by the secret police of Communist Russia, Nazi Germany, and other assorted totalitarian regimes of several continents.

The geographical area in which Lenin, Trotsky, and Stalin would institute and maintain slave camps and make their own contributions to the evolution of political terrorism also has a singular heritage of violence.

The Scythians, warlike nomads who spoke an Indo-Iranian language and roamed the plains north and east of the Black and Caspian Seas from the ninth to the third centuries B.C. had as their main deity the god of war. Represented by a sword struck into the ground, it was wetted by the blood of prisoners. The Scythians also drank this blood. Like American Indians, they scalped their captives and attached the scalps to their bridle reins as signs of prowess. They often skinned their prisoners alive, believing that human skin collected in this manner was superior to animal hide.

Yet in time the Scythians were paid in their own coin. In the thirteenth century A.D., the Mongols of Genghis Khan overran the last remaining domains of the descendants of the Scythians in Central Asia. They hauled the conquered populace into the fields, where they placed the captives on the ground face down—men, women, and children in separate neat rows. The Mongols then marched along the rows, methodically cutting off all heads. After a few days they would suddenly return to flush out and kill the survivors who had escaped the first roundup.

In the fourteenth and early fifteenth centuries, Tamerlane, who claimed descent from Genghis Khan, assembled pyramids of human heads, each pyramid containing skulls by the scores of thousands. Although such pyramids had been piled up before by the Maliks of Herat and other conquerors of earlier centuries, Tamerlane's were on a far vaster scale. Yet these and other victors on occasion did keep at least some of their captives as live property—a dubious form of mercy that took man thousands of years to evolve.

Conquerors sweeping out of the East to plague and plunder the West also displayed this questionable progress. In the fourth and fifth centuries the Huns, in their invasions of Central and Western Europe, not only massacred men and their families but also took slaves. The Vandals in the fifth century, in addition to murdering multitudes and destroying precious works of art, kept captives, if not statues, as their property.

When, early in his career, Temuchin, the future Genghis Khan, led his Mongols against the neighboring Tatars, he consolidated his victory by destroying nearly all of that people's males, but spared boys if they were no taller than a cartwheel's linchpin. All women and surviving children were enslaved, and even the name of the victim people was adopted by the victors, who were from then on known as both Mongols and Tatars.

After the initial butchery of the conquered Russians in the mid-thirteenth century, the Mongol-Tatars made prisoner-taking a form of taxation. As the era's doleful song lamented:

> If a man has no money,
> The Tatar takes his child;
> Should there be no child,
> The Tatar takes the wife;
> If there is no wife to lose,
> The Tatar takes the man himself.

During ensuing wars and raids the Tatars would return with many roped and chained Russians. Once safely out of the reach of Muscovite troops, the raiders would sort out their human booty. A French witness of one such episode in the depredations by the Crimean Tatars in 1664 recorded that before their departure for their Crimean homes the victors went through their 20,000 captives and "cut the throats of all those who were over 60 years of age and thus unfit for labor. Men of 40 were spared for the galleys, young boys for delights, and girls and women for procreation and eventual sale."[1]

It has been thought by some historians that until the Mongol-Tatar invasion the Russians were a mild folk, not given to cruelty against one another or even toward foes, that they must have learned their atrocious ways from those Tatar intruders and usurpers. Yet we know that long before the hordes from Asia struck at them, the Russians used savage and unusual punishment of their own during both peace and war. Their slaves, serfs, and freedmen were subject to ingenious, blood-chilling cruelties. One method was to bury prisoners and criminals (among the latter, women accused of adultery) up to their heads. This left the bodies to unbearable pressures of the earth and the heads exposed to sun or frost as well as to the gnawing by hungry dogs.

But the oppressed, when rising, were also cruel. When serfs and Cossacks rebelled against the Tsar and his nobles, terrible vengeance was theirs. In 1670, Stenka (Stephen) Razin's capture of Astrakhan and his "great slaughter and robbery" of many noblemen, foreign officers, and mariners was observed by an English chronicler:

> [Prince Ivan Prozorovsky, Astrakhan's governor] was . . . made to goe up that high square Steeple, which stands in the midst of the Castle of *Astracan*, for a Beacon to direct those that Navigate the *Caspian Sea* . . . From this Steeple the said Governor was cast down head-long. . . . The Brother of the Governor, and many Noblemen and others, that would not come to him [Razin], he put to the sword, as also many Dutch and other Officers, and some Holland Mariners. . . . The Churches, Cloisters, and the Houses of the richest Citizens were plunder'd; the Writings of the Chancery burnt, the Czar's Treasure of the Kingdom of *Astracan* carried away, many Merchants strangers, being there at that time, as Persians, Indians, Turks, Arminians, and others, were put to death . . . both the Sons of the Governour he caused to be hung by the Legs upon the Walls of the Town, and to be taken down again, putting one of them, after much torture, to death, and causing the other to be beaten half dead. . . . His [the governor's] Lady and Daughters he delivered to the Soldiers, his Companions, to take them for their wives, or, if they pleased, to abuse them.[2]

As Razin marched west and north to take other cities along the Volga, peasants' uprisings preceded his army; serfs killed off their landlords with their entire families, putting their severed heads in sacks and bringing them to Razin, flinging the bloody bags at the leader's feet as they petitioned to join him.

One hundred years later, in the revolt of 1773-75 led by another Cossack of the Don, Yemelian Pugachev, as one after another Tsarist fortress in the steppes fell, officers, along with landlords and priests and visiting foreigners, were tortured and slain. Anyone wearing Western clothes was doomed. A German botanist was captured near one estate as he was peacefully gathering flowers and grasses. The gleeful rebels stripped off his clothes and impaled him. Whole families of nobles were hanged on their mansion gates. Parents and children were suspended in rows according to age. Decades later, in *The Captain's Daughter*, a tale of those times, Russia's great writer Alexander Pushkin, while delineating Pugachev's character in faintly sympathetic strokes but harshly deploring the atrocities for which he was responsible, presented a thought to be remembered and repeated for generations: "God save us from witnessing a Russian rebellion, senseless and ruthless!"

Each of the rebel leaders was defeated: Razin in the 1670s by the troops of Tsar Alexis, and Pugachev in the 1770s by the army of Empress Catherine II. After being apprehended, both Razin and Pugachev were tortured and executed. Their followers were knouted and branded, many tongues and ears were cut off, and thousands were hanged. Rafts filled with limp bodies dangling from gallows were sent down the Volga and other rivers. These, as intended, left a lasting impression on the miserable masses.

From the heritage of the Mongol-Tatar enslavers and torturers, carried on and improved upon by such native insurgents as Razin and Pugachev, derives much of the terror of that giant bloody upheaval, the Russian Revolution. And from that Revolution stems much of the political terror in the world today.

II

East or West, what is the cause of violence, of the destructiveness of human beings?

Hannah Arendt remarks that given "the enormous role violence has always placed in human affairs" it may seem surprising that writers on history and politics have devoted to it so little of the close study it surely deserves. But on second thought it is not so surprising. As Arendt says, "This shows to what an extent violence and its arbitrariness were taken for granted and therefore neglected; no one questions or examines what is obvious to all."[3] Yet if writers on history and politics have not pondered it sufficiently, novelists and psychologists have.

While declaring that his fellow Russians were pure and would yet bring their light from the East to the benighted Western world, Fyodor Dostoyevsky wrote of the universal violence in man's nature. In 1866, in *The Gambler*, he reflected: "Savage, limitless power—even over a fly—this is a kind of enjoyment. Man is a despot by nature; he loves to be the torturer." In 1879, two years before his death, after a tumultuous life of suffering and of witnessing the torment of others, he said: "There is much good in man, but also so much evil that, were it to surface, we would find it difficult to breathe anywhere in the world." In part this was so because man was not only a sadist but also a masochist. Man wanted to be tortured, he derived a keen delight from being whipped. Man's joy is in the whip (we read in *The Gambler*), "when the knout scourges his back and tears his flesh to pieces."

In more recent times Sigmund Freud wrote and taught that aggression was a basic instinct that could be destructive not only of others, but also of the self. It was, he declared, part of a pattern of man's natural instincts, some positive and others not. To Eros, or the life instinct, Freud counterpoised Thanatos, or the death drive. In this dichotomy Freud saw the principal drama of man's subconscious, of man's whole being.

In an elaboration of Freud's theory, Carl Jung believed that even if aggressiveness does not emerge in us as individuals, it is still an inborn part of us that can and does surface when we form a collective, particularly when we form a mob. Jung states:

> We are blissfully unconscious of those forces because they never, or almost never, appear in our personal dealings and under ordinary circumstances. But if, on the other hand, people crowd together and form a mob, then the dynamics of the collective man are set free—beasts or demons which lie dormant in every person till he is part of a mob. Man in the crowd is unconsciously lowered to an inferior moral and intellectual level, to that level which is always there, below the threshold of consciousness, ready to break forth as soon as it is stimulated through the formation of a crowd.[4]

In her brief but meaningful book *On Violence*, Arendt pays particular heed to the interconnection of violence and power. She convincingly argues that power—the gaining and the exercise of it—is all-important in the many kinds of violence we know, including those of greed, passion, crime, riots, revolution, and terrorism. Violence: to many, its other name is power.

Often, however, it is the very realization of a person's powerlessness that leads him to violence. If a human cannot be powerful enough to be creative, he becomes destructive. In *The Anatomy of*

Human Destructiveness, Erich Fromm writes: "If man cannot create anything or make a dent in anything or anybody, if he cannot break out of the prison of his total narcissism, he can escape the unbearable sense of powerlessness and nothingness only by affirming himself in the act of destruction of the life that he is unable to create."[5]

Then, paradoxically, violence itself can become creative, or, in Fromm's words, "Destruction is the creative, self-transcending act of the hopeless and crippled, the revenge of unlived life upon itself."

But this elevation of violence into something creative or otherwise positive is surely subject to doubt. Such praise causes damage to mankind. Whether or not political violence has been manifested as a lust for power or as a reaction to the fear and frustration of powerlessness, it has, while being clearly excessive, been unduly—and harmfully—glorified, romanticized, and legalized. This worship and legalization of violence is a tradition that has inspired terrorists and enabled them in part to justify their actions undeservedly.

III

Is all aggressiveness, be it individual or collective, necessarily bad? Konrad Lorenz argues that aggression, although definitely something we are born with, need not be all negative. (Here, to an extent, he agrees with Fromm.) Lorenz says that humans, unlike animals, manifest their aggression too indiscriminately. Animals fight to kill in order to preserve their specific group's territory and thus their food and females, to survive and reproduce. Humans kill not only for these goals but also for many counterproductive reasons.

For this failing, Lorenz blames thousands of years of inventive, human civilization, which have derailed man's natural instinct of moderate aggression and have caused him to become a mass murderer. As being particularly pernicious, Lorenz cites technological developments that are increasing the power and the remoteness of the slayer. It is the evolution of human ingenuity, so terrifyingly represented by the nuclear bomb, that debases the survival value of aggression, that has brought the hatred and mutual destruction so characteristic of our era.[6]

But B. F. Skinner, the behaviorist, asserts there is no such phenomenon as man's inherent nature, bad or good. He believes we are born blank. As we grow, social influences mold us. Our violence and other outcroppings of aggressiveness are a result of social conditioning. There is nothing in our so-called nature to prevent us and our society from emerging into something just and peaceful and altogether positive.

Emphatically disputing Skinner while accepting some premises of both Freud and Lorenz, Fromm stresses two completely different kinds of man's aggression: defensive or benign, and offensive or malignant: "The first, which he [man] shares with all animals, is a phylogenetically programmed impulse to attack (or to flee) when vital interests are threatened." Fromm calls this aggression good because it serves "the survival of the individual and the species, is biologically adaptive, and ceases when the threat has ceased to exist." The malignant aggression, however, manifests itself even when our vital interests are not threatened. It constitutes the real problem because it imperils man's very existence.

But Fromm equivocates when asked to categorize either form of aggression as an innate instinct. Branding the word "instinct" as old-fashioned, he substitutes the term "organic drive"—such is usually his answer to the issue of whether man's violence and destructiveness may be defined as part of the nature we are born with. Yet, Fromm pronounces finally, these are not irremediably innate; "hence, they can be substantially reduced when the socio-economic conditions are replaced by conditions that are favorable to the full development of man's genuine needs and capacities." Thus, in fact, Fromm comes very close to Skinner's position on social conditioning of blank humans.

In common with many social critics, past and present, Fromm explains malignant aggression in terms of the "exploitation and manipulation" of man by man. Once these evils are removed, he promises, man will cease being "a psychic cripple . . . a sadist or a destroyer." This is quite similar to what many terrorists, including Marxists, proclaim.

Indeed, among history's leading terrorists there has often been this Fromm-like assurance—the confident promise that the inevitable extirpation of human injustices will end aggression and violence once and for all. Thus Lev Trotsky wrote, in the midst of mass shootings he was ordering in July 1919, that aggression and war—and, by implication, terror—should not be viewed as permanent. War, he argued, would someday disappear just as by his time cannibalism had faded away. "Struggle [force, aggression] will remain, but only as mankind's collective struggle against nature's hostile forces," he prophesied.[7]

To this day, revolutionaries and terrorists of all shades and levels declare, sincerely or not, that, come the giant upset resulting in a new, brave, and just world, terror will no longer be necessary and man's violence will be only an unpleasant memory. For, they vow, with the eradication of personal greed, of man's misuse of man, in the halcyon by-and-by when the cruel state at last withers away and the planet blooms forth as a never-ending garden of justice and love, violence will surely be gone.

But en route to that perfection, terror is a must. If, according to Marx, a revolution, particularly a proletarian revolution, is the loco-motive of history, the fuel of that locomotive is terror.

2

Terror: An Overall View

When terrorists striving for power attack the Establishment, men and women are kidnapped, airplanes are hijacked, bombs are exploded, and ransoms are collected. Such extreme political action usually appears to be motivated by visions of human improvement, and as a consequence some observers regard it as "messianic" or "convictional" terrorism. Although terrorists give innumerable explanations of their violence, these rationalizations are frequently related to three basic concepts:

1. Society is sick and cannot be cured by half measures of reform.

2. The state is in itself violence and can be countered and overcome only by violence.

3. The truth of the terrorist cause justifies any action that supports it. While some terrorists recognize no moral law, others have their own "higher" morality.

II

Terrorists believe society is sick and does not realize the gravity or even the nature of its own illness. They are convinced they will provide mankind with a cure before the hour is too late. Knowing they are members of what would otherwise be an ignored minority, terrorists reason that the use of bombs and bullets, skyjackings and kidnappings is the only way of awakening the stupid majority to what is urgently needed. Seldom do terrorists receive widespread support, yet they usually remain confident that their audacity will eventually stir up the sluggish or indifferent majority to a higher morality, to a drastic and moral action of violence.

Second, terrorists insist that they really do not initiate violence—they respond only to already existing forms of aggression. Latin American guerrillas, for instance, are wont to distinguish between "negative" and "necessary" violence. The former is the alleged or real (as in Chile) viciousness and immorality of the right-wing Establishment; the latter is their own terror directed at capitalist governments, whose very laws, terrorists claim, constitute a kind of violence. They eschew peaceful ways of changing such laws even when such ways are available. They insist that in bringing true justice they have no choice but to break the unjust coercive laws of what they regard as repressive states.

This militant reasoning is not new. Before he was executed in 1797, François Noël ("Gracchus") Babeuf, that fiery but luckless French predecessor of Marx, appealed to the oppressed: "Cut without pity the throats of the tyrants, the patricians . . . all the immoral beings who might oppose our common happiness." In 1840, Pierre Joseph Proudhon pontificated, "Property is theft," thus giving revolutionary absolution both to his contemporaries and to future generations who would rise against the "thieves" and the go-ahead to wield terror against them. In Russia, in 1917, Lenin urged the masses, *"Grab' nagrablennoye!"*— "Rob that of which you have been robbed!" Historically this was the very first official Bolshevik invitation to mass terror of the haves by the have-nots. Initially it was confined to the seizing only the property of the rich, but soon the rich themselves were threatened with jail and death. This was the counterblow of the masses, their answer to what they perceived as the violence, oppression, and immorality of the state apparatus, which had been controlled by the upper and middle classes. The irony of it, so often escaping those who do not bear the brunt of this revolutionary answer, is that in the final outcome the masses of the revolution do not become the masters; instead, out of their midst rises a new class of oppressors.

We may concede to the revolutionaries that the state—any state—can indeed be violent and often is. And yet, if the state engages in violence, its people can, at least, try to restrain it in ways short of violence, such as by mass-scale passive resistance. But that remarkable nineteenth-century theoretician of anarchism, Mikhail Bakunin, like many modern revolutionaries, viewed terror on the part of the exploited as the sole possible and proper response to the violence of the state. He regarded *any* state as organically pernicious, against the iniquities of which any and all nonviolent remedies were useless. Only bombs and blood would cleanse the socio-political environment.

Marx considered capitalism, rather than any particular state, inherently cruel, the fountainhead of injustice. He proclaimed that it would have to be swept away by the rising proletariat, which would then create a nonviolent socialist state that would in the course of progress wither away, resulting in the wonderful stateless Communist society.

His followers adopted his vision and have followed it into modern times. In a Maoist periodical published in the early 1970s by an American student group, we read: "The capitalist society is violent by its very nature. The exploitation of workers, causing them to live on the edge of poverty, is a form of violence. To assume that wage-slavery is not violent is patently false." Professor Herbert Marcuse taught Angela Davis ("the best student I ever had in the more than thirty years of my teaching") that the "institutionalized" violence of capitalism had to be answered with the "defensive" violence of radical students. In her very first lecture at the University of California in Los Angeles, she proved the professor's apt pupil when she asserted: "The first condition of freedom is an open act of resistance—physical resistance, violent resistance."

George Jackson, the revolutionary black convict, while in Soledad prison, wrote to Angela Davis: "Dialectics, understanding, love, passive resistance, they won't work on an activistic, maniacal, gory pig." Only violence by the blacks, he went on, can "take the murder out of their system, their economics, their propaganda." Thus believing, George Jackson soon died in gunfire.

Even as the terrorists attack, they insist that their aggression is (in Professor Marcuse's definition) nothing but "defensive." In February 1974, in San Francisco, the self-styled Symbionese Liberation Army, which kidnapped and converted Patricia Hearst, proclaimed that their terrorism was a reply "to the murder, oppression, and exploitation of our children and people." Theirs was a righteous "Revolutionary War against the Fascist Capitalist Class and all their agents."

On March 15, 1974, when Clark E. Squire, the handsome 36-year-old member of the Black Liberation Army, was sentenced to life imprisonment for the slaying of a New Jersey state policeman, he spoke to the judge: "The Black Liberation Army has been accused of killing policemen. All we do is stop the police from killing us. If the police don't want to get killed, they should stop murdering blacks and Third World people. The poor people of the nation are being victimized by the system. The Black Liberation Army has been fractured, but it will continue until the oppression is stopped."

To Marcuse, to Jackson, to the Symbionese and the Black Liberation Army, it was moral to kill the immoral society.

III

But there is another revolutionary view of morality: no less a leader than Lenin himself categorically denied the existence of absolute morality altogether.

Today, adhering to Lenin's dictum, certain leaders and followers in extremist parties throughout the world frankly and bluntly voice their credo that no inherent morality exists in human custom and law; that law is only an instrument used by the state for its own purposes, that its so-called morality is a means of manipulation.

Still, at the same time, other violent revolutionaries have claimed for themselves a higher morality, devoutly believing in their own virtue. The Soviet and other orthodox Communist press laud Communist justice as surely superior to what exists in capitalist lands, as well as in Mao's China and Albania. And in the same vein, the Maoist and other non-Soviet spokesmen deride both bourgeois and Soviet law and morality while praising their own subversion, terror, and suppression as the only morality true and inherently lawful.

Some of the clearest pronouncements on what is moral for the revolutionary can be found in two nineteenth-century sources, one Russian, the other German.

The Russian document is *The Catechism of a Revolutionary,* ascribed to the authorship of the anarchist Bakunin and his wild young friend Sergei Nechayev, although recently it has been claimed that the work was written by an obscure disciple of Nechayev.[1] In our times *The Catechism of a Revolutionary* made a powerful impression upon some of the Black Panther leaders: Eldridge Cleaver wrote in *Soul on Ice* that he used its text's premises "along with some of Machiavelli's advice."

The salient sections of the *Catechism* describe the revolutionary as having "no interest of his own . . . no feelings . . . no belongings," as a man for whom revolution is the only interest, thought, and passion. "He will be an implacable enemy of this world, and if he continues to live in it, that will be only so as to destroy it more effectively." The boast of the American terrorists of the late 1960s and the Arab commandos of the '60s and '70s that the world's moral revulsion to their deeds does not dismay them is an affirmation of a postulate in the *Catechism*: The revolutionary "despises public opinion; he despises and hates the existing social ethic in all its demands and expressions; for him, everything that allows the triumph of the revolution is moral, and everything that stands in its way is immoral." It follows that "merciless destruction" by revolutionaries is moral. With this ruthless and total annihilation of society as the revolutionist's aim, "he must always—tirelessly and in cold blood—be prepared to die and to kill with his own hands anyone who stands in the way of achieving it."

The Anti-Dühring of 1877, by Friedrich Engels, Marx's faithful alter ego and collaborator, is even more extreme than the *Catechism*.

In his *Anti-Dühring,* Engels pitted himself against the ideas of his contemporary, the German philosopher and economist Eugen Karl Dühring. Engels vehemently proclaimed that "we [the Communists] reject any dogmatic morality as an eternal . . . henceforth unchangeable moral law, allegedly having its permanent principles standing above history and national difference." He denounced morality as a tool of class suppression. Was the triumph of the revolution (in its violent Nechayevist sense) moral? Nonsense, implied Engels. Necessary and inevitable, but neither moral nor immoral. There was no such thing as absolute morality.

And, as we know, Lenin agreed. In 1920 he wrote: "We don't believe in eternal morality. We expose the fraud of all sorts of fairy tales about morality."[2] Proceeding from Engels' theory on morality, Lenin (who had within him much more of the violent Bakunin than the bookish Marx) held that, since violence was the crux of the capitalistic system, violence against the system was wholly justifiable. While being unconcerned with questions of morality, Lenin was frankly for revolutionary violence and vehemently for revolutionary terror.

In our times, Dr. George Habash of the Arab terrorists, leader of the Marxist-Leninist Popular Front for the Liberation of Palestine, has explained his raiders' brutality by saying that they are involved in a revolution, and that in a revolution any and all means are permissible. Mark Rudd, the fugitive Weatherman, was quoted by the Liberation News Service as having said: "A worldwide revolution is happening. A revolution is not a dinner party. Revolution happens through force of arms." And this, from both the Arab and the American (the former nominally a Christian, the latter born a Jew), is surely an echo of Lenin's famous dictum: "Revolution is a difficult matter. It cannot be made with gloves or manicured nails . . . should not be measured by the narrow standards of petty bourgeois morality."[3]

Some modern criminologists and academicians agree with Engels and Lenin that there is no such thing as absolute morality. Among others is Professor Peter Schafer, from 1946 to 1950 chairman of the prison commission of the Ministry of Justice in Hungary. Now living in the West, he still insists, in his book *The Political Criminal* (1974), that if a violent revolutionary represents himself as moral and his antagonists as immoral, we must concede him his claim; for what, in truth, are morals? What is moral to me or to you may well be immoral to others. And who are we to judge—especially since the morals of the revolutionaries become the morals of the state, once the revolutionaries have seized it?

Apparently Professor Schafer's departure from Communist Hungary has taught him little.

IV

Along with the extremists' belief that society is sick and violent and deserving of any act that would change it, is their abhorrence of gradual reform.

This complete rejection of gradualism is typified by the attitude of the Argentinian-Cuban, Dr. Ernesto Ché Guevara. His first wife, Hilda Gadea, recalls that in 1954—early in his career as a revolutionary, before he joined the Castros and helped them win Cuba—Guevara argued heatedly that "the only way . . . was a violent revolution" of drastic socio-economic dimensions and that "any other solutions" offered in Latin America by moderate liberation movements "were betrayals." On this point, he was hot with rage. Hilda records in her memoir: "I did try to quiet Guevara a little, but he rejected me brusquely: 'I do not want anybody to calm me down!' he almost shouted."[4] This was entirely in keeping with Lenin's hatred of liberals, not because they were not doing enough for the people, but because they were doing too much, and thus postponing, if not wholly obviating, the revolution. All the Guevaras yet to come would honor Ché's implied slogan: The Worse, The Better.

The worse, the better: Diana Oughton was a rich girl from Dwight, Illinois, a Bryn Mawr graduate who was destined to become a Weatherwoman and to perish at 28 while attempting a make a bomb. She died in the basement of a house on West Eleventh Street in New York on March 24, 1970. Her biographer tells us how, in the mid-1960s, while she was still working with the Quakers, she had tried to help the poor Indians of Guatemala, and how a fellow North American, a radical, acridly admonished her: "You're only delaying the revolution." A Guatemalan intellectual agreed: "What this country needs is to line up the fifty first families against the wall."[5]

Thus Bakunin and Nechayev had spoken, and Marx and Lenin had preached, and Guevara had acted, and in time Diana heeded, to her own tragic end.

V

Regarding themselves as the possessors of the only possible remedy to the evils of the Establishment, terrorists assert the "legality" of their actions and the "illegality" of the state to which they are opposed. They solemnly claim sovereign rights for their organizations as they flaunt sovereignty's trappings and mannerisms.

Many call themselves "the Army." The Irish Republican Army set the precedent in taking such a name. Various Latin American guerrilla groups were among the first to use the terms "People's Army" and "People's Armed Forces." North American terrorists, such as the Black Liberation Army and the Symbionese, followed this practice of military pomp, and in the case of the Symbionese Liberation Army its picturesque but formidable leader, Donald D. DeFreeze, elevated himself to the post of "Field Marshal General."

The word "People's" is incorporated into their organizational names to demonstrate the alleged source of their sovereign power. The hideaway apartments or cellars in which they hold their kidnapped captives are designated as "people's prisons." They announce "trials" and "sentences" for their victims. When they kill or threaten to kill their prisoners, they shun such words as "shooting" or "strangling," using the far more governmental and military term "execution" instead. And they become a sovereign entity indeed when they successfully force newspapers, radio, and television to publicize their manifestoes and ultimatums word for word.

In addition to sovereignty, terrorists maintain they represent an assortment of philosophies that to us often have almost religious connotations.

What Crane Brinton, in his *A Decade of Revolution, 1789-1799*, wrote about the essence of the Great French Terror is largely true of all the movements of terror and outbursts occurring since the late eighteenth century. "The Terror," Brinton asserts, "like much milder and less interesting political situations, is the interaction between a social environment and men consciously attempting to alter the environment."[6]

Violent revolutionaries consciously attempt to change their time's and area's socio-political and economic environment, and in doing so proclaim that their program is based on a superbly rational philosophy. Yet, terror is not the manifestation of a genuine philosophy but of a rage that is sometimes rationalized in philosophical terms. In this rationalization of terror there is a theological element. Brinton rightly calls terror's justification (by terrorists) a religious emotion on the part of an ecstatic minority. With religious zeal, Robespierre and all the other terrorists with him promised Liberty, yet deprived their fellow men not only of that precious gift but of life itself—in Liberty's name. (Ironically, the Jacobins, the most extreme of the French terrorists, derived their name from a peaceful Jacobin—Dominican—monastery in Paris, which they used as a meeting place.)

In the Jacobin view, terror furthered freedom. Brinton explains their—and Robespierre's—peculiar logic: "Freedom consists, not in doing what one wants to do, but in doing what is right. The general will of the republic is right. The Committee of Public Safety knows what that general will is. To obey the Committee, therefore, is to obey one's better self, to be really free. To disobey the Committee is to obey one's worse self, to be a slave.'' Terror frees its victim; when ''it cuts off the head of a very recalcitrant citizen, it is presumably also freeing him.'' Robespierre himself defined his reign as ''the despotism of liberty against tyranny''—because the guillotine unfettered those doomed men and women from the errors that had so tyrannically gripped them.[7]

Without a genuine philosophy and a true morality, terrorists in their infinite fallibility abuse others and themselves while rationalizing their acts in a way that seems to have validity only for them—a way that reveals terrorism's awful ''theology.''

The wicked must be killed to protect the virtuous. And the wicked should be grateful for being given this chance to serve the cause of the Revolution by dying: indeed, it is an opportunity to save their souls from damnation. In speaking of Robespierre and his terrorist entourage, Brinton most fittingly cites a statement by St. Robert Bellarmine, the fanatical Italian cardinal of the sixteenth and seventeenth centuries (canonized in 1930), in which he said that ''it was a positive benefit to a heretic to kill him, because the longer he lived the more damnation he acquired.''

The religious (or pseudoreligious) fanaticism of the terrorists also involves the punishment of revolutionaries themselves. They must accept violence against themselves no less than inflict it on others. Even the Revolution's ardent leaders and followers must serve the Revolution by dying on the scaffold when the Supreme Leader deems such executions necessary.

As Brinton observes, the bloodthirsty Jacobins were exultingly religious not alone by accident of the derivation of their name: ''The devotional language of the Jacobins, their frequent accesses of collective emotion, their conviction of righteousness, their assurance that their opponents are sinners, direct agents of the devil, their intolerance, their desire for martyrdom, their total want of humor—these are unmistakable signs of the theological temperament.''[8] Since Robespierre's time most terrorists have displayed a similar religious zeal.

Brinton reminds us that Robespierre in his own time survived as long as he did ''because the Terror was in large part a religious movement, and Robespierre had many of the qualities of a second-rate religious leader. . . . His speeches were sermons, edifying to the faithful, quite empty to the unbeliever. . . . His churches were the Jacobin clubs. . . .'' And inevitably, as in any sect or political movement, when ''the Terror became more and more a form of religious intoxication and less and less of a government of national defense, dissension broke out'' between at least two sects of the faithful—the twin bodies in charge of executions: the Committee of General Security and the Committee of Public Safety, each one far less a body of politicians than a band of religious fanatics.[9]

3

Terror as Aberration

Are terror and terrorism manifestations of mental disturbance in those who engage in such violent practices?

The reader is asked to remember that the author is a socio-political writer and a historian, not a trained psychologist. Whatever his un-tutored views, he at all times defers to professional psychologists, whose findings will be scrupulously quoted. But this is the author's own opinion:

The world at large accepts to only a very small degree the phenomenon of terrorism as something normal. On the contrary, the world views it as abnormal—"sick."

A war may be cheered by the majority of a given nation, at least in its very beginning, but terror—never. Even if, in recent times, thanks to electronic and other media, certain terrorists may appear glamorous, they are still neither heroes nor martyrs to the general populace.

Terror is sometimes applauded by that ineffectual intellectual who takes every fad seriously, or perhaps, timid as he may be, admires a tough man or woman whose murderous activities are political and thus "not really criminal." An outstanding example is the little-concealed applause or at least sympathy for the terrorists of the Symbionese Liberation Army of San Francisco and Los Angeles in early 1974 and for their fiery end that May.

But as for the masses, they want peace from both war and terrorism. Political terror sometimes—not often—may be met with their passive acceptance, even if not with vigorous praise, because, as someone has observed, the masses are better able to understand courage than wisdom. They may also be afraid to protest, as has happened in recent years in Ulster and Lebanon.

This does not mean that I divide the world into just two categories—intellectuals and nonintellectuals—in all earthly matters. The division is used here only with regard to the acceptance of, or cheers for, terror because, singularly enough, these two categories seem to react to this phenomenon of violence somewhat differently from each other.

Yet, on occasion, the attitudes of both toward this problem appear to converge. Intellectuals and nonintellectuals may be impressed, without necessarily approving, not only by the lone daring of revolutionary terrorists, but even by the sweep of such wholesale murderers of the past as Attila and Torquemada, Robespierre and Napoleon, Stalin and Hitler. But this is not the usual reaction of the popular mind and heart. Passive acceptance is not really adulation. It is merely dull indifference.

Violent revolutionaries and their idealistic supporters or witless sympathizers sometimes argue that by and large the mass is uninformed or plain stupid, that it does not know its own good, for whose sake the terrorists sacrifice their own and others' lives. Even if we grant this premise (which I, for one, do not), the sheer fact remains that most people do not want terror, do not applaud it, and certainly do not join with the terrorists in enthusiastic numbers.

This writer lived in his teens through the Russian revolution and its terror, both Red and White. ("Lived" is the correct word here, for on one occasion, at the age of 19, I was taken to be shot.) From my ample experience I can testify that neither side of gunwielders, torturers, and executioners was cheered by most citizens, no matter what those luckless people's political views or inclinations were. And from my many subsequent years of study of the terror avalanches of other nations and periods I can affirm that much the same plague-on-both-your-houses attitude prevails practically everywhere and always.

So we come to the question of what is normal and what is not. If we regard this antiterror or nonterror feeling as being typical of the majority, then for better or worse the attitude can be assumed to be normal and any practice of terror or praise for terror to be abnormal. The argument that people are against terror because they are not politically conscious or are simply uninformed is not to the point. What matters here is that it is apparently normal to be against terror if only because the majority feels that way.

If it is not likely for most of us to cheer terror, it is even less likely for us, the majority, who do not care for terrorism, to engage in murderous activities ourselves. Violence may in truth be inherent in human nature, as so many socio-psychologists and anthropologists postulate. In every one of us there may be a murderer. Yet the overwhelming majority of us do not kill—or at least try not to. What the majority feels and wills and the way the majority behaves constitutes the norm. Thus murder and any other violence are a deviation from the norm and most murderers and terrorists are to one extent or another abnormal. No amount of hair-splitting justification and rationalization can make such departures normal.

Of course, by calling them abnormal, we will not make terrorists vanish. But it is nonetheless important to establish the mental deviation or sheer aberration of many terrorists, both to understand what ails them and to caution many of us not to be swept into approval of the terrorists as they applaud themselves for transgressing conventional morality.

We can recognize two definitions of the abnormal: one in the sense of being "unusual"—in not conforming to the characteristics of the majority; the other in the sense of being psychologically disturbed. But it requires neither a jump nor a giant step to connect the two. Being psychologically disturbed often involves, or starts with, a state of an *acute* lack of characteristics of the majority.

And we must be careful in defining the majority. At times, in sharply separated areas, there can loom what paradoxically appear to be two distinct and opposing majorities. Thus, one majority can wildly cheer Yasir Arafat as a liberationist leader (as he was at his appearance at the United Nations in November 1974), while another majority elsewhere demands that he be thrown into an insane asylum or jailed. This is where sheer numerical count fails. Even as the Communist and Third World delegates at the United Nations roared their welcome to Arafat, they—not being truly elected in their respective home countries, some of which are seething with dissidence, others of which are half-starved into a sluggish indifference—did not in fact represent the multitudes for which they presumed to speak.

Astonishingly, in the West, some recent writers on political crimes manage to avoid the question of how much actual backing among the populace of the Communist and Third World countries the Arafats do have. Such writers also manage to slide over the question of terrorists' mental deviation or aberration. Thus Professor Schafer in his book touches upon this aspect only briefly and lightly. In his discussion of political crime and morality there should have been more than a few casual and unenlightening pages on political crime and mentality.

Today's terrorists may differ from their predecessors in history but early or late, then or now, most political terrorists have not been normal. In this respect there is no gap between our own era's murderous-suicidal Symbionese man or woman on the one hand and a guillotine enthusiast of Robespierre's days on the other.

At all times the root of the terrorists' so-called idealism is a deep psychological disturbance. Naturally, this does not mean that all people who do not agree with the majority are psychologically disturbed. But we emphatically include among the psychologically disturbed those dissidents who are violent, who try to prove their nonconformity by bombings, killings, skyjackings, and kidnappings.

Terror is a double-edged word: It is what the terrorist uses against his victim. It is also the mortal fear felt by the victim. Sometimes the terrorist acts out of his own terror, or, as Friedrich Engels once shrewdly put it, terror is "the domination of men who are themselves terrorized." What Engels should have added, but did not, is that such men's and women's transition from *feeling* terrorized to *acting* as terrorists tends in itself to be a sign of aberration—a paranoiac manifestation, a string of systematized delusions, a projection of personal conflicts ascribed to the supposed hostility of others. That is, such terrorists usually are not oppressed or terrorized; they only imagine themselves victims of hostility.

Terrorists themselves will not agree they are so crazed. Unlike many nonpolitical criminals, messianic terrorists seldom claim insanity as their defense, even if this is the sole way to escape major penalty. In America we know of only two notable instances in which terrorists admitted that something was indeed awry with their mentality: Samuel Melville, the New York bomb-planter, wrote to his former wife Ruth shortly before he was killed in the Attica Prison riot of September 1971 that he was "a nut" who "freaked out," wasting his life; and his girl friend Jane Alpert, on emerging from the underground and surrendering to the authorities in November 1974, seemed to agree with her lawyer when he told the judge that her terrorism of four years back "was an aberration in an otherwise exemplary life."*

But the overwhelming majority of political terrorists picture themselves as virtuous and their foes as evil. When captured, interrogated, and tried, they proudly and defiantly declare that they alone are sane and the rest of mankind is crazy.

This claim is elevated into governmental practice when the revolutionaries seize the state and become the all-powerful Establishment. For instance, the Soviet secret police categorize political dissenters as mental cases and send them to insane asylums apparently on such a premise as, You don't like the Soviet regime? You must be crazy!

---

* The case of Patricia Hearst is somewhat different: the affidavit she signed after her capture in San Francisco in September 1975, and the initial plea she entered, stating that she had been practically crazed into terrorism by her Symbionese captors, stemmed from her family's and lawyers' plan to exonerate her, rather than from her own belief that she had been made insane by the torture and sundry drugs used on her by her kidnappers. It is clear that as a terrorist, at the time of her capture and subsequent trial, she considered herself sane. By December 1975 her lawyers also decided to discard a plea of insanity and to use as her defense that she had been coerced and frightened by the Symbionese.

At least a few of the political dissenters in the Soviet Union today may indeed be mentally ill, but many of them are not—they are peaceful oppositionists, not violent terrorists.

The question may be asked: Why don't we class them as mentally disturbed since they do not agree with the Soviet majority? The answer is: They do not agree with the *submissiveness* of the Soviet majority, rather than with the Soviet majority itself. We are entitled to our suspicion that these dissidents and the Soviet majority do agree in their dislike of the Soviet government and the Communist Party. Only the majority is too afraid to voice its opposition. The dissidents are not afraid.

After committing these harmless humans to mental institutions, those secret policemen who masquerade as psychiatrists try to drive them insane not alone by confining them with genuinely insane patients but also through injections of the brain-cell-destroying reserpine, among other drugs. The testimony of Dr. Norman Hirt of the University of British Columbia Medical School, in his studies of Soviet abuses of psychiatry, established that the doctors in the employ of the Soviet secret police misuse this drug widely. Ordinarily, reserpine is a tranquilizer, but in huge doses it damages the "foundation structures of the brain," as Professor Hirt stated in his deposition to the staff of a Congressional subcommittee in Washington in October 1972. He explained: "What happens is that portions of the brain collapse on themselves, and you get what looks like atrophy of the brain in the so-called psychiatric units" of the Soviet Union. He also called it "a deliberate form of chemical lobotomy," adding: "This treatment they [the Soviet secret police doctors] have apparently perfected." Other drugs used by the KGB doctors on political prisoners are, according to the eminent Canadian psychiatrist, aminazin and sulfozin. The first produces destruction of the memory system and a violent lack of control of muscular movements (athetosis). The second, a 1 per cent solution of purified sulphur in a peach-oil base, "is never employed in ethical practice," but, says Dr. Hirt, is often used by the KGB on its prisoners.[1]

Conversely, however, the Soviet authorities admit, even if not publicly, the real insanity of their own terror-wielding secret police. This is when, most guardedly, and usually in such rare periods of frankness as Nikita Khrushchev's reign, they allow certain details to be published about the sheer abnormality of such of their secret police chiefs as Vyacheslav Menzhinsky[2] and Nikolai Yezhov; or when we learn, from defectors, about the existence in the USSR of special, well-concealed insane asylums maintained exclusively for former members of the Soviet secret police. And yet, a strange phenomenon: The notorious Soviet secret police chief Lavrenty Beria has often been described as a sadist, both by his top Soviet associates who eventually killed him and by many of his surviving victims, but, curiously, seldom as an outright madman. Even the most reliable of Western experts on Soviet terror, Robert Conquest, in his monumental book *The Great Terror,* does not make any explicit charge of insanity or other forms of abnormality regarding Beria, who was aberrant enough.

II

We are fortunate to have some medical studies of terrorists as madmen, even if such analyses are lamentably scarce. They differ from psychological theories about violence insofar as discussions of violence are necessarily more general than are those on terrorism, the latter being a more specific form of violence.

Dr. Lawrence Z. Freedman, professor of psychiatry at the University of Chicago, has written of political terrorism as "the polistaraxic crime par excellence."[3] He coined the term "polistaraxic" by combining the Greek words *polis*—community—and *taraxic*—upsetting. These community-upsetters are to be distinguished from nonpolitical terrorists. Their compulsion to act violently involves four psychological factors.

Dr. Freedman cites these four factors "in the order of increasing psychic depth." He does not state on what information his theory is based. Nor does he stipulate whether all four factors presented by him are to be found in any one terrorist. Thus, if we understand Dr. Freedman correctly, a terrorist may suffer from all four, or from only one or two, perhaps even three, of the four. It is possible that some or all of these factors also apply to people who are not terrorists. But in terrorists these factors or drives are accentuated to the point of danger, making these men and women what they are—terrorists.

And so, the four factors:

First, the political terrorist is motivated by his desire to reaffirm his masculinity, for in his "preterroristic situation there have been severe blows to self-image." Dr. Freedman speaks of male terrorists only, but we may presume that women terrorists suffer from a similar feeling of earlier blows and a wish to assert themselves menacingly.

We should add that in many cases terrorists' abnormality can be traced to unhappy childhoods, to the hurt of illegitimacy, to broken homes. And in other instances, what appear to be a comfortable and placid childhood and a well-protected adolescence, on closer examination seethe with the son's or daughter's protest against the real or imagined domination or, contrariwise, inadequacy of the mother and especially of the father, as is usually pointed out in discussions of

Freud's theories. When such a child grows up to throw bombs or shoot guns, the attack is against the resented parent rather than the hated state, despite Jung's doubts on the subject.

On the surface such a child-adult may be rich; inside he or she is poverty-stricken. Dr. Robert Harrington, director of the Hampden District Mental Health Clinic in Springfield, Massachusetts, is noted for his work with many white young women, affluent and intelligent, but disturbed. In September 1975, speaking of some such women who turn to violence, he observed: "Their inner life is one of impoverishment, and everything becomes external to them. They never look inside themselves. Some try to solve problems, some act violently, but they never contemplate their own responsibility. They just play out their impulses on society all over the place."

Extending his thought, Dr. Harrington declared: "I think it becomes a kind of fusion of sexuality and violence when these kids find someone of a different group like [Charles] Manson, or the Symbionese Liberation Army led by a black—someone from a 'foreign' group that represents something alien to their own family, some kind of cultish, crazy, occult figure. And then you start getting the things like Patty Hearst holding a neat big rifle, or the [Lynette] Fromme girl with her .45."[4]

The more intelligent of those terrorists who come from the upper classes sometimes do look deeply enough into themselves to find roots of their murderous aberration. Thus Mikhail Bakunin himself explained his rebellious spirit by his early suppression by his despotic mother. Those of his friends who knew him well also accounted for his violent preachments and acts as caused by his sexual impotence, a pathetic failing in this enormous and imposing physical frame.

But others, rich or poor, nobles or commoners, do not look inward at all, nor do their friends and associates give us true reasons for the terrorists' behavior. It remains for outsiders to spell out the deep causes.

We know from outside sources, for example, that Johann Most, the German-American anarchist of the nineteenth and early twentieth centuries, the author of a celebrated manual on bombing the rulers and the rich, from childhood on suffered from the shame of his illegitimacy, the persecution by his stepmother, the brutality of an employer in his youth, and the disfigurement of his face by a clumsy operation.[5]

In our own times, the bloody conduct in 1973-74 of the self-styled "Field Marshal General Cinque," born Donald David DeFreeze, who died in a hail of bullets and a ring of flames as chief of the Symbionese Liberation Army, was foretold in the probation report of the 1960s on him as a "schizoid personality with strong schizophrenic potential,"

gripped by "a fascination with regard to firearms and explosives"[6]—all
of this implacably springing from his ill-starred ghetto origin and early
family maladjustments. Here truly was a sociopath on a warpath,
dubious courtesy of his childhood.

As the second of Dr. Freedman's four factors, he sees the terrorist's desire to submerge his individuality in a group. "Individuality
requires acceptance of a burden of responsibility," Dr. Freedman
states. "It can create a sense of impotence. . . . Depersonalized man is
able, in a sense, to abandon his individuality and his status as a person
and to act only as the instrument of a larger group." This awesome
group is the refuge of an impotent, irresponsible terrorist.

As if echoing and reaffirming Dr. Freedman, Dr. Lewis Yablonsky,
a sociologist of California State University at Northridge, declared in
September 1975, at the news of the capture of Patty Hearst in San
Francisco and of Lynette (Squeaky) Fromme in Sacramento, where
the latter pointed a loaded gun at President Gerald Ford, that both
women acted like depersonalized robots: "With no definite ego of their
own, they placed themselves in a totally subservient position, following orders. They have low or no self-esteem, and they are desperately
seeking recognition and approval." Patty was following the orders of
her Symbionese kidnappers and brainwashers, even though most of
them were long since dead. Lynette was still under the spell of Charles
Manson and his murderous cultist "family," even if he and the most
tenacious of his disciples were long since in prison. So desperate were
Patty's and Lynette's craving for attention, Dr. Yablonsky pointed
out, that they had "no regard for their own safety," and so were
"more dangerous because of that."[7]

Third of the factors analyzed by Dr. Freedman, and surely linked to
the first, is the seeking by the terrorist of an ambivalent closeness to his
victim. Such a terrorist, an individual who refuses to be an individ-
ualist, seeks—in terror—intimacy not only with his fellow terrorists,
but also with his victims, especially when they seem so powerful and
so high above him. "The terrorist is recognized, and is negotiated with,
and is able to prove his power to bring the most powerful and admired
figure . . . to his knees."

The fourth and final element Dr. Freedman identifies is "a kind of
terroristic sacrament," an act of violence "that is not merely the dedication of human powers to the service of the gods." Here Dr. Freedman quotes Professor Abraham Kaplan of the University of Haifa who
imagines a terrorist as saying: "In spilling of blood, there is not only a
dedication to the service of the gods, but a device to compel the gods to
my service. I have been a channel for them. . . . I provide a way for
them to enter my being, and make themselves effective." Professor

Kaplan comments: "In this transvaluation . . . it is precisely the need-lessness of the act and, from the outsider's viewpoint, the despicable features of the act, the killing, which are essential to it."

This fourth factor in the Freedman-Kaplan analysis was among the topics I discussed in early February 1975 in Jerusalem with Professor Yehoshafat Harkabi of the Department of International Relations and Middle Eastern Studies at the Hebrew University. A general in retire-ment and former chief of Israeli Army Intelligence, author of *Pales-tinians and Israel* (1974), he spoke to me of the "terroristic sacrament" as it pertained to the Arab fedayeen or guerrillas. Said Professor Harkabi:

"Even if this mystical blood feeling of the fedayeen is not their own inherent idea, the repeated preachment of it to them by their leaders eventually makes it their own. They come to believe it through indoctri-nation. And so it doesn't really matter whether or not it is inborn—the fact is they believe in this blood magic of violence fanatically."

He recalled that Frantz Fanon's sermon of how good it is to purge oneself through shedding blood is enormously popular among militant Arabs. Tied to this is such Arabs' purging of themselves through ver-biage. "They spill words as easily as they spill blood," Professor Har-kabi remarked. "The Arab terrorists are graphomans—they write much and often, revelling in words."

In this discussion of the mystic feeling of blood sacrament, not only Professor Harkabi but other Israeli experts on terrorism to whom I talked in early 1975 mentioned the role of drugs. Time and again vari-ous drug pills are found on the bodies of dead or captured Arab guer-rillas. "These pills are regularly issued to the fedayeen and also to some regular Arab army men by their superiors to put these fighters into a mystic mood, a mood of exaltation, of fearlessness of death," one Israeli expert said to me. "At one time the question was raised among us whether we, too, shouldn't provide our soldiers with some such pills. Wisely we decided against it."

It is pointed out that the word "assassin" is of Arabic origin and derives from the word "hashish." The original assassins were Moslem fanatics in Syria and Persia in the eleventh to the thirteenth centuries whose self-chosen mission was to assassinate Crusaders. Their Arabic name was *hashshashin,* or "hashish eaters."[8]

Dr. Freedman, in his analysis, puts an assassin far beyond the time and place of his historic Mideastern origin. He speaks of him as a latter-day terrorist, East or West, who kills a President or other head of state in a kind of fanatical euphoria, in a mystical exaltation of blood sacrament. He views such an assassin of a head of state not only as a man or woman who suffers the consequences of a bungled childhood;

the psychiatrist also sees this individual's awful gaps on growing up:
"As an adult the assassin suffered an intensity of self-loathing, a sense
of humiliation and abasement, an absence of self-esteem, profound
awareness that he received inadequate approbation by those who were
significant to him in his environment." In blood sacrament he seeks his
salvation.

The blood feeling sometimes relates to or subconsciously suggests
an actual blood kinship. Dr. Freedman suggests that the enemy to be
killed by the assassin, the terrorist, the guerrilla, the commando, is his
father or is fancied as the oppressive father, who is also guilty of taking
the child's mother away from the child. Here we recognize the well-
known Freudian message that at all times terror against the Establishment has been in the rubric of parricide a hateful, death-carrying
wish and action to destroy the father, be he arbitrarily authoritarian or
benevolent, be he full of *machismo* or a weakling, but ever the posses-
sive husband of the mother—of the womb and the motherland desired
by the frustrated son for himself.

Not that this concept is universally accepted by other psychologists. Jung wrote: "To explain the murderous outburst of Bolshe-
vistic ideas by a personal father complex appears to me as singularly
inadequate." As we have seen (in our chapter on Violence), Jung
rejected the explanation of the human psyche as a personal affair only.
Instead he stressed "the uprush of collective forces" resulting in
bloody aggressiveness.

Dr. Freedman emphasizes that, in their violence, humans strike
out not alone at their fathers or father-figures, but also at their own
selves. He points out that terrorists and nonpolitical aggressors are,
particularly in one respect, very much alike. "The terrorist murderer,
no less than the personal [nonpolitical] killer, strikes the mirror. He ob-
literates an intolerable image of himself which he himself has when he
strikes out at his victim."

But the terrorist group, in which an assassin, a guerrilla, an urban
commando tries to lose his unbearable individuality, is sometimes of
not much, if any, help. To their very end, these terrorists remain—in
Dr. Freedman's definition—"maladapted pathological isolates."

Another valuable approach to the terrorist as a demented personality may be gleaned from Dr. David Wechsler's classic study, *The Measurement and Appraisal of Adult Intelligence,* with its fine clinical
portrait of what is called "the sociopath," or the socio-psychological
deviate. Dr. Wechsler writes of adolescent sociopaths, the young
American deviates whom he studied mostly in New York, but his
description also fits those adults who are messianiac terrorists, as can
be seen from these observations:

"Sociopaths generally have a grasp of social situations, but they are inclined to manipulate them to their own advantage in an antisocial way." Extreme sociopaths (we may include as extreme, by the very nature of their activity, practically all messianic or convictional terrorists) "are not only perverse in their behavior, but distorted in their social comprehension." But they are not mere neurotics: "The sociopath's test performance as a whole is characterized by a breeziness and self-assurance which contrasts markedly to that of a neurotic. He is not bothered by contradictions and, when not ornery, takes everything in his stride. His abstract thinking is generally below average."[9]

Dr. Russel V. Lee, clinical professor emeritus of the Stanford University Medical School, goes further when he classes as abnormal or "not mentally sound" all the leaders of the twentieth century who started wars or launched massive campaigns of terror, or both. "Hitler," Dr. Lee points out, "could well have been used in the medical classroom as a classic example of paranoia." Stalin "was a sociopath, a moral imbecile." Dr. Lee rightly defines Hitler and Stalin as insane terrorists but, into the same category of clinical madness, he also places those nondictatorial and nonterroristic leaders in history who started—or joined in—cataclysmic wars.[10] (This, we may add, would reinforce the run-of-the-mill terrorist's view of the state, particularly the capitalistic state, as guilty of violence.)

Sometimes terrorists themselves, high and low, join in the chorus by accusing their leaders and one another of being mad, crazy, insane. Some such analysts in the underground are peculiarly qualified to make these appraisals. Thus, in 1927, three years after Lenin's death, Dr. Alexander Bogdanov, a psychiatrist who had been an early top-rank Bolshevik and had known the sacrosanct leader intimately, said to a trusted friend: "When for several years I observed certain of Lenin's reactions, I as a doctor came to the conviction that Lenin was at times overcome by psycho-states with definite signs of abnormality." Another oldtime Bolshevik physician, Dr. Konstantin Takhtarev, who had known his leader well, wrote that as early as 1903 Lenin was "deeply shaken by the struggle" at the Second Congress of his Party in London resulting in the Bolshevik-Menshevik split: "At the end, even his iron nerves could not endure, and he fell ill with a nervous collapse." This, the doctor explained, "was expressed in a singular form of a disarray of his vessel-motivating nerves under the impact of the central brain shock."[11]

The periods of *razh* (rage), of which Lenin's wife Nadezhda Krupskaya was to reminisce, and which were quite frequent in his life, bore all the earmarks of dementia that should have been, but were not, medically treated. Upon his death in 1924, the autopsy revealed "sclerosis of his brain's blood vessels" and the general deterioration of the brain "which best of all explains the causes of his extraordinarily demonic genius, his impulsiveness, fanaticism, despotic nature, the hatred and ideas of destructiveness that possessed him."[12]

In China, the Communist leader Lin Piao and his anti-Mao co-conspirators, in a manifesto drafted by Lin's son and a few Air Force officers, denounced Mao Tse-tung as "a paranoid and a sadist"—states of personality demonstrated by the Mao regime's mass-scale arrests and executions kept up for years. Interestingly enough, this revealing manifesto was made public by the Mao government itself, even if in a restricted way, to the faithful cadres only, soon after Lin had perished.

One may well argue that this accusation was mere propaganda, not based on any solid medical evidence gathered by Red China's doctors. Yet the very use of the medical term "paranoid" suggests that, consciously or not, someone high in Mao's entourage (if not Mao himself) realized that the essence of the behavior of their elite may border on the aberrant.

In many instances the mental aberration of terrorists is fairly apparent. In other cases the illness is adroitly camouflaged by the claimed or seeming idealism of the kidnappers and bomb-throwers as well as by the businesslike efficiency with which they organize and carry out their brilliantly inventive coups.

Sometimes efficiency in terrorism is combined with effective expertise in legitimate commerce. Such was the astonishing case of Giangiacomo Feltrinelli, the Italian millionaire publisher, the eccentric radical who was a wonder as a money-maker and an elusive perpetrator of revolutionary crimes until that March day in 1972 when his mangled corpse was found near a sabotaged power-grid pylon outside Milan. In Feltrinelli's case, while his efficiency as a businessman appeared to endure to his very death, his efficiency as a terrorist finally failed—illustrated by the manner in which he died. And that manner underlined the basic insanity lurking beneath his idealism.

In certain life stories, such as those of the Russian, French, and Italian terrorists of the late nineteenth and twentieth centuries, irrational behavior is patently evident. Insanity was medically certified for Pyotr Tkachev in France and Carlo Cafiero in Italy when, in acute forms, it caught up with these theoreticians and practitioners of revolutionary violence in their later lives, landing them in mental institutions at the end, both in the 1880s.

As to the exact forms of their eventual madness: There is general agreement among Tkachev's biographers that he died insane, but no indication of what his delusions were. One of the most thorough studies of Russia's populist, socialist, and terrorist movements, *Roots of Revolution* by Franco Venturi, describes Tkachev's end: "In 1882 he became ill and his state rapidly became extremely serious. He spent the last years of his life in a lunatic asylum and died on 4th January 1886."[13] Cafiero, the Italian, went mad when he acquired the guilty feeling that he was literally consuming more than his rightful share of sunshine of this planet.

III

On the other hand, there are those deranged criminals who, although apolitical, try to ennoble their deeds with totally false pretensions to political motivation. Occasionally, they are hailed by radicals. Some Weatherpeople, including their prominent leader Bernardine Dohrn, cheered—even if briefly—the brutal Tate-LaBianca murders in Los Angeles in August 1969 by Charles Manson and his harem. They cheered until the rank insanity of the "Helter Skelter" (as Manson called his group) became all too evident. Even if belatedly, the Weatherpeople realized the total absurdity of Manson's scheme. He had wanted to kill whites, blame blacks for the massacres, thus arousing the nation against blacks, and so causing the "Helter Skelter" of a racial white-black holocaust, which Manson's followers alone would survive.[14]

In other instances, insanity of such pseudopolitical nature is not welcomed by radicals at all, for its sheer abnormality is evident from the start. No terrorist group cheered when, on March 20, 1974, the tall, thin 26-year-old Peter Sydney Ball, alias Ian Ball, tried to drag Britain's Princess Anne from her chauffeur-driven limousine on the Mall near Buckingham Palace. Wounding four men but bungling his kidnapping scheme, he was captured. In his car nearby was found his letter to Queen Elizabeth, Anne's mother, demanding three million pounds sterling ($7,200,000) in ransom, as well as the government's promise not to pursue him in Switzerland, whither he had planned to flee for a life of ease.

On investigation he was discovered to have had a long history of mental illness. In 1967 and again in 1969 he had sought psychiatric treatment in a London hospital, where he was diagnosed as schizoid— a mentally disturbed subject with tendencies toward schizophrenia, already suffering from disintegration of the personality.

After his capture he attempted to make a political virtue of his sickness. On April 4, 1974, standing between two plainclothesmen in London's Bow Street Magistrates' Court, he had his alibi: "I did it because I wished to draw attention to the lack of facilities for treating mental illness under the National Health Service." On May 22 at the Old Bailey, the central criminal court, Peter Sydney Ball was sentenced to confinement in a mental institution "without limit of time," his plea of the socio-political motive wholly and properly disregarded.

Throughout history men have tortured and killed ostensibly for political reasons but actually driven by their nonpolitical lust for violence. A slayer's mental disturbance becomes evident when he runs amok on both sides of the political divide with equal readiness, changing from one camp to its opposite at a moment's urge. We see this in Louis Malle's film of 1974, *Lacombe, Lucien,* based on the real case of a 17-year-old Frenchman who, during the Second World War, wished to join the Resistance and, on being rejected, was enrolled as one of the Gestapo's torturers and murderers. Malle has explained his anti-hero: "He is a violent lad, he likes to brawl, but he is very complex, very secretive, very alone. It isn't that he is stupid. He is no more stupid than a university professor, but he sees the world in a quite different way. There are always people like that. I did my military service in Algeria, and I saw young French soldiers torturing. . . ."

Certain of history's most renowned assassins would kill for any political ideology, not for pay but on an indiscriminate insane impulse. Thus, though never legally found mentally ill (there proved to be no time for this), Lee Harvey Oswald was motivated, most likely not by politics, but by insane urges as he attempted to murder the extreme right-wing General Edwin A. Walker on April 10, 1963, before finally, on November 22 of that year, succeeding in assassinating the liberal President John F. Kennedy.

In April 1972, a morose unemployed bus boy and janitor from Milwaukee, 21-year-old Arthur Herman Bremer, stalked President Richard M. Nixon, the Republican, on his visit to Ottawa, and awaited Senator Hubert H. Humphrey, the Democrat, in New York, before shooting and paralyzing Governor George C. Wallace, the enemy of both, on May 15 in Laurel, Maryland. As Bremer was led away, he asked his captors: "How much do you think I am going to get for my autobiography?" But money was not really his goal; this would do him little good in his many years in prison. Nor was his aim political. This gunman's craving was for dubious glory, clearly an aberration, one of the many forms of mental disturbance gripping history's terrorists.

In the same category was the person and the act of the 45-year-old Sara Jane Moore, who attempted to assassinate President Ford in San Francisco on September 22, 1975: with her record of many years of mental imbalance, she had once tried to help in (but was dismissed from) the food give-away program wrested from the Hearsts by the Symbionese Liberation Army; had later associated with various radical groups on the West Coast; had been an informer for the FBI and other law-enforcement agencies; and finally fired that shot at the United States President—a tragic picture of a confused mind lost in the political vortex of modern times.

But to return to those terrorists who appear to be definitely political and in the service of one certain cause:

In sum, not all such political terrorists are insane or mentally disturbed, but most are. Such messianic or convictional murderers and kidnappers seldom if ever admit their abnormality (in contradistinction, as has been pointed out, to nonpolitical slayers who are wont to plead "temporary insanity" in their defense). The politicals are prone to intellectualize their aberrant trait in themselves.

Despite their lofty protestations, many political terrorists are acting out of the disturbances of their minds and souls rather than out of political reasons. If it is possible to explain all human behavior in terms of emotion, so it is logical to ascribe much of terrorism to the influence of emotion upon the terrorists—to postulate that many terrorists are disturbed in extreme ways mentally.

For their insane violence, blame their families, blame society, if you will. But the true cause is deeper, in a configuration of fear and hatred, in their own innermost drive to do violence. In nonpolitical violence the dark drive is sheerly criminal. In political terror it is prettified with programs and slogans.

PART II

History

VERY SOCIAL

First D. H. Conspirator—"After we have killed all kings and rulers, *we shall be the sovereigns.*"

Second D. H. Conspirator—"And then we will kill each other. What sport."

(Cartoon by Thomas Nast—Public Affairs Press)

4

Robespierre's Bloody Virtue

What is happening now is related to what has happened in the past. And because terrorism so threatens our lives today, it is important for us to know its history and tradition.

Historically, terrorism's main stages have taken place in Western Europe and Russia; then, North America, and latterly, Asia and Latin America, followed by Africa.

For two main reasons the canvas unrolls with the Reign of Terror of the French Revolution of the late eighteenth century.

First, this was the phenomenon chosen by Karl Marx, Friedrich Engels, and Vladimir Lenin as the subject of their intense study and the foremost model for their own preachments and activities. Since, overwhelmingly, Marx, Engels, and Lenin are the prime sources of inspiration for modern terrorists throughout the world, it is through them that these terrorists owe their beginnings to Maximilien Robespierre and his Reign of Terror.

Second, this Great Terror of 1793-94 was the first in history to attempt the elevation of primitive passion into a high-flown political philosophy, and to create an organization that tried to systematize murder and other lawlessness into a set of rules.

Of course, political slayers had, for thousands of years, tried to manipulate people through violence and fear. But Robespierre's reign was the first terror organized nationwide by revolutionaries actually seizing power and becoming a punitive government proclaiming murder as the law of the land. The very terms "terror," "terrorism," and "terrorists," used in their modern sense in so many languages, have come to us mainly from Robespierre's Reign of Terror—one more confirmation that today's exercises of terror trace their lineage to Robespierre.

And yet Robespierre as a political executioner was no complete surprise to mankind. In Paris, the wholesale massacre of the Protestant Huguenots on Saint Bartholomew's Night and Day, August 24, 1572, was a political bloodbath no less than an outburst of religious intolerance. Elsewhere in Western Europe, during that century, as before and after, political strife was not accompanied by any tender mercy. In Germany and Austria the Peasants' War of 1524-26 raged amid brutal atrocities—more, in this case, on the part of the suppressors than on that of the rebels, even though Thomas Muenzer, a Lutheran preacher, exhorted his peasant followers before his death in 1525: "At them, at them while the fire is hot! Don't let your sword get cold! Throw their tower to the ground! So long as they are alive you will never shake off the fear of men."[1]

In 1532 the Westphalian city of Muenster was captured by a fanatic faction of the otherwise peaceful Anabaptists. A megalomaniac tyranny was introduced—with murder and polygamy, among other features—led by John Boeckeler, also known as John of Leyden. In 1535, the forces of the deposed Prince Bishop Francis freed the city, and the leaders of the rebellion were put to torture and death.

Back in France and closer in time to her Great Terror, the mysterious and possibly mythical Abbé Jean Meslier, in his *Testament* (published by Voltaire, who was perhaps the real author of the document), roared his thunder in the spirit and phrases of all the Muenzers and Boeckelers of Europe's past: "Let all the great ones of the earth and all the nobles hang and strangle themselves with the priests' guts, the great men and nobles who trample on the poor people and torment them and make them miserable."

At last, as if in long-delayed response to these appeals, came the French Revolution with its guillotine—history's first campaign of political terror to be legislated by a people's duly elected representatives into a state-authorized system. And so, though terror had been used by individuals and groups before Robespierre's rule, his Reign of Terror systematized violence, hallowed it by the state's prestige, and created an intense fear in a way and on a scale heretofore unknown, a way that gave rise to the concept of modern terrorism.

II

The Revolution began in 1789, climaxed into the Great Terror in 1793-94, ebbed into the period of the Directory from 1795 to 1799, and ended with the rise of Napoleon, who became First Consul in November 1799 and crowned himself Emperor in 1804. He fell ten years later, and the Bourbon Kings were restored to the throne of France.[2]

Historians differ on the precise causes of the Revolution. Some see it as mainly an uprising of the French peasant masses and other under-privileged against the feudal regime of oppression that had for centuries fattened the kings, nobles, and clergy at the expense of the downtrodden. Others view the cataclysmic upheaval as a revolt of the new and growing middle classes, the bourgeoisie of France, seeking their place in the sun. Still others stress the influence of liberal, humane ideas of the so-called Enlightenment fermenting in France and elsewhere in Western Europe throughout the eighteenth century, emanating from the era's mankind-loving philosophers and pamphleteers, and finally reaching the apex of radicalism and bloodshed not quite expected or welcomed by those authors. We may conclude that all these major factors (and a host of minor ones) played their roles at a rapidly increasing tempo.

We agree with many historians that the sins of the old regime had been greatly exaggerated. Yet there was no doubt that the grievances of the lower and middle classes of the time—in 1789 and before—were real. The numerous wars of the Bourbon regime had been costly to the people. Taxation was unequal, corruption rife, and the burden of other injustices heavy.

In both the cities and the villages a proposal for fiscal reforms, advanced by Jacques Necker, a banker and a thoughtful financial expert, met with popular acclaim. The King agreed to it reluctantly. On May 5, 1789, the deputies representing the nation's three main estates (classes)—the nobility, the clergy, and the common people—met at Versailles. At once the deputies of the commons (the so-called "third estate") demanded socio-political reforms far more drastic than were those they were initially empowered to make. In these demands, such deputies were joined by some of the lower clergy and even by a few nobles. When the King balked, the deputies, on June 17, renamed themselves the National Assembly and took an oath not to rest until a constitution had been evolved and adopted.

Fearing bloodshed, the King acquiesced, but his court nobles were indignant. Blaming Necker for what was happening, they pressed Louis XVI into dismissing him as minister of state. A revolutionary mob in the streets took this is as pretext enough to storm the Bastille, the royal prison in Paris. A 29-year-old journalist, Camille Desmoulins, by his revolutionary speeches, helped incite the mob on its march. That Day of the Bastille, July 14, is generally considered the beginning of the French Revolution.

The King, terrified by the mob's success, immediately reinstated Necker. In July 1789, the revolutionaries established their soon-to-be-famous Commune of Paris as the city government and organized the National Guard to protect their victories. On August 4 the National

Assembly abolished all feudal privileges of the King, the nobility, and the clergy.

As it drafted the promised constitution, the Assembly renamed itself the Constituent Assembly. Some clergy and many nobles fled abroad. In part under the influence of these émigrés, the Emperor of Austria and the King of Prussia issued in 1791 a call to the European governments to restore the King of France to his former power. On June 20 and 21 King Louis and his wife Marie Antoinette tried to flee Paris to foreign lands, but were recognized at the village of Varennes and brought back.

The constitution was ready in 1791, and the King recognized the document. Its preamble was the celebrated Declaration of the Rights of Man and Citizen, based partly on Jean Jacques Rousseau's theories of man's equality and sovereignty and in part on the American Declaration of Independence.

The tumultuous Constituent Assembly ended in September 1791 and was succeeded by the Legislative Assembly, which lasted one year and was dominated by three groups of deputies: the extreme radicals, the Jacobins; a smaller faction of the Cordeliers, rapidly changing from moderates to become more and more uncompromising (their name, like that of the Jacobins, stemming from a sequestered Paris monastery, the original meeting place of these revolutionaries); and the middle-of-the-road republicans called the Girondins (because their early members were deputies from the province of Gironde). Since the Jacobins happened to occupy the higher rows of seats in the Convention hall, they were also called the Mountain. The Girondists, seated below, were known as the Plain. They were particularly outraged by the call of the Austrian and Prussian monarchs to restore the French King's power. On April 20, 1792, war was declared against the Austria of the Hapsburgs, from whose dynasty Marie Antoinette had come.

So began the French Revolutionary Wars, in which so much of Europe was eventually involved. The initial reverses suffered by the French armies gave rise to rumors of treason at the court, most of them on the part of Marie Antoinette. On August 10, 1792, a mob attacked the Tuileries palace, and the Paris Commune seized all police authority in the city. Among the Commune's leaders were two fiery Cordeliers, Georges Jacques Danton, a lawyer, and Jean Paul Marat, a physician.

In August 1792, the royal family was imprisoned in the cells of the Temple. The Assembly suspended the King and issued orders to elect a new body, the National Convention. In September, mass murders swept the French capital under the guidance of the Paris Commune, particularly of its *Comité de Surveillance* in which Marat played his role as the inciter of the mob.

In his journal *L'Ami du peuple* (Friend of the People), Marat stridently denounced not only the King but every institution and vestige of the old regime. On September 21, 1792, largely under the impact of Marat's agitation, the Convention abolished the centuries-old monarchy and the next day proclaimed the First Republic. Tried by the Convention for treason, Louis XVI was sentenced to death by a majority of one vote. He was guillotined on January 21, 1793. His Queen, Marie Antoinette, daughter of the Austrian Emperor Francis I, followed her husband to the scaffold nine months later, on October 16. Their young son died in prison under the brutal treatment of the child's jailers. (He never reigned, but the reverent monarchists of France later called him Louis XVII.)

In the three astonishing years of its sessions from September 1792 to October 1795, the Convention did much that was bad and some that was good. History's first parliament arose out of universal suffrage; it was this full-fledged representative body of revolutionary France that legalized the Great Terror. And it was this Convention that finally, in July 1794, voted the Terror's cessation.

The stiflingly hot July day of 1794—the Ninth of Thermidor by the new revolutionary calendar—definitely marked the fall of Maximilien Robespierre and was thus the last gasp of the Reign of Terror. But exactly when that bloody period had begun is a matter of disagreement among historians. Some define the Great Terror's start as far back as the storming of the Bastille on July 14, 1789. Others, more logically, date its beginning as of the mass killings of September 1792.

Touched off by the news of the French defeats on the foreign war fronts and by the rumors of treason by royalists, those September massacres raged in and around the jails in which a variety of the outlawed were held. As so often happens in a spontaneous mob action, the attackers in their fury hauled victims out of their cells indiscriminately. Not only aristocrats and priests, but also thieves, forgers, and whores were dragged to the self-appointed tribunals in the corridors and nearby rooms. Two verdicts were possible: guilty, or not guilty. Those condemned were forthwith taken into the prison courtyards or adjacent streets to be slain by the revolutionaries. During this nightmare the severed head of Princess de Lamballe, the Queen's maid of honor, was paraded in front of the prison in which the royal family awaited its fate. The toll of the September Days was estimated at some 2,000 lives.

Still other historians call the September Massacres only a foretaste to the Great Terror, which, they reasonably maintain, began with the seizure of power in late May and early June 1793 by the enraged Jacobins prevailing over the more moderate Girondins. Not that the Girondins were truly restrained. On occasion they also could and did murder and repress, but as a sustained policy—as a countrywide fact— terror was the tool of the Jacobins. Before the latter's full ascendancy, both sides had been responsible for terror, organized or not.

Foremost of the Jacobins, Robespierre was grabbing terror's steering wheel.

III

"He will go far because he believes everything he says." This faith in his own verity and honesty was "the secret of his influence." Thus, early in the Revolution, spoke Count Honoré Gabriel de Mirabeau, who until his death in 1791 was himself one of the most prominent men in revolutionary France. The subject of his remarks was Maximilien Robespierre.

Robespierre, born in 1758 to middle-class French family of Irish extraction, was a frail child in his native town of Arras. Going to Paris on a scholarship given him by the bishop of Artois, he proved an exemplary schoolboy at the Collège Louis-le-Grand—studious, gentle, shy. His Jesuit masters loved him, mostly because he was excellent in rhetoric, a skillful orator, though of scant emotionalism.

Later, at the law school of the University of Paris, he was a classmate of Camille Desmoulins, destined to be his fellow revolutionary and one of his many victims. Returning to Arras to practice law, Robespierre won his very first important case and was appointed a criminal judge, but soon resigned because, he said, he could not bear to hand out death sentences.

At Arras he also indulged himself in literary pretensions, as a dilettante member and director of the Rosati, a society dedicated to the cultivation of wit and letters. In the spirit of his time he composed verses that were remembered as "gallant and Bacchic."

On the serious side he read all of Rousseau's works religiously, called on the great sage in person, and considered himself a thoroughly understanding and faithful disciple of that philosopher's vision of an ideal society. In 1789, at 30, Robespierre was sent to Paris as an elected deputy to the Estates-General. There, and later in the Constituent Assembly, he gradually lost the last traces of his timidity. Joining extreme radicals, he delivered numerous speeches, evading no issues, hammering the same persistent points again and again. All of his plodding and increasingly fanatical self he put into his oratory, his ideas, his work.

At first some of his colleagues and many of the public laughed at his idealistic theories and personal traits. But he walked and talked through all this as if these jests and insults were of no matter. With his perseverance, his tremendous capacity for work, he was making headway. His frenetic praise of Rousseau helped. As the more conservative of his fellow members in the Jacobin Club withdrew in 1791, Robespierre became its head. When, in December 1792, Louis XVI was brought to trial at the Convention, it was Robespierre's cold and murderous speech more than any other factor that decided the 387-to-334 vote of death for the King.

Becoming first among the equals, killing thousands in the name of virtue, Robespierre spoke in sorrow about his own sacrifices and sufferings. Women burst into sobs, and more and more idolizers hailed him as "The Incorruptible," while those close to him called him "kind friend."

In appearance, although he dressed well, he was rather unremarkable. His hair was neatly powdered; his clothes were immaculate, appraised by some connoisseurs as of sober and tasteful elegance, but by others as foppish: knee breeches and silk stockings; a nankin-yellow or blue or brown coat and a chamois waistcoat; and a huge pleated bow tie, arranged with painstaking care to practically smother his neck. Small-statured, his poses unimpressive, his stride jerky, he had a harsh voice. His chin was short and sharp; his skin a sickly yellow. His eyes were piercing but half covered by the eyelids, deep in the sockets. Their look was described as *verdâtre,* possibly because of his green-tinted spectacles. His fine but small forehead bulged somewhat above his temples. His nose was small, narrow and pointed, but with very wide nostrils; his mouth large but the lips thin, pressed at the corners unpleasantly, with an indecisive smile verging on sarcasm.

He was sparing in his food habits, and walked instead of riding to and from his clean and modest lodgings. These were in the house of the intensely admiring Maurice Duplay, a prosperous and bourgeois but radical-thinking carpenter, who together with his wife and four daughters waited on him as much as he would allow. The girls sometimes played the harpsichord for their illustrious lodger, in the respites between his orations and writing, and his running of France under the giant shadow of the guillotine. Three of the four daughters were unmarried, and one—Eléonore—was particularly worshipful. Fond of her, he was rumored to be her lover, but in fact (perhaps) was no more than her proper and austere fiancé.

"Sinister sweetness" and "macabre-tragic significance" were among the phrases applied by later historians of the Revolution to Robespierre's figure, face, clothes, and habits.

IV

In the momentous year of 1792 Robespierre, this lawyer who hated law, rose to leadership in the Convention slowly, almost imperceptibly. In July 1793, upon his joining the Committee of Public Safety, it was immediately apparent that he was the undisputed chief of the French Revolution. Under him, terror erupted in earnest. His first targets were the Girondins.

The Girondins, with no true unity among themselves, lacked a definite attitude to terror. On the one hand they publicly deplored the September Massacres, branding them as sheer anarchy, thus confirming the Jacobins in their ardent support for the very same Massacres and so widening the chasm in the Convention and in French revolutionary politics in general. On the other hand, the Girondins, after pleading for a milder sentence for the King, finally voted his death.

But even the execution of Louis XVI in January 1793 did not wholly unleash the historic Terror. The bloody wave rose high beginning in June 1793, when the Girondins were expelled by the Jacobins from the Convention and, in the next few months, were sent by Robespierre to the guillotine. The Jacobins were then aided by that small but virulent club of the Cordeliers, led by the fiery lawyer Danton and the flamboyant journalist and orator Desmoulins.

As for the theory of terror, it was Danton who, among the first, formulated its purpose: Terror was a most desirable, most urgent weapon to defend the young Republic against its foes, both foreign and domestic. To an extent he was echoed by Lazare Carnot, the revolutionist who had been trained as a military engineer, and who from 1792 on was to go into history as the organizer of the new revolutionary armies of France and the architect of her eventual military victories over the Austrians and other foreign enemies. Carnot proclaimed that the Great Terror was the explanation of these triumphs. In truth, however, the principal successes of the French armies came before, not during, the Terror's sharpest crests.[3] The Great Terror did not inspirit the citizen-soldiers; it frightened not the invaders, but the French themselves.

Danton, in his speech at the chaotic session of the Convention of August 12, 1793, urged, as one of the measures of stepping up the Terror, the arrest—as hostages—of all "suspects" in Paris and the provinces. In the Convention's session of September 5 commemorating the first anniversary of the Massacres, it was decided to expand the Revolutionary Tribunal and to form a special army of 6,000 infantrymen and 1,200 cannoneers to carry terror throughout the nation.

In addition, Danton proposed revolutionizing all worthy men, particularly in Paris, by providing every worker with a rifle. Revolutionaries everywhere were to have arbitrary power to detain, judge, and execute any and all "suspects."

Bertrand Barère, an ardent Jacobin, summarized: "Let us make terror the order of the day!" Terror was not to be an exception to the new life—it was to be its ambiance and prime rule. People would have to accept it for their own welfare. Another Jacobin rationalized: "Since neither our virtue nor our moderation nor our philosophic ideas have been of use to us, let us be brigands for the good of the people." This was the phraseology that would live for generations, and with such pithy excuses generations of men would be made to suffer and die. These excuses would reappear in the slogans of Lenin and Trotsky, of Hitler and Mussolini, of Mao Tse-tung and Ho Chi Minh, of Castro and Guevara, of DeFreeze and Arafat.

Thus, in France in 1793-94, terror was justified not alone as a means of the survival of the French people threatened by its enemies, but also as a path to the people's welfare and virtue. In November 1793, Jean Nicolas Billaud-Varenne, the secretary of the Jacobin Club, elucidated the principles of a complete revolutionary centralization of state power to be based on the smiting ax, so that the French government could be "purified" instead of remaining "a volcano of villainy." On December 4 these postulates were formally incorporated into a law of terror.

Finally and authoritatively, Robespierre himself invoked the good of the people as the paramount reason for terror. In his speech of December 25, 1793, on "the Principles of the Revolutionary Government," the advocate from Arras intoned that the theory of this government was as new as the very revolution that gave it birth—it could be found in no books but only in the life and strife of that specific era. Robespierre explained the difference between two regimes as he saw them—the revolutionary and the constitutional. The former regime had as its task the creation of a republic; the latter, the safeguard of that republic. Robespierre viewed the world of politics quite narrowly: to him there were only two positive kinds of governments. He elucidated these two regimes: A revolution meant war by the legions of freedom against their adversaries. A constitution came after the triumph of the revolution—it was the regime of a victorious and peaceful freedom. This specific time in France was one of war. Therefore the nation's revolutionary government must defend good citizens with all possible force, implacably dealing out death to the enemies of the people.

These concepts were enough, Robespierre declaimed, to make clear the origin and nature of revolutionary laws. But the opponents of these concepts and these laws, the captious persons who called these laws tyrannical, were either stupid individuals or vice-ridden sophists. Robespierre asked: "If the revolutionary government must be more energetic in its actions and freer in its steps, does this mean that it is less just and less lawful?" He answered: "No! For it bases itself on the holiest of all laws—the good of the people; and on the most inalienable of all rights—necessity."

This argument served as an all-important part of almost every public statement by Robespierre, always ending in his call to improve yet further the work of the Revolutionary Tribunal and to bring to the guillotine blade yet another rollcall of persons, yet more categories of men and women.

Through all this, Robespierre claimed to be the truest of all the disciples of Rousseau. He reminded his listeners that Rousseau had described man as good by nature but corrupted by civilization. This idea was twisted by Robespierre into his burning conviction that man could be saved from himself, from his meanness and criminality, by the guillotine. Robespierre would help man get rid of the evil not recognized by man himself; he would restore man's pristine purity by the death penalty. By executing them en masse, this provincial lawyer would be doing his victims the valiant favor of restoring virtue to them and to society. Their execution would be less of a punishment, more of a gift—the gift of the original, inborn sinlessness returned to them as their heads rolled off the bloody block. This Republic of Virtue via Blood, ushered in by Robespierre, would surely be blessed by the Supreme Being, by Robespierre's own version of the Supreme Being, the new revolutionary deity whose worship Robespierre decreed as a new state religion, in whose honor he arranged his peculiar pageants of worship.

Because of this singular fanaticism, he has been called by some a mistaken idealist. In sober reality he was mistaken, but he was not an idealist. To apply this noun to him is an insult to idealism. Robespierre was a sick, demented man who caused wholesale deaths while emitting high-sounding but vapid phrases. His was not an ideology; it was a phraseology.

And yet, at first, many Frenchmen and Frenchwomen took his oratory for an ideology as well as for a viable revolutionary religion. Many willingly, even enthusiastically, followed him. As an illness often overcomes an individual by degrees, so the Grand Terror, charged up and maintained by this extraordinary zealot, grew in phases so insidious that even decent persons sometimes failed to notice they were being drawn in as his followers; too late did these followers realize that soon they were to join his victims on the tragic scaffold.

Their hysterical applause for the tyrant was replaced by sheer fright when, alas, nothing was left for them to do but mount the steps and submit to the blade.

V

Nor did the mechanics of the Great Terror emerge all at once. This was a piecemeal process, covering a span of months. Three institutions shared the awful task of revolutionary punishment: the Committee of General Security, the Committee of Public Safety, and the Revolutionary Tribunals, all three owing their existence and power to the Convention.

Of the two committees, that of General Security was formed by the Convention earlier than the other. Shortly, however, the Committee of Public Safety became the stronger; it was soon terror's main tool.

The Committee of Public Safety, established on April 6, 1793, had evolved out of yet another and milder committee, functioning since New Year's Day of 1793. Until April this original committee no more than marked time, agitating and threatening rather than being truly punitive. In the April reorganization the original committee was streamlined down to nine members, all of them rabid Jacobins. From April on, this Committee of Public Safety, with Robespierre as its head was the actual revolutionary government of France. Its might as the Republic's smiting ax grew with the fortunes of foreign war and domestic uprisings then churning against the Jacobins.

The Prussian, Austrian, and English armies, under indifferent leadership, had their moments of success but never pressed their advantage to anywhere near Paris, as under abler generalship they might well have done. Nonetheless, the first alarming news from those fronts, rather than the later Grand Terror, did serve to rally many Frenchmen to the cause of the Revolution. The main and bloodiest wave of the Terror rose after the French revolutionary armies had begun to prevail on the battlefields. But even after these foes had been pushed back and ceased being a peril, Robespierre and his Jacobins continued to use the threat of foreign invaders as the Terror's excuse. Of internal threats to the Revolution, in 1793-94, there was even a lesser specter, but this, too, was used by the terrorists in power, in perhaps an equal measure as was that of the external danger, to control the people and keep themselves in power.

After June 2, 1793, some of the outlawed yet surviving Girondins made their way to the provinces and raised banners of revolt, not so much in any general protest against terror or to attack Robespierre and his Jacobins as in sheer self-defense: for Robespierre had resolved to exterminate the Girondins as unruly eccentrics too intent on occasional tempering of the era's violence.

Robespierre's campaign against the Girondins was aided by Jean Paul Marat, who hated these would-be moderates of the Revolution with all his ill and bitter being. He demanded that the Girondins must go the way of the King. Instead, it was Marat's turn to go: on July 13, 1793, the eve of the anniversary of Bastille Day, the beautiful 24-year-old Norman noblewoman Charlotte Corday assassinated Marat by plunging a knife into his heart unerringly while he was sitting in his medicinal bath.

The sympathy that Charlotte Corday admitted for the Girondins gave Robespierre his chance to intensify his hunting and killing of them—no difficult task, as the Girondin resistance in the provinces was feeble and thus swiftly suppressed. Most of the escaped Girondins were eventually found in their hiding places or futile wanderings. Many of them were executed, while some cheated their pursuers through suicide. At the Great Terror's end very few would come out alive.

A sharper problem for Robespierre was the revolt in the province of Vendée, in western France on the Atlantic coast. Devoutly Catholic and loyally monarchist, the Vendéean peasants were shocked by the persecution of the clergy and particularly by the execution of Louis XVI. In the summer of 1793 they joined with the local nobles, priests, and artisans to rise and fight for King and Church. These insurgents were hardier than the Girondins, and for a time they were successful, controlling most of northwestern France (except the city of Nantes). But they were steadily losing, even as their rebellion sputtered on through mid-1794, until Robespierre's fall.

These attempts by the Girondins and the Vendéeans, as well as the threat of the foreign armies, gave the Committee of Public Safety the continued excuse for gathering more and more power. Month after month, from the spring of 1793 on, its machinery of terror expanded until the Convention's decree of December 4 summarized all the latest laws on the subject, making the government a monster of cruelty and blood.

And what of the Committee of General Security? It was established by the Convention on October 2, 1792. Originally consisting of 30 members, it was gradually reduced by the Convention in numerical strength until, in early September 1793, it had only nine members, all of them with deputy seats in the Convention. It tried, periodically but not too successfully, to compete with the Committee of Public Safety. Both committees were responsible to the Convention, but soon this was mostly on paper. In stark reality, Robespierre—not the Convention—controlled both, as well as other, lesser committees.

The Convention itself was fast becoming a nullity. Particularly after the Girondins' disaster, many remaining deputies played safe by staying away from the Convention sessions, and those who came cheered Robespierre and his men less out of agreement than out of fear. Others were frequently absent on missions to the provinces and the army. Thus the two committees, but especially that of Public Safety, ascended as the totally unhindered government itself.

At first the Committee of General Security was in charge of the police and prisons throughout the country. Its local *Comités de Surveillance* held the power of life and death; arrests were made on their warrants with neither constitutional nor other legal restraints. But none of this committee's members in Paris had the striking personalities and political renown of the committeemen of Public Safety.

These Public Safety leaders were the celebrated Carnot, Danton, Barère, Billaud-Varenne, and Jean Marie Collot d'Herbois. The yet more important men on the Committee comprised the so-called Triumvirate: Robespierre, Georges Couthon, and Louis de Saint Just. All the leaders, but especially those of the Triumvirate, had come to the top through their energy, cruelty, fanaticism—and their ready oratory, which mesmerized the Convention and the mobs alike.

Robespierre himself cast a spell that was uncanny. A mystic far more than a cool intellect, he quickly came to command so much power because the simple and the naïve below him beheld in him an almost supernatural quality, while the sophisticates around him soon recognized and feared the unbending despot who would brook no opposition. So all bent before him, genuflected, else death be their penalty.

On October 10, 1793, all authority in France was subordinated to Robespierre's main committee. The two bodies, those of Public Safety and of General Security, were in theory still equal and cooperative. Occasionally they did meet as one administrative unit. But as early as the spring of 1794 this harmony was no longer even a pretense. The Committee of Public Safety now had its own police. Its rise was clear and frightful—the historic precedent and pattern for the emergence and gradual strengthening of the terror machines in the various twentieth-century totalitarian states.

Debates in the Convention, which officially continued as the ostensible pinnacles of wisdom and justice in the Republic, became perfunctory. Only rarely did the Convention come to life—when Robespierre, Saint Just, or other celebrities reported for their committees. Nonetheless, the Convention lived on as a nominal symbol of the Revolution. And, in a larger sense, it permitted the new state's terrorism to appear entirely legal and just. Thus the modern totalitarian states use their puppet parliaments, sham courts, and formally existing ministries to be similar shields and screens for those nations' practitioners of terror—for their dictators and secret police.

As the French Revolution evolved, the nation's cabinet ministers were soon completely powerless—no more than obedient clerks. Finally, in the spring of 1794, April 1 proved a veritable fools' day for the Executive Council of Ministers when, on Lazare Carnot's initiative, all the ministries were abolished.

In the provinces, districts, and municipalities the Committee of Public Safety had its so-called "national agents" as permanent resident representatives, fully empowered to coerce and terrorize any and all "suspects." In addition, the Committee sent out special delegates on particular missions of violence. In this they were aided by volunteer gadflies from the local Jacobin clubs. Some such volunteers, drawn from among the superenthusiastic natives of departments (provinces) or districts or cities, in time became the almighty revolutionary masters of their areas. They—and the "national agents"—were sometimes accountable only nominally to the Committee of Public Safety in Paris; in actuality they functioned as self-willed murderers, plucking their victims with no warrants from the capital. Out of the institution of such proconsuls were to rise the future prefects of the 80-odd departments or provinces of France. Some of the Committee's bloodthirsty agents stayed on to become Napoleon's administrators in the country. Himself an offspring of the Revolution, Napoleon was practical enough not to abolish all its institutions and by-products. He would use that which he found useful. The Revolution had produced enough able executives even if, en route to their local or otherwise limited power, they had also proved ruthless executioners. Napoleon, whose hands were more than amply blood-spattered, kept these satraps in their posts despite their gory pasts. "Prefect" was his nicely sounding name for such an administrative official of the Empire, sufficiently camouflaging the man's prior revolutionary excesses.

In 1793-94 the provincial counterparts of the Paris Committee of Public Safety were known as "revolutionary committees." The same name was used for similar organs in the neighborhoods of Paris, for, propagandistically, the people had to be reminded again and again of their glorious Revolution. At times this soul-stirring appellation was abandoned, and, instead, local Committees of Public Safety were set up; then, once more, the Red-flag name "revolutionary committee" would return, either together with, or in place of, a local Public Safety body. In both cases the joyful duty of such a unit was to work with the "national agents" and the main Committee in finding and arresting all kinds of suspects, and handing them over for trial.

The trials (if they could be called that), customarily brief and resulting in death sentences, were the prerogative of the omnipresent Revolutionary Tribunals. The highest Tribunal, in Paris, was first established in March 1793 and assumed its final form the following October. So voluminous did its one-way traffic become that the earlier somewhat decorous trappings (the presence of defending lawyers, requirement of evidence, and the right to cross-examine) were soon discarded. Acquittal or any moderate sentence was extremely infrequent. The road from the Tribunal was usually to the guillotine. In Paris the most sinister figure at the Tribunal was its chief prosecutor, Antoine Quentin Fouquier-Tinville, more commonly known as "the archangel of death."

A native of Picardy, a petty ne'er-do-well tradesman under the monarchy, embittered by his failures, he was to find revenge in the Revolution. Some slight training as a lawyer helped him rise from minor legal office to that of the nation's principal nemesis. An early Jacobin, a friend and relative of Desmoulins, he was among the intense admirers of Robespierre and would zealously serve his idol and the Cause. Thomas Carlyle described him with the geologic term "plutonic," meaning stony-hearted, and also "ferret-visaged." Contemporaries spoke of Fouquier-Tinville as dressed always in black, his hair black, his eyebrows black and thick, his small, round eyes continually darting, his thin lips neatly shaven, his chin willful, and—an awesome contrast—his mouth loud with a constant stream of jokes and puns while he prosecuted his cases, "wallowing in blood," as the many who hated him whispered in fear.

He sent to the guillotine not only Queen Marie Antoinette but also such revolutionaries fallen from grace as the Girondins and the Cordeliers, including (unwaveringly) his kinsman Desmoulins. His manner of questioning at trials was brutal; he offended female honor as he hammered at the captive women brought into his presence; he denigrated the republican pride of the revolutionaries under judgment. He increased the batches of defendants facing the Tribunal until there would be 150 of such unfortunates at a time. His eventual boast was that all told he prosecuted more than 2,400 "counterrevolutionaries," sending to the guillotine an overwhelming majority of them.

Nor must we forget yet another historic personage of the epoch: Dr. Joseph Guillotin, the public-spirited physician who contributed to the Revolution his improvement of an old head-chopping knife-apparatus. The naïve medico fancied himself a true humanitarian when he provided that sharp blade; he sincerely thought he was *helping* the doomed in making their deaths so quick and relatively less painful. Yet, in historical fact, the deadly machine had been known in earlier versions in the Germanies and elsewhere in Europe, and Dr. Guillotin's variant was but a slight advance in efficiency.

The doctor had been elected to the Constituent Assembly in 1789, and he used his legislative seat to laud the merciful swift-killing quality of his contraption to his fellow deputies who, at one point of his speech-making, burst out in uproarious laughter when they realized it was his own invention he was praising. Little did many of them dream how close their own acquaintance with the fearsome blade would be!

First tried out in 1792, the guillotine was to gain worldwide fame as the most chilling memory of the French Revolution. For generations to come it would be a dreaded symbol. But in our own 1970s a weird North American counterculture entertainer, Vincent Damon Furnier, better known as "Alice Cooper," drew a mindless laugh out of his audiences by including a guillotine in his stage show: he would stick his repugnantly untidy head into Dr. Guillotin's machine, the stage crew substituting a fake head before the blade would fall. Thus old terror thrilled the mob of our violence-filled times. Fun, not fright, was the new response.

5

The Guillotine Athirst

In any land and at any time an entire nation may watch violence with equanimity and even enjoyment, provided that coercion and murder are remote enough in time or place (or both)—when they do not intrude upon or threaten the headline readers and television viewers. But when terror strikes near, when it ceases being a spectacle, it is a vastly different matter—it becomes a fearsome peril. A revolution as such may be popular with the majority. But when terror is the main feature, never—not when it hits close to home.

The French Revolution and its Great Terror is a prime example. The fall of the old regime was met with general acceptance and even cheers. The roll of the heads, not so. The nineteenth-century historian Hippolyte Taine estimated that, as the bloody wars rose, the total number of terrorists did not exceed 300,000. Crane Brinton increases this number by another 200,000 of those who apparently sympathized with, and actively supported, the Great Terror: he writes that in 1794 the aggregate membership of the "popular societies" (that is, the Jacobin clubs) throughout France was 500,000—out of the total adult male population of eight million.

Much of this violent activism was concentrated in Paris. Many provincial cities and towns, and particularly villages, lacked any sizable terrorist contingents. In many a locality the enthusiasm for arrests and executions had to be generated and kept up by a handful—sometimes only five or six—of Parisians sweeping in on missions from the capital and ordering the locals to step up the terror.

These emissaries had the right, in the name of the Convention and Robespierre's Committee of Public Safety, to dispense with any trial whatever for certain categories of suspects. One revolutionary general described in a report to the Convention his method of dealing with the émigrés snared by his men: "No court sentence is needed. My saber and my pistols do their job.'' The Convention greeted this with thunderous and repeated applause.

At Lyons, an emissary ordered a tribunal to arrest, interrogate, and try a youth. As the official sat at his luxurious dinner, the tribunal's judge came in to report that the youth had been found innocent. Between his forkfuls the emissary shouted: "I have already told you to shoot this man this very day! Go!" The youth was shot.

The traveling satraps were informed by Robespierre, and some apparently even believed, that there was no such thing as an excess of revolutionary power in the service of the people's weal. But as they journeyed, most of them robbed people of their food, of the best of wines, of furniture and clothes. Little of this was handed over to the needy—most was kept for the traveling officials and their aides (and the women with them), who, as they went, sowed death and ruin. Those of the minor officials and other terrorists who survived the Revolution to become servitors of Napoleon and, still later, even of the restored Bourbons, often came into the nineteenth century with fortunes gathered for themselves and their progeny during the Reign of Terror.

Some were dizzy with their new power. One functionary, on entering a theater and seeing that the women in the front section did not rise before him, actually went mad. Running up and down the aisles with his bared and swinging saber, he cursed the audience for its lack of respect for him, the people's representative.

Taine emphasized that among these terrorists were individuals embittered by life under the old regime and just plain and fancy psychopaths now winning a release from their hurt and passion: the criminals and the demented of all kinds and levels, particularly those bursting forth from the lower classes; subordinates full of envy and vengeance; petty tradesmen burdened with failure and debt; idle and drunken workers and artisans; tavern and café habitués never partial to humdrum toil; tramps of the countryside and the city; prostitutes cheap and costly—all who could aptly be defined as antisocial parasites now having their day and especially their night of orgies, robberies, and death sentences.

And over and above such flotsam and jetsam stood the shrewd, cool opportunists of that tragic era's terroristic personnel, eager and able to grasp power and possessions through their fellow humans' misery and death. They took care to echo Robespierre as they mouthed their pious generalities about the people's cause, always keeping their eye on their own personal advantage.

But there was also a small minority of those who truly, fanatically believed they must kill for the greater good and ultimate salvation of all Frenchmen and Frenchwomen. Here were the heirs of the Spanish Inquisitors who were happy that they were saving the sinners' souls as they burned their living, screaming bodies. Here were the predecessors of the socialist Narodniki and of the Marxist-Leninist urban guerrillas of later centuries with their utter certainty that murder is a prerequisite for paradise on earth.

II

What of the victims—their numbers, their backgrounds?

It is calculated that, on the eve of Robespierre's fall, the "suspects" in the nation's prisons were nearly 400,000 men, women, and even children. For most of them the Ninth of Thermidor came none too soon.

The exact total of the Terror's victims remains unknown. It is nevertheless estimated that in Paris alone, in just the two final months of the Great Terror, 2,663 men and women were guillotined, and that in the entire period of 1793-94 the lists of the victims of 178 tribunals reached nearly 17,000. The modern reader must smile wryly at this pale shadow of the millions killed on the orders of Lenin, Stalin, Hitler, Mao and other dictators and tyrants of the enlightened twentieth century, not to count the millions more surviving for years in this era's totalitarian prisons and slave camps.

But the 17,000 of Robespierre's victims were by far not all the toll. Many more thousands were slain outside the curt procedures of the tribunals; many died by saber, shot, or noose. At Nantes, the Jacobin deputy Carrier crammed his victims into old ships, which were then towed into the middle of the Loire and sunk with their human cargo. Others perished of disease and malnutrition in the jails. At Nantes, of the 13,000 prisoners, 3,000 died of typhus and hunger.

The list of the most illustrious lives snuffed out by the revolutionaries, begun with King Louis XVI on January 21, 1793, was continued by his widow, Queen Marie Antoinette, who knelt to the blade with fortitude and dignity on October 16. In between came the series of executions spurred by the stabbing to death of Marat on the evening of July 13. The time's nonpolitical sadists showed their kinship with the political terrorists when Count (better known as Marquis) Donatien Alphonse François de Sade delivered his most celebrated public oration as a funeral eulogy of Marat, of him who had once demanded no less than 270,000 counterrevolutionary heads.

Despite the revolutionaries' profession of love for their fellow

humans, especially for their fellow revolutionaries, it is the basic hatred and fear inherent in revolutions that makes their bloody practitioners inevitably turn on one another.

That summer of 1793 the Revolution began to devour its own children—first, the Girondins. We have seen how those of them who had
escaped the June imprisonment were now being hunted in the streets
and the countryside. On October 31, of the Girondins in jails since
June, 21 were carried off to the guillotine. Through the winter of 1793-
94 the Cordeliers were added to Robespierre's proscription ledgers.
The main target was Jacques René Hébert, who led the extremist
Cordeliers after Marat's death. This particular attack by Robespierre
was welcomed by the middle classes of France who were apprehensive
of the violent anti-property views and actions of Hébert and his
followers. It was true that Hébert, like Robespierre, was all for terror
against nonrevolutionaries, yet his domination of the Paris Commune
threatened Robespierre's personal power. And so a charge of conspiracy was concocted against these Cordeliers, and on March 24,
1794, Hébert and his entire group were guillotined.

Next, Robespierre struck at the less extreme of the Cordeliers—at
such of his erstwhile allies as Danton and Desmoulins. These two
luminaries of the Revolution saw their influence wane when that skillful intriguer, Billaud-Varenne, turned against them, especially against
Danton. It was Billaud-Varenne who advised Robespierre to finish off
Danton. A colorful yet cruel figure, Billaud-Varenne was born near
Port-au-Prince in Haiti, a lawyer's son and himself a lawyer as well as a
teacher and pamphleteer, a rabid revolutionary in spite of his Jesuit
schooling. In September 1792, he harangued the mob amid the corpses
of the Massacres: "Brave citizens, you are extirpating the enemies of
liberty: you are at your duty!" He promised the murderers monetary
rewards from the "grateful Commune and country." He exhorted:
"Continue your work!" On the twenty-second of that September it
was on his motion in the Convention that the First Republic was proclaimed. In August 1793, he led the mass arrests at Dunkerque and
Calais. In early 1794, he kept telling Robespierre that Danton was too
right-wing for the Jacobins and that Danton, and Desmoulins with him,
must die.

At last, on April 4, 1794, Danton and Desmoulins, with 13 of their
associates, were carted off to the guillotine. Desmoulins died in cowardly fear, but among the braver Danton's last words was his calm
philosophizing: "Robespierre will follow me; he is dragged down by
me. Ah, better be a poor fisherman than meddle with the government
of men!" Four months later the prophecy came true, on that stifling
July-Thermidor day. Some historians feel that had Danton been spared

and continued in power, he might have saved Robespierre on the Ninth.

Antoine Laurent Lavoisier, the great chemist, then only 51 (what marvelous discoveries could yet have been given by him to mankind!), was guillotined on May 8, 1794. The president of the tribunal that condemned him was said to have rejected a petition for mercy with these words: "The Republic has no need for scientists."

Perhaps the revolutionary tribunal mistook science, this aristocracy of man's mind, for the aristocracy of inheritance, of socio-political power—and all aristocrats of the *ancien régime* were supposed to be among the prime targets of the Great Terror. But did those aristocrats of inheritance pay the heaviest penalty? Here is the actual record:

Through the entire duration of the Great Terror, a total of 1,158 aristocrats perished. This was but a little more than one-quarter of one percent of the numerical strength of the era's French nobility, which then counted some 400,000 men, women, and children. Unlike the subsequent practice of the Lenin-Stalin decades in Russia, when social origin was sufficient reason for upper- and middle-class individuals to be jailed and even shot, Robespierre's terror did not doom the French nobility solely by virtue of blue blood. In a most haphazard way, men and women of all classes were guillotined or otherwise slain not only on charges of wartime treason or other antistate activities, be such charges true or not, but often because of the sheer personal greed or grudge of the executioners.

Indeed, when later historians of France examined the lists of 12,000 guillotined men and women whose social status could be ascertained, it was discovered that 7,545 of these were peasants, workers, artisans, lowly soldiers, valets, domestics, seamstresses, and craftsmen's wives and daughters. They were not royalists or even Girondins or Cordeliers, surely not all or most of them. But any transgression of the Revolution's laws of economic austerity was considered treason. And so a Parisian was guillotined because he had in his possession several small loaves of bread baked for him on a doctor's prescription. The 17-year-old daughter of a painter was executed after she was found to have some 5,000 candles given to her by former palace officials in settlement of her father's old bill for services.

Entire families—grandparents, great-grandparents, children—were sometimes jailed along with the accused fathers or mothers. The prison at Arras held, among others, a coal merchant with his wife and seven children, ages 7 to 17; a noblewoman with her nine children; and six children with neither fathers nor mothers.

When an emissary was asked what to do with the children of some guillotined Vendéeans, he barked out: "Guillotine! Guillotine them!"

And then personally watched as boys of 13 and 14 were placed under the knife, which, because the bodies were so small, smashed their skulls instead of chopping off their heads at the neck.

Terror expanded and lasted, for one reason among others, as Mark Aldanov was to observe, because "not all as yet had gotten rich through the Revolution—not everything was as yet robbed, not all the land taken away from the landlords had yet passed over to the new owners, and not to everyone the Revolution had become sufficiently repugnant."[1]

III

Why and how did the Great Terror come to its end? Why and how did Robespierre reach his?

The Ninth of Thermidor was brought about by several combinations of Robespierre's adversaries; the most significant of them came from the terrorists' own midst. The less fanatical of these perceived increasingly that sooner or later their own end would come; that their names might in fact be on Robespierre's very next proscription list. More pragmatic than others around the dictator, they were far less plagued by the blinding curse of this quasi-religious self-intoxication with Terror the Great and the Good.

Such men as Bertrand Barère and Joseph Fouché, although high-ranking members of the almighty Committee of Public Safety, feared for their own safety when, in that decisive summer of 1794, they formed a conspiracy against the tyrant.

Barère, from a family of middle-class lawyers and clergymen, was himself a lawyer and a magistrate under the monarchy. Coming to Paris from Toulouse as a member of the Estates-General, he early joined the Jacobins. In the Convention and on the Committee of Public Safety he declared himself an adherent of Robespierre, calling for terror as "the order of the day," and urging the King's execution. His demands also included the expulsion of all Bourbon princes from France, the confiscation of the émigrés' estates, and the destruction of sacred tombs.

Fouché, born near Nantes, was originally a schoolmaster trained by the Oratorians, a French religious order whose monks believed in rationalistic theories of education. In the Convention since 1792, he was distrusted by everyone, yet in his uncommon shrewdness he outsmarted all, mainly because very early he developed his own, private network of spies.

These two men, just as the other Public Safety committeemen, had been guilty of mass murders. Now they would add Robespierre's blood to their record. Now, before Robespierre could kill them, they would kill him.

Their timing was right. Joining them were the men of the Committee of General Security, when they realized that Robespierre had just established a special secret police bureau, answerable to him alone, the main function of which was to hem in their own Committee's police.

As he faced his new and sudden enemies, for once Robespierre appeared hesitant. He trusted the power of his vague oratory, of his very presence in the depleted and frightened Convention. But—the surprise of it—the Convention now came to life and displayed courage, joining with his foes.

Far too long had its remaining members trembled, waiting for their names to be called in the Terror's awful lottery. In fact, Collot d'Herbois, the president of the Convention, now for the first time used his authority against Robespierre. This former actor, who together with Fouché had in the fall of 1793 organized the bloodbath to drown the anti-Jacobin rebellion at Lyons, when that city was partly destroyed and hundreds of its people were put to death, and who in the spring of 1794 had helped Billaud-Varenne and Robespierre destroy Danton and Desmoulins, now, in these crucial hours of July-Thermidor, linked hands with the new conspirators. As the Convention's president, Collot d'Herbois guided the proceedings of its historic session like a skilled master, checkmating and thwarting Robespierre and his handful of diehards at every move.

In despair Robespierre hoped for the armed rally of a Parisian mob, particularly workers who had in the past seemed to cheer him and his Terror. But in this time of need only a few came forth. Perhaps the heavy rain discouraged them. More likely, the workers—like so many other Parisians—were too hungry, too dispirited, too mindful of their own victims fallen to Robespierre's guillotine. Some, from the capital's poorer sections, for a while filled the square before the Hôtel de Ville, in which the last act of the drama was being played out. But they did nothing, if only because there was no one even to try to lead them against Robespierre's enemies.

Fortunately for the coup, Paul Barras, a terrorist who knew military art, threw in his lot with the plotters. A viscount from Provençal, he had as an officer of the King fought in India against the British, and had later quarreled with the royal minister of the navy over best ways of colonial administration. In the great French upheaval, his revolutionary credentials included an early Jacobin membership, a vote in the Convention for the King's execution, and leading the suppression of an anti-Jacobin revolt at Toulon. Now, in July 1794, joining the foes of Robespierre, he proved his worth. On the momentous Ninth of Thermi-

dor, charged with the defense of the Convention against possible rescuers of Robespierre, he acted with vigor and dispatch, organizing the
supporters of conspiracy.

Other able terrorists who turned against their chief were Carnot and
Billaud-Varenne. Thus the curtain crashed down: the fallen tyrant was
wounded in the jaw (in a rumored attempt at suicide, though possibly
shot by one of the attackers in the scuffle), and put under arrest.

There was no trial either for Robespierre or for the score of his
diehards. They were simply outlawed, and were brought to the Tribunal only to have their identities confirmed. The "archangel of death,"
Antoine Quentin Fouquier-Tinville, as always black-clad but now
deathly pale (he was sensing his own imminent doom), merely nodded.
On the Tenth of Thermidor—July 28—Maximilien Robespierre was
guillotined.

With him were executed 21 of his faithful. Among them were his
brother Augustin Robespierre (with a broken thigh, suffered in the last
fight when he had tried to escape by jumping from a window); Georges
Couthon (who, in that same fight, had been thrown down a staircase
and thus immobilized); Louis de Saint Just (who had quietly surrendered at the Hôtel de Ville). In the next two days, the major part of
the membership of the Paris Commune was brought to the blade.

Prisoners of Robespierre—if found still alive—were being released,
some swiftly, others slowly. At that, some missed deliverance by only
a few days. Thus, on the fifth of Thermidor, a mere four days before
the Terror ended, Alexandre de Beauharnais was guillotined. However, his young widow Josephine, then 31, was spared through that
brief, fateful span, and emerged after the Ninth from the death cells.
Later she was to marry Napoleon and be crowned Empress of the
French.

Yet, for some of her less lucky fellow prisoners, the Terror did not
stop even with the downfall of Robespierre. In the jubilant confusion
no one gave the necessary orders to free the last of his victims awaiting
execution, to go counter to Fouquier-Tinville, who refused to halt the
guillotining but instead sent this word to the chief ax-wielder; "Do
your duty!" And so, on the day of the Ninth, even after the good news
of the dictator's fall spread all over Paris, the prison guards on their
appointed rounds were busily shearing the hair of the condemned and
otherwise preparing them for the scaffold. In the late afternoon of that
day, 42 persons were guillotined—the Great Terror's "last heads rolled
down," as the French historian Louis Madelin has written, "the heads
of little people, almost all of them small shopkeepers, and also the head
of a poor woman, a widow."

Little notice, however, was taken of such sad mishaps. The main news was the tyrant's end, the Great Terror's termination. And whether or not the Thermidor conspirators wished it, they had in fact written a finale to the Red Terror as a whole. Relief and rejoicing rose in great surges in Paris and the rest of the nation as well as all over Europe.

And now a new terror soon boiled up: the White Terror, to punish Robespierre's still-surviving aides. Somehow this did not frighten the French people as a whole, but only those smaller numbers who had ties with the Red terrorists now being rounded up and executed.

It was generally felt that, unlike Robespierre's victims, these new condemned were guilty and thus deserving of their fate—which was not necessarily true in every case. Nor were they excessively numerous. In truth, some of the Red terrorists were spared and even honored because they had had a part in Robespierre's downfall. They were now entitled not only to their lives and freedom but also to new power and wealth.

With much respect they were called Thermidorians, after that historic month of the revolutionary calendar. Beginning with 1795, these Thermidorians were also known as the men of the Directory—the new French government established in 1795 in the wake of the receding Revolution. Two new legislative chambers elected five members of the Directory to be the executive branch of the post-Terror power in the nation. Very soon inflation, corruption, and inefficiency were the Directory's sorry record. It lasted four short years. In November 1799, two of the directors helped Napoleon overthrow the Directory, making him First Consul.

In those post-Robespierre times, Joseph Fouché rose to unprecedented heights—first under the Directory, then with Napoleon, who in 1809 made him Duke of Otranto, and finally—until his death in 1820—as the restored Bourbons' favorite. This Fouché, this "butcher of Lyons," the ruthless chief of the police under several French regimes, is often called the father of the modern police state. To him the future Berias and Himmlers owed their debt.

Paul Barras came forth as a principal member of the Directory. Ever the military man, he crushed a revolt of the Parisian populace in 1794-95; always a suave charmer, this former nobleman enjoyed the favors of Josephine de Beauharnais before turning her over to her future husband Napoleon. Though in 1799 he helped Napoleon to power, he did not have Napoleon's entire trust and did not derive sufficient advantages from his aid to the Corsican. Still, thoroughly immoral and corrupt, Barras the whilom terrorist lived on until 1829, dying at the ripe and safe age of 74.

From 1795 to 1799 Lazare Carnot, the supreme molder of the French revolutionary armies, also flourished as a member of the Directory, and later served under Napoleon. Although exiled after the Bourbon Restoration in 1815, he lived eight more years following this misfortune, at last dying in 1823 at 70.

In contrast, others of the surviving Jacobins were not permitted too long a respite and were punished soon after the Ninth of Thermidor notwithstanding their role as the smiters of Robespierre. Their merit as the terminators of the Great Terror granted them but very short leases on life. The uprisings of hungry people in the spring and autumn of 1795, while almost at once suppressed by the Directory, nevertheless gave the newly invigorated Convention an excuse to finish off a number of the old terrorists. Among others, Collot d'Herbois and Billaud-Varenne were transported to Guiana in 1795. On May 7 of that year the "archangel of death," Fouquier-Tinville, was guillotined. Of the deportees, Collot d'Herbois was one of the first to die—in Guiana in 1796.

Three years later Napoleon, following his assumption of power on November 9, 1799, offered pardon to Billaud-Varenne, but the old revolutionist would take no risks. Declining the offer, he remained at Cayenne, marrying a black woman and busying himself on his small tropical estate. In 1816 he traveled to New York, then settled in Haiti, where he died in 1819.

Barère, proscribed by his fellow Thermidorians in April 1795, escaped from his prison the next winter and for five years hid out in Bordeaux. Later he was a secret agent for Napoleon. He wrote his memoirs and, destitute, was compelled to sell the last of his few belongings. The Restoration made him an exile at Brussels, for he was remembered as a regicide who had voted for the King's execution, but in 1830 he returned to France, where he died in 1841 at 86.

The year 1795 marked the fullest sweep of the first White Terror. While many of the former associates of Robespierre were exiled, others were put to death by the new courts' sentences, and still others were dragged out of the prisons (particularly in the provinces) and slain by mobs, bringing back the memory of the September Massacres of 1792. Some of the doomed tried to cheat the blade, if not the mob. As six of the court-condemned Red terrorists awaited their execution, they made a suicide pact. Three succeeded; the other three failed. With their self-inflicted wounds, the second three were carried to the guillotine, their own old weapon.

A yet more determined campaign of the White Terror had to wait until 1815-16 and the Bourbon Restoration. This was far more of a spontaneous outburst on the part of the royalists than any policy of the government itself, which in fact was too weak to restrain the avengers. The royalists would turn the wheel of history back to pre-1789 times, to what seemed to them a halcyon era of law and order; they would be more Bourbonists than the Bourbons themselves. Napoleon was to be cursed no less than Robespierre. In the White Terror of 1815-16, vengeance was inflicted on the Bonapartists no less than on those still desiring a republic. For full measure, Protestants were also included among the victims—as scapegoats, as a symbol of those French who had rejected the Church, which was now to be brought back to its old power and glory.

Particularly in Marseilles and other southern cities, hundreds were killed by the ugly mobs, in many cases instigated by the returning émigré nobles and the unforgiving clergy. Fouché, now minister of the police to King Louis XVIII, drew up proscription lists of his old fellow revolutionists and Bonapartists, and these were the men found guilty by the royal judges. By such sentences Lazare Carnot was exiled and Marshal Michel Ney (of Napoleonic wars' fame) was shot, both in 1815. Another marshal and two generals were murdered by mobs. As if to mock any future Marxist explanations of history as a battle of the lower classes against the upper, one of the most vicious royalist mobs—that in the city of Nimes, where it held sway for several terrible weeks—was headed by a worker.

If any overall socio-political lesson can be discerned in the Great Terror and its White aftermath, it is this:

Perhaps no nation is ever guaranteed against such inhuman horrors, and indeed, in Crane Brinton's words, on many a historical occasion "what began as a movement of liberation could easily end as terrorist autocracy"—could end and, in fact, did end as such.

And when not prevented or halted in time, terror as a policy of revolutionaries either striving for power or finally achieving it can erode the people's will and the opportunity for true democracy.

Terror does not result in equality, except in the matter of a heightened chance of death for many. It thoroughly destroys man's liberty and it annihilates his fraternity.

The terror of the French experience seemed to prove to the demos that it—the people—could not rule through its representatives, that first an oligarchy and then a sole despot would arise through this very terror. Terror frightened and subdued the French people. It accustomed them for decades to a single tyrannical will: it made possible, almost inevitable, the appearance of—and submission to—Bonaparte and later the returning Bourbons and, yet later, Napoleon III.

A republic of any democratic substance could not prevail even when, briefly, it did take shape. Thus the Second Republic lived but four short and ineffective years, from 1848 to 1852. The memory of the First Republic with its Great Terror was too vivid, too chilling. The French needed time to realize that a republic did not have to be bloody. For its more peaceful and longer-lasting Third Republic, the nation had to wait until 1871.

And whatever deeply liberating or reforming effects were bequeathed by the French Revolution, its Great Terror surely was not responsible for any such profound beneficence.

Still, to the violent revolutionaries of the nineteenth and twentieth centuries the French Terror held lessons quite different from any sobering influences—wrong lessons. Marx, Bakunin, Lenin, and a long procession of their varied followers studied Robespierre's record with passionate devotion and worshipful approval. To the anarchists of the last century and to the guerrillas, commandos, and totalitarians of our age Robespierre showed the only true way. The problem for today's terrorists is only where and how to improve upon Robespierre's trail-blazing, so that each new Great Terror rages longer than did the historic French experiment in those two brief years.

6

In the Name of Marx

Every bloody inch of Robespierre's short but significant path in history was closely and eagerly studied by Marx and Lenin. Yet, our own current crop of terrorists take not Robespierre but Marx and Lenin as their infallible mentors. Even if their original debt is to the Great Terrorist of France, they proudly call themselves not Robespierrists, but Marxist-Leninists.

When, on May 15, 1974, three Arab guerrillas of Nayef Hawatmeh's organization, centered in Beirut, attacked the Maalot school in Israel, causing the deaths of more than a score of teen-agers and several adults, including themselves, they did this in the name of Marxism-Leninism.

One month earlier, on April 11, three suicide raiders from Ahmed Jebreel's Arab "General Command" had perished in the Israeli town of Qiryat Shemona after killing 18 men, women, and children. These terrorists, too, and their Captain Jebreel, in the safety of Beirut, proclaimed their motive as the very same Marxism-Leninism.

Still earlier, in the two massacres of 1972, at the Lydda airport in May and at the Olympic Games in Munich in September, George Habash's Popular Front men and Yasir Arafat's Black September group announced the glory of Marx and Lenin as they murdered.

In September 1970, as the Arab fedayeen hijacked and dynamited three West European and American airplanes, they swore by the wise beards of Marx and Lenin. In Jordan, while foreign newsmen were interviewing the leaders of the Arab guerrillas who were detaining plane passengers as hostages, Lenin's portrait stared at the journalists from the wall of the commando information center at Amman. A slogan nearby read in its clumsy English: "Marxist-Leninist ideas—and practice accordingly!" In the ensuing war between King Hussein's army and the Palestinian commandos, the terrorists holding the North Jordan city of Irbid declared that the form of their city government was "Soviet," in the best tradition of Leninism as derived from Marxism.

In North America, the 18-year-old David Sylvan Fine, one of the four fugitives accused of the bombing at the University of Wisconsin in Madison in August 1970 that killed a peaceful researcher at his desk, was said by a former classmate to be "capable of quoting Marx or Lenin to support any hypothesis." As the Weathermen, Black Panther, and Symbionese terrorists insisted that they were the devotees of Karl Marx and Vladimir Lenin, so did the Quebec separatists assert that they kidnapped and slayed under the same Marxist banner.

In Latin America, the Tupamaros and other urban and rural guerrillas stressed their fealty to Marx and Lenin. So did the Turkish, Japanese, and West German terrorists, and even in North Ireland the most militant of the Catholic rebels said that *Das Kapital* was the ultimate answer.

But how much of this violent inspiration does in fact spring from the words and deeds of Marx and Lenin?

II

Let us start with Marx. Some surprises await us here. In 1974, Dr. Lawrence Z. Freedman, the American professor of psychiatry specializing in causes of terror as a polistaraxic crime, stated categorically: "Historically, Marx and Engels were very much against terror. They saw it as a form of revolutionary suicide."[1]

However, just as the modern guerrillas and commandos are not exactly right in sanctifying their murders and kidnappings with the name of Marx, so does the American professor err in absolving both Marx and Engels as terror's spiritual fathers. The actual allotment of such responsibility is more complex:

Today's terrorists are of course correct in their insistence on Marxism as their root, insofar as the general essence of their claimed ideology is concerned. As Marx did in his writings and speeches, so they in their programs and practice stand for a total cataclysmic end to capitalism.

The major difference between their position and that of Marx is, however, that while Marx predicted and threatened terror, it was seldom that he prescribed its use exactly or consistently. He did write and speak freely about the necessity of terror during two phases of his activities: one, early in his preachment, during the German and other European revolutions and unrest of 1848-50; the other, late in his life, at the time of the Paris Commune uprising. But for most of his long years he was rather guarded on the subject. In no other than these two periods do we find in his texts many such outright calls to assassination and other terror as those that shrill at us from the pages of the anarchists, of the Narodniki, of the Socialist Revolutionaries, of the post-1917 Communists, and of the yet later terrorists the world over.

Nor was Hannah Arendt quite precise in asserting that "Marx was aware of the role of violence in history, but this role was to him secondary; not violence but the contradictions inherent in the old society brought about its end."[2] In fact Marx did believe in terror, its inevitability and unavoidability as a prime—not secondary—factor in the revolution to come, but more often than not this was a muted belief. Except for his famed *Circular* of March 1850, which he himself repudiated a mere six months later but which was rescued from oblivion and used triumphantly by Lenin in the next century, Marx was either reticent or vague on the all-important question of exactly how the dispossessed of the earth were to arrive at power. Uprisings, guerrilla campaigns urban or rural, all that which is so much on the agenda of modern revolutionaries, were not spelled out by Marx. But they must have been very much on his mind, and did indeed surface turbulently, even if not in great detail, in 1848-50 and 1871, when he used history as an example for his time.

In no other than these instances does terror figure much in his collected works. One explanation for this reluctance or omission is that in the first six decades of the nineteenth century, certainly up to the Paris Commune of 1871, "terror" was not a nice word. The memory of Robespierre's reign of the guillotine was ugly and revolting rather than nobly revolutionary. Professor Oscar J. Hammen, the noted biographer of Marx and Engels in their early phases, remarks in a letter to me:

> Marx, as a master of tactics, did not want to scare the public too much. You have to bear in mind that the "terror of the terror," as Benedetto Croce called it, dominated men's minds in that age. People did not want a repetition of anything like the French terror of 1793-95. They recoiled from it. This fear was most pronounced among the Germans in 1848-49, and accounts to a considerable degree for the failure by the Germans to resort to more extreme measures, which would have perhaps assured a greater degree of revolutionary success.[3]

Yet, as he endorsed various episodes of terrorism in history, it seemed at times as if Marx would disregard this fear. Such endorsements were more than academic statements, revealing that occasionally he did not worry overmuch about losing followers through his praise of Robespierre. Part of the reason is that the fear of terror, although it did exist, was not all that pervasive in Europe.

Terror was not completely avoided by the Red side in the early nineteenth century, either before or after the White Terror of 1815-16, that Bourbon madness of vengeance for the hurts and losses sustained during the Revolution. Indeed, terror was the means used by the irregu-lar, ragged, volunteer forces of the Spaniards against the French in-vaders, the lower-class Spanish guerrillas who sapped Napoleon's strength even prior to his grandiose failure at Europe's other end, at Moscow in 1812. The very word *guerrilla*, or "little warfare," came from the Spain of that heroic period from 1808 on. Terrorist tactics were also among the methods employed successfully in the 1820s by the Carbonari ("charcoal burners"—from their disguise in hideouts in groves and fields), the secret revolutionary societies of Italians against their own lords as well as against their Austrian masters. (The guer-rillas and the Carbonari rebels rose up against their foreign usurpers more often than against the native Establishments of Spain and Italy.)

Between the time of the Carbonari and the era of Marx—about a quarter of a century—there lived any number of radical prophets and activists, but none was to reap Marx's fame or gather his followers. Born in Germany in 1818, two decades later Marx was ready to an-nounce that only his brand of socialist thought was truly scientific and thus destined inexorably to succeed, ushering in a true millenium on earth. His chief idea was that human progress came not out of any Judeo-Christian harmony and love, but out of the brutal struggle and hatred that are always with us. In this belief in hatred lay his oblique prophecy of terror.

If at times this prophecy was more than oblique or implied, Marx, during the two periods of his fierce militancy, not only praised some past terrors, particularly that of Robespierre and his entourage. He also deplored the absence of terroristic habits among his own radical contemporaries in the German uprisings of 1848 and the Paris Com-mune of 1871, pointing out that this timidity was one of the main reasons for the fiasco of those revolts.

In 1848-50 he castigated the "humanity of weakness" of the Ger-man insurgence of February and March 1848. The German and other West European upheavals of the time, he wrote, should have taken the decisive course of the English and French revolutions of 1648 and 1789. Those two revolutions were not narrowly English or French, he said; they set valid lines for all of Europe, whose masses should emu-late those predecessors by taking over power violently.

Marx declared that he regretted the lack of a German with the determination and fortitude of Cromwell, a German who would order the feeble Frankfurt Parliament to disperse. In 1848, in his article "The Bourgeoisie and the Revolution" in the *Neue Rheinische Zeitung*, he wrote approvingly of the French proletariat of 1793-94 and the Great Terror as a wonderfully good "plebeian way of smashing the enemies of the bourgeoisie—doing away with absolutism, feudalism, and philistinism," thus helping the temporarily positive force of the bourgeoisie to clear the ground for the future victory of the proletariat.

He raged at the bloodbath let loose in Paris in June of 1848 by General Louis Eugène Cavaignac, whose soldiers killed many workers in street battles, executed several hundred more on the Champs de Mars, and transported thousands more to the suffocating penal colonies overseas. Marx threatened revenge of a Red counterterror.

One of his most drastic and direct preachments of Red terrorism appeared in the *Neue Rheinische Zeitung* of November 5, 1848, when he wrote, underlining his key words: "There is only one way to *shorten* the murderous death agonies of the old society, only one way to shorten the bloody birth pangs of the new society . . . only one *means*—revolutionary terrorism." Desperately Marx hoped for better luck in the new year, boldly predicting in the *Neue Rheinische Zeitung* of January 1, 1849: "*Revolutionary upheaval of the French working class, World War*—that is the table of contents of the year 1849."[4]

In his *Circular* to Europe's workers, issued by him in London in March 1850, Marx gave the only explicit instructions on insurrection he ever authored. In this text he urged the workers to arm themselves, ostensibly to help the liberals in their struggle against the old order—but to keep the weapons even after that order's fall, so as to turn them against those liberal allies and other bourgeois and win the morrow for the workers' revolution. But in September 1850 he retreated from that position paper—a position paper that became the precise scenario for Lenin to put into effect so decisively in 1917.

For two ensuing decades, from the fall of 1850 to the spring of 1871, Marx's hopes were low and his appeals more academic than revolutionary. But with the establishment of the Paris Commune in March 1871, he once again saw flames and forecast victory amid Red terror. After the Commune's fall in May, from his London study he sorrowfully praised the Communard leadership for its decree of April 7, "ordering reprisals and declaring it to be its duty 'to protect Paris against the cannibal exploits of the Versailles banditti, and to demand an eye for an eye, a tooth for a tooth.' " His sorrow stemmed from the fact that the Commune leaders did not live up to their threat of terror. Adolphe Thiers, heading at Versailles the effort of suppressing the Commune, "did not stop the barbarous treatment of prisoners," yet, noted Marx, "the shooting of prisoners was suspended for a time" by Thiers because of the Commune's threat. But when Thiers and his generals realized "that the communal decree of reprisals was but an empty threat, the wholesale shooting of Communist prisoners resumed and [was] carried on uninterruptedly to the end." This was the death of the Commune. Terror triumphed. But alas for Marx, it was White terror, not Red.

III

Yet the Commune's leaders were not the only ones to hold back. Time and again, Marx also restrained himself on this problem of terror. Despite his various boasts that he would scorn to hide his views out of tactical considerations, he hedged on certain subjects. Basically, both Marx and his faithful Engels had ambivalent attitudes toward terror. As human beings they did not think terror as desirable. But both felt that history demanded it. Professor Hammen elaborates:

> I believe that both *normally* would want as little of that as possible. But they both thought historically, and I believe that they considered terror and force as inevitable, at least in some degree. Where class was arrayed against class, what else could you expect; it was just in the natural order of things.[5]

Both expected war to hasten revolutions, and wars would be justification of terror, wars being, in their opinion, terror in themselves. In Marx's famous statement to his fellow revolutionaries in London on September 15, 1850, he declared that workers had to experience as many as "15, 20, 50 years of civil wars and international wars," not only to change the world's socio-political and economic conditions, but also to transform the workers themselves "in preparation for the exercise of political power."

In later years, in their exchange of letters, Marx and Engels never expressed a word of concern over the sufferings of the masses. And we know that such suffering must result, should a great depression and a crisis come, followed by a revolution with or without wars, but a revolution surely full of human disasters. Hammen writes: "They always welcomed signs of such crises. The workers just had to go through it all. If mass suffering was an acceptable situation, it is possible to conclude that Marx and Engels were just as ready to accept suffering of other sorts, unto terror."[6]

It would be edifying for some diligent researcher to count up the number of times Marx and Engels mentioned the words "terror" and "terrorism" in their writings and orations. Historically, yes, they would use the words—with their continued praise for Cromwell and especially for Robespierre: numerous favorable references to the Frenchman are scattered through their works. But less often than might be supposed would they use these two words in relation to their own times, and still less would they recommend terror bluntly as a necessary revolutionary tool of today and tomorrow. Instead, they used such words as "revolution" and "revenge," such phrases as "war of the classes" and "the people, this final, sovereign judge." On one occasion Marx said: "For the informed no more need be said."

But when describing revolutionary action of some West and Central Europeans against the Tsar's reactionary steamroller, Marx employed the word "terror" far more frankly. Of the Hungarian revolt of 1849 he spoke eloquently: "For the first time since 1793, a country surrounded by overwhelming counterrevolutionary power opposed the *terreur blanche* with the *terreur rouge*, with the rage of revolutionary passion." And if and when the final battle of the West against the Tsar's troops came, the Germans, along with the Poles and the Magyars, would bring about a fraternity of peoples via a thoroughgoing revolution and its bloodshed—"only through a most determined terror against these Slavic peoples," the Russians and others chained and driven by the Tsar. In sum, it was all right to urge *terror*, using the semitabooed word, when speaking of a campaign against the Tsar and his Slavs.

As for Engels himself in the role of theoretician of revolution, aside from his celebrated partnership with Marx, his view of violence was that of the accelerator of economic development; in this sense, like Marx, he hailed violence. But, Engels added, if violence is used by a country's power structure unwarranted by its economic development, then such a political power will suffer defeat in its use of violence.

Here we have a rare glimpse of Engels as a doubter of the virtues of violence and terror. On one occasion he even questioned the proper socio-economic origin and wisdom of Robespierre's experiment as well as the desirability of terror if it exploded in the Paris of his own time. Engel's antiterror statement is found in his letter to Marx of September 4, 1870, a few months before the Commune, when Engels was worrying about the likelihood of workingmen's Red terror in Paris getting out of hand:

> From these perpetual little panics of the French . . . one gets a much better idea of the Reign of Terror. We think of it as the reign of people who instill terror. But quite the contrary, it is as the reign of people who are themselves terrified. *La Terreur* is for the most part useless cruelties perpetrated by people who are themselves fright-

ened, for the purpose of reassuring themselves. I am convinced that the blame for the Reign of Terror, Anno 1793, falls almost entirely on the over-nervous bourgeois acting the patriot, on the little, philistine petit-bourgeois soiling his pants in fright and on the riff-raff mob, making a business out of the terror. The present little terror comes from precisely the same classes.[7]

This was the most definite antiterror statement he ever made, and possibly the basis for Dr. Freedman's sweeping assertion that historically "Marx and Engels were very much against terror," that "they saw it as a form of revolutionary suicide."

There is no evidence that Marx agreed with these doubts of Engels. To the contrary, we know that in his appraisal of the failure of the Paris Commune during the following spring Marx felt there was not enough Red terror.

Nor did Engels himself persist in his sudden negation of violence. In the late 1870s he attacked Professor Emil Dühring for telling the Socialists of Berlin that force had an evil potential and that the proletariat should be careful in using it, since it could corrupt the new society the workers would be building. Engels in his angry onslaught reminded the professor of Marx's famous maxim that force played a revolutionary role as "the midwife of every old society that is pregnant with a new one." Yes, Engels echoed Dühring, "every use of force may demoralize its user," and this was indeed unfortunate. But violent force "is the instrument with which the social movement realizes itself and shatters political forms which have grown rigid and moribund." Particularly in Germany, "a violent clash . . . has the advantage of extirpating the servility that has permeated the national consciousness as a result of the humiliation of the Thirty Years' War."[8]

The greatest single contribution made by Engels to the use of terror among other violence by a revolutionary party or government was his vehement rejection in 1877 of any morality. This was what Lenin in 1920 would most avidly seize upon as the main premise of his young Soviet government, as the principal justification of his secret police, with its mass arrests and executions.

Elsewhere in his writings Engels also provided Lenin, Mao Tsetung, Castro, and other conquering revolutionaries of the generations to come with their rationalization of the use of terror not only en route to power but after achieving it. In early 1873 Engels asserted: "A revolution is certainly the most authoritarian thing there is; it is the act whereby one part of the population imposes its will on the other part by means of rifles, bayonets, and cannon—authoritarian means if such there be at all; and if the victorious party does not wish to have fought in vain, it must maintain this rule by means of the terror which its arms inspire in the reactionaries.''

But to what ultimate goal is this rule of terror? On one memorable occasion Engels dolefully admitted that, with all the terror employed, the aims originally declared by revolutionaries are usually miscarried. In 1885, two years after the death of Marx, in reply to a question by the Russian revolutionary Vera Zasulich, Engels wrote: ''The people who boasted that they had made a revolution have always seen the next day that they had no idea what they were doing, that the revolution did not in the least resemble the one they would have liked to make.''[9]

This was probably the wisest point ever made by Engels. But this is not the kind of axiom latter-day terrorists and revolutionaries would notice in the works by Marx and Engels—if, indeed, they read such sacred literature as they claim they do.

IV

Intertwined in all discussions of Marx and Engels must be that remarkable Frenchman, Georges Sorel (1847-1922). By too many has Sorel been unjustly blamed as an influence upon, practically a spiritual father of, Benito Mussolini. Rather should he be remembered and re-read as an apologist of revolutionary—not fascist—violence stopping short of terror.

At one time something of a Marxist, and in its early phase a supporter of the Soviet revolution, Sorel was on the whole an original thinker in his own right whose ideas on force were definitely different from those of Marx, Engels, and Lenin. His celebrated *Reflections on Violence* do not supply us with any detailed or profound analysis of violence in human nature. He took for granted man's impulse to violence; his concern was how best to use it for the good of mankind.

Generally, Sorel was a pessimist who sadly recognized the steady increase of corruption and other unlovely human traits all around him. Since violence was inevitable, he would control it, at least in part, by letting mainly the workingclass use it for virtuous ends. This violence was to be employed in industrial strikes of his fellow Syndicalists opposed to the Marxist Socialists. He wrote: ''Syndicalists speak of . . . revolution in the language of strikes.'' Strike violence, he insisted, was a positive phenomenon:

Proletarian violence, carried on as a pure and simple manifestation of the sentiment of the class war, appears thus as a very fine and

very heroic thing; it is at the service of the immemorial interests of
civilization; it is not perhaps the most appropriate method of ob-
taining immediate material advantages, but it may save the world
from barbarism.[10]

In proletarian strikes and their violence Sorel promised fairness and
justice, with no resemblance to the terror of a Robespierre or of any
cruel, arbitrary state. "Proletarian acts of violence" would be no terrorism but "purely and simply acts of war," bound by time-honored rules
of civilized hostilities, with no hatred or vengeance, with no executions
of prisoners or other vanquished persons.[11]

He was repelled by the glorification of the Grand Terror by even
such mild Socialists as his contemporary, Jean Jaurès: "I do not feel
the same indulgence toward the guillotiners as he does; I have a
horror of any measure that strikes the vanquished under a judicial
disguise." He saw no glow in the "acts of savagery" committed by
"the revolutionaries of '93."

He saw no need for the proletariat of his time and of the future to
repeat Robespierre's bloody error, particularly since that monstrous
guillotiner in no way represented the workers of his era. Very much
like Engels in his September 1870 letter to Marx, Sorel, decades later,
viewed the Grand Terror as the handiwork of ignorant, frightened members of the middle class. But, unlike Engels, Sorel gave documenta-
tion. He quoted Taine, who in his *La Révolution* noted that, of the 577
deputies of the Third Estate in the Constituent Assembly, many were
lawyers, notaries, bailiffs, and other exploiters—not workers. Sorel
would also prove that Engels was right in his fears of the non-
proletarian nature of the Parisian terror in 1870-71. He quoted another
French historian about the Commune: "It was the middle-class element that was most ferocious in the Commune, the vicious and bohemian middle class of the Latin Quarter," while the workers and
artisans amid this horrible crisis "remained *human*, that is, *French*."

Contrary to the threats and dire predictions by Marx and Engels,
and notwithstanding the bloody practice by Lenin (of which Sorel was
fully aware before his own death in 1922, two years before Lenin's),
Sorel would present mankind with a wholly pure revolution: "We have
the right to hope that a socialist revolution carried out by pure Syndicalists would not be defiled by the abominations that sullied the
middle-class revolutions."

And because the middle class everywhere was as cowardly as it
was cruel, the takeover of the state and society by the striking Syn-
dicalist proletariat would be simple. The middle class—the bourgeoisie
ruling the System—would give in even in the face of moderate vio-

lence. Not even moderate violence, but merely a threat of violence, would suffice. Thus, in the Sorel version of the use of force, there would be no need for the civil wars and terror envisaged by Marx and Engels, the false prophets.[12]

7

Anarchists: Philosophers
with Bombs

While for the most part the terrorists of the 1960s and '70s have represented themselves as Marxist-Leninists, a significant number trace their heritage to Trotsky and Mao. But they also owe their creeds and bombs to other influences, notably those of the old anarchists.

In the 1960s, Eldridge Cleaver's Black Panther group in Berkeley republished as a pamphlet the no-holds-barred *Catechism of a Revolutionary*, the authorship of which is ascribed to Bakunin, the anarchist, and his fiery pupil Nechayev. In his *Soul on Ice* Cleaver recalls that when he first read it he "fell in love" with it: "I took the *Catechism* for my bible and, standing on a one-man platform that had nothing to do with the reconstruction of society, I began consciously incorporating these principles into my daily life, to employ tactics of ruthlessness in my dealings with everyone with whom I came into contact. And I began to look at white America through these new eyes."[1]

In the spirit of the destructive *Catechism*, Nechayev's actions included a murder, that of Ivan Ivanov, a Moscow student and a fellow conspirator who had dared to disagree with him. In late 1869, Ivanov was killed on Nechayev's orders. More assassinations directed by Nechayev would surely have followed but he had to flee West, where he worked—and quarreled—with Bakunin, and where in 1872 he was finally arrested by the Swiss police and handed over to Tsarist Russia as a common criminal. Tried in 1873 for Ivanov's murder, Nechayev was sentenced to 20 years. He died a prisoner in the Peter and Paul Fortress in St. Petersburg in 1882.[2]

Two documents owe their origin to Nechayev: his own (or at least inspired by him) *The Catechism of a Revolutionary*, which has had a lasting influence; and Dostoyevsky's great novel *The Possessed* (in the original Russian, *Besy* [Devils]), based on the revolutionary theories and practice of Nechayev and his group, so well understood and bitingly satirized by the author, who had himself in his youth tried to plot in the name of socialism.[3]

Even after Nechayev's arrest and sentence, his bitter message of massacre lived on for a time in Western Europe more than in Russia. Pyotr Tkachev, once a close associate of Nechayev, declared when he was an émigré in Switzerland and France that, come the revolution, all the earth's inhabitants over the age of 25 would have to be killed because they would never be able to accept the new regime. Tkachev died in 1885, insane, in a public hospital in Paris,[4] but his sermon about those over 25 was remembered and quoted in subsequent decades, among others by Albert Camus in his book *The Rebel,* so popular among the American campus elite of the 1950s and '60s. Is this where the semijesting, semi-earnest warning by America's New Left—"Don't trust anyone over 30"—originated? If so, our New Left was more generous than Russia's Old Left by five years as well as more humane by not threatening to kill.

(Camus, in *The Rebel* and other writings, although seemingly disapproving of any violence, largely on moral grounds, did make an exception for revolutionary violence if it was either in response to violence by the state or an attempt to forestall such violence from above.)

II

Before meeting Nechayev, Bakunin[5] was rather haphazard in his explosiveness: he orated brilliantly in praise of revolution and mounted the barricades wherever in the West these were available, but he did not often strive to organize conspiracies or rebellions with any forethought and care. Nechayev brought to Bakunin his own systematic fanaticism. Those who knew the pair felt that Nechayev, while deceiving and almost victimizing Bakunin on a grand scale, had nevertheless an effective and sinister impact eagerly accepted by the older man. It was thanks to Nechayev that Bakunin reached his apogee—and utter failure—as an active revolutionary, preaching anarchy and terrorism. His apogee was the challenge he flung at Marx for the control of the First International. His failure was climaxed by Marx's engineering Bakunin's expulsion from the International (an expulsion that fatally wounded the International), and by Bakunin's own defeats in Europe's revolutions.

But what Bakunin failed to accomplish in the prime of his revolutionary career he did achieve in the last few years of life and most emphatically after his death in 1876, at 62. It was largely his influence that set the growing and spreading groups of West European anarchists, particularly in Italy and Spain, upon their paths of action: on to anarchism by deed—by dynamite and guns.

To comprehend fully the personality and role of Mikhail Bakunin in the annals of terror we must invoke a glimpse of the Russia from whose unquiet loins he came. Born in 1814, he was 11 years old when Tsar Nicholas I ascended the throne amid the revolt of the Decembrists, the idealistc noblemen-officers whom the sovereign's loyal troops soon and easily downed. A long night of reaction fell upon Russia, to last throughout the entire reign of Nicholas I, the 30 years from 1825 to 1855. Civil government, military service, education, the Church, the life of the masses and the classes, all felt the heavy stamp of the Tsar's jackboot.

The Tsar's long-time (1833-49) minister of education, Count Sergei Uvarov, proclaimed the slogan of Orthodoxy, Autocracy, and Nationalism as the basis of all teaching and learning in the Empire. He appointed army generals as district school superintendents, and curtailed the autonomy of Russia's universities. Censorship was tightened into absurdity. Permits to travel abroad were obtained with great difficulty.

Peasant serfs were restive. In the Tsar's three decades of reign more than 500 rural uprisings occurred, but all being local and impulsively uncoordinated, they were suppressed quickly and ruthlessly. Now and then the Tsar would order committees to investigate the peasants' problems, with stacks of reports and no reform as the result. In 1842, in a speech to his State Council, Nicholas I delivered himself of this weighty thought: "There is no doubt that serfdom as it now exists in Russia is a flagrant evil, of which everyone is aware, but to attempt to remedy it now would be an evil even more disastrous."[6]

Educated persons were allowed to read, write, and discuss theology, philosophy, and other subjects, provided their political implications were not mentioned or, if dwelt upon, only in conformist, conservative terms. Nevertheless, from 1845 to 1849, a group of intellectuals dared to gather in the home of a nobleman, Mikhail Petrashevsky, a minor employee of the Ministry of Foreign Affairs, a follower of Charles Fourier and Count Claude Henri de Saint-Simon, to talk of socialist and other radical ideas. Dostoyevsky and other young writers were members of what became known as the Petrashevsky Circle. When the West European revolutions of 1848 deepened the Tsar's alarms, his police intensified their search for, and rooting out of, dissent. The Circle was uncovered and its members were arrested. Several of them, including young Dostoyevsky, were sentenced to death, but their reprieve was read to them as they stood on the scaffold, in sight of the firing squad and their own coffins.[7] Years of forced labor in Siberia was their fate.

A few noblemen-intellectuals had managed to cross into Western Europe before the Petrashevsky calamity. In 1834, at the age of 20, in his first protest against Tsarism, Bakunin resigned as an officer of the privileged guards, and in 1840 left Russia for the West. And Alexander Herzen, the radical writer, after nine months in prison and several years of exile in the provinces, used his large inheritance to move himself and his family to Western Europe in early 1847. For decades afterward both men, each in his own way, exerted a significant effect upon Westerners as well as upon Russians.

Bakunin's extreme radicalism was in sharp contrast to Herzen's militant liberalism. Bakunin's preachment was more than anarchism: it often emerged as a curious alloy of anarchism and Pan-Slavism. But, foremost, Bakunin was against the state of any kind, nationalist or not. His longing for collectivism was accented with a belief in violence, and he practiced his teaching: he took an energetic part in Western uprisings, at Prague in 1848 and in Dresden in 1849, among others. Arrested in Saxony, he was condemned to death, but was given a reprieve and handed over to Austria, whose government at first also sentenced him to death, but ended up by happily sending him back to the Tsar.

For six years he was a prisoner in the dungeons of two of the Tsar's fortresses, losing his teeth and most of his health. For a time he also lost some of his revolutionary integrity when, from his Peter and Paul Fortress cell, he addressed to Nicholas I his *Confession,* an astonishing document in which he not only tried to justify himself as a rebel but also groveled before the Emperor and extolled the crushing mission of the Empire. This was, however, only abject lip service; in his heart Bakunin remained a bitter rebel. Eventually transported to Siberia, in 1861 he made his sensational escape on an American ship, first to Japan, and thence to America and Western Europe. In London he became a friend of Herzen, Marx, and other revolutionaries—with most of whom he in time argued and broke.

In 1863 Bakunin attempted to aid the Polish rebellion against Tsar Alexander II by sending volunteers and arms on a British ship, unsuccessfully. In 1864-68 he fomented revolutionary activity in Italy; in 1871 he participated in an uprising at Lyons, France; in 1874 in a revolt in Bologna, Italy. All through the 1860s and into the mid-'70s he kept up his frantic activity.

Unlike Marx, Bakunin had no faith in the historic virtue of the proletariat. He insisted that the proletariat could be bought by the crumbs off the capitalists' tables. Nor did he share Marx's contempt for the peasants as "rural idiots" and for the declassed ragged ruffians of the urban *Lumpenproletariat* as hopeless scum. On the contrary, Bakunin blared his blood-curdling calls to, and placed all his high hopes on, the destructive instincts of the peasant masses and the city riffraff, led by desperate students and other radical intellectuals. In the apt analysis by Professor Paul Avrich, Bakunin "insisted that the revolutionary impulse was strongest where men had no property, no regular employment, and no stake in things as they were." Bakunin "foresaw that the great revolutions of our time would emerge from the 'lower depths' of comparatively undeveloped countries. He saw decadence in advanced civilization and vitality in backward, primitive nations."[8]

Our own contemporary Herbert Marcuse, in his refusal to deify the proletariat and in his trust in the revolutionary mission of students leading a nondescript mob to the barricades of tomorrow, is definitely more of a Bakuninist than the Marxist he claims to be, and this is why Moscow's propagandists attack the professor so frenetically.[9]

Similarly, the outburst of the Maoists in the West, as well as in the Middle East, against the current Kremlin line is strikingly like the Bakuninist rage against Marx one century ago. It has much the same substance and phraseology.

In the view of certain non-Soviet Marxists, Bakunin's only fault may have been that he was too much ahead of his time. Herzen was so right in commenting that Bakunin habitually "mistook the third month of pregnancy for the ninth." Indeed, as Professor Avrich puts it, Bakunin is proving more relevant for our century than he was for his own. So many modern terrorists, even if claiming to be Marxists (of non-Soviet kinds), are in fact in agreement with those anarchists of today who live and fight by Bakunin's credo, including his postulates about the uselessness of the proletariat and the usefulness of peasant masses. In the process they do not even notice that they thus cease being Marxists.

III

Following the sad-heroic experience of the Paris Commune of 1871, the new generations of revolutionaries would no longer be timid—they saw both reason and romance in a wholesale extermination of lives. More and more such terrorists felt a perverted pride in their execution of men for political aims.

The Paris Commune had failed. The White terror that ended it had proved more effective than the Red terror of the Communards. But in the minds of Europe's revolutionaries the Paris failure did not mean a final funeral dirge. Revolts would yet come and be triumphant. And they would rage not alone against exploitative capitalistic states—the target would be any state whatever. Many revolutionaries held that the socialists of Karl Marx were wrong when they meant to smash the capitalist state—only to replace it with a socialist state, which, as would any state, be unjust. To them Bakunin the anarchist was overwhelmingly right.

Thus it came about that the revolutionary convulsions in Western Europe (and, to a much lesser extent, in America), in the 43 years between the Paris Commune and the Sarajevo shots that triggered World War I, were dominated by anarchists. Years later, in 1953, Max Nomad, a reflective anarchist of a nonviolent species, defined the violent anarchist of the pre-1914 era as "the pure-in-the-heart revolutionist who honestly believes he is not out for power." With gentle irony Nomad compared the anarchist bomber to "the romantic wooer who is convinced that his only aim is to serve his beloved."[10] But in reality the anarchist—like any other political terrorist—is far less romantic and much more selfish. He has always served not his darling mankind but only his own half-insane (if not totally deranged) ego, cursed by his drive of destruction. Anarchists, like other terrorists, are no humanitarians.

Beginning with the early 1870s the anarchists were raring for action. It would not do for them to wait patiently for leaders to establish new political parties that would prepare insurrections slowly. Moderate Socialists could and would bide their time, but true rebels would burst out. To such quick-tempered men and women in the West, Bakunin was infallibly right. He was then living his last few years, and more than ever he was incapable of any genuine organizational verve. But if he could not organize, he could inspire.

As he called for bloodbaths and hurled thunder, Bakunin did not, however, have much of a following in the industrial north of Europe, where the proletariat now listened to the orderly Socialist parties, with their reliance on a gradual wresting of reforms from the capitalist states. But in the south, particularly in Italy and Spain, the more miserable and less patient proletariat, and especially the wretchedly poor peasantry, did respond to the militant summons.

In the early 1870s that summons was carried to the disaffected by such young Italian anarchists as Enrico Malatesta and Carlo Cafiero. But since the few mass insurrections they tried to ignite were not successful, these men and others like them would, for the next few decades, well into the twentieth century, engage in their "propaganda by the deed"—by sporadic guerrilla uprisings in the countryside and, increasingly, by terroristic acts in the cities. Kings, presidents, governors, and other rulers were targets, and a number were indeed slain by bomb and pistol.[11]

In their attempts at mass insurgence, the anarchists had some limited success in the beginning, but they soon met with failure. Late in 1876 (the year Bakunin died), Malatesta and Cafiero were joined by a picturesque Russian revolutionary, Sergei Kravchinsky-Stepniak, along with his Russian lady friend. A house was rented in San Lupo, a mountain village northeast of Naples. Ostensibly the lady's lungs were in need of mountain air; but in fact the group had gathered to plan a peasant rebellion. A sizable quantity of ammunition was brought in, camouflaged as the lady's luggage. Kravchinsky had briefly been a Bakuninist, joining any rebellion, under whatever flag and theory. The year before, in 1875, he had fought with the Serbs rising against the Turks in Bosnia and Herzegovina. He was disillusioned by this Slav cause; still, the valuable experience gave him the opportunity of writing one of the first handbooks on guerrilla warfare.

But the Italian police files on Malatesta, Kravchinsky, and their associates were well kept. The anarchists were watched as they gathered at San Lupo. Gunfire was exchanged when some of the group were arrested; a policeman died of wounds. However, many lesser rebel leaders succeeded in escaping.

In the spring of 1877 a peasant revolt was begun in Lentino, another village. Again Malatesta and Cafiero were involved. A noteworthy feature of this insurgence was a solemn anarchist ritual of a public bonfire wherein the local records of property ownership and peasant debts and taxes were burned to ashes. A proclamation was read declaring King Victor Emmanuel II deposed. Yet, although the peasants of Lentino and the vicinity cheered the anarchists, and even the village priest joined the rebels, the movement petered out ingloriously when the King's soldiers encircled the cold and hungry insurgents with hardly any fight, taking them off to jail.

The world barely noticed. But the telegraph wires hummed and newspaper headlines shrieked when, in 1878, two bomb and knife attempts were made in Italy again. In February, in Florence, a young man flung a bomb into a parade being held in memory of the recently deceased Victor Emmanuel. At the year's end, in Naples, a 29-year-old cook tried to knife the new King, Humbert I. The knife bore the inscription, "Long live the international republic!" No one was killed either at Florence or Naples. On the second occasion the King was merely scratched, while his prime minister, who was with him on that ride, suffered a slight wound. Both times the Italian anarchists disclaimed any connection with the attempts, and none was in fact established by the police. Yet when monarchists celebrated the King's survival and the Queen's birthday, and bombs were thrown into the parading crowds at Florence and Pisa, resulting in several deaths and a number of wounded, the anarchists' terroristic influence, if not their direct involvement, was generally taken for granted.

Curiously, feeling either intimidated or magnanimous, the Italian government made no objection when in August 1878 a sympathetic jury acquitted Malatesta and his fellow anarchists for the uprising in the spring of 1877.

Though he was acquitted, Malatesta was to last through many more years of repeated imprisonments and exile, to die in Fascist Italy in 1932 at 79, at his last making a living as an obscure electrician, no longer active in terror or articulate about its theory.

Cafiero came to an early end in the 1880s, going insane with the idea that he was appropriating more than his equitable share of sunshine on earth.

Kravchinsky returned to Russia, to assassinate almost immediately—in August 1878—the chief of the Tsar's political police, to escape to Western Europe once more, there to write novels glorifying the era's terrorists, and finally to die in London in 1895 at 44—run over by a railroad train.

IV

It was in 1876, the year of Bakunin's death, that yet another Russian nobleman-revolutionist appeared in the West to cast his spell upon Europeans for many decades to come. This was Prince Pyotr (Peter) Kropotkin, then only 34, a scion of an ancient family tracing its roots to the Ryuriks, the first dynasty of Russia sprung from the vikings.[12]

In his youth he served the second dynasty, the Romanovs, as a worshipful page to Tsar Alexander II, and later as an army officer, explorer, and geographer in Siberia. He read much, and in 1872 became deeply impressed with Bakunin's writings. As a consequence, he renounced his allegiance to the Tsar and abandoned his brilliant career. He would serve the people as a convinced anarchist.

Today, we commonly regard Kropotkin as the peaceful, nonviolent author of the message that spontaneous, brotherly communes of good will would gradually do away with both capitalism and the state. In actuality he was an aggressive spokesman of terror for a long time before he finally gave up his advocacy of violence. In the 1870s, before he was at last arrested and incarcerated by the Tsar's gendarmes, he not only published and distributed illegal literature among Russian workers but, in his opposition to any liberal reformism, urged peasants to form armed bands. After his spectacular escape from a Tsarist prison in 1876 and on becoming an émigré in Western Europe, he took pride in calling himself a disciple of Bakunin, agitating and plotting with the anarchists. True, unlike the late master, Kropotkin did not himself climb any barricades, but he was soon widely acknowledged as the foremost theoretician of anarchism and terror, exerting a tremendous pull on the emotions of all those West European (and later, American) revolutionaries who were ready to sacrifice lives—those of their victims as well as their own.

In 1879, in Switzerland, Kropotkin launched a periodal, *Le Révolté,* in which a typical editorial proclaimed the necessity of terror, of "permanent revolt," not alone by oral and printed propaganda, but also "by the dagger, the rifle, dynamite." In 1881, while not sharing the belief of the Narodniki in the preservation of the state by its drastic reform through revolution, he hailed their murder of Tsar Alexander II as a blow at the System. That year Kropotkin joined with Malatesta and other anarchist leaders meeting in London to advocate the use of bombs for both offense and defense against the exploiters, and thus the need for revolutionaries to study chemistry and other physical sciences so as to improve their explosive-making skills.

Toward the end of the 1880s, particularly after permanently settling in the rather relaxed England of the time, Kropotkin grew less stormy, more pensive. In the words of James Joll, "From being a conspirator and agitator he became a philosopher and prophet"—a philosopher without a bomb. Since the turn of the century he allowed but two exceptions for extraordinary situations where he felt violence was inescapable: during the Russian revolution of 1905, when in his London home he took up rifle practice to prepare for his possible return to his turbulent homeland; and in the First World War, when he ardently supported the Allied cause against Imperial Germany, and thus blessed the mass slaughter. Until his death in 1921 at 79 in Russia, to which he returned after the revolution of 1917, he continued to preach his gentle, noncoercive brand of Communism-anarchism.

V

In the latter 1870s, within a span of a few months, not only was an attempt made to assassinate King Humbert of Italy, but there were also two tries at killing the Emperor of Germany and one at slaying the King of Spain.

Other attempts at murder and actual assassinations followed in the years and decades to come, some by amateurs who were not convinced revolutionaries or professional anarchists, but many inspired by the theories and techniques of the era's anarchists. The leaders of Europe's anarchists were often blamed by the authorities and the press for this or that outrage when, in fact, these leaders would learn of such attentats after they had occurred.

Nevertheless, the anarchists, while disclaiming their responsibility and sometimes even their role as inspirers, cheered the gory deeds and doers. Thus a Swiss anarchist newspaper paid high-flown homage to the German worker who had attempted to assassinate the Kaiser: "Humanity will preserve the memory of the tinsmith Hoedel, who was prepared to sacrifice his life to make a superb act of defiance against society, and, as his blood spurted beneath the executioner's ax, was able to inscribe his name on the long list of martyrs who have shown the people the way to a better future, toward the abolition of all economic and political slavery."

No less than the rulers and the rich, the state's and society's institutions were targets for the guns and explosives of that period's anarchists. They proudly hoisted their new emblem—the black flag.

In 1886, one Charles Gallo, a young anarchist, from his vantage point in the visitors' gallery of the Paris Bourse, threw a bottle of vitriol at the stockbrokers and clerks below, then fired three wild revolver shots at them. By lucky chance he harmed no one, which failure he unrepentantly deplored in his utterances at his subsequent trial. As he was led off to his 20 years of hard labor, he shouted: "Long live revolution! Long live anarchism! Death to the bourgeois judiciary! Long live dynamite!"

Also in Paris, on December 9, 1893, Auguste Vaillant, a restless ne'er-do-well, hurled down a bomb from a balcony at the assemblage of the Chamber of Deputies. Again no one was killed, although a number were wounded or injured. The ultraleft hailed Vaillant's attempt as a *beau geste,* the radical poet Laurent Tailhade declaring that "the victims do not matter so long as the gesture is beautiful." Some thoughtful observers felt that Vaillant actually wished to commit suicide and longed for immortality. Yet Vaillant protested against his impending execution; he went to his death exclaiming: "Long live anarchy! My death will be avenged!"

Each terrorist bomb or shot was followed by a wave of police searches, arrests, trials, prison sentences, or much-publicized executions. Inevitably the response came in new attentats and explosions. One week after Vaillant's execution in February 1894 a lone avenger, Emile Henry, set off a bomb at a café near a railroad station in Paris, but was quickly caught. When it was pointed out to him that the café's habitués were petty shopkeepers, clerks, and even workers, that the 20 people his bomb had wounded (one of them soon dying) were truly innocent of any capitalist sins, Henry calmly objected: "There are no innocent.'' This statement is truly characteristic of the extreme protester's attitude at all times and in many lands: man's entire social structure is rotten, all its participants are to be blamed. Nor did Henry's death sentence unnerve him. He said, for himself and his fellow terrorists: "We inflict death; we will know how to endure it.''

Deaths of innocents were many. In Spain in 1892 a young anarchist threw a bomb at a general to avenge the execution of four anarchists implicated in an insurrection at Juarez put down the year before. And then a friend of the bomb-thrower hurled a bomb into a Madrid theater, killing 20 men and women. A short time thereafter, a bomb was flung from a window into a religious procession, wounding the innocent.

There was a suspicion that this bomb was thrown by the Spanish police to gain an additional excuse for wholesale arrests of anarchists. In other countries such sins of the police were quite transparent. The French police were known to form quasi-anarchist groups consisting of *agents provocateurs* in order to find and ensnare true anarchists; the police even published an anarchist newspaper in Paris, and in 1881 sent a delegate to the anarchist meeting in London at which Malatesta and Kropotkin spoke. The Italian police maintained two agents in Paris in the early 1900s. Nicknamed Virgil and Dante, they displayed an impressive knowledge of anarchist ideas and life-style.

The police of several countries would have liked to prove conspiratorial connections linking such leaders as Kropotkin and Malatesta to the explosions and gunshots. Never were these—or any high-level theoreticians—found guilty of having direct responsibility, though they were often arrested following attentats or violent industrial strikes. (At one point Kropotkin drew a three-year French jail sentence because he was in France at the time of a miners' riot at Montceau.) Yet the intellectual inspiration of Kropotkin's books, journals, and speeches upon the rank-and-file activists was indisputable.

On the West European left, anarchism was fashionable among at least some artists and writers. A few of these became convinced anarchists, even though they never tossed bombs. Gustave Courbet was a close friend of Proudhon, participated in the Paris Commune of 1871, and the following year came to an anarchist congress in the Jura Mountains—to drink wine and sing his monotonous French peasant songs rather than discuss theory or plot. Camille Pissarro participated in the anarchist movement more actively: he did lithographs for anarchist periodicals and a cover for one of Kropotkin's pamphlets. In fact, he read and admired the master's writings, particularly *The Conquest of Bread* (1888), expressing his hope in a letter that Kropotkin's "beautiful dream,'' this utopia of mankind becoming a lovely network of anarchical communes, might yet turn into a reality.

In 1894, in Paris, 30 editors and writers, some far more bohemian than anarchist, were put on trial on charges of forming a criminal association. A number of these were the time's famous names. A few had fled before the trial; the rest were acquitted. And indeed, they had only talked and written. Most of these men of art and letters did not agree with the late Bakunin's exhortations and predictions of a world-wide catastrophe. They agreed, rather, with the gentler Kropotkin and his new vision of a quick and bloodless transformation of humanity. But among the true activists of anarchism the Bakunin line of blood and ruin prevailed.

Some criminals, while not actually belonging to the anarchist move-ment, were facile at using its language. "The policeman arrested me in the name of the law; I hit him in the name of liberty," said Clement Duval in Paris in 1886 when apprehended for burglary. In court he explained his crime as his way of redistributing wealth. Taken from the courtroom with a death sentence, he cried out: "Long live anarchy! Long live the social revolution! Ah, if ever I am freed, I will blow you all up!" His sentence commuted, he escaped from jail in 1901, and he was practically adopted as their own by the admiring Italian anarchists in New York, where he died at an old age in 1935.

Less fortunate were François-Claudius Ravachol and Emile Henry, both of whom were executed in France in the early 1890s. Both were of twisted minds, the former clearly a common criminal, the latter an intellectual with a fierce hatred of the existing order, and both using their homemade bombs with a senseless disregard for innocent lives. Both insisted on what seemed to be an anarchist philosophy, and both died with rare courage. The anarchists of Western Europe were puz-zled as to whether to accept these two as their brothers in spirit. Such doubts were particularly strong in the case of Ravachol, who at one time had been known as a police informer as well as a petty thief who murdered for money. But the seemingly ideological pronouncements made by Ravachol and even more explicitly and cogently by Henry, as well as the unflinching manner in which they faced their executioners, finally convinced the anarchists of the West that here were their breth-ren indeed.

VI

In those decades before the fateful August guns of 1914, the roll call grew longer. Many attentats miscarried, but many resulted in the spec-tacular deaths of sovereigns, presidents, and prime ministers.*

* Of the miscarried attempts, most sensational was the attempt in 1858 by an Italian nationalist, Felice Orsini, to throw a bomb at Napoleon III. The French Emperor es-

The year 1881 opened the bloody list when, on March 13, Tsar Alexander II of Russia was blown to fragments and on September 19 President James Garfield of the United States died of the wounds inflicted upon him on July 2.

The Tsar was killed not by anarchists but by the Narodniki, a socialist party that, unlike the anarchists, did believe in the institution of the state once it was thoroughly cleansed through revolution. Nonetheless, the anarchists of Western Europe and America, including Kropotkin, applauded the Tsar's murder. The President fell to the bullets of a wholly nonideological, near-insane, disgruntled office seeker, but the anarchists accepted this death also with satisfaction.

In 1894 President Sadi Carnot of France, a direct descendant of Lazare Carnot, the famed "architect of victory" of the French Revolution, was murdered in Lyons by an Italian anarchist whose knife was sharp and precise.

In 1897, in Spain, at the baths of Santa Agueda in the Basque Provinces, Prime Minister Canovas del Castillo was assassinated, also by an Italian anarchist.

The next year, in 1898, it was a third Italian anarchist who, in Geneva, stabbed to death the melancholy, nonpolitical Elizabeth, Empress of Austria and Queen of Hungary, by then virtually separated from her husband, Franz Joseph II.

And again it was an Italian anarchist who killed Italy's King Humbert I in 1900.

Across the ocean, in 1901, President William McKinley of the United States was mortally wounded while shaking hands with visitors at an exposition in Buffalo, New York—his assassin, although not affiliated with anarchists, had avidly read their literature and had been definitely influenced by them.

In 1908 King Carlos I of Portugal and his heir apparent, Prince Luis Filipe, were slain by two assassins while riding in the streets of Lisbon in an open landau. The two regicides were members of a secret political society, so secret or at least so vaguely programmed that its presumed connection with the anarchists or even its precise revolutionary coloration was never ascertained.

In Russia, the Tsar's Prime Minister Pyotr Stolypin escaped anarchists' attempts to murder him but finally, in 1911, a Socialist Revolutionary Party member, who had served as a police informer as well,

---

caped, but a number of others around him were killed or injured. For this, the famous revolutionary Giuseppe Mazzini was blamed by the authorities in both France and Italy, because Orsini was one of his followers, although Mazzini was not at all involved in Orsini's act. Other bungled attentats, by nonrevolutionaries, included an attempt on the life of England's Queen Victoria in 1872.

killed him in the Kiev opera house in the presence of Nicholas II himself.

And on June 28, 1914, at Sarajevo in Bosnia-Herzegovina, the most celebrated murder of the era took place: Archduke Franz Ferdinand, nephew and heir of Austria-Hungary's Emperor Franz Joseph II, was assassinated, along with his wife Sophia, not by anarchists but by young Serb nationalist revolutionaries.* Thus, the First World War.

The lights went out all over Europe as guns thundered. For four years millions of lives were lost or maimed—far more than the terrorists of the pre-1914 decades could destroy, and in the end Europe's three mighty empires—those of Russia, Germany, and Austro-Hungary—fell, an accomplishment certainly beyond the capability of Bakunin and his followers. What the terrorists could not achieve, the rulers themselves brought about.

And still the anarchist dream was not fulfilled: the state not only survived, but in large and important parts of Europe and Asia it grew into a totalitarian monster, a monster so terrible that it has become one of the greatest perils humanity has ever known.

* Prior to 1914, the most outstanding regicide in the Balkans was the savage murder in Belgrade in 1903 of Serbia's King Alexander Obrenovich and his Queen Draga. But the motive for this was neither nationalist nor revolutionary. It is true that the King's nine-year rule was illiberal and highhanded and his Queen was unpopular, but their assassins made their act a sheer palace coup, for dynastic reasons more than any other. In both 1903 and 1914 the Serb slayers, though not anarchists, were indeed their spiritual kin in the sense that, nurtured by the violence of their times, they believed in "quick" solutions.

8

America's Pie

"Violence," the black activist Rap Brown once remarked, "is as American as cherry pie." Indeed, violence of many varieties was America's Anglo-Saxon and Irish tradition even before it was augmented by the abuse of black slaves and joined and altered by the influx of Central and East Europeans with their particular passions.[1]

The very first landing of the white man on the North American shores meant clashes with the native Indians. Crowding the red men off their hunting and fishing grounds was soon attended by bloodshed, of the resisting Indians against the encroaching whites, and of the aggressive whites striking at the red resisters.

But there was also violence of whites versus whites. Early in the life of the new nation there was the manhandling, the deprivation of property, the expulsion and flight to Canada and England of the Crown's loyalists losing out to the patriots of independence.* In the next century, the nineteenth, came political mob murders, such as that

---

* In his speech of November 13, 1974, at the United Nations Assembly, Yasir Arafat, head of the Palestinian terrorists, tried to equate his murderous organization to "the American people in their struggle for liberation from the British colonialists." If these Arabs are now being called terrorists, he said, then those eighteenth-century Americans should also be classed as terrorists. He compared himself to George Washington, the "heroic Washington whose purpose was his nation's freedom and independence." Answering Arafat on November 21 at the same forum, the chief American delegate John A. Scali rejected this equation of the historic American record with the Arabs' "indiscriminate terror." Said Scali: "If there were instances during the American Revolution where innocent people suffered, there was no instance where the revolutionary leadership boasted of or condoned such crimes. There were no victims, on either side, of a deliberate policy of terror. Those who molded our nation and fought for our freedom never succumbed to the easy excuse that the end justifies the means." In sum, there is terror and there is terror. The Arafat variety is surely a far cry from the American brand of George Washington's era.

of the abolitionist writer and editor Elijah P. Lovejoy at Alton, Illinois, on November 7, 1837. Another mob, this one driven by religious zeal, killed the Mormon leader Joseph Smith and his brother Hiram at Carthage, Illinois, on June 27, 1844.

In the 1830s and again in 1853-54 anti-Irish and generally anti-Catholic riots flared in a number of American cities. In the 1840s and '50s the Know-Nothings of the Northeastern cities as also in the South had a self-cultivated sinister reputation of advocating, if not actually or extensively practicing, a systematic terror against "the Papists."

And all the time the savage beat of the repression of Negroes and Negro uprisings throbbed through American history. The slaveowners' terror held the blacks in their bondage, and periodically the slaves rose against their masters with a terror of despair, an outstanding (but by no means sole) example of which was Nat Turner's Southhampton Insurrection in Virginia in August 1831.

. Three decades later the Civil War broke out between the North and the South, and its terror was not only on the many battlefields but also behind the lines, of citizen against citizen, and often of brother against brother.

When, on Good Friday, April 14, 1865, John Wilkes Booth fired his shot in Ford's Theater in Washington, he was confident that many of his fellow countrymen and certainly the coming generations of Americans would hail his murder of Abraham Lincoln. That assassination of national leaders was at times approved by some Americans may be seen from the bitter remark by Thaddeus Stevens, the radical Republican congressman from Pennsylvania, as the efforts to convict the impeached President Andrew Johnson failed in 1868: "I have come to the fixed conclusion that neither in Europe nor America will the Chief Executive of a nation be again removed by peaceful means. If tyranny becomes intolerable, the only recourse will be found in the dagger of Brutus."

And after the Civil War, the hooded and bedsheet-shrouded Ku Klux Klan rode in the South, venting on its victims the losers' brutal revenge.

From the mid-century on, the winning of the Southwest and the West meant a displacement or subjugation of the Mexicans, and this, too, was far from peaceful. Later in the century, in the same prairies, raged the continuous mutual terror of the cattlemen and the farmers; and the raids of the have-not desperadoes upon the banks and trains of the haves, with the violent response of vigilante riders and hanging judges. Everywhere in the forming, sprawling nation lynching erupted, not alone of blacks by whites, and of whites by whites, but presently also of Orientals by whites.

In the 1870s and '80s the "Chinese-Must-Go" campaign against the coolies, who had been brought mainly to build America's railroads, spilled blood in California, Wyoming, and elsewhere in the Far West. At the continent's other end the anti-Italian riot in New Orleans in 1891 boiled over.

But greatly more significant and longer lasting was the new brand of terror introduced to America by her young industrial age—the terror of capital and labor warring upon each other.

Outstanding was the lengthy strife of the Molly Maguires, a secret organization of Irish coal miners in Pennsylvania from about 1865 to 1875, murdering the oppressive policemen in the employ of the companies, waylaying and slaying mine superintendents and other bosses, but themselves getting caught and killed in turn.

The economic panic of 1873 spewed forth thousands of unemployed. Particularly in large American cities, it drove hordes of the jobless and their families homeless and hungry to sleep on the streets and under the bridges. Riots and demonstrations erupted. The one at Tompkins Square in New York on January 13, 1874, was attacked by the police ferociously. Some demonstrators fought back, one German immigrant splitting a police sergeant's head open with a claw hammer.

In the summer of 1877 a wave of railroadmen's strikes, beginning in the East, spread into general riots across the entire continent. Slogans of socialism and anarchism were proclaimed. To strengthen the failing police, militia units were called out, but at some crucial points the militiamen refused to fire and joined the rebels.

II

Nevertheless, acts of deliberate political terror of Socialist or anarchist category, such as were then beginning to make press headlines in Europe, were as yet absent from the American scene. The two most significant assassinations of the nineteenth century in the United States, those of Presidents Lincoln in 1865 and Garfield in 1881, differed sharply from the European pattern. Lincoln's murderer was an overwrought Confederate sympathizer; Garfield's killer, a half-crazed job-seeker; neither was a revolutionary.

Yet it is an error to hold (as is sometimes done in American literature) that the militant Socialism and violent anarchism in this country owe their origins entirely to importations from Europe. The influence was at least mutual.

The American strikes and riots of the 1870s attracted the attention of radicals in Europe almost at once. Bakunin, who had first visited the United States briefly in 1861 (en route to Europe after his escape from Siberia via Japan), and who had then even toyed with the idea of becoming an American citizen, planned to return to this country in 1874 but was too ill for the journey. Two years later he was dead. Kropotkin, at that time as yet thinking and writing in terms of violence, declared in the *Bulletin* of the Jura Anarchist Federation that the news of the American disturbances filled Europe's revolutionaries with admiration and hope. He saw marvelous signs for the future in the very spontaneity of the American explosions at so many geographic points at once, as well as in the participation of industrial workers of a wide range of trades and skills, and in the ferocious and determined mood and behavior of the rioters. It was this revolutionary promise that seemed to dawn in America which, in 1882, prompted the mercurial German anarchist, Johann Most, to migrate to these shores.[2]

Most began his stormy life as the illegitimate son of a governess and a minor army officer who later was a low-paid copyist for a lawyer. The claim was that the father would have married the mother, and the son would not have been born a bastard, had there been money for a wedding ceremony. The boy grew up in utter poverty, sick in his puny body and ever wounded and rebellious in spirit.

Irefully surveying his fellow humans out of his deceptively mild blue eyes, with hatred for all the world in his heart, young Most joined the radical varieties of Marxists in Germany. Of little formal schooling, a bookbinder since 17, he had access to learned tomes and read voraciously. He soon wrote for publication, lecturing and agitating as he wandered all over Central Europe. For a grim total of five years, he saw the inside of German and Austrian prisons. One such stay was in connection with someone else's attempt on the life of Kaiser Wilhelm I. Expelled from Austria and finally from his native Germany, he moved to London, where he started *Freiheit* (Freedom), a German-language weekly.

The turbulence of his appeals to his readers soon revealed him as a Bakuninist, and he was thrown out of the German Social Democratic Party. In 1881, he greeted the news of the assassination of the Tsar with joy, and his threats of more terror brought him a 16-month jail term. Released in late 1882, he sailed for America, landing there on December 12, to stay until the end of his life nearly a quarter of a century later, and to be remembered as the greatest single influence on American terror in his time.

Most's fame had preceded him. While moderate Socialists at once repudiated him, farther-left radicals welcomed him with delight. He addressed them with fire and brimstone at the very first mass meeting arranged for him at New York's historic Cooper Union hall. There followed a tour of the United States, and almost everywhere his speeches of brilliant anger inspired the formation of new anarchist clubs or fresh life for the old ones.

On return from his tour, settling in New York, he resumed his *Freiheit*. His constant cry was to destroy mankind's exploiters, "Extirpate the miserable brood! Extirpate the wretches!" As a practical guide toward this aim he published, in English, a pamphlet entitled, *Science of Revolutionary Warfare: A Manual of Instructions in the Use and Preparations of Nitroglycerine, Dynamite, Gun-Cotton, Fulminating Mercury, Bombs, Fuses, Poisons, Etc. Etc.*

The text gave detailed instructions on how to plant explosives for best results in churches, palaces, ballrooms, and other places of festive gathering; it also included a dictionary of most effective poisons to be used against capitalists, politicians, spies, and "other traitors."

Here was a true predecessor of all the celebrated twentieth-century manuals and guides to guerrilla war and terrorism by Mao Tse-tung, Ché Guevara, Carlos Marighella, and others, down to our time's anonymous brochures of instructions on how to make an atomic bomb for revolutionary action.

III

Native Americans, who had earned their anti-System spurs well before Most's arrival, now joined him as his virulent aides and were further radicalized by his leadership. One such was Albert R. Parsons, a native of Alabama and a Confederate Army veteran, who had come to Chicago in time to take part in the riots of the summer of 1877.

In the next few years, together with August Spies and other firebrands, Parsons headed a split away from the Socialists, who seemed too tame for them. They established a series of Revolutionary Clubs, which, true to this name, assumed an increasingly anarchist character. Thus was an ardent following ready for Most on his arrival in 1882. Less than one year later, in October 1883, at a convention in Pittsburgh, Most, with Parsons, Spies, and other radicals, formed the International Working People's Association. Its central office moving to Chicago, it became commonly known as the Black International, not because of the Negroes in its membership (there were hardly any), but because black was the color representing European anarchists—in contrast to the red of the Socialists.

The manifesto issued by the new organization called all the down-trodden of the earth, particularly those in America, to instant revolutionary action aimed at the "destruction of the existing class rule by all means." As intense agitation by followers spread to many urban centers, and as the continued spasms in the American economy in the 1880s deepened unemployment and the people's restiveness, the nation's upper and middle classes were gripped by alarm and fear. The press opened its furious onslaught upon Most and his anarchists. His shaggy beard gave rise to the stock character of an anarchist in the cartoons—a wild, hairy man with a smoking bomb in his threatening hand, a foreigner bent on destroying this paradise called America.

Little heed was paid to the circumstance that Most's energetic friend and top aide Parsons was a native American, and that there were also other natives in this supposedly anti-American movement. Even less cognizance was taken of the fact that anarchism as a philosophy had indigenous roots and proponents even before Most and Parsons first loomed large on American soil, and that a prominent variant of it was thoroughly peaceful.

Indeed, Most's contemporary and antithesis in the movement was the nonviolent, contemplative, scholarly Benjamin R. Tucker, whose intellectual inspiration was Henry D. Thoreau, and who found his practical teacher in Josiah Warren. Tucker described himself as "a consistent anarchist . . . an atheist, a materialist, an evolutionist, a prohibitionist, a free trader, a champion of the legal eight-hour day, a woman suffragist, an enemy of marriage, and a believer in sexual freedom." All this may have needed manuals too, but not of the kind Most and Parsons were busily compiling. And so Tucker created far fewer headlines than the Black International could—and did.

The climax came in May 1886 in Chicago, in what was destined to become sadly celebrated as the Haymarket Square Riot.[3]

IV

The preceding winter had been a harsh one. Unemployment was high, and thousands of the jobless wandered the streets and listened to indignant speeches by Socialists and anarchists. The Knights of Labor and other, lesser unions grew in membership as demands for more jobs, shorter hours, and better wages sounded yet more insistently. On May 1, nearly 300,000 workers all over the country struck for an eight-hour day. Most warned that the wage-and-hour struggle alone would not bring the lower classes their victory; again and again he stressed the need for revolutionary violence. Yet—a curious lapse for them—

for a time Parsons and Spies were in favor of more propaganda and less explosiveness, of gradual infiltration into the labor unions for peaceful gain.

But Spies changed his mind once more when, on May 3, the Chicago police fired into a crowd of strikers at the McCormick Harvester Plant when these jobless attempted to manhandle scabs. One striker was killed and several were wounded, some seriously. Spies, a witness of the shooting, ran to the office of the anarchist *Alarm* (edited by Parsons), and in his extreme anger dashed off an appeal, beginning: "REVENGE! Workingmen, to Arms!!!" In his burning text he charged that six strikers had been killed "because they, like you, had the courage to disobey the supreme will of your bosses." This blood must be avenged: "If you are men, if you are the sons of your grandsires, who have shed blood to free you, then you will rise in your might, Hercules, and destroy the hideous monster that seeks to destroy you. To arms we call you, to arms!" The appeal was set and printed in English and German, and 5,000 copies were handed out in the Chicago streets.

The police knew the style of *Alarm*. The periodical had often lauded Alfred Nobel's invention of dynamite as a sweet gift to the oppressed: "It will be your most powerful weapon; a weapon of the weak against the strong." The masses were urged to "use it unstintingly, unsparingly." So the police were on the alert when, the day after the shooting, on May 4, an evening meeting of workingmen's protest was announced by men close to *Alarm*.

Some 3,000 men, women, and children gathered near Haymarket Square (actually on a street two blocks away). Speeches by Spies, Parsons, and other agitators seemed rather moderate when a force of 180 policemen arrived to order the crowd's dispersal. A rain had started, diminishing its numbers to some 500. One of the orators tried to assure the captain in command that "we are peaceable." Then a large bomb exploded.

Thrown from a nearby alley, it landed between two companies of the police. One policeman was killed and many were wounded. In their panic, and blinded by smoke, the police began to shoot at the crowd and some even at one another. Part of the crowd that had taken the Spies advice seriously and had come armed now fired back at the police. The police, reforming their ranks, charged. The battle was over in a few minutes; seven policemen lay dead while some 60 of their comrades were wounded. No accurate count of the workers' casualties has come down to our time, but these losses were generally recognized as much greater than those of the police.

Nor was it ever ascertained just who it was that had tossed the bomb. But in her outrage and hysteria, the middle and upper America of the time demanded vengeance. Police raids and arrests swept the homes and editorial offices of Chicago's radicals, both militant and mild. The grand jury returned indictments against nine men, one of whom was never apprehended. This was Rudolph Schnaubelt, a labor organizer, in time celebrated on two counts: He was vastly and inaccurately romanticized in Frank Harris's novel *The Bomb*. And he succeeded in escaping to Latin America where, changing his name, he became a rich coffee planter.

From his safe haven, through various anarchist publications, Schnaubelt denied any connection with the Haymarket bomb. Of the remaining eight, several proved that they were not at the Square on May 4. Nonetheless, at the quick trial that opened on June 21, all eight were found guilty of instigation, which in the judge's eyes was tantamount to perpetration. Seven were sentenced to death; the eighth, Oscar W. Neebe, drew a 15-year term in the penitentiary.

Higher courts turned down the men's appeal. A campaign for mercy was launched by prominent personalities at home and abroad. William Dean Howells, George Bernard Shaw, and Oscar Wilde circulated and signed petitions or otherwise supported the plea. But Henry George and Robert Ingersoll declined to add their signatures.

Two of the seven asked Governor Richard J. Oglesby of Illinois to spare their lives, and just before the time of execution he commuted the pair's sentences to life imprisonment. A third, Louis Lingg, the only one of the original eight who truly knew the ways of dynamite, used his knowledge to explode himself to death in his cell by setting off a capsule between his teeth the night before the hanging. His woman friend was believed to have smuggled the fusecap to him.

Four were hanged on November 11, 1887. Two of these were Albert Parsons and August Spies. All four died courageously, Spies saying to his executioners, the black hood already around his head: "There will be a time when our silence will be more powerful than the voices you strangle today."

On June 26, 1893, John Peter Altgeld, the new Governor of Illinois, pardoned Neebe and the two others still in jail. His *Pardon Message* of 18,000 words was an acrid denunciation of the 1886-87 miscarriage of justice. This courage of Altgeld's liberal convictions brought him savage rebuke from such leaders as Theodore Roosevelt, who branded him a man who "condones and encourages the most infamous of murders." The vituperation of Altgeld, intensified by his opposition to President Grover Cleveland's use of federal troops in quelling the strike at the Pullman works in 1894, resulted in the end of his political career.

V

Through all this, Johann Most, although having his share of American prison experience, remained legally uninvolved in the Haymarket affair. For in May 1886 he was 840 miles away from Chicago: shortly before the Haymarket tragedy he had been taken to Blackwell's Island in New York on a year's jail term for incitement to violence.

From then on, particularly in the early 1890s, his role became quite erratic. This was the period when moderate Socialists began their ascendancy among America's radicals, while the ebbing anarchist action was gradually taken over from the natives and the Germans by immigrants from Eastern Europe or the latter's sons and daughters. Of these newcomers Most was resentful, disapproving, and jealous. But also, by this time, he may have by degrees genuinely become far less violent than he had been before.

Two young anarchist leaders emerged, both of Russian-Jewish origin: Emma Goldman and Alexander Berkman.[4] Like many other radicals, they were much exercised by the news of the all-day battle between the hired Pinkerton guards and the Carnegie Steel strikers on July 6, 1892, at Homestead near Pittsburgh, in which the two sides lost a total of ten men killed and some 60 wounded. The strikers won, the Pinkerton force retreated, but six days later several thousand Pennsylvania militiamen were sent to Homestead, and the strikers were defeated.

Hearing of this, Berkman decided on a sacrifice for justice. On July 23 he stormed into the Pittsburgh office of Henry Clay Frick, Andrew Carnegie's imperious deputy chief, and fired revolver bullets at him that wounded him in the neck, then stabbed at Frick's hip and legs with a dagger. When aides rushed in to overpower this thin, desperate intellectual, they noticed that Berkman, while struggling, was also chewing something frantically. His subduers forced his mouth open, extracting a capsule of explosive before he could detonate it with his teeth and so blow up both himself and his captors.

Frick miraculously recovered. Berkman was sentenced to 22 years in the penitentiary. It was then that Most burst forth with his aversion for the young challengers of his influence: writing in his *Freiheit,* he denounced Berkman's attentat as unneeded and untimely. Whereupon, incensed, Emma Goldman horsewhipped Most at a public meeting in Cooper Union, the very scene of Most's first American triumph of a decade before.

Losing much of his charisma, especially with the younger anarchists, Most almost welcomed one more term of imprisonment on

Blackwell's Island meted out to him in the government's general retribution for the assassination of President William McKinley in September 1901 by Leon Czolgosz, who had admired Emma Goldman but had also read some of Johann Most's writings. But even this penalty did not restore Most's prestige among radicals. During the last few years left to him he drank heavily. In March 1906 he died in Cincinnati while on a lecture tour.

A few months later, in May 1906, in consequence of a public campaign for his pardon, Berkman was released. From then on he confined himself to writing and speeches, never again lifting his hand to shoot or stab.

Generally, in the 1890s and 1900s, the anarchism of Russian Jews on New York's East Side and elsewhere in North America was reduced to hair-splitting theorizing in cafés and little periodicals rather than any actual terror. Many still insisted that they believed in propaganda by the deed; grandly they professed to be Bakuninists, yet in practice they followed the Kropotkin of his later, relaxed phase. A few in fact settled on land in the East and Northwest in communes whose love-thy-brother pattern was taken from Kropotkin's peaceful preachment. Immediately before and during the First World War, nonviolent anarchist tendencies were voiced, in print and oration, also by new non-Jewish Russian and Ukrainian immigrants who settled as factory workers in New York, Detroit, Chicago, and other large cities. In their case, too, Kropotkin, not Bakunin, was the prophet.

VI

Anarchism as a violent movement in America had virtually expired at Haymarket in 1886. Fifteen years later, in September 1901, when McKinley died of bullets fired in Buffalo by Czolgosz, the terroristic action was the result not of a conspiracy but of one man's derangement, indeed inspired by anarchist publications and speeches, but not organized by any group or team. Essentially, it was an act not by a movement but by a loner.[5]

In 1894 the United States Congress had passed a law designed to keep foreign anarchists from landing on these shores. But this of course did not stop native-born Americans from becoming dangerous anarchists. Leon Czolgosz, although of foreign origin, was a native American. The fourth child of Polish immigrants, he was born in Detroit in 1873. His father was a common laborer. His mother died when Leon was 12, and the father remarried. Leon did not get along with his stepmother.

The family moved from one Michigan town to another as the father sought menial work. They had little money and meager food. Finally they settled in Cleveland where Leon, as he grew up, found a job as a mill hand. Although proving himself an exceptionally good worker, and never once losing his job despite the recurrent depressions, Leon was a solitary figure; he apparently chose not to have friends.

He took to reading, chiefly Socialist and other radical periodicals; he frequented Socialist meetings. Once, when Emma Goldman visited Cleveland, he heard her speak, and was much impressed. He later traveled to Chicago to talk to her, but could not meet her. Both in Cleveland and Chicago he tried to approach anarchist groups, but these were suspicious of his vague, emotional talk, of his insufficient knowledge of their theory. So he remained very much alone, soon becoming tense and cranky; then, in 1898, he suffered a nervous breakdown.

He rejoined his father's family but was moody and uncommunicative, sporadically quarreling with his stepmother, at times going out into the fields to shoot rabbits, but mostly staying in his room to read anarchist literature for hours at a spell. When, on July 29, 1900, Italy's King Humbert I was assassinated by an Italian anarchist, a silk weaver who had come from Patterson, New Jersey, Leon Czolgosz read and reread newspaper accounts of the murder, and he carried those clippings with him for weeks.

In 1901 he decided to kill President McKinley, not because of any hatred for him, but on the general premise that no capitalistic ruler was any good. Czolgosz, then 28, traveled to Buffalo and planned his deed coolly. Buying a short-barreled revolver that could almost be concealed in his huge hand, he also took care to wrap a large handkerchief—more like a scarf, really—around his palm, fingers, and wrist. And so, on September 6, he joined the line of people wishing to shake hands with the President at a reception held in the Temple of Music of the Pan-American Exposition in Buffalo, New York.

Many precautions were taken that day to safeguard the President at his Buffalo appearance, for the fear of anarchists was great on both sides of the ocean, King Humbert's recent murder being remembered especially keenly. But apparently no one suspected this ordinary-looking young man in his simple dark clothes, his wide-set eyes calm, his face bearing a childish and almost vapid expression. As Leon Czolgosz neared the President, he struck aside the hand the President offered, and fired his two shots.

After eight days of pain and final agony, McKinley died on September 14. America, stunned and outraged, gave Czolgosz a swift trial. On September 26, found sane in the eyes of the law, the assassin was condemned to death. He was executed on October 29, 1901, in the prison of Auburn, New York.

Police raids swept Cleveland, Chicago, Detroit, New York, and other large centers. Hundreds of radicals were questioned, and scores were arrested, among them Emma Goldman and Johann Most.

Throughout the subsequent decades America was the scene of political attentats, most of which did result in deaths, but all of these shootings were acts by loners, not by organized movements and team-conspiracies. Nor was anarchism to be blamed as a definite influence. Consider, indeed, these acts of terror and their exact motivations:

On October 14, 1912, the time of his third-party Bull Moose presidential candidacy, Theodore Roosevelt was shot in the chest while delivering a speech in Milwaukee, Wisconsin. The lone gunman's bullet hit Roosevelt's eyeglass case and his folded manuscript, which slowed the missile and saved Roosevelt's life. Bravely he got up and delivered his speech of one hour and a half before agreeing to be taken to the hospital. He recovered, but remained incapacitated almost to the campaign's end.

On February 15, 1933, in Miami, Florida, President-elect Franklin D. Roosevelt's car was riddled with bullets, but the President escaped miraculously while cradling in his arms the mortally wounded Mayor Anton J. Cermak of Chicago.

On September 8, 1935, at Baton Rouge, Louisiana, that state's Senator Huey P. Long was killed in a volley of shots.

On November 1, 1950, in Washington, some Puerto Rican extremists tried but failed to murder President Harry S. Truman.

On November 22, 1963, at Dallas, Texas, President John F. Kennedy was assassinated.

On April 4, 1968, in Memphis, Tennessee, the black leader Martin Luther King was murdered.

Two months later, on June 5, 1968, in Los Angeles, President Kennedy's brother, New York's Senator Robert F. Kennedy, fell dead to a killer's gunfire.

On May 15, 1972, at Laurel, Maryland, Alabama's Governor George C. Wallace, campaigning in his Presidential aspiration, was shot down and paralyzed for life.

In all these historic attempts and murders we see a mixed bag of gunmen's motives; we find only one organized group, that of Puerto Rican nationalists attempting to kill Truman, but all the rest of the assassins and would-be assassins were loners and sundry kinds of psychotics or bearers of personal vengeance, as in Long's case, but few (excepting the Puerto Ricans and the racist murder of King) with any definite political ideology.

VII

Standing rather aside from the above list there was the terrorism by native Americans in the period 1900–1920, chiefly in the Far West, which was motivated by immediate economic no less than by political considerations. In that prolonged episode, desperate union men evolved into daring terrorists, and a few of these half felt or even openly avowed that they were convinced anarchists. But even if these few were indeed anarchists by conviction, theirs was not truly a wide and well-rooted political movement. They were too few, even if some of their deeds were sensational.

The world at large first learned of them on December 30, 1905, when Idaho's ex-Governor Frank Steunenberg was killed by a bomb, which was soon traced to Albert E. Horsley, alias Harry Orchard, a member of the Western Federation of Miners, a fighting union with a grudge against Steunenberg for his crushing a strike of 1899. Horsley-Orchard was induced to confess and to implicate three of the Federation's top officials, among them its secretary-treasurer William D. Haywood, an anarcho-syndicalist of some renown.

Two of the three were tried but acquitted. Clarence Darrow, the famous lawyer, was Haywood's attorney; he gained his client's freedom by proving that there was no evidence other than Horsley-Orchard's charge. Haywood, one of the founders of the Industrial Workers of the World and a member of the American Socialist Party (from which he was expelled for his advocacy of violence), was later jailed again, accused of sedition during the First World War. In 1921, while awaiting one more trial, he escaped—and turned up in Soviet Russia. He spent his last few years there, unhappily. When he died in 1928 his ashes were placed in the Kremlin wall.

Horsley-Orchard, who before his trial had also confessed the murder of 26 other men on the Federation's orders, was rewarded for his seeming repentance: his death sentence was commuted to life imprisonment, and he died in an Idaho jail in 1954 at the ripe age of 88.

Nearly five years after Steunenberg's slaying, there occurred the no less celebrated dynamiting of *The Los Angeles Times* building. In this explosion, soon after the midnight of October 1, 1910, 20 persons were killed. The newspaper was owned by Harrison Gray Otis, widely known for his extreme antiunion policies. He now blamed labor leaders for this act of terrorism. A private detective in the Otis service succeeded in pinning the charge on John J. McNamara, secretary-treasurer of the Bridge and Structural Iron Workers' Union. He and his younger brother James were brought to trial. Darrow was engaged for the McNamaras' defense, and a stiff court battle was expected when, in a sudden drama, the two brothers confessed, John protesting that he "did not intend to take the life of anyone." He was sent to the San Quentin Prison for life, while his brother James was sentenced to 15 years, of which he served ten, being released in May 1921.

In 1916, in San Francisco, a bomb was thrown into a patriotic war-preparedness parade, killing ten and wounding 40 persons. Its origin was never conclusively proven, but a private detective hired by the city's power companies accused two men: Thomas J. Mooney, a radical labor agitator who was rather a loner in the San Francisco union movement; and Warren Billings, an adventurous young man who had once served a short jail term for transporting dynamite. At their trial, which attracted international attention and caused worldwide protests by liberals and radicals, Mooney was sentenced to death, and Billings to life imprisonment. In 1918, through President Woodrow Wilson's intercession, Mooney's sentence was commuted to life imprisonment, and in 1939 he was pardoned, dying three years later.

The years 1919 and 1920 were the period of a major Red scare in the United States. In April 1919 a package arrived at the house of a senator in Georgia; when a servant opened the package, her hands were blown off. Thirty-six other packages, addressed to prominent persons, were halted in post offices across the country and found to contain bombs. No clues were discovered as to the identities of their senders, nor of the origin of the dynamite planted and exploded on September 16, 1920, in New York's Wall Street in front of J. P. Morgan's banking house, as the result of which 34 people were killed and more than 200 injured, the interior of the building wrecked and the damage totaling two million dollars.

A campaign of governmental repression followed. Attorney General A. Mitchell Palmer ordered arrests of thousands of radicals, many of whom, being of foreign origin, were deported to Soviet Russia. The exile ship *The Bufford* carried Alexander Berkman and Emma Goldman, among others. But the terror by then being conducted by the new Soviet government against its subjects did not meet with these anarchists' approval. In 1921 both were back in the West, a thoroughly disillusioned pair of revolutionaries. In 1936 Berkman committed suicide; in 1940 Goldman died.*

* Max Nomad, in his *Dreamers, Dynamiters, and Demagogues* (New York: Waldon Press, 1964, pp. 207-09), disputes the official and generally accepted version of Berk-

The era truly closed in 1927 with the execution in Boston of two Italian-American radicals, Nicola Sacco and Bartolomeo Vanzetti, charged and convicted six years before in a case of murder and robbery at Braintree, Massachusetts. Little or no evidence was brought out against the two, but a certain mighty part of the Establishment chose to smite them as a symbol rather than an actual agency of that oldtime anarchistic terror which in historical reality had long since spent its force, opening the stage to far different forms of political killing that would begin in the 1930s and last well into the 1970s.

----

man's death in France as a suicide. He states that Berkman was killed by his young Hungarian mistress in a fit of jealousy. Nomad knew the girl. He writes: "This happened during the period of the Popular Front regime, and the French authorities were not anxious to stir up a scandal involving elements of the Left, even though the people involved were outside the regular Left. So the police—most likely upon the wise suggestion of Leon Blum, then Prime Minister—declared that it was a case of suicide, and enough money was raised to enable the girl to leave France and settle in some other country. I never heard of her again." According to Nomad, the girl was jealous of Emma Goldman who, though 67 years old in 1936, still had a hold on her erstwhile lover Berkman.

9

Hunting the Tsar

In the latter 1960s, a splinter group of America's youthful Weathermen proudly called themselves the Narodniki. In Western Europe, too, in recent times those Populist terrorists of Russia's 1870s-80s have been recalled as among the influences upon modern political violence. At least some of the revolutionaries in one land or another have taken their inspiration from the Narodniki. The Narodniki's main mission was to slay Tsar Alexander II; finally, after long travail, they chased him down to death.

The details of this macabre hunt of the Narodniki are unique:[1]

In 1855, in the midst of his unsuccessful Crimean War against the British, the French, the Turks, and the Sardinians, Tsar Nicholas I died, according to some reports (including those of his loose-tongued doctors) not of any natural causes but of poison taken by the Tsar when he could no longer bear the shame of his defeat at Sevastopol. His young and liberal son Alexander II ascended the throne. He planned to free the serfs and introduce other much-needed reforms.

But he would take his time, some six years in fact, until his first important change. Meanwhile, the young of Russia were in ferment. Nihilists had appeared in the late 1850s. The word "nihilist," first coined from the Latin *nihil*—"nothing"—in the 1830s by an obscure Russian journalist, was revived by Ivan Turgenev in his novels to describe the new breed of young radicals of the latter 1850s and early '60s who valued or recognized nothing as restraining their morals and behavior.

A galaxy of brilliant young publicists seemed to speak for or support such new views of the world. In and out of prison, such writers as Nikolai Dobrolyubov, Dmitry Pisarev, and Nikolai Chernyshevsky preached what to the elders was worse than nothing—materialism, professional revolutionism, denunciation of art for art's sake, and sacrifice of everything so as to benefit the deprived masses. The influence of these books and magazine essays upon Russia's young intellectuals was enormous. It was amid such ideas that Nechayev and his Nechayevists would form their ranks for terrorist action.

Compared with these drastic appeals, Alexander Herzen's books, periodicals, and leaflets, smuggled into Russia from his West European printeries, were mild. He was for freedom and the dignity of man. The state must be reformed, not demolished. Society was gravely ill, yes, but curable. In London, with his close friend Nikolai Ogaryov, Herzen started a Russian press and at his own expense (his large fortune in Russia had never been confiscated by the Tsar) published his libertarian journals, first *Polyarnaya Zvezda* (The Polar Star), 1855-62, then *Kolokol* (The Bell), 1857-67. Through their pages Herzen's program for Russia was clear: Serfs must be freed and given land of their own. Censorship must be ended. Corporal punishment was to be abolished. True justice should be the rule for all.

With most of its 2,500 to 3,000 copies at the magazine's peak going illegally to Russia, Herzen's *Kolokol* was soon the most influential periodical in that country. All the outstanding writers and editors in Russia eagerly awaited each new issue. High Tsarist officials, and even the Tsar himself, read its attacks on autocracy and its bold proposals of reforms.

But in the 1860s, among the young, Herzen's appeal and prestige declined. Even as the Tsar, in 1861, at last did free the millions of serfs, Russia's rising young radicals demanded yet deeper and wider socio-political changes. Herzen's and Ogaryov's ideas were too tame for them. Nihilists were clamoring for a real revolution.

In the next decade, the 1870s, more and more of those young intellectuals left their comfortable homes *idti v narod,* to go into the people, as the time's phrase had it. (From this came the word *Narodniki,* meaning "Populists.") They were not only of noble families, but also *raznochintsy,* meaning "persons of various ranks"—that is, sons and daughters of merchants, clerks, priests, and others of the middle class.

They went as schoolteachers, doctors, nurses, midwives, not only to teach and heal those wretched ex-serfs, but, more importantly, to agitate for more land and against the Tsar and his officials. Along with their daring talk they brought to the villages brochures printed underground or abroad. Written in a pseudopopular style, these extolled the memory of Stenka Razin and Yemelian Pugachev—those cutthroat leaders of the peasant insurrections of the seventeenth and eighteenth centuries—and called for similar mass revolts immediately.

But many peasants were suspicious of these smooth-talking strangers. The Tsar had given serfs their liberty, even if without enough land—and now these intruders spoke against the Tsar the Liberator! Here and there agitators were seized and delivered by the peasants themselves to the police. And now the police were on the alert, arresting the wandering talkers without waiting for the peasants' aid.

There followed large-scale trials, such as the famous case of 193 in 1877. But to the judges and the juries these men and women seemed romantically naïve and harmless. These rebel Narodniki, as yet of a nonviolent variety, were either acquitted or deported north and east, to live as political exiles under lax police supervision. They soon escaped, or completed their terms, and returned to St. Petersburg and Moscow to plot in earnest.

Of the new and more intensively revolutionary organizations, *Zemlya i Volya,* or Land and Liberty, soon became very active. In August 1879, meeting underground, it evolved into the still more radical *Narodnaya Volya,* or the People's Will. These Narodniki proclaimed their business: terror.

By killing off governors, chiefs of police, and, above all, the Tsar himself, these intellectuals aimed to bring about a new society of complete justice and breath-taking beauty. Their program: Take all the land away from the landlords and give it to the people. Depose and, if need be, destroy the Tsar and all Tsarist officeholders. In place of the Tsarist state, create a new and free state of autonomous communes with elective and always replaceable executives of the people's will. The text of their typical manifesto reminded fellow Russians: "Such was the program of the people's socialists of yore—of Razin, Pugachev, and their men." It declared: "Such is the program of today's masses. Such is our program, of us—revolutionaries-populists."

II

With their unprecedented persistence and ingenuity these young, angry Narodniki schemed and tried one assassination plot after another. But the highest target on their agenda was Tsar Alexander II himself—a manhunt remarkable in its duration, stubbornness, and inventiveness.

Although the most liberal of sovereigns in Russian history, Alexander II did not satisfy the aspirations of that nation's extremists. If anything, his reforms were dangerous: they pleased, or gave hope to, entirely too many of his subjects who, in the revolutionaries' desiderata, should have been seething with anti-Tsarist ire, should have been rising to the rebel call and battling toward the future socialist republic. But the Tsar's assassination would surely awaken the oppressed and rally them to the red flag of the People's Will—or so thought these terrorists.

The beginnings of this manhunt had actually antedated the People's Will. Until the latter 1870s, the several attempts on the Tsar's life had been the work of loners or small, ill-organized groups. The mighty People's Will would change all this.

In the pre-People's Will phase, the first attentat against Alexander II occurred on an April day in 1866 when a 26-year-old student, Dmitry Karakozov, fired his pistol at the Tsar as he was re-entering his carriage after a walk in the Summer Garden in St. Petersburg. The terrorist missed, and was immediately seized. A peasant in the crowd was credited with making Karakozov miss by striking his arm just as the student had aimed his weapon. Whether or not this had actually happened, it became a useful legend: a plain man of the soil, the Tsar's savior! Think of it! The peasant was brought to the Tsar and solemnly made a noble. But the legend misfired when the peasant soon proved to be a dolt and eventually died in drunken obscurity.

No uprising of the masses against the Tsar, expected by Karakozov and his friends, took place in the wake of the attempt. When Karakozov was seized, he shouted at the simple people in the crowd who assisted the police in grabbing him: "Fools, I've done this for you!" After an investigation, more than 30 associates of the terrorist were found and captured. All were tried. Karakozov alone went to the scaffold the following October. The others were sent to Siberia in chains, some, in time, going insane.

Before that April day in 1866 the Tsar had been toying with the idea of following his freeing of the serfs (1861) and liberalization of the courts (1864) with a rudimentary parliament. Now, abruptly, this project was abandoned. Instead he ordered large-scale arrests, stringent censorship of press and books, suppression of academic freedom, and other such acts based on fear and control. From then on, for several years, the Empire lay still.

It was only toward the very end of the 1860s that revolutionary stirrings reappeared in Russia, particularly as represented by Sergei Nechayev. But Nechayev, although truly wild as a terrorist, did not appear to be engaged in a plot against the Tsar himself. Had he eluded the police long enough, he might have come to that; indeed, in one of his leaflets Nechayev promised to wipe out the entire Imperial House (later to be quoted with approval by Lenin); but he had no chance to try this, spending the last decade of his life in the dungeons of the Peter and Paul Fortress, where he died in 1882.

Throughout the middle 1870s, as new revolutionaries took up the bomb and the bullet against the Tsarist state, these men of the Land

and Liberty organization shot at and sometimes killed informers and minor officials. The Russo-Turkish War of 1877-78 quickened the nation's pulse and, as any war does, brought some disaffection despite the victory of the Tsar's armies.

The war made it easier for terrorists to raise their gun sights. Returning from his foreign adventures, Sergei Kravchinsky-Stepniak in August 1878 killed General Nikolai Mezentsev, chief of the Tsar's political police. He did this on behalf of the Land and Liberty group, showing his customary bravery by stabbing the victim in broad daylight on a central street of St. Petersburg, and, at that, facing the general as he wielded his knife, for, he felt, only hired murderers were unchivalrous enough to strike in the back. Kravchinsky-Stepniak escaped, his fellow terrorists holding a fast carriage in readiness for him, with the very same racehorse in harness that had helped Prince Peter Kropotkin flee prison two years earlier.

In February 1879, Grigory Goldenberg shot and killed Prince Dmitry Kropotkin, Governor of the Kharkov Province in the Ukraine and a cousin of Peter Kropotkin, the anarchist. And in April 1879, for the first time since Karakozov's shot of 13 years before, bullets were again fired at the Tsar.

This attempt was made by a Land and Liberty member, Alexander Solovyov. He acted alone, although he was supported in his intent by certain of his fellow members. Five times he fired at the Tsar as he was taking his habitual walk on the grounds of the Winter Palace in St. Petersburg. All five bullets went wild. The Tsar ran, stumbled, fell, but was not hurt. The police escort nabbed Solovyov at once. He swallowed poison, but this was quickly neutralized medically by his captors. Solovyov was tried and, later that spring, publicly hanged.

Some Ukrainian members of the Land and Liberty made extensive preparations in 1878-79 to dynamite a street in the city of Nikolayev that the Tsar was expected to cross. But these plotters were caught and hanged before they could achieve their aim, and their dynamite wound up in the hands of the police. (A similar tunnel to the middle of a street for the same regicide purpose would be tried again by Narodniki in March 1881, to be abandoned for another method. But as a coincidence or a case of parallelism, many years later, in December 1973 in Spain, several Basque terrorists did kill Prime Minister Luis Carrero Blanco by patiently tunneling from a house basement to the middle of the street where they blew up the prime minister's automobile.)

Other Narodniki, implicated in lesser acts of terror or propaganda, were rounded up and executed or deported to Siberia in the last three years of the 1870s. But determined new members and leaders continued to arise in the underground. In August 1879, as the People's Will organization announced its existence, its men and women at their very first formal meeting passed a solemn resolution that henceforth they would bend all their efforts toward killing the Tsar, a priority above all priorities.

III

The enterprise from then on would be far more systematic than the attempts by Karakozov, Solovyov, and the Ukrainian group. The People's Will would now clearly exercise its full authority.

The outstanding personalities in charge of this manhunt that brought down the prey were two young lovers: Andrei Zhelyabov, a serf's son, 29 years old in 1879; and Sofiya Perovskaya, a 26-year-old daughter of the nobility, whose father was a general and had once served as Governor of St. Petersburg. Other principal terrorists were Stepan Khalturin, a peasant cabinetmaker, aged 23; and Nikolai Kibalchich, 25, a priest's son and an expert bomb-maker who also dreamed of inventing a "rocket airplane."

This group's initial try was planned for the fall or winter of 1879, when the Tsar would travel by train from his vacation in the south back to the capital. The conspirators would blow up the Tsar's train as it was en route. Caches of dynamite would be planted at three widely separated spots; if one did not go off, the second or third charge would be detonated. The three places were at Odessa on the Black Sea, at Alexandrovsk in the Ukraine, and in Moscow.

Heaven seemed to be on the Tsar's side: bad weather caused him to change his route, eliminating Odessa. So the first trap was canceled. The second charge, at Alexandrovsk, failed to explode as the Tsar's train passed over the deadly mine: something had gone wrong with the plotters' wires. The third charge, near Moscow, planted at the end of a tunnel dug by the terrorists from a cellar to the railroad, did go off—but under a wrong train, causing no damage except for the smashing of a freight car loaded with Crimean fruit. The Tsar escaped again.

The next major move would be to arrange an explosion inside the Tsar's palace in St. Petersburg. In September 1879, Khalturin succeeded in being hired by the Tsar's own household as a cabinetmaker and carpenter. He was given lodgings in a basement dormitory of the Winter Palace. When two floor plans of the palace were found in the possession of an arrested fellow revolutionist, the police became highly suspicious—but not of Khalturin. He looked too guileless; he was too industrious to arouse any doubts.

One day in the course of his woodworking duties he realized he was in a palace room alone with the Tsar. A thought flashed through his mind: How easy it would be to bring down his hammer on the sovereign's skull and so end the manhunt! But he had to clear his idea with Zhelyabov, who immediately objected, saying that this form of murder would make Khalturin's getaway impossible. He insisted on a remote-control explosion that would allow the dynamiter to escape.

And so, each evening, Khalturin would return from his secret meetings with Zhelyabov in the city to his bed in the palace basement, carrying with him additional small quantities of dynamite. He stored the explosive under his pillow, where, despite all the police and guard searches, it went undetected.

But Khalturin had problems. For one thing, sleeping on his nightly dynamite cache gave him headaches and he had to transfer it to the more exposed chest containing his linen and clothes. But, he decided, in a way the chest was an advantage as the hiding place: when the time came, he would use it as a mine to be detonated.

His artful pretense of innocence and his diligence as a carpenter soon presented him with another difficulty: an elderly gendarme, one of those who had been moved into the carpenters' quarters to watch the workers, so greatly trusted and liked Khalturin that he began to fancy him as as excellent prospect for his young daughter. The terrorist had to summon all his patience and courage to keep playing his role of this skillful but simple artisan.

At last, on a February evening in 1880, all was ready. The Tsar was scheduled to enter a dining room with his guests and entourage; Khalturin, knowing this timetable and the palace floor plan, set off his dynamite from the basement.

But an audience with two visiting German princes had delayed the Tsar. When the powerful charge went off, he was nearby but only severely shaken, while 11 persons were killed and 56 wounded, mostly soldiers of the guard.

Once more the Tsar emerged unharmed. Actually, it was the guards' room on the level between the basement and the dining room that was demolished. The explosive charge, although strong, had not been massive enough to reach upward into the dining room above the guards' quarters. Even if the Tsar had been in the dining room at the time, he would most likely have escaped death or even serious injury.

Khalturin and Zhelyabov stood outside the palace, observing the confusion and listening to screams. For the nonce both evaded arrest.

IV

But Alexander II knew the revolutionaries would not rest. He now knew how a hunted animal felt. By this time, his Empress having peacefully passed away, he had at last married his long-time mistress, his deeply loved Princess Catherine Dolgorukaya. She and their children were finally legitimatized. He was planning to crown his Catherine, but in moments of depression he wanted to escape the terror once and for all, musing on how wonderful it would be to abdicate in favor of his eldest son and retire with Catherine and their young children to private life in some faraway corner of the planet.

On their part, despite the continuing arrests, the main members and leaders of the People's Will were as yet at large and feverishly active. Having carefully restudied the Tsar's daily habits, the terrorists resolved anew to blow him up on one of his rides or walks through the capital.

In the winter of 1880-81, they chose as one of their most feasible areas Malaya Sadovaya Street, the route along which the Tsar's carriage usually traveled to and from his reviews and parades. Two terrorists, a man and a woman, pretending to be a merchant couple, and looking the part, rented under a false name a two-room basement on that street, ostensibly for a cheese shop. While one room was used for the store, the other served as the pair's living quarters, and it was from this room that a tunnel was begun to the middle of the street. When ready, the tunnel's end would hold the dynamite to be detonated under the Imperial carriage or sled. The revolutionaries had experience in this kind of digging: it will be remembered that they had once burrowed a tunnel near Moscow to the railroad and the Tsar's train, which nevertheless they had failed to explode. They hoped for better luck this time.

But the Malaya Sadovaya neighbors, noticing certain strange goings-on about the shop, particularly so many young men visiting the place (the diggers), grew suspicious and alerted the police. And a nearby tradesman, fearing competition, started rumors against the new store. In the guise of sanitary inspectors the police came, but, inefficient as they were, stopped short of the ill-concealed entrance to the tunnel. The terrorists weathered this peril by a hairbreadth.

The tunnel was almost ready when the People's Will leadership decided, in addition, to place bomb-throwers along the Tsar's route on March 13, that Sunday the terrorists had selected as their target date. This was done because of the possibility that the tunnel charge might not go off at the crucial moment or that, even if it did explode, the Tsar might survive, or his route might avoid the Malaya Sadovaya block altogether. In any of these cases the bomb-tossers would strike at the Tsar aboveground, should he still be alive.

But suddenly and unexpectedly a calamity overwhelmed the terrorists when, on Friday evening, the eleventh, less than two days before the time set for the attentat, Zhelyabov was seized during a police ambush in the lodgings of another revolutionary who had behaved incautiously and had been under surveillance. This put the terrorists under extraordinary pressure. Before the police could trace and find all the others of the group, the People's Will had to strike with all the force it could muster. More bombs must be made quickly; both the tunnelers and the surface terrorists must do their jobs without hitch.

Sofiya Perovskaya, the woman leader who knew all the details arranged by her lover, Zhelyabov, took his place as head of the operation. Suppressing her grief, she went about surveying the streets of the Tsar's probable passage, choosing the bomb-throwers, and distributing the bombs freshly made by Kibalchich, who had labored on them for 15 hours through the night. Thus came the fateful Sunday.

That murky snowy afternoon the Tsar decided to drive to the Manege as planned. Despite the tension in the wake of Zhelyabov's capture and the rumors about the peculiar cheese shop, he wanted to see the maneuvers of men and horses and the marching of two Guards battalions he liked so much. Inexplicably, the police failed to return to the shop and search it more carefully. But the Tsar was informed of the cheese shop and told his wife about it. He promised his worried Catherine that he would avoid that suspicious Malaya Sadovaya block both coming and returning, and indeed did so.

Perovskaya, loitering around the Manege and seeing that the Tsar had arrived unharmed, still thought he might pass the shop on his way back. But, the parade over, the Tsar gave last-minute instructions to his coachman, and the carriage, with its armed escort, again swung away from the tunnel. At once Perovskaya figured out his alternate route—correctly.

She acted swiftly, giving her four bomb-throwers new orders. Only three took up their changed positions along the Tsar's route. The fourth, losing courage, carried his bomb package back to the underground headquarters and went home. It was a wonder that neither he nor the other three drew any notice from the police as they walked or lingered with their deadly packages. The first explosion came as a total surprise.

The first volunteer to hurl his bomb was the 19-year-old Nikolai Rysakov. He threw it between the legs of the horses of the Tsar's coach. When the spurt of the snow, earth, pavement, and flesh subsided and the bluish smoke cleared, a Cossack lay still on the ground and a butcher's delivery boy writhed and groaned, both mortally wounded, both soon dying. Several others were injured. But the Tsar was unhurt, although there was a small cut on one of his hands. A police chief helped him out of the shattered vehicle.

The sovereign crossed himself, as if thanking God for his escape, then walked to where the injured lay moaning and a crowd was holding the terrorist. Recovering from his shock and daze, the Tsar inquired about the bomber's identity, then turned away. In answer to an officer's question, the Tsar said:

"Thanks be to God, I am safe."

The terrorist, in the tight grip of his captors, looked at the Tsar and remarked:

"It may still be too early to thank God."

Indeed, the second terrrorist was now nearby, leaning against a railing with a parcel in his hand. This was Ignaty Grinevetsky, an engineering student, a Polish noble aged 24. The Tsar, not knowing the danger, walked a few steps toward him. Grinevetsky turned toward the Tsar, and, facing him, threw his bomb. The august target was reached.

After the deafening explosion, the smoke lifted. Amid the debris lay a number of wounded, among them both the Tsar and the terrorist Grinevetsky. The Tsar was on his back, bleeding profusely, his body and limbs hideously torn. By the Tsar's side lay the terrorist, unconscious.

The Tsar, his words barely audible, begged: "Help me, help me. . . . Cold, cold." He was lifted and taken to the Winter Palace. There, within an hour, he died. A flag hoisted over the palace signaled his end.

Grinevetsky, carried to the palace infirmary, regained consciousness but refused to tell his questioners his name. He soon died.

V

The supreme irony of that bloody March day was that on that very morning Alexander II had at last signed a document promising a first step toward a parliamentary government. His son and heir, Alexander III, hesitated only briefly before abandoning all such liberal intentions. Instead, he instituted a reign of reaction.

Nor did the people rise in revolt against the new Tsar and his nobles as the revolutionaries had so fervently hoped. The masses were silent. If they spoke up at all, it was in sharp indignation against those misguided murderers of their Tsar the Liberator.

Rysakov, the first bomber, having survived, was now frightened and talkative in his interrogation. With these clues, the police rounded up such terrorist leaders as Perovskaya, Kibalchich, and others. They were tried and sentenced to hang. From his prison cell Kibalchich petitioned for a postponement of his execution so that he could finish the blueprints of his "rocket airplane." The request was denied; his plea, along with his drawings, was discovered in the Tsarist archives after the revolution of 1917.

In April 1881, five principal terrorists—among them Perovskaya, Zhelyabov, Kibalchich, and the repentant Rysakov—climbed the scaffold. Before the hanging, the four embraced one another but shunned Rysakov.

Khalturin the carpenter was caught and hanged in 1882, after he had topped his career by taking part in the assassination of the military procurator of Odessa.

For a few weeks after the Tsar's assassination the surviving terrorists thought they could advance their cause and perhaps even save their comrades from the gallows by offering a compromise to the new Tsar. If Alexander III would grant certain liberties, they would call off their terrorist war. But they exaggerated their power, which was now gone. The war was over; the new Tsar, with the stern advice from his tutor, the statesman Konstantin Pobedonostsev, a friend of that former revolutionary Dostoyevsky, was launching his policy of repression.

Among their other sentiments, the terrorists of the People's Will who were still at large—underground or emigrated to West Europe—cared for the world's opinion. They did not want to be accused in the West of inspiring terror where it should not be occurring. When, in the distant United States, President James A. Garfield was shot by the crazed office seeker Charles J. Guiteau on July 2, 1881, dying on September 19, the Executive Committee of the People's Will issued a statement condemning terrorist activities in a democratic country such as America. Unlike the despotic Tsardom, in the United States "the free popular will determines not only the law, but also the person of its administrators." These Russian terrorists denounced "all such deeds of violence as that which has just taken place in America . . . a land where citizens are free to express their ideas" in speech, print, and ballots rather than bullets and bombs.

One of the surviving Narodniki terrorists did eventually reach American shores to enjoy this country's freedom to the end of his long and curious life. This was Sergei Degayev, an army captain who left the military service at an early age to enroll in an engineering school where he first met revolutionaries and soon became one himself. He was in his mid-20s when he participated in the plot on the life of Alexander II by being one of the diggers of the cheese-shop tunnel. Arrested in late December 1882, he was beguiled by a shrewd gendarme, Lieutenant Colonel Georgy Sudeikin, into thinking that the two of them together—Degayev and Sudeikin—would yet hand over Russia to the People's Will. En route to this goal Degayev was to become an informer and betray his comrades. After a year or so of such service, Degayev realized he had been duped by the colonel into this betrayal, and, on December 28, 1883, he murdered Sudeikin.

Fleeing abroad, Degayev and his wife successfully vanished in the United States. Resuming his studies, he earned his doctorate in philosophy under another name at Johns Hopkins University. As Professor Alexander Pell, jolly and immensely popular with his students, he taught for ten years at the University of South Dakota, where he was also Dean of the College of Engineering. His past a well-guarded secret, his whereabouts unknown to any Russian, this former terrorist was intensely interested in campus athletics and served as a class father and an indefatigable dinner host to innumerable students. Later he taught at Chicago's Armour Institute of Technology. He died at the age of 67 in 1921.

A close friend of his and a fellow Narodnik terrorist, Lev Tikhomirov, was also an émigré, in Western Europe, but did not remain there. Eventually he was to return to Russia. Losing his faith in revolution, he publicly declared his change of heart in a pamphlet, *Why I Have Ceased to be a Revolutionary*. He proceeded to what he thought was his journey's logical end: in September 1888 he petitioned Alexander III, the son of the murdered sovereign, to forgive him and allow him to come home. The Tsar granted his request. On returning, the ex-terrorist became a most loyal subject, a pious communicant of the Russian Orthodox Church, and an important journalist in the service of the dynasty. In time, the last Tsar, Nicholas II, gratefully presented him with a golden inkpot.

VI

Dostoyevsky died a few short weeks before Alexander II's murder. For the three last decades of his life he was an ardent supporter of the throne and the Russian Orthodox Church, having renounced the revolutionary ideas and actions of his youth that had earned him ten years as a convict and an exile in Siberia. It was these years that transformed his views on radicalism into bitterness, expressed so powerfully in *The Possessed*.

Now, just before his own death, while relaxing one day in the capital's Summer Garden, he happened to overhear two men discussing their plans to kill the Tsar. Apparently they were members of the People's Will. They did not realize they were being heard; they were frank in their talk. It did not take Dostoyevsky long, experienced in such matters as he was, to recognize precisely what these two men and their talk were. He listened, horrified; he was as if under a nightmarish spell, impaled on the bench on which he sat.

At last, shaking himself loose, he fled the Summer Garden. As a zealot of the Tsar he should have hastened to the police to report what he had heard. Instead, he sped to a reactionary friend of his, an editor-publisher, and told him; neither one did anything about it. If there was a struggle in Dostoyevsky between the need to warn the police and the Russian intellectual's innate reluctance to be an informer, the latter won.

10

Azef: Terror Chief as Double Agent

After that March Sunday of 1881, as the course of repression was chosen and the previous reign's reforms were halted, slowed, and some—particularly those in education—reversed, one of the angriest orders of the new Tsar was to smash the People's Will once and forever. Besides the five regicides who were hanged, many terrorists were jailed or exiled to Siberia. Comparatively few escaped to foreign lands or hid in the underground.

Even liberals, shocked and afraid, would not extend their former sympathy and aid to those in hiding. Still, a small group of young students would try terror again. They chose March 13, 1887, to mark that date of six years earlier, by attempting to assassinate Tsar Alexander III. But the conspirators never came near their target: a careless letter was intercepted by the police, who arrested the plotters in time to prevent the attempt. Five of the conspirators were hanged. Among them was Alexander Ulyanov, the elder brother of Vladimir Ulyanov-Lenin.

Not till the beginning of the 1900s would terror again find adherents among Russian revolutionaries. These would come forth at the very dawn of the twentieth century from the membership of a freshly formed party, the Socialist Revolutionaries, their ranks recruited in Russia and among the Russian political émigrés in Western Europe. Their Terror Brigade (in the original Russian also known as "The Fighting Organization") has gone into history for one astonishing reason above any other: the chief of the Terror Brigade was a double agent, and his service to the Tsar's police was not discovered by the revolutionaries for years. No other case of such daring duplicity has to this time been known in all the annals of political terror. Not even today, a time so replete with double agents in intelligence services and terrorist organizations, has this amazing phenomenon of the early 1900s been approached by the depth of its treachery.[1]

II

These Socialist Revolutionaries were non-Marxist socialists, heirs of the Narodniki, full of the same strong faith in the revolutionary potential of Russia's peasant masses, with their allegedly communal instincts. As the Narodniki before them, so these new Socialist Revolutionaries believed in the efficacy of the bomb and the bullet as the means to bring about an immediate millenium for peasants as well as for all other humble subjects of the Tsar.

But, turning their disdainful backs upon the peasants and placing their main trust in the urban proletariat (then just appearing in any number), there surged those Russian intellectuals who had by the late 1880s and early 1890s read and embraced Marx and Engels. Together with Marx, they viewed peasants everywhere, but particularly in Russia, as "rural idiots" (in Marx's own phrase), hopeless herds who would not help their own salvation but would have to be dragged by their ignorant necks into the brave new world of the socialist future. Only workers, class conscious and generally wise, would rise in a proper revolution led by these intellectuals. At the end of the 1890s they established their Social Democratic Party. Among them young Lenin was an ascending authority. Favoring mass rebellion, he saw little use for any heroic terror by loners or small teams.

The time was ripe for both the Socialist Revolutionaries and the Marxists to emerge. Tsar Alexander III died in 1894; his young son Nicholas II was on the throne, trying to continue his late father's forbidding policies, but with little success. Under its lid the nation was stirring after a long stupor. Now, not only revolutionaries but liberals too were raising their voices in speeches, books, and periodicals. Native merchant money was going into expanding factories. West European capitalists brought their investments into Russia. Thus capital, domestic and foreign, was changing and energizing the old semifeudal economic scene. The new rising classes felt they were deserving of political rights that had not been granted them. The new century opened in turmoil: in the cities, demonstrating students and striking workers filled the streets; in the countryside, peasants were trying to shake off the remaining grip by the deteriorating nobles through both land purchase and sporadic rebellions.

The Socialist Revolutionaries launched their terror by assassinating high officials. In April 1902, Dmitry Sipyagin, the Tsar's minister of the interior in charge of the police, was shot. Following this murder the Socialist Revolutionaries solemnly explained: "Each terroristic blow tends to deprive the autocracy of part of its strength, handing this strength over to the side of the fighters for freedom." Rather than threatening the Tsar himself, they would attack his ministers.

For this, they gave two reasons. First, more than the Tsar, they blamed the cabinet ministers for the misdeeds of the System. Second, it was easier to reach the ministers with bullets and bombs, whereas the Tsar could and did withdraw to the far recesses of his palaces. But there may have been a third and more important factor: Although the peasantry and many lower-class townsmen were becoming increasingly antiregime, they were, in the main, still of a monarchical mood. To them, the person of the Tsar was as yet mystically awesome, even if the System was less and less so.

Sipyagin's successor, Vyacheslav von Plehve, was then quoted as saying that what Russia needed to thwart the revolutionaries and wean people away from them was a small victorious war somewhere on the Empire's fringes. The Russo-Japanese War, breaking out in February 1904, seemed to be the answer to his prayer. But in July, von Plehve, too, was assassinated, a terrorist bomb blowing him into nothingness.

The defeats of the ill-prepared Russian armies and navies by the Japanese fanned the fires of domestic strife. The fall of Port Arthur at the year's turn brought a wave of antigovernment demonstrations, climaxed by the Bloody Sunday of January 22, 1905.

That Sunday a vast but orderly throng of St. Petersburg's workers marched to the Winter Palace with a naïve petition, phrased loyally, for a redress of their miseries. The Tsar had left the capital the day before. Grand Duke Vladimir ordered the troops to fire. Some 1,500 workers were killed and many were wounded—not only men, but women and children as well. The revolution of 1905 had begun.[2]

In February 1905, Grand Duke Sergei, Governor General of Moscow and the Tsar's uncle and brother-in-law, was murdered by the Terror Brigade. In June, the crew of the battleship *Potemkin* rebelled at Odessa, killing some of its officers and taking the warship to asylum in Rumania. Everywhere, week in and week out, workers struck, peasants rioted, landlords' mansions went up in flames. In St. Petersburg, with Lev Trotsky as one of its leaders, the first soviet (council) of workers' deputies was formed in the fall. That October a nationwide strike was called. It was a stunning success. Industry, commerce, railroads, post and telegraph came to a standstill. At the insistence of Sergei Witte, the prime minister, concessions were offered by Nicholas II.

These were: the granting of a constitution; the expansion of the Duma, the previously promised parliament; and a pledge of civil liberties—freedom of speech, of the press, of meeting and association. But still the riots, bank robberies, and outbursts by troops disobeying their officers continued.

At this time, in 1905–06, the so-called "circles" of anarchists in various Russian cities grew in membership and changed from reading and talk to forays in terrorism.[3] The new enrollees were mainly converts from the Social Democrats and other Marxist groups, and some from the Socialist Revolutionary Party. In their programs these "circles" combined Bakuninist violence with a touching faith that, once the System was destroyed and its debris cleared, peaceful communes of Kropotkin's prescription would replace the state. (The communes envisioned by the Narodniki and the Socialist Revolutionaries would have preserved, and coexisted with, the state—an abomination to anarchists at all times.)

The two strongest organizations of Russian anarchists were *Chyornoye Znamya,* or Black Flag, so named to honor their movement's international symbol; and *Beznachaliye,* or Without Authority, to reaffirm the anarchists' principal tenet. The former was active in the Empire's western and southern cities, but gradually spread to St. Petersburg and Moscow too. The latter started out for the most part in those two cities. In both, many of the terrorists were extremely young, some of them boys of 15 and 16. Sons and daughters of the nobility fought and died side by side with those of the middle and lower classes, as well as of nondescript, declassed elements.

Like the Terror Brigade of the Socialist Revolutionaries, these anarchists shot and killed various officials, bombed governmental offices, and staged armed robberies of banks, such money-seeking raids becoming popularly known as "exes"—from the word "expropriation." But, rather differently from the SR Terror Brigade, the anarchists also engaged in what they proudly dubbed "economic terrorism": lethal attacks on the persons of industrialists and other prominent businessmen (a startling prevision of terror practices of the 1970s in the West).

Still, throughout the period, it was the SR Terror Brigade rather than the anarchists' violence that caused this Russian earth to shake and nearly shatter.

At long last the high revolutionary tumult began to ebb. Two more strikes, called to gain new concessions from the Tsar, petered out. The armed uprising of December 1905 in Moscow was badly handled by its leaders, and, unsupported by the rest of the nation, was crushed by the elite Semyonovsky Guards regiment, which stayed loyal to the throne.

The Terror Brigade tried to continue, but by that time it had been bled white by its commander, the traitor Azef.

III

In 1901 a daring and enterprising young man from the southern city of Rostov on the Don was among those radicals who helped organize the Socialist Revolutionary Party. Two years later he enrolled in the Party's Terror Brigade and the very same year, 1903, became the Brigade's chief.

He was Yevgeny (Yevno) Azef, 34 years old when he took over the Terror Brigade. From then on, diligently and skillfully he planned assassinations of high Tsarist personages. Even though many of his terrorist subordinates were apprehended and usually executed, he somehow managed to elude the police net time after time.

It was Azef who organized, among other blows at the Tsarist regime, the murders of Minister of the Interior Vyacheslav Plehve in 1904 and of Grand Duke Sergei in 1905. From mid-1906 on he was a member of his party's Central Committee, yet he insisted on—and won—an independent status for his Terror Brigade. Impressed by his successes, the Committee placed funds and arms at his personal uncontrolled disposal.

What the Committee and the Brigade's terrorists did not know, and even his wife—an ardent revolutionary—did not suspect, was that Azef had been doubling as a Tsarist police agent ever since 1893 when, a student of electrical engineering in Karlsruhe, Germany, he had been paid to spy on his fellow Russians in foreign schools and cafés. Continuing as an informer on his return to Russia, and rising high in the Socialist Revolutionary Party, he was able in the early 1900s to prevent, practically at their very final moments, some of the assassinations he himself would plan. He betrayed to the Tsar's police many of his best bombers and other friends. In 1901 he tipped off to the police the identities and whereabouts of the Social Revolutionaries gathered in secret congress in Kharkov; in 1905 he handed over to the gendarmes the list of almost the entire personnel of his Terror Brigade; in 1908 he sent to execution seven more Brigade members.

But when he decided that a certain attentat must proceed without hitch to its deadly conclusion, he would have some difficulty in explaining to his Tsarist employers his rare "inability" to thwart such murders. Given his astounding cleverness and luck, his excuses were invariably accepted.

Thanks to the money that streamed to him both from the Party and the police, he became a high spender. His night-spot habits in company with fast women were soon noticed, but his fellow revolutionaries were only awed and even pleased by this mode of life, explaining it by the requirements of his intricate plotting against the Tsarists. His sinning was conspiratorial, they reasoned.

In early 1908 one of the café women was chosen by him as his steady mistress. She was a German, a cabaret dancer-singer, and an expensive courtesan, favored by at least one Grand Duke and perhaps by more than one. Before long it was jestingly remarked that Azef was a self-elected kin under the skin to the Imperial family. He and the woman grew very fond of each other; even then Azef might have been planning eventual quiet retirement with her somewhere in Western Europe.

His physical appearance was unusual. As described at the time by a former police chief, he was "fat, round-shouldered, above medium height, small arms and legs; thick, short neck; round, pudgy, yellowish-swarthy face; narrow cranium; dark hair, straight and stiff; low brow, dark eyebrows, eyes gray and slightly rolling; big, flat nose, protruding cheekbones, very thick lips, prominent chin." Ugly, and strangely magnetic.

He was a neat and even elegant dresser. As he traveled on the combined business of the police and the Terror Brigade, he masqueraded as a rich merchant. Quite early he converted from his original Judaism to the Lutheran faith, so as to avoid the restrictions the Tsarist regime had placed on the Jews. But there was no trace of any religious feeling in him, even less of any true political conviction. He joined and served the police because, the son of a very poor family, he was obsessively avid for money. But he also craved adventure and danger.

IV

By 1906-07 the increasing failures of terrorist acts and the multiplying arrests of the revolutionaries led to a growing suspicion that there was a traitor in the Party's very command. However, all through the disasters, no one thought that treachery stemmed from Azef himself. When at long last the very first suggestions pointing to him reached the Party's leaders, such hints and later outright accusations were indignantly dismissed as an adroit police maneuver meant to undermine one of the most fearless and effective battle commanders in Russia's revolutionary history.

But in time the thought of Azef as a double agent possessed a bold and persistent Socialist Revolutionary leader, Vladimir Burtsev. Doggedly he followed the growing body of his clues and deductions until he succeeded in confronting a former high chief of the Tsar's police,

Aleksei Lopukhin. Meeting him on a railroad journey, Burtsev questioned Lopukhin politely but determinedly until the man, after some hesitation but governed by his moral sense (he had long been outraged by Azef's role), finally confirmed Burtsev's information about Azef.

In 1908 Burtsev began to advance accusations against Azef in direct talks with the Party's top leaders. Aghast, these high personages countercharged the accuser with disruption of the revolutionary cause. That October they summoned Burtsev to a court of honor in the Paris apartment of Boris Savinkov, Azef's second-in-command. Among those judging Burtsev was Kropotkin himself, who, although an anarchist still, and surely not a Socialist Revolutionary in any sense, was nonetheless greatly respected by socialists as a veritable patriarch of the anti-System movement. Kropotkin came to the proceedings from his London home, and it was hoped that with his decades of experience in the underground he would certainly be capable of judging Burtsev's clues and proof and, if need be, help condemn the accuser.

As the judges assembled and heard the statements and saw the documents presented by Burtsev, they were livid with disbelief. Several of them, feeling sure his charges would "inevitably collapse," demanded that Burtsev commit suicide. Savinkov later reminisced:

> Azef was my friend. Our long terrorist activity brought us close to each other. . . . I knew Azef as a man of tremendous will power, strong practical mind and great executive ability. I saw him at work. I saw his unbending consistency in revolutionary action, his devotion to the revolution, his calm courage as a terrorist, and, finally, his ill-concealed tenderness for his family. I regarded him as a gifted and experienced revolutionist and as a firm, resolute man. This opinion, in general, was shared by all comrades who worked with us, men and women of different character and temperament, the credulous and the skeptical, old revolutionists and youths.[4]

But now Burtsev was arguing that this supreme revolutionary was a superagent of the Tsar's police, a shockingly unprecedented traitor. Displaying proof after proof, Burtsev stood his ground and pressed his charges. When the judges were still unconvinced, he produced his final document—Lopukhin's statement. The judges were stunned.

Kropotkin was among the first to believe. Burtsev's trial was stopped at once. Instead, a full-scale investigation of Azef was launched. As its very first step, Azef was given a chance to clear himself. Later Savinkov felt this was a mistake: "Azef should have been killed." Delaying this punishment, his former comrades unwittingly gave him the brief time necessary for him to make his escape.

And so he survived. From January 1909 on, Azef traveled and hid out with his German mistress in Germany, Egypt, Italy, Greece, and Scandinavian countries under a sequence of false identities and passports supplied him by the Tsarist police. He finally settled with her in Berlin as Herr Alexander Neumeier, a German businessman. The Socialist Revolutionary Party leadership officially sentenced him to death wherever he might be found. Periodically its operatives searched for him, at times coming very close to his new cover. In the summer of 1912, his newly grown small beard notwithstanding, he was recognized at a German resort. Advised of Azef's whereabouts, Burtsev wrote to him, requesting a meeting and promising secrecy and safety. Apparently Burtsev could not resist his desire to see how this appalling man would behave toward him who had exposed this incarnation of evil. The victor wanted to savor the insect on the sharp end of his pin. But he also possibly hoped to draw out of Azef some hitherto unknown details of his dark deeds.

Curiously, Azef agreed. Why did he? Most likely, in a Dostoyevskyan mood, the fallen man wanted to see his nemesis. They met at Frankfurt am Main, and for two days Azef poured out to Burtsev a pseudojustification of his treason. Among other points he claimed that in 1908 he had been about to complete his preparations for the assassination of Tsar Nicholas II when Burtsev had so inconsiderately interfered with his accusations. "If not for you, I would have killed him," he chided Burtsev.

Playing safe, Azef vanished from Berlin for the winter of 1912-13, but in the spring he was back. His business in Berlin was the stock market, with periodic trips to Europe's various gambling casinos. His life with his mistress was happily and prosperously bourgeois, but he would take risks in the bourse and at the roulette wheel as if to approximate the perils and razor-edge thrills of his yesteryears as a double agent.

During the First World War, on a June day in 1915, he was recognized at a Berlin café. The very next day he was arrested on a street by a German police detective. The government of Kaiser Wilhelm II charged him with being an "anarchist" and thus subject to extradiction to Russia once the war ended. In vain did Azef protest against "this ridiculous accusation." He was kept in prison for two and one-half years, in solitary confinement, first in a damp cell, then in a hospital. He was released in late 1917, but he was mortally ill, and in April 1918 he died.

Back in Russia, Lopukhin was arrested by the Tsarist authorities when the Azef case broke into the world's headlines. He was charged with the crime of harming the Imperial interests by helping Burtsev's exposé of Azef. In 1909 Lopukhin was tried and sentenced to hard labor, but this was lessened to exile to Siberia. Two years later he was given clemency and restored to all his civil rights. He died 11 years after the revolution, in 1928.

Although Savinkov had taken over the Terror Brigade in early 1909, the awful publicity of the Azef case dispirited many revolutionaries, particularly the movement's young men and women. The morale of most terrorists was broken.*

V

Sergei Witte had done Nicholas II an inestimable favor by terminating the disastrous war with Japan in September 1905 and by wresting from the Tsar his promises of political reforms in October. But as the revolutionary fevers went down, Witte lost out to reactionary generals at court. In April 1906, Pyotr Stolypin was appointed minister of the interior, Witte resigned as prime minister in May, and Stolypin took over this post in July. He was the new strong man.

The diminishing disturbances were harshly quelled by loyal soldiers and Cossacks; revolutionaries were court-martialed and hanged, the noose becoming grimly known colloquially as "the Stolypin necktie"; the Duma was tamed. Yet, to subdue whatever popular impatience still smoldered, certain reforms were offered from on high.

Foremost among Stolypin's peaceful changes was a land reform that many peasants had wanted for generations: their freedom from the *mir,* or the commune that chained them to their village—their new and welcome opportunity to leave that stagnant commune at will for individual farms of their own. Thus would the millions of Russia's peasants become the middle class of the countryside they were so eager to be.

---

* Boris Savinkov's subsequent years are instructive. He survived the revolution of 1905-06 and played a major role in the events of 1917. But the lesson of his fight against the Communists is this: History, as it were, should be firmly on your side as you mount a campaign against your enemies. The past experience that you as an individual or a group or even a government may have had in this horrendous business of violence will mean little or nothing if you have not kept up with the fast-changing times, with your lifetime's new situations and new terrorists. Savinkov in Tsarist times was a superb organizer and daring commander of the Socialist Revolutionary terror against the Imperial might. After Lenin's seizure of power, Savinkov tried to fight the new Communist terror—and failed. In the early 1920s, from Poland, Savinkov attempted to wreak terroristic vengeance upon the Communists, whom he viewed as usurpers of his beloved revolution. But Red Moscow's secret police outfoxed him easily and captured him ignominiously, later killing him by throwing him down several stories from a prison staircase window. The lesson of his capture and death was plain and so remains for our day and the future: to annihilate modern terrorists with their superior methods of battle, the counterblows must be a hundredfold smarter and stronger than the terrorists' own ways and weapons.

Thus would Stolypin destroy the appeal of the terrorists and other revolutionaries to the rural masses.

The revolutionaries correctly appraised this land reform as an ominous threat to their cause. So in September 1911, at an opera house in Kiev, in the Tsar's presence, Prime Minister Stolypin was shot to death by a student, Dmitry Bogrov. Like Azef, but on a minor scale, Bogrov had been a double agent. Discovered as a police spy, Bogrov had been ordered by his former comrades of the Socialist Revolutionary Party to redeem himself through this assassination. Bogrov succeeded, but was caught at once and soon hanged.

After Stolypin's death the land reform was not carried out as rapidly as it would have been had he administered it. But the creation of the rural middle class went on. Only the outbreak of the First World War bogged it down. The revolution of 1917 stemming from the war finished it.

Had Stolypin lived into 1914 he might have prevented the outbreak of the war, and thus of the eventual revolution. For he was against wars, and did prevent a war in 1906-07, when Austria's boldness in the Balkans had nearly caused it.

In February 1914, in a memorandum to the Tsar, one of his high aides at the court (of little actual power, however), Pyotr Durnovo, warned Nicholas II against going to war, predicting a revolution and the dynasty's downfall, followed by a failure of liberals and other moderates before an upsurge of the masses led by extremists—a precise scenario of the events as they actually happened from August 1914 to November 1917.[5] Durnovo had singular clairvoyance.

Not heeding this prophecy, late in the summer of 1914 the Tsar plunged his Empire into that cataclysmic war. The result was as Durnovo had forecast: In March 1917, the three centuries of Romanov rule ended in one week of riots in Petrograd, formerly St. Petersburg, the war-fatigued capital. With that incredible swiftness, not only did the proud dynasty fall but the older phenomenon of Tsarism itself died, and with it one thousand years of autocracy.

The war had destroyed most of the well-disciplined regular troops of the Empire. The new soldiers, hastily drafted from villages and factories, did not fire at the March 1917 rioters but, on the contrary, joined them. Even the Cossacks, those watchdogs of the throne, those sworn foes of the common people, came over to their side for the first time since 1775 and Pugachev's rebellion.

But neither did the soldiers and the Cossacks rally to the banner of Alexander Kerensky's Provisional Government when its liberals and moderate Socialists were deposed, jailed, or hunted down by the extremists of Vladimir Ilyich Lenin a few months later, in November

1917. The margin of Lenin's success was at first blade-thin, but he held on to his power ruthlessly, and won.

And so the Romanov dynasty was succeeded first by Kerensky's well-meaning but feeble liberals and then by Lenin's Bolshevik-Communists, who proceeded to build the new Soviet state and society that became a unique autocracy of terror in the footsteps of Robespierre and Marx.

11

Lenin: High Priest of Terror

The centrality of Lenin to modern terror is by now beyond dispute. How many political terrorists of recent years have proudly, and correctly, called themselves Leninists! In Alexander Solzhenitsyn's monumental encyclopedia on Soviet terror, *The Gulag Archipelago*, there is conclusive proof that it was Lenin, not Stalin, who first installed the meat choppers of the secret police; that Stalin was but the inevitable inheritor and expander of the tragic system.

In Lenin's writings and speeches are countless orders and exhortations to kill individuals and groups dissenting from Communist dogma and action. It is a mistake to think, as some scholars do, that while worshipping the memory of his brother Alexander Ulyanov, hanged in 1887 for the plot to murder Tsar Alexander III, Lenin disapproved of his brother's terrorism. In reality, Vladimir frowned only upon Alexander's timing; terror was to be used when the seizure of power was imminent—and afterward.

Since Lenin believed capitalism to be violence, the revolutionary use of violence was no more than a wholly proper counterviolence. If there was any question of its use, it was one of degree and timeliness. This precept, then, came to be the basic tenet of the Weathermen and the Symbionese Liberation Army; the Quebec desperadoes and the Irish Provos; the Uruguayan Tupamaros and many other Latin American urban guerrillas; as well as the Arab, Turkish, Japanese, and other terrorists. A striking demonstration of debt to Lenin was the worshipful laying of a wreath at his tomb in Moscow on November 27, 1974, by two visiting Arab terrorist leaders, Yasir Arafat and Nayef Hawatmeh—a gesture of gratitude for their recent triumph at the United Nations, gratitude to the great teacher of wholesale political murder by two of his outstanding disciples.

These and many more like them are the heirs of the revolutionary tradition laid down for modern times by this extraordinary Russian.

Far more than any other prophet or leader in history, even more than Marx (although using Marx, along with Robespierre, as sources of inspiration and as models), Vladimir Lenin showed the way to millions of believers throughout the world, making large-scale terror the tool of thousands and tens of thousands of Red activists both in his own time and for decades after his death. Nor should his influence upon certain of his enemies be discounted: Hitler and lesser fascist dictators were quick to borrow some of Lenin's techniques of mass terror.

But only a few studious intellectuals among recent terrorists have read Lenin to any extent. As they assemble their bombs and oil their guns, most terrorists seldom quote Lenin precisely, if at all. They know Lenin, as they know Marx, mainly from a few slogans taken from secondary works.

Nonetheless, they are genuine Leninists. It is in the spirit of his world-shaking teachings that they are bent on destroying the state and society as these now exist. However, whether they realize this or not, they do differ from their revered master in one significant respect. As they raid and kidnap, kill and demolish, they flaunt their supreme conviction that they alone are moral—the only moral force in the world today—and that everyone else is not. Lenin (in this at least, though not in much else) was more honest: he wrote and proclaimed that there is no such thing as absolute morality among humans, that each class holds as moral only that which suits its purposes. This includes the class of proletarians and revolutionaries no less than the middle and upper classes of the privileged.

II

The many Western books on Lenin,* banned in the Soviet Union, will tell you that there was little Russian blood in him—so much Finno-Ugric (Volga Chuvash tribe) or even Mongol (Kalmuck) was there on his father's side; so much German and Swedish on his mother's. A few biographers even speculate on a possible Jewish strain in that German stock. Why else are the Soviet archives so curiously reticent about Lenin's maternal grandfather, Dr. Alexander Blank?[1]

---

* Born Vladimir Ulyanov, he first used "N. Lenin" as his pen name for articles written in his Siberian exile, 1897–1900. This disproves the occasional assertion that he renamed himself Lenin in honor of the hundreds of striking Siberian gold miners shot on the Lena River shores by Tsarist troops in April 1912. But may I propose this theory: It is known that in his young bachelorhood he had once proposed to a Marxist schoolteacher of St. Petersburg, Appolinaria Yakubova, but that the lady had declined the honor. Could it be that by her friends she was called Lina or Lena, and that that is how Lenin (meaning "I am Lena's") chose his revolutionary pseudonym?

From his father's side came not only Lenin's deep-set, slanting eyes and high cheek bones, but also the wild anarchical spirit of the Asian steppe, the ruthlessness of a rebelling serf, the nomad's impatience. From his mother's people he inherited the self-discipline of a prodigious worker, the systematic mind of a Western intellectual.

How does a middle-class youth, suddenly, with no prior notice, become a violent revolutionary? There is neither common rule nor easy explanation, but in Lenin's case we can see four catalysts.

First, his father's death. Ilya Ulyanov, an energetic, strict, God-fearing Tsarist school official in the Volga town of Simbirsk had, for reasons of status, among others, insisted that his gifted children (Lenin was the third of six) study hard and behave well—which they did until his demise in January 1886, when Vladimir was not quite 16. It was then that the two elder children, Anna and Alexander, students in St. Petersburg, became revolutionaries. The influence in the capital of their new friends and books aided the removal of whatever restraint they had felt while their father was alive. Similarly, that same year, according to Lenin's own later statement, he himself became an atheist.

Second: His brother Alexander's execution was, as a catalyst, far more decisive. In May 1887, when Alexander at the age of 21 was hanged, Vladimir was 17 and in his last year of high school. His brother's execution turned him into a convinced political rebel. In December, not quite 18 and a first-semester freshman at Kazan University, he was detained and expelled for taking part in a demonstration against a campus administrator. As he was exiled to the family estate, legend has it that the police officer who had him in tow chided: "Why did you engage in this revolt, young man? Don't you realize you're up against a wall?" "Yes, a wall, but a rotten one," Vladimir replied. "One kick and it will crumble."[2]

It was about this time that he came under the third influence. This was his discovery of Nikolai Chernyshevsky, particularly of that writer's high-strung novel *What Is To Be Done?* In time, Lenin would attribute to it his own initial socialism, dialectics, and materialism.[3]

A priest's son and a non-Marxist radical, Chernyshevsky predicted, and his disciples echoed, that socialism would come first in agrarian, semifeudal Russia—not in the industrialized West. Here was the demand to nationalize land, factories, and commerce; to confiscate Church riches; to form one strong, centralized revolutionary party that would institute a dictatorship, manipulate elections to bar from power any adherents of the overthrown regime, and lay the foundations of an entirely new society. The one major element lacking in Chernyshevsky and his followers was the Marxian faith in the holy mission of the proletariat.

Then, in 1889, the year Chernyshevsky died, the 19-year-old Lenin saw his fourth and most important light: Karl Marx. He read *Das Kapital* and other works by both Marx and Engels and declared his allegiance. He also paid homage to Georgy Plekhanov, the haughty aristocrat who explained Marx so convincingly.

Lenin's exile to the rustic region ended in 1888. Not allowed to re-enter a university, he studied at home, passed his bar examinations in 1891, and became a lawyer. But he practiced not the law he had learned and despised—rather, the revolution he idealized. He and other young rebels formed an underground group to agitate among the factory workers of St. Petersburg. In December 1895, eight years and four days after his first detention, he was again arrested. In the total of nearly 14 months he spent in prison, he read and wrote intensively, the Tsar's police obliging him with the many books needed for his research.

It was almost with regret that in 1897 he left the St. Petersburg jail—the one place in Russia where no distractions took the scholar away from his work. He was even pleased with the three years of Siberian exile that followed. His fiancée, Nadezhda Krupskaya, was permitted to join him there; they were soon married. The hunting, fishing, swimming, ice skating, and chess were good diversions from the long writing sessions. He completed his first major opus, *The Development of Capitalism in Russia;* it was published while he was still in Siberia.

The Social Democratic Party had been founded by a handful of intellectuals meeting in Minsk in March 1898, nearly two years before Lenin's release from exile. In late July 1900, he went abroad to join Plekhanov and other Social Democratic leaders; he was not only a member of the Party but, through his publication and correspondence, a rising star in its galaxy. That December he, Plekhanov, and other émigrés saw the first issue of their paper, *Iskra,* roll off the press in Leipzig, ready for smugglers to take to Russia. Its title promised a great flame to shoot forth from this small beginning—*Iskra* is the Russian word for "spark."

In the paper's columns, in the heated arguments behind the editorial scene, in mansard and café debates, Lenin pronounced himself a better Marxist than Plekhanov. At first they worked together in providing Russia's revolutionary underground with directives, but they soon quarreled bitterly. In Lenin's interpretation of Marx there was more violence than either Marx had ever preached or than Plekhanov, that prudent radical, approved. In the early 1900s, Lenin believed that a Marxist Social Democrat must work toward his Party's dictatorship.

He invoked Robespierre and the Jacobins, insisting: "Without Jacobin violence, 'dictatorship of the proletariat' are words emptied of all content."[4]

Lenin's Marxism always preserved much of Chernyshevsky's urgent tocsin: "To the ax!" To his famous program-pamphlet of 1902 Lenin gave the title of Chernyshevsky's old novel: *What Is To Be Done?* In 1903 he broke with Plekhanov and other moderates, cleaving the Party between his own extreme Bolsheviks and the milder Mensheviks. Updating Archimedes, he said: "Give us an organization of real revolutionaries and we will turn Russia upside down."[5] He evolved his concept of a full-time, elitist, professional revolutionary party, a highly centralized body with one political line of ideology and action, with one man at the top who would command unquestioned obedience. And that man would be Lenin.

In 1904, Lev Trotsky, then among Lenin's critics, foresaw the scheme's deterioration: "The organization will replace the Party, the Central Committee will replace the organization, and finally, the dictator will take the place of the Central Committee."[6] Thus, years in advance, Trotsky forecast Joseph Stalin's role no less than Lenin's course—the role and the course by which Trotsky himself would perish.

Thinking he was being only paternally protective, Lenin did not believe that Russian workers could organize and rise by themselves. He and his intellectual elite had to guide them. Indeed, Lenin would be the despot over all, including his allegedly beloved workers.

III

Early in his career, Lenin rejected terror by small groups, such as the ones to which first Nechayev, and then his own brother had belonged. In Lenin's firm view, terror must not consist of isolated, unrelated events, but must be a vast mass action, well coordinated by a central revolutionary authority standing and moving high above the people. Under such circumstances Lenin would encourage terror even before the actual takeover of power by revolutionaries—just before, in the very process of smiting down a bourgeois government and establishing a revolutionary one, but surely not far ahead of the final barricades.

And yet he admired those grim and volatile conspirators of the 1860s and '70s, Nechayev and Tkachev, who had called for immediate action, for calumny, amorality, and the murder of dissidents; who had held that any means were right in furthering a revolution, and that a revolutionary leader must have complete mastery over his followers.

His admiration for Nechayev became widely known in January 1934, 12 years after Lenin's death, when his close associate, Vladimir Bonch-Bruyevich, reminisced in a Moscow magazine[7] that in his intimate talks with his aides Lenin had praised Nechayev, on one occasion saying: "We must publish all of Nechayev's work. He must be researched and studied. We must find all his writings, decode his pseudonyms, collect it all and print it." Similarly he prescribed Tkachev's writings for his Bolsheviks. In Tkachev's insistence that a revolutionary minority, with the help of the masses, direct or indirect, should seize power and then transform Russia's society, using propaganda and brutal force, can be seen a striking prevision of Lenin's course.[8]

But it was Nechayev above all who gripped Lenin. In his talks with Bonch-Bruyevich, Lenin said that it was unfortunate that, beginning with Dostoyevsky's *The Possessed,* Nechayev was so denigrated in Russia, even by revolutionaries who "completely forgot that this titan of the revolution possessed such strong will and enthusiasm that even in the Peter-Paul Fortress, incarcerated amid impossible conditions, he succeeded in influencing the soldiers of the guard into obeying him entirely."

He lauded Nechayev's belief that, come the revolution, all the Romanovs should be executed—the job done by Lenin in 1918, even if not completely. Lenin would remind his faithful that Nechayev was a genius, that he "had a special organizing talent, an ability of introducing singularly new conspiratorial habits, and could express his ideas in such astonishing formulations that you remembered them all through your life." And Lenin did remember. In much of his writing we find the same insistence as in the Nechayevist *Catechism* that a revolutionary organization be strictly centralized, that by means of such a tool and unfettered by any morality, the revolutionaries can and should turn, not only Russia, but the whole planet upside down.

As Lenin saw early, neither Bakunin nor the Narodniki were effectively organized, and the Socialist Revolutionaries seemed to have inherited the same unpragmatic traits. But Nechayev and Tkachev, because of their ruthlessness and their belief in the absolute authority of a revolutionary leader, had been superbly practical in a way of which Lenin thoroughly approved, though he had his own definite ideas as to when and how terror should be used.

In 1899, in a draft of a program he wanted the Social Democratic Party to adopt, Lenin wrote, underlining some words as was his wont: "In my personal opinion, terror *at the present time* is an inexpedient method of struggle." The Party must shy away from it until a change in the political situation might call for a corresponding change in tactics. Meanwhile this new Party must concentrate all its forces on the strengthening of its organization and its distribution of printed material.[9]

Two years later, in an *Iskra* issue of 1901, he gave one of his most detailed and clearest indictments of premature terror:

> In principle we have never rejected terror nor can we reject it. Terror is one of those military means that can come in handy and be even necessary at a certain moment of a battle, when the troops are in a certain shape under certain circumstances. But the crux of the matter is that terror is being urged now [by the Socialist Revolutionaries] not at all as one of the operations of an army in action, one that is closely connected and coordinated with the entire system of struggle, but as an independent method of individual attack, isolated from any army whatever.[10]

Terror is of no advantage in this war against the Tsar and his minions when the revolutionary warriors lack a sufficiently strong centralized organization and while local revolutionary units are still weak. "This is why," declared Lenin, "we categorically declare that such a method of struggle under present conditions is neither timely nor expedient." At this juncture, terror only takes brave fighters away from their more important tasks; "it disorganizes the forces not of the government but of the revolution."

Lenin painted a dismal picture of the situation in Russia, a situation not at all favorable for the Red cause:

> We see the broad masses of urban workers and plain city folk rushing into battle, but the revolutionaries showing a lack of any headquarters of leaders and organizers. In this state of affairs, as the most energetic revolutionaries leave to engage in terror, does not this mean a weakening of those fighting units which alone can give us real hope? Does it not portend a break in contacts between revolutionary organizations on the one hand, and those disunited masses of the dissatisfied protestors on the other—those who are ready for the battle but are weak precisely because of their disunity?

As they venture forth to kill the Tsar's officials, Lenin argued, those Socialist Revolutionary terrorists are completely out of touch with the masses and with their needs of the moment. Through constant coordination with the people "lies the only assurance of our success."[11]

He paid tribute to the terrorists' bravery, by inference bowing his head to his brother's martyred memory, but issued his stern caveat:

Far be it for us to deny any significance whatever for an individual
heroic blow, but our duty is to warn most energetically against too
much fascination by terror, against regarding it as the main and
basic means of struggle, something to which so many are inclined at
this time.

He cautioned: "Terror can never become a regular method of military action: at best it is useful only as one of the ways of a decisive
assault." He posed the question: "Can we at this moment *issue a call* to
storm the fortress?"[12]

The Socialist Revolutionaries answered, Yes! Lenin cried out, No!
In those early 1900s the Socialist Revolutionaries insisted that terror
caused people to think politically and correctly much more surely than
could be done by months and months of propaganda. In 1902, in *What
Is To Be Done?* Lenin argued that terror as a substitute for political
propaganda was regressive. That year he branded the terror policy of
the Socialist Revolutionaries as "wobbly" and "devoid of solid
ground." He chided those of his Marxist comrades who would be
seduced even briefly by the halos of the self-sacrificing pistol-wielders
and bomb-hurlers. In 1902 a worker tried to kill the Governor of the
Vilno Province, drawing praise from both Yuly Martov and Vera Zasulich, then two of Lenin's closest Party associates. Lenin was furious
with them.

Ever and again Lenin insisted: The yesteryear's Tkachevs should
be remembered with reverence, and much could be learned from their
grandiose designs and awesome heroism, but their end was tragic and
should not be imitated. In *What Is To Be Done?*[13] Lenin warned: "If
the original of an historic event is a tragedy, its copy is but a farce." He
lauded Pyotr Tkachev's preachment as "sublime"; he acknowledged
that its implementation as terror had in its time indeed frightened
the autocracy, but the "excitative" terror of the latter-day pseudo-
Tkachevs was simply laughable. Terror, he wrote, would be effective
only when the mob loosed it in an armed insurrection, and the army,
instead of quelling the mob, joined with it in its temptuous onslaught.

He cited the 1902 strike and mass demonstration of workers in
Rostov on the Don as proof enough that piecemeal terror favored and
practiced by Socialist Revolutionaries was wrong, and that Social Democratic agitation among such masses as those of Rostov would lead to
better results in bringing Tsarism and capitalism to their perdition.
Again and again he hammered home his sermon: Terror would not
trigger off the desired revolution; assassinations only wasted valuable
lives of revolutionaries. "Not even a hundred regicides are as produc-

tive in their stirring, educational impact as just one participation of tens of thousands of working people in meetings discussing their vital interests." Not in individual acts of terror, but in such meetings and demonstrations did he see the foreshadowing of the final uprising.

He praised the Social Democrats of the Don because in their famous proclamation of 1902 they "put demands to the government in the name of the working class and the entire people and not as threats of more attentats and murders." They would use terror "as one of auxiliary methods" but not as the main tool of struggle against Tsarism.[14]

With fury and venom he never tired of denouncing the Socialist Revolutionaries as sheer adventurers whose terror was "naught else but the combat of loners, entirely condemned by the experience of history." Repeatedly he spoke up against the ease with which other revolutionaries were carried away by their admiration for those daring attentats of the early 1900s. When, in April 1902, Stepan Balmashov, a student terrorist, murdered Minister of the Interior Sipyagin and one month later was hanged in the Schluesselburg Fortress in St. Petersburg, Lenin was sorry to note that this caused "a new turn in favor of terror in the mood of some revolutionaries." What useless loss of Balmashov's life, he said, only to see the replacement of one scoundrel minister, now dead, by another scoundrel minister, now very much alive and on the rampage!

Thoroughly disagreeing with Lenin, the Socialist Revolutionaries glorified their terroristic acts as noble duels against the Tsarist forces of darkness, duels that woke the masses. Not so, Lenin shot back in 1902, such "duels" produce sensations that soon fade, giving place to the apathy of the populace, to its "passive waiting for the next duel." Could not the Socialist Revolutionaries understand that, by concentrating on terror, they distracted the few organizational talents in the movement from their difficult and as yet unachieved task of forming a revolutionary workers' party? In so many parts of Russia, Lenin insisted, the proletarians do want to fight the Tsar and the capitalists, but their leaders are few, and handicapped by lack of money and Red literature. And some of those needed leaders waste their shots and at times their lives instead of joining the people as organizers, agitators, and strike chiefs.

In 1903 he prepared a draft of a resolution, to be adopted by the Second Congress of the Social Democratic Party meeting that year in London, strongly condemning terror.[15] Although the Congress ended in the historic split of the Party into the radical Bolsheviks led by Lenin and the moderate Mensheviks headed by Plekhanov and Martov, both factions continued to agree on certain weighty themes, including their opposition to Socialist Revolutionary terror. For 14 years thereafter they said in unison: Terror, but not now!

Yet they did make an exception for the Tsar himself. At that Congress of 1903, not only the Bolsheviks but the Mensheviks as well spoke up for a death sentence for Nicholas II, if and when came the Day. Years later, when Lenin seized power and instituted the mass terror that the Mensheviks decried in horror, Lenin would delight in reminding them of that erstwhile bloodthirstiness.

As revolutionary rumbles rose higher and higher in Russia in 1904, Lenin began to add other qualified exceptions to his "terror but not now" dictum. Thus he declared that sometimes it was absolutely necessary for workers to kill spies infiltrating their midst, but that it would be an error to make a regular practice of this. Instead, a special organization should be created capable of spotting such informers and rendering them harmless without resorting to anything resembling habitual terror.

When, in July 1904, Sipyagin's successor, Minister of the Interior Plehve, was assassinated by the Terror Brigade of the Socialist Revolutionaries, Lenin commented that this success "must have cost the terrorist organization enormous efforts and prolonged preparatory work." Surely "this experience warns us away from such ways of struggle as terror." For "Russian Social Revolutionary terror was and remains a specific method of struggle by the intelligentsia"—not by the people. Only the proleteriat with its class consciousness and eventual rising will provide Russia with a genuine revolution. It was not surprising to Lenin that sympathy for terror was so frequent "in the radical— or playing-at-radicalism—circles of the bourgeois opposition" to Tsarism. Nor was it surprising to him that, among Russia's revolutionary intellectuals, infatuation with terror was typical of "precisely those who do not believe in the vitality and strength of the proletariat in its proletarian class struggle."[16]

As the year 1905 ushered in Russia's first modern revolution, and Lenin in his West European exile read about the increasing murders of the Tsar's officials, he kept on asserting that all such terror was premature. When, that February, Grand Duke Sergei was assassinated, Lenin once more disapproved—if only because it cost "tens of thousands of rubles and a great deal of revolutionary strength" that should have been used instead to organize the masses under his Social Democratic leadership. Besides, by his reactionary policy, the Grand Duke had been "revolutionizing Moscow better than many revolutionaries" of the Terror Brigade could ever do. He should have been spared thus to continue!

Early in 1905 Lenin wrote that as a rule terror expanded in the lulls between mass movements, and such slayings were "absurd." Terror, he reiterated, was good only when the terrorists were not individual pioneers separate from, and too much ahead of, the revolutionary mob, but right *in* the mob—"sunk" in it as part and parcel, flesh and blood of it. As it was being practiced at the time, it was but a weakness of the intelligentsia.

IV

Nonetheless, as the year's revolutionary flood swelled, he was changing his mind.

In the spring of 1905, at the Third Congress of the Social Democratic Party held in London, Lenin quoted Marx's statement of 1848 that the Great French Terror of 1793 had been a good plebeian way of eradicating both absolutism and counterrevolution. Lenin declared: "We prefer to put an end to the Russian autocracy by this 'plebeian' method." Nothing short of mass terror would now do. "Were we even to capture St. Petersburg and to guillotine Tsar Nicholas, we would face several Vendées."[17] To avoid such promonarchical resistance, to nip it in the bud, the new revolutionary government must launch wide-scale executions.

Later in 1905, with obvious relish repeating this phrase of Marx, Lenin threatened: "If our revolution achieves its victory, we will smash Tsarism in a Jacobin way, or, if you please, in the plebeian way" of which Marx had written—that is, via mass terror.[18] He hailed such Marxist terror when, in September, a group of 70 revolutionaries attacked the Riga prison and, despite their casualties, killed one detective and wounded several policemen, but freed two revolutionaries who had been condemned to death. Only in such group action would terror justify itself, exulted Lenin.[19]

He was rapidly acquiring a taste for this wide-range terror against the autocracy with the ultimate hope of toppling it. In the fall of 1905 he drew up a set of instructions, entitling it "The Tasks of the Units of the Revolutionary Army."[20] These units' activities should be of two kinds, he recommended: 1. Independent military action. 2. Leading a mob. The units could be of any size, starting with as few as two or three members. He listed their possible arms: a rifle, a revolver, a bomb, a knife, a knuckle-duster, a stick, an incendiary rag soaked in kerosene, a rope or a rope ladder, a spade to help in barricade building, pyroxylin, barbed wire, and nails to cripple the onrushing cavalry. Guns could be acquired by swooping down unexpectedly upon a lone policeman or Cossack.

For such workers' formations, Russian revolutionaries should acquire ever mightier explosives, perhaps learning from the Japanese who, Lenin recalled, had proved so much smarter than their Tsarist opponents in the war of 1904-05 (then just ended). He suggested the two new weapons emerging from the conflict: the hand grenade and the automatic rifle.

In his instructions Lenin now praised (and further urged) the increasing murders of spies, policemen, and gendarmes; the bombing of police stations; the freeing of the arrested; and the armed seizure of the government's funds, to be used for the needs of the uprisings. He urged the units to adopt and widen such techniques. He advised the insurgents to climb to roof tops and upper stories, from there to pelt the Tsar's troops with stones and to pour boiling water upon them.

In the Moscow workers' uprising of December 1905, its failure notwithstanding, Lenin saw a vindication of his new views on terror and other revolutionary tactics. Here was an example of mass terror that his Social Democratic Party should recognize as viable, should accept and adopt, but "of course while organizing and controlling it, subordinating it to the interests and circumstances of the labor movement and the general revolutionary struggle," so as to guard such terrorist acts against nonideological excess.[21]

V

While his foes argued against him, his own Bolsheviks followed him almost blindly. Until 1917 only a few thousand radicals were aware of Lenin, but even in his thin émigré years, the loyalty of those who believed in him was limitless and, to those outside the fold, incomprehensible. "No one had this ability to infect others with his plans," wrote Alexander Potresov, a cofounder of *Iskra* who broke with Lenin in 1905, "to awe others with his will, to subjugate with his personality that this man possessed, this man who at first glance was so insignificant and rather rude, lacking polish, so devoid of the quality of charm. . . . He had a kind of secret hypnotic effect emanating from him. . . . Only Lenin represented the rare phenomenon, rare particularly in Russia, of a man of iron will, unbridled energy, the energy that combined this fanatical belief in the movement, in the cause, with the no lesser belief of Lenin in himself."[22]

Lenin was conscious of his growing charisma, but he also recognized the resentment and even hatred he inspired. He knew how to use the people who loved him and whom he needed; and he was thoroughly ruthless with his antagonists.

So shrill and vehement were his assaults that many doubters paused to say that perhaps he had a case after all. In his polemics he did not stop at personal and dirty fighting. Once his sister Anna had to "clean up" one of his book manuscripts before letting even his friends see it. He sneered at any niceties in a debate. A revolution demanded roughness, a pitiless onslaught, curses and bullets (the last after power was won) for liberals and timid Socialists no less than for conservatives and reactionaries.

More than anyone else in the young Social Democratic Party, Lenin was responsible for the split in its ranks into the Bolsheviks and the Mensheviks. The split proved to be a grave fault in the momentous years of 1905-06: when the revolution of that time burst in the Tsar's domains, the divided Party was far less influential than it might have been.

Lenin himself, returning to Russia in late 1905, was singularly ineffectual. He was still too much of a man of the underground and the Western cafés, of quibbling over texts, a Marxist monk too dazzled by the intense fire of the revolution facing him on his sudden emergence from the émigré cloisters to be able to master and guide the flames. The revolution failed. Lenin went back to his foreign mansards, his writing desk, his speeches and wrangling before his tiny émigré audiences.

What had gone wrong? We Social Democrats were not cruel and amoral enough, said Lenin. Next time we should be far tougher. To a Bolshevik intellectual, Lenin mused: "A Party is no girls' dormitory; Party members should not be measured by the narrow standards of petty-bourgeois morality."[23]

VI

In the latter part of 1906, as the revolutionary volcano was so catastrophically subsiding, but as isolated attentats by the Socialist Revolutionaries still exploded, Lenin persisted in condemnation. In September he branded those "loners alienated from the masses" as demoralizers of Russia's workers and other broad sectors of the population.

He continued to watch the news of the now rare instances of the Terror Brigade's activity, and in November 1907, just before he moved from Finland to Switzerland, he sent his scornful message to the Socialist Revolutionaries: "Your terrorism, gentlemen, is not a result of your revolutionary conviction. Your revolutionary conviction is limited to terrorism." In 1908 he saw nothing but decay in the Socialist Revolutionary Party still trying to live with its slogans of terror. Those terrorists were petit-bourgeois, Lenin said. In his view, they were as petit-bourgeois in their desperate character as their liberal nonterrorist brethren were petit-bourgeois in their psychological depression, now that the heroic, hopeful period of 1905-06 had miserably ebbed.

In 1908 Lenin looked around the world for revolutionary fuel, ticking off with joy the demonstrations in India, the insurgence in China, and the barricades in France. In early March 1908, he wrote approvingly of the assassination of the King of Portugal as a correct step toward an overwhelming social upheaval that might yet dawn in that country. But, true to his concept of what makes genuinely good terror, he added that he regretted in the Portuguese case "the element of [the individual] plotters' category of terror, that is, terror that is weak and essentially falls short of its goal." The goal should be terror of the real sort, he emphasized, terror in which the entire people and not merely single bomb-throwers and pistol-shooters would participate, "the kind of terror that genuinely renews the country, the terror that made the Great French Revolution famous."[24]

In the few years remaining before the First World War, Lenin centered his attention and venom on what was going on in his quieted homeland. He ceaselessly branded the Mensheviks as too timid and the Socialist Revolutionaries as too independent and satanic. But above all, he was disturbed by the tidings that the workers of Russia were so quiescent after their recent outburst.

However, in January 1913, the latest news of Russian workers' strikes lifted his spirits. He declared that "time is passing when terrorist loners could speak of 'inciting' people by terror." Russia's proletariat had found a new and truer incitement—"the revolutionary strike, stubborn, jumping from place to place," as strikers aroused the other exploited elements of the population from their stupor, and as the strike evolved into a revolutionary street-and-plaza demonstration by hundreds of thousands.[25] In his text of the resolution adopted by the Central Committee of the Social Democratic Party in the summer of 1913 he castigated the Socialist Revolutionaries for continuing "to advocate terror, whose history in Russia has fully justified the Social Democratic criticism of this method of struggle and has ended in terror's complete failure."[26]

VII

As an émigré steeped in the narrow cauldron of doctrine-mongering, Lenin was isolated not only from the Russian reality of the time, but also from the larger issues of the world. The war of 1914 thundered as a great surprise for him, and the defection of so many Socialists—Russian and West European both—from the official pacifism of the Second International shocked him. In this sudden patriotism of his ex-comrades, now cheering for the armies of their countries, he saw heinous treason to the cause of internationalism.

Not that he himself was a pacifist. Far from it. On October 17, 1914, he wrote: "The slogan 'peace' is not the right one at this moment. This is a slogan of priests and philistines."[27] Two weeks later he elaborated: "War is no accident and no 'sin,' as the Christian reverends think. They preach humanitarianism and pacifism. The strikes of conscientious objectors and similar opposition to war are but pitiful, cowardly, idle dreams."[28]

That October he urged his followers in Russia to work subversively with the main aim of "turning a national war into a civil war," but not to urge Russian soldiers to shoot at their officers *individually* (he underlined this word). Terror, as in peacetime, had to be of mass-scale variety only, not of the individual category that would smack of the Socialist Revolutionary policy.

In May-June 1915, in his pamphlet on the demise of the Second International, he postulated that "wars, with all their horrors and calamities, are of a certain usefulness, mercilessly exposing and destroying as they do much that is rotten, outlived, moribund in human institutions." This imperialist war was particularly useful because it was so vast that it would lead to civil wars, to a world revolution. He urged all who would read and hear him to press their propaganda toward this end. The longer the war, the surer the Red outcome.[29]

12

Now Is the Time

At last, in March 1917, came the awesome news from Petrograd. Once again, Lenin was taken by surprise.

In 1916, on the very eve of the great upheaval in Russia, he gloomily told his fellow émigrés in Switzerland that no Russian revolution in his and their lifetime was possible. But now that the Tsar was overthrown, the future was clear and sharp to Lenin.

Suddenly, in 1917, his feel for timing clicked superbly. In some of this there was cold logic, keen calculation. But much of it he was born with, an animal's inherent instinct of precisely when and how to jump in attack or defense.

His longer view told him it was all right to accept large sums of money from the Kaiser's government to subvert Russia's soldiers and civilians—provided he left no incriminating documents behind, but used shadowy go-betweens and signed no receipts.[1] It told him, too, that it was all-important that he return to Russia *now*, before Russia's emerging middle classes could consolidate their hold on the political framework of the state and reform it. And so the Germans, hopeful that revolution within Russia would ease the pressure on their Eastern front, arranged for him to travel on the famous "sealed" train across Germany, then on by way of Sweden and Finland to Petrograd.

On his return he sniffed the air of post-Tsarist Russia and decided unerringly that the appearances of power were deceptive, that the liberals, who were then the government, only thought they were ruling but actually were not. He sensed correctly that, although his followers were a mere handful, his many foes were not organized, and that most people were inert onlookers. And so he won, not through his strength or sterling qualities, but by his opponents' scandalous default. His genius was in knowing that default.

This default first dawned on him in July 1917, when Lenin and his Bolsheviks half-led an abortive uprising of workers, sailors, and soldiers against Kerensky's government. It was a foolish revolt, poorly prepared and haphazardly attempted. "We made some blunders," Lenin later admitted.[2] The July revolt was put down quickly, and Lenin went into hiding.

Kerensky then had his best and last chance to finish Lenin and his men. Lenin expected this, almost fatalistically: "Now they will shoot all of us."[3] But they did not. The moderate Socialists in the government would not think of repressing the naughty Bolsheviks. Weren't these Leninists their fellow Socialists? In David Shub's delicious phrase, Kerensky's Socialists displayed their "dainty caution,"[4] and so Russia's freedom and democracy were lost. Later, after his November triumph, Lenin explained: "Power was lying in the street; we picked it up."

But it was not that simple. He met opposition in his own Party hierarchy; fear and hesitation before the drastic step of the November insurrection hovered among them. From his nearby hiding place, he had to overcome this resistance by his urgent and near-cursing notes to his men in Petrograd. He won.

II

That summer and fall, en route to power, what did Lenin say about his own future use of terror?

In June 1917, writing in *Pravda*, he praised the historic role of the Jacobins in France and proclaimed that his Bolsheviks were the new Jacobins—except, he promised, they would not resort to terror. He and his Party "would not guillotine the capitalists," but employ other effective measures: "It would be enough to arrest 50 to 100 magnates and aces of bank capital, the chief knights of Treasury-robbery . . . holding them a few weeks *to expose their bad deeds* . . . then release them," meanwhile placing the banks and other capitalistic enterprises under workers' control. But no shooting, no hanging, not even any prolonged imprisonment, he avowed. At the same time he denounced the few feeble measures taken against the Bolsheviks by the Kerensky authorities.[5]

In mid-July, after the quelled street rebellion, came some stronger repressions: Trotsky and a few other Bolshevik leaders were arrested, their newspapers banned, and capital punishment was nominally restored. From his secret quarters Lenin protested the reprisals, which, he claimed, included not only the closing of *Pravda* and the disarming of his adherents, but also "the execution of a certain number of soldiers." This last charge was a vast exaggeration, for hardly any Bolsheviks, either soldier or civilian, were then being killed. The murder of

Ivan Voinov on July 19 was the only authenticated case. This worker, an old-time Bolshevik, was slain by the *yunkera*, officer-candidate trainees, on a street in St. Petersburg, where he was selling copies of *Pravda*. (In Communist times, the name of this street would be changed from Shpalernaya to Voinov.) Lenin, meanwhile, made preparations for his own sudden death, which many people in Russia then considered quite possible (and, many, most desirable). He asked his aides to publish some of his recent writings on Marxism and the state, later a part of his *The State and the Revolution*, "in case they bump me off."[6]

But soon enough, seeing that he had survived and was now safe in concealment, he took heart and issued new threats. Once his revolution came, he wrote in August, his Party would close the bourgeois newspapers and take other steps to render the exploiters harmless. Early that month he swore that in the July bloodshed his adherents were totally innocent and Kerensky's forces despicably guilty: the Bolshevik demonstrators were not the first to open fire; they had only responded to the government's fusillade. If true lists of those fallen were published by the Kerensky side, Lenin quibbled from his hideout, they would show many more Bolsheviks killed than their adversaries. This would prove, he said (illogically), that the Leninists were not the first to shoot.[7]

That summer the Petrograd Soviet, with its non-Leninist majority, tried to pass a resolution against capital punishment. In early September, from his secret hole in Finland, Lenin wrote that the resolution was good if only because one of its paragraphs "contained the excellent, true thought that capital punishment was a weapon against *the masses*." In parentheses he added: "It would have been different had the subject been a weapon against landlords and capitalists." This was ominous. Here was Lenin's first hint in 1917 that he would use the death penalty against the rich merely because they were rich.

Immediately afterward, in the same month of September, he bluntly promised just that—violence, death, to all his foes. No revolutionary government "can avoid using capital punishment against *the exploiters*," against "landlords and capitalists."[8]

III

And so, on November 8, 1917, having emerged from hiding, having at last seized the reins from Kerensky's fumbling hands, Vladimir Lenin appeared as Russia's new ruler at the Congress of the Soviets in Petrograd.

We have a vivid portrait of him by the American rebel, John Reed, who saw Lenin in his high moment of triumph that November evening in the Congress hall. The historic page in *Ten Days That Shook the World* reads:

"It was just 8:40 when a thundering wave of cheers announced the entrance of the presidium, with Lenin—great Lenin—among them. A short, stocky figure, with a big head set down in his shoulders, bald and bulging. Little eyes, a snubbish nose, wide, generous mouth, and heavy chin; clean-shaven now, but already beginning to bristle with the well-known beard of his past and future. Dressed in shabby clothes, his trousers much too long for him. Unimpressive, to be the idol of a mob, loved and revered as perhaps few leaders in history have been. A strange popular leader—a leader purely by virtue of intellect; colorless, humorless, uncompromising and detached, without picturesque idiosyncrasies—but with the power of explaining profound ideas in simple terms, of analysing a concrete situation. And combined with shrewdness, the greatest intellectual audacity."[9]

The promise of liberty and justice was here. On that very day, the Congress made its eloquent but empty gesture of abolishing capital punishment. Red terror was launched almost at once.

During those chaotic days, while some brief resistance to the Bolsheviks sputtered out in Moscow, and before a full-scale civil war flared up in the southern and eastern provinces, a weak sign of opposition to the new Red masters was the strike of the old state's office staffs. On December 11, Lenin called upon his Bolsheviks to start "revolutionary terror" against "the saboteurs and the striking functionaries."[10] That winter he blamed his foes for "the civil war, the bribery, and the sabotage" now rampant against his regime. Such were the circumstances, he declared, that made it necessary for his government to institute terror. "Therefore we must not repent using it, we must not renounce it."

After Kerensky's fall, few Russians fought the Bolsheviks in his name—so discredited was he by his complete failure to stop Lenin while the stopping was possible. Other, far more energetic anti-Bolshevik forces now came forth. Lenin's enemies taking up arms against the Soviets were a rainbow of political faiths. Although the Mensheviks were for the most part against any armed resistance to Lenin, right-wing Socialist Revolutionaries were very much in the battlefield against him. They were led by such colorful men as that old-time anti-Tsarist terrorist, Boris Savinkov, as well as by certain bold members of the dispersed Constituent Assembly. Their units were made up of middle-of-the-road peasants, moderate Socialist workers, and also rightist Cossacks, but most of these troops were soon taken over by promonarchical generals and officers. Soon known under the catchall name of White Guards, they were in time the main threat to Lenin's new regime.

On December 20, 1917, Lenin established his Cheka as the first official arm of Bolshevik terror, placing it under the chieftancy of that Polish-Russian monster, Feliks Dzerzhinsky. Described by a fellow Bolshevik as "even a narrower fanatic than Lenin," Dzerzhinsky had a tremendous influence on Lenin. A tall man, in high boots and dirty tunic, the rest of his clothes just as slovenly, Dzerzhinsky had "unpleasant transparent, sickly eyes, which it was his way to 'forget' lengthily on some object or person. He would fix his glassy eyes with their widened pupils on a target, and leave them there. Many feared that stare. Even among the Bolshevik leaders no one liked Dzerzhinsky."[11] But Lenin did. He now had his Torquemada. Executions intensified in late December, a new and awful turn in the churning events.

When Plekhanov and other moderate Socialists protested, Lenin in a special article, "Plekhanov on Terror," in *Pravda* for January 4, 1918, recalled his former friend's passionate oration of 1903 in praise of revolutionary suppression. *Salus revolutionis suprema lex*—had Plekhanov not spoken these very words 15 years earlier?

True, in 1903, in London, at the Second Congress of the Russian Social Democratic Party, Georgy Plekhanov had spoken of the necessity to subordinate everything to the grand aim of the coming revolution; if a basic democratic principle or an individual's inherent right stood in the revolution's way, the principle and the right would have to be suppressed. Plekhanov had cited the ancient principle, *Salus populi suprema lex* ("The good of the people is the supreme law"), and interpreted it as *Salus revolutionis suprema lex*—"The good of the revolution is the supreme law."

Under certain circumstances, Plekhanov had continued, it would be possible for us Social Democrats to declare ourselves against universal suffrage. And should the good of the coming revolution call for a dispersal of an unfriendly parliament, this would have to be done even after two years of such a parliament—yes, even after a mere two weeks!

In his 1903 oration Plekhanov had stopped short of justifying the revolution's terror against its enemies, but now, in early January 1918, Lenin used Plekhanov's old words to justify the Bolshevik terror. It was for the good of their revolution that Lenin and Dzerzhinsky were now executing (in Lenin's words) "the saboteurs, the organizers of the officer-candidate uprisings" and closing "the newspapers kept by the bankers."

Lenin asked Plekhanov and other Socialists: "When your Kerensky restored capital punishment at the front, gentlemen, was it not terror?" He failed to mention the fact that Kerensky's order had for the most part remained on paper.

Asked Lenin: "When your coalition government used [General Lavr] Kornilov to shoot to death whole regiments for not enough spirit in fighting the war, was it not civil war, gentlemen?" In reality, no such wholesale execution of disobedient regiments occurred under Kerensky and Kornilov.

Lenin also referred to Kerensky's jailing of 3,000 soldiers at Minsk for using "pernicious propaganda" (a dubious charge on Lenin's part, not supported by historical evidence), as well as Kerensky's "strangling of *workers'* newspapers" (by this Lenin may have meant the occasional, timid banning of his *Pravda* in the summer of 1917). With pathos Lenin hammered: "Was this not terror, gentlemen?"

Yes, fumed Lenin, this was terror, and so now it was his turn to reply with his own Red terror. The difference was, he wrote in his attack on Plekhanov, that the terror waged by Kerensky and Company was directed *"against workers, soldiers, and peasants* in the interests of a handful of landlords and bankers, while the Soviet power applies its decisive measures against the landlords, the marauders, and their servitors *in the interests of workers, soldiers, and peasants."*[12]

Early and late, Lenin used the "Stop thief!" technique, accusing others of his own sins. His attacks against the Kerensky-era death penalty, which was rarely (if at all) used, were followed by Lenin's orders to kill multitudes, which were in fact carried out. In the summer and early fall of 1917 he had fumed at Kerensky's government for postponing the Constituent Assembly, this age-old dream of Russian liberals and socialists. But in mid-January 1918, when the Assembly finally convened and when Lenin saw he lacked a majority in it (75 per cent of the delegates were non-Bolsheviks), Lenin dismissed it abruptly. He gave it not even the two weeks, once suggested by Plekhanov for "an unfriendly parliament." He gave it less than two days. When unarmed workers and intellectuals demonstrated on Petrograd streets for the Assembly, Lenin had his troops fire on them. Numbers fell dead and wounded.

That January 1918 he wrote his celebrated instructions to his followers, "On How to Organize Competition,"[13] which many years later were quoted by Solzhenitsyn to prove Lenin's primacy as the founder of modern terror. The "competition" urged by Lenin was in ferreting out those "vile insects," the human "fleas and bedbugs," the nonconformists of all classes, the opponents of the Red cause wherever in the vast nation they could be found, rich men or poor, from the despicable bankers to those traitorous proletarians who shunned work, such as the Petrograd typesetters who, Lenin complained, refused to work on Bolshevik newspapers. Shoot them "on the spot, every tenth of them guilty of parasitism," Lenin prescribed; jail the rest and make them scrub toilets, and if you release any, do so conditionally, with special identity papers branding them as suspects under constant surveillance, subject to rearrest and firing squads.

One class or group of classes did not even have to be guilty of any specific offense to be marked for extinction. Thus it was in strict accordance with Lenin's dicta and Dzerzhinsky's directives that one of their principal Cheka aides, Martyn Latsis, wrote an article entitled "Red Terror," published in the October 1918 issue of *Yezhenedel'nik Ch. K.* (The Cheka Weekly). Therein he instructed the secret police personnel:

> We are destroying the bourgeoisie as a class. When you interrogate do not search for data proving that the defendant acted or talked against the Soviet regime. The very first question you must pose to him is, To what class he belongs, of what origin, education and profession he is. Only these questions will determine his fate. Here is the sense and substance of Red terror. . . .[14]

But who were the interrogators and the executioners? The same Latsis frankly noted in 1921 that plain and fancy psychotics had made their way into the Cheka personnel, which also contained "swindlers and simply the criminal element who use the title 'agent of the Cheka' for blackmail, extortion, and lining their pockets."[15]

IV

Destruction of his era's society was Lenin's chief call and one that appalled many Russian Marxists. Soon after Lenin's seizure of power, a prominent Bolshevik remonstrated with him: "You are only destroying. . . ." Lenin hastened to agree, "his eyes suddenly alight with malice," that his fellow revolutionary was "correct, entirely correct." The old comrade-in-arms protested: "But all of us old-time revolutionaries never preached destruction for the sake of destruction. Particularly as Marxists we have always stood for the destruction only of that which is doomed by life itself, which is coming down by itself. . . ." "But I believe that everything existing now has rotted, has outlived its time!" cried Lenin. "Take the bourgeoisie, take democracy, if you like this better. It's all doomed, and by destroying it we only complete the inevitable historical process."[16]

He knew how to hold power after seizing it, as he continued to destroy. Again it was by his foes' default. Even now, in the months of their mortal danger, they would not unite. While the left anti-Leninists would not rise up against what they thought were their fellow Socialists, the rightists failed to press their action begun in the south and east of Russia either boldly enough or with any thoughtful popular programs. Many opponents chuckled: they would bide their time, they would give the Communists (as the Bolsheviks renamed themselves in March 1918) all the rope they needed to hang themselves. It was the same mistake the German Communists made about Hitler in the early 1930s.

At first they did not realize that relentless terror, Lenin's main message and medium, would defeat all. Later, his inner circle admitted that without terror Lenin would not have endured. In 1917-21 he had no real constructive plan, but he was a superb organizer in the face of surprises and setbacks. He liked to quote Napoleon about first plunging into a battle and only then "seeing" the thing to be done. Even if he did foresee the civil war in the wake of his coup, he did not imagine it would be so long and bitter. Nor could he apparently see that not only the middle and upper classes would perish through his terror but that the vast lower masses would also bleed in volume.

Not that this would have bothered Lenin. Vladimir Woytinsky, who knew him intimately in 1906-07, wrote of him: "Cold, like a steel blade . . . no compassion . . ."[17] Maxim Gorky, during his brief but fierce disapproval of Lenin in late 1917, charged him with cynical callousness toward both workers and peasants: "Toward the masses of people Lenin behaves like a veritable pitiless lord of the manor. He is a leader, but he is also a Russian lord; he has in him these characteristics of this privileged category of old Russia."[18]

At the height of the civil war unleashed by him, Lenin remarked that no people in the world other than the Russians could bear so much without breaking down or breaking loose from the authority above them. Actually, in those bloody years there were widespread revolts of peasants and workers against him, but they were poorly armed and feebly organized. His few picked troops slaughtered them. No mercy for the masses if they stood in history's way.

Nor would he mourn the great intellects who were massacred. He was annoyed with Gorky's intercession for the gentle professors now awaiting their execution in Dzerzhinsky's cells; he was astonished that Gorky would waste his breath and time pleading for this detritus of the old regime. Sometimes he would grant Gorky's requests, but often they were fruitless. Thus, just as Robespierre's guillotine killed one of the world's greatest chemists, Lavoisier, so Lenin's firing squad killed one of Russia's finest poets, Nikolai Gumilyov.

At times the mass snuffing-out of lives was as accidental as it was senseless. At a meeting of his top commissars Lenin sent a note to Dzerzhinsky in his seat: "How many wicked counterrevolutionaries do we now have in our prisons?" Dzerzhinsky scribbled back: "About 1,500." Lenin read the answer, grunted, put a cross mark opposite the number, and returned the note to Dzerzhinsky, who at once got up and left. All 1,500 were executed that night, since Dzerzhinsky took Lenin's cross for a wholesale death sentence, not realizing it was the dictator's habit to put a cross mark on the margin of any document as his sign that he had read it.[19]

V

Passionately Lenin desired polarization. Always he did his utmost to bring it about when it did not exist, to foster it wherever he spotted its beginnings. He did not want compromise that might have brought civil peace. Terror was an inevitable part of the polarization he strove for. In April 1918, as the civil war was increasingly savaging the land, he wrote: "Any great revolution, particularly a social revolution, is unthinkable without a civil war"—and a civil war inescapably spelled terror.

The trouble with all previous revolutions was their short-gasp quality. "The revolutionary enthusiasm of the masses . . . did not last long" in those old-time upheavals, he noted. Yet it is only such enthusiasm that keeps up "the tense state" of the masses and "gives them strength to apply merciless suppression" against all those in the way. He intended to hold the Russian masses under long-term tension, to make them kill and destroy for years, if need be. It would be impossible, he declared, to "defeat and root out" capitalism without the physical destruction of capitalists, without "a ruthless downing of the resisting exploiters." To slay the foes, to kill the carriers of unrevolutionary ideas, such as thieves, hooligans, bribe-givers, and black marketeers, "*an iron hand is needed.*" He reveled in being berated as a dictator. "Dictatorship is an ironclad power, acting with a revolutionary boldness, full of speed, merciless in suppressing the exploiters and the hooligans."[20]

He was not only incensed by the continuous carping of the still-surviving moderate Socialists, some of them his former fellow members in the Party, but also by others—such as the Socialist Revolutionaries, or the Ess-Ers, so known by their Russian initials—who were his old implacable enemies. The nerve of *them* objecting to *his* terror!

On April 7, 1918, in his speech at a Moscow mass meeting, he castigated the Mensheviks as beastly hypocrites: "When we resort to executions they turn into Tolstoyans, shedding crocodile tears, screaming about our cruelty. They have forgotten how together with Kerensky they sent workers into the war's holocaust, hiding secret pacts [with the Allies] in their pockets. This they have forgotten while becoming tenderhearted Christians, advocating mercy." He spoke of the foreign interventionists helping the Whites against the Soviets. "And at this difficult time the Mensheviks and the right-wing Ess-Ers, these loving lambs, shout about our cruelty"—they who "erect gallows" for captured Bolsheviks. "In reply I say to them: Yes, we do not deny our violence against the exploiters. These tears of the Mensheviks and of the right-wing Ess-Ers, caused by our severity, is their last attempt to participate in the nation's political life and, at the same time, the symbol of their weakness. We will give them short shrift."[21]

In his speech to his commissars of labor on May 22, 1918, he pointed to the White terror, those "unprecedented brutalities and seas of blood" with which "the bourgeois and its adherents," among whom he classed liberals and right-wing Socialists, "were flooding the cities" of the Ukraine and Finland. He warned: "All this shows what awaits the proletariat if it fails to carry out its historic task." Half countermeasures would not do. Class-conscious workers must organize a crusade; Red terror must not abate.[22]

In the heat of this gargantuan battle, some young Socialist Revolutionaries would emulate the lone courage of their Party's old terrorist heroes. On June 20, 1918, Moisei Goldshtein-Volodarsky, a high commissar, was assassinated in Petrograd by a new-generation Ess-Er. Six days later Lenin protested to Grigory Zinovyev the lack of prompt retribution: "We are placing ourselves in an embarrassing situation: in our resolutions . . . we threaten with mass terror, but when it comes to action, we *apply brakes* to the *entirely* correct initiative of the masses" who, according to his information, demanded precisely this terror. The Socialist Revolutionary "terrorists would consider us mere softies." Red terror must be stepped up, particularly in Petrograd, whose fighting spirit must be a decisive example to the Red executioners all over the country.[23]

These new Ess-Er assassins were not supported by the masses of Soviet Russia, Lenin declared on July 1, just as their predecessors of the Azef-Savinkov Terror Brigade had no following among the workers of Tsarist Russia.[24] Yet this did not mean that the new anti-Soviet terrorists deserved mild treatment. Death must be the penalty. In early July 1918, Lenin recalled how in November 1917 the Bolsheviks, having defeated General Pyotr Krasnov near Petrograd, had let him go free and unharmed "because the intelligentsia were against capital punishment." And now look at Krasnov—at the head of his White Cossacks of the Don, hanging and shooting workers and peasants. "No," insisted Lenin, "a revolutionary who does not wish to be a hypocrite must be for capital punishment. There has never been a single revolution and a single civil war without executions."[25]

He was outraged by those Communists who were proving to be weak-kneed: "Throwing fits of hysterics, they shout, 'I will leave the Soviets!' " Such faint hearts implored Lenin to honor the Soviet decree of November 1917 abolishing the death penalty. Forget that law, Lenin admonished. "Weak is the revolutionary who at a time of sharp struggle is stopped by law's sanctity. In a period of transition, laws have but a temporary significance. If a law hinders the revolution's pace, the law must be abrogated or corrected."[26] No comrade should hesitate using terror, execution of the foe, as the revolution's supreme weapon.

In mid-July 1918 the local Soviet of the Ural city of Yekaterinburg (now Sverdlovsk), where the deposed Nicholas II and his family were imprisoned, did not hesitate when White troops came near: lest the Tsar be rescued, the Soviet ordered the execution of the royal prisoners. On July 16, the Tsar together with the Tsarina and their four children, were shot and bayoneted to death in the cellar of the house of their captivity. The children included the former Heir Apparent Alexis and three grand duchesses, all young. With them, the family physician and three servants were murdered. In Moscow, Lenin and his associates approved the execution, possibly *post factum*.

Constantly, tirelessly, Lenin expanded his proscription lists.[27] In August 1918 he noted the rising wave of peasants' revolts against the Soviet regime and decided that these were kulaks or richer muzhiks— surely a minority of Russia's peasantry, but a determined minority who, allied with the landlords and capitalists, were already using and would further increase their White terror against the proletariat. Against these rebel peasants, these "mad enemies of the Soviet power," he promised unflinching Red terror. Either—or! "Either the kulaks will murder a multitude of workers, or the workers will stamp out the kulak, this robber, this insurgent minority daring to rise against the toilers' government. There can be no middle solution."

To a local Communist leader in Nizhni Novgorod on the Volga, on August 9, he wrote urgently that a White Guard uprising was evidently in preparation in that city, and that it must be thwarted by "mass terror at once." He ordered "*shooting and deportation of hundreds* of prostitutes who made soldiers drunk, of former officers, and the like"; he dictated massive searches, execution of those found with arms, and wholesale deportations of Mensheviks and other "unreliables." The same day he telegraphed his commissars at Penza and Vologda to launch "a merciless smashing" and "a ruthless mass-terror against the kulaks, the priests, and the White Guards," and to lock up all suspicious elements in concentration camps outside the city limits.* The next day, the tenth, he prodded Alexander Tsyurupa to take hostages in the fertile countryside of Saratov, some 25 or 30 rich peasants in each subdistrict, and these were "to answer with their *lives*" if grain deliveries were not made to the Red state.

Momentarily he diverted his stern eyes West. The outside world's view of his regime must somehow be won over. In his "Letter to American Workers" of August 20, 1918, Lenin repeated his familiar argument that no revolution or civil war could be waged without terror. He excoriated "the saccharine clergy" of the West for "not understanding this necessity" of Red executions. He recalled the terror used by Americans in winning their War of Independence of the 1770s-80s** and their Civil War of the 1860s. How much greater than those historic American necessities "is the task of the overthrow of the *hired* capitalistic slavery, the overthrow of the power of the bourgeoisie" in which the Russian Communists were now engaged and for which they had to exercise their terror.

* The term "concentration camp" dates back to the Boer War when, on December 27, 1900, Lord Horatio Herbert Kitchener, the British commander, ordered their establishment to hold and hem in the families of the Boer guerrilla fighters. The official British rationale was not to punish those families but to prevent them from helping their fighting men who would come home between battles to rest and resupply themselves. The introduction of these camps did contribute to Britain's eventual victory in South Africa, but in the process some 18 to 26 thousand of the camp inmates died of dysentery, measles, typhoid fever, pneumonia, and poor diet. (Spanish detention pens for Cuban rebels had been established in 1895, but these were not called "concentration camps.")

In Tsarist Russia the first concentration camps were established and called by that name late in the First World War for the Austro-Hungarian and German prisoners, to absorb their overflow from the regular military barracks, particularly after the so-called Brusilov Breakthrough of the Austrian lines in the summer of 1916, which had resulted in a tremendous number of captives. I recall that at the time (when I was a boy in Russia), the term "concentration camp" did not have an ugly sound at all. In the civil war I first heard the term in November 1917, when I saw captured Cossacks being marched by Red Guards to the "concentration camps" awaiting them on the outskirts of our city. This was a shock to the populace: How could Russians "concentrate" fellow Russians? Later, the shock became a horror, especially in Stalin's time, when the concentration camps multiplied to constitute a veritable network—"the archipelago"—of barbed-wired islands on the map of the Soviet Union.

** This argument was also used by Yasir Arafat, the Arab terrorist leader, in his tumultuously cheered speech to the United Nations Assembly in New York on November 13, 1974.

He was, in his "Letter," sarcastic about the West European bourgeoisie—"oh, how humane and just!"—whose "servitors now accuse us of terror." Here, too, he delved into history:

> The British bourgeois forget their year 1649, the French their 1793. Terror was just and legitimate when the bourgeoisie used it to its own advantage against the feudals. Terror became monstrous and criminal when the workers and the poorest of peasants dared to apply it against the bourgeoisie! Terror was just and legitimate when used to replace one exploiting minority by another exploiting minority. Terror became monstrous and criminal when it began to be used in the interests of the overthrow of *every* exploiting minority, in the interests of the really great majority—of the proletariat and the semiproletariat, of the working class and the poorest peasantry.[28]

He reminded American workers that by mid-1918 this unjust World War of the imperialists had cost mankind 10 million lives and 20 million invalids, all for the sake of deciding which predators, British or German, would rule the planet. He went on: "If *our* war, the war of the oppressed and the exploited against the oppressors and exploiters, costs half a million or one million victims in all lands, the bourgeois will say that the former victims are legitimate but the latter are not. The proletariat will say something entirely different." For the proletariat knows "the truth that no successful revolution is possible without *the suppression of the exploiters' resistance*."[29]

VI

Lenin's own turn to be a victim came on August 30, 1918, when Dora (also known as Fanny) Kaplan, a Jewess, a 35-year-old right-wing Socialist Revolutionary with a pre-1917 record of anti-Tsarist terror and terms in Tsarist prisons, fired two bullets into him. He was in a Moscow factory yard, leaving a workers' meeting, when she approached him, shooting. She was at fairly close range but too nearsighted to aim well. Gravely wounded, he nevertheless survived.

Krupskaya, privately, said she was horrified that her dear husband's assailant, this woman revolutionary Kaplan, might be executed in this revolutionary country. She was hoping her husband would pardon Dora. But he did not. Dora Kaplan was executed four days after her attempt. "The shooting of a person, particularly of a woman, is not an easy thing," her Red executioner piously recalled in print 40 years later, in 1958.[30]

Her death was accompanied by an intensified campaign of shooting hundreds of hostages and prisoners all over the nation. Even as he was still recovering in bed, Lenin directed the bloodshed. On September 10 he telegraphed in code to Trotsky at the latter's field headquarters at Sviyazhsk outside Kazan, then occupied by the Whites but under Red attack, that he was worried by Trotsky's slowness in deciding to shell that Volga city. Trotsky "must not feel sorry for the city" but subject it to an artillery bombardment and other onslaught, since "merciless destruction is necessary."[31] But Trotsky did try to spare at least what he considered to be the righteous part of Kazan's populace: in a special appeal to the workers of Kazan, he warned them to get themselves and their families out of the city before the final Red drive started.

As Lenin continued to order new executions, he did not refer to his own wounds as his justification. That fall, in his tirades against Karl Kautsky, the grand old man of the German Social Democratic Party, who was bitterly denouncing the Soviet terror, Lenin went far afield as he bade Kautsky to pay heed to such bourgeois-capitalist terror as "the Dreyfus Affair in republican France, the lynching of Negroes and internationalists in the democratic republic of America, the case of Ireland and Ulster in democratic Britain, the harassment of the Bolsheviks and the organization of pogroms against them in April 1917 in the democratic republic of Russia."[32]

On November 7, 1918, the first anniversary of his coup, while addressing a meeting-concert of Cheka personnel in Moscow, he acknowledged that not only the foes of the Communists but often friends as well criticized the Cheka's harshness. He argued: "We have assumed a heavy task. On taking over the nation's government we have naturally made errors, and it is natural that the Cheka's mistakes are most apparent." The philistine intelligentsia seizes upon these errors, not wishing to fathom the crux of the matter. But this matter of the Cheka should be seen in a larger perspective than pointing the accusing finger at its sundry errors, "weeping and fussing about them." The Cheka operatives will themselves learn to avoid mistakes. He promised to purge the Cheka personnel of elements alien to the revolution and its needs—to lessen, if not eliminate, the terror's excesses. But the terror and the Cheka as its revolutionary weapon must go on "decisively, speedily, and, above all, truly," by finding and destroying real foes of the revolution.

He then invoked Marx's axiom: "Between capitalism and Communism lies the revolutionary dictatorship of the proletariat. The more the proletariat will press upon the bourgeoisie, the more ferocious will be the bourgeois resistance." He cited the White terror in France of 1848, the anti-Red rising of the Russian officer-candidate schools in November 1917, and the shootings of the workers in Finland in 1918 as reason enough for the Cheka terror.[33]

Yet, hardly a fortnight later, on November 20, 1918, he cautioned his Party against the use of suppression and terror as the only tactics in dealing with the petit bourgeois if circumstances compelled the latter toward rapprochement with the Communists. Other, more peaceful methods—propaganda, agreements on common action against big business and rich landlords—were to be tried. By "the petit bourgeois" he must have meant Russia's peasants, then rising in massive insurrections against the Communists. These uprisings were engulfing whole provinces. Sheer terror was not enough; simultaneously with executions, cajolery had to be attempted.[34]

13

Thought Waves of Hatred

The First World War had just then ended in the Allied victory. It was widely expected that the Allied troops, already landed on Russia's fringes in the north, east, and south, would soon proceed with the Whites toward Moscow, to deliver the final blow against Lenin's Party and government.

This possibility was a real threat. The Communist terror was stepped up. Lenin looked West toward the defeated nations that might yet revolt and join Red Russia in her struggle.[1] But in January 1919, as the second year of his civil war got underway, he mourned the reverses suffered by his friends in Germany; he raged at the killing of her radical leaders by reactionary army officers; he called upon the German proletariat to launch its counterterror. On January 19, at a special Moscow meeting of protest against the murder of Karl Liebknecht and Rosa Luxemburg in Berlin, he cried out: "Death to the executioners!"[2] In March, at the First Congress of the Communist International, he pounded: " 'Freedom' in the German republic . . . is the freedom to go unpunished after slaying the leaders of the proletariat."[3]

On May 27, in his "Greetings to the Hungarian Workers," he called upon them to destroy those Socialists or petit bourgeois who, after joining their Red revolt, were vacillating: "Executions by firing squads—here is the legitimate lot of a coward in the middle of a war."[4] Again and again he lied that after the monarchy's fall he was not the first to start terror in Russia. In July he told an American journalist that the Bolsheviks had not followed their November 1917 takeover with any terror whatever. "We freed not only many of Kerensky's ministers but even Krasnov, who had fought against us." Red terror, he claimed, came only after the capitalists had tried to resist the new Soviet government.[5] In August he mocked certain of the moderate Russian Socialists then offering an alliance with the Communists if they would end terror. It was not the Communists who were responsible for terror; it was "the bourgeoisie of the entire world" who forced the Soviet side to answer terror with terror. "Here is where the source of terror lies. . . . Those who sermonize us against terror are naught but agents—a weapon, witting or not—in the hands of those imperialist terrorists who are strangling Russia with their blockades. . . . But their cause is hopeless." The Mensheviks, the right-wing Socialist Revolutionaries, and the capitalists, hatching their plots to regain power, "try to tell the Soviet government to stop using terror."[6]

Eye for eye, tooth for tooth! In September 1919, when Lenin heard that the anti-Communist government of Estonia might execute 26 of that country's Reds, he threatened "to shoot all the hostages being held by us." No White leader was to be trusted—Admiral Alexander Kolchak's White terror of those months was a lesson to those who believed him: "For their trust tens of thousands of Siberian workers and peasants have paid the price of being shot or birched to death."[7]

In the same month of September, as German Social Democrats accused Lenin's Communists of betraying their own principles in first opposing capital punishment and then instituting mass executions, Lenin flung back that the proletarian opposition to the death penalty was never meant for revolutionary times: "Is a revolutionary party of the working class thinkable that would not punish with death, in this harshest of civil wars, the actions and plots of the bourgeoisie to bring foreign troops for the purpose of overthrowing the workers' government?" He scorned the liberals and Socialists, who kept on denying the necessity for Red terror, as "hopeless and laughable pedants."[8]

He was self-righteous about Red terror; rarely would he be apologetic about it. In December 1919, in his speech to the Seventh Congress of the Soviets, he jeered at former friend and now Menshevik leader, Yuly Martov, for saying that he, Lenin, "was defending himself on the problem of terrorism." He also berated the moderate Socialists for their demand that the Cheka be "either abolished or improved." He was indignant: "We don't pretend that everything we do is the best. We are ready and glad, without the least prejudice, to learn [to do better]." But those moderate Socialists were too inept to teach the Communists exactly how to improve their Cheka units. "No, our Cheka units are organized splendidly!" To accuse the Communists that they practice "too much terror"? How foolish! Not while there were still underground White plots at home and White terror abroad, particularly in Germany where "leaders of the Communists are being murdered" and the murderers go unpunished.[9] The Congress delegates punctuated his speech, especially his hymns to the Cheka terror, with thunderous applause. (How many of them lived only to be executed by Stalin's terror some 15 years later!)

In the heat and bloodshed of those months few dared to argue with Lenin that he was contradicting himself on terror—that he was avoiding the basic realization that those engaged in terror were not motivated by the "justice" of the Cause. They were motivated by fear and their desire to stay in power.

II

Increasingly, his thoughts, speeches, and writings turned upon the West. Would it war upon his revolution in earnest? Would its proletariat rebel against its bosses and thus expand his experiment into a worldwide conflagration?

In December 1919 he spoke angrily, yet with hope, about the repressions by the French military of the insurgent French sailors and of the French Communist agitators at Odessa—about the sentencing of the men of the French navy to hard labor for their refusal to aid the Whites of South Russia; and about the execution of Jeanne Labourbe, the fearless propagandist among those French on the Black Sea. He was sure the news of these interventionist atrocities against their own French would revolutionize the West. In his mind, this White terror further justified Lenin's Red terror.

That month, repeatedly, he stressed that his terror was but a consequence of Western terror—"the terror of the almighty worldwide capitalism that has tried to strangle, to doom to death by starvation, the workers and peasants struggling for their country's freedom." And again: "We say: Terror has been foisted upon us. . . . Is it not terror when the world's navies blockade this hungry land? Is it not terror when foreign agents, claiming their diplomatic immunity, organize White Guard uprisings?" Red terror was a must. "Had we tried to respond to these [enemy] troops with words, with persuasion, had we attempted to influence them somehow other than with terror, we would have been stupid, we would not have survived even two months."[10]

In January 1920 he inveighed against the White terror of the bourgeoisie, then raging, according to him, in Germany, Switzerland, and North America. Not to resort to Red violence and terror under such circumstances would mean "to become a weepy petit bourgeois, to sow reactionary philistine illusions about a social peace"—a peace that was impossible while capitalism reigned.[11]

In a speech in February he blamed the Allies who, with their terrorism, "compelled us to wage terror," without which the Soviets "would not have lasted even two days." At this time he tried nonetheless to reassure the West: he claimed that early in January of 1920, particularly after the recapture of Rostov on the Don from the Whites of General Anton Denikin, "we no longer used capital punishment,"[12] apparently feeling more secure in such victories, even though the civil war was not yet over. He claimed too much. In early 1920 the Red terror abated somewhat but did not cease; executions, although in smaller numbers, continued.

Yet it was clear that Lenin felt he had to temper his terror to a degree, perhaps in answer to Karl Kautsky's treatise on *Terrorism and Communism,* which Lenin denounced as full of anti-Communist falsehoods, but which apparently disturbed him nevertheless. In fact, in his speech that February he coupled his boast about abandoning executions with one more attack on Kautsky. But an indication of the meaning of this purported cessation of the death penalty could be seen when a new antiterror law was introduced—no doubt on Lenin's own orders—by no less an executioner than Dzerzhinsky, the Cheka chief himself. The Communist leaders were rather more honest when, in the new law's text, a reservation was included that executions would be resumed in all their severity if a changed situation demanded it.

Lenin deliberately exaggerated the anti-Communist measures taken by the Western governments in the postwar period. He decried such measures as "White terror," whether or not these were indeed mass-scale repressions of radicals. Throughout the years 1920-21 he was particularly incensed by what was happening in Kautsky's Germany. He accused the German Social Democrats, now governing their country, of being White terrorists: "They still call themselves Social Democrats and yet they are the most despicable executioners who, allied with the landlords and the capitalists, have murdered the leaders of the German working class, Rosa Luxemburg and Karl Liebknecht, along with fifteen thousand German proletarians." At another time he claimed that all those 15,000 victims were Communists. Red violence and terror, he said in July 1920, were inevitable as the workers' response to the Liebknecht-Luxemburg murders by German army officers, as well as to Krupp's buying up of the press. In August 1921, in his "Letter to German Communists," Lenin justified proletarian violence by saying: Not just 15,000, but "tens of thousands of Germany's best people, her revolutionary workers, have been slain or tortured to death by the bourgeoisie. . . . The armed bourgeoisie has trapped the unarmed workers, killed them en masse, murdered their leaders, ambushing them systematically one after another."[13]

III

In the centuries of the Tsarist reign many naive Russians ascribed the government's injustices to the cruelty and corruption of Tsarist officials, but absolved the Tsar himself: the sovereign, it was said, was kept in ignorance of the people's sufferings by the wiles of his bureaucracy.

No such mistake could be made about Lenin. He fed the broad masses of Soviet Russia a constant stream of his own speeches and writings, urging violence and threatening death in the plainest possible terms: "It is better to destroy one hundred innocent people than to let one guilty one escape," and, "If for the sake of Communism it is necessary for us to destroy nine-tenths of the people, we must not hesitate."[14] And yet, because of his will, his direction, and his astonishing personality, the masses accepted his leadership even as it was dooming and destroying them. Or did they? The answer is: Not universally, not always.

But in 1920, Lenin's inner strength began to slip. In September he lost Inessa Armand, that colorful contrast to Nadezhda Krupskaya. Through his adult life, Krupskaya was his comrade-secretary more than his wife. She was reticent, devoted, and dull. But Inessa, whom he first met when she was 30 and he 40, an ebullient Russian revolutionary of French and Scottish origin, proved his one absorbing woman. Now she was dead of cholera. At the ceremony of her burial under the Kremlin wall Lenin was utterly shaken. He reeled; "we thought," Alexandra Kollontai wrote, "he would fall any moment."[15]

That autumn the main battle against the last White general, Baron Pyotr Wrangel, was being won in the Crimea. But the entire nation lay in ruins; even Moscow, the proud Red capital, was starving. Two Britishers, a man and a woman, called on Lenin in his Kremlin office on separate visits and for different purposes.

H. G. Wells, the prophet of the future, came to talk. He went away in a mood of deep skepticism, almost of derision. He defined Lenin's Communism as plucky and honest but with no practical plan, "like a conjurer who has left his pigeon and his rabbit behind him, and can produce nothing whatever from the hat." Lenin exposed the main chink in the armor of his confidence when he admitted to Wells: "To make it a success, the Western world must join in. Why doesn't it? . . . Why does not the social revolution begin in England?"[16]

The other English guest was Clare Sheridan, the young, beautiful sculptress, a cousin of Winston Churchill, then secretary for war and air and distinctly anti-Communist. Lenin consented to sit for her without halting his work. She thought Lenin looked very ill; his skin was the color of ivory. Dora Kaplan's bullets had left their ravages after all. And his routine was now too sedentary; he had little fresh air or exercise. Mystically, she mused that Lenin was doomed—"dying, choking, suffocating from thought waves of hatred" aimed at him by millions of his foes and victims.[17]

IV

His last rally of spirit and action was his sharp turn, in 1921-22, from War Communism to the New Economic Policy. By this limited return to private capitalism, Lenin saved his Party as well as his country. Yet it was an admission of failure. In March 1922, at the Party's Eleventh Congress, Lenin admitted as much when he sadly declared: "The automobile breaks loose from one's hands, as if despite the driver's will the car rolls in quite another direction. . . . The car rolls not quite the way, and often not at all the way, fancied by the man sitting at the wheel."[18]

Still, in those last few years of his life he worked on, and at times would even relax, mostly by hunting. Almost to his end he liked singing and music. Revolutionary songs sometimes moved him to tears. Love songs, too, seemed to grip him with youthful memories.

Of music he preferred Beethoven's *Pathétique,* which Inessa used to play for him. The year after her death, while listening to a pianist play the sonata, he said to Gorky: "I know nothing greater; I would like to listen to it every day. It is marvelous superhuman music. But I can't listen to music too often. It affects your nerves, makes you want to say gentle stupidities and stroke the heads of people who could create such beauty while living in this vile hell. And now you mustn't stroke anyone's head—you might get your hand bitten off. You have to hit them on the head, without any mercy. . . ."[19]

He would continue this hitting of people on the head, this terror, even as he launched the seeming respite of the New Economic Policy. He stormed against the persistent malfunctioning of the Soviet state apparatus; he blamed most, if not all, of Red corruption and particularly the state's antipeasant excesses on "old-regime officials, the landlords, the bourgeois, and other scum" who had crept into the Communist ranks and were now doing their worst in exploiting the farmers and enriching themselves. Once more he demanded shooting: "Here is where we need a purge through terror—trial on the spot and unconditional execution."[20]

As an occasional substitute for shooting, Lenin stressed strict concentration camps and insane asylums. Late in 1921, in his address to the Party's Central Committee, he said: "Comrades, I ask you to heed my words in all seriousness. We must dot the country with camps of correctional labor, and their regime is to be most harsh, not at all liberal. . . . We face one more dilemma: What to do with those petty intellectuals, the dissenters who are with us and yet against us at the same time. Psychiatric hospitals should play a tremendous role in their education. I think, comrades, that in this problem you will support me. . . ."[21]

But, best of all, shoot them—to answer their challenge, whatever that challenge be. In March 1922, once more he repeated his tired fiction that just before his November 1917 takeover it was Kerensky and his men who had first challenged the Bolsheviks "in a most extreme manner," and that it was only in response to that challenge that "we launched terror and triple-dose terror." And were such opponents to try a challenge once more, *"we will launch terror again."*[22]

He brazened that Russia's workers and peasants favored Red terror, that only the hysterical intelligentsia opposed it. He castigated moderate Socialists, such as Yuly Martov and Viktor Chernov, who denounced terror; he mocked them as beating their breasts and intoning, "Praise O Lord that I am not like 'them,' that I have never adhered and do not now adhere to terror." He branded as "petty fools" such Socialists who in the recent past had "caused the masses to find themselves . . . under the White Guard terror." Stupid world, choose your terror, said Lenin: "Either the White Guard kind, the bourgeois sort of the American, English (in Ireland), Italian (Fascist), German, Hungarian, and other types, or the Red proletarian terror. There is no middle. There is no 'third' kind nor can there be."

Neither during nor after the civil war did Lenin really apologize for his Red terror as something inhumane and horrible, even though so essential to the survival of the Cause. Only in one public utterance, in November 1918, had he admitted that the Cheka was committing certain errors of excess that would, however, be avoided in the future. The promise was never kept, of course. The clearest admission of the awfulness of this glut of blood was made neither by Lenin nor Trotsky but by their top associate, Grigory Zinovyev—and this not in Russia but abroad, under the pressure of foreign Socialist indignation.

This occurred in mid-October 1920, at the congress of the Independent Social Democratic Party of Germany, held in Halle. Sent to the congress by Lenin to represent and praise the Russian Communist Party, but met with much anger of these German Socialists, Zinovyev at one point of his speech said with most unaccustomed contrition: "We never anticipated that we would have to resort to so much terror in the civil war and that our hands would become so bloodstained."

But contrition and steady mellowing were not in Lenin's plans. In 1920, as a rare exception, he let Martov, his old comrade of the *Iskra* days, leave Russia for Western Europe. Soon afterward, he made a few more exceptions, ordering the deportation to the West of several batches of liberals and even of some peaceful anarchists. But no such mercy was to be shown to the Socialists who opposed him and decried terror. Chernov had to escape westward at great risk to his life, hunted as he was by the Cheka. Lenin issued instructions to keep all such Socialists under surveillance, to arrest them, to deport them to Siberia, to shoot them, even though the civil war was over.

In his notes for the speech he was to deliver on March 7, 1922, to his Party's Eleventh Congress, Lenin wrote: "As for the Mensheviks and Socialist Revolutionaries: *they should be shot as traitors.*" In the actual speech this came out as "For the public advocacy of Menshevism our revolutionary courts must pass death sentences." In May of that year he personally drew up a law that meant firing squads for the Mensheviks and the Socialist Revolutionaries. In time, most of these Socialists of Russia died by Communist bullet or from overwork and starvation in Soviet jails and slave camps.

In those May days of 1922 he put much thought into his law legitimizing terror. As he forwarded his draft to the Commissar of Justice Dmitry Kursky, Lenin appended a significant letter, in which he wrote: "The courts must not ban terror— to promise that would be deception or self-deception—but must formulate the motives underlying it, legalize it, as a principle, plainly, without any make-believe or embellishment."[23]

Robespierre had made his Grand Terror a sanctified legality; so would Lenin elevate his terror through a special, detailed, solemn law. So would in their time pontificate juridically Stalin and Stalin's heirs, Hitler and Mussolini, Mao and Castro, DeFreeze and Arafat.

At long last, all this hectic expenditure of will and energy, this constant, merciless beating of multitudes of people over the head, cost Lenin his own life. His paralysis of 1922-23 and his death on January 21, 1924, came not solely as the delayed reaction to Dora Kaplan's shots of August 1918. He died at the age of 53 because he had exhausted his sturdy physique and implacable mind by those self-inflicted burdens of incessant hatreds and schemings; by the self-chosen task of willing, exaggerating, and finally leading this unprecedented revolt and the massacre of the millions; by the sheer exertions of years that no morning calisthenics could repair.

V

Before, during, and after 1917, Lenin not only used calumny and every kind of unscrupulous conniving and contriving against anyone who dared to oppose him—he demanded the same conduct from his followers. Sometimes he was frank to the point of writing instructions such as these on penetrating hostile trade unions: "The Communists must, if necessary, distort the truth and resort to subterfuge, cunning, and mental reservations."

Angelica Balabanova, that pristine-pure revolutionary from her youth into her eighties, tried to work with Lenin as secretary of the Communist International but finally gave up, saying that "no one contributed more [than Lenin] to degrade and profane the idea for which so much has been sacrificed." She said of Lenin that, in Goethe's words, "He desired the good and created evil," and that therein lay his tragedy.[24] But she missed one vital point: He did not see this as a tragedy. For he never viewed *his* evil as evil.

This inevitably led to the moral and psychic deterioration of many of his followers. For here was a singular paradox: While teaching his cadres the permissibility—even the necessity—of engaging in cynicism, lies, slander, plunder and, finally, mass murder, Lenin at the same time demanded of them civil honesty, devotion to duty, service to the populace. To his life's close he did not perceive this contradiction. He thought that he personally knew where to draw the line between destruction and construction. He took it for granted that all other Communists would know too. But, of course, most of them did not.

Some of his Western biographers hint that he was assailed by doubts as he lay dying. Doubts he had, yes, but about details, never about his main ideas and actions. There is not the slightest proof that in his last months Lenin regretted his life's work. The doubted or deplored details had to do with the clumsy functioning of the new Soviet state, and—importantly—with Stalin's inheritance of Lenin's power. This unfortunate development the dying Lenin wished to prevent, but could not. He who had fought and won so many battles lost this one. He gradually saw the enormity of Stalin's cruelty and duplicity and the power Stalin had been gathering, but it was too late for Lenin on his deathbed to halt and demote him. But if ever there was logic in the life and work of Lenin, it was in the fact that Stalin inherited his idea and his system.

Trotsky wrote: "It was not Stalin who created the apparatus, but the apparatus created Stalin."[25] This should be revised to read: "It was not Stalin who created Leninism, but Leninism that created Stalin.'' The Georgian and his monstrous terror machine were no perversion of Lenin. They were the direct, inescapable results of Lenin's dicta on and practice of terror. And Stalin's heirs have, in the main, been the pair's inevitable consequence, even if in varying degree.

14

Trotsky: Target of Boomerang

All leaders—terrorist or not—must have their seconds-in-command. Hitler had Heinrich Himmler; Mao Tse-tung, Chou En-lai; Fidel Castro, his brother, Raúl. Lenin had Trotsky. In their time they wielded enormous power, derived, on the whole, from their masters. How, then, did Trotsky differ from the others?

He is the only second-in-command who became, in his own right, almost first. Even today, throughout the world, the Trotskyite movement survives—not in the name of his leader, but in his own. No other secondary chief has an International still named for him, still following his aims.

Certain terror groups of the 1970s make a point of proclaiming their fealty to Trotsky's memory. They do this to deny any allegiance to, or connection with, the present leadership of the Soviet Union, which, although avowedly Leninist, still regards Trotsky as anathema. Some such terrorist organizations either call themselves Trotskyite officially or are known as Trotskyite unofficially. A few, not Trotskyite, establish and maintain loose ties with the Trotskyite Fourth International.

An outstanding example is Argentina's *Ejército Revolucionario del Pueblo*, or the People's Revolutionary Army, which was first formally established in July 1970 at the Fifth Congress of the Trotskyite *Partido Revolucionario de los Trabajadores*, or the Workers' Revolutionary Party. It is true that in 1973 this important guerrilla organization split into three groups, two of which nominally moved away from the Trotskyite credo (one becoming officially pro-Castro, the other temporarily pro-Perón), but the third—*ERP—Fraccion Roja*, or Red Faction—remained staunchly Trotskyite.

In Europe, one of the two groups of Spain's *Euzkadi Ta Askatasuna*, or Basque Country and Freedom, has connections with the Trotskyites. The Provisionals of the Irish Republican Party are known to seek links with the Fourth International of the Trotskyites centered in

Brussels. The press of the Trotskyites everywhere voices moral support to practically any guerrilla organization in the world, and many terrorists appreciate this applause and succor.

This, then, is the main tenet of the Trotskyites today: even those of them who do not practice terror themselves are openly and sometimes vociferously in favor of terror. The theoreticians among them seem to know the historic position of Lenin on the question of terror—when it is permissible and even necessary and when it is not. In these 1970s, in most recent and current situations, terror to them is a "must." Many of them also like to quote approvingly China's Mao Tse-tung on the modern necessity for terror. In fact, the guerrillas and commandos who call themselves Trotskyites have much in common with the Maoists, some interchangeably using both names. But the stricter of the Trotskyites object to Mao because they cannot forgive him his oft-advertised Stalinism.

As much as they abhor Western capitalism, today's Trotskyites hate the Soviet regime. For this to them is the regime that had hounded Trotsky in the middle and late 1920s and through the 1930s until its agent murdered him in 1940. To them this is the renegade System that betrayed Socialism and Communism by erecting a state and society of the new inequality. Today in the Soviet Union the means of production belong to the state, but the state does not belong to the workers and peasants—it is, alas, the property of the new Communist privileged. So say the Trotskyites as they trumpet their summons for one more revolution, this time against the capitalists and the Brezhnevs both.

Denouncing today's Soviet terror, the guerrillas and commandos in Argentina, Ireland, Spain, and elsewhere praise the memory of Lev Davidovich Trotsky because, like Lenin, he had stood for what was to them a pristine-pure revolutionary terror, and had practiced terror in what these new followers say was a true Marxist way.

Similar to Robespierre, Trotsky fell victim to the terror he had helped Lenin launch. In this, to many young revolutionaries of our times, there shines the halo of a selfless rebel. Rather than any ideological theory, his martyrdom appeals to modern terrorists perhaps more than even Lenin's life and work. Unlike Lenin, Trotsky was more bombastic than bitter as he ordered mass executions. Amid the bloodshed he caused, he struck romantic poses. This has made him human—not humane—to many terrorists of the new generation.[1]

II

Born in 1879, son of a prosperous Jewish farmer in the Ukraine, Lev Davidovich Bronshtein became a Social Democrat revolutionary at 17 and changed his name to what was destined to be his celebrated political pseudonym at 23. Many years later, as an exile in Mexico, he proudly explained: "My political name has been my genuine name since 1902. It is Trotsky."*[2]

It was in 1902, when he reached London on escaping from Siberia after nearly five years of prison and exile, that Trotsky made his first major statement on terror. In an article on Russia's oldtime revolutionaries, he wrote that the memory of those long-gone terrorists called for vengeance, but added: "Not for a personal but for a revolutionary vengeance. Not for the execution of cabinet ministers but for the execution of the autocracy."[3]

He joined Lenin on the *Iskra* staff, although in 1903, at the Party's congress in London, he sided with the Mensheviks against Lenin. One of his main points of difference was his insistence that Lenin's willful ideas and practices would result in a one-man dictatorship.

But, like Lenin, he continued to oppose individual terror. Late in life he would recall: "From 1902 to 1905 I delivered, in various cities of Europe, before Russian students and émigrés, scores of political reports against terrorist ideology, which at the beginning of the century was once again spreading among the Russian youth."[4]

He meant the Ess-Ers. He declared that to a degree he respected, but disapproved of, "the heroic adventurism" of the legendary People's Will, in his own time emulated by the Socialist Revolutionary terrorists. He personally knew many of both the old and the young terrorists, and had learned from their "tragic lessons." Even in his earliest years as a Marxist, he and his fellow radicals rejected the terrorists as ideologues, while being sorrowfully solicitous about them as humans:

> For us, a terrorist was not a character from a novel, but a living and familiar being. In exile we lived for years side by side with the terrorists of the old generation. In prisons and in police custody we met with terrorists of our own age. We tapped our messages back and forth, in the Peter and Paul Fortress, with terrorists condemned to death. How many hours, how many days, were spent in passionate discussion! How many times did we break personal relationships on this most burning of all questions![5]

* Some of his biographers suggest he took this, as a whim, from a Tsarist jail guard so named whom he had known in his imprisonment before the revolution. Generally, the name "Trotsky" is not uncommon in Russia; it is thought to mean "a man from Troki"—a small town in Lithuania. But it may also be a contraction of "Troitsky," derived from *Troitsa*, or Holy Trinity, which name was often encountered among Russian Orthodox priests and their descendants.

Terror, Trotsky then held, was a *sine qua non* in certain situations, but sanctifying terror was inadmissible. At times, practical reasons demanded that terror, sanctified or not, not be used at all.

Even, as in the abortive revolution of 1905, Trotsky seemed to have a chance at terror, he declined it. That momentous fall in St. Petersburg, when Trotsky took charge of Russia's very first Soviet as its chairman, the Socialist Revolutionary members of his executive committee proposed that the Soviet respond with terror to each new repressive measure of the Tsarist government. But the Social Democrat members rejected this course. Trotsky, as the Soviet's head, was explicit about it.

After its 50 days of cresting the revolutionary tide, the Soviet was suppressed, and Trotsky was arrested and tried. The trial, delayed, took place in October 1907, and on the seventeenth of that month, in his celebrated speech to the court, Trotsky denied that his Soviet's agenda had contained any call for an armed uprising, although he proudly acknowledged that Socialists such as himself did believe in the use of force. In any state, he said, no matter what its form, "the monopoly of brute force and repression belongs to the state power." Through force the state fights for its existence and survival. In any state, "repression is quite inevitable." He went on: "We are not anarchists, we are Socialists. The anarchists call us 'statists,' because we recognize the historical necessity of state repression."[6] The Soviet he had guided took the place of the disabled Tsarist state.

Yet, in all its 50 days, Russia's very first Soviet applied no force. In his oration Trotsky did not touch on the reasons for this. We may surmise that his Soviet did not have, or felt it did not have, real power; the Tsarist state was mauled but not yet paralyzed. In 1905 the army, despite its frequent restiveness and even mutinies, was on the whole still the Tsar's loyal pillar.

Afterward, once more an émigré in Western Europe, Trotsky looked back, and was not sorry about his rejection of terror as a revolutionary weapon before its proper time. In 1909 he wrote: "Terrorist work in its very essence demands such a concentration of energy upon 'the supreme moment,' such an overestimation of personal heroism and, lastly, such a hermetically concealed conspiracy as . . . excludes completely any agitational and organizational activity among the masses."[7] Very much like Lenin, Trotsky held that terror made victims not only of its Tsarist targets but also of the terrorists themselves, so courageously yet futilely sacrificing themselves or at least their liberty, and, above all, punishing the working class that would have profited from the revolutionaries' efforts had they been less explosive.

Russian terrorism in the century's initial years betrayed the nation's backwardness, Trotsky asserted. According to him, the revolution of 1905 showed how fruitless was the intellectual with his non-viable terrorism, and how, in contrast, incipiently strong and promising the country's proletariat was proving. What with the needlessness of the Socialist Revolutionary terror, and with the rot exposed by the Azef debacle, the phenomenon of individual attentat was doomed. Fading in Russia, Trotsky insisted, "terror has migrated far to the East—to the provinces of Punjab and Bengal. . . . It may be that in other countries of the Orient terrorism is still destined to pass through an epoch of flowering. But in Russia it is already a part of the heritage of history."[8] At its most virulent or seemingly successful, Trotsky concluded, it had been but a blind alley.

In the years before the First World War, Trotsky warned that killing a cabinet minister meant overestimating that minister, whereas the real enemy, still unreached, was the System represented by the minister. In 1911, as terrorist moods spread among young Austrian workers, Friedrich Adler (himself a terrorist-to-be) asked Trotsky to contribute his views on this theme in the pages of *Der Kampf*, the theoretical monthly of Austria's Social Democratic Party. Trotsky eagerly obliged, declaring in his article that even a so-called successful attentat could produce but a short-lived confusion in a given nation's corridors of power. He wrote:

The capitalist state does not rest upon [cabinet] ministers and cannot be destroyed along with them. The classes whom the state serves will always find new men—the mechanism stays intact and continues to function. But much deeper is the confusion which the terrorist attempts to introduce into the ranks of the working masses. If it is enough to arm oneself with a revolver to reach the goal, then to what end are the endeavors of the class struggle? If a pinch of powder and a slug of lead are ample to shoot the enemy through the neck, where is the need of a class organization? If there is any rhyme or reason in scaring titled personages with the noise of an explosion, what need is there for a [political] party? What is the need of meetings, mass agitation, elections, when it is so easy to take aim at the Ministerial bench from the parliamentary gallery? Individual terrorism in our eyes is inadmissible precisely for the reason that it *lowers the masses in their own consciousness*, reconciles them to impotence, and directs their glances and hopes toward the great avenger and emancipator who will someday come and accomplish his mission.[9]

III

Six years later, in April 1917, "the great avenger and emancipator" did come to Russia in the person of Vladimir Lenin, and now Lev Trotsky ended his many years of captious independence in the revolutionary movement.

That spring Trotsky, having spent most of the First World War in France and a few months in the United States, sailed from New York for his turbulent but jubilant homeland. Immediately upon arrival he allied himself with Lenin's unremitting attack upon the crumbling liberal Establishment of war-weakened Russia. In July he formally joined the Bolshevik Party, and was elected to its Central Committee. In the eyes of the stirred-up masses of 1917, Trotsky was clearly an avenger and emancipator second only to Lenin, and at times even equal to him in drive and fame. Agreeing with Lenin in practically everything, he was soon as much of a terrorist nemesis as was Lenin himself. In tune with their pronouncements of so many previous years, this terror had to be on a giant scale, not at all pettily individualistic.

Like Lenin, Trotsky greatly exaggerated the extent and strength of the few anti-Bolshevik measures attempted by Kerensky in the summer and early fall of 1917, underservedly decrying those pinpricks as "the mad White terror reigning in the streets of Petrograd." Later, precisely as had Lenin, he extolled the virtues (so-called) of the Red terror instituted by the Bolsheviks on seizing power. Heading the newly formed Red Army, Trotsky became a principal terrorist in the land.

Terror was necessary, Trotsky wrote in February 1923 as he looked back at the civil war of 1917-21, because this was the only effective method of bringing the bourgeoisie to its senses. "The petit-bourgeois, taking the bit and bolting, wishes to bow neither to any limitations nor to any yielding whatsoever nor to any compromise with the historical reality—until this reality stops him short with a club over his skull. He then lapses into prostration and meekly capitulates to the enemy."[10]

Trotsky viewed the Red terror of 1918 as an imperative tool against Red Army deserters and "those social groups that feed and inspire desertions—the kulaks, some of the clergy, and the remnants of the old bureaucracy." He praised those revolutionary tribunals whose "few exemplary sentences serve notice to all that the socialist fatherland, mortally imperiled, demands of all and sundry their unconditional obedience." Terror (here he used the fig-leaf word "repressions"), in conjunction with propaganda and proper organization as improved by his command that summer of 1918, brought about in the Soviet fortunes the needed change for the better in a matter of a few weeks. The Red warlord was pleased.[11]

He denounced as kulaks those peasants who refused to give up their bread to the Red requisitioning units. In a speech in Moscow on April 21, 1918, Trotsky threatened to make short shrift of the stubborn rustics, for "the subject now is life and death of the toiling masses." He proceeded to carry out his threat. Many were the executions.

There would be, Trotsky said, "special measures" and "double-dose ruthlessness" toward those oldtime generals and officers who would dare to use the Red Army for their counterrevolutionary plots. He promised such men's swift executions, and kept his promise cruelly. He called upon the Russian workers to be brutal: "We must not repeat the errors of previous revolutions. . . . The working class is too quick to forgive. All too easily does it forget the violence of the noblemen's regime, which for centuries enslaved the serfs, which robbed, destroyed, and raped. The working class tends to be magnanimous and soft-hearted. But we say to it, 'No! Until the foe is broken completely, we must handle him with an iron hand.' "[12]

In a speech on June 4, 1918, he claimed that although Russia was now plunged into a civil war, "the Russian revolution has so far not known terror in the French sense of this word." (This was not true: by then fierce Red terror had been in effect for several months.) He brandished his gun still more menacingly: "The Soviet power will henceforth act more decisively and radically." He warned the opponents, particularly such Mensheviks as Martov, at that time still free and active in Moscow: "Your game may end most tragically." From his seat in the audience Martov cried back: "We were not afraid of the Tsarist regime—nor will we be frightened by you!"[13] Soon Trotsky would prove that the Lenin-Trotsky regime would indeed be more frightful than that of the Tsar.

In May he ordered the execution of any member of the insurgent Czechoslovak Legion in Eastern Russia who would not willingly lay down his arms. In August he arranged for some of Russia's very first concentration camps to be set up in a number of cities for "murky agitators, counterrevolutionary officers, parasites, and black marketeers." In late September, as the seesaw of the civil war momentarily turned against the Red side, and as the forcibly mobilized officers increasingly deserted to the Whites, Trotsky in a special order reminded the defectors that "they betrayed their own families: fathers, mothers, sisters, brothers, wives, and children."[14] He instructed one of his staff's high commissars to gather all the necessary information about the fleeing officers' kin and to arrest them.

Yet, three months later, he cautioned his subordinates to use restraint, for, he said, not all the officers nor all civilian experts were saboteurs. The proletariat must not say, "I will destroy all of you and will get along without specialists." The Red warlord admonished: "This would be a program of our hopelessness and downfall." The Russian proletariat, while arresting and executing any plotters who were indeed guilty, must say to those not guilty but as yet reluctant, "I shall break your will because my will is mightier than yours, and I shall force you to serve me."

He further explained to his soldiers and civilians: Were this Red terror to degenerate into a wholesale deportation and execution of the trained bourgeois experts needed by the new Soviet society, the Communist revolution would have to be sadly judged as "a phenomenon of historical regression." But he reassured his faithful: "Fortunately, this is not so. Terror, as a demonstration of the will and the strength of the working class, is justified precisely by the fact that the proletariat has succeeded in breaking the political will of the intelligentsia, in calming down the professionals of various categories and areas of work, and in gradually subordinating them in their skills to the purposes of the proletariat."[15]

Trotsky listed saboteurs subject to harsh repressions: physicians, professors, high-school teachers, engineers, and telegraphers, among others. But avoid shooting them! Regretfully, the new Soviet state had need of them. They must be subdued and made to work for Communism. Terror must not be used "in advance" but only when necessary. Alas for Trotsky's singular moderation: soon terror was used in advance—and wholesale.[16]

As he announced stepped-up terror on certain key occasions, he luxuriated in ecstatic, would-be poetic phrases. On July 22, 1918, in his communiqué on the executions in the wake of the crushed anti-Communist revolt in Yaroslavl on the Upper Volga, he wrote: "The stern hand of the Revolution struck the heads of the criminal enemies of the people."[17] The Soviet regime, he proclaimed on August 3, 1919, shall burn treason and disorder out of Russia's body "with a red-hot iron." No one will go unpunished—"we will leave not a trace of impunity."[18] On December 7, 1919, he compared his soldiers and commissars to the ancient Japanese samurai: each such Red fighter "knows how to die and teaches others to die" for his cause—"the cause of the working class."[19]

Yet, even among these Red soldiers and their commissars, each moment of ill fortune on the battlefields of this civil war produced weaklings. Trotsky was quick to recognize this, and took steps. In August 1918, he decreed firing squads for cowardly soldiers and faltering commissars. On August 14, he broadcast: "If any unit retreats without an order to do so, the first to be executed will be the unit's commissar, the second—its commander."[20] As an example he put to death the Communist commander of a regiment who fled from the Kazan battlefield and tried to sneak away on a steamer for the safety of Nizhni Novgorod. In a speech to some newly graduated Red Army officers, waiting for their battle assignments, he praised the man's execution as "entirely just, this stern, merciless measure."[21]

In November 1918 he acknowledged that "certain comrades say our actions are too harsh, too devoid of mercy," but his answer to this was twofold: Such are the times we live in—cruel and merciless. Our survival demands this terror.[22]

Not all deserters were to be shot: plain soldiers were needed at the front. But if such a simple man, when caught, attempted to resist, he was to be shot on the spot. In late November 1918 he ordered wide publicity for all executions of deserters, spelling out in full the names and units of the condemned men "and where possible also the where-abouts of their families."[23] Not only resisting deserters, but also those who incited these men to desertion or to "disobedience of a battle order," were to be shot. The same for anyone discarding his rifle or selling any part of his equipment. Those who sheltered Red deserters were also to be executed, and their houses burned.[24]

The following spring, in April 1919, Trotsky stipulated to his revolu-tionary tribunals: the higher a deserter's post, the steeper must be his punishment. High or low, "Woe to the deserters!" he declaimed.[25] His inclusions were sweeping: In his order of July 8, 1919, orderlies and nurses found guilty of neglecting the Red Army's wounded and sick were equated with front-line traitors. "Scoundrels of this kind," he decreed, "must be shot dead equally with deserters fleeing from their battle posts."[26]

Again and again he stressed the despicable sin of the Whites' terror and the sublime virtue of his own Red brand of execution. In his untir-ing stream of battle orders, speeches, and articles, he tried to educate everyone to the full beauty of Red terror. Propaganda was to accom-pany Communist execution, and vice versa. Each punitive sentence handed down by a revolutionary tribunal "must have an agitational character," he urged on April 23, 1919—it should "frighten some while enhancing the faith and vigor in the hearts of others."[27]

IV

As was Lenin, so Trotsky, too, was outraged when in January 1919, the Spartacist uprising in Berlin was quelled and the two leaders of left-wing Germans, Liebknecht and Luxemburg, were murdered by their army captors.

Trotsky contrasted the proper Marxist conduct of Liebknecht in going out into the streets to agitate among the German workers with the capricious and surely non-Marxist behavior of Friedrich Adler two years earlier, on October 2, 1916, when that Austrian Social Democrat assassinated the Austrian prime minister, Count Karl Stuergkh, in a Vienna restaurant, for Adler was "unable to find any other outlet for his indignation and despair." Trotsky condemned Adler as "an opportunist" and "a skeptic from head to foot" who did not believe in the historic, heroic mission of the working masses, but who "by his solitary shot vainly attempted to put an end to his own skepticism." The result was sad: his hysteria spent, Adler "fell into a still more complete prostration." No true Marxist would be an individual terrorist; Adler was a neurotic, an emotional intellectual, not worthy of Marx's wisdom bestowed only upon his faithful pupils, the Communists; a shocking deviation from the ideal represented by Liebknecht and Luxemburg.[28]

Now, in 1918-19, the many Russian counterparts of Adler and other Western neurotics, all these Mensheviks and similar anti-Communist leftists, for the time being as yet spared by the Soviet terror, made brave effort to protest against the Red firing squads. Their clamor was particularly strong when the victims were not capitalists, but radicals. This protest had to be answered.

On July 9, 1918, the day after the left-wing Socialist Revolutionary rebellion against the Communists was put down, Trotsky in a public speech admitted that not only those Ess-Ers, but also anarchists were being executed.[29]

> I am asked, "You consider yourselves Socialist-Communists, yet you jail and execute your own comrades, the Communist-Anarchists?" This question, comrades, indeed deserves an explanation. We, Marxist-Communists, are profound opponents of the anarchist doctrine. It is a mistaken doctrine, but in no way does it call for arrests, imprisonment, and especially executions.

Trotsky went on to analyze in detail the errors of the anarchist ideology, and reiterated that such falsehood does not merit repression, yet—

> Under the flag of anarchism there has gathered during the revolution a large crowd of hooligans and vultures, of bandits and other knights of the night, all with their lengthy criminal records of rape,

thievery, and robbery. These pseudo anarchists who break laws should be apprehended and punished. The Soviet order must be of durable fiber. We have assumed power not to be robbers, hooligans, bandits, and drunkards, but to establish a common work-discipline and honest life of toil.

And this meant shooting these pretenders of radical ideology—executions with neither mercy nor repentance.

Most expressive of Trotsky's stand on this problem was his angry brochure *Terrorism and Communism*, in reply to Kautsky's attack under the same title.[30]

Karl Kautsky, the patriarch of Western socialism, the foremost German-Austrian Marxist who in his young years had known both Marx and Engels and for decades was a literary executor of both, now led the ideological fight of the Second International against the Lenin-Trotsky Third, or Communist, International. His first weighty salvo was *The Dictatorship of the Proletariat,* published in the summer of 1918 and denouncing the Russian Communists as thoroughly un-Marxist and even anti-Marxist. Late that year Lenin, in his usual dull phrasing, responded with his *The Proletarian Revolution and Renegade Kautsky*. In 1919 Kautsky continued his onslaught with his *Terrorism and Communism*.

This time Trotsky, rather than Lenin, would answer at length. In his vibrant style he began writing his impassioned rejoinder during the same bloody months of 1919, traveling in his command train along the civil war fronts. He finished the manuscript in June 1920 on the Polish front, and had it printed and circulated at once. In years to come, as new editions and many translations of Trotsky's *Terrorism and Communism* kept on appearing, he would add introductions with new explanations, excuses, pleas, and bitter attacks on Kautsky and other foes of Soviet terror.

One of his major points was that neither he nor his associates ever advocated terrorism *per se*. He asserted that he was against the coercion and terror employed by the bourgeois. Terroristic methods had always been used by the capitalists and their governments far more widely, and to much greater effect, than by the oppressed, that is, "up to now." But now the glorious Russian Revolution was reversing this ratio, Trotsky thundered, for mankind's good.

Between the old Tsarist terror and the new Soviet variety there was a sharp difference, he went on. "The terror of Tsarism was aimed at the proletariat. The gendarmerie of Tsarism throttled the workers who were fighting for a socialist order." Therefore it was pernicious terror. But we Communists "shoot landlords, capitalists, and generals who are striving to restore the capitalist order." This is beneficial terror. Trotsky jeered at Kautsky: "Do you grasp the distinction? For us Communists it is quite sufficient."

But there was one important feature of Red executions on which Trotsky chose to keep silent: even then the myriad victims of the Communist terror included not only landlords, capitalists, and generals whose executions Trotsky approved so self-righteously, but also—increasingly—the intellectuals, workers, and peasants who disagreed with the Communists or were merely suspected of such dissent. These, too, were shot as dead as were the landlords, capitalists, and generals.

Nor was Trotsky truthful when he protested to Kautsky that the Communists never shot prisoners taken in battle. The historic fact remains that both sides, the Red and the White, executed many of their military captives.

Furthermore, Trotsky showed scant logic and little scholarship when he coupled his own Red terror with every historical instance of "good" terror—the seventeenth-century English, the eighteenth-century French, and even whatever repression the Unionists undertook in the American Civil War. He likened the terroristic acts of the Southerners in the 1860s to the ugliness of the White Guard cruelties of General Denikin and Admiral Kolchak of 1918-19. Ludicrously he elevated the Soviet terror into the noble rubric of Abraham Lincoln's rule.

For once Trotsky did not repeat his earlier fulminations about the alleged "White terror" of Kerensky's forces in 1917. On the contrary, wonder of wonders, he agreed with Kautsky that in November 1917 there was barely any resistance from the troops of the bourgeoisie to the Bolshevik takeover (except in Moscow, where the fighting against the Bolsheviks did last several days but mainly, Trotsky explained, because the local Red leaders were inept). The bourgeoisie of most of Russia did not resist because they were caught by surprise. But, soon recovering, the bourgeois began their civil war against the Bolsheviks—and the latter had to use terror in self-defense.

Here Trotsky distorted the sequence of events. Not for a moment would he concede the historical fact that it was the Bolsheviks, not their adversaries, who had started the civil war by attacking and overthrowing Kerensky's Provisional Government in November 1917. In Trotsky's arguments, as in Communist invective of all periods, the fault was ever that of their foes, not of the Communists.

At that (Trotsky lectured Kautsky), the Russian bourgeoisie would not have had the will or even the weapons to launch its resistance if not for the powerful instigation and help received from the Western capitalists. Russia's Red terror would have been much less severe, almost nonexistent, had the Western Socialists overcome and deposed Western capitalists, had they established true Socialist-Communist regimes a few months or even weeks before the Russian revolution. It was all the horrible failing of Kautsky and his ilk. But among Trotsky's arguments, this was surely one of the feeblest. Terror by the Russian Reds would have been inevitable under any circumstances. The history of the Soviet regime through its nearly six decades shows this inevitability clearly enough.

Trotsky did spot one glaring weakness in Kautsky's arsenal: the German Socialist accepted as necessary, even praiseworthy, the terror of revolutions of the past. In particular Kautsky lauded the Great Terror of the French Revolution, saying that the Jacobins had no other way to save that revolution except through terror. In addition, while berating the Soviet practice of shooting hostages, Kautsky was a staunch admirer of the Paris Commune of 1871, and how could he be, Trotsky questioned, when the Commune also took political hostages?

In other words, according to Kautsky, terror had to be safely in the past to be applauded and even hallowed. Trotsky savagely tore at this Kautskyism. If the moralistic Kautskys were against terror, they had better be against any terror at all, or, for that matter, against any violence, including that of war. Trotsky argued: "The state terror of a revolutionary class can be condemned 'morally' only by a man who, as a principle, rejects (verbally) every form of terror whatsoever—consequently, every war and every insurrection. For this, one has to be merely and simply a hypocritical Quaker."

Essentially Trotsky saw little difference between a war, an uprising, and a campaign of terror. He hectored Kautsky and, with him, all Socialists, liberals, and pacifists:

> *Intimidation* is a powerful weapon of policy, both internationally and internally. Like revolution, war is founded upon intimidation. A victorious war, generally speaking, destroys only an insignificant part of the conquered army, intimidating the remainder and breaking their will. The revolution works in the same way: it kills individuals, and intimidates thousands. In this sense, the Red Terror is not distinguishable from the armed insurrection, the direct continuation of which it represents.[31]

Several years later, in December 1922, writing in another connection, Trotsky once more came to the same conclusion: "War and revolution are extremely cruel and destructive methods of solving social problems. But there is no other method!"[32]

Even as the hostilities ceased, and Russia's peaceful reconstruction was seemingly begun by her Communist victors, war and terror remained their ever-present threat and recurring action. On December 1921, discussing the concessions granted by the New Economic Policy, Trotsky wrote: "We, the proletarian party, decide to what limits we will descend in our agreement with the bourgeoisie: here, down to this line, is the agreement, but beyond it . . . the machine gun is in our hands."[33]

V

In a few more years the machine gun proved to be firmly in Stalin's hands—turned against Trotsky.

It is so much drivel to say, as some ill-informed historians of the Russian revolution pontificate, that the rift between Stalin and Trotsky was ideological, that Stalin wanted the revolution to succeed first in the Soviet republic before its torch was carried to other nations, while Trotsky wanted a worldwide revolution at once. In fact, both wanted the very same thing: a thoroughly revolutionized Russia that would, simultaneously, in the process of her radicalization set fire to other countries as well. The enmity between the two men was solely of personal character. It was a struggle for power, no more and no less.

By the late 1920s, Trotsky was expelled, first from the Communist Party, then from the Soviet Union he had helped to found. On August 20, 1940, he was murdered in his Mexican exile by an assassin sent by Stalin. If Lenin had fallen as an indirect victim to the waves of hatred he released, Trotsky, like Robespierre, was a direct sacrifice to the terror he himself had fashioned, Robespierre's head rolling from under his own guillotine, Trotsky's skull sundered by a Communist's alpine ax.

In the last years of his life, in his Western exile, Trotsky had felt it necessary to defend himself against the Stalinist charges that he was directing a diabolically clever campaign of his followers' terroristic acts all over the Soviet Union. Distraught, angry, he tried to assure the world that he had never been for such non-Marxist individualistic terror. In late December 1934, after a young disgruntled Communist killed Sergei Kirov, the top commissar in Leningrad, Trotsky protested: "The terrorist organization of the Communist youth is fostered not by the [Trotskyite] Left Opposition [to Stalin] but by the bureaucracy, by the internal decomposition of the Stalinists. *Individual terrorism in its very essence is bureaucratism turned inside out.*"[34]

As, in his helpless foreign exile, he read in horror the news of the subsequent purge trials in Moscow, as he raised his voice and pen against the accusations and false confessions involving him, he still failed to realize fully that in fact there was no such "terrorist organization of the Communist youth" or of their elders as charged by Stalin's secret police, that Kirov's assassination had most likely been organized by the secret police on Stalin's orders, and that other terrorist acts had been of similar origin or even had never happened.

Nor did he, dying his violent death, comprehend that Stalin the supreme terrorist had been made possible by Lenin primarily and by himself—Lev Davidovich Trotsky—secondarily.

In Russia, in those awful 1930s, Trotsky's two married daughters and his son Sergei were exterminated by Stalin's secret police. In Paris, in February 1938, his second son, Leonid, was murdered by a Stalin agent. Through all this, Trotsky should have understood, but did not, that these deaths had been decreed not alone by Stalin but also by himself, Trotsky, as well as by their dearly beloved leader Lenin, all the way back in 1917-18, when they had first launched their massive terror.

In his final years, again an émigré in the West, frantically Trotsky appealed to Europe's and America's liberals and democrats, those spiritual kin of the Russian liberals and democrats he had jailed and shot in his time of power. Pathetically he implored them to join their anger to his against the torture and imminent death of his children left in Stalin's Russia.

But history said to Trotsky (as it would have also said to Lenin, had he lived beyond 1924): Once you trample on civil liberties and on lives while turning your sarcasm on the Kautskys, your potential allies, your rescuers from your errors and sins, you must take the consequences. But Trotsky, while electing to be a warrior of revolution on his own terms of mass terror, became indignant in the latter 1920s and all through the 1930s when bullets of his own molding came flying at him and his family, well into that August 1940 day when the ax blade of his own honing swung at him.

Even in the 1930s, though he branded Stalin's behavior as oppressively undemocratic and even terroristic, he still denounced his early opponents of the oppression he himself had stood for in company with Stalin. Thus, at a date late enough for him to know better, while he fought his last long-distance battle against Stalin behind the vainly barricaded Mexican doors of Coyoacan, Trotsky besmirched the memory of the anti-Communist rebels of Kronstadt of 1921 by calling them "reactionary." They were simple soldiers and sailors, peasants and workers. He admitted this much. They were in search of honesty and liberty, of surcease from terror. Nearly two decades after he had them ruthlessly shot down by his terrorist henchmen, executing even those who had finally surrendered on a promise of leniency, he would not grant them this motive.

Thus his failure to heed history's plainest lesson, to acknowledge his and Lenin's cardinal error.

15

Stalin's Archipelago

From Lenin and Trotsky the path of terror led to Stalin and Stalin's heirs. Over these decades the character and organization of Soviet terror underwent certain changes. The transformation can be traced through the vast literature by survivors and scholars, available not in Russian alone but also in other languages, especially by such writers as Alexander Solzhenitsyn, Roy Medvedev, and Robert Conquest.[1]

In the reminiscence of one little-known survivor of the Lenin-Stalin camps, Nikolai Otradin, now residing in the United States, we find a concise analysis of the Red terror from Lenin on up to the end of Stalin's rule as consisting of essentially three periods.[2]

During the first period, that of the civil war of 1918-21, the arrests, executions, and other repressions were the combined result of both the spontaneous anger of the lower classes against the middle and upper ones and the calculated action of the revolutionary government. Many shootings were done by men of the masses, on the spur of the moment, with neither trials nor formal sentences. Yet there is no doubt that Lenin and Trotsky deliberately fanned such mob outbursts so as to create and intensify the revolutionary atmosphere.

As in Robespierre's terror, so in this first Lenin-Trotsky period, all classes were represented in prisons and on execution rolls. Otradin recalls: "We were rounded up both selectively and nonselectively." And so numerous were the arrested that during the civil war there were not enough old Tsarist jails to hold these new Soviet captives. So, in addition, barges moored on the rivers, monasteries lost in the forests or on northern islands, and other makeshift detention sites were used.

Amid the cruelty of it all there was still a chance and thus a hope. If a victim escaped the firing squad by drawing a 10- or 20-year sentence, and if somehow he did not succumb to starvation or epidemic in those cells, barge-holds, or barracks, he could perhaps gain freedom in just a few months—thanks mainly to the energetic pleas, influence, or bribes by their kin or friends still at large. In many cases, Cheka commissars accepted (or even demanded and received) bed-services of the female relatives of the political convicts as payment for the latter's release.

The terror's second period lasted from the end of the civil war in 1921 to the First Five Year Plan of 1928. Early in this period, with the Red victory[3] won over the Whites and foreign foes, voices were raised by the more humane Communist leaders that perhaps the Cheka should be abolished and the Red terror at last terminated.

These would-be humanists were overruled. Yet through the 1920s and their New Economic Policy until 1928-29, there were in the Soviet Union but two large concentration camps: in the sequestered monasteries of Solovki, the island in the White Sea north of Arkhangelsk with branch barracks on the nearby mainland; and on the Vishera River shores on the continent, in the Perm region of the European slope of the Urals. From these two camps thousands of men were sent to various railroad- and canal-building or other work areas throughout the north. The total of all such convicts up to 1919 was no more than some 20,000, although outside the camps, all over Russia, the numbers of those shot by the Cheka were by that time in the hundreds of thousands.

Compare this with the estimated millions of victims in Stalin's time, most of whom were killed during the third or main period of the Soviet terror, lasting from 1928-29 to the dictator's death in March 1953. Otradin states that the mass terror of this third phase was no sudden development. It had been carefully prepared during those comparatively mild 1920s when the New Economic Policy gave the Communist leadership an opportunity to pretest and organize the terror of the succeeding decades quietly. Thus the gigantic Archipelago of Solzhenitsyn's description—of thousands of concentration camps, of millions destined to die of slave work and malnutrition if not by firing squad—would become the awful reality of the third period.

To these three periods we should add the fourth, from 1953 well into these mid-1970s, the time of Nikita Khrushchev and Leonid Brezhnev, which Otradin does not discuss and which stands quite distinctly separate from the first three phases. At a later point of this narrative it will be discussed.

II

Born on December 21, 1879, as Iosif Dzhugashvili, the son of a hard-drinking Georgian shoemaker in the small Caucasian town of Gori, Stalin[3] in his boyhood was sent by his pious mother to a theological seminary in Tiflis (now Tbilisi). He later claimed he was expelled for his early revolutionary activity, but his mother denied this, saying she removed him from the seminary because of his weak health.

Becoming a clerk in the Tiflis observatory, he devoted most of his effort to underground work for the Russian Social Democratic Party, which he joined in 1898, when he was not yet 19. The Tsarist police soon knew him as an agitator and strike organizer; his first arrest came in 1902. It was in Siberia, to which he was exiled in 1903, that he learned of the split between the Bolsheviks and the Mensheviks, and chose the former as the more militant. Escaping from Siberia in early 1904, he returned to the Caucasus to resume his revolutionary activity. He adopted the name Stalin, meaning Man of Steel.

He first met Lenin in 1905 at the Party conference in Finland. Two years later, with Lenin's secret approval, Stalin organized the first major Bolshevik terrorist act: on June 25, 1907, in Tiflis, his men attacked and robbed a State Bank carriage, causing bloodshed and getting away with 340,000 rubles ($170,000). Arrested in April 1908 in Baku, he was exiled again. Altogether, the years 1902-17 meant for Stalin six arrests, repeated imprisonments and exiles, and several escapes. The revolution and fall of Tsarism in March 1917 freed him from his last Siberian exile. He came to Petrograd to take charge of the Bolshevik newspaper *Pravda* and to join Lenin on his return from Switzerland in April.

In years to come, from his position of power, as he rewrote history, Stalin asserted that from the spring of 1917 he was Lenin's closest aide. In fact it was Trotsky, not Stalin, who shared Lenin's fame as his second-in-command and often as his equal. Stalin was obscure throughout the civil war, as Commissar of Nationalities; he also collected food supplies for the Red Army and played a role in the defense of Tsaritsyn on the Volga against the White offensive. (On becoming the Soviet dictator, Stalin renamed Tsaritsyn Stalingrad. After his death in 1953 and denigration by Khrushchev in 1956, Stalingrad became Volgograd.)

Stalin's gradual rise to power began in 1922, when Lenin made him secretary general of the Communist Party, with the task of bringing it out of its post- civil war disarray. Stalin shrewdly used the job to pull his aides—mostly nonintellectuals—up the bureaucratic ladder, thus creating his own political machine. This alarmed Lenin but, already on his deathbed, he could do little except to urge, in his last will, Stalin's removal. Lenin wrote: "He is too rude . . . insufferable." Stalin, now in command, suppressed the document.

Lenin died on January 21, 1924. From then on, for nearly 30 years, until his own death at the age of 73 on March 5, 1953, Stalin wielded his untrammeled and terrible tyranny over the vast empire. Sending multitudes to slavery and death, he was quoted as saying: "One death may be a tragedy, but millions of deaths are only statistics." He was frank about his sadism, on one occasion remarking that he derived the greatest pleasure from planning in detail precisely how he would do away with an intended victim and then going off to bed for his sweet and sound sleep, knowing that in the morning he would put the death sentence into effect.

At a whim, Stalin reclassified comrades as enemies to be executed. He turned upon his aides and staunchest supporters, either on what Khrushchev was later to call "distrustful" and "sickly" suspicion or on the coldblooded premise that intimidation works best when terror is highly indiscriminate. Not a single one of Stalin's favorites was ever sure of his continued favor, nor of his own liberty or even life. These favorites were in mortal fright, trembling each time they were called into Stalin's presence. When thus summoned, they said their grim farewells to their families, not knowing whether they would return. Some, in fact, did not. Aware of their fear, Stalin played on it with relish, asking a henchman: "Why do you turn around so much today and avoid looking at me directly in the eye?"

Increasingly in his three decades of dictatorship, as he ordered a mass chorus of praise from the people high and low, he at the same time formalized on a grand scale the insanely cruel terror initiated in Russia by Lenin and Trotsky. Through the swirling madness of mass murder, he displayed for all the world to see the irrational purposes of this terror that, in a much more flagrant way than any other Soviet leader before or after him, Stalin used as the main basis of his power.

Not that the two leaders before him, Lenin and Trotsky, should be absolved to any degree. Nor should we concede that in their terror Lenin and Trotsky were more rational than Stalin. All three should be judged as one phenomenon. And far from being a late or sudden development, their rule of mass-scale murders from 1918 to 1953 had been largely predetermined by the trio's psyches (at the root of their politics), inherent and unfolding long before their coming to power.

And yet, in modern literature, very little has been done to show the necessary connections between the mentalities of Lenin, Trotsky, and Stalin. Thus, in *The Anatomy of Human Destructiveness* by Erich Fromm, we find that Stalin is classed with Hitler and Himmler in the chapters on "Malignant Aggression." Stalin and the two Nazis are described as sadists; in addition, Stalin is defined as possibly suffering "from paranoid tendencies in the last years of his life." With all that, Fromm's analysis of Stalin's aberration is quite inadequate—surely not

so full or original as are his depictions of Hitler's necrophilia and
Himmler's sadomasochism. Lenin is not even included in this company. Astonishingly, all that Fromm has to say about Lenin is that, like
Marx, Engels, and Mao Tse-tung, Lenin had "a sense of responsibility." As for Trotsky, there is not a single mention of him in all the
526 pages of Fromm's book.

While we wait for a truly expert study of the dementia of the founders of the Soviet state and terror, we see that at least on the surface
the aims of the Soviet secret police over their nearly six decades have
been soberly practical. They have been threefold: First, to remove
actual and potential enemies of the Communist dictatorship. Second,
through this to intimidate the rest of the population. Third, to secure
manpower for the work projects run by the secret police.

The "show trials" of the 1930s, where terrorized and often innocent defendants vied with one another to heap slander and malice
upon themselves while confessing the most fantastic "crimes" invented by the secret police, did intimidate most of the populace. But
they also convinced some gullible citizens that wholesale arrests and
harsh punishment were truly deserved—until that time, of course,
when these naive men and women were in their turn themselves arrested, starved, beaten, tortured, and sent to slave camps or shot dead.

An explanation of that terror was once given by a perceptive victim. A Russian engineer sentenced to a long term in a Stalinist concentration camp (we do not know whether he survived it) said to a fellow
inmate (who did survive and brought his reminiscences to the West):
"We are accused of wrecking. Wrecking there is, in fact, but it is the
regime's own wrecking, not ours. Those power-hungry amateurs,
those incompetents, have made such a mess of the nation's political
body and above all of the nation's economy that they need scapegoats.
We are the scapegoats for the years and years of their mistakes. Hence
this terror."

At the same time we must remember that this terror, this slavery,
was more than a purely political tool. It was and still is an important
economic resource of the Soviet regime, or at least an attempt to make
it such a resource.

The Red regime's need for labor was at certain times a predominant
reason for terror. From a secret 750-page book of Soviet economics,
published in Moscow in 1941, that fell into Nazi hands during the initial
Soviet retreat in the Second World War and was eventually found in
Germany by the American victors, we glean the following:

On the eve of that war, slave labor cut and finished 12.5 per cent of
all Soviet timber, built 22.5 per cent of the country's railroads, and

mined 75 per cent of its gold, 40. 5 per cent of its chrome, and 2.8 per cent of its coal. The secret police were also in charge of all capital construction.

From other reliable sources we know that it was common for the headquarters of the secret police in Moscow to apportion in periodic instructions to its provincial offices the arrest of so many engineers of a certain specialty, so many lumberjacks or tailors or railroad men, so many skilled hands for whatever the secret police enterprises needed in the coming months of their own Five Year Plans.

Special slave laboratories, established for captive scientists and engineers, were meant to contribute toward the Soviet Union's technological progress. Thus, in the 1930s, one of the most valued Soviet sites of radioactive ore mining and processing was made into a property of the secret police, with large numbers of professors, engineers, and other experts arrested for the express purpose of this particular production. The extraction and processing of radium by highly qualified slaves was done in the extreme Arctic north of European Russia, in the Pechora region near the White Sea. The concentration camp contained radium mines, eight chemical plants, and three laboratories—chemical, radiometrical, and physiological—among other units.

The slaves manning this huge compound included Professors F. A. Toropov and G. A Razuvayev, both celebrated chemists; engineers A. N. Kazakov, G. S. Davydov, S. A. Savelyev, and M. D. Tilicheyev; and many others, almost all eventually perishing in their cages. Kazakov was a renowned flyer and specialist in aeronautics; Davydov was a metallurgist, sentenced to ten years of hard labor on his return from a mission to the United States; Savelyev had pioneered in radio; Tilicheyev was well known in oil mining. Together with nonexperts, the number of prisoners here reached 1,000. Yet their total production was ridiculously low: by the testimony of a surviving slave of this camp who later reached the West, the annual output of radium totaled 4.7 grams in 1936 and 6 grams in 1937.

In 1938 the world-renowned Soviet aircraft builder, Andrei Tupolev, was arrested. On trumped-up charges he was sentenced to five years in jail—first in Moscow, then at Omsk in western Siberia where a *sharashka,* or a special design and test laboratory-prison, was established by the secret police for him and more than 100 other scientists and engineers to help Tupolev create his efficient airplanes for both war and civilian purposes. Mikhail Gurevich, one of the two inventors of the celebrated MiG plane, was among these slaves. So was Sergei Korolyov, the famous pioneer of Soviet rocketry.[4]

Solzhenitsyn's great novel *The First Circle* is about one of these prison-laboratories for Soviet slave-scientists and engineers of Stalin's era. It is based on the novelist's own experience as a mathematician-physicist incarcerated in a slave pen and forced to do research.

III

Today, side by side with such regular Soviet law agencies as the court system, the network of state attorneys known as procurators, the Ministry of Justice, and the Ministry of the Interior, but in actuality overshadowing all of them, there reigns the Soviet institution called KGB, which is the current embodiment of the secret police and which, as an organization, though under other names, realized its greatest power under Stalin.[5]

The initials stand for *Komitet Gosudarstvennoi Bezopasnosti,* or Committee for State Security; it is nominally attached to the federal Council of Ministers, but in reality subject to the Politbureau, which is the supreme organ of the Communist Party, and to its Secretary General Leonid Brezhnev. The head of the KGB is Yury Andropov, a personal friend of Brezhnev and a neighbor of his: Andropov's apartment is one floor below that of Brezhnev in one of Moscow's best sectors, on Kutuzov Prospect (Number 24). The two and a few of their intimates often get together in one or the other of the pair's apartments for supper parties, at which Brezhnev likes to cook.

Let us look back at the list of the predecessors of the KGB and Andropov. The first such security force with arbitrary powers of life and death was established by Lenin on December 20, 1917, six weeks after his seizure of power. It was usually referred to as the Cheka, or Ch. K., after the Russian initials of the first two words of its long name, the Extraordinary Commission for Combating Counterrevolution and Sabotage. Dzerzhinsky, its first chief, was soon widely dreaded as a cold-blooded, ruthless exterminator. No regular trials were held by the Cheka; death sentences were decreed either by a three-man tribunal (*troika*) or by a provincial or regional head of the agency, each such powerful individual acting on his own. One report estimated the total of those executed in the four years of the Cheka's existence at more than 1,760,000. Sentences were usually carried out by shooting, in prison basements. (Executioners on the White side during the civil war sometimes used firing squads but, quite often, gallows as well.)

The adjective "Extraordinary" in the Cheka's official name was a near-ironic Red promise that terror was a temporary tool, to be discarded when the civil war ended and the new Soviet republic was certain of its survival. Indeed, on February 6, 1922, the Cheka was disbanded, but, as it turned out, only nominally. Now it was the GPU, later called OGPU, for the name *Ob'yedinennoye Gosudarstvennoye Politicheskoye Upravleniye,* or the United State Political Administration. In fact, it was the same Cheka merely rechristened in the direction of greater permanency, with the same deadly staff and under the same Feliks Dzerzhinsky.

After Dzerzhinsky's death in 1926, the OGPU was headed by another Russian-Polish Communist, Vyacheslav Menzhinsky. This man, a devotee of mathematics and Persian art, was once called by Lenin "the decadent neurotic." Between executions he read pornographic novels and wrote erotic poetry. His own death, in 1934, was reportedly arranged by his assistant and successor, Genrikh Yagoda.

On July 10, 1934, the OGPU was made part of the People's Commissariat of the Interior, at once feared as the sinister NKVD, the initials of the Commissariat's Russian name (*Narodny Komissariat Vnutrennikh Del*). Under Dzerzhinsky and Menzhinsky the old Cheka and the OGPU had already added to the terror at home an elaborate system of espionage in foreign lands. Now, under Yagoda, the new NKVD expanded its activities abroad and at the same time extended enormously the use of slave labor in concentration camps in the country's northern and eastern provinces.*

The son of an artisan, Yagoda first joined the Bolsheviks in 1907 at 16, was arrested by the Tsarist police at 20, and was drafted into the army during the First World War. In the civil war he held a noncombatant post in the Red forces and shifted to the secret police in 1920. Rising to the very summit, he became known and feared for his ingenious cruelty. It was he who prepared the first two major trials of such fellow Communists incurring Stalin's displeasure as Zinovyev, Kamenev, and others. Under Stalin's own guidance, Yagoda succeeded in exacting from these high-rank defendants astonishingly abject confessions of crimes they had not committed against Stalin and the Party— so starkly depicted in Arthur Koestler's novel, *Darkness at Noon.* Yagoda picked his staff shrewdly; one of his assistants was known to boast that with his methods of interrogation he could force Karl Marx himself to admit his guilt as Bismarck's agent.

Yagoda was removed by Stalin in September 1936, in Stalin's usual

---

* In addition, in 1934 a Main Administration of State Security was formed (within the NKVD) that, in time—February 1941—was made into the NKVD's twin—the NKGB, which after March 1946 became MGB, now KGB. At the same time the name Gulag emerged, for *Glavnoye Upravleniye Lagerei,* or the Main Administration of Camps; hence the title of Solzhenitsyn's book, *The Gulag Archipelago.*

pattern of demonstrating his power by demoting and killing his most loyal aides. In March 1938, Yagoda was tried, along with some of the top-level Communist leaders he himself had earlier arrested and harassed. Among other charges of Stalin against Yagoda was that he had poisoned the writer Maxim Gorky. Soon afterward Yagoda was shot, along with those other fallen Old Bolsheviks.

His post at the NKVD pinnacle was assumed by Nikolai Yezhov, whom Stalin had discovered at a provincial post and brought to Moscow. A native of St. Petersburg, of humble origins, Yezhov joined the Bolsheviks in March 1917 at 23, later served as a Red Army political commissar, and moved into the secret police in the mid-1930s. Because of his phenomenal sadism and his short stature (only five feet), Yezhov was called—in frightened whispers—"the bloodthirsty dwarf." Among his practices was that of personally killing his victims in his office.

Always the secret police had the right, introduced by Lenin and continued by Stalin, to kill people at will. But in the great campaign of terror launched by Yezhov on Stalin's orders in 1936-38, death or jail sentences were formalized in a show of legality, which, however, was limited in its pretense. Even before the Yezhov period, Stalin gave the NKVD's Special Board the authority to mete out "administrative" terms of up to five years in exile or forced-labor camps, in the defendants' absence and with no counsel present to plead the victims' cases. In the purge period of '36-'38, the Board increased such sentences to 25 years. Death sentences were numerous. The entire mind-boggling span of these years became known colloquially as *yezhov-shchina:* "the horrible time of Yezhov."

Then came Yezhov's own doom. In 1938 he was transferred by Stalin from his NKVD post to head the Soviet Union's water transport, and in 1939 he disappeared. Soon he was executed by his successors, although Stalin had the rumor spread that Yezhov had died in an insane asylum. This was clearly Stalin's clumsy attempt to disassociate himself from the terror he was in fact responsible for and to explain Yezhov's mass tortures and murders by Yezhov's sheer madness.

In 1938 the secret police chieftancy devolved upon Stalin's fellow Georgian, Lavrenty Beria.[6] He remained at this job until a few months after Stalin's death in March 1953.

A peasant's son, Beria had some minor technical education and became a Bolshevik in 1917 at 18. In secret police work since 1921, within ten years he was Stalin's merciless satrap for all of Transcaucasia. Like Yezhov, he particularly enjoyed having important victims—Communists and others—shot in his presence in his own office. In 1935 he ingratiated himself with Stalin by writing a fraudulent history of the Caucasian revolutionary movement with outrageous flattery for Stalin's role. This proved to be the main factor in his transfer to Moscow and his replacement of Yezhov.

Thin-faced, wearing a pince-nez, Beria seemed an austere figure, but even before the promotion he had been notorious for hard drinking and lechery. Now, in Moscow, he gave full vent to his proclivities. Among other pastimes he would on afternoons cruise the streets of the Red capital, spot a pretty girl of a good family in her early teens hurrying from school or to her music lesson, and order his guards to seize and bring her to his bedroom. He would violate the captive, at times—in case of desperate resistance—first drugging her or making her drunk. After several days of his pleasure he would sometimes release the girl, upon warning her and her family to be quiet about it, but sometimes he would kill her and the family so as not to leave any possible complainants.

Prominent in Beria's activity was his organization of Trotsky's murder in Mexico in 1940. In time he received in his Moscow office and personally thanked on their return from Mexico his two chief aides in the assassination, one of them the Spanish Communist Caridad Mercader, the murderer's mother. He then presented her to Stalin, who bestowed a decoration upon her.

When, in March 1946, all the Soviet commissariats were renamed ministries (after the old Imperial and general Western custom), the NKVD became the MVD, or the Ministry of the Interior. By the MVD's side, the MGB, or the Ministry of State Security, grew into a mighty organ, the distribution of the police functions between the two never entirely clear, but both under Beria until just before his death in 1953.

On Stalin's death there was a distinct possibility that Beria, with the help of his plentiful special secret police troops, would seize all power in the land. But somehow he lacked the nerve to do this.[7]

In June 1953, Beria was grabbed by Khrushchev and his associates, charged with treason (including an accusation that he had spied for the British!), and condemned to death, his execution taking place in December 1953, according to an official communiqué, or several months earlier—in the summer of that year, immediately upon his arrest—according to other, informal accounts.

Heartbreaking reminiscences by survivors and by relatives of victims exist now for every phase of the Lenin-Trotsky-Stalin terror. But the greatest sufferings appear to have been experienced when, under Stalin's guidance, Yezhov was in charge. In his *The Great Terror,* Robert Conquest states that at the peak of the Stalin-Yezhov purges in 1937-38 some 8,500,000 people, or 5 per cent of the nation's population, were arrested, and that most of these were sent to slave camps where the annual death rate was 20 per cent. Nor was Yezhov's successor Beria much milder. At the height of the Beria period, the concentration camps held as many as 20 million people—according to the statement made on April 4, 1955, by John H. Noble, an American released from a Soviet slave camp after more than four years of imprisonment. This is more than three times the figure given later, for the same time, by Solzhenitsyn. As his source, Noble cited a statement he had heard from a Russian prisoner with access to such statistics because of his employment as a bookkeeper at the central Gulag headquarters.

Other Stalin-era reports estimate that about 10 per cent of this human mass of misery were women (most of them sentenced for being wives, daughters, and other kin of the imprisoned or executed men); and that 90 per cent of the captives were men of working age, representing 15 to 30 per cent of the country's total male working population. From his experience as a long-time American diplomat in the Soviet Union, George F. Kennan declares that in the purges of the 1930s there were destroyed "a full 75 per cent of the governing class of the country, a similar proportion of the leading intelligentsia, and over half of the higher officers' corps of the Red Army."[8]

A distinguishing characteristic of the Stalin reign was its mass slaughter of Communists by Communists, which had not been so common in the years of Lenin and Trotsky. So all-embracing, in the mid-1930s, were the arrests and executions of Communists in the Soviet Union that a French magazine printed a cartoon showing a demented man in a desert chasing himself with an ax, the caption below reading: "The Last Communist."

Torture of prisoners by the Soviet secret police, interrogators, and guards had already been known in the Lenin-Trotsky period, but under Stalin it was refined and expanded into regular, incessant practice. The methods of torture were many:

Placing a prisoner on the so-called "conveyor"—keeping him or her sleepless for days and nights at a stretch while being questioned by a series of interrogators taking their turns, until the victim signed a false confession.

Tearing off the prisoner's nails. Crushing his fingers between doors. Holding him and other prisoners in a tightly packed cell, with standing room only, for several days and nights, with neither food nor water, until the few survivors were taken out to sign whatever was demanded of them. Or putting the prisoner against a wall with arms raised, the guards beating him each time he dared to move, until the man's legs swelled and after several fainting spells he collapsed completely.

Urinating into the prisoner's mouth during his interrogation.

Administering brutal beatings to the children of prisoners in the parents' presence until "confessions" were signed.

Raping the prisoners' wives and daughters in the prisoners' full view, with similar results.

In the camps, allowing and even encouraging nonpolitical criminals to beat, rob, and rape political prisoners. One method of abusing a woman prisoner was *poslat' yeyo pod tramvai,* or "send her under a trolley car"—subject her to mass rape by 20 or 30 nonpolitical criminals and sometimes by guards.

IV

Following Stalin's death in 1953, arrests decreased greatly, a limited amnesty was announced, and, after Beria's downfall, measures were taken to treat prisoners more humanely. Gradually there came reviews of sentences and numerous "rehabilitations" of victims, in many cases—alas—posthumous. The reasons for the new Khrushchevian policy of mitigation and even apology were several:

Concessions to the people were essential, for hardly a family in the land had by 1953 remained unaffected by the state-decreed and -maintained terror. The many years of Soviet repression had had its calculated effect of intimidating the populace—but it had also rendered them so terrorized as to make them listless. People did their work poorly and ineffectively. Particularly in the slave camps productivity was low. Stalin's heirs in the Kremlin now knew that, economically, slavery did not really pay. Besides, the hardest job of pioneering in the north and east had already been accomplished—by the millions of slaves, so many of whom were by then dead. Free labor could now be induced by wages and bonuses, not by armed guards and vicious dogs, to migrate to those remote, poor-climate areas, to live in relative comfort in barracks built by slaves and to work in mines dug and improved by those who had perished.

The slaves' strikes and rebellions in Vorkuta in the northeast and in Karaganda in Central Asia in 1953, although bloodily quelled, were one more reason for Stalin's heirs to relax the repressions. For in those slaves' insurrections they saw a specter of nationwide uprisings.[9]

And there was the world's opinion, too. Stalin had not worried about it; so powerful he had deemed himself to be, and had indeed been. But the new leaders were not so sure. And by then, unlike Stalin's time (and the earlier Lenin-Trotsky years), the world knew and at last believed the stories brought West by the escaped survivors of the unprecedented terror.

Nor were only the people living in fear. The leaders were also afraid. Stalin's high-placed aides too, as it now became known, had not felt safe in the face of the terror machine they themselves were managing. Respite and assurance were needed by everybody in the nation, of all classes and stations. Beria's downfall was brought about by his Kremlin colleagues' apprehension that, unless eliminated, he would become another Stalin. And Khrushchev and his group also needed a scapegoat to offer to the now restless Soviet masses and classes for Stalin's crimes—and their own. What handier scapegoat than this hated chief of the dreaded secret police?

Thus in 1953 a new, milder policy was introduced, reaching its height in February 1956, when Khrushchev delivered his famous "secret" anti-Stalin speech to the Twentieth Congress of the Communist Party.

The danger of new arrests was diminished, first of all, for Communist Party members who, from the initial post-Stalin time on, could no longer be seized by the secret police without the knowledge and clearance on the part of their Communist superiors. The ill-famed *troika,* the three-man MVD tribunal with arbitrary powers to sentence Soviet citizens in secrecy and in the victims' absence, was abolished. As numerous surviving prisoners were released and fewer new slaves were brought in, certain forced-labor camps were closed. In some of the remaining ones, army guards took over from the MVD slave drivers, and the prisoners' treatment became noticeably more bearable.

From the mid-1950s, the KGB, or the Committee for State Security, as the successor of the MVD and MGB (and of the earlier Cheka, OGPU, and NKVD), has been the top organ of the Soviet secret police, in implacable charge of the continuing arrests and their victims as well as the never-ceasing espionage and sabotage in foreign countries the world over.

A watershed in the renewal of terror was the Hungarian revolt and its suppression by Soviet tanks in late 1956. Soon after the Budapest events, arrests of suspect or restless Russians and non-Russians were resumed in the Soviet empire. By 1958 such arrests, although not publicized, were occurring *en masse.* The new wave included not only "first offenders," but also rearrests of many of those freed only a short time before. Western researchers of the phenomenon estimated that in 1961 there were some three to four million prisoners in Soviet concentration camps. This figure was in time judged to remain constant for the next 14 years, except that by 1976 it also included the growing numbers of those political dissenters who were kept in the KGB's special insane asylums, even when such prisoners were entirely sane. Nor should we forget the additional contingents of prisoners in the jails and camps of Czechoslovakia (particularly numerous after the suppression of that country in August 1968 by Soviet tanks), Poland, East Germany, and other so-called "people's democracies," where the native secret police usually act with the guidance or at least cooperation of the Moscow KGB.

It is true that, although the prisoners' beatings, tortures, and killings in the prisons and concentration camps of the Soviet empire have not stopped completely, these now occur less frequently and in most cases are not perhaps as brutally sadistic as they commonly were in Stalin's era. On the other hand, the number of fresh arrests is higher, and the treatment of prisoners is harsher than in Khrushchev's time. Instances of inmates' suicide are on the increase.

The dominant role of the KGB over the nation's regular courts is once more quite definite. It is the KGB that decides which of the political trials in these mid-1970s are to be conducted behind closed doors, even if held in regular courts. Sentences by such courts in the defendants' absence are on the increase, sternly reminding the population of Stalinist times. A regular court sometimes swiftly turns over a prisoner to the KGB's keeping. Often there is not even a formal charge and any legal condemnation—only the court's finding that the prisoner must be demented since he does not like the Soviet regime. Such was, for instance, the case of the poetess Nataliya Gorbanveskaya when, in July 1970, the Moscow city court committed her to the infamous Serbsky Insane Asylum, which is within the KGB network, staffed by "psychiatrists" officially employed by the KGB, and even wearing their KGB uniforms and insignia as colonels and majors of the secret police beneath their unbuttoned white coats. Since 1970 such commitments of political dissidents to mental hospitals have been common. Treatment of these perfectly normal prisoners include forcible injections of drugs, in the KGB's hope that this will soon make the unfortunates truly insane.

The maximum term in present-day concentration camps appears to be 15 years, but cases are known where prisoners are being held well beyond this limit. The death penalty is still on the Soviet law books, for treason to the state (such as caused Colonel Oleg V. Penkovsky's execution in May 1963), and for major economic crimes (the law of May 5, 1961), as well as for murder and banditry. While a high court of the Ministry of Justice may be the agency that passes a sentence of capital punishment, the penalty is carried out by a firing squad of the secret police, as in the Stalinist era.

By the middle 1970s the protesting voices of Amnesty International and other Western organizations on behalf of Soviet dissidents became a strong chorus. The Soviet dictatorship has responded to it reluctantly and sparingly. Often it has disregarded the protests of Western intellec-

tuals completely, though at times it has yielded by allowing a few
dissidents to leave the Soviet Union for good. Sometimes it has deported them against their will. Thus, in February 1974, the KGB arrested Alexander Solzhenitsyn and at first threatened him with execution. Then, realizing the furor this would arouse abroad, the KGB
expelled him to Western Germany.

Some Soviet and Western intellectuals attempted to use the
détente, then being negotiated by the United States President Richard
M. Nixon and the Soviet leader Leonid Brezhnev, toward the lessening
of the Soviet terror in its latest phase. In late June and early July 1974,
as Nixon and Brezhnev met in Moscow and Yalta, the Soviet nuclear
physicist Andrei D. Sakharov appealed to them:

> Do what you can, at least for some of the prisoners—the women,
> the old people, those who are ill, those who have been tried more
> than once (the courts punish them with special perversity). Bring
> about the immediate release of all who have been incarcerated for
> more than 15 years, the maximum term fixed by law. Encourage
> international supervision of places of confinement in all countries—
> in these places human rights and humanitarian principles are vio-
> lated most often.[10]

To strengthen his plea, Professor Sakharov went on a hunger strike
that he kept up for almost a week. The only response from Brezhnev
was his order to the Soviet television technicians to cut off at its very
beginning the interview with Sakharov that American broadcasters
tried to relay from Moscow to the world at large.

As for President Nixon, there is no evidence that he interceded with
Brezhnev in any way on behalf of Soviet prisoners and other dissidents. On the contrary, in a public speech prior to his flight to meet
with Brezhnev, the President warned that there should be no interference with the domestic affairs of any nation, no matter how much
we may sympathize with the victims of such a nation's terror.

From August 1974 on, the new President Gerald R. Ford, having
inherited Secretary of State Henry Kissinger, has on the whole continued this Nixon-Kissinger policy of noninterference with the severe
repressive course of the Soviet government within that country.

But a welcome contrast came in October 1975, when a special
committee of the Norwegian parliament awarded Sakharov the year's
Nobel Peace Prize, citing the Russian scientist for his fearless advocacy of human rights, particularly the right to dissent and the right to
freedom from oppression and terror: "His basic principle is that universal peace cannot have a lasting value if not based on respect for
every individual in society."

V

There remains for humanitarians and demographers as well as for historians the grave problem of the exact or even approximate total toll of Soviet terror from Lenin's seizure of power in November 1917 to Stalin's death in March 1953.

On the eve of the revolution of 1917, political prisoners in Tsarist jails totaled fewer than 800. In the first volume of his *Gulag Archipelago*, Solzhenitsyn estimates that as many as six million political convicts were held in Soviet prisons and concentration camps at any one time (while another six million were nonpolitical inmates and slaves). This high figure, according to Solzhenitsyn, was reached just before Stalin's death. In his second volume, Solzhenitsyn writes that from late 1917 to early 1953 between 40 and 50 million humans passed through Soviet jails and slave camps, including men, women, and children who never came out alive. Those dead totaled between 15 and 25 million.

Hitler's victims of gassing, gallows, firing squads, and other means of extermination (not counting those lost in battles and bombings) totaled between 10 and 12 million, of whom six million were Jews. But then, the Nazis had only 12 years to establish their grisly record, whereas the Lenin-through-Stalin period lasted more than 35 years.

In early 1974, Western intelligence sources put the Soviet prison population under the Brezhnev-Kosygin regime as anywhere between one million and 2,500,000, of whom only 10,000 were considered political convicts. But defectors and émigrés from the Soviet Union in 1974-76 ridiculed this figure as entirely too low.

The number of those politicals who are unjustly confined to Soviet insane asylums is unknown.

Thus the grand promise of Russia's terrorists, from the Narodniki through the Terror Brigade of the Socialist Revolutionaries to Lenin's launching of mass murders, which sought to justify their bloodshed by their aim of making mankind happy, was never even close to realization. In the Soviet Union and other Socialist-Communist countries there may have been economic gains, but even these could have been achieved by peaceful means. The human rights of the original dream and promise—equality, justice, personal liberty—have not been enhanced. Far from it; whatever such rights did exist in preterror times have by now been trampled into the bloody mire by the hobnailed boots of torturers and firing squads.

16

Hitler's Holocaust

Because of the similarities of the ideologies of Nazism and Fascism, it is sometimes held that Hitler learned his techniques of terror from Mussolini. Nothing can be further from the historical truth. Hitler learned mostly from Lenin, Trotsky, and Stalin, not from Il Duce. The Gestapo, as it first emerged in early 1933, adopted many of its methods from the Cheka and its successors, and practiced them consistently in all the 12 years of its existence.[1]

Mussolini's terror was weak and rather amateurish. Only one outstanding political murder marked its start: the killing by the Fascists in 1924 of Giacomo Matteoti, the Socialist leader and fearless opponent of the Black Shirts. Later, in a far more prolonged and systematic campaign, came arrests, years of imprisonment, and exile to the desolation of the volcanic Lipari Islands and other such dreary locales for many adversaries of Fascism. Jews were not seriously harassed until late in Mussolini's reign, when the Second World War brought the pressure and actual occupation of Italy by Il Duce's Nazi ally.

The tortures and gas chambers for millions of victims of the Nazi concentration camps in Germany, Poland, and elsewhere in conquered Europe had no true or massive antecedents in Fascist Italy. Not Mussolini, but Soviet dictators developed the camps and tortures that eventually Hitler's Germany expanded upon.

Yet there were also native German roots. Germany's was a sad, mad tradition. The Nazi terror did not spring hydraheaded, unexpectedly, with Hitler's ascension to power in January 1933. Nor was it new even in the preceding five or six years of the storm troopers' bloody rampage on German streets in defiance of the Weimar Republic's police.

Murders by right-wingers of persons who did not agree with them had earlier beginnings. After the failure of the left-extremist Spartacist revolt of 1919, its leaders, Karl Liebknecht and Rosa Luxemburg, were killed by their captors, German army officers, in Berlin's Tiergarten. The loss of the First World War by Imperial Germany had prompted nationalist fanatics to band together in Free Corps organizations bent on murdering liberals. They killed the Bavarian Prime Minister Kurt Eisner in 1919, the signer of the Versailles Treaty Mathias Erzberger in 1921, and Foreign Minister Walter Rathenau in 1922. Such terror was called *Feme-Morde,* after *Vehme,* an illegal secret tribunal of medieval times. Martin Ludwig Bormann was among these Free Corps members, most of whom later joined the Nazi Party as storm troopers. During this period, as one of his pastimes, Bormann specialized in plans to persecute churches. He loved to read accounts of Christian martyrs, apparently looking for ideas of torture to be tried once the Nazis came to power.

Such were then the immediate forerunners and initial comrades of Adolf Hitler; such was the background of the Nazi Party. The name Nazi was an abbreviation of the *Nationalsozialistische Deutsche Arbeiterpartei,* or National Socialist German Workers' Party, which was joined and taken over by Hitler and a handful of his fellow malcontents in 1919-20, soon after its establishment. On November 8 and 9, 1923, they tried to take over Bavaria in a beer-hall putsch at Munich, but were put down by regular army units. Sixteen Nazis were dead, and some of the leaders were captured and tried. On April 1, 1924, Hitler began his comparatively short term of imprisonment in the fortress of Landsberg. In his cell he wrote his book *Mein Kampf,* which combined a program of violent anti-Semitism and anti-Communism with some vague promises of socialism.

In time the United States Ambassador in Germany, William E. Dodd, rightly observed about the Nazis: "They did not invent anti-Semitism. They simply were the first to organize it so it could be used as an effective weapon of the state."[2] Indeed, hatred of Jews as "Christ-killers" had been preached in the churches of Europe, particularly in Germany, for centuries. This medieval religious animosity had been strengthened by a sense of socio-economic and cultural separateness of the Jews as strangers in many peoples' midsts. The Nazis would exploit this age-old alienation in new ways. Here was a link, too, with the antiruling class focus of the German Communists competing for the allegiance of the same masses. Here likewise was a weird connection with the religious motive of Robespierre's terror and the primitive mystic faith of so many other terrorist leaders and movements in human annals.

The anti-Communist slogans of the Nazis early attracted to Hitler the support of such military figures as General Erich Ludendorff, hero of some of Germany's victories over Tsarist troops in the First World

War, and the money of such Rhineland industrialists as Fritz Thyssen and Gustav von Bohlen Krupp. The German masses and inflation-ruined middle classes gave Hitler their allegiance, not only because of his pretended socialism and raving anti-Semitism, but also through the revengeful emotions of the losers' patriotism he aroused (to lose the war after such victories!). Thus did they allow themselves to be misled by some of the most deranged terrorists history has known.

En route to power Hitler proclaimed himself the Leader (*Fuehrer*) of the Germans as the fair-haired, blue-eyed Nordic master race destined to rule over Europe and even the world. The swastika, a crooked cross of prehistoric origin, with its clockwise arms, became the Nazi symbol. Well-financed by the industrialists and others, Hitler soon had two private armies: the brown-shirted SA, or storm troopers (*Sturmabteilung*—Storm Section), founded in August 1921; and the black-shirted-with-silver-trimmings SS, or elite guards (*Schutzstaffel*—Protection Unit, to assure Hitler's personal safety), established in December 1924. These groups, particularly the storm troopers, began a reign of terror on the streets and roads of Germany, molesting the Jews and battling those German workers who tried to stay faithful to the once-influential Social Democrats and the Communists.

Gradually, the vulgar and derisive word "Nazi" assumed frightening meaning. It inspired terror. The Nazis themselves were using it not as a word of opprobrium but proudly, smugly. "Heads will roll!" they threatened, and heads began to roll.

The closing tragedy of the democratic Weimar Republic was ushered in as early as 1925 when Field Marshal Paul von Hindenburg, hero of the First World War, was elected by the incredibly misguided German voters as their second President. He was already 78 and increasingly senile. On January 30, 1933, at the age of 86, in a complete daze, Hindenburg obeyed the schemers around him by handing Germany over to Hitler, appointing him Chancellor.

Now the Nazi terror moved from the rowdyism of the streets to the solemn aegis of the state. Soon all other political groups were abolished, and the Nazis became the nation's only party. On December 1, 1933, Hitler declared: *"Partei und Staat sind eins"*—the Party and the State are One. Hitler had learned well the lesson of Lenin, Trotsky, and Stalin—those men who first made use of their Party as the tool by which to take over the state completely.

II

The Gestapo, which was in charge of Hitler's terror, emerged early in 1933, in the very first phase of Hitler's rise to state power. The name of Hitler's dreaded secret police came from the first syllables of each of the three parts of the name *Geheime Staats Polizei,* or the Secret State Police. At its inception it was under the general supervision of Hermann Goering.

Rolf Diels was the Gestapo's first chief. During the Weimar Republic he had been a minor functionary in the Ministry of the Interior (1930), later becoming a high official in the Prussian police (1932). Originally siding with the Social Democrats, Diels watched Hitler's growing success and became a Nazi. Hitler, on assuming power, made Diels chief of the Berlin political police, and, in July 1933, head of the secret police for all Germany under Goering.

He was soon replaced by Heinrich Himmler, who came out of Munich with Hitler, and who had been an early associate of the Leader since the beer-hall putsch days. Himmler had served briefly in the German army at the war's very end, then becoming a drifter, with tenuous ideas of migrating to Russia or Turkey or South America to study agriculture; for a while, on a plot of land in Bavaria, he tried unsuccessfully to raise poultry for a living—hence the mocking name of "chicken farmer" applied to him by his foes.

The son of a Munich high-school teacher and administrator, he was both dull and pedantic, ambitious and shrewd, and withal definitely a sadomasochist. Brutal toward those below him, he was worshipful and servile to any authority above him—first and foremost, since the 1920s, to Hitler.

Reared as a Roman Catholic, Himmler, along with other early Nazis, left Christianity for a primitive Teutonic paganism of their own devising. At the same time, like his Party comrades, he said he professed socialism. One of his first jobs in the movement was that of secretary to Gregor Strasser, a left-wing Nazi then second in the Party only to Hitler. A milestone in Himmler's advancement was his appointment by Hitler in 1929 as chief of the SS elite guards. Their black shirts with silver trimmings were decreed by Himmler in fond memory and imitation of the uniforms of some young Bavarian noblemen he had enviously known in his high-school days.

In March 1933, Hitler made Himmler police chief in Munich. One year later, on March 15, 1934, he took over as head of the Gestapo—Diels, because of his former Social Democrat connections, was not sufficiently trusted.

In Munich almost everyone was awed. Even Himmler's family was impressed. True, before Hitler's ascension, old Papa Himmler had occasionally complained about his "black sheep Heinrich" and his belonging to the rambunctious Nazis. "My wife and I," the schoolmaster used to say, "are ashamed that our son is involved with those gangsters.'' Playing safe, old Himmler would not join his son's Party even after its triumph and Heinrich's dazzling elevation, although he and other family members did derive satisfactions and advantages from their young man's rise.

From 1933 on, Himmler's power was second only to that of the Leader, and his honors were endless. Typical of the kudos he collected, Frankfurt's Paul Ehrlich Strasse, commemorating the discoverer of a cure for syphilis and a Nobel Prize laureate, was renamed Heinrich Himmler Strasse. In 1939, in addition to his other multiplying titles, he became Commissioner for the Consolidation of the German Race, in which office he was to supervise the "Germanization" of most of Europe, soon to be conquered. During the war he expanded his activities into the military realm by creating a military elite guard (*Waffen SS*) as an autonomous force within the Reich's armed forces, and at one point even commanding an Army Group, supposedly at the front. In 1943 he also became the minister of the interior. After the attempt on Hitler's life in July 1944, Himmler gathered ever more power into his hands, taking charge of the army's entire reserves. In the last few months of the Nazi regime he even tried to take over from Hitler.

Wherever he appeared, peering icily through his eye glasses, his awkward figure was viewed with trembling and fawning. Yet, as in his youthful years, so now at his pinnacle, this terrorist-in-chief was ill at ease with women, and on one occasion conceded that he detested them. He nevertheless had a grand plan for them. He called upon German girls to go to bed with his SS guardsmen even if out of wedlock, so as to produce blond Nordic babies "for the good of the race," and for this purpose he meticulously organized *Lebensborn* ("Fount of Life") maternity homes. He himself had two families—one by his fat and insipid wife, eight years his senior, who tried to henpeck him; and one by his mistress, an attractive young secretary whom he bedded at the height of his power. He was bourgeois—treating the younger woman well, as he did his children by both.[3]

Reinhard Heydrich was Himmler's chief aide. In the pre-Nazi years he had been in navy intelligence on the Baltic shores; it was rumored that one of his grandmothers was Jewish, and that after his rise in the Nazi service he had ordered a new tombstone for her grave, with the name "Sarah" omitted. Some described him as willowy, with an oval-shaped face, almost girlish-looking. A German-Jewish woman journalist who saw him in his forbidding black uniform at a diplomatic party in Berlin in February 1935 described Heydrich thus: "He is six feet tall, lean, trim, yellow-haired. His eyes are blue, yet remind one of a frog. His appearance is ascetic, and he rarely, if ever, smiles. They say he is the brains of the Gestapo, merciless, brutal, despotic, and has

more power than his master, Himmler. He is hated by the army even
more than his superior."[4] On May 27, 1942, in Prague, Czech plotters,
with the aid of British intelligence, assassinated "Hangman" Heydrich. This was avenged by the Nazis on June 10, when they wiped
out the population of the Czech town of Lidice.

In January 1943, Heydrich's job was filled by Ernst Kaltenbrunner,
who became Himmler's right hand. The son of an Austrian attorney
and himself a former lawyer, he was early known as a cruel and excit-
able Nazi, a scar-faced lecher, and a murderous coauthor with Hitler
and Himmler of the "Final Solution" for millions of Europe's Jews.

Also among the men who helped design and implement Hitler's
terror was Adolf Eichmann, who from 1940 on was the head of the
Gestapo's Jewish section, in charge of organizing the deportation to
their deaths of multitudes of Jews. Born in Solingen in the Rhineland,
the city famous for its steel cutlery, he was, as a child, taken to Austria
where he grew up as an Austrian. He was supposed to have followed
his father's profession as an electrical engineer, but, having failed in his
studies, became a traveling salesman. He got one such job through the
influence of a Jewish director of the firm that employed him—a man
who was a distant relative of his stepmother. His own face sometimes
looked Semitic, and it was perhaps this that made him accept the
suggestion of Kaltenbrunner, his fellow townsman of Linz, to join the
Austrian Nazis. By his Party membership and his subsequent wholesale murders of Jews, Eichmann quite likely tried to negate his Semitic
looks. He was bandy-legged, thanks to his early hobby of horse-
manship; swaggering, and hard-drinking; and at his Gestapo work most
minute with card-filing. Yet he took wild joy in his gory job, boasting to
his Jewish victims, "I am a bloodhound," his eyes queer and glittering.

III

All through 1933, that first year of Nazi rule, the Brown terror
increased in intensity. Agents of the Gestapo swooped down upon
homes, offices, factories, and resorts, dragging away Jews, Communists, Socialists, and liberals. On April 26, 1933, while discussing with
two high German prelates of the Roman Catholic Church, "in the
friendliest terms," his policy of combatting liberals, Socialists, and
other adversaries, Hitler said that "he was only doing to the Jews what
the Church had done to them over the past fifteen hundred years."

Men and women, Jews and non-Jews, were beaten and tortured in
barracks, jails, and the newly established concentration camps. Newspapers, magazines, book publishing houses, and libraries were seized
by the Nazis and purged or closed. On May 10, 1933, Dr. Josef Goeb-

bels, Hitler's club-footed, bitter, yet talented vulture of culture, ordered the burning of 20,000 books to "cleanse German literature of alien elements."[5]

Then came the bloody purge of June 30, 1934, when, as had happened so often before in history, terrorism took the terrorists as its victims. On Hitler's explicit instructions, a number of former officials and some prominent Nazis were murdered. Foremost among the victims were the Von Schleichers, husband and wife. General Kurt von Schleicher had held a series of important posts in the German army after the First World War. In 1932 he was war minister, and two months before Hitler's final climb he became Chancellor; through all that vital year, however indirectly, he had helped Hitler in his rise to power. Yet, known for his intriguing wiles, Von Schleicher was feared by Hitler—the reason he and his wife were assassinated. Other top-ranking Nazis murdered by the Gestapo that June 30 included Gregor Strasser, whom Hitler suspected of plotting with Von Schleicher, and Captain Ernst Roehm, one of the founders of the Nazi Party, organizer and leader of the storm troopers, who, although unconnected with Von Schleicher, had fallen from Hitler's favor for a variety of political reasons. Yet Hitler, after the murder of Roehm, gave as his explanation not politics, but Roehm's blatant homosexuality. Many other Germans, Nazis and non-Nazis, were slain that June night, for Hitler's men used the opportunity to settle a broad range of personal scores. Heydrich was one of the busiest executioners in the June purge; it was said that he personally arranged Strasser's hanging.

Hardly a month later, on July 25, the Nazis in Vienna murdered Austria's Chancellor Engelbert Dollfuss, thus preparing the way for Hitler's eventual takeover of that country. On October 9, Croat Fascists furthered Hitler's policy in the rest of Europe when, at Marseilles, they assassinated King Alexander of Yugoslavia, then on a state visit to France. With him was murdered his host, French Minister of Foreign Affairs Louis Barthou. In Hitler's eyes King Alexander's sin had been his attempt to revive an alliance of anti-German powers that could have possibly checked the Nazis.

In 1935 a set of special laws prohibited marriages between Jews and "Aryans" (white non-Jews), deprived the Jews of all civic rights, and restricted them in several other ways. These were called the Nuremberg Laws, as the Bavarian city of Nuremberg had become the site of the Nazi Party's congresses and spectacularly theatrical mass rallies—a city in itself almost a symbol of Nazism. In November 1938, a period of "broken glass" was staged by the Nazis in many German cities and towns, when Brown Shirts smashed and looted Jewish stores and homes, burned synagogues, and killed or injured many Jews.[6] The excuse for the pogrom was the assassination of a minor German diplomat in Paris by Herschel Grynszpan, a 17-year-old Jewish boy, on November 7 of that year. Though arrested, Grynszpan miraculously survived the war.

From then on, starting with the "Crystal Night" (another name for the "week of broken glass"), the anti-Semitic feature of Hitler's terror was in the fore. Anti-Semitism, traditionally lurking in many Germans, was increasingly used by the Nazis as a technique for manipulating the masses toward the success of this Brown terror—just as the popular antielite and antirich attitudes in France and Russia were used as techniques by Robespierre and Lenin in their Red terror.

The coming of war with the Nazi attack on Poland in September 1939 signaled the transition of the Brown terror from thousands of victims to millions upon millions. The ensuing conquest of Europe extended the terror geographically and ethnically. The sadism of the Nazi torturers, slave drivers, and executioners reached a depth and scope that was often unprecedented.

LA MORT DE ROBESPIERRE

D'après une peinture de John Beys, gravée par James Idnapila.

Robespierre gets his own medicine.
(Culver Pictures)

Tsar Alexander II, his sled dynamited by a Narodniki bomb, emerges unharmed, but is killed by a second bomb, March 13, 1881.

(*Above:*) The Haymarket
Riot: A dynamite bomb
explodes amidst police,
Chicago, May 4, 1886.
(*Harper's Weekly*, May 15, 1886—Picture
Collection, Branch Libraries, the New York
Public Library)

(*Left:*) Four Chicago
anarchists, blamed for the
Haymarket Riot, are hanged,
November 11, 1887. Their last
words, reported by a police
captain present:

"You may strangle this
voice but my silence will
be more terrible than
speech."—August Spies
"*Hoch die Anarchie!*"—
Adolph Fischer
"Hurrah for anarchy!"—
George Engel
"O men of America, let
the voice of the people be
heard. . . ."—Albert
Parsons

And the trap was sprung.
(*Leslie's Illustrated Weekly*, November 19,
1887—Picture Collection, Branch Libraries,
the New York Public Library)

Grand Duke Sergei is assassinated by the Terror Brigade, Moscow, February 17, 1905.

Terror in the Russian Civil War: Captured Bolsheviks are ordered to disrobe before execution, their clothes thereby remaining free of bullet holes or blood-stains so they can be sold.

"Whoever painted that hasn't suffered enough. Send him to Siberia."
(Drawing by B. Wiseman; © 1954 The New Yorker Magazine, Inc.)

Scene in a Stalinist concentration camp.

(Drawing by Sergei Korolkov, survivor of a Stalin-era slave camp, who later lived in the United States;
the Library of Congress)

(*Above:*) A Nazi shoots a Jewish
mother and child.
(Courtesy, YIVO Institute for Jewish Research)

(*Left:*) A Jew awaits death
on the edge of a corpse-filled
pit, 1942.
(Bildarchiv Preussischer Kulturbesitz)

(*Right:*) A Jewish victim is
stripped and photographed
before execution, Poland, 1942.
(Bildarchiv Preussischer Kulturbesitz)

(*Top:*) Maoist Terror:
Beheading in Red China.
(Courtesy, Chinese [Nationalist]
Information Service)

(*Above:*) Executed Mainland
Chinese washed ashore at
Hong Kong.
(Courtesy, Chinese [Nationalist]
Information Service)

(*Right:*) Chinese prisoners,
awaiting execution, on
display in a public square.
(Courtesy, Chinese [Nationalist]
Information Service)

Ché Guevara.
(Courtesy, United Nations)

*"We also have a nonstop flight, Houston-Washington,
due to arrive in Havana at 3:44 a.m."*

(*Left:*) Argentina: Dead Marxist guerrilla is rushed to morgue, August 13, 1974.

(Wide World Photos)

(*Below:*) Weathermen's explosion: The house on Eleventh Street, New York City, March 1970.

(United Press International Photo)

HUEY NEWTON
'MINISTER OF DEFENSE
BLACK PANTHER PARTY

Royal portrait.

(*The Black Panther Magazine*, January 4, 1969)

(*Above:*) Symbionese pyre: The house of the last stand, Los Angeles, May 17, 1974.

(*Below:*) LaGuardia Airport aftermath: Victims of bomb explosion in temporary morgue set up in lounge, December 29, 1975.

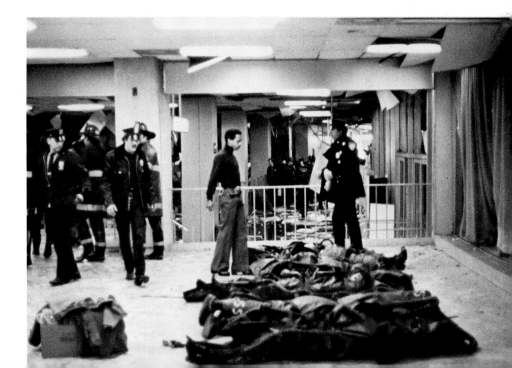

'we hereby proclaim the Irish Republic as a Sovereign Independent State, and we pledge our lives and the lives of our comrades-in-arms to the cause of its freedom, of its welfare, and of its exaltation among the nations.'

Extract from "The Proclamation of POBLACHT NA H EIREANN"

(*Above:*) IRA Provisionals proclaim their historical tradition. An Underground poster.

(Courtesy, British Army Headquarters, Belfast)

(*Below:*) On a street in Belfast, 1974.

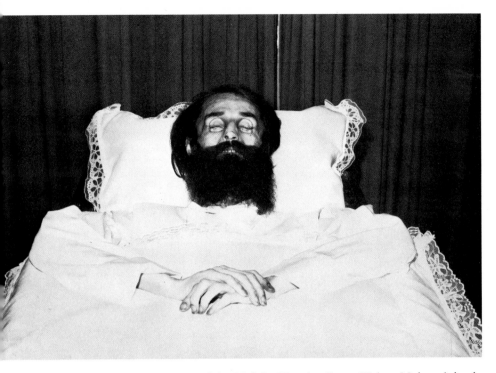

(*Above:*) Captured member of the Meinhof-Baader Gang, Holger Meins, dying in hunger strike, November 1974.

(Reinartz—Black Star)

(*Below:*) Lone survivor of terrorist attack on West German Embassy in Stockholm is stripped and searched by Swedish police, April 24, 1975.

(R. Adler Creutz—Black Star)

(*Left:*) Maalot, May 1974.
(I. Simyonsky—United Press International Photo)

(*Below*) Yasir Arafat addresses the United Nations, November 13, 1974.
(T. Chen—Courtesy, United Nations)

(*Right:*) Arab guerrillas captured by Israeli troops, Golan Heights, May 23, 1974.
(United Press International Photo)

(*Below:*) Israeli trooper (his face blacked out by censor) returns to Tel Aviv from rescue operation at Uganda's Entebbe Airport, July 4, 1976.

(Wide World Photos)

17

The Final Solution

During the war Hitler began what he called the Final Solution for the Jews—their total extermination.

Some scholars of Hitler's terror are of the opinion that he first conceived his massacre of the six million Jews under the impact of his military defeats from 1942 on, and that the deterioration of his personality may also have contributed to the monstrous idea. But this view is incorrect. The first mass murders, of thousands of Jews in a single day, had already occurred in 1941. And the germ of this decision dated even further back. Joachim C. Fest, one of Hitler's most perceptive biographers, rightly holds that the Final Solution had been in his blueprints from the very start of his political career; it was "fully consistent with Hitler's thinking, and was, given his premises, absolutely inevitable."[1]

Genocide, starting with the Jews, later claimed Gypsies and envisaged an eventual destruction of Poles, Ukrainians, Belorussians, Russians, and other Slavs. Had the war been won by the Nazis, their victorious *Drang nach Osten* would have yielded them the whole vast East—all the way to the Ural Mountains and possibly beyond—as the new *Lebensraum* for no one but this ideal superrace of blue-eyed, fair-complexioned Germans. Of the annihilated Slavs, only the fairest babies would have been kept alive, to grow up as adopted Germans, completely ignorant of their Slavic origin (exactly as the oldtime sultans of Turkey ordered many captured Serb and Bulgar boys to be brought up as ferocious Slav-hating janissaries). And some comely blond Slav girls would also have been preserved as likely breeders to replenish the master Germanic race.

Well into the war, many Poles remained indifferent and some even approved as the Nazis destroyed the Jews and put down the last desperate uprising of the Warsaw Ghetto. Certain Ukrainian toughs helped the Nazis shoot Jews in East European towns, fields, and death camps. But gradually, more and more Poles found themselves prisoners in

Nazi enclosures. Many Ukrainians were not spared either, nor were Belorussians, particularly those who rose against the occupiers or assisted the partisan guerrillas in the forests and swamps. Russians were already dying by the tens of thousands in Nazi military prison camps, mostly of starvation and medical neglect, for the Soviet government had refused to sign the Geneva Convention on humane treatment of captives, and Stalin regarded all his surrendering soldiers and officers as low-life traitors. In this policy he even sacrificed his own son, Yakov Dzhugashvili, an artillery colonel captured by the Germans early in the war: the Communist dictator refused a Nazi offer to exchange him for some high-ranking German prisoners, and the hapless colonel died in a prison camp. (As accounts by survivors would have it, Yakov committed suicide either by throwing himself against the camp's electrified barbed wire fence or by dashing toward that wire in his wish to be shot by the guards, which he reportedly was.)

As the crisis of the German side became acute and manpower was needed in the munitions factories, some surviving prisoners were taken from concentration camps to do slave labor in various enterprises. These were, however, mainly non-Jews. But the bulk of such non-Jewish slave labor was not dragged through the concentration camps. These men and women were rounded up in the villages and cities of the Nazi-occupied Ukraine, Belorussia, and other Eastern lands, and carried directly to the barracks, plants, and fields of Germany to contribute to the Nazi war effort under living and working conditions somewhat better than in the death camps. Still, many of the slaves eventually died of overwork and malnutrition, or in prisons and on gallows for insubordination, or under the Allied air bombing of German industries and cities.

II

The greatest holocaust was played out in the concentration camps for civilian victims of both sexes and all ages, from babies to the very old, with Jews as their principal population, most of them rapidly and efficiently processed to their deaths.

At first the camps were of several varieties and under different jurisdictions. There were the main ones directly under the Gestapo, but others were set up by ambitious storm troop leaders and regional Nazi chiefs known as *Gauleiter*. Later in the war the vassal henchmen in Rumania, Hungary, and other occupied countries established their own camps for Jews, dissidents, and targets of personal grudges or blackmail. In time all camps were brought into Himmler's Gestapo network.

The earliest of the most important camps was at Dachau near Munich. Other large and frightful camps on German soil were those of Buchenwald, Belsen, Ravensbrueck, Sachsenhausen, and Mauthausen (this one near Linz in Austria). In conquered Poland were the notorious mass-extermination camps of Auschwitz (Oswiecim), Majdanek, Treblinka, Sobibor, and Chelmno, among others. Cruel medical experiments were conducted on prisoners at Dachau, Buchenwald, and Auschwitz. Gassing and cremation of men, women, and children were carried out at Auschwitz, Treblinka, Belsen, Sobibor, and Chelmno.[2]

In September 1939, at the war's start, the total of Nazi concentration camp inmates was 21,000; in 1945, at the war's end, it was 714,000. But in the years between, four million unfortunates died in these camps, and five million others were killed by the Nazis outside the camps. This is a conservative estimate; the true total may be ten to twelve million.

Jews perishing in the Final Solution are counted as six million, of whom more than 1,600,000 were children. Professor Raul Hilberg comes to the conclusion that three-quarters of all the victims in the camps were Jews, and that almost one half of them perished at Auschwitz and Treblinka.

Jews, gathered from all over Nazi-held Europe—all the way from the south of Greece to the north of France—were gassed and fed into the giant ovens or shot in ditches. But there were also those Gypsies, Poles, Estonians, Russian military prisoners, obstreperous *Ostarbeiter* ("workers from the East"), and even Jehovah's Witnesses of sundry nationalities who were shot, hanged, and gassed.

For some the journey to death was a long and harrowing agony. Packed into suffocating or freezing freight cars, they were hauled from their homes to far-off concentration camps thousands of miles away. En route and particularly on arrival they were beaten, tortured, raped, and humiliated in ingenious and unspeakable ways. Senseless methods of work were devised for them, such as carrying heavy stones to cliff tops, only to be carried back to the bottom, then carrying them to the top again, as in the ancient Greek myth of Sisyphus; and this for days, until these prisoners died of exhaustion or took their own lives by jumping from the cliffs into the abyss below. And over the captives were not only the brutal Nazi guards but also the so-called *Kapos*, or auxiliary camp policemen, chosen by the Nazis from the prisoners themselves to supervise and torture their fellows, friends, and relatives.

For others the end came close at home and swiftly. Thus, on September 29, 1941, the entire Jewish population of Kiev in the Ukraine, 50,000 men, women, and children, were marched by the Nazis to the city's outskirts where, in a huge ravine called Babiy Yar (Women's Pit), they were shot and buried in a mammoth common grave. The operation took two days, 35,000 executed on the twenty-ninth, the other 15,000 made to wait their turn until the thirtieth. Everyone was ordered to undress, and, as Anatoly Kuznetsov described it from the words of a 14-year-old boy who miraculously escaped (only to be recaptured and killed by the Nazis later that day), people "would be lined up, one behind the other, so as to kill more than one at a time; . . . the bodies were then piled up and earth thrown over them, and then more bodies were laid on top; . . .there were many who were not really dead, so that you could see the earth moving . . . some had managed to crawl out, only to be knocked over the head and thrown back into the pile."[3]

Nor was this the end of Babiy Yar's service as a gigantic execution and burial site for the victims of the Nazis. In the two years of the German occupation of Kiev, a total of 200,000 people perished in that enormous ravine, Jews being brought there again and again as they were found hiding in and near Kiev, and being supplemented with Russians, Ukrainians, and other "undesirables."

In many occupied areas Jewish girls and women were taken for the Nazi soldiers' brothels, but in time most of these were also shot or gassed and sent to the ovens.[4] Watches, jewelry, gold tooth fillings from the mouths of the thousands of the doomed were removed, hair was shorn for wigs or industrial uses, human fat was at times rendered to make soap. Mounds of shoes, clothes, and suitcases were collected and shipped to Germany for sale or as the government's gifts to its people.

Musicians were easily found among the Jews, and orchestras were formed by the Nazi wardens, who ordered them to play merry Viennese waltzes and rousing military tunes as they preceded the condemned to the gas chambers. Expert engravers were separated from the rest of the prisoners for special teams organized on Hitler's and Himmler's orders to forge Allied paper money, particularly British pounds sterling. Strong-muscled Jews, from Slovakia and other areas, were put together in *Sonderkommandos,* or special burial teams. As they dumped the dead into the graves, they sometimes noticed that certain fleshy parts of the corpses, such as buttocks, had been cut out with knives—flesh stealthily carved out by surviving starved prisoners trying to keep alive by cannibalizing their dead. And periodically, the musicians, the engravers, the burial men, and even many of the *Kapos* were also exterminated.

Outside the camps, as Jews about to be executed were herded into the ghettos such as the one in Warsaw, the Nazis appointed councils in such areas from among the Jews themselves, to assist the German administrators of these slaughter pens. In their season the councillors were also executed by their Nazi masters.[5]

III

The outside world seemed either to have forgotten or neglected these millions of victims. Many of the condemned, awaiting their turn at the gas chambers and the crematoria, could have been saved. But mankind at large appeared to be devoid of humanity. In effect, it told the condemned to abandon all hope. By the middle of the war the Allied governments had done nothing specific to rescue the millions of victims. The rationale was that only a complete victory over the Nazis would stop them, and all effort was bent toward that end.

During the war the Allies did not bomb the gas chambers and ovens or any other parts of the concentration camps, as their airmen could have done with comparative ease. At various times there were unused possibilities of international protest, of energetic diplomatic action, even prospects of deals (this, later in the war) ransoming the victims for money, trucks, food, or other goods needed by the Nazis. No such transactions were seriously considered by the Western powers. In fact, before and during the war the British, then in charge of Palestine, did much to hinder the progress of Jewish refugees to its shores. The fierce zeal with which the Jewish terrorists of the Irgun and other such organizations would eventually combat the British was at least in part explained by the terrorists' outrage at this callousness of London. After the war, serious charges were brought, too, by certain liberal writers against the Vatican for not doing what surely was within its prestige and power—to rescue some of the millions of the doomed, particularly the Jews.

On the contrary, in some outside lands the Nazis found eager admirers and imitators of the Final Solution. In Hungary, Rumania, and other countries native anti-Semites rose to form for the Nazis those vassal governments and armies that contributed to the persecution and execution of the helpless Jews in those parts of Europe. In France, the hitherto repected Louis-Ferdinand Céline wrote books proposing to massacre all Jews. In Italy the expatriate American poet Ezra Pound sent forth much the same message in his radio broadcasts on Benito Mussolini's behalf.

But there was also a positive aspect. In Germany, France, Holland, and Poland, among other countries, there were cases of Christian love and heroism when non-Jews, at fearful risk to themselves, concealed Jews from the Gestapo. Some such Christians perished with their Jewish friends once they were discovered by the Nazis or betrayed by neighbors. Others succeeded. An outstanding instance of peril and triumph was the effort of thousands of Danes to ferry almost all their country's Jews under the cover of night across the water to safety in Sweden.

And yet millions of Jews and others went to their horrible deaths unaided, not even by their faith in God. The Jews of Europe, accustomed though they were by the memory of centuries past to their lot of persecution and pogrom, were nevertheless staggered by the enormity and totality of their slaughter decreed and carried out by the Nazi Germans. While many died with God's name on their lips, others rebelled, mostly in unsuccessful ways. At a synagogue in Lodz, Poland, a solemn court of the faithful was convened to forbid God to punish Jews any more. In another East European town a group of Jews judged God and found him guilty of letting this ghastly, all-embracive catastrophe overwhelm His chosen people.

Certain postwar writers, notably Hannah Arendt, faulted the Jews themselves for being so sheeplike on their mass marches to the slaughterhouses, with hardly a finger lifted in resistance. But we know that the Warsaw Ghetto did rise to fight the superior German soldiery for days and to die heroically with their pitiful makeshift weapons in emaciated hands. There were also a few other collective and individual attempts to withstand the implacable Brown tide. Of the individual cases was a Jewish butcher who, while standing in a pit with his brethren waiting to be shot, suddenly leaped out and sank his teeth into a Nazi officer's throat, not releasing it amid the other Nazis' shouts until the German was dead. The butcher and all the Jews in that pit died in a hail of bullets, but at least that one executioner died with them.

But not all the men who implemented this terror, among them the guards, gas pumpers, oven tenders, and other executioners of the concentration camps, were sudden or deliberate sadists. Many indeed were, but some had drifted into their grisly work by degrees, at first little imagining their future role in the service of Hitler and Himmler. After the war, Willy Brandt, the future Chancellor of West Germany, but then a Norwegian press attaché amid the ruins of Berlin, was in a group of diplomats taken to see the infamous Sachsenhausen concentration camp. In 1972 he told an American interviewer:

> I talked with some of the former guards who were waiting to be tried. Several of them had been my age, nineteen, in 1932, shortly before the *Machtergreifung* [Hitler's seizure of power]. They couldn't know what was going to happen—had no idea that millions

of human beings would be exterminated like vermin. They fell for the speeches, the slogans, the flags, the songs. I am sure there was no thought of crime among them at that time. I remember one man, who had been a barber in Spandau. He told me how he'd become involved. It was simply a matter of standing at attention, saying "Yes, sir," and obeying orders. In the beginning, the orders were simple and relatively harmless. Then came more speeches, more indoctrination, still more speeches, special security rules, and *very* special orders. Gradually, the man felt himself driven almost inexorably toward the very center of crime. I asked him whether it had ever occurred to him to disobey his orders. He looked at me as though I were mad. He said, "One of us, just one, refused to join an execution squad. He said he could not kill women and children. The next day, he was executed." And so the young man went on "doing the job," as he called it. I asked him what he told his wife when he came home on leave. "Good heavens," he said, "I told her nothing. She wouldn't have looked at me any more."[6]

In retrospect Brandt philosophized: "Apparently, we are able to distinguish clearly between man and beast, but we are unable to see the line that goes straight through some men and makes them part man and part beast."

The part that was human, minimal as it proved to be, sometimes gave a rude awakening shock to the man despite his bestiality. Frequently when a Nazi executioner suddenly began to brood, he ended by taking his own life. Himmler himself was known to warn his Black Shirts against such unseemly weakness. Other Nazi executioners went insane. (In the Soviet Union there were precisely the same phenomena of suicides and insanity among Communist secret policemen, particularly those interrogators who tortured their victims. As already mentioned, some defectors revealed the existence of special well-appointed mental institutions in which the crazed Stalinist interrogators and executioners were confined in great secrecy.)

After the war many Germans protested not only their innocence but even their ignorance, saying they had never known about the Nazi concentration camps and those myriads of atrocities and millions of deaths. But they could not explain just how it was that they had missed the stench of the gas chambers and the ovens even as they lived nearby or served in the German troops in the vicinity. Some even denied knowing that the millions of the *Ostarbeiter* were slaves—they said they took these laborers to be willing volunteers from the conquered East. Neither did they know, they said, that between the failed attempt on Hitler's life of July 20, 1944, and the war's end in May 1945, some 200 German officers and officials had been executed for this plot, many of them hanged most torturously on butchers' hooks like so many carcasses, and that 6,800 others of Hitler's political enemies, also non-Jews, had been killed by Himmler's police.

When in 1945 retribution finally came, Hitler and Goebbels took their own lives in the Berlin bunker, not in repentance, but in desperation over the loss of the war. The other criminals of the Third Reich were cornered elsewhere. Of the four highest Gestapo personages, only one found himself judged and condemned at Nuremberg. This was Kaltenbrunner. Two others had died before that historic trial, one by avengers, the second by his own hand. The fourth eluded capture for 15 years and execution for 17.

The first of the four to die, as we have seen, was Heydrich, assassinated in Prague in 1942. The second was Himmler. In early May 1945, as Nazi Germany fell, Himmler wandered amid her ruins in disguise, wearing an eye patch and carrying the false papers of a corporal. His British captors failed to recognize him. But he could not stand a plain soldier's humble status in a prisoners' camp. "I am Himmler," he announced. Even then he was not searched thoroughly enough and thus succeeded in swallowing concealed poison, dying a suicide at Lueneberg on May 23, 1945.

In 1946, at the Nuremberg Trials, Kaltenbrunner, the third of the four, used all his wiles to draw a prison sentence instead of the noose he so amply deserved. He tried to blame others, particularly Himmler and Heydrich, for the millions of deaths in which he had had a share. His frantic efforts failed. On October 1, 1946, Kaltenbrunner was among the 12 Nuremberg defendants sentenced to death. But one of the dozen, Hermann Goering, escaped hanging by taking poison smuggled to him in his cell. On the night of October 16, Kaltenbrunner and ten others were hanged at the Nuremberg prison.

The fourth Gestapo leader's death, that of Eichmann, did not come until 1962. Having escaped from the Allies in 1945, Eichmann was finally traced to Argentina by Israel's secret operatives. Kidnapped and brought to Israel in 1960, he was publicly judged and condemned in 1961 and hanged in 1962, the only case of capital punishment in Israel since its establishment as a state. During the trial Eichmann said: "I carried out my orders. Where would we have been if everyone had thought things out in those days?"

Many lesser Gestapo officials and concentration camp functionaries were caught in 1945 and thereafter. They were tried by a wide range of Allied and new German courts. In the East most of them were hanged; in the West, others of them were imprisoned for terms of various lengths.

In his manic drive to exterminate millions of innocents, Hitler dismissed the possibility of the world's censure—he depended not only on what he thought was his inevitable victory, but also on the brevity of human memory. "Who remembers the Armenians?" he scornfully asked his confidants midway in the Second World War, referring to the genocide of vast numbers of Armenians by Turks during the World War I.

He proved to be wrong about his war's outcome, but right about man's remembrance of his mass terror. Some—in fact, many—people had to be reminded of Hitler's holocaust while the echo of the war's guns still reverberated. In 1946 in Iowa a small-town businessman pulled a stack of horrifying photographs from his desk drawer. Showing them to me, he explained: "I took these pictures when I led some of our American troops into Munich and we liberated the Dachau concentration camp nearby. These dead and dying prisoners of the Nazis were the ones we found there. Now when one of my Iowa townsmen tells me that we really shouldn't have gone to war against the Nazis who, says he, weren't so bad after all, I pull out these snapshots and show them to him. This usually shuts him up."

The question is: For how long?

IV

These historic Brown and Red terrors do not stand each by itself. There is a connection between the insanities of Lenin, Trotsky, Stalin, and Hitler. And there is a similarity in the behavior of the millions doomed by the Communist and Nazi terror machines. In both cases the submissiveness of the victims was quite alike. Hannah Arendt for the German tragedy and Alexander Solzhenitsyn for the Russian voiced their indignation over the docility of all those millions shuffling to their tortures and death.

Particularly in his *Gulag Archipelago*, Solzhenitsyn devotes remarkable pages to people's cattlelike submission to arrest, exile, and eventual perdition in secret police dungeons and concentration camps. Solzhenitsyn wonders if each victim was so inert and meek because in his heart and mind he knew that he was innocent and that this nightmare could not happen to him—not for long, anyway—for his innocence would soon be proven. But they were also so submissive because the Leninist-Trotskyist-Stalinist terror on the one hand, and the people's dumb, numbed reaction to it on the other, constituted two parts of one thing—mass psychosis, rare even in Russian history. Solzhenitsyn feels that desperate resistance by the victims, their attack, or rather counterattack against the arresters and tormentors, would have succeeded even if not organized—if spontaneous and frenetic enough.

But survivors of the Leninist-Stalinist death camps do testify to the last-minute revolts of the slaves at the mines of Vorkuta in the Arctic wastes of northeastern Russia and of Karaganda in the deserts of Central Asia. And we know that in the camps and ghettos run by the Hitlerites there were indeed some uprisings of the Jews and other prisoners, who died valiantly with those pitiful weapons in their thin, convulsive hands. In both instances the rebel strength was too unequally pitted against the Communist and Nazi suppressors, and this is why the rest of the world even to this day knows so little of that woeful resistance.

The fact remains that in both historical cases the revolts against the mass terror were a rare exception, that generally the condemned went to their doom obediently. And Solzhenitsyn is entirely right in saying that the victims' sheer innocence made for their herdlike march to the camps and graves. Similarly the Jews and other bewildered inmates of the Nazi camps were inert and almost hopeful, often to their last breath. For they knew they were neither criminals nor Hitler's real political opponents. Not only could they disbelieve that this nightmare was happening to them—they expected the good Allies in the outside world to rescue them. In Russia, the multitudes of Lenin's, Trotsky's, and Stalin's sacrificial offerings to Marx knew no guilt of their own. The overwhelming majority of them had not been in active opposition to the Communist regime. They had no past, no training, no experience in resisting or outsmarting the Red secret police and slave-labor guards with their snarling dogs.

In both cases, the professional political foes of the Reds and the Browns had either fought it out and fled to the safety of foreign soil early enough or had been destroyed at the very beginning of the struggle. The millions of Jews in Germany and in Nazi-conquered Europe, and of the Russian and non-Russian victims in the Soviet Union, were quite unlike those initial resisters. They did not know *how* to put up a fight for survival; most of them never even thought of either resistance or timely escape.

PART III

Modern Times

(*Ludas Matyi*, Budapest, reprinted in *Atlas*, August 1970)

18

Mao's Muzzle

These were the greats of terrorism in the past: Robespierre, Lenin, Trotsky, Stalin, Hitler. Have others now come to continue the chain?

One especially has arisen. He comes out of the East. His name is Mao Tse-tung. While so many of today's terrorists proclaim themselves Marxists-Leninists or Trotskyites, some of them march under the banner of Maoism to boot.[1]

Among the New Left there is a widespread notion that it was Mao Tse-tung who, back in the 1930s, soon after his Long March but still fighting toward power, wrote the world's earliest manual on the strategy and tactics of terror. In reality, Mao's instructions of 1938 on how to combat the enemy dealt with rural guerrilla warfare rather than with urban commandos. And Johann Most's handbook on dynamiting the rich had come much earlier.

Moreover, modern terrorists have not learned much from Mao about Marxism or any other kind of socialism. Such is the learned opinion of Professor Karl A. Wittfogel of Columbia University, a former Communist who knows both his Marx and his China.[2] According to him, Mao Tse-tung brought to East Asia not socialism but a new variety of Oriental despotism. In Dr. Wittfogel's view, there was more freedom in China under the oldtime and comparatively inept Oriental authoritarianism than there is now under Mao's efficient totalitarian system.

What Mao has molded in China is not the socialism of the Marxist theory but a repressive state capitalism of military and industrial complexes. Professor Wittfogel holds that Mao never really knew what socialism or Communism could or should stand for: "Mao did not betray the principles of socialism, for the simple reason that for him these principles never had any meaning." And by the same token, today's leftist activists in the Americas, Western Europe, and the Middle East who declare themselves Maoists are similarly innocent of either allegiance or treason to Marx: "Today's New Left extremists, who call for the creation of a more just and free society and who in their campaigns invoke Mao Tse-tung, are, of course, even more ignorant than he." Despite their constant recital of Marxist slogans, their knowledge of Marxist thought—if any—is not applied by them at all to the reality of totalitarian power in Russia and China. Neither Marx nor Lenin nor Mao taught amply enough on how to employ terror en route to power.

But the use of terror on coming to power is a different story. In this area Mao has been adept both as a borrower of grisly techniques and a bold innovator. Here he really has something new to teach current terrorists.

Among radical leftists, especially the terrorists, Mao's pungent dictum that political power begins at a gun's muzzle is justly famous and popular. He has of course always preferred the gun to be in Red hands, not in those of his adversaries. And the gun is to be used with ferocity and dispatch within China itself no less than against his regime's foreign foes.

Paradoxically it would seem as if, on the eve of his takeover of China, Mao gave credit to ideas rather than guns. On July 1, 1949, he wrote: "We owe thanks to Marx, Engels, Lenin, and Stalin, who gave us weapons. These weapons are not machine guns but Marxism-Leninism."[3] But in all his other statements on the subject, and foremost of all in practice, he stressed not ideas, but guns and other means of brute and bloody force.

In this, Lenin was indeed Mao's teacher. As early as March 1927 he paraphrased Lenin when he wrote: "A revolution is not the same thing as inviting people to dinner, or writing an essay, or painting a picture, or doing fancy needlework; it cannot be anything so refined, so calm and gentle, or so mild, kind, courteous, restrained, and magnanimous. A revolution is an uprising, an act of violence whereby one class overthrows another." Promising revolutionary excesses, Mao thus explained the need for untrammeled terror: "To right a wrong it is necessary to exceed the proper limits, and the wrong cannot be righted without the proper limits being exceeded."[4]

On the very threshold of triumphing over all of China, in his significant brochure "On the People's Democratic Dictatorship" of July 1949, Mao asserted that "the machinery of the state is an instrument of oppression" against the new regime's enemy classes. "It is violent, and not benevolent. 'You are not benevolent,' we are told. Exactly so," he agreed smugly. And this violence, this malevolence, of the Red army, the police, and the courts was not only to wipe out the old and hostile classes—it was also to be a weapon of long-range, deep-reaching change. He called for the strengthening of these Communist instruments for the mammoth task ahead.

On February 27, 1957, after years of Red China's mass executions, Mao paused to rationalize and glorify his campaigns of terror. All those many death sentences were "absolutely necessary; it was the demand of the people; it was done to free the masses from long years of oppression by counterrevolutionaries and all kinds of local tyrants." This Red terror "set free the productive forces" of the Chinese people. "If we had not done so, the masses would not have been able to lift their heads." Continued vigilance was the price China had to pay. Mao mocked those who said that after all this bloodletting there were no counterrevolutionaries left, and that "all is at peace; that we can pile up our pillows and just go to sleep." Far from the stark truth, Mao protested.[5] Many were the people's foes still lurking in China; they must be hunted, judged, and shot.

Yet it was shortly before this urging that Mao had startled the world, causing it to hope for his regime's liberalization, when he seemed to invite freedom of discussion through his slogan, "Let a hundred flowers blossom and a hundred schools of thought contend." But he quickly silenced the naïve hopeful when on February 27, 1957, he added that "the broad masses of the people" should distinguish "between fragrant and poisonous weeds." The business of terror must go on as usual. In fact, some melancholy observers commented that Mao had purposely encouraged those hundred flowers of discussion and dissent to bloom so as to know what and where they were, to be chopped off by his security officers that much more handily.

His eager aides elaborated on the Great Pilot's thoughts. Thus it was explained in the Red press and on the Red radio that civil liberties and the so-called rights of the individual had to bow before the revolutionary necessity of terror. No warrants from any courts or procurators (state's attorneys) were needed for searches and arrests by security officers. Bloodshed was imperative to achieve the goals of the Communist Party. Wrote Minister of Public Security Lo Jui-ch'ing in *People's Daily* on September 28, 1959: "In suppressing the resistance of the counterrevolutionaries, the dictatorship of the proletariat cannot, of course, avoid the shedding of blood. But the nature of such bloodshed is entirely different from the bloodshed under the dictatorship of the exploiting classes; here the blood that is shed is not the people's but that of counterrevolutionaries." Terror was a historic necessity. "No dictatorship can be realized and maintained without the direct use of force, "said *Hung Ch'i* (Red Flag), the Central Committee's theoretical organ, on November 1, 1960.[6]

If anyone in China still failed to comprehend what was going on, a

Communist writer in a Peking journal patiently explained: "Execution means fundamental physical elimination of counterrevolutionaries, and is of course the most thorough measure for depriving counterrevolutionaries of the conditions for counterrevolutionary activities." In no case was mercy to be given. Those in Red power indulging in undue clemency were weaklings to be punished for "the deviation of boundless magnanimity," as Minister of Public Security Lo Jui-ch'ing put it. A Chinese woman Communist coined a slogan, "Mercy to enemies is cruelty to the people."

II

Though Mao, like Lenin, used terror as a tool, unlike Lenin, he did not bother to excuse his Red terror as but a reluctant answer to White terror.

And surely there had been right-wing terror in China before 1949. Its record goes back to the 1920s, notably to that night of April 12, 1927, when the young and vigorous Chiang Kai-shek, by his sudden coup, defeated the left or Communist wing of the Kuomintang and made it exclusively his own party. Thousands of Communists and other radicals were arrested; hundreds were executed; the rest fled to their bitter underground and eventually achieved their Long March to refuge in Yennan, and then, in 1949, their triumph over Chiang and China. Communists, who once had been legal as a political entity and as full-fledged members of the Kuomintang Party, were for years outlawed by Chiang's Nationalists. Thousands of Communists, when apprehended, were tortured and killed, among them Mao's wife Yang K'ai-hui—"a brilliant woman," Edgar Snow wrote, "a student of Peking National University, later a leader of youth during the Great Revolution, and one of the most active women Communists." If Mao's terror was a response in vengeance, he answered thousands of deaths with millions of them.

In 1949-50, when China's Red terror began in earnest, there was no real resistance or threat to the regime. Chiang's defeat had been too complete. Uprisings or any other belligerence by the remnants of Nationalists holed up in the mountains of China's fringes were few and sporadic. But the Mao government made a deliberate decision to institute mass-scale terror so as to destroy such classes of the population as it judged to be not assimilable then or ever into the new Red scheme of things.[7]

As earlier in Russia, so now in China, landlords were among the first on the list. Officially only those landlords who had been exploiters were to be tried and executed. In practice, any landlord was the target, followed by anyone whose father or grandfather was a landlord. Then came village elders, propertied or not.

From the very start, Mao's was more than putative or preventive terror. It also had to serve a variety of propaganda aims. The enemy was punished even when he meekly submitted. He had to be an object lesson unto death. The old Leninist axiom was applied: If there is no enemy left, an enemy has to be invented in order to deflect the anger of the masses from the new Red system as that anger's possible target. In one village, a rich peasant thought he would survive by giving up his land to the community and becoming a worker in a distant city. But he was found and hauled back to his original habitat, there to be tried and condemned; he must be used as human fuel for the fiery campaign of introducing the peasants of that locality to the class struggle of Communist decree.

The land reform of 1950 was not alone an economic redistribution—it was also, and mainly, a political retribution. Even when a peaceful division of land was possible, it had to be avoided as a harmful illusion. "The more violent is the peasant movement, the more complete is the collapse of the feudal system," read the Politburo's instructions for the Central-Southern Region in December 1950, reinforced by these directives from one of the leaders: "Give the masses the opportunity. . . . Give free course to their passions. Do not hold them back, do not intervene. Even if their actions have gone too far, do not throw cold water for the time."

In the middle 1950s the terror was turned against the peasant mass itself—to collectivize it into communes despite its will. This particular brand of terror consisted of two phases. The first came when, on the eve of the collectivization, many peasants showed their opposition by witholding their grain from the government collectors. Numerous farmers were shot, and the delivery of grain and other food improved dramatically. The second phase was ushered in when the collectivization actually began, and many farmers expressed their unhappiness with it.

In the village of Liuchiatsun, province of Ahwei, a farmer named Liu mourned the state's seizure of his three-acre holding and vaguely spoke of resistance. He was arrested and publicly tried on charge of being a reactionary by the Circuit Tribunal in the new brick Public Security Station, to which the local peasants were summoned to witness the proceedings. A few other similarly charged offenders were brought in. The procurator asked the audience:

"Comrades, what do we do with these inhuman counterrevolutionaries, these criminals, bandits, secret agents of capitalism, and organizers of Taoist sects?"

From the assemblage came the shout: "Kill them! Kill them!" By their strange accents it was clear that the shouters had been transported for the occasion from another area. Now the local peasants had no choice but also to call out: "Kill them!" Liu and the others were thus condemned and shot.[8]

Nor did cities have long to wait their turn. Businessmen and managers, as well as intellectuals who seemed to be too independent in thought and habit, were soon the victims. And they were joined by those who were religious or known or suspected to have been critical of Communism, and by those who had in any way associated with foreigners, as well as by any Nationalist officials or officers who had unwisely stayed behind.

As terror was made nationwide, the successive purges were called "campaigns" of cleansing, with multiple "Anti" slogans. Thus the "Five-Anti" campaign was officially aimed at bribery, tax evasion, cheating in contracts, theft of state property, and theft of state economic secrets. Under this capacious catchall practically anyone could be arrested and charged in one way or another—especially merchants, industrialists, and professionals.

China's state terror emerged full-blown in less time after the Red takeover in 1949 than it had taken state terror to emerge in Russia after 1917 and in Germany after 1933. Two reasons for this speed and perfection stand out: There were, after all, those ready-made Lenin-Stalin-Hitler models to emulate and expand. And, in the case of the Chinese Reds, there were those many years from the mid-1920s to 1949 in the underground and on the march that gave Mao's men time and opportunity to prepare their terror apparatus so thoroughly.

III

Unlike Dzerzhinsky or Beria with their sinister fame in the annals of the Soviet terror, or Himmler and Heydrich in Nazi history, there has been no world-renowned figure in China's purges. The closest in notoriety, though not so widely recognizable and proverbial, is Lo Jui-ch'ing, Mao's terrorist-in-chief, the minister of public security from 1949 to 1959, and afterward—with the rank of general—chief of staff of the People's Liberation Army. It was he who organized the very first secret police for Mao and has left his deadly and efficient mark upon the apparatus.

A native of the Szechwan mountains, the son of a landlord, Lo was trained at the Whampoa Military Academy, once commanded by Chiang Kai-shek. Lo joined the Communist Party in 1928 in his twenties, and went to the Soviet Union to work with its secret police.

A participant of the Long March of 1934-35, he used his Soviet terrorist experience in purging anti-Mao elements in the Fourth Front Army. "Crude," "savage," "malicious" were the epithets applied to him by the high-ranking survivors of his early purges who managed to escape to Hong Kong. Because of an old battle wound in the face, he could not smile; a grimace of his twisted mouth was the substitute. Yet he loved life, particularly whatever alcohol and women came his way.[9]

By the late 1950s Lo had built a formidable People's Armed Police of 700,000 arresters, interrogator-torturers, spies, guards, and other functionaries of Public Security neatly compartmentalized into seven divisions: forced labor camps, general police, antiguerrilla work, intelligence, counterespionage, frontier defense, and economic defense, the last specializing in tax-collecting and strike-prevention.

A special Household Office with its own police force was part of each Public Security Station. The Household units had a complete dossier on every person within the Station's bailiwick, and the unlimited right to enter, search, and arrest. Denunciation of citizen by citizen was encouraged. Informing was done either by mail or in person. Special offices were set up to supervise such correspondence and the filing of oral reports. In August 1952, a publication of governmental directives on this activity revealed the existence of People's Denunciation Reception Rooms, where the informers apparently came to make their charges. The directives stated: "All accusations and appeals from the masses, whether in written or oral form, should be received and seriously dealt with. To facilitate the people's prosecution, procedures of reception must be simple and disposal of cases must be speedy." In addition, the Ministry of Public Security organized special denunciation committees, each of three to 11 members, in every school, factory, office, and neighborhood. Citizens were urged to report suspicious behavior or even lukewarm loyalty to Communism on the part of their relatives, co-workers, neighbors, and doctors (patients on leaving hospitals were to hand in critical appraisals of their physicians and nurses). Many responded with alacrity. In a North Chinese city of 50,000 inhabitants, 1,500 letters of denunciation poured in within just one month. In Shanghai, one man denounced 60 persons. A Manchurian was said to have walked 100 miles to make one denunciation.

A lull in terror might seem to settle in; then a sudden outburst would puncture it. Thus, on a spring night in 1951, multitudes were taken from their beds in Shanghai in a well-prepared dragnet. The number of the arrested was never divulged, but in the survivors' estimates it ranged from a few thousand to 100,000.

The Great Leap Forward of 1958-60 resulted in a carnage all its own, both in terms of the victims it claimed during the nationwide effort to form communes and in terms of the peasants and functionaries blamed and punished for its failure.

Certain categories of non-Chinese also perished in the repeated terror campaigns. Among such victims were White Russians in Harbin and Shanghai, some European Jews who had come to Shanghai and Tientsin as refugees from Nazism, and Uigurs and Kazakhs in Sinkiang. Many Tibetans were added after that country's subjugation. In 1960, refugees from Lhasa reaching Nepal reported that thousands of lamas were in special camps where they were whipped to do manual labor on road- and airport-building, and that more than 1,000 of these had been starved to death.

The Cultural Revolution, beginning in 1965, exacted its own toll. First, there were members of the administrative organs of the Communist Party, whom Mao signaled the young Red Guards to disturb, humiliate, and even destroy; then, those youths and workers who in Mao's subsequent opinion went too wild and had to be tamed by the army; and, at all phases of the Cultural Revolution, all sorts of criminals (in the Western sense) and personal-grudge victims who were eliminated amid the turmoil. The top layers of both the Party and the army, no less than their middle and even lower echelons, contributed their shares of the condemned to trials and executions.

Students protesting against being torn away from school to work on remote farms or on the river dikes were lucky not to be shot but merely sent to concentration camps. An old professor received an eight-year sentence for wondering in a casual conversation about how long Mao might yet live. His crime, officially, was "spreading rumors of an antigovernment nature and attacking government policy." In the camp he was not too badly treated by the guards but soon died—"of loneliness," it was explained.

As in the Stalin-Trotsky conflict, and in Hitler's purge of Captain Roehm and Roehm's associates, so in Mao's China Communists fell from high favor, were declared renegades, heretics, and plotters, and were annihilated in particular purges. Thus many were liquidated on the charges that they were followers of Liu Shao-ch'i, and from the summer of 1972 to this day a special campaign is raging against the cursed memory of Lin Piao, said to have perished in an airplane crash after a coup attempt against Mao in September 1971. Hundreds and possibly thousands of Chinese have been imprisoned and executed in the wake of Lin, as earlier so many were sacrificed in the baleful name of Liu.

IV

At times, while exalting terror, China's Red leaders nonetheless have tried to pretend a modicum of moderation. Not everyone arrested was shot, they said; in fact, they claimed, the majority was spared to be sent to the camps.

On October 23, 1951, in his report to the National Committee of the Chinese People's Political Consultative Conference, Chou En-lai confirmed that by the end of the previous spring "the movement for the suppression of counterrevolutionaries had reached a high tide throughout the country." Many counterrevolutionaries "owed blood death debts" to the people and had to be wiped out: "only death could satisfy the people's anger in these cases." But there were other instances in which the people's vengeance could wait: "We have adopted the policy of pronouncing on those criminals who have merited the death penalty but who owe no blood death, who are not great objects of the people's anger, and whose crimes against the national interests, though serious, are not in the most serious category, a death sentence suspended for two years, and [we are] putting them to compulsory labor for that period so as to see how they turn out."[10]

In 1957, in another public speech, Chou En-lai divided all the arrested into four categories. Without citing any absolute figures or the date of the start of the period covered, he gave the following percentages: In the first category were those executed, comprising only 16.8 per cent of the apprehended (which meant that one out of every six was shot). These had to be put to death, Chou remarked, because "public wrath was extremely strong against them." The second category, those "sentenced to reform through labor," were 42.3 per cent, of whom 25.6 per cent had eventually been released, after serving their terms, but 16.7 per cent of whom were still (in mid-1957) in custody. The third category, who were not in prisons but under police surveillance, numbered 32 per cent, but, of these, 22.9 per cent had apparently earned their clean bill of ideological health and were therefore—by mid-1957—released from surveillance, but 9.1 per cent did remain under such watch. The fourth category, 8.9 per cent of the total arrested, were released unconditionally. In all, Chou calculated, more than one half of those arrested, or "57.4 per cent of these counterrevolutionaries have been released or are no longer under public surveillance after undergoing reform through labor or after being shown clemency."[11]

As to the labor camps for those lucky enough to be spared, these have followed the Leninist-Stalinist-Hitlerite models fairly closely. Today Red China's Corrective Labor Establishments are of three varieties: the Labor Reform Camps for long-term prisoners, which are used for hard labor, heavy construction, railroad- and other road-building, and basic agriculture; the Education Through Labor Camps for shorter-term convicts, in which lighter toil is assigned, such as the manufacture of consumer goods, often for export; and the Forced Labor Camps for petty criminals and the habitual unemployed or drifters, some of whom are not formally sentenced but are classed as "volunteers," in which tasks and treatment are less stringent. Still, despite the range, in all of the camps life is harsh.

A survivor reaching Macao reported that in his "reform farm" camp the working day was 11 hours long, with one brief break for a meal, and the labor load twice the ordinary farmer's norm. Those who were thought to be slow were beaten by the guards with canes. Only two days a month, usually alternate Sundays, were considered free—that is, free of heavy toil but still devoted to some lighter duties. In this camp of 3,000 prisoners, some six or seven deaths occurred daily, but replacements arrived constantly. A prisoner falling ill had only a ten per cent chance of recovery.

In practically all three categories of camps, excessive work, malnutrition, and tuberculosis are causing a high mortality. Prisoners are ceaselessly moved from cot to cot in their barracks to prevent friendships from developing. Periodic self-criticism meetings add to the hardships. The guards are usually southern Chinese in northern camps, and northerners in the south; thus leniency is discouraged. Even when released, the former prisoner knows no peace; he is under unremitting surveillance, and his family and other relatives are responsible for his behavior.

The thoroughness of the terror has made for a universal submission of these hundreds of millions of people, not to the idea of Communism, but to its ironclad system. The miracle is that some thousands still risk their lives attempting to escape to Hong Kong or Taiwan. Such efforts are punishable by prison and camp terms of three years. If caught offshore, the freedom-seeker is usually shot.

Whether on coast or inland, only a few try to resist when seized. Occasionally official announcements mention wounds received by arresting officials. More of the people about to be apprehended seek surcease in suicide rather than fight, usually just prior to arrest, when those marked for this fate know what is coming.

In the early 1950s especially, suicides of citizens, particularly of businessmen who had not escaped to Taiwan or Hong Kong in time, were frequent. For months, people walking on the streets of Shanghai shunned the sidewalks in front of tall buildings to avoid being hit by falling bodies. Some roofs were guarded by soldiers.

In one April day of 1952, in Canton, 17 merchants and managers ended their lives. Two of the businessmen, knowing they had been denounced and were to be arrested and executed, climbed to the roof of a business building, locked a metal gate behind them, and, using megaphones, shouted to the crowd gathered below: "No matter how innocent you may be, the Communists will ruin you! Death is less painful than Red persecution!" When the police finally broke through the gate and were about to grab them, the pair jumped from the roof to their deaths.[12]

Other suicides were found drowned in rivers and pools, or hanging from park trees—in one case a little boy dangling by his father's side. In some cities mass rallies and newspaper and radio exhortations against suicide were launched by the Red authorities. An Australian arriving in Hong Kong from Shanghai described one such rally: "The loudspeakers advised the crowd, 'Never commit suicide. Just go and confess your crimes. Confession isn't so bad. Your fine won't be too big. It's better than committing suicide.' After that, they had a parade and the sound trucks boomed out all over town the advice not to commit suicide. The papers printed it the next day."[13]

19

Three Innovations

In Red China's terror we find three horrendous innovations that were either totally or largely absent in Robespierre's France or Communist Russia or Nazi Germany, inhuman as the terror machines were in all those countries.

One innovation was designed to strike at the very heart of Chinese society—the family. Not especially church-oriented, the Chinese have for centuries been ancestor- and family-centered. To destroy the fabric of the family—its cohesiveness, its interdependence of one member on the other, the love of the aged for the young, the obligations of the young toward the old—would be terror of itself. By encouraging and often compelling the young's betrayal of their elders, and of the elders' informing on their young by making such behavior extraordinarily public, for all to see and applaud, Mao was carrying that terror to an ultimate degree.[1]

Before Mao, Stalin had tried to ennoble a son's "unmasking" of his father into a nationwide campaign of adulation for the boy, but the country, although frightened and submissive, did not quite join in the decreed chorus of praise. This was the case of the 14-year-old Pavlik Morozov during the collectivization of Soviet farms in the early 1930s. The boy denounced his father as "falling under the influence of his kulak relatives," and the man was shot. Outraged, the villagers, led by the boy's uncle, killed Pavlik. The killers were rounded up by the Communist authorities and executed. Monuments to Pavlik Morozov dot the Soviet Union to this day, but to date there have been few emulators of his deed, nor has the Soviet government exerted itself to find, among the nation's children, many—if any—carbon copies of Pavlik.

Not so Mao's government. From its very inception, it has made this incitement of sons and daughters to denounce their parents a persistent, continuous policy of the state. Particularly in the 1950s and '60s children were practically ordered to accuse their elders, and so send them to trial and execution. At one public mass trial, a girl condemned her mother: "I do not recognize this woman, a special agent who has sabotaged our student patriotic movement, as my mother. I ask the government to execute her so that she will no longer be a menace to the people." In Canton, a 20-year-old student, the son of one such victim, publicly vouched his satisfaction: "My father should have been killed long ago. For the security of the people, for the permanent destruction of the old system, for truth, for peace, I must firmly approve his execution."[2]

To instruct younger children the state prepared special comic strips, one of which showed a boy wangling out of his kin the location of his hunted father's hideout, then leading the police to the secret place and calling out, "Father, I am going to the latrine. Will you accompany me?" The beguiled father emerges and is arrested. The boy's mother is shown to be pleased, saying to the boy: "What you have done as a member of the Youth Corps is right." Not in a comic-strip fancy, but in stark reality, there was one occasion to prove that family betrayals could also include a parent turning in his child: a father tracked down and delivered his runaway son, declaring, "My son is a criminal to the people, he should be killed."

Such filial and parental ferocity was often made an important part of public trials, the swifter to drive home the lesson that the old Chinese reverence for the family had to be wiped out, so the state could have complete control. The family was a hindrance in the state's and the Party's way; as such, it had to be destroyed, and its destruction demonstrated publicly.

II

These mass public trials, with thousands and tens of thousands summoned to abuse the doomed and to witness their executions, was Red China's second innovation in terror.[3]

Lest we probe for the root of such mass trials in ancient Rome's Coliseum shows, let us recall that the Christians torn to bloody pieces by the lions before the cheering crowds were not on trial—they had been condemned in advance, and on those arenas were not subject to any pseudojudicial procedures.

Nearly two thousand years later Hitler and Stalin attempted public trials of some of their victims, but these instances were comparatively few, with only limited numbers of defendants and abusing spectators. The proceedings were indoors, in courtrooms. Mao took his doomed to stadia, with multitudes brought to curse the wretches. This was truly a new technique in terror.

Such mass public trials did not begin with Mao's takeover of China in late 1949. They antedated this victory by a decade or more; it was a device used by his Communists in the sizable areas of the country gradually won by them during the civil war. But at that time the Communists claimed that such public judgments were on comparatively minor charges and resulted not in the death penalty, but in fines, brief confinement or supervision, and loss of civil rights. Major cases were heard by tribunals, not in crowded stadia, and did often bring death.

Actually, the death penalty was pronounced and carried out in mass trials even before 1949, although perhaps only sparingly, as, for instance, in clear cases of landlord oppression. But after 1949 both the mass trials and their executions were widely used and publicized.

The first great wave of public trials rolled across China from 1949 to 1953, reaching its intensity with the Korean War. The second came in 1969-70, a by-product of the Cultural Revolution. The difference in the second wave was that this time the mass trials were not only photographed and broadcast by radio but also televised, frequently including the executions themselves. If a third wave is ever to occur, the wonders of technology may supply it with color and satellite transmission, so that the blood would be vividly crimson on the myriads of screens in homes and offices and factories throughout the world.

In the first campaign, a typical mass trial of some 200 defendants occurred at the Canidrome, once used for Shanghai's famed dog races. A stage was erected in the field's center; this was surrounded by a human sea brought to curse the victims, and to hear and cheer the accusations, confessions, and death sentences.

A loudspeaker was used to recite the victims' alleged or real crimes and to incite the crowd to its cries of denunciation. Dutifully the crowd, when instructed, yelled in unison: "Death to them! Death to them! Take them back to the scene of their crimes and kill them!"

To one side of the defendants and separate from the crowd stood a group of bound or shackled men: these were being prepared for their own trials to be held the next day; here they were given a foretaste of what they were to endure.

At another mass execution in Shanghai, 208 doomed, their arms tied behind their backs, appeared under the escort of their executioners; the crowd yelled (with prior prompting and rehearsal by the Party organizers): "Kneel down! Kneel down!" Some of the victims cried out their innocence and even struggled, but most were silently trembling and knelt obediently. They were shot dead by soldiers walking past their backs and firing into their bent heads. On command, children in front of the crowd began to sing revolutionary songs. Adults pressed forward to see the corpses; one blue-clad worker was heard to say, "Quite right to get that squint at 'em. Cheers you up."

So many wished to see the execution and the corpses that hundreds had to take five-minute turns.

Some public trials were on a smaller scale but of the same technique. One day in 1951, in the courtyard of Shanghai's National Textile Mills, a worker with his wife and their son stood trial as counterrevolutionaries amid a crowd serving as a jury. The prosecutor asked, "Shall we shoot them?" and the crowd shouted back, "Shoot them!" The prosecutor pressed on, "Do the people want to shoot them immediately?" The mob echoed, "Shoot them immediately!" The doomed family, on their knees, faces pale and bodies shaking, were shot at once as the mob bellowed, "Kill them!"

A colossal show was staged in the early 1950s in Canton, where 198 prisoners were held in the square before the Sun Yat-sen Memorial Hall in the presence of some 500,000 citizens jamming the square and overflowing to the adjacent side streets. Those who could not see the performance could hear it on the 229 loudspeakers installed for the occasion, with the state radio broadcasting the proceedings to points yet farther away, Communist functionaries everywhere organizing many "tuning-in" parties.

In the square, on the central platform, a Communist judge, through a microphone, advised the spectators of their rights: "As these prisoners pass before you, you may beat them, bite them, or spit on them to wash away your hatred." Many did so. Many screamed, "Shoot them!" "Vengeance for the people!"

One of the hapless 198 was accused of signaling Nationalist planes during a raid; another, a school administrator, of being "a cultural spy" who had mistreated his students; a third, of having been a Chiang Kai-shek terrorist who in 1927 had killed 40 Chinese Communists and 24 staff members of the Soviet consulate in Canton. Now the judge declared that all the 198 had already been tried and sentenced to die but that this immense crowd was to confirm the verdicts. The following dialogue ensued between the leaders on the platform and the mob around it:

"Shall we shoot all these counterrevolutionaries?"

"Shoot them all!"

"Should these counterrevolutionaries be made targets for our guns?"

"Make them targets!"

"These verdicts are entirely correct and righteous. They are according to the people's opinion."

The 198 were then taken to the Floating Blossom Bridge over the Pearl River and shot at once, the crowd witnessing the massacre, some lingering to kick and spit at the corpses.

Among those publicly tried and executed in the early 1950s were former Nationalist officials, merchants, factory managers, various property owners, as well as Christian clergy, non-Communist labor union leaders, teachers, students, and newspapermen. In 1969-70 simple workers and peasants were frequently victims.

In more recent campaigns, public trials were first resumed in mid-December 1969 in Shanghai, Harbin, and at sundry places in the province of Sinkiang. From January 1970 on, they were also reported to be occurring in Peking, Tientsin, Wuhan (the three-city area of Hankow, Hanyang, and Wuchang), and in the provinces of Fukien, Honan, Kwantung, Kwangsi, Heilungkiang, and Inner Mongolia. At each such trial the average compulsory audience-"jury" was 10,000. In the spring the trials in Kwantung were prudently suspended because of the annual Canton Trade Fair, so that the many visiting foreigners would not learn of the morbid phenomenon. From other sources, however, the news reached Hong Kong that throughout China in the first six months of 1970 at least 5,000 defendants were thus judged, of whom at least 1,000 were executed.

On a bitterly cold morning in January 1970, six prisoners, their arms bound, their heads shaven, were brought to the sportsground near Peking's West Gate before a crowd estimated at 20,000. The proceedings opened with a band playing "The East is Red." Each of the six bore a placard on his chest proclaiming his crimes: bribery, embezzlement, corruption, and conspiring with that revisionist and traitor Liu Shao-ch'i. The five judges (two women, two men in military uniforms, and a civilian from the secret police) and the firing squad were ready. Witnesses screamed their charges through a bullhorn, waving their little red books of Mao's *Thoughts*. It was announced that the six had confessed their transgressions. On command the mob roared: "Guilty! Death!" The sentences were then passed and the six were executed on the spot. Many of the crowd passed the bodies, spitting at them and some urinating on them. By noon, all was over. As the crowd dispersed, the band played "Sailing the Sea Depends Upon the Helmsman."

For the public trials of both eras, the early 1950s and 1969-70, instructions on mustering an audience-"jury" were widely distributed. Published in an official periodical, they read:

The enthusiasm of active elements in making accusations and passing sentences can be prepared among selected groups beforehand. It is desirable to regulate the degree of tension. The masses can be stimulated right from the beginning; then pressure can be slackened to allow time for ideological precept and discussion; finally tension must be again strengthened so that the feeling of mass indignation can last until the end of the trial.

In certain cities ingenious embellishments were added to this business of mass incitement. In Shanghai, as victims were marched to their trials and deaths, high-school students escorted them with drums and gongs, chanting, "Kill nice! Kill them well! Kill all of them!" An official report of a public trail in Mukden proudly divulged the detail that many people on the way to the executions not only beat gongs but also performed the Communist Yangko dance.

Yet, on the decent side, in the incautious eyes of some onlookers, tears could be seen. This was a furtive sight, for to sympathize with the doomed was in itself a gross and punishable crime. Others would not shed any tears, neither would they shout curses at the victims vociferously enough or press to the front to see and kick the corpses. And this behavior, too, was suspect to Mao's public security men.

Early in this bloodbath there were, in fact, rare instances of public courage. At a trial in Szechwan some peasants rose to defend a prisoner. In Nanking an audience-"jury" refused to shout for execution repeatedly enough. One can well imagine the ultimate fate of such brave ones.

The purpose of the mass public trials was not alone to punish the wrongdoers and do away with the scapegoats and human hindrances, real or imaginary. The main aim was to shake the nation to its very foundations, to revolutionize it, to commit the masses to this violent Communism, this savage change. For, in common with many revolutionaries of many nations and periods in history, Mao's men believe that change comes only through violence. And only extreme, shocking violence, and the coerced participation of the masses in this violence, would genuinely shatter and annihilate the old state, the traditional society, and the venerated family of China. After such a cataclysmic experience and their own part in it, the nation's masses would never dare to go back to any milder forms of coexistence with their fellow men, if only for the fear that this might show their sense of guilt for their cruel share in Red terror.

As in the Russian and German cases, so it was in that of China: at least some strata of the population initially accepted terror and participated in it willingly and even enthusiastically—as long as they did not suffer from the terror and could possibly profit from it.

The profit has often been material, at the victims' expense in property, position, power. More generally it has been psychological, giving vent to long dammed-up personal, social, or nationalistic frustrations. In China the organizers of mass public trials were shrewd to include, especially in the initial phase, landlords with true sins of exploitation and thieves and bandits with real criminal records. Hence, among other reasons, the acceptance and participation by the masses.

There is this factor: The many centuries of Oriental authoritarian rule, of no civil liberties or a genuine understanding of and longing for them, all so typical of the Oriental despotism of which Professor Wittfogel discourses aptly, made the mass public trials uniquely Chinese.

Have there been Western imitations of Mao's mass trials? It is known that very early in his triumph Fidel Castro arranged a few such gory circuses in Havana, but Cuba was no China, her Western population could be neither that docile nor that bloodthirsty, and soon Castro reverted to trials behind closed doors and executions at lonely dawns.

III

Red China's third innovation has been the frankness with which from the start of their terror Mao's men spoke for all the world to hear of the millions they killed—something that even Lenin, Stalin, and Hitler had not publicly boasted overmuch.[4]

In 1952, in his long article on "Great Achievements of the People's Republic of China," published in English in the official organ of the Cominform (Communist Information Bureau) in Bucharest, the Red Chinese leader Po Yi-po, then an alternate member of Mao's Politburo, declared: "In the past three years we have liquidated more than two million bandits." His announcement was even more explicit when broadcast on the Peking radio: "Now the bandits are all dead."

The Western world gasped. *The Manchester Guardian,* commenting on Po Yi-po's statement, pointed out that no government had since Tamerlane's mass murders of the fourteenth century openly bragged of such slaughters: "Countries at war may boast of the armies they have destroyed, but that is destruction of foreign enemies, not of their own subjects. Who has ever before made a statement, in print and on cool consideration, like this of Po Yi-po?"

In the first half-dozen or so years of the Red rule in China, how many were arrested and imprisoned or killed? How many more were yet to be rounded up? On June 10, 1955, *People's Daily* of Peking estimated that more than 90 per cent "of our revolutionary ranks are good people." But how many were not counted as revolutionaries?

Even if those 90 per cent were considered by the rulers as revolutionary, this left slightly less than ten per cent of China's population in the nonrevolutionary and not-so-good minority, to be kept under surveillance and perhaps under arrest and even given the death sentence. Indeed, *People's Daily* went on, the minority were "covert counter-revolutionaries and bad characters, and we must get rid of them with a firm hand. Otherwise they would grow in size and multiply in number." Let us complete this calculation by Peking: Slightly less than ten per cent of China's 750 million (a figure accepted for the mid-1950s) would mean some 70 million suspects at the very least.

In late 1952 a report by the American Federation of Labor totaled those killed in China's Red terror at more than 14 million. On November 3, *Time* Magazine mused: "The Western mind, traditionally skeptical of imprecise estimates, might question the AFL's figures, but there could be no doubt that, whatever the count, murders by Mao & Co. represent an enormity that the human mind cannot take in."

In February 1957, Mao informed the Chinese Communist Party leaders gathered in Peking that from late 1949 to early 1954 some 800,000 were executed. But Western sources concluded that for that period about one million per year had been a more credible figure. In mid-1957, officials of the United States State Department appraised the human toll of Red China's terror as between 18 and 20 million. Some Western calculations were based on such official Peking statements as that by Chou En-lai in 1957 that up to that time one out of every six Chinese arrested by Public Security was shot.

In the American and West European euphoria of the early 1970s, when non-Communist businessmen and governments sought trade and diplomatic exchanges with Red China, it suddenly became unfashionable to continue speaking and writing of Mao's terror. In the words of a well-known saying, "You do not mention rope in the house of a hanged one."

But in July 1971, one American professor did dare to utter the freshly forbidden word. In a report entitled "The Human Cost of Communism in China," prepared for a Congressional committee by Dr. James L. Walker, director of the Institute of International Studies at the University of South Carolina, and released to the press, the curious and the thoughtful could read:[5]

The high Chinese Communist Party leaders who sit down at convivial banquets with visiting Americans may be guilty of as great crimes against humanity and their own people as were Hitler and Stalin and their followers.

Those who wish to rationalize public assassinations, purges of classes or groups or slave labor as a necessary expedient for China's progress are resorting to the same logic which justified a Hitler and his methods for dealing with economic depression in the Third Reich.

The cost of progress achieved under Communist rule is too high for the conscience of the world to absolve its perpetrators. In terms of human life and human suffering and in terms of destruction of moral and cultural values this cost cannot be condoned by any rationalization.

Mankind should know the truth about Mao's terror, and should not so easily forget or forgive. Professor Walker reminded the United States that Mao and Chou had welded themselves to their goal for more than half a century, "and in its name they have not hesitated to commit any act." Those eager to have the Red Chinese as commercial and diplomatic partners should remember this mass slaughter, done for "a doctrine long discredited in the world, both in terms of performance and intellectual respectability." The question that most concerns humanity "is not whether this or that figure is exaggerated, but the extent to which mass unstructured killings have been and continue to be a part of the mode of rule in Communist China."

He then presented, with admitted uncertainty about his calculations, this summary of China's human losses as a consequence of Mao's movement:

The first civil war, 1927-36: 250,000 to 500,000.

Losses during the Sino-Japanese War, 1937-45: 50,000.

The second civil war, 1945-49: 1,250,000.

Land reform prior to 1949: 500,000 to 1 million.

Political liquidation, 1949-59: 15 to 30 million.

The Korean War, 1950-53: 500,000 to 1,234,000.

The drive for communes (the Great Leap Forward), 1958-60: 1 to 2 million.

Campaigns against minority nationalities, including Tibet: 500,000 to 1 million.

The Cultural Revolution, 1965-69, and its aftermath: 250,000 to 500,000.

Deaths in forced labor camps and frontier development: 15 to 25 million.

In all, the human toll up to mid-1971 was 34,300,000 at the least or 63,794,000 at the most. Critics of the report have taken vigorous exception to the size of practically every category, and even to the inclusion of certain categories, such as the losses during the Sino-

Japanese War, which should not have been blamed on the Communists. Critics have also said the the Congressional committee authorizing this report was itself suspect as grossly partisan: it was none other than the Senate Judiciary Subcommittee on Internal Security, chaired by Senator James O. Eastland, surely not known for any liberalism. It has also been pointed out that Professor Walker is a staunch conservative and a long-time friend of the Chinese Nationalists.

Indeed, we could well wish that liberals, rather than conservatives, would denounce the massacres on the Left as they usually do the slaughters on the Right. But liberals fail to do so, leaving this particular stage to their right-wing opponents. More is the pity.

As for Dr. Walker, conservative though he definitely is, there is no question as to his academic honesty and thoroughness. Facts are facts, and he presents them scrupulously, with all the footnotes needed. And many of the sources cited by him are not alone Red China's own boasts anent this terror and Radio Moscow's indignation on the subject (the red kettle calling the red pot black), but also such liberal American newspapers as *The New York Times* and *The Washington Post* of the pre-euphoria years, when the awful truth about Mao's terror was not as yet swept under the beautiful rugs of the banquet halls.

20

Wanton Romantics:
Guevara, Debray, Marighella

To leftist political terrorists everywhere, Ernesto Ché Guevara is a symbol more immediate and relevant than Marx, Lenin, Trotsky, and Mao. While these four are the root and inspiration of modern guerrillas and commandos, all four are awesomely remote. But the Argentinian, who with the Castro brothers won Cuba for the revolution and died heroically alone in the Bolivian jungle, truly belongs to the terrorists of the 1970s. Ever young, he is of their flesh and blood and time. He can be, and is, glorified in a singularly intimate way by today's activists identifying with him.[1]

Guevara's portraits are like Red icons on the walls of guerrilla hideouts; books by and about him are dog-eared paperback bibles in radical haunts; his clothes and hair are copied; guerrilla units are named after him, and in Beirut, following the Maalot massacre of May 1974, a Western correspondent met an Arab fedayeen proudly calling himself Guevara. Has any terrorist of our epoch renamed himself Marx, Lenin, Trotsky, or Mao?

Ché died a failure, yet this endears him to the terrorists and other radicals all the more. For in their eyes his death redeemed his failure. Daniel James, his astute biographer, defined Guevara, two years after his death, as "the anti-hero," the man "who never wins but enlists our sympathy." James went on to say of today's youth: "They, like him, are the losers in our society, but they intend to go down fighting just the same. What matters to them is not that Ché failed—indeed, that enhances his attraction for them—but that he did so fighting to the last."[2]

Early in his Marxist youth Guevara read and knew his Lenin. He also came across the Nechayevist *Catechism*, and quoted it approvingly. Guevara wrote and spoke in the Lenin-Nechayev spirit when he extolled the professional revolutionary as the highest type of humanity—the man or woman who sacrificed all for the revolution, who had no personality and no life outside this full-time occupation of destruction, to whom death itself, either his own or that caused by him, held neither fear nor regret.[3] In his own case Guevara was to live and fight and die with no real concern for his two wives and the five children he left behind. Occasionally he thought of them, at times tenderly, but he thought and cared far more intensely about the revolution.

Yet, unlike Lenin, he attached little importance to a revolutionary party or a political program. His guerrilla force was his life and his party, and its violence—his personal violence, too—was all the program he needed.

But though he lost in the end, it cannot be said of Guevara that in his colorful 39 years his triumphs were few. On the contrary, the winning of Cuba and the subsequent homage paid to him by the Communists and others of the left as he toured the world so cockily would have been sufficient for many another man's ego. Even in his lifetime, his published theories of revolutionary action, his manuals of guerrilla warfare, and his own deeds of terror were hailed by thousands upon thousands of his worshippers and imitators. In the middle 1960s, still in his thirties, he thought he was secure in history, his name ringing awe to both friends and enemies. But he wanted more, and so perished.

II

Ernesto Guevara de la Serna was born in Rosario, Argentina, on June 14, 1928, the first child of an impoverished upper-class family. Both his parents were radicals of no definite party, but they were constantly and generally incensed at the state and society of their time and country. The father tried to be an architect and later a businessman, but with poor results. The mother was a stronger character and, as a protester, far more mercurial.

She concentrated more of her love on Ernesto than on his siblings. One reason for this greater care was the asthma from which he suffered since early childhood. The boy reciprocated by a deep admiration for his mother. The father, to him, hardly mattered. In his youth and manhood Ernesto would court similarly strong-willed girls and women, eventually marrying two of them in succession, and having brief affairs with a number of others.

He was an intensive and rapid reader and a good student. He was three months short of 25 when he completed his medical course and became a doctor. But healing was not his passion. He would rather roam and adventure, preferably with a gun. He would kill, not cure. In his first guerrilla months in the Cuban mountains of the Sierra Maestra he was annoyed when his new friend Fidel Castro called upon him to be the rebels' physician. He wanted to be a guerrilla, not a doctor, and—even more—a guerrilla commander, which, indeed, he soon became. His resentment was even sharper when Castro ordered him to tend the wounds of some Batista men they had captured.

In the late 1940s-early 1950s his terrorist days were still ahead of him when, first as a student and then as a young doctor, Ernesto, in company with a vagabond friend, crossed much of Latin America by wheel, raft, and foot. He learned the mountains, the jungles, and the pampas of Chile, Peru, Colombia, Venezuela, Bolivia, Panama, Costa Rica, and Guatemala. He met natives of a wide social range, but particularly of the lower classes. With his friend or alone he worked as a stevedore, a dishwasher, a salesman, and a medico, or just begged for the day's food and the night's shelter. He knew hunger and thirst; he mastered the art of survival, despite his chronic asthma, in many a strange and forbidding terrain. All this would prove useful in his later and yet more perilous years.

In 1954 he found himself in Guatemala. He was then a convinced Marxist but not yet a Communist; and he was ardently sympathetic to Guatemala's ultraleft government of Jacobo Arbenz Guzmán. It was in Guatemala that his radical friends gave Guevara the name Ché (this word, of Italian origin, was used in Argentina and nearby countries to mean a fond "pal," "buddy," or "Mac"). And it was in Guatemala that he met Hilda Gadea, a Peruvian leftist of Andean Indian ancestry. She became his mistress and, later, his first wife.

In rage and utter dismay he watched as Guatemala's anti-Communists, with the aid of the United States Central Intelligence Agency, organized and carried out the overthrow of President Jacobo Arbenz and his Communists. For a very brief while Guevara was in a leftist paramilitary unit but saw no action—there was no time for it, since the trained Guatemalan army sided not with these amateur radicals but with the right-wing rebels, and all was soon over.* Thus would Guev-

---

* At the airstrip outside the Guatemalan capital, Guevara was briefly a prisoner of the anti-Arbenz forces and their CIA mentors. The CIA agent in charge of these particular captives was E. Howard Hunt, Jr., who 18 years later, in 1972, was a White House aide and one of the main organizers of the notorious Watergate break-in in Washington. Another aide, who in 1971-72 shared an office suite at the White House with Hunt, reminisced after the Watergate scandal: "I thought Howard was a nice enough, if somewhat foppish, sort, until one day when he told me about his great regret in life. When he was a CIA agent presiding over the 1954 overthrow of President Arbenz of Guatemala, he had held a group of prisoners on the airstrip just as he was about to leave the country. He decided to show mercy and freed them. A few years later, he learned that one of the

ara bring from Guatemala one of the most important of his convictions: a nation's standing army is not to be trusted by revolutionaries; among their first tasks en route to Red power, and especially immediately after seizing power, they must destroy the country's regular armed forces.

From late 1954 on, Ernesto and Hilda were political refugees in Mexico. It was through her friends among the Cuban exiles in Mexico City that he met Fidel and Raúl Castro, presently joining them in their schemes and plots.

Ché was 28 when in 1956 he enrolled in the Castro expedition on the *Granma*. The little yacht landed its 82 rebels at Niquero on Cuba's southeastern coast, in the foothills of the Sierra Maestra, on December 2. The next morning, in the town of Alegria de Pio, the soldiers of Dictator Fulgencio Batista attacked them. Only 15 of the 82 escaped. Ernesto, suffering a minor wound, was among the survivors.

Two years of desperate struggle followed; in its fire, against incredible odds, the Rebel Army was forged into maturity. The upward path from Alegria de Pio was harsh and bloody. It was at that first battle's end that Guevara was faced with the momentous choice; in his own words: "I had before me a field pack filled with medicines and a case of ammunition—the two were too heavy to be carried together; I took the case of ammunition, leaving behind the field pack."[4]

This young asthma-racked physician was a bold soldier from the start. Fidel Castro quickly saw his friend's potential: as new volunteers swelled the small band in the rugged hills, he gave Ernesto increased responsibility in the field of battle, until he named him Ché Comandante and entrusted a significant part of his fighters to his leadership.

During this period, Ché was developing into a brilliant tactician and ruthless disciplinarian. He led his soldiers in clever defenses and daring ambushes. He did not hesitate to order executions of captured enemies when he thought them deserved or necessary. If at any point any of his own guerrillas disappointed him by showing faint hearts, he had them shot too.

As Batista's inept troops faltered and retreated or surrendered, as the Rebel Army pushed its way toward Havana, many men rejoicing or panicky offered their allegiance to Castro or laid down their arms. Some were accepted as volunteers, others not. When at long last Cuba's Communists came forth to join the rebels, Castro took their help and alliance, but Guevara sneered.

---

prisoners he had let go was Ché Guevara, the Cuban revolutionary; he said that had been enough to convince him never to allow himself to become compassionate again." (Douglas Hallett, "A Low-Level Memoir of the Nixon White House." *The New York Times Magazine*, October 20, 1974, p. 39.)

Ché had no use for these wily talkers of the revolution, some of whom at certain junctures of Cuba's recent history had even collaborated with Batista. Guevara's contempt for what was called the Old Guard of the Cuban Communist Party was to last well into the 1960s, even as Castro, after accepting the Communists, himself became a Communist, bringing his guerrillas—including Guevara—into their fold, and fusing the two elements into Cuba's new Communist Party. Ché's contempt and distrust proved to be weighty factors in Guevara's later career, finally causing his defiance of the Moscow line and the break or at least the cooling of his friendship with Castro.

III

Meanwhile, on January 4, 1959, there was the uproarious welcome by the people of Havana as the Castro brothers' and Guevara's *barbudos*, the bearded warriors who had smashed Batista's forces, rode and marched into Havana. There was Ché's and his men's swagger along the city's delirious avenues and boulevards—and the reign of terror Ché instituted at the La Cabaña fortress, where he executed many of Batista's officers. Later he was placed at the head of the nation's economy and at the top of the many delegations the new Red Establishment sent to capitals the world over. There were Guevara's incessant speeches and publications—and from them came trouble.

For in time Guevara, although high in the command of the new Cuban Communist Party, still would not forgive its Old Guard for its collaboration with Batista. Moreover, he would not excuse its—and its Moscow patrons'—hesitancy in promoting the world revolution with its rebel armies and uprisings, most especially in Africa and Latin America. In his impatient view, the Communists of the Soviet Union were not doing enough. And his friend Fidel, although launching his export of the revolution from Cuba to other Latin American shores, seemed to bend too readily to the cautionary will of Moscow.

Along with so many revolutionaries of the 1960s, Guevara increasingly saw Red virtue in Peking rather than in Moscow. The men of the Kremlin frowned on what they were beginning to consider as Guevara's Maoism, which was mixed, they believed, with Trotskyism. Castro, dependent as he was on the military and economic aid from the Soviet Union, was ever more distant from Ernesto.

So, in the spring of 1965, Ché was no longer Fidel's principal comrade and in charge of Cuba's economy. From then on, and for more than two years until Guevara's death, Ché disappeared from public view.

Castro chose to be taciturn and enigmatic about Guevara's whereabouts. It has since been divulged that for six months in 1965 Guevara, with a band of well-tested Cuban guerrilla veterans, tried, unsuccessfully, to help the rebels of the Congo, and that in 1966-67 he was on his last and tragic adventure in Bolivia.

Castro did assist Guevara in the preparation and initial stages of the Bolivian episode. But just as Guevara's pitifully small contingent was about to strike at the Bolivian armed force, Castro sided with Moscow and the Bolivian Communist Party, leaving Ché without support. Thus, from November 7, 1966, when Guevara first arrived in Bolivia with his four companions as the vanguard of his rebel unit, to that October 1967, when his Bolivian captors executed him (despite the reported attempts of CIA operatives present at Guevara's last moments to spare him), Guevara's effort to create "one more Vietnam" (as he called it) in those unfriendly jungles proved nothing but a dismal disaster.

In Havana, Fidel delivered heroic eulogies, offering to the La Paz government the release of 100 political prisoners from the Cuban dungeons in exchange for Guevara's body, but La Paz refused. To date even Guevara's grave and cremation site remain a secret, for his Bolivian executioners did not want his last resting place to become a revolutionary shrine.

IV

What did Guevara leave behind besides his effulgent legend and his dashing image on portraits and posters?

In one of the very last entries in his diary, Guevara regretted the loss of a book by Trotsky, which had been found by Bolivian soldiers shortly before Ché's capture and execution. This provided his foes in Moscow with one more confirmation (if any more were needed) of their suspicion that Ché believed in Trotsky's permanent revolution thesis—that the Argentinian opposed Moscow's and Castro's latter-day policy of shrewd, even if temporary, compromise with the capitalists.[5]

Above all, in his own speeches and writings, there was Guevara's intense stressing of the necessity and efficacy of unremitting revolutionary terror. Specializing in the countryside variety of guerrilla warfare, paying little heed to the problems of urban terror, he nevertheless dwelt on terror in general when he wrote: "Terror should be considered as a valuable element [of revolutionary struggle] when it is used to execute some noted leader of the oppressive forces who is characterized by his cruelty, his efficiency of repression, by a number of traits that make his elimination useful. . . ." This would seem to make him an admirer of Lenin's brother who tried to assassinate Tsar Alexander III in 1887 rather than of Lenin himself, who in all his many underground years until 1917 had fumed against the Socialist Revolutionaries and their campaign of individual terror. But Guevara was certainly a follower of Lenin in the program and action of mass terror just before and surely right after the revolutionary victory was won.

It was, for one, his resolve, carried from Guatemala after the downfall and flight of Arbenz in 1954, that even though in the Russia of 1918-21 oldtime Tsarist officers were used by Trotsky to build his Red Army, in modern times and in all countries the standing armed forces must at once be destroyed by the revolutionaries. Guevara had other proof for his thesis beyond the Guatemalan experience: he was still alive in late 1965 when Indonesia's army drowned the Communist coup attempt in blood. Had he survived to 1973, he would have seen a similar blow administered to the left by Chile's generals; more than ever he would have been strengthened in his belief.

In January 1959, Guevara had the power and the will to act on his belief. As commander of the La Cabaña fortress he sent scores, perhaps hundreds, of Batista's captured officers to the wall and the firing squads. To him, the degree of the guilt of this or that lieutenant or captain was of no matter. The old regime, particularly its military, must go, in this giant pool of blood.

The Castro brothers were of the same mind, and thus Guevara was not the only executioner-in-chief. In fact, introduction into Cuba of the frightful Chinese-style public trial was Fidel's idea. One of the most spectacular of such shows was the judgment of Major Jesus Sosa Blanco, brought before a festive and approving mob of 17,000 in Havana's multimillion-dollar Sports Palace built by Batista. Guevara, however, operated less in such circuses and more through the wholesale drumhead verdicts behind La Cabaña's heavy doors.

This side of Ernesto Ché Guevara as a terror theorist and practitioner is generally less known than is his romantic reputation as a guerrilla chieftain and prophet. But his portrait would be incomplete without it. Nor should we forget the readiness Guevara expressed to see much of mankind perish in atomic warfare should "many Vietnams" finally lead to such desperation on the part of the North American rulers that they would use A-bombs against the rising masses. So many would die, yes, Guevara conceded, but it would be a necessary historic price to pay—for the survivors to emerge as a new, brave, socialist society.

But what of his far more voluminous writings on guerrilla methods as his legacy to the coming generations? There are his *Guerrilla Warfare*, first published in 1960; *Guerrilla Warfare: A Method*, 1963; and his most celebrated essay, "To Create Two, Three . . . Many Viet-

nams," of April 1967. Of these, his two guerrilla manuals, although in
the years to come so worshipfully studied by all those Irish, Arab, and
other terrorists, mainly borrow from, or echo, Mao Tse-tung's, Ho Chi
Minh's, and General Vo Nguyen Giap's writings on the subject. The
parts in his texts that stemmed from Guevara's own experiences in the
Sierra Maestra and en route to Havana are more original, naturally, but
even these only reinforce the classic Red Chinese and Vietnamese
prescriptions.

The overwhelming point, however, is that first in his Congo expedition and then fatally, in his Bolivian attempt, Ché violated almost
every one of the rules laid down in his own manuals. In that jungle in
1966-67 he went against his own practical precepts as if driven by a
suicidal desire to fail and die.

Mao, Ho, and Giap never dreamed of staging their revolts in lands
not their own. But Guevara chose not his native Argentina but this
alien Bolivia for his stand. His argument—that all of Latin America
was his land—might have been valid in the time of Simón Bolívar a
century and a half earlier, but not in the 1960s of the jealous national-
isms below the Rio Grande. In bleak reality, the circumstance of Ché's
being an Argentinian, while others in his guerrilla handful were Cubans
and so few were Bolivians, served to doom his enterprise in the eyes of
the natives as an invasion by foreigners.

Further, Guevara shared the Mao-Ho-Giap postulate that peasants,
not proletarians or dropout intellectuals, must be the backbone of a
guerrilla force. Yet Bolivian peasants refused to volunteer for Ché's
cause, viewing his group as outsiders. Instead of joining, they often
fled at the band's approach. Worse, they proved to be informers, carrying to the soldier-hunters the latest news of Ché's whereabouts and
doings.

Not too far away were thousands of restless tin miners, but they
also would not contribute any recruits or other help, while the Communist leaders, who so influenced these miners, never kept their half-
promise to rally them to Guevara. Nor did he seem to worry much
about it.

Every guerrilla-manual rule of seeking and using allies was either
disregarded or broken by Guevara in that crucial period of 1966-67.
Even the liaison with whatever urban terrorist support could conceivably come from La Paz was kept up poorly, if at all. And so, early or
late, no help arrived from the city.

In the jungle, the theater of Ché's action, those phases of preparation, reconnoitering, bold attack and smart recoil, so carefully spelled
out in his 1960 and '63 texts, were honored in gross breach only.

In addition, Guevara failed to take the simplest precaution of checking up on the glamorous female guerrilla Tania, the Argentine-born German Communist, who joined him at the very last. Some elementary effort at intelligence-gathering by him or his aides would have revealed that she was neither a true believer in his cause nor with him because of personal love or admiration; she was an agent of the KGB, most likely sent by the Soviet secret police to keep tabs on this Maoist and near-Trotskyite until his very end. (She herself was killed by the Bolivian soldiers a brief time before Ché's capture and execution.) There is even a possibility that, by design or not, it was she who brought the soldiers closer to Guevara, their elusive quarry.[6]

But before his death, most disappointing to him was the miscarriage of his prophecy that the Bolivian foray would flare into one more Vietnam, and then yet another and another. For some time he was certain that, with the Bolivian army in distress and panic, the United States would intervene to save the situation, that the Marines and other American troops would be landed as they were in Vietnam, only to be bogged down; that other Latin American countries, their revolutionary patriotism aroused, would rise in a glorious guerrilla sweep, causing more North American interference and continent-wide conflagration. More and yet more Vietnams!

The Americans did not fall into this trap. They contributed training, arms, even advisers and CIA agents in the field, but no troops. And the Bolivian overlords and their soldiers were not the dissolute panicky rabble of the Batista kind; their land was not the Cuba of that petty dictator's era, not at all "a brothel surrounded by the sea," as Batista's Cuba had been called. The Bolivians—after their brief initial fumbling—recovered. They struck, pursued, and trapped Guevara and his band, a feeble group of never more than some 40 men and one woman. One of the chief hunter-captors, the rough, tough Colonel Joaquin Zenteno Anaya of the Eighth Division skillfully interrogated Guevara; then—on instructions radioed from La Paz—ordered Guevara and two of his principal aides to be shot.

So Ernesto Ché Guevara perished, only to live in the memories and on the posters of terrorists soon to arise in the Middle East and Japan and in the back streets of Montevideo, Buenos Aires, Hamburg, and Ankara.

The most direct vengeance for his death had to wait nearly nine years: on May 11, 1976, in Paris, the Bolivian ambassador to France was slain as the envoy was about to put a key into his car parked beneath a bridge over the Seine. The victim was Guevara's nemesis, Colonel Zenteno.

The gunman escaped. Soon a telephone call came to Agence

France-Presse. Speaking in unaccented French, a male voice declared that Guevara's slayer had been killed by the "International Ché Guevara Brigade."

V

Jules Régis Debray's was a lesser fame and a greater failure because, among other factors, although captured in the same campaign as Guevara, he was denied his martyrdom.[7]

This precocious Frenchman gained his widest celebrity when still in his twenties, in the early and mid-1960s. A member of a wealthy, intellectual, but conservative Roman Catholic family, the son of a lawyer-industrialist and a prominent Paris councilwoman, he began his radical career as a brilliant student of Jean-Paul Sartre. He closely followed and loudly cheered the Algerian rebellion against France. Above all, he was influenced by the events in Cuba.

He spent a year teaching at the University of Havana, met Fidel and Raúl Castro, and was warmly befriended by them. Later he interlarded his trips throughout Latin America with long stays in Cuba, and by his lectures and writings was soon recognized as the chief explicator of the Castros.

His style was often oblique and verbose; he used a thousand words where a hundred clear ones would have done. Yet the Castro brothers elevated him into their court philosopher. On their directive his long essay-book *Revolution in the Revolution?* was hailed as the regime's new holy text and printed in many editions. Given this cue, the New Left all over the world took Debray to its collective heart.

But when reduced to its essentials, Debray's message was rather simple. He was for terrorism, but said little about urban terror as he discoursed at length on guerrilla warfare; in this he was very much like Guevara. And like so many other terror ideologists, Debray was for a total class war with no compromise or power-sharing with any moderates whatever.

Debray insisted that each country must find the best way of revolution most suited to itself. He was for improvization in revolution, for, he held, no revolution repeated the pattern of any previous one. He argued against what he branded as Trotskyite confusion when he wrote: "What is good for a factory or capitalist metropolis is not valid for the Indian community, which dates back to Mayan or Inca society." Whether "Peru or Belgium," there must be a uniqueness, a particularity, about the country's guerrillas and commandos. But in each case he stressed the importance of first establishing a rebel *foco*—

a terrorist base from which to start. Yet his critics pointed out that at various times in his lectures and publications Debray contradicted himself by differentiating very little between one country and another.

Occasionally he downgraded a political party as such, even a most radical one. He wrote: "The vanguard party can exist in the form of the guerrilla *foco* itself. The guerrilla force is the party in embryo." He stood at rapt attention before Fidel: "This [the *foco*] is the staggering novelty introduced by the Cuban Revolution." He projected Castro's experience and triumph into the revolutions to come: "The people's army will be the nucleus of the party, not vice versa." That a guerrilla force is the vanguard of a revolution, replacing a Leninist party, was in truth Guevara's theory. Debray was only elaborating on it.

As Debray prescribed his rules for guerrillas, he emphasized the need for tenacity, for a continued resistance in the face of all possible failures. He reflected Fidel's thinking when he laid down these three stages as guerrillas' guidelines: Stage of establishing the *foco*. Stage of development even as the enemy attacks. Stage of revolutionary offensive, both politically and militarily.

VI

At last, in March 1967, Jules Régis Debray sallied forth into the field, to join Guevara in the Bolivian thickets and to test theories in practice.

Ché was now fond, now slightly contemptuous, of Régis. His names for Debray—"our Frenchman" and "Danton"—were at times uttered in a friendly way, at others derisively. He soon suggested that Debray leave the jungle, that he return to France to rally intellectual support for this Bolivian venture, particularly by such cause-pleaders as Sartre. Debray protested that he could yet be useful at Guevara's *foco*, but Ché, with some irony, entered in his diary that the Frenchman protested too vehemently—that is, apparently not really wishing to be believed.

Debray left on April 20, after one month with Guevara and his men. But he did not make it to the safety of the outside world. Almost at once he was captured by the Bolivian soldiers along with two others, one a guerrilla, the other a British journalist. Debray claimed to his captors that he, too, was a newspaperman (with the aid of forged credentials obtained by Tania through her underground connections in La Paz), that he had not fought, that he had been ill and thus did no combat as a Guevara guerrilla. Later he asserted, mainly for the benefit of his radical admirers, that he had left Guevara because of this illness. From Guevara's diary entries and his dispatches to Havana that spring comes an impression that Debray had at that time manifested a lack of stamina, and that it had been more than physical stamina that was wanting. Daniel James bluntly comments: "The author of the fiery essay on *Revolution in the Revolution?* was, in other words, a coward in the face of the reality of revolutionary warfare."[8] That was why he left Ché.

His captors beat Debray brutally and took him to prison. In October 1967 he was tried as an intellectual author on guerrilla warfare (which accusation Debray denied as so much nonsense), and on formal charges of murder, robbery, and treason. He was brave at his trial. Declaring himself innocent of such charges, he nevertheless asserted: "I affirm my political and moral coresponsibility in the acts of my comrades which motivate the present trial." Eloquently he philosophied:

> Each one has to decide which side he is on—on the side of military violence or guerrilla violence, on the side of the violence that represses or violence that liberates. Crimes in the face of crimes. Which ones do we choose to be jointly responsible for, accomplices or accessories to? You choose certain ones, I chose other, that is all. . . .
>
> Naturally the tragedy is that we do not kill objects, numbers, abstract or interchangeable instruments, but, precisely, on both sides, irreplaceable individuals, essentially innocent, unique for those who have loved, bred, esteemed them. This is the tragedy of history, of any history, of any revolution. It is not individuals that are placed face to face in these battles, but class interests and ideas; but those who fall in them, those who die, are persons, are men. We cannot avoid this contradiction, escape from this pain.[9]

Indignantly he disputed his captors' triumphant statements that it was he, Debray, who had—unwittingly or not—drawn the hunters to Guevara's trail and eventual end. He said that the Bolivian security force had known earlier, from some deserters, precisely where Guevara was hiding.

On hearing during his trial that Ché was dead, Debray said: "My greatest sorrow is not having died at his side." A death sentence was expected for Debray, but instead he drew a 30-year prison term.

VII

The courage of his convictions did not last long beyond the courtroom. In his cell he was gloomy, pessimistic about ever being amnestied, and contradictory and occasionally even defeatist in his letters or during interviews with the press. Now he relished his renown no more, remarking sadly that his fame happened "for reasons independent of my will."

But throughout the world a well-orchestrated chorus of liberals and radicals arose in fervent pleas to the Bolivian government to amnesty Debray. His influential friends and highly connected family enlisted help that weighed much. Among those who appealed to the government at La Paz were Pope Paul VI, General Charles de Gaulle, André Malraux, François Mauriac, and Jean-Paul Sartre. In the United States and elsewhere Cuban exiles proposed the exchange for Debray of Comandante Huber Matos, once Castro's comrade but now his prisoner and facing execution for opposing Communism.

At last, in October 1970, the left-leaning nationalist General Juan José Torres, having ousted Bolivia's right-wing military leaders and toppled their President Alfredo Ovando Candia, himself became President and was willing to respond to the pressures of those radicals who had made his success possible. Among their demands was Debray's freedom. On December 23, 1970, President Torres amnestied the Frenchman, along with a number of Bolivian guerrillas and other revolutionaries. Debray was flown to Allende's Chile in a military plane. He was free after a confinement and despair of three years and eight months. And he was still young—only 30 years of age.

He proceeded to surprise his admirers by declaring in a series of press statements that he was no longer a believer in terrorism, be it rural or urban, as the sole Marxist pattern for revolutionaries. He praised Chile's President Allende and his program of gradual takeover from the capitalists through democratic institutions. In 1971 he wrote an enthusiastic book about Chile's peaceful path to socialism.

The events at Santiago in September 1973—Allende's violent death and the crushing of his regime by the military—left Debray more melancholy than ever. Still, he would not return to his old advocacy of revolutionary coercion and destruction. In early 1974, from his Mexico City residence, with a heavy heart he criticized the Symbionese Army's terror then unfolding in San Francisco. There must be other ways—saner and kindlier ones—to make humanity happy.

VIII

A celebrated Latin American theoretician and practitioner of guerrilla terror, who nearly but not quite matched Guevara in his worldwide impact, was Carlos Marighella, the Brazilian. He came to notice in the latter 1960s, just about the time of Guevara's death. It was as if he had picked up the banner fallen into the blood and mud of the jungle from the hand of the stricken Argentinian.[10]

Unlike Guevara, despite his own sizable contribution to terrorism, Marighella remains a shadowy figure. At the decade's end his guerrilla career, although extremely violent, was cut short by policemen's bullets. Not much is known about Marighella's origins, his preterror life, nor about his fighting years and the exact circumstances of his ambush and death in November 1969. Here is the little we do know:

We know that, as a former army captain, a member of Brazil's Communist Party and even on its Executive Committee, he resigned from the latter in late 1966, decrying the Committee as "ineffectual" and "lacking mobility." Marighella shared Guevara's hostility for the Old Guard of professional Communists grown pompous and cautious. The Party completed this process of alienation in late 1967 when it expelled Marighella from its ranks as too violent a man.

Carrying his cause into the field, Marighella began to collect like-minded militants around him, at first mainly in the countryside.

In Brazil two guerrilla groups were particularly active in 1968-71: *Acao Libertadora Nacional* (ALN), or National Liberation Action, and *Vanguarda Popular Revolucionaria* (VPR), or the People's Revolutionary Vanguard. Not meeting with success in rural areas, they transferred their activity to cities, becoming urban guerrillas from 1968 on.

Their inspiration was Maoist; their training and arms came from Cuba. Three leaders were outstanding: Carlos Marighella, Joaquim Camara Ferreira, and Carlos Lamarca. They hit at Brazil's military dictatorship with a series of raids on arsenals, of bombings, bank robberies, seizures of radio stations, and kidnappings of foreign diplomats.

Soon Marighella was deferred to by both Ferreira and Lamarca. The former army captain became the guerrillas' main spokesman. In August 1968, in Havana, Marighella published a study of the Brazilian terror movement that was also a manifesto. In it he declared that the guerrillas' goal was "the expulsion of United States imperialism and the total destruction of dictatorship [in Brazil] and its military forces in order to establish the power of the people."

One of the first bold acts of terror in Brazil that year was the machine-gun murder of Captain Charles Chandler of the United States on a street in São Paulo in October 1968, by the VPR under Lamarca—to avenge Guevara's death, it was said. Near the captain's body leaflets were left with a paraphrase of Ché's threat: "Brazil is the Vietnam of America."

Marighella's activities reached their height in the second half of 1969. In August he led a dozen guerrillas armed with submachine guns in a raid on a radio station. Taking it over, he broadcast a virulent denunciation of the nation's military dictatorship. On September 4, Marighella's ALN kidnapped United States Ambassador Charles Burke Elbrick. At the end of 78 hours the Brazilian government submitted to Marighella's demand, exchanging 15 political prisoners for the ambassador's safe return. The prisoners were flown to Mexico City, whence most of them soon departed for Cuba.

The record of Marighella's men also includes the hijacking of a Brazilian airliner to Cuba, the fire-bombing of the home of the Archbishop of São Paulo, and at least eight successful bank holdups.

But in early November Marighella and several of his men were surrounded by federal policemen in a house near the American consulate at São Paulo. In the shootout one terrorist and three policemen were wounded, and Marighella was killed.

Other men, somewhat lesser than Marighella but able in their own ways, carried on the fight in 1970 and 1971. Both the ALN and the VPR cooperated in June 1970 in the abduction of West German Ambassador Ehrenfried von Holleben. In December 1970, the Swiss Ambassador Giovanni Enrico Bucher was captured by the VPR. A Japanese diplomat was also kidnapped. All were freed in exchange for political prisoners flown to Cuba: 40 for the German, 70 for the Swiss, and five for the Japanese.

IX

The foremost significance of Brazilian terror is, however, the famed *Minimanual of the Urban Guerrilla,* written by Marighella and treasured in its many translations by modern terrorists all over the world.

In his *Minimanual* he set down concisely the rule that terrorists must be different from bandits by being strictly political: "The urban guerrilla follows a political goal and only attacks the government, the big capitalists, and the foreign imperialists, particularly North Americans."

The police, the army, and the security officers are the enemy's first line of attack and defense; the urban guerrilla "systematically inflicts damage" on that line and beyond. He is "to distract, to wear out, to demoralize" the class foe and his servitors; "to attack and destroy the wealth and property" of the enemy; to start and escalate "a war of nerves" through raids, sabotage, and armed propaganda; to know exactly and in what terrain to ambush, to strike, and, if need be, to retreat, to free jailed comrades and to take and handle prisoners and the kidnapped; to be aware of the personal qualities and style of life the terrorist should have.

The commando must be talented and well trained. He is to be "a good tactician and a good shot," to "know how to hide and to be vigilant," to be versed in the proper use of ammunition and explosives—of guns, bombs, Molotov cocktails, and other weapons. An echo of Nechayevism was in Marighella's stipulation that the "firing group" should be no larger than four or five. However, he also suggested that two such groups could, when necessary, be brought together into "a firing team . . . directed and coordinated by one or two persons."

Surprise and violence are the two powerful weapons in the commando's arsenal: "To compensate for his general weakness and shortage of arms compared to the enemy, the urban guerrilla uses surprise. . . . To prevent his own extinction, the urban guerrilla has to shoot first."

Violence must be deliberate and thorough: "We are in full revolutionary war and that war can be waged only by violent means." Spies and informers must be killed ruthlessly, as must be certain other designated prisoners; "the urban guerrilla must execute with the greatest coldbloodedness, calmness, and decision."

As a former army officer Marighella knew—and taught his men—where and how to obtain arms readily. It was by raiding military installations. The procedure was for a group of commandos to don soldiers' and officers' stolen uniforms, and even to crop their hair in a barracks manner, then enter a post, quickly disarm the surprised sentries and other personnel, and shoot those resisting. A thorough looting of the arsenal was to follow, including scooping up all the drugs available at the installation.

We have an account of a typical raid in Brazil carried out in accordance with Marighella's instructions. First his men stole an army vehicle that they knew contained uniforms. They found four uniforms, one of them a colonel's. Four terrorists put them on and drove the stolen car to a camp. A French journalist, trusted by the guerrillas to a point of being taken on some of their expeditions, reported: "Chance had it that the only man at the guard post with any rank was a corporal. The vehicle entered the camp without difficulty. The 'colonel' got out, chewed out the corporal, and made him line up men for inspection. When the ten men were lined up, the militants took out their weapons, took those of the soldiers, undressed them, and took their uniforms as well."[11]

In the wake of the Brazilian example, such deceits have been reported throughout the world. In practically all cases it is clear that in their latest use of a variety of methods, terrorists have followed the instructions of the *Minimanual,* Marighella's simple, lucid, destructively practical work, which draws not only from his old army training but also from his experience as an activist of terror.

As Brazil's students rioted against repression, the terrorists linked their own outbursts with those of the eager men and women of the campuses. But Marighella's vision was also to attract the workers and other lower classes of the cities and, in time, to try again for the allegiance and participation of the peasants.

In that, Marighella and the other guerrilla leaders of Brazil failed repeatedly. The movement remained that of disaffected intellectuals and pseudointellectuals. This was its main weakness.

Nor would the Establishment bow and surrender so easily. Through new draconian legislation, by stringent and cruel military and police action, with ghastly torture of those captured, the dictatorship counterattacked. At length it won.

The ebbing of the terrorist movement in Brazil from its high point of late 1969 was quickened by the death of its chiefs: following Marighella's end, Camara Ferreira died in 1970, and Carlos Lamarca in 1971. The capture of terrorists, the torture and killing of prisoners, and the intimidation of those liberals at large who sympathized with, and tried to aid, the decimated guerrillas, all these and many similar measures did their work. In 1976, Marighella's teachings were still alive and being applied by his disciples in Argentina and Ulster, in the Middle East and Eritrea, but they are only a memory and a theory in Brazil.

21

The Morbid Tango

In February 1974, four Latin American terrorist organizations came together in Buenos Aires, Argentina. They represented the militant revolutionaries of Argentina, Uruguay, Bolivia, and Chile. All four were illegal in their own countries, having been outlawed by rightist or military regimes. They were extremist organizations that refused to cooperate with moderate leftists or even orthodox pro-Moscow Communists. At their meeting on February 13, the delegates issued a belligerent statement reaffirming Ché Guevara's message of the impossibility of compromise and of the need to fight to either victory or death.[1]

They established a Junta of Revolutionary Coordination, with the aim of interconnecting and expanding through Latin America "a prolonged revolutionary war" that would in time make the entire continent that One More Vietnam urged by Guevara. The common front of the four organizations would mean joint operations, including an interchange of personnel and arms.

At this writing, the Argentinian *Ejército Revolucionario del Pueblo* (ERP), or the People's Revolutionary Army, is the strongest of the four terrorist groups represented at the February 1974 conference.

How did Argentina's terrorism come to be?

On the eve of the Second World War, Argentina was predominantly agricultural, and the main profit of its rich produce accrued to a powerful handful of landed aristocracy who luxuriated on great estates and in the resorts and night clubs of Western Europe. Farm hands and cattle herders stayed poor; factory workers, state employees, and other urban lower and middle classes had a hard time making ends meet.

In the late 1930s and early '40s the country's sudden industrialization swelled the slums of Buenos Aires with a huge influx of rural folk and they, as textile, metallurgic, and automobile workers, were restive. When Colonel Juan Perón emerged to power in 1945-46, he had their support. Perón and his dynamic actress-wife Evita promised and then gave the lower classes a wide range of pay raises and other boons. Yet Perón was not a socialist. An admirer of Mussolini and Hitler, he was a demagogue and near-fascist whom the upper classes applauded, for their own wealth and privileges remained untouched. However, his policies and the corruption of his regime soon exhausted the nation's treasury. More and more Argentinians came to resent him.

In 1952, Evita died of cancer. Without her, Perón further lost in popularity. In 1955, the military, with the aid of the Catholic Church, ousted him. Yet for years to come the country could not recover. Its many problems were too complex. Unrest deepened. Finally, in early 1973, the military bowed to the pressure of the nostalgic masses (and even of some of the middle and upper classes) who clamored for Perón's return from his exile in Spain.

But his new presidency was a mere shadow of his pre-1955 might. He was old and ill. His new wife Isabel, whom he made vice-president, vainly tried for the late Evita's charisma. When, in July 1974, Perón died and Isabel became President, terror and other chaos on both left and right shook the state to its dubious foundations.

Between his return in June 1973, after 18 years of exile, and his death on July 1, 1974, Perón disclaimed violence. "I never killed any-one." And: "I am a vegetarian lion." But there is a record. When in 1969 Peronist guerrillas murdered Augusto Vandor, an influential labor leader who might have kept the country's workers out of Perón's column, the man's slayers boasted: "We followed one of Perón's sayings, 'In politics you cannot wound the enemy, you must kill him.' "[2]

Four years later, Perón-inspired killings were still a fact. "If I were fifty years younger I would understandably go about planting bombs," the 77-year-old Perón said in early 1973 while still an exile in Spain. A few months later, back in Argentina and in power, he gave the signal to fight against his formidable enemy, the ERP. So the war of the terror-ists, in and out of the government, went on.

The ERP was formally established in July 1970 at the Fifth Con-gress of the Trotskyite *Partido Revolucionario de los Trabajadores* (PRT), or the Workers' Revolutionary Party. However, in 1973, on the eve of Perón's return, the PRT and the ERP split into three groups. All three preserved the name ERP, yet all three were different. The main ERP, in its allegiance to Castro, had to mute the Trotskyite ideas and phraseology so repugnant to Havana (obedient to Moscow). The sec-ond group, ERP-*Fracción Roja*, or the Red Faction, remained loyal to the Trotskyites, but its influence was minimal. The third group, ERP-*Augosto 22*, at least for a time tended to cooperate with the radical

Peronist formations and even supported Perón for the presidency. It is in part from among these "August" men that some of the Montoneros sprang, the most cohesive and dedicated of the Peronist terrorists. (Their name came from the common Spanish noun *montonero*, meaning "bushwhacker," "guerrilla.") But most of the "August" group either remained under, or soon resubmitted to, the main ERP command.

In March 1973, at the time of the Peronists' rapid ascension to power, the more conservative of the Montoneros confidently predicted the ebbing away of any and all terrorism in the country once Perón landed from Spain. In late May the new President, Hector J. Campóra, the dentist-turned-politician, who held office while waiting for Perón's arrival and takeover, proclaimed an amnesty for some 1,500 political prisoners, including many convicted guerrillas. He called a conference with the heads of several terrorist organizations to ask suspension of their activities. While the Montoneros and several other terrorist groups agreed, the main ERP refused categorically. Its revolutionary zeal would not allow any compromise with the Establishment, Peronist or not.

Nor were all the Peronistas willing to wait patiently for the millenium promised by the aged leader. Many young Montoneros and other militant Peronistas would not restrain their guns or turn them exclusively against the ERP adversary. There were early signs of Peronist infighting, which finally, on June 20, 1973, broke forth in a mass shootout among the rival groups of the Peronistas, right and left, who had come to greet Perón's return from Spain that day, only to leave in the field more than 100 dead and over 400 wounded.

Yet the principal terrorist group in the Argentinian drama was, and still is, the People's Revolutionary Army—the anti-Peronist and anti-any-Establishment ERP.

II

From its inception in 1970 the ERP had recruited its devotees from among the city young, both the well-to-do and the workers. In 1972 it was estimated that some 500 staunch members were controlled by the PRT's Military Committee and so-called "general staff." In early 1972 the ERP consisted of 17 cells in six Argentine provinces. The ERP's leader, Cuban-trained Mario Roberto Santucho Juarez, was the PRT secretary-general. By January 1974, after the division into three groups, the main ERP numbered more than 2,000 activists and some 12,000 cryptomembers in numerous auxiliary cells. Their fanaticism or, as they would loftily put it, their ideological dedication, as well as their courage, discipline, and meticulous attention to detail in their operations, have won for them an almost unbroken series of successes.

Santucho, the ERP top leader (until his violent death in July 1976) was a man of daring enterprise and cool nerve, with a long record of shootouts, imprisonment, and spectacular jail breaks. On August 15, 1972, Santucho was among the six guerrillas who broke out of a prison camp, hijacked a commercial jetliner at the Trelew airfield in southern Argentina, and commanded the pilot to fly it to Chile. But 19 of Santucho's comrades, including his pregnant wife were caught at the airfield. A week later 16 of these, among them Santucho's wife, were executed by guards at the Trelew naval base jail, while (it was claimed) attempting to flee.

Soon Santucho stole back into Argentina to resume his ERP chieftancy. In December 1972, his guerrillas gunned down Admiral Emilio Berisso (retired). In April 1973, the same fate befell Admiral Hermes Quijada. Both these men were held responsible by Santucho for the killing of the 16 terrorists in the Trelew prison. It was in memory of the date of the Trelew slayings that the ERP's special commando team in charge of most important executions was named "the August 22 Unit."

From the spring of 1973 on, emboldened by the downfall of the military government and the initial permissiveness of Dr. Campóra, the ERP met journalists in impromptu press conferences. These were called in suddenly seized private quarters, on one occasion on the second floor of a social club and dance hall in a northern suburb of Buenos Aires, whose owners, an entire family, were kept under guard in another room of the building through the three hours of the meeting. On the wall behind the trio of guerrilla leaders answering newsmen's questions were two posters, one of Guevara, the other of General José de San Martin, the nineteenth century South American leader of the war of independence against Spain. Between the posters hung the terrorists' blue-and-white flag with a red star. Everywhere at the doors and windows were well-armed men, as well as a submachine gun and shotguns in open cases ready for action.

That spring of 1973, mocking President Campóra's plea for a nation-wide reconciliation and continuing its raids, kidnappings, and murders, Santucho's group declared that Campóra's program was a contradiction in terms: "a national unity between the army oppressors and the oppressed, between exploitative businessmen and the exploited workers, between the oligarchs who own the fields and the ranches and the dispossessed peons." By late summer it was amply clear to the ERP and the entire nation that since his return on June 20 Perón had been encouraging and rallying conservative elements around him. The ERP declared that there would be no peace between it and Perón, who at best was but "a bourgeois reformer" and at his worst a hireling of the capitalists. In August, Santucho asserted: "Ample sectors of progressive and revolutionary Peronism, who have sincerely believed that Perón was a revolutionary, are now disorganized." Santucho appealed: "Our guerrilla army calls on these to unite with us." Bloody business as usual.

When first the dentist Campóra and then the dictator Perón asked for a popular vote of confidence to put a stamp of legitimacy on their power, the ERP came out against any elections whatever. For the ERP was always opposed to all parliamentary systems or any hints thereof; not elections but fierce class war constituted its only program. "Power is not born from votes, power is born from gunpoint," it proclaimed in a bluntly Maoist public statement. As long as weapons were in the hands of the Establishment, votes would not help the repressed, who would enjoy true freedom and power only on seizing arms. On March 8, 1973, with the double-barreled purpose of making its antivote-stand known and of doing this at gunpoint, the ERP kidnapped the owner of a mass-circulation daily *Crónica* of Buenos Aires, in order to compel the paper to publish this antielection manifesto. The newspaper complied and the owner was released.

In April 1975, Isabel Perón urged Argentinians to vote in the local election in the small province of Misiones. The Montoneros agreed, although their vote proved to be a poor third. But the implacable ERP stayed away from the polls, and instead, on April 13, the election day, it purposely chose to send a strong terror group to attack an army garrison, killing a colonel and rounding up a supply of weapons while losing two ERP members.

The ERP would vote by gunfire and no other way. To this day they ride high. This is so because of their inventiveness, their daring, their remarkable efficiency, and their calculated readiness to shed anyone's blood—including their own.

As an example of the way they operate: For a typical kidnapping, the ERP activists are divided into five teams. The first thoroughly surveys the locality where the abduction is to take place. The second carries out the actual kidnapping, delivering the victim (stunned, sometimes wounded, often rolled into an innocent-looking rug) to the third, which in turn transports him to the fourth—the team in charge of "the people's prison." The fifth team stealthily returns to the victim's home to observe and report back to the leaders whatever can be learned of the reaction of the police and the mood of the victim's family.

To replenish their arms, the terrorists raid military installations. A notable episode caused by one such raid started on August 11, 1974, when 70 ERP guerrillas attacked an infantry regiment's headquarters in Catamarca Province. The raid failed. Two of the raiders were killed, while the government forces suffered only a few wounded. Soldiers and police pursued the fleeing ERP into the mountains, a full-scale battle was fought, and 16 guerrillas were killed. In Buenos Aires the ERP leadership angrily protested that the government was lying, that the 16 had been slain not in combat but after they had surrendered. The ERP declared its vengeance: 16 army officers will be killed, one by one, to match the 16 fallen comrades.

From then on, for weeks and months, ERP commandos hunted army officers on the streets of Buenos Aires and elsewhere, displaying astonishing ingenuity in tracking and trapping their victims. No precautions and no bodyguards were able to save the officers. As the killing continued, word spread that the ERP was singling out those officers who had received special counterinsurgency training in the American-sponsored school at Panama.

III

Since the latter 1960s the onslaught of all messianic terrorism in Argentina, and especially of the ERP, has been three-pronged: against the armed forces and the police; against businessmen, both foreign and native; against labor leaders and other political opponents, right or left. Thus in 1972 murders by various guerrillas included those of General Juan Carlos Sanchez, who was in charge of the antiterrorist campaign in Rosario; of Oberdan Sallustro, the Italian manager of the Fiat-Concord concern in Argentina, killed after the demand by the leftists of a million-dollar ransom was agreed to by Fiat while the condition or release of numerous political prisoners was refused by the Argentinian government; and, last but not least, of several trade union men.

Political kidnapping, though said to have originated with the Uruguayan Tupamaros, has been brought to its present sophistication in Argentina by the ERP. In the five years from 1968 to mid-1973 almost all groups of terrorists in Argentina, but most aggressively the ERP, collected between 15 and 20 million dollars in ransoms, covering more than 60 foreign and domestic victims. Of these sums, nearly two million dollars were exacted in April 1973 for the release of Francis Victor Brimcombe, an executive of the British American Tobacco Company; and, it is rumored, three million dollars in July of that year were paid to free John R. Thompson, president of Firestone-Argentina. But the highest payment ever made to the ERP was for the life of Victor E.

Samuelson, an Exxon oil executive, who was kidnapped by the ERP on December 6, 1973, while lunching in his company refinery's dining room. After 144 days in captivity, he was released in late April 1974, for a record ransom of $14,200,000.

The "Robin Hood" approach has also been profitable, especially in terms of propaganda. Usually this has involved a demand that the companies or the relatives of the abducted donate food and medicine to the poor. This technique has been widely practiced by the ERP and other Argentinian guerrillas and in time emulated by terrorists elsewhere, including the Symbionese Liberation Army in San Francisco, the kidnappers and brainwashers of Patricia Hearst in 1974. Typical was the case of the Ford Motor Company in Buenos Aires, forced in May 1973 to donate one million dollars' worth of food, medicine, equipment, and educational materials to children's hospitals and needy schools, after the guerrillas threatened to kidnap or kill a number of Ford executives in Argentina.

Propaganda in the course of abductions is important to the ERP. On July 23, 1974, one of its teams kidnapped Eric Breuss, the Austrian manager of a steel factory, but spared his life. Finally, on December 6, the terrorists released him in Córdoba on nothing more than his promise to sit down and negotiate with his workers—but as he was freed, he was not only bound and gagged, but also wrapped in the ERP flag.

Yet, despite the customary clockwork methods of the guerrillas, some Argentinian kidnappings have been tragically bungled. Thus on Thanksgiving Day in November 1973, John Swint of the Ford Motor Company in Córdoba was killed, together with his two bodyguards, during an attempt to capture him. Also in Córdoba, on Good Friday in 1974, the American consul Alfred Laun 3rd fought his kidnappers and was so gravely wounded that the terrorists decided he would be only a burden to them. So they dumped him near a riverbed, wrapped in a blanket, along with serum bottles thoughtfully included. He was, however, soon found by rescuers and in time recovered, although the call was indeed close. Not so fortunate was John Patrick Egan, U.S. consul in Córdoba, kidnapped by the Montoneros on February 27, 1975, and killed the next day, his body dumped on a dirt road wrapped in a banner inscribed, "Perón or death. Long live the Fatherland. Forever my general."

IV

The main support of, first General Perón, then his widow Isabel, came from Argentina's powerful labor unions, whose leadership has long been anti-Communist, antiterrorist, and antibusiness. From Perón's death in July 1974 on, even as they realized the lightweight inadequacy of President Isabel Martínez de Perón, these labor chiefs would still keep her in office despite all the left-wing guerrillas and right-wing extremists shooting or clamoring to get her out of the presidency. The labor heads simply had no one else to serve as a screen for their ambitions. The most they conceded to the opposition was to make Isabel, in July 1975, force her corrupt favorite, Minister of Social Welfare José Lopéz Rega (a specialist in astrology, among other things), out of his post and into European exile. But frail Isabel must continue as their useful camouflage.

Labor leaders in Argentina were being slain left and right. What should be added, importantly, is that this seeming evenhandedness early revealed an ominous split between the right-wing conservatives and left-wing radicals within the Peronist movement no less than the continued warfare by the ERP upon the unionists, whether conservatives or not, supporting Peronism.

It was the ERP's "August 22 Unit" that murdered José Ignaci Rucci, head of the General Confederation of Labor, a strong supporter of Perón. This occurred on September 25, 1973, as Santucho's answer to the outlawing of his guerrilla organization the day before. (So awed was the Establishment by the ERP that this formal outlawing had been delayed that long.) Well into 1975, the killings of other labor leaders continued, either by the ERP to discourage the unions from siding with Juan and Isabel Perón or by the rightists to punish those who were on the left. In the early fall of 1973, soon after Rucci's death, Perón declared "a frontal war on Marxism."

But as the year 1974 dawned, it became clear that Perón was losing his grip on the left wing of his own movement. Angrily he denounced his leftists as "stupid shouters." But they were shooters no less than shouters. His own Montoneros were soon turning their guns upon the Peronist conservatives. In June 1974, just before Perón's death, they reminded the nation that they supported Perón but not his wife and vice president—because she so definitely identified herself with those despised conservatives, particularly with the venal Rega.

In July 1974, right after Perón's funeral, the Montoneros split into two factions, the leftist of which proceeded with a novel series of murders. From the fifteenth to the thirty-first of July, a former cabinet minister, a newspaper executive, and a congressman fell under their gunfire. All three were moderate Peronists. On August 3 a communiqué proudly claiming the authorship of the third of the slayings, "for the usurpation of the name of our leader General Perón," was issued to the radio stations and an afternoon newspaper in the city of Córdoba. It was signed, "Montoneros—Soldiers of Perón."

This extremist faction of the Montoneros was headed by Mario Firmenich, a guerrilla figure who had been imprisoned until May 1973 and who, freed in that month's mass-scale pardon of politicals by Campóra, at first was willing to wait while Perón seemed to be trying to make up his mind between the left and the right within his movement. But in the uneasy months between Perón's return and death, as the old dictator was forced by the situation to make his choice, Perón backed the right against the left. And after his death on July 1, 1974, his widow Isabel, as the nation's President Isabel Martinez de Perón, lacking even the last shreds of his appeal, was definitely on the rightist path.

So, in the last week of August 1974, Firmenich of the Montoneros declared "the people's war" upon Isabel Perón's regime, which, he charged, represented the capture of her late husband's political heritage "by imperialists and oligarchs." On September 6, in a clandestine news conference, he claimed his group's responsibility for the latest string of bombings, burnings, abductions, and killings, and promised more of the same. He said that his valiant Montoneros were concentrating on businessmen and on nongovernmental antiguerrilla elements, but would soon be strong enough to take on the military and the police as well.

By the spring of 1975 these Montonero terrorists numbered several thousand gunmen. They still insisted that, unlike the ERP, they were not Marxists. In reality they were a curious alloy of Marxists and non-Marxists, the latter including vague left-wingers, sheer adventurers of all stripes, and plain criminals. Marxist or not, the Montoneros' methods and exploits were bold, not only matching those of the Marxist-Trotskyite ERP, but even at times exceeding them.

That spring the Montoneros kidnapped two high executives of Argentina's richest multinational company, Bunge & Born, and demanded 60 million dollars as ransom. The victims were Jorge and Juan Born, sons of one of the firm's founding families. On June 20, 1975, the Montoneros called a clandestine news conference. Mario Firmenich presided. Announcing that the ransom had been paid, he presented to the journalists one of the two kidnapped, Jorge Born, and released him at the end of the conference. Juan Born was freed elsewhere.

The $60 million was the highest ransom ever paid in modern kidnappings, political or otherwise. It equaled one-third of Argentina's annual military budget. With this much money, Firmenich said, the Montoneros would be able to step up their terror into victory.

In vain did Isabel Perón's government try to prevent Bunge & Born from paying the ransom. The best it achieved was the arrest in March, at the international airport of Buenos Aires, of four employees of the firm as they landed with $4,800,000 they were bringing from Swiss banks toward the ransom price.

The firm, with its annual sales in grain and other commodities of two billion dollars, of which some $350 million originated in Argentina, made plans to curtail its operations drastically. For, from then on, it simply lacked ready cash for its business.

V

Inevitably came the right-wing reaction. The rightist counterterror was intensified with the emergence of a vigilante organization calling itself the Argentine Anti-Communist Alliance, which struck at both the ERP and the Montoneros as its two principal targets, with lesser blows at minor leftist guerrillas and their sympathizers. It soon became known that the Alliance was organized and its murder program directed by the Peronist government.

This anti-left campaign began in earnest in January 1974 as a backlash to the raid by the ERP upon the tank garrison at Azul and the killing, among others, of the commanding colonel and his wife (in the presence of her two children). At that time the right-wing vigilantes bombed offices of leftist groups in Buenos Aires. The bombings were followed by other such attacks. In February, rightist youths fired shots at the building of the leftist *El Mundo,* the only newspaper daring to print the ERP's statements. Hardly a week later the large industrial city of Córdoba was seized and controlled for several days by the police and right-wing workers rising against the governor of the province and his staff, accused by the rightists of being Marxist-oriented and passing weapons to leftist terrorists. In Buenos Aires, in July, soon after Perón's funeral, a young woman-leftist was raped and murdered by rightists, and a building with the offices of the leftist Lawyers' Guild was bombed.

On September 16 the activists of the Anti-Communist Alliance killed Atilio Lopez, a left-wing Peronist and prominent transport workers' union leader. The next day, bus and subway crews struck throughout Argentina for 24 hours in outrage and mourning. This, however, did not deter the rightist terrorists 11 days later from dragging out of his apartment and murdering the 67-year-old lawyer Silvio Frondizi, brother of former President Arturo Frondizi of Argentina, as punishment for Silvio's well-known defense of guerrilla suspects and political prisoners. On September 30 a bomb blast in their car killed a Chilean émigré, General Carlos Prats Gonzales, and his wife. He was the former commander in chief of the Chilean army in the Allende era who, after the coup by that nation's junta, had had the dubious wisdom of seeking political asylum in Buenos Aires.

Between the summer and early December 1974 the Anti-Communist Alliance killed more than 40 students, labor union leaders, lawyers, and congressmen. That December the toll reached ten victims a week. The Alliance itself boasted that in a ten-month period it assassinated 200 people, in one case wiping out an entire leftist family.

In the continuing massacre of the left and the right, more than 300 persons were slain in the time from July 1, 1974, when Isabel Perón inherited her husband's presidency, until mid-April 1975. It was estimated that from January 1 to October 26, 1975, the terror toll was nearly 1,000.

The army, for so long leaving antiterrorist operations largely to the police and the vigilantes, went into action in earnest beginning in early 1975. A task force of 2,500 moved into the mountains above the sugar plantations of Tucumán Province in the north, where an ERP contingent of 200 was entrenched. The intent of the guerrillas was to create here a "free" territory from which to expand gradually into the rest of Argentina, until the entire nation would be taken over. One of their methods was to seek out and murder the families of the army officers fighting them. No prisoners were taken in the ensuing battles by either side. Between February and early November the military claimed killing 116 guerrillas while losing 31 officers and men. To the southwest of Tucumán, in the city of Mendoza, on one November night another army unit, raiding left-wingers' homes, arrested 1,300 guerrilla suspects and sympathizers.

Still, for some military, this drive was not enough. Demanding Isabel Perón's resignation and an outright military rule with a total war upon all terrorists, parts of Argentina's air force rebelled in December 1975. They seized bases and airports, and for five days appeared about to win, when other military remaining loyal to Isabel succeeded in putting the rebellion down.

The day after the air-force rising was quelled, guerrillas struck in unprecedented numbers—as if to prove to both factions of the armed forces that they, the terrorists, and not the military, mattered in Argentina. Two days before Christmas 1975 some 500 commandos attacked an army arsenal, an army regimental compound, and several police stations in and around Buenos Aires. For once, this was a combined offensive of both the ERP and the Montoneros. But the government troops rallied, and the massive onslaughts were repulsed. Navy jets helped by bombing the guerrillas trapped in the arsenal. Two days after Christmas, a smaller group of terrorists hit again, now at an army communication base in La Plata, and lost once more. On both occasions, scores of the attackers were killed, many of them mere boys and girls in their teens, some executed on the spot after they had surrendered to the defenders.

But the army's loyalty to Isabel Perón was tenuous—the top military command did not see the time as yet ripe for her removal. At last, on March 24, 1976, it did seize and depose Isabel, sending her into exile at a lake resort. The junta, headed by General Jorge Rafael Videla, loosed an avalanche of arrests of labor union chiefs and other Peronist leaders. The antiterrorist drive was stepped up.

And still the guerrillas of the ERP and the Montoneros pushed on with their terror, killing and being killed. Between March 24 and early June, some 320 on both sides were slain. On May 30, at La Plata, commandos abducted Colonel Juan Pita, appointed by General Videla to run Argentina's trade unions. Right-wingers went on to kidnap and murder scores of leftists, among them refugees from Uruguay and other Latin American lands. On June 1, one of the most prominent exiles, Bolivia's former President Juan José Torres Gonzales, was seized and killed by "parties unknown."

VI

By mid-1976, so many killings and other atrocities were being committed daily in Argentina by so many allied or conflicting organizations that at times it was difficult to ascertain just who was slaying or abducting whom and why. Was it by then a full-sized civil war? No, said some citizens wryly. To have a civil war a nation must have a sharp-cut polarization, and here in Argentina we have no such polarization, but a chaotic fragmentation, with each fragment justifying its murderous actions, its terror.

As leftist leaders were increasingly chosen to be the victims of the right-wing junta, they sought not the underground haven with the ERP and the Montoneros but the surer safety of asylum in the Mexican embassy—and flight out of the country.

At what point of their program do the guerrillas stand now?

If, by their diehard policy and violent action, the ERP, or the People's Revolutionary Army, and the Montoneros aim to bring about a real, all-enveloping civil war in Argentina of the scale and intensity once unleashed by Lenin and Trotsky and so eloquently urged by Guevara, these terrorists may yet have their wish. And should they win in such a monstrous conflict, the result would be a Soviet Argentina of their dream and of so many others' nightmare.

If, by their bold and incessant campaign of kidnapping and murder of businessmen and diplomats, they mean to strike down and drive out capitalists both domestic and particularly foreign, the terrorists are succeeding. By 1976 there was a wholesale exodus of North Americans and West Europeans from Argentina—first of their families, then of the executives themselves. In September 1972 several hundred American businessmen were stationed in Argentina; two years later fewer than 50 remained. Native managers were delegated to take over many offices and enterprises. Two large companies, International Business Machines and Otis Elevator, moved out of the country altogether. The flow of investments diminished. Of the $1.4 billion representing the United States stake in Argentina, only $200 million were new investments during the period 1969-73. Even less was freshly invested in 1974-76. And the native capitalists and managers were also gradually (but some speedily) losing their nerve. The cost in ransoms, security-guard upkeep, and sheer worry, sometimes bordering on nervous breakdown, was proving too much.

The ERP—and, lately, the Montoneros as well—were the near-winners, becoming a state within the state, offspring of disruption in this huge land, and themselves increasing the chaos in this nation of twenty-five million.

22

Heirs to Tupac-Amaru

The terrorist organizations of the three other countries meeting in Buenos Aires in February 1974 to form their international Junta—those of Uruguay, Bolivia, and Chile—were by then very much unlike their Argentinian host, the ERP. All three groups had fallen on parlous days, and in 1974-76, the blood-soaked shoe was on the other foot. In all three countries military dictatorships ruled, ruthlessly ferreting out guerrilla and commando units, imprisoning and killing the activists and their sympathizers by the thousand.

Uruguay's Tupamaros, only a few years before, had been one of the best-organized and most-publicized terror organizations in Latin America. In 1970 they kidnapped and murdered an American police adviser, Daniel Mitrione. The subsequent film *State of Siege,* directed by Constantin Costa-Gavras, has, since its completion in August 1972, gained a worldwide sympathy (at least among intellectuals) for the slayers of Mitrione but not for the victim and his family. In early 1971 the Tupamaros abducted Geoffrey Jackson, the British Ambassador, and held him in a dungeon for 245 days before finally releasing him. His 1973 memoir, *People's Prison,*[1] is a calm and thoughtful indictment of his jailers. But by early 1974 the Tupamaros as an organization were virtually extinct, even if a handful of its surviving members tried to speak bravely in its name at the Buenos Aires meeting of the four terrorist formations.

Wherefrom this name, the Tupamaros? A succinct answer is given by Ambassador Jackson in the foreword to his book:

> My Uruguayan kidnappers, known as the *Movimiento de Liberación Nacional,* had adopted their alternative designation of "Tupamaros" from another century and another corner of Latin America. Tupac-Amaru was the last scion of the Incas, brought up in eighteenth-century Peru as a Spanish hidalgo. Outraged by the

oppression of his fellow Indians—by Spanish settlers conceivably no more authoritarian than his own ancestors—he launched a belated movement for indigenous rights.

Inevitably it failed; and in 1784 Tupac-Amaru was executed in Lima, torn apart by four cart-horses. His name, in the more Spanish-sounding abbreviation of Tupamaro, became a synonym for "trouble-maker" throughout the scattered Spanish settlements of eighteenth-century Latin America. Almost two centuries later that term of opprobrium was adopted by a small group of Uruguayan urban guerrillas, dedicated to the overthrow of the present order of society, as a badge of honor.

The Tupamaros were first organized in 1963, a restless time when it was evident to many that something had gone astray in this former model democracy, so often called the Switzerland of South America.

The continent's smallest republic, wedged between Brazil on the north and west and Argentina on the south and west, Uruguay now has nearly three million inhabitants unevenly distributed within the country: almost one half of them live in Montevideo, the capital and largest city. A tradition of free public education, including the university level, has resulted in a 91 per cent literacy rate, among the highest in the world. As early as the dawn of the twentieth century Uruguay's political democracy was, among other things, expressed in a well-developed welfare network, which owed its advances to the country's large-thinking reformer, President José Batlle y Ordoñez. Pensions were especially generous, many people retiring at 50 years of age, some even at 45.

But the nation's prosperity and social benefits came from a lopsided economy, dependent on the fluctuations of the world's markets for Uruguayan cattle, sheep, meat, wool, hides, skins, and wheat. During the two World Wars and the Korean conflict the world's demand for these goods was high and the prices stayed healthy. But after 1955 the markets and the prices slumped. The 20 per cent of the Uruguayan population that supplied the agricultural produce on which the other 80 per cent counted began to balk at their burden. Farmers started to ship their yield across the border to Brazil, where higher prices awaited them, rather than deal with Uruguay's state purchasers and their low rates.

The more than a score of state industrial and trade corporations, employing one-quarter of Uruguay's labor force, were inefficient and increasingly corrupt. The costly bureaucracy ballooned while the birth rate dropped to the lowest in Latin America. This meant that not enough new producers were growing up to support the aging population on those ample pensions. The country could no longer afford its vaunted welfare system and its many officials. Inflation, added to lower- and middle-class unemployment, caused widespread unrest.

Yet at first this unrest was confined mainly to Montevideo and other urban areas, and, at that, to only one or two strata of the population. Farmers still ate; the prices they received from Brazilian middlemen and domestic black markets paid for the manufactured goods they needed. But more and more factory workers suffered; the middle classes were also miserable. However, unlike some other Latin American countries, Uruguay had few slums or militant proletarians. Thus, almost since their inception, the Tupamaro terrorists were a minority middle-class phenomenon, active almost wholly in Montevideo.

II

Numbering at their height some 1,000, the Tupamaros were Cuban-inspired and Cuban-trained elitists who displayed a disdain for the workers and the farmers and for the Uruguayan Communist Party, which, they felt, talked but did not act.

In this the Tupamaros shared Guevara's contempt for the Old Guard Communists, whom he dismissed as too timid and fumbling. Indeed, founded shortly after the Russian revolution of 1917, Uruguay's Communist Party in all its decades had made barely a dent in the country's politics. By the early 1970s, the 35 to 40 thousand members of the Communist Party, recruited from labor unions and among university students, showed their total obedience as they followed their leaders' orders in refraining from militancy, while the nation's political scene was traditionally dominated by the two bourgeois parties, the Colorados and the Blancos, which cooperated in ruling the country.

Thus violence became the Tupamaros' monopoly. "We are the answer to an unjust system," said a Tupamaro when interviewed in a 1972 documentary film. The Communist Party surely was nowhere near such an answer. In one instance the Tupamaros announced a wait-and-see phase during the country's national elections, but resumed their bloody agenda when a popular coalition embracing the Communist Party came in a poor third, thus confirming once more the basic Tupamaro disbelief in the efficacy of any parlimentary system.

Yet, until 1970, the Tupamaros shed little blood, confining themselves to bank and casino robberies, kidnappings for ransom, and raids upon arsenals. Then, on July 31, 1970, they abducted Daniel A. Mitrione. Father of nine children, Mitrione was an American with an efficient record as a police chief in Richmond, Indiana. He had been sent to Montevideo by the United States Agency for International Development, officially to help the native police in traffic control and communications but, as the Tupamaros charged, actually to train the Uruguayan security force in the techniques of torture.

The Tupamaros demanded the release of 150 political prisoners as ransom for Mitrione. The Uruguayan government refused to accede. The United States government, true to its policy of opposition to complying with any terrorist terms, would not pressure the Uruguayan government into giving in to the Tupamaros. And so, ten days after his kidnapping, Mitrione was murdered ("executed," in the lofty Tupamaro phrase) by his captors.

Other kidnappings and killings by the terrorists followed, both foreign and native victims swelling the frightful roster. Proceeds of some of the ransoms and bank raids were shared with Uruguay's poor. A few names of Tupamaro leaders became known and were widely publicized amid the increasing panic. Foremost in the headlines was that of Raúl Sendic, the chief founder of the Tupamaros.

Sendic had begun as a member of the Socialist Party while still a university student. Dissatisfied with the Socialists' placidity, he left them for organizational activity among the depressed sugar-refinery workers in the country's north. At first he helped to form a labor union; then he brought his people to Montevideo for street demonstrations. But government officials only smiled indulgently as Sendic called for urgent reforms. So, in the early 1960s, his terrorist phase began, and the Tupamaros were formed, according to some sources, out of the handful of those devoted members of the radical sugar-plant workers. But by 1970 these and other proletarians were definitely outnumbered by middle-class intellectuals of Sendic's type.

Sendic proved a fearless as well as an enterprising guerrilla chieftain. Once, after having been captured and having escaped, he underwent plastic surgery on his face that made him unrecognizable; with a new face and another man's name and documents, he calmly resided in the center of Montevideo, directing his formidable organization.

The police and prison guards were not only inefficient—many were venal. Jail-breaks were easy and many, the most sensational of them occurring in September 1971, when 106 Tupamaros were led to freedom by Sendic himself through a tunnel from the Punta Carretas maximum security prison, not without the bribed assistance of the guards.

The movement was also aided by certain liberals, some of them highly placed in the nation's government and society, one of these publicly declaring that he was guided by no less a personage than the Pope, who once said that violence was justified against tyranny.

Within the organization, in time, a closely knit and efficient hierarchy was developed by Sendic and his aides. The Tupamaros were ruled by a Central Committee and a Secretariat; the rank and file were divided into "columns," with strict delineation of specialties and duties. For instance, a well-meshed sector of men and women ran "people's prisons" where the kidnapped were kept. An International Affairs Committee took care of cooperation with terrorist groups outside Uruguay.

Within the country sporadic contacts were maintained with other radicals. For a period, in 1971-72, the Tupamaros accepted help from a minor anarcho-syndicalist group calling itself "the Popular Revolutionary Organization 33." But the Uruguayan Communist Party was not courted, nor could it make up its own mind about the Tupamaros. While officially it condemned their "adventurous behavior" (almost in the same abusive terms that 70 years earlier Lenin had used against the Socialist Revolutionary terrorists), one spokesman for the Party suddenly, in 1971, praised Sendic's contingent as "sincere, honest, and courageous revolutionaries."

III

In early 1972 the Tupamaros seemed to be nearing their apex when they made a cardinal error: though not entirely prepared, they struck at the nation's armed forces with a fresh and unprecedented ferocity. They had misjudged their own strength and that of the foe. Thus came a drastic change in the fortunes of the Tupamaros.

On March 1 the newly elected President Juan Maria Bordaberry, a wealthy cattle rancher, took office. Having devalued the Uruguayan peso and instituted other bold economic measures, he appeared on television with an appeal to the people to support him in improving exports and in fighting inflation. The people remained passive; not so the Tupamaros, who feared the reformers would cause them to lose the little support they had among the masses.

On April 14 the Tupamaros assassinated a former government official and three security guards. That mid-April, 15 Tupamaros and ten other prisoners made a successful break from Punta Carretas through a tunnel dug from the prison hospital to the city sewers. President Bordaberry asked the Congress to declare a state of "internal war" against the terrorists for 30 days. After much angry debate, by a vote of 68 to 56, the Congress complied, and a state of war was proclaimed on April 15, suspending certain liberties specified in the constitution and granting the police and the army considerable leeway of action.

At once free-lance right-wing action erupted from civilians organized into a so-called "Squadron of Death," who on April 16 caused a dozen explosions, wrecking the headquarters of leftist newspapers as well as the apartments of the liberal legislators who had voted against the "internal war." One bomb was thrown into the Soviet embassy, but without wreaking great damage.

On April 17 the police went to the Communist Party building on the pretext that some Tupamaros were hiding in its clubhouse. The Communists denied any Tupamaro presence. Ordered to come out, seven non-Tupamaro men, aged 21 to 45, stepped on the sidewalk and were mowed down by police fire. Their subsequent funeral was attended by 40,000 marchers. A two-day protest strike by the Communist-controlled labor unions did not, however, halt Bordaberry's determination.

With the army taking over from the police, the Tupamaros were put on the defensive. On May 16 Bordaberry extended the "internal war" for 45 more days. In the middle of that year—1972—within a four-month period, 5,600 searches and anti-Tupamaro ambushes were organized, 29 terrorists were officially announced as killed and 28 wounded, 1,994 suspects were netted, and, in addition, 147 out of the 180 Tupamaro escapees from prisons were recaptured. Torture was used during interrogations, and as one of its results a broken prisoner led the soldiers to a Montevideo house where Sendic and his girl friend, with one more Tupamaro, were found.

The house was surrounded. Refusing to give up, the trio opened fire. Gravely wounded, the leader finally surrendered, and with him the two others. Earlier, on June 22, his second-in-command had been captured on a downtown street. This was Jorge Manera Liuvras, who had worked as an engineer for the state telephone company, and had been one of the famed 106 escapees from Punta Carretas.

Harried and badly crippled, the Tupamaros tried to fight back. Within that very same four-month span in the middle of 1972, when scores of Tupamaro bases were located and destroyed, the terrorists carried out eight more kidnappings, 35 armed raids on police stations, and 60 assaults against offices, factories, and homes, killing 15 and wounding 24 policemen, while scooping up large amounts of money and many weapons.

In late May, two "people's prisons" were found by the army. The second and the more important one of these was ringed on May 28 by hundreds of soldiers in a residential district of Montevideo, two miles from the capital's center. The eight guerrilla guards had instructions, if surrounded, to kill their two captives and themselves. Instead, after 45 minutes of negotiations with the soldiers, they gave up at the very last moment, preventing one of their number, a woman who was a dedicated terrorist, from murdering the prisoners.

The two freed men, thin and haggard, were Ulysses Pereyra Reverbel, chairman of the state power and telephone company, and Carlos Frick Davie, a former minister of agriculture. The first captive, sentenced by the Tupamaros to life imprisonment, had been in the dungeon 14 months; the second had been kept a prisoner for more than a year. This "people's prison" was camouflaged as the private dwelling of a family consisting of a man, his wife, and their four children, aged 4 to 11. They lived peacefully, near-normally, above the cells. Like most other Tupamaro installations, this house was connected by a tunnel with the city's sewers. It was betrayed to the army by a previously captured Tupamaro, probably after torture.

IV

By the end of 1972 the army announced the defeat of the Tupamaros. And with their crushing victory members of the military acquired a taste for power. More and more, President Bordaberry was their tool rather than his own man. After a brief try to retain his independence, he acquiesced, becoming a willing and even eager instrument of the generals. Ironically, the Tupamaros ultimately caused the opposite of what they had wanted.

Now the victors were antiliberal no less than antiterrorist. On June 27, 1973, President Bordaberry closed both houses of Congress, accusing their members of corruption and obstruction. From then on, he would rule by decree. The nation's 19 municipal councils were also abolished; the National Workers Confederation of the Communist-led labor unions was outlawed. Strict censorship was clamped down on the press.

In July, troops with tanks and tear gas dispersed an attempt by students and workers to march in protest. By October 1973 it was widely observed that the civilian President reigned but did not rule, that his all-powerful mentors and Uruguay's real bosses were two generals: Hugh Chiappe Posse, army chief of staff, and Esteban Cristi, commander of the Montevideo garrison.

On October 28, 1973, the government closed the country's only university, branding it as "a center of Marxist indoctrination and incitement to armed struggle." Some 150 students, instructors, and administrators, including the rector and nine deans, were arrested. On December 2, Bordaberry ordered the disbandment of the Uruguay Communist Party and the ending of its two newspapers. Also terminated were the Socialist Party, the Student Workers Resistance Party, and several leftist campus groups.

In 1974, on March 5, Bordaberry decreed a ten-week suspension of the well-known leftist weekly magazine *Marcha* (Progress) and the arrest of several of its staff members for publishing a story presenting a Uruguayan police inspector as a torturer-rapist. In June, at the United Nations, Niall MacDermot, Secretary General of the International Commission of Jurists, reported that a fact-finding mission to Uruguay ascertained that in the nearly two years since July 1972 some 3,500 to 4,000 men and women had been interrogated in the campaign to stamp out the Tupamaros, and that one half of that number had been tortured.

In December 1974, however, some of the surviving Tupamaros and their friends emerged in Paris—to demonstrate to Bordaberry that the fight was far from over. On the nineteenth of that month Colonel Ramon Trabal, the military attaché and intelligence specialist at the Uruguayan embassy in France, was found dying in his car in the basement garage of his Paris apartment house, six bullets in his body. He had been shot by unknown attackers as he was returning home for lunch.

Soon a representative of the killers telephoned a Paris news agency office to announce that the slayers were French associates of the Tupamaros, joined together in the Raúl Sendic International Brigade to avenge those whom Trabal was hunting both at home and in Europe. His murder was described by the caller as a warning to other manhunters and repressors to cease and desist.

The very next day, on the twentieth, at Soca, 34 miles east of Montevideo, five bullet-ridden bodies were found. These were Tupamaro terrorists, either taken from their jail cells or freshly captured at large, and murdered in payment for Trabal's death.

In February 1976, Amnesty International estimated the number of political prisoners in Uruguay at nearly 6,000, and of those killed since 1972 at 22. It also reported beatings, electric shocks, forcibly administered hallucinogenic drugs, and other tortures used on captives by the Uruguayan police.

The embers of the epochal Tupamaro fire still glow. Yet, in the history of modern terrorism, we do have cases of hardened professional revolutionaries ceasing their activism—some after the seeming peak of their success, some through their sudden defeat, and others after a gradual change of mood. Whatever brought their collapse, not all the Tupamaros are now either dead or in the dungeons of Montevideo or in their Havana or Paris exile. Many remain in their homeland, but not in any underground preparing to rise once more; they are busy in all sorts of humdrum occupations, resigned to a life of peace, if not of happiness, their stormy past but a receding memory.

V

The story of the other two Latin American terrorist groups that attended the meeting in Buenos Aires is one of sporadic outbursts followed and surely eclipsed by the counterterror of the military.

In Bolivia, the troops and the police of Colonel, later General, Hugo Banzer Suarez, the country's President since August 1971, needed but some eight months to wipe out the scant shards of the *Ejército de Liberación National de Bolivia* (ELNB), or the National Liberation Army, the remnants left behind from Ché Guevara's disaster.[2]

These ELNB activists were centered in La Paz and other cities, where in 1966-67 they had feebly tried to lend support to Guevara and in 1968 to his few survivors in the jungle. Among the leaders were the three Peredo brothers, but Coco and Inti Peredo, who had once fought in Guevara's group, were killed by the Bolivian security forces, while Chato Peredo lived and battled into the 1970s as the ERNB's sole surviving chieftain.

Chato Peredo thought he would avoid Guevara's error—he would not rest his hopes and operations on the peasants. But in the cities, too, some would-be followers turned out to be weaklings and even informers. In March 1972, President Banzer's searchers discovered the main ELNB base in La Paz and 20 "safe houses" in the capital, as well as in Cochabamba and elsewhere. Some 150 men and women, activists and accomplices, were rounded up, while 15 were shot dead during the searches.

Other ELNB guerrillas were ambushed, captured, or killed through the rest of 1972 and early in 1973. The total number of those arrested for political reasons—mostly on no formal charges—from Banzer's takeover in August 1971 well into 1973, was estimated at more than 2,000 men and women.

In early 1974 the Reverend Eric de Wasseige, speaking for the Bolivian Commission for Justice and Peace, a body composed of Catholic clergymen and laymen, acknowledged some lessening of torture and repression in the country "thanks to important pressure from national and international organizations," but pointed out that, although somewhat diminished, torture still went on: "We have ample evidence from families and freed prisoners that torture is still being used and there is no fundamental change in the arbitrary and repressive system."

However, feeling that the backbone of the guerrilla movement was being gradually broken and that other opposition was diminishing, the dictatorship quietly released many of its prisoners, chiefly in late 1973, so that in early 1974 the Commission for Justice and Peace could say that only about 300 remained in Bolivia's prisons.

The Commission's brave efforts against repression and torture continued through 1975 and 1976.

VI

As to the last of the four nations represented at the February 1974 meeting of Latin American terrorists in Buenos Aires:

In Chile,[3] leftist terrorists have never been much of a force. If anything, vigilante or rightist terror predominated even before President Allende's downfall in September 1973. As an example, of the three major assassinations of the Allende era, two were perpetrated by right-wingers and but one by leftist extremists: in October 1970, General René Schneider, the army chief, was killed by rightists in a bungled attempt to kidnap him, which was part of an unsuccessful plot to overthrow Allende; in late July 1973, a submarine officer and military aide to Allende, Captain Arturo Araya Peters, was murdered by rightists; and in June 1971, a vice president in a previous government, Edmundo Perez Zukovic, while in his car on a side street, was ambushed and slain by leftists.

On June 29, 1973, it was a rightist conspiracy of members of an armored regiment that erupted into an abortive rebellion against Allende, causing the death of 22 persons. But that summer's leftist try to infiltrate two units at the Chilean navy's main base near Valparaiso fizzled before it could grow into any violence.

That summer, in the first two weeks of the truck owner-drivers' strike begun on July 26 against Allende, more than 200 terrorist attacks resulted in five deaths, but again the aggression was anti-Allende, not leftist—a lower middle-class kind of terror by the truckers. In their strike the truckers were greatly helped by funds secretly provided by the United States government through the CIA, with the aim of (as American officials later, in September 1974, put it) "destabilizing" Allende's Marxist government. Altogether, in the years 1970 to 1973, these funds ran up to eight million dollars. Not only truckers, but also other anti-Marxist organizations and elements in Chile were aided from these sums.

Allied to the truckers, the principal organization of the right-wing terror was the Fatherland and Liberty group. Opposed to them, but not linked to any other revolutionary formation, was the *Movimiento de Izquiera Revolucionario* (MIR), or the Left Revolutionary Movement, which early in 1974 would send its delegates to the Buenos Aires meeting.

But the MIR, with all its vaunted militancy, avoided a head-on collision with the rightists. At one time it had indeed been terrorist; it had begun its guerrilla activities in the late 1960s as a young Castroite movement, but even then it had been rather insignificant. The election of Salvador Allende Gossens to the presidency by a plurality of 36 per cent on September 4, 1970, presented the MIR with the perplexing dilemma of either continuing its terror or damping it down as not to embarrass the new Popular Unity of the left. The MIR never fully resolved this puzzle, pulled as it was in different directions all through the three Allende years, until his overthrow and death on September 11, 1973.

Nor was the Allende regime, through its existence, entirely clear in its attitude toward the MIR. The President's Socialist Party was less under his control than it was generally thought. Few outside observers realized that it contained not alone its old, respectable Social Democrats, but also a newly formed admixture of Trotskyites, Maoists, and Castroites. The Communist Party, the Socialist Party's ally, was considered too moderate or timid by some of these extremist neo-Socialists, who now took the side of the MIR as its members argued heatedly but fruitlessly against the moderate policies of the Chilean followers of Brezhnev. The MIR was, for the most part, lost and ineffectual in the midst of the intellectual infighting within the Socialist-Communist milieu, though many of the MIR members did try to prove their viability: by organizing and leading Chile's Indians and other rural poor in land seizures, and by heading urban squatters and nonunion factory workers in hunger marches and forcible takeovers of wholesale firms dealing in food and other consumer essentials. And looking back, in September 1974 the CIA publicly admitted (not without some reluctant admiration) that, of all the leftist organizations in Chile in 1970-73, the highly fanatical MIR was the only one its agents had failed to infiltrate.

Had Allende finally flashed a signal for the MIR to rise en masse against the capitalists and the recalcitrant middle classes, its leaders and impatient followers would have been foremost in mounting the barricades and shooting the privileged. But no such summons was issued by the chief of Popular Unity. Plainly, Allende was no Lenin or Trotsky. And surely the MIR lacked a Castro and especially a Guevara of its own to lead the dispossessed to Santiago's posh blocks to initiate an all-encompassing massacre of the rich.

Thus was the opportunity missed, or, rather, yielded to the anti-Reds. On that September 11 in 1973, the junta struck and won. Since then, in the grim feast of the rightist conquest, thousands of leftists and suspects have been arrested, and many of them executed, often with no trials and sometimes after hideous torture.

Currently, among other victims, the MIR activists, who have never matched the ferocity of the Argentinian ERP or the Uruguayan Tupamaros, are nevertheless paying the same price of jail and death when caught by the junta's men or, if they are lucky enough to escape, of a dolorous existence as émigrés in strange lands.

23

Siempre la Violencia!

In Latin America, terrorism has been caused not only by socio-economic conditions and political struggle but also by the nature of the people involved.

Siempre la violencia! Always violence! is a common saying—almost a motto—in Latin America. "They shoot one another over soccer scores," is the observation of my friend Richard Severo, who, while working for *The New York Times,* has had extensive experience in Central and South America. "This is true of practically all of Latin America," he adds. "Especially so of Guatemala."

And it was in Guatemala[1] that one of the most recent major chapters of Latin America's leftist terrorism opened in 1968. On January 16 of that year two American military attachés were killed by Guatemalan terrorists. On August 28, a group of guerrillas murdered the United States Ambassador John Gordon Mein in his car on a Guatemala City street. This was, in part, the long-delayed vengeance of the country's left for America's role in the 1954 overthrow of the Arbenz government.

However, from 1954 to 1968 Guatemala had not enjoyed serenity. Battles had flared up on the streets and in the jungles; there had been assassinations of rightist leaders and guerrilla chieftans. But all this was considered minor or routine when compared to the crescendo of slayings reached in the middle 1960s. By 1966 considerable forces of leftist guerrillas had concentrated in the Sierra de las Minas, which which had become a veritable rebel stronghold. That summer, army units had invaded the area with a determined ferocity. They had been helped by civilian vigilantes of a right-wing terrorist group known both as the White Hand and An Eye For An Eye. In 1967, some 1,000 deaths were attributed to these rightists. This was, in effect, a civil war.

The killing of the three American diplomats in 1968 was not only the left's vengeance for 1954 but also a counterblow for the White Hand murders of 1967. Through 1969 the left kept up the momentum of its offensive and ascendancy. Its principal terrorist organization was the *Fuerzas Armadas Rebeldes* (FAR), or the Rebel Armed Forces.

Alarmed, the right formed a coalition that on March 1, 1970, made an energetic colonel, Carlos Arana Osorio, the nation's President. He had come to the right-wingers' attention by commanding a bloody suppression of a peasant guerrilla uprising in which up to 3,000 rebels had been killed.

But, despite Arana's declaration of a state of siege, the left kept up its massive attack. Between late February and April 1970, the terrorists kidnapped Guatemala's Foreign Minister Alberto Fuentes Mohr; United States embassy aide Sean Holly; and West Germany's Ambassador Count Karl von Spreti.

In the first two cases the Guatemalan government yielded, releasing a number of political prisoners in exchange for Fuentes and Holly. But in the third episode, the new President Arana refused the guerrillas' terms for Ambassador Spreti: release of 22 political prisoners and payment of $700,000. The terrorists then killed their German captive. The Bonn government bitterly blamed President Arana's stubbornness for the Ambassador's death; there was a coolness between the two governments, both of which withdrew their diplomats.

Between April and July 1970, prominent citizens of both right and left were assassinated. Among others, the left-wing leader Victor Rodriguez was murdered. The World Confederation of Labor charged that in just the first two months of President Arana's state of siege, as many as 600 trade union members were killed by the government and its right-wing toughs. In that bloody war, not only terrorists and other radicals but many liberals and other moderates also lost their lives.

For 1971 the Guatemalan press listed some 1,000 violent deaths, including those of 15 mayors and several legislators. There were also 171 kidnappings and 174 missing persons. In June and July 1972, the FAR launched fierce attacks, and many rightists were killed. But when, on June 25, a few hours after welcoming President Arana at the airport from a trip abroad, First Vice-President of Congress Olivero Castanedo Paiz was assassinated in a restaurant, it remained unknown whether his murderers were leftists or rightists—so chaotic by then was *La Violencia* of its many men and factions.

The right struck in various ways. In September 1972, eight Communist Party leaders disappeared. In February 1973, a Cuban news agency quoted a Guatemalan policeman, who had been kidnapped by leftists, as saying that the eight were dead, that they had been tortured by their rightist kidnappers and were about to be thrown from an air force plane into a volcano; but when this proved impossible due to bad weather, the eight were dumped into the shark-infested waters of the Pacific.

On the other hand, in June 1973, the rightist Congress deputy Hector Solis Juarez was assassinated—he had been accused by the left of the 1970 murder of Victor Rodriguez.

The years of 1974 and 1975, although more peaceful, were viewed by many Guatemalans as but a pause before battles still to come. The conundrum of Guatemala remains far from being solved.

II

In neighboring Mexico[2] the year 1968 was also marked by a major revolutionary tumult—by that summer's student riots in the capital, accompanied by the looting of stores and burning of cars in the streets, all of which was apparently aimed at the disruption of the Olympic Games held that year in Mexico City. On the following October 2, more than 300 demonstrators and bystanders were killed and wounded by the police and security forces, and numerous arrests were made. Later, Mexico's ultraleftists declared that more than anything this bloodshed and repression had convinced them that reformism led nowhere, that only outright guerrilla warfare was the answer.

Some of these disorders seemed spontaneous, but the inspiration soon proved to be Cuban while the actual guidance was traced by Mexican intelligence experts to a few KGB officers within the Soviet embassy. These Soviet agents were accused of the earlier recruiting of young Mexicans for training at Lumumba University in Moscow for just such flare-ups. Other Mexican youths, both boys and girls, had been sent to North Korea and North Vietnam for similar preparation. On returning to Mexico, all three detachments were fused into a brigade of some 30 specialists on street fighting. They called themselves the Revolutionary Action Movement—in Spanish, *Movimiento de Acción Revolucionaria* (MAR).

The earlier Soviet and North Korean connection of some of these revolutionaries became known to the Mexican authorities in 1971 after the arrest of several MAR members during a bank robbery. The Soviet involvement was confirmed on another occasion in 1971 when a policeman strolling in the countryside accidentally discovered a group of four terrorists in a hut studying the maps of what turned out to be a plan for an uprising. The group's arsenal was captured, and its Soviet source ascertained in the process of the police investigation. Despite Moscow's denials and protests, five members of the Soviet embassy in Mexico City were expelled.

This may have been one of the last instances in which Soviet agents were so directly involved in Latin American subversion. From 1971 on, increasingly, the Soviet policy emphasized a peaceful diplomatic and commercial relationship. The year 1972 in particular, ushering in the Kremlin's campaign of détente with the West—especially with the United States—also saw the Soviet discouragement of Castro's well-known export of revolution to other Latin American countries.

Castro's efforts diminished—in the Western Hemisphere, but not elsewhere. In October 1973, soon after the latest Middle East war, a Cuban armored brigade of 4,000 men was airlifted to Syria to participate in the attrition campaign against Israel on the Golan Heights until that campaign's halt in May 1974. The brigade remained in that area as the Syrians' ally, waiting for Castro's new orders. These came in October 1975, when Moscow and Havana decided on active intervention to help the pro-Soviet faction of blacks in Angola, which became independent of Portugal on November 11. Of the five to seven-and-a-half thousand Cubans brought to Angola by air that autumn, about one-half arrived directly from Havana, while the other half proved to be from the armored brigade already poised near the Golan Heights. Eventually, the total of Cubans in Angola reached 16,000.*

In Latin America, though, in the mid-1970s, the orthodox Communist parties everywhere had their new Moscow-Havana directives to keep a low profile—to shun and oppose those leftists who urged immediate revolts and organized kidnappings and murders. In their turn, the terrorists denounced Moscow and its now-tame Communists in Latin America as traitors to the Cause. The guerrillas and commandos swore their allegiance to Marx and Lenin, not to Brezhnev and Kosygin.

And even as Mao Tse-tung and Chou En-lai, while castigating the Soviet leaders as despicable revisionists of Marx and Lenin, were themselves becoming friendly with American and other Western capitalists, the terrorists in Latin America (as elsewhere) still proclaimed their programs as Maoist. More and more, however, as if realizing that Mao, too, no longer stood for worldwide revolution, the terrorists described their groups and tenets as neo-Trotskyite.

On its part, the Mexican government has claimed that the nation's terrorists are not revolutionaries at all, but merely bandits and robbers bent on personal enrichment. To concede their ideological character would be, for the government, a partial admission of the lack of socio-economic and political justice in Mexico, an indication that the system

---

* Terror at home has in the meantime been continued by Castro. In 1967 he publicly spoke of 20,000 political prisoners in Cuba's jails. This number, thereabouts, has remained constant down to 1976.

has hardly changed since the revolution of 1910, its promise to the people not lived up to.

Personal greed and political goals, however, can be intertwined. In September 1971, Mexican terrorists kidnapped Julio Hirschfield Almado, and soon freed him for a ransom of $240,000. Money was of importance to these kidnappers, but there was also a political element in the fact that Señor Hirschfield was the Mexican government's director of airports. In November of the same year Dr. Jaime Castrejohn, the millionaire rector of the Guerrero State University, was ransomed by his wife paying $200,000, but, in addition, the Mexican government agreed to the kidnappers' other demand—freedom for nine prisoners who on the twenty-eighth of November were duly flown on a Mexican Air Force plane to Havana.

In early May 1973, both a call for money and a political demand were presented by the terrorists of FRAP (*Fuerzas Revolucionarias Armadas del Pueblo,* or the People's Revolutionary Armed Forces), who had kidnapped Terrance G. Leonhardy, the United States consul general in Guadalajara. The $80,000 ransom was paid. The political condition was the release of 30 prisoners from seven jails across the country. The guerrillas issued a political statement "to the proletariat of Mexico," accusing "the privileged caste" of the nation of "enriching itself for hundreds of years at the cost of the workers who had labored under subhuman conditions." As the 26 men and 4 women were at once released and flown to Havana, the government of President Luis Echeverria Alvarez disputed their political purity, branding them as "common delinquents" who had been committed for robbery and murder. Yet at least one of the released 30, a Venezuelan named Raúl Anaya Rosique, was an experienced political terrorist who, previous to joining the Mexican guerrillas, had done some bloody toil for the Arab Fatah. It is true nonetheless that the Mexican terrorists use ransom money and the proceeds of bank robberies not only to buy more arms and to share a little with the country's poor, but also to line their own pockets.

In terms of international connections of terrorists, there is little (if any) presence of North American revolutionaries in the Mexican organizations—this, despite the geographic proximity of the two countries. Richard Severo commented to me: "Generally, Mexican guerrillas avoid the areas bordering on the United States. In this they are not very smart. Border cities like Tia Juana and Juarez would be ideal as their targets, for here are tremendous concentrations of dissatisfied and restive people who flock to the border from all over Mexico to cross illegally into the States in search of a living. Our immigration control catches at least a half-million of them a year and sends them back. And most of these do not return to their homes in the Mexican interior. They stay along the border, waiting for another chance and yet another to steal across into the United States. What a pool of the dispossessed and the rebellious from which the terrorists could try recruiting! But no, in this area the guerrillas are very few and mostly on the run.''

Severo also notes that among Mexico's various terrorist organizations there is a minimum of liaison or other means of coordination. The reason, he feels, is not an ideological rivalry, but jealousy of a personal nature suggesting a war-lord or robber-chief mentality.

Still, until its catastrophic crushing in late November 1974, the Party of the Poor seemed to maintain some loose contact with the 23rd of September Communist League,* and the latter's members as well as other terrorists appeared to accept, even if reluctantly, the general notion in the country that Lucio Cabañas, a former teacher, the charismatic chieftain of the Poor, was the symbolic leader of Mexico's terror.

Because of its rough terrain and isolation, Cabañas chose the state of Guerrero as his theater of action. Here, this teacher-turned-terrorist chief gathered a nucleus of fighters and the worshipful admiration of the lower classes as for seven years he made his lightning raids, descending from the mountains to rob and kill the rich and reward the poor. The peasants of Guerrero, wretchedly destitute, receiving mere pittances from the dealers who bought the marihuana they were raising, were all for Cabañas. But in actual fact, despite their admiration, they gave him little support as he raided the banks and abducted the rich and fought it out with soldiers. They were too afraid.

In May 1974, Cabañas kidnapped the 74-year-old Senator Ruben Figueroa, a millionaire transportation magnate and an important member of Mexico's ruling party, by luring him to a meeting ostensibly to discuss the terrorist's surrender. That summer the government sent to Guerrero some 16,000 soldiers, estimated to be one-third of the entire Mexican army, to catch Cabañas or, at least, to find Figueroa, who was finally freed in September. But Cabañas remained elusive. At last, toward the end of November, the former teacher and his men were

---

* In early 1973, the 23rd of September Communist League was formed from the remnants of several terrorist groups that had in part deteriorated. The name was in honor of September 23, 1965, when some guerrillas made an abortive attack on a military barracks in the state of Chihuahua in Mexico's north. In August 1974, this 23rd of September League was reputed to have grown strong to a point of being the closest to a national urban commando organization in Mexico, while the best known of the various rural guerrilla bands was the Party of the Poor, active in the mountains of Guerrero near Acapulco.

cornered, for by then as much as one-half of the Mexican army had converged on these mountains. In December, in a fierce battle, 27 Party of the Poor fighters were killed, including Lucio Cabañas. He was then in his mid-thirties. The poor of Mexico lost their folk hero; the terrorism, however, persisted.

In 1974-76, the 23rd of September League continued to fight it out with the Establishment. On December 10, 1974, its terrorists struck at two Mexico City banks at once, killing six policemen and getting away with $200,000. On April 25, 1975, guerrillas, most likely also of the League, shot their way into a Mexico City bank, slaying some 15 persons, including ten policemen, while taking only $12,000. On August 12, 1975, urban commandos, surprising a group of policemen and government inspectors at breakfast in a marketplace, killed two policemen and three inspectors. Eleven days later, terrorists slayed two naval guards. In each case the dead bodies were quickly stripped of their weapons, the Mexico city police chief explaining: "The League is desperately short of guns. They kill my men to get their arms." (Shades of Lenin, who in 1905 recommended precisely this method of replenishing the revolutionaries' arsenal.)

In late May 1976, the League kidnapped Nadine Chaval, the 16-year-old daughter of the Belgian ambassador to Mexico, demanding $800,000 as ransom, but in a few days freeing her for slightly more than one-half of this sum. On May 6, terrorists machine-gunned to death a wealthy family's seven private guards, surprising them at breakfast, as well as two government security men as they tried to stop the gunmen's getaway car. On June 4, 1976, in a Mexico City suburb, guerrillas fired submachine-guns from two speeding cars at rows of policemen standing in a morning roll call. Six policemen were killed and six others wounded. Speeding off, the slayers flung out leaflets declaring the League's authorship of this massacre.

The boldest kidnapping of recent times was done by the FRAP, or the People's Revolutionary Armed Forces, when, on August 28, 1974, at Guadalajara, four gunmen of that group seized the 83-year-old father-in-law of President Echeverria himself. The victim, J. Guadalupe Zuno Hernández, was well known, having been Governor of Jalisco State, and founder of the University of Guadalajara. He still taught some part-time courses and kept up his influence in state politics.

The FRAP intended to repeat its success of May 1973 when it had abducted Terrance G. Leonhardy, the American consul general, and demanded—and got—a ransom of $80,000 and freedom for 30 political prisoners who were flown to Cuba. Now, for the President's father-in-law, it specified 20 million pesos, or $1,600,000, and the release of 15 captives.

But it was right after the Leonhardy episode that the Mexican government had decided to follow the example of the United States and Israel: never again to submit to terrorists' terms. Categorically President Echeverria refused to ransom his wife's father. The FRAP realized he was implacable. So, late in the night of September 7, the kidnappers set Señor Zuno free, receiving nothing in exchange, but perhaps consoled by the thought of the President's humiliation—they did prove they could be almost anywhere.

As for Señor Zuno, relaxing at his home once again, the erstwhile victim startled the interviewers surging around him by loudly praising his kidnappers as true humanity-lovers and denouncing his son-in-law's government as a clique of reactionaries. The kidnappers, Señor Zuno said, were surely nobler than these rulers who serve the CIA and "the Yankee imperialists and capitalists who have no respect for anything" and are the ones who "want the wealth of Mexico" for their own greed.

His son Vincente Zuno remarked, "My father has been a revolutionary all his life." But there may be yet another explanation; Señor Zuno was proving himself a sly and shrewd *hombre*. Let other Mexicans of wealth and position, in their fear of terrorists, surround themselves with costly security guards; he would insure his person against a renewed seizure by mouthing the kidnappers' own lingo. A simpler recipe, this, and less costly, and quite amusing at that.

Not to forget Señor Zuno's son-in-law: President Echeverria, as if to erase his humiliation, kept on mouthing his pseudorevolutionary phrases while continuing to send his army and police to hunt and shoot leftist terrorists. The depth of his hypocrisy was reached in late September and early October 1975, when the President of Mexico joined the worldwide campaign of protest against the execution of terrorists in Spain by Generalissimo Francisco Franco's government. Echeverria even demanded Spain's suspension from the United Nations "for violations of human rights." A month later, on November 10, he instructed the Mexican ambassador in the United Nations to vote in favor of the Arab-sponsored resolution to brand Zionism as "a form of racism." Thus, while terrorists of Mexico were shot down by her Establishment, terrorists in the Middle East hailed her President as their eccentric yet staunch ally.

III

In Peru,[3] a rare and ominous drama is being played out. There, army generals decided to turn left, as if to thwart any possible native Castro and particularly any would-be Guevara bringing revolutionary end to them. Some years ago there was a genuine guerrilla movement in Peru, and until 1965 it made serious headway, especially because it was supported by peasants. At that time, though, the army, which had received training in counterinsurgency, demolished the rebels and by the decade's end a unique government of leftist-oriented generals was firmly in control. It was headed by General Juan Velasco Alvarado who, in October 3, 1968, first seized power in a bloodless coup, and who in his turn, after nearly seven years of power, was overthrown on August 29, 1975, by his second-in-command, Francisco Morales Bermúdez.

From 1968 on, these high-rank military stealers of Marxist thunder have been opposed by leftists who claim to be purer radicals, as well as by right-wingers, mostly teachers and other intellectual civilians. For a time both the left and the right, separately but at times in a curious alliance, tried to combat the generals by strikes and demonstrations rather than by outright terror. Yet the leftist generals of Peru themselves engaged in terror by incarcerating their antagonists in horrible penal colonies in the steaming jungle. In late July 1974, President Velasco took over eight major newspapers in Lima, the capital, thus smothering the last independent voices in the nation. Protests by the weakened opposition were of no avail.

But the takeover of the press served as a catalyst for more definite rebel action. That summer, for three successive nights, demonstrators stoned government buildings and burned vehicles in Lima. Velasco's forces arrested more than 500 people. In mid-August, eight prominent opposition leaders were detained on charges of attempting "to create chaos." At last, terrorists appeared. They were perhaps of the left opposition to the generals, but perchance with some assistance from the right as well.

On December 1, 1974, unknown assailants opened fire, from a car drawing alongside, at an automobile carrying Velasco's Prime Minister and two generals. The Prime Minister (who was also Peru's war minister and commander in chief of the army) escaped injury, but the two generals were wounded.

Six days later, on December 7, a group of terrorists raided a Lima hotel where foreign ministers of seven Latin American countries were housed as guests at a Velasco-sponsored celebration. The audacity of the attack was underlined by the fact that the hotel was heavily guarded by Peruvian troops and police. Two of these guards were wounded as the terrorists fled under the answering fusillade.

Since late August 1975, Peru's new President Morales has lessened his predecessor's repressive regime somewhat, but not appreciably enough to signal a return to democracy. As did Velasco in his seven years, so Morales in his reign is showing uncommon skill at utilizing some of the left's methods of suppression no less than its slogans of socialism as he stands ready to meet the challenge of the ultraleft and the ultraright—both.

By their actions, the leftist military dictators of Peru have joined the traditional rightist generals and admirals of Brazil, Paraguay, Chile, and other depressed Latin American countries who have gained and held power through bloody coups, through their utter repression of students, teachers, labor unions, and the press, and by their readiness to disallow the most essential human rights. Under such regimes it is almost impossible for a rural guerrilla group or an urban command team to organize, to grow, to strike back.

Interestingly, in their violent turn to the left as they seized and held power, Peru's generals may have set a significant pattern for other parts of the world to follow. Witness the case of Portugal, where army officers, in 1974-75, on overthrowing a half-century's fascist dictatorship, drove high-handedly toward a totalitarian Communist regime of their own, failing in their objective by a hairbreadth.

IV

In Colombia,[4] two guerrilla organizations have been active: the Castroite-Maoist *Ejército de Liberación Nacional* (ELN), or the National Liberation Army—the same name as Bolivia's terror group; and the pro-Moscow *Fuerzas Armadas Revolucionarias de Colombia* (FARC), or the Revolutionary Armed Forces.

For years neither of the two made much headway as they centered their insurgence in a countryside where peasants did not respond to the terrorist message. The *campesinos* preferred action of their own as they moved onto large estates, squatting on the land and cultivating it with no aid from any guerrillas. Then, as they stubbornly resisted the landlords and the army, they lost a few lives here and there and thousands in arrests. But after being expelled, they implacably returned in ever new invasions.

Finally, in 1974 and 1975, the peasants did reach an understanding with the guerrillas of the ELN. In August 1974, the newly sworn-in President Alfonso Lopez Michelson faced a widespread peasant revolt in the northern state of Bolivar, led by ELN guerrillas. He sent troops against them; clashes grew into regular battles, with many dead; other parts of Colombia were soon affected. On June 26, 1975, a nationwide state of siege was proclaimed.

Recently there have been other, isolated instances of terror in Colombia. On January 21, 1974, a young Ecuadorian militant successfully skyjacked a Colombia domestic airliner, forcing the pilot to land it in Havana. Not so successful, however, were the three gunmen who, on May 10 of that year, seized a Colombian jet, demanding a ransom of $400,000 and a passage to Cuba. After nearly 20 hours in the air and at a small airport, the guerrillas lost when policemen posing as a relief crew jumped the hijackers and overpowered them. In the scuffle, a pilot helped with a karate chop, despite the wild last-minute shooting by one of the gunmen. In the end the only casualty was a wounded hijacker. Still less successful was the escapade by a hijacker who, together with his young wife, their baby in her arms, on July 24 of the same year forced a domestic flight to land at Cali, some 190 miles southwest of Bogotá. Before the gunman could state his demands, the 122 passengers aboard the plane, now waiting on the ground at Cali, managed to escape, and the police, through a ruse, entered the cabin and killed the man. He turned out to be a repeater—a skyjacker who once before, in 1969, had forced a Colombian plane to Havana. In early September 1975, General Ramon Rincon Quinones, one-time commander of Colombia's antiguerrilla forces, was machine-gunned to death from a passing car by terrorists ambushing his automobile in Bogotá's rush-hour traffic. His driver was seriously wounded. Within hours the passing vehicle was found, and three suspects were arrested.

In March 1976 the FARC guerrillas kidnapped a wealthy industrialist, Octavio Echavarria, and as soldiers tried to rescue him in the jungles where they had found him, killed him with two shots in the head. At the same time a woman suspected of traitorous intentions was slain by her commando comrades.

But hardly to be repeated in these mid-1970s are the Colombian events of 1965-66, when an unusual Roman Catholic priest, Father Camilo Torres Restrepo of Bogotá, forsook his calling for guerrilla warfare, finally dying in the jungle, gun in hand. (His odyssey is unfolded in a later chapter.)

V

Venezuela's[5] terrorists were a worry to her rulers in the early and middle 1960s. At that time the country's guerrillas seemed to be the continent's best organized and most formidable rebel movement. The main formation was *Fuerzas Armadas de Liberación Nacional* (FALN), or the Armed Forces of National Liberation, supported by the small but aspiring Venezuelan Communist Party and certain lesser but active terror groups, including the student revolutionaries of the Central University in Caracas.

But the rulers were neither asleep nor panicky. On the one hand, they let North Americans come in to train picked Venezuelan troops in special counterinsurgency tactics that were soon applied in the field energetically and successfully. On the other, reforms and concessions to the masses were cleverly offered, notably in the pacification program of 1969, whereby the limping Communist Party was legalized by the government, most of the political prisoners were freed, and even terrorists were given amnesty.

Although slums continued to fester in areas that adjoined the luxurious apartment houses rising out of oil-field prosperity, the steps taken by the successive Venezuelan regimes, particularly in their left-of-center phase, against excessive North American economic domination seemed to offer hope to the proletariat. Support for the guerrillas nearly disappeared, while the continued policing of the country helped keep things quiet.

Occasionally, however, isolated terrorist bands have shown their endurance. For instance, a certain Federico Buttini flamboyantly led a guerrilla group called *Punto Cero,* or Zero Point, but in the course of 1972 the police wiped out the band, and Buttini was jailed. Late that year he escaped from prison by exchanging places in his cell with his accommodating brother, who was visiting him. On May 18, 1973, his group hijacked a Venezuelan airliner, ordering it to Panama. Whether Buttini himself was on that plane is not known. In November 1973, another guerrilla band abducted a West German honorary consul, Kurt Nagel, but the national guard was quick to trace the kidnappers and shoot it out with them bloodily, freeing the slightly injured victim.

But the most celebrated Venezuelan terrorist of modern times prefers to be active, not in his native land, but far afield. This is the 26-year-old Ilyich Ramírez Sánchez, known as "Carlos" or "the Jackal," the son of a wealthy Caracas lawyer who in his Communist enthusiasm gave each of his three sons one of Lenin's names. While the two other sons are named Vladimir and Lenin, this terrorist received Ilyich, Lenin's patronymic. In 1974-76 "Carlos" gained unique fame leading his international band of Arabs, Japanese, West Germans, and other terrorists in a series of kidnappings and murders.

VI

Farther north and west, Nicaraguan terrorists defy the long-time dictatorship of President Anastasio Somoza.[6] Their Sandinist National Liberation Front is so named in memory of Augusto Oscar Sandino, the famed guerrilla chief who fought against the ruling Somoza family and the United States occupation forces in the 1930s and was killed in 1934.

Founded by university students in Managua (Nicaragua's capital) in 1961, the Front is now led by Cuban-trained intellectuals and peasants. The chief commander is Carlos Fonseca Amador, a man in his late thirties. In early 1975 the Front was so strong that on March 21 its force for a while occupied the town of Rio Blanco. Against the Front, President Somoza pits his special antiguerrilla unit of 400 National Guardsmen. As the guerrillas come to villages for food and then withdraw, the Guard battalion rushes in to punish the peasants, arresting many villagers and executing others. Then the guerrillas return and force male survivors into their ranks. The result is that many villages are now empty, as peasants flee both sides in panic.

In late 1974 the Sandinista Front invaded Managua itself: on December 27, a well-armed group raided a Christmas cocktail party in the capital. The host, a former cabinet minister, was killed; so were two policemen guarding the suburban mansion. For more than two days, 13 hostages were held, among them two cabinet ministers and three ambassadors. Somoza gave in; on the thirtieth the guerrillas were flown to Cuba, together with 14 political prisoners freed from jails on the terrorists' demands. In addition, one million dollars in ransom was paid to the group, and their violently anti-Somoza manifesto was obediently published and broadcast in Nicaragua. As they boarded the plane at Managua, the terrorists and the freed prisoners were warmly applauded by a crowd.

Yet, nearby in the Caribbean, rulers are sterner and there is little popular support for guerrillas. Thus for many years Haiti's[7] terrifying dictator, François "Papa Doc" Duvalier, was able to rule that country not only because of his dreaded secret police, the *Tontons Macoutes* (a Creole term for "bogeymen"), but also because of the stupor of the great majority of his subjects. These days, under his quieter son and heir, Jean-Claude Duvalier, the Tontons Macoutes officially no longer exist, and the young dictator's terror does not seem as frightful as it was under his late father. Perhaps it need not be, for the subjects, illiterate and intimidated, neither dare nor care to help the very few resisters.

The small resistance in Haiti came to the fore on January 23, 1973, when the United States Ambassador Clinton Knox and the American consul general were abducted. Both were freed 18 hours later after the Haitian government paid $70,000 in ransom and released 12 political prisoners who were flown to Mexico City. In June and July several bombs were exploded at Port-au-Prince, the capital, where the presidential palace was gutted in an ensuing fire. In September a guerrilla group proclaiming itself Marxist tried an invasion in the Baie Saint-

Nicolas area, but was repelled by a coastal patrol. But these few attempts were pinpricks, not deep slashes.

The events in the adjacent Dominican Republic[8] in late September and early October 1974 proved once more how little support Caribbean terrorists have recently had from the population at large and even from their fellow radicals. On September 27, five armed men seized an American woman diplomat, Barbara A. Hutchison of the United States Information Service, on a street outside her office. At gunpoint they forced her into the Venezuelan consulate, where they rounded up seven more hostages. Announcing that they were members of the Freedom Movement of 12th January, they demanded, as ransom, one million dollars from the American government and the release of 36 political prisoners from the Dominican President, Joaquin Balaguer.

Not only did Washington and Balaguer refuse to yield, but at least 10 of the 36 prisoners declared they wanted no part of the deal. Moreover, the leaders of the country's *Movimiento Popular Dominicano,* from which the January 12th group was a split-off, denounced the kidnappers. It had by this time attempted to live down its extremist past, wishing to become a legitimate political party in opposition to Balaguer.

The gunmen dropped their demand for money but kept insisting on freedom for the 36 captives. Still Balaguer would not submit to the terrorists, and, as the terrorists knew, public opinion was also working against them. Finally, after 13 days of siege, the terrorists accepted the offer of a safe passage and flight to Panama in return for the release of Miss Hutchison and the other hostages.

Similarly, in nearby Puerto Rico,[9] the state is not repressive and there is a noticable lack of sympathy for the terrorist minority. Nevertheless, the terrorists have been and continue to be bent on winning the island's total independence from the United States. Back in the 1930s, the violent Nationalist Party under Pedro Albizu Campos staged protest marches, riots at the University, the assassination of a police chief, and other disorder and bloodshed. In Washington, on November 1, 1950, Puerto Rican terrorists tried but failed to murder President Harry Truman. On March 1, 1954, in the House of Representatives in Washington, several Nationalist Party members shot and wounded five congressmen. In San Juan and other Puerto Rican cities there were terrorist bombings in 1971. In New York in 1973 a Puerto Rican group calling itself *Furia* placed incendiary devices in department stores. As always, the actions were done in the name of revolutionary independence.

A major outburst occurred on October 26, 1974, when five powerful bombs were exploded at various business sites in New York—one in the financial district, two in Rockefeller Center, and two on Park Avenue. Much property damage but no casualties resulted. From their underground, Puerto Rican terrorists declared that their *Fuerzas Armadas de Liberación Nacional,* or FALN, was the perpetrator. Later these explosions were followed by a number of bomb detonations in Puerto Rico itself, mainly at American-owned industrial plants and offices, but again with property damage and no human injuries.

However, on January 24, 1975, three persons died and some 40 were injured when a private luncheon club in New York's Wall Street financial district was bombed by the FALN. The club was an annex to the historic Fraunces Tavern, where in 1783 George Washington had addressed his troops. Then, on April 3, 1975, explosions shook a bank, an insurance company, and two restaurant sites in midtown Manhattan. In the early morning of October 27, 1975, nine well-coordinated explosions occurred at government buildings, corporate offices, and banks in New York, Washington, and Chicago. These included the United States Mission to the United Nations (New York) and the State Department (Washington). Structural damage but no human casualties resulted. The FALN proudly claimed responsibility, and again made its two demands: independence for Puerto Rico, and release of five terrorists still in federal prisons, serving sentences for the Washington shootings of 1950 and 1954.

And yet, throughout this terror, no supportive fury could be discerned among the many Puerto Ricans in the United States or among the people back home. Here violence has been by the few, not by the many.

The whole Caribbean area, however, remains a potential hotbed, with a looming specter of wider, more intensive, more significant outbursts to come.

24

Fanon and the Black Panthers

In the Caribbean, on Martinique, an island that itself has never been a scene of modern guerrilla warfare, Frantz Fanon was born.[1] A light-skin black, he had fought valorously in World War II for the Free French in France and Africa. After being trained as a psychiatrist, he gave his medical service to both whites and non-whites, but in the 1950s became an outstanding ideologue of revolution against the whites. This and not medicine would be his main work.

In Algeria he was a leading member of the *Front de Libération Nationale* (FLN), which had been formed by Algerian Arabs who were fighting their French overlords. And though the French government and the *Organisation Armée Secrète* (OAS), a secret army of French settlers, steadfastly opposed him and his cause—on several occasions there were attempts to assassinate him—he rose to become one of the three most notable black revolutionaries in Africa, standing beside Patrice Lumumba and Felix Moumié (called "the Ho Chi Minh of Cameroun"). However, Fanon died in late 1961 of leukemia in Washington, D.C.,* before the ultimate victory of the *Front,* which occurred on July 3, 1962, when France officially withdrew from Algeria. The victory itself led only to a replacement of the European elite with a native elite: the socio-economic justice, for which Fanon had battled, did not after all dawn over the dark continent. Yet the impact of his ideas is still felt.

* At the suggestion of Soviet physicians he had seen in Moscow, Fanon went to Washington, D.C., to receive anti-leukemia treatment at the National Institutes of Health. In arranging for his visit, he accepted assistance from the CIA. At that time, the United States had an interest in reducing French and British involvement in the Arab world, and though for different reasons, so too did Fanon.

II

In the United States, black militants such as Eldridge Cleaver, Bobby Seale, Huey Newton, and thousands of their followers enthusiastically read and took to heart Fanon's books: *Black Skin, White Masks; A Dying Colonialism; Toward the African Revolution;* and particularly his final effort, written just before he died, *The Wretched of the Earth.*[2]

In these volumes, the English translations of which were published in the late 1960s, the Black Panthers found a message they felt they had been waiting for: a call to abandon and denounce the white culture foisted for centuries upon the blacks and people of other colors by white conquerors, masters who not only enslaved them but also destroyed or mangled and debased their original cultures.

There were also Fanon's angry exhortations to the blacks, the browns, and the swarthy (such as Arabs) to rise and attack not only in the name of nationalism, so as to form their own sovereign states, but also, and more importantly, in the name of a socio-economic revolution that would give true power to the masses.

In addition, he had a grand vision of a united Black Africa, with each tribe and nation helping one another in the fight to throw off the white yoke, and then, upon victory, to create a political and socio-economic union of the entire continent. This splendid dream also appealed to the Black Panthers.

For America's blacks, Fanon had a specific sermon. He knew and wrote of their plight. He branded the United States this "nation of lynchers," this "monster in which the taints, the sicknesses, and the inhumanity of Europe grew to appalling dimensions."

As for the method to be used in achieving freedom, bluntly, unabashedly, Fanon recommended violence. In so doing, he advanced two principal points:

First, their violence would be—in fact, already was—the just answer of the trodden to the exploitation, atrocities, and other violence perpetrated upon them by their enslavers. He, as a doctor in French-ruled Algeria, had seen colonialists torturing and shooting Arabs; he, who had witnessed the sickness and hunger caused by the white overlords elsewhere in Africa, and even in his own Martinique, which was comparatively more peaceful and humane than those other arenas of white oppressions, knew only one method for achieving freedom: violence.

Second, he proclaimed, violence was psychologically beneficial. As a psychiatrist, this revolutionary physician declared that violence provided the oppressed with a salutary release, with a means of affirming themselves.

Puristic Marxists, while praising Fanon for much else in his writings and revolutionary activities, censured him severely for his hymns to violence. They would not acknowledge that, while their Moscow and Peking mentors piously were rejecting violence, these mentors' own record was filled with terror. The Black Panthers of America, whatever their other faults, would have none of such hypocrisy. Like Fanon, they were for violence openly and articulately, no matter what Marxist pundits pretended to preach.

Violence, then, was Fanon's message. Small wonder that later on, in his extremity, Eldridge Cleaver chose Algeria as his refuge when he fled from the United States, and that a number of other American blacks, as fugitives and skyjackers, followed him to that North African shore. For Algeria was not only willing to give them asylum—Algeria was to them a memory of Fanon, who had fought for her independence. They were in effect coming not to an alien land, but home to Fanon.

III

Chronologically the Black Panthers[3] were preceded by the Student Nonviolent Coordinating Committee of the early 1960s, which began on a North Carolina black campus as a part of the aggressive but nonviolent civil rights movement. When violence did erupt, it was initiated by the belligerent whites of the South, outraged by the blacks' demands for integration and by their effort to register black voters. From 40 to 50 marches and demonstrations a week occurred throughout the South, with young white idealists enthusiastically streaming in from the North to help the blacks against the repressive Southern whites.

But in 1964 the focus shifted from civil rights to black power. Sympathetic white liberals were no longer welcome as allies. Among the leaders, the humanistic black students were replaced by fierce militants, such as Stokeley Carmichael and H. Rap Brown. The organization, although still bearing its famous name, was now neither student nor nonviolent. In time the word "Nonviolent" was dropped, substituted by "National."

But to some blacks, the Committee, even in its new phase, was not potent enough. In October 1966, two activists in Oakland, California, started another organization. They were Huey P. Newton (named by his parents in honor of Louisiana's late Senator Huey Pierce Long,

whom they admired)[4] and Bobby G. Seale. They called their group the
Black Panthers, taking their dramatic symbol—a lunging black pan-
ther—from an obscure Alabama organization of blacks, the so-called
Lowndes County Freedom Party.

They made public a ten-point platform and program of the Black
Panther Party, Seale stressing in particular that part of Point 10 which
stated: "We want land, bread, housing, education, clothing, justice,
and peace." An important official purpose of the founders was to
defend blacks against police brutality. But from the beginning it was
clear that the Black Panthers were themselves on the offensive. Armed
onslaught upon the white Establishment was their announced method;
gaining black power through a revolution was their aim, although they
were vague about the actual forms and extent of such black power once
they won it.

A certain amount of naive pomposity was manifested early in the
movement as its leaders assigned titles to one another, such as Minister
of Foreign Affairs, Minister of Finance, Minister of Information, and
the like. Before George Jackson, the "Soledad Brother," was killed in
August 1971, while attempting a prison break, he had been appointed a
General and Field Marshal of the Black Panthers.

In place of "We Shall Overcome," the low-key slogan and song of
the civil-rights movement, they introduced their shouts of "Power to
the people!" and "Black power!" along with the chant:

> Revolution's begun! Off the pig!
> Time to pick up the gun! Off the pig!

They popularized the abrasive "pig"—policeman; they originated
the ebullient "Right on!"*

Some of the Black Panthers' liberal critics accused them of fusing
Mao-Marxist ideology with fascist paramilitarism. In fact, their ideology remained inchoate; but their paramilitarism was clearly visible

---

* "Power to the people!", supposedly of pure black origin, may have in fact been
inspired by Lenin's cry in the summer of 1917, "Power to the Soviets!" (Cleaver and
other Panthers have written of their reading of Lenin's life and works.) "Pig" for the
policeman may, or may not, have come from the black ghetto. On more research it may
well prove a Whitey invention, possibly brought to the American scene by those who
have read George Orwell's *Animal Farm,* with the most negative role assigned by the
author to the pigs oppressing the other animals. But the high-pitch "Right on!" does
appear to be a Black Panther original. Its exact meaning is still rather uncertain. In the
random research I have done, hardly any blacks I questioned, and none of the whites I
asked, knew its literal sense. Does it mean, I queried, You are so right, or, You are right
on the dot, stay there. Finally a likely explanation came from a black friend: "It says you
are to go right on, forward—keep on going, leftward and forward against all Whitey's
opposition!"

from the start, as Black Panthers strutted around in their black jackets, black berets, and tight-fitting black pants, their pockets bulging with side arms, their clenched fists high above their defiant heads.

A dramatic show of their gun-toting bravado came on a May day in 1967, when a contingent of Black Panthers burst into a session of the California state legislature in Sacramento, shotguns and rifles in hand. This, they asserted, was to prove their right to bear arms in self-defense. A variation of this performance was given in 1969 at Cornell University, where black students leaving a building they had seized were photographed and televised brandishing rifles and wearing cartridge-studded bandoleers. These students said they had been provoked by some white students threatening them with guns.

In Oakland, with blacks constituting one half of the city's population, the Panthers made an immediate impression; and from among their leaders, who were greeted with awe and cheers by many, emerged the strangely magnetic Eldridge Cleaver.

His fame was international in scope with the publication of his autobiographical *Soul on Ice,* which explained the early and late frustrations of his life as a young black, boasted of his career as a rapist and robber of whites, and reiterated the inevitability of mass revolts such as the one he believed would be launched by the Black Panthers. The influence of Frantz Fanon was yet in the offing, but as early as 1966-67, the Nechayevist *Catechism of a Revolutionary* had its powerful appeal to Cleaver.[5]

IV

Shootouts with the police in Oakland and elsewhere began. More and more people learned that "Off the pig!" meant "Kill the policeman!" In their turn the police contributed to the folklore the phrase, "Up against the wall, you motherfuckers!", which they used when ordering the Panthers to stand facing a wall where they would be frisked.

The Panthers glorified bloody encounters as part of an incipient civil war. In early 1970, Cleaver spoke with relish of "the running guerrilla war of rooftop sniping, midnight ambush, the mass shootouts that the Panthers and police have been waging in a number of cities." The exact statistics of policemen killed or wounded in such battles cannot be ascertained, since the authorities often bunched their Panther-caused casualties with those suffered by the police in non-Panther shootings. As for the blacks' losses, it was asserted in December 1969, following the police slaying of Chicago's Panthers Fred Hampton and

Mark Clark, that in two years—1968 and 1969—police throughout the country had killed 28 Black Panthers.

This was stated in San Francisco by Charles R. Garry, chief counsel and spokesman for the Black Panthers, a white, and immediately repeated by the white and black press from coast to coast, together with an indignant charge that there was a nationwide and centrally directed drive by the police and the Federal Bureau of Investigation to decimate and perhaps even annihilate the Black Panther Party through outright, unprovoked killings.

A careful analysis of all the available factual data by Edward Jay Epstein in *The New Yorker* of February 13, 1971, established that not 28, but 10 Black Panthers were killed by the police in that two-year period—five in 1968, and five in 1969. No Black Panthers were slain by the police in 1970, insofar as Epstein could determine. Nor was there any central authority responsible for these ten deaths. Epstein made clear, however, that, even without any such extermination orders from Washington, there was a spontaneous feeling among the police across the country that the Black Panthers were indeed the enemy they boasted they were. Hence the policemen's ferocity.[6]

There were other Black Panther deaths, nevertheless, incurred during battles with other black militant organizations. Two Panthers were killed in the gunfight of January 17, 1969, on the Los Angeles campus of the University of California, and two more were slain later that year in San Diego. All four were victims of the Panther rivalry with US, also known as the Simbas (after a celebrated Congo tribe of warriors), an armed black group hostile to the Panthers.* There were also killings of Panthers by Panthers, such as the murder in New Haven on May 21, 1969, of Alex Rackley, accused by his fellow Panthers of being a police informer.

Of the ten Black Panther deaths actually caused by the police, two episodes stand out.

The first occurred in Oakland on April 6, 1968, when two policemen were wounded by a group of Panthers. Later, the Panther leadership argued that the shooting started when several Panthers in automobiles "were approached by two pigs and menaced with guns." Whoever did the initial menacing, it was evident that the Panthers unleashed the first shooting. Soon police reinforcements surrounded a house in which a number of Panthers had holed up. A 90-minute battle ensued; a third policeman was wounded; and as Panthers filed out from the building,

---

* In early January 1976, proof was made public by the United States media to show that the enmity between the Panthers and the other black militants, particularly in California, was deliberately incited by agents of the FBI, who, however, claimed that they merely wished thus to disrupt the black insurgency without meaning to cause deaths.

one of them was killed and another wounded. Later it was said that at least one of them—and possibly both—came out naked or at least stripped to their shorts, with hands over their heads, when the police started to shoot. Bobby Hutton, age 17, Panthers' minister of finance, was the one slain. It was Cleaver who was wounded, and, along with seven other Panthers, arrested. After having been indicted and released on bail, he avoided the trial by fleeing the United States.

The second episode occurred in Chicago where, close to five o'clock in the morning of December 4, 1969, 14 plainclothes policemen of the state attorney's office stormed the apartment of Fred Hampton, the 21-year-old chairman of the Illinois Black Panther Party. Surrounding the building, kicking in the flat's front door, they began to fire—the police would claim (after the event) a shotgun blast from within had greeted them. When all was over, two Panthers were dead: Hampton, killed in his bed, and a fellow Panther, Mark Clark, slain sitting in a chair.

Subsequently it was shown that the police had held a search warrant for illegal weapons that, according to the information they had received from the FBI, had recently been moved to Hampton's apartment. But it also turned out that in the savage fusillade of December 4 only one bullet may have been fired by a Panther, while anywhere between 83 and 99 were poured into the apartment by the police. A federal grand jury, empaneled in 1970, using the findings of the FBI ballistics experts, dismissed the statements of the police department's own investigators of the affair as "seriously deficient" and bordering on "purposeful malfeasance." An indictment and trial of Edward V. Hanrahan, the state attorney, and of 13 others connected with the raid, followed.

Eventually, they were all acquitted. The families of Hampton and Clark then brought a multimillion-dollar civil suit for damages against Hanrahan and the others. In the process, in early 1974, it was revealed that the information about the arms in Hampton's flat and the flat's detailed layout had been brought to the authorities by a Panther, William O'Neal, who had served the FBI as its secret agent. With the Panthers, O'Neal had been a security chief, responsible for the arming of his fellow members and the proper care for, and use of, the Party's weapons. He was also in charge of safeguarding the Panthers against infiltrators and informers.

V

The assassination of Martin Luther King in Memphis, Tennessee, on April 4, 1968, signaled an outbreak of mass violence in the United

States. A wave of riots and fires rolled across the land. There were killings; stores were smashed and looted; city block after city block was aflame. The time seemed to have come for the Black Panthers, foremost among other revolutionary troops, to mount not only rooftops but also barricades.

From then on, for two years and more, white rebels no less than blacks played their tumultuous role. This was the time of the student rebellions and attacks on campus administration buildings, of the fire-bombing of military installations, of the raids on induction centers, of the increasing stormy anti-Vietnam-war demonstrations, and, finally, in May 1970 , of the killing of white students at Kent State University in Ohio and of black students at Jackson State College in Mississippi.

Through all this, white rebels hailed the Panthers; would join them whenever the blacks would let them, which was not always, since by degrees many Panthers were growing more and more anti-honky and segregationist. Yet the white revolutionaries persisted. Character-istically, the Students for a Democratic Society, at their National Coun-cil meeting held in Austin, Texas, on March 30, 1969, in a special resolution on the Black Panther Party, praised it as "the vanguard force" in the black liberation movement:

> The fundamental reason for the success of the Black Panther Party is that it has a correct analysis of American society. They see clearly the colonial status of blacks and the dual oppression from which they suffer: national oppression as a people and class exploi-tation as a superexploited part of the working class. The demand for self-determination becomes the most basic demand of the op-pressed colony. And nationalism becomes a necessary and effec-tive means for organizing the black community and forging unity against the oppressor.[7]

In the summer of 1969 the SDS-Weathermen's organ *New Left Notes* lauded the Panthers as the "model for all who will fight." And yet, that very August, Chairman Bobby Seale and Minister of Informa-tion and Chief of Staff David Hilliard criticized their white admirers. Seale castigated the SDS as "a bunch of those jive bourgeois national socialists and national chauvinists." Hilliard fulminated: "We don't see SDS as being so revolutionary. We see SDS as just being another pacification front. . . . SDS had better get their politics straight because the Black Panther Party is drawing some very clear lines between friends and enemies. . . . We'll beat those sissies, those little school-boys' ass if they don't try to straighten up their politics."[8] All this because at the United Front Against Fascism conference called by the Panthers in Cleveland in mid-July 1969, the SDS delegates had dared to disagree with their black hosts on a rather minor detail of common policy.

But still the white radicals persisted in their eagerness to cooperate. In some earnest groups of America's liberals, too, the Panthers were now fashionable. In New York, in early 1970, Mr. and Mrs. Leonard Bernstein gave their much-publicized cocktail party in honor and financial aid of the Black Panthers. All through that period, for several years, it was a sign of good and progressive taste for the press and intellectuals to be indignant about the police role in the continuing shootouts with the Panthers. As Panthers, singly and in groups, were taken to trial, more and more meetings and cocktail parties were held by white sympathizers, defense funds were established, and attorneys provided.

At a mass rally in New Haven in 1970, President Kingman Brewster, Jr. of Yale University declared that he doubted whether there could be a fair trial for black revolutionaries anywhere in America. Yet the Establishment, although alarmed by this Red storm lashing the land, was at the same time fearful of treating the rebels too harshly. With all those liberal voices raised in defense and even praise of the Panthers, the nation's courts bent backward to prove that no one was being punished unduly.

Thus, in the very same New Haven of President Brewster, the trial of Bobby Seale, Erika Huggins, and other Panthers on charges of murder ended in a dismissal after a hung jury. Seale went on with his organizing and speechmaking; Mrs. Huggins was free to become an elected member of the Berkeley Community Development Council, an antipoverty agency. In New York, after a long trial (February 1970-December 1972), 21 Panthers, accused of a conspiracy to blow up buildings, bridges, and tunnels, were acquitted. Huey Newton's three trials on charges of killing an Oakland policeman ended in three hung juries, and Newton peacefully proceeded to write one more book.

While some Panthers fled to foreign lands or went underground, only a few were sent to jail, most prominently David Hilliard, for threatening President Richard Nixon's life. With the new decade, the Panthers kept up their successes. In the early 1970s their emissaries, mostly black but a few white as well, proliferated in Western Europe and the Middle East. For a time, in her rather confused involvement, Jean Seberg, the film actress from Marshalltown, Iowa, worked for the Panthers as their Paris representative. As she later put it, she was "the honky representative of the Panthers. I was doing some translations and political things. . . . I officially broke with them, though. I've analyzed the fact that I'm not equipped to participate absolutely and totally. I had a very bad mental breakdown."[9]

Europe was keenly interested. In country after country, press and television publicized the Black Panthers as if they were about to triumph and take over all of America. After a trip to Sweden and a survey of that nation's television, an American editor reported in early 1972: "The Black Panthers are given so much time that many Swedish people believe it is the only American organization that speaks for blacks."[10]

The compliment of imitation was paid in such places as Israel, New Zealand, and India. In Jerusalem and Tel Aviv, young Jews of Sephardic or Oriental origin complained that they were being discriminated against in jobs and housing by the Ashkenazi or European Establishment of the new state. As a consequence, they formed a volatile and aggressive but short-of-terror group and named themselves Black Panthers. In May 1974, in Auckland, New Zealand's largest city, a few Maoists announced their newly organized Polynesian Panther Party. Meeting regularly in a shabby church hall in a poor suburb, they demanded a change in the white racist policy of New Zealand, plotted a revolution, and confidently predicted their party's violence and victory within five years. In India, in the Bombay area, a group of young writers among the Harjans, or the untouchables, called themselves the Dalit Panthers, the word *dalit* meaning "the oppressed" in Marathi, the local language, and the word Panthers used in honor of America's Black Panthers. Poetry, plays, and fiction, containing angry sociopolitical protest, were produced by these Panthers of India.

In the United States, one non-black counterculture group dubbed itself the White Panthers. In addition, juvenile Puerto Ricans in New York and one or two other large cities, adopting paramilitary dress and brute-force methods, calling themselves Young Lords and professing Maoism, declared they were an affiliate of the Black Panther Party. In 1969-70, in Chicago, the Young Lords joined with the Panthers in some political action. On a somewhat humorous side, in Miami and New York, some mildly protesting white elderly people took the name of Gray Panthers as they demanded more aid.

The expression "Black Power" had innumerable echoes: senior citizen power, woman power, gay power, Polish-American power, Italian-American power, and the like. The clenched fist as a salute-threat, widely believed to have been introduced by the Panthers, but in fact an oldtime gesture of white radicals in Europe, was now also raised by the Chicanos and other ethnics of America.

VI

And yet, surprisingly to some, but not so to others who knew better, the support among the blacks themselves for the Panthers was less in actuality than it appeared on the surface. The number of activists was not so large as were the boasts and fears. A sage police officer in Oakland once remarked that their rhetoric and rioting created for the Panthers more semblance of power than the strength they in truth possessed. Even at the height of their seeming prowess, in late 1969, the total membership of the Panthers in all their chapters across the country was no more than 1,200. Some experts placed it as low as 800, and in mid-1972 at about 700.

Middle-class psychology continued to grip vast segments of America's blacks. They had no wish to destroy the Establishment: they simply longed for more crumbs from its sumptuous tables. The experience of Watts and other burning and wrecked ghettos showed that riots only left their homes, stores, and jobs in charred ruins. Silently, almost sullenly, they disagreed with Cleaver and Fanon: black was not that beautiful—not to many of them, not always. They still wanted to identify themselves with the white culture that had subjugated them so cruelly but that was so desirable, if only in part—the part they had long ago accepted and would not give up.

Far from turning to a Nechayevist or any other kind of violent revolutionary belief, many blacks still went to church, listened to their preachers, and sought hope and solace in the Bible. By late 1972 Bobby Seale himself recognized this as he spoke to an interviewer: "Probably forty per cent of the whole black population in this country is sitting in church every Sunday morning. It's absurd to ignore all of the black people sitting there. If you think they are getting brainwashed, then why don't you go in there? If you can relate some aspect of your philosophy to theirs, then check it out."

In 1972 there were clear signs of a change in the nation's political climate. The war in Vietnam was being phased out; violence at home subsided. The Weathermen, underground since late December 1969, now seemed explosive only sporadically. Stokeley Carmichael, the erstwhile stormy chief of the Student Nonviolent (National) Coordinating Committee, in 1972-73 claimed to have formed a new peaceful black party aimed at forging strong bonds between America's and Africa's blacks, apparently with no barricades in the program.

So came a change for the Panthers, too. While Cleaver still had support in New York for his militant calls from his refuge in Algeria, Seale and other Panther leaders on the Pacific Coast drastically forsook him. The split was completed as the California Panthers began to mold a new image for themselves: of gradualists rather than extremists, of philosophers with no guns, of peaceful agitators.

Gone with the guns were the black berets, black jackets, and tight black trousers. "Gun is not necessarily revolutionary," averred the Party's supreme commander, Huey Newton, in his most startlingly non-Maoist statement of all.* In came more and more of those benevolent breakfasts for black children, free clothes, tests for sickle-cell anemia, joint programs with churches, and escorted buses for the elderly to guard them against muggings. The Panthers now wore suits, sports jackets, and conventional trousers as they went about their philanthropy.

Subsequently, Seale even became a candidate for mayor of Oakland in 1973. Neatly dressed, sensibly spoken, this was a strikingly different man from the Bobby Seale who, it seemed such a brief time ago, had screamed at Judge Julius Hoffman in the conspiracy trial of the Chicago Seven and had been gagged and bound in the courtroom.

Seale lost the election, but was nonetheless cheerful and optimistic afterward. Despite his landslide defeat, the vote for him had been impressive, he said; he viewed it as a base for further progress; the Panther policy would not revert to the old violence. Anyway, Seale and his supporters asserted, those blood-curdling threats "Off the pig!", "Death to the pigs!", and "All power to the sniper!" had been mostly oratory and misinterpreted; they should not have been taken literally, and surely were not meant to be regarded or remembered seriously. Even the name Black Panthers was no longer stressed; it was being eased out.

But many policemen in various American cities had lasting memories. They did not trust the Panthers' new stance. They went on the alert each time young blacks tried to start a new Panther chapter in one more city. By threat more than by shooting, the police prevented such chapters from becoming active or from even coming into being at all.

---

* However, after a seemingly peaceful phase, Newton reverted to violence, even if of a rather non-Maoist kind, when in the summer of 1974 he stopped his car at a downtown Oakland street corner, beat a young black girl with a revolver, and then shot her in the head, wounding her gravely. She later died. As murder charges awaited him for this, he pistol-whipped his elderly tailor when the man fondly called him "baby" during a fitting in his luxurious penthouse. Summoned to court, Newton disappeared underground. Before long, he sent communications from Havana, where he had found asylum.

VII

In early August 1972, the annual FBI report estimated the aggregate Black Panther membership at 710 full-time activists in 38 chapters, of whom a mere 100 sided with Cleaver.

Eldridge Cleaver fled from the United States in 1968 when he was not only on bail but also on parole from a California prison, at the time his parole was about to be revoked. He wandered from one Communist or Third World country to another until September 1970, when he established in Algiers what he loftily called the International Section of the Black Panther Party. His wife Kathleen and a group of followers were with him.[11]

At this point he did not have much money. Back home, the United States Treasury had prevented him from receiving royalties from his highly successful books, *Soul on Ice* and *Post-Prison Writings and Speeches*. In doing so, it had used the 1950 regulations derived from the 1917 Trading with the Enemy Act, the Treasury branding Cleaver as an enemy national of Red China, North Korea, and North Vietnam, which he had visited since 1968.

But now in 1970 the government and the press of Algeria hailed him as a revolutionary hero. Algeria's President Houari Boumedienne, head of her sole political party, the National Liberation Front (for which Fanon had once propagandized and labored), extended ample help to Cleaver and his Black Panther fellow exiles.

Cleaver's group was given a fine white-and-blue villa at El Biar, a choice suburb of the capital. Not only a generous subsidy for the group's day-to-day expenses, but also numerous amenities and facilities were provided, including a costly Telex, which Cleaver grandly dubbed the Revolutionary Peoples' Communications Network.

But over the ensuing months and years, the showy and noisy style of the Cleaverites' behavior began to grate on the nerves of their Moslem hosts. Boumedienne also disapproved of Cleaver's tireless seeking of worldwide publicity. Of the 20-odd rebel contingents from all over the world to whom Algeria was then extending political haven and financial support, these Black Panthers appeared to be the most strident and tactless.

A rather unwelcome furor was caused in June and August 1972, when two hijacked planes from the United States landed in Algeria and the abductors declared that they were Black Panthers, in spirit if not in prior membership. These new, bold blacks wanted to be integrated into Cleaver's group. Cleaver was pleased. The hefty $1,500,000 the skyjackers brought in ransom (a half-million in one case, and one million in the other) was claimed by Cleaver—for further Afro-American revolutionary activities, he said.

But Boumedienne had no intention of handing the ransom money to Cleaver. The Algerian leader shocked not only the Panthers but many other revolutionaries in other countries by returning all the ransom to its American corporate owners, Western and Delta airlines.

By then rebels everywhere felt that Boumedienne and his Algerian nationalists were betraying their revolutionary principles, formed so significantly by Fanon's teachings and sacrifices. The rebels saw Algeria cuddling up to American and other Western capitalists. And there was something to this charge. Algeria needed foreign loans; she wanted deals with oil companies and other Western investors; and the government was then developing a national airline of its own and did not want to aid and abet skyjackers, particularly non-Arab ones.

A campaign of isolation and harassment against Cleaver was stepped up considerably. Telephone calls from outside often failed to reach the Panthers; Arab voices intercepted the calls. When Cleaver tried to complain, he found he could not get through to Algeria's higher-ups who formerly had responded so eagerly. Now he had to talk to reluctant and even rude underlings.

On August 10, 1972, as a part of what now seemed a deliberate effort to get rid of the Panthers, the police raided the villa. Next, the police cancelled the reception announced by the Panthers for August 18, the Day of Solidarity with the Afro-American People. That month, for a while, the authorities kept a police guard around the villa, but soon removed it, thus ending the Panthers' virtual house detention. In September these wards of the Algerian government could again receive visitors and circulate in the city at will.

But a new blow fell when, in late August or early September (the exact time is unknown), Boumedienne ordered the villa's Telex and telephones cut off. The reason given was the inordinate expense run up by the Panthers in their flood of revolutionary communications to every far-flung point on the globe.

Knowing they were no longer welcome in Algeria, the black exiles wished to leave. But they were far from certain as to what country would accept them. The fedayeen camps in the Middle East might have been a logical destination, but a well-founded report has it that as early as 1970-71 the half-dozen Panthers sent by Cleaver to Yasir Arafat's headquarters did not get along with him and his men: the Panthers were denied the publicity they sought, and the Arabs were unpleasantly surprised when these black American revolutionaries showed little stomach for any real fighting alongside the Fatah commandos on the several raids that occurred during the visit.

By the spring of 1973 all the Panthers seemed to have scattered from Algeria and not always fraternally—there have been signs of the group's internal quarrels, one or two of the men leaving behind their bitter public letters of disassociation with the organization.

For a time, in Algeria, that other fugitive from California justice, Timothy Leary, the psychedelic guru, and his third wife Rosemary had found shelter with the Cleavers. The experience, according to later testimony by Leary, was sheer gloom: "Often it was sorrowful to be with E. C. and sense our mutual dilemma. We were both charismatic shamans now trapped by our images." The isolation was novel and frightful, with no chance for either "to hang around in the new creative chaos" where "a new generation was taking over," with nothing but disillusionment for such old leaders or prophets as Cleaver and Leary.

Leary later went to Europe, where political asylum was not granted. He traveled from Switzerland to Afghanistan, where he was soon seized and extradited as a criminal to California and jail. Subsequently the Cleavers moved from Algeria to Paris, where Eldridge's French lawyer battled the bureaucracy for Cleaver's right to political asylum. But in May 1975, Cleaver publicly declared that he would return to the United States "before July 4, 1976, the nation's two hundredth anniversary," to stand trial for his part in the Oakland shootout—provided he was not imprisoned until trial.

He said he was peaceful now, no longer desiring to take off anyone's head, no longer a Panther, no longer welcome in Communist countries where, he said, there was no room for popular will. He spoke of his new faith in a democratic process that he believed did exist in the post-Nixon America. He said that the Panthers had contributed to the salutary change in America's System. Now, in America, he asserted, "institutions don't have to be blown up but only perfected." But he, too, had changed. Bravely he conceded his old error: "Now, several years and many Communist countries later, I find the grass not greener on the Communist side of the fence. So, now, here I stand, locked outside the gates of the paradise I once scorned, begging to be let back in."[12]

He returned to the United States on November 18, 1975, and was taken in custody by the FBI on arrival at New York's Kennedy Airport. In Oakland his successor as the Panthers' information minister, the still-militant Elaine Brown, warned the few remaining faithful that the black community should not give any support to Cleaver until by his behavior in jail and court he proves "that he is not playing the Judas role" in return for preferential treatment and early freedom.

But it was open to question if Miss Brown herself had much support among American blacks for her cautionary remarks on the subject of

Cleaver. In the mid-1970s, as extremist black movements in America receded, faded, altered, or disappeared, a New York journalist wrote: "Followers of separatist and ultramilitant messiahs, never numerous, have all but vanished. Unlike five or ten years ago, no one is expecting either the millenium or the apocalypse any time soon."[13] Some black leaders recalled what Malcolm X had once said: "Power is best used quietly, without attracting attention."

But, ominously, even in the calmer mid-1970s not all blacks agreed with this. In 1973-74 there were blacks as well as whites in the terroristic Symbionese Liberation Army. Early in 1974 the so-called Zebra killings in San Francisco were part of a war of blacks upon whites. Most significantly, in the early and middle 1970s a new militant grouping, the Black Liberation Army, made headlines across the nation. Its sole business: to kill the police.

VIII

These young American blacks initially emerged in the declining phase of the Panthers, which was marked by Bobby Seale's turn to peaceful tactics and Eldridge Cleaver's flight to Algerian exile. The Liberationists rejected what they felt to be the failure of the older leaders to guide them toward black power explosively enough.

The Black Liberation Army was a loosely organized cop-killing union of a few score to a few hundred consisting mostly of men but with some women too. Their earliest nucleus was a faction of Cleaver's followers, said to have been formally expelled from the Panthers by Huey Newton. This group murdered its first policeman in the spring of 1971.

Traveling across the continent in small teams, from San Francisco to St. Louis to Atlanta to New York, they financed themselves by bank and store robberies and, to a lesser extent, by sales of narcotics, as they made their main task the slaying of policemen. They felt, and also occasionally proclaimed in their letters to the media, that the police were the chief enemies of the downtrodden. Only when these pillars of the capitalistic System were smashed would a true and thorough revolution be possible.

Some warpath blacks were not affiliated with the Black Liberation Army at all, yet claimed this increasingly terrifying name for their assaults. On the other hand, one of the most spectacular killers, Mark Essex of New Orleans, probably not a member of the Black Liberation Army, was claimed by its leaders posthumously for their ranks.[14]

His exploit was too deadly and headline-filling not to be appropriated by the Black Liberation Army. Mark James Essex, 23 years old, a former United States Navy sailor, came from his Kansas hometown of Emporia to New Orleans to stage in a downtown hotel on a January day in 1973 a 30-hour massacre and shootout with the police, in which six persons were slain, including a police superintendent, and 14 wounded. Essex was finally shot dead, but there were indications that at least two more blacks, a man and a woman, had been with him, firing bullets. A black man, perhaps Essex but perhaps that other desperado, had informed a black chambermaid in the hotel that this was "a revolution," assuring her: "Don't worry, sister, we're only shooting whites today." In a small New Orleans apartment where Essex had lived before going amok, the police found these graffiti on the walls:

"My destiny lies in the bloody death of racist pigs."

"The quest for freedom is death, then by death I shall escape to freedom."

"Revolutionary justice is black justice, shoot to kill."

"Hate white people, beast of the earth."

That not only white policemen, but black ones as well were to be destroyed was declared in this one: "Kill black pig devil." And, last but not least, was the classic Maoist inscription: "Political power comes from the barrel of a gun."

A New Year's eve killing of a police cadet on a New Orleans street preceding the hotel slaughter was later also ascribed to Mark Essex.

Much more definitely in the forefront of the Black Liberation Army, and alive but in prison at this writing, have been these four leaders: Henry S. (Sha Sha) Brown, Mrs. Joanne Deborah Chesimard, Clark E. Squire, and Robert Hayes (calling himself Seth Ben Ysaak Ben Ysrael), all in their twenties except for Squire, who is in his mid-thirties.

In February 1972, in St. Louis, along with Ronald Carter, a fellow Black Liberation member, Brown was in a gun battle with the police. Carter fell dead, while Brown was captured and later tried and sentenced to 25 years in jail. But he was returned to New York to be judged for the ambush murder of two policemen on the Lower East Side on January 27, 1972. This trial, in early 1974, resulted in his acquittal, but he was kept in New York prisons on other charges.

His prominence in the meantime was gained mainly by his repeated and ingenious attempts to escape. On October 23, 1973, he coolly walked out of a hospital room whither he had been taken for an X-ray. He was recaptured in Brooklyn a week later. In April 1974, a team of Black Liberation men unsuccessfully tried to free Brown by breaking into a Manhattan jail with the aid of an acetylene torch. On August 15, 1974, Brown was scaling a Brooklyn prison wall when he was wounded in the right shoulder, dropped to the ground, and was recaptured.

Mrs. Chesimard was apprehended on May 2, 1973, in a chase and shootout on the New Jersey Turnpike in which Werner Foerster, a state trooper, and a black militant were killed. The series of her trials began in December 1973, the first one on a charge of an armed bank robbery in the Bronx in September 1972. She and her codefendant, Fred Hilton, constantly interrupted the judge, Mrs. Chesimard being particularly imaginative in calling him not only a "racist" but also a "fascist pig in a black nightgown," and suggesting to His Honor loudly: "I should direct you to go jump out of that window."

But the jury said they could not believe the witnesses against the pair, and both Mrs. Chesimard and Hilton were acquitted. Her other trials, among them the one in New Jersey in connection with the trooper's slaying, were yet to come when it developed that, while in jail during her first trial, she had become pregnant, but with whose willing help she would not tell nor would any male in her proximity boast.

On March 15, 1974, after a trial in New Brunswick, New Jersey, Clark Squire, age 36, was sentenced to life imprisonment for murdering Werner Foerster, the state trooper in the battle of May 2 of the previous year. The judge then pronounced an additional sentence of 24 to 36 years for assault, robbery, and gun possession, to be served consecutively beyond the life sentence, should the latter be shortened by parole. Plainly the judge meant this Black Liberation man never in his lifetime to taste freedom again.

Without looking at the judge, Squire addressed him:

"I don't ask any consideration. There is no justice. I will give my life for the poor people.

"The Black Liberation Army has been accused of killing policemen. All we do is stop the police from killing us.

"If the police don't want to get killed, they should stop murdering blacks and Third World people.

"The poor people of the nation are being victimized by the System. The Black Liberation Army has been fractured, but it will continue until the oppression is stopped.

"I say: the Black Liberation Army still lives."

A policeman was shot dead in the Bronx, New York, on July 5, 1973, his body bearing 14 bullets. Robert Hayes, a Black Liberation Army man, was suspected. When, on September 17 of that year, the police went to his apartment to arrest him, he fired a sawed-off shotgun at them, wounding two officers slightly. On March 28, 1974, a jury including one black man and one black woman found him guilty of the

July 1973 murder. He bowed to them deeply as he was taken back to jail to await his sentence. This, handed down on May 10, was 35 years to life in prison. On July 9 he was tried additionally, this time for the attempted murders of policemen of the previous September. Now his sentence was five concurrent life terms, to correspond in number to the five policemen he had attempted to kill.

On the other hand, another New York jury of 11 men and one woman, six of whom were black, was deadlocked, thus resulting in a mistrial for five other reputed Black Liberation Army men accused of ambush killing of two policemen, one white and the other black, in Harlem on May 21, 1971. The trial, in 1974, had lasted two and a half months; the jury deliberated 26 hours for three days in mid-May. A black jury member later said: "Some people in the jury don't trust the police." Another of the jury agreed: "They didn't want to believe fingerprints, photographs, nothing. They came into the jury room with their minds made up." Nor would they believe any hostile witnesses, one black juror sadly remarking that his fellow jurors "figured these witnesses were programmed to say what they had to say—that they were under pressure, that they were threatened with losing their children."

And the five defendants, even as they awaited a retrial, were duly grateful to the jury. Their spokesman echoed the March speech by Squire as he addressed the jury: "Our main concern is survival of black and Third World people. Our only crime is working in our country to help our own people."

In the 1970s a number of Black Liberation Army members fell in gun battles with the police. The personality of one of these was particularly noteworthy in the sense that he was a synthesis of so many rebel strains.

This was the militant killed in the New Jersey Turnpike fusillade of May 1973—James F. Coston, age 32, a leader in the Black Liberation Army but also holding a past Black Panther record, having served in the Cleaver faction as minister of information. In addition, he had been a Black Muslim, using the adopted Islamic name of Zayd Malik Shakur.

On May 7, despite the protests of some patriotic or would-be patriotic organizations and individuals, Coston-Shakur was buried at the Long Island National Cemetery on the basis of his honorable discharge after four years in the United States Navy. At the funeral service, conducted in an Islamic rite, his father praised Coston-Shakur as "a struggler, a revolutionary," who "died for a good cause." The father proudly stated that he and his two sons had been Black Muslims for 15 years.

On the chest of the corpse six bullets were arranged. The coffin was flanked by the flags of the Black Liberation Army, the Black Panthers, and a Puerto Rican independence group. A Black Liberation representative eulogized the fallen member: "He was using revolutionary violence to end all oppression that our people are subjected to." A Black Panther also praised the dead man as their own, a delegate of Cleaver in an eloquent oration quoting Coston as saying in his lifetime: "I shall not compromise. And to the last pulse in my veins I shall resist."

Some 80 people attended Coston's funeral, but hundreds had viewed the body in the mortician's parlor, urged as they were beforehand by leaflets signed by the Black Liberation Army and widely distributed in New York's black neighborhoods.

As if in a competition of mournful display, more than 3,000 policemen from many points came to the last services in East Brunswick, New Jersey, for Werner Foerster.

Early in 1973 the FBI made public these statistics of policemen losing their lives in the line of duty throughout the nation: 86 in 1969, 100 in 1970, 125 in 1971, and 112 in 1972. But precisely how many of these deaths could be ascribed to either the Black Panthers or the Black Liberation Army was not disclosed. In August 1973, in New York alone, the authorities blamed the Black Liberationists for five policemen's slayings of the early 1970s.

Defying the U.S. Supreme Court's decision against capital punishment, several state legislatures restored the death penalty, confining it mainly to the murderers of policemen and other members of law-enforcement agencies. Some judges, while waiting for their states to bring back hanging or electrocution, made sure that police-killers would never get out of prison. In Texas, in May 1973, a San Antonio judge, voicing his regret that he could not sentence a policeman's slayer to death ("the Supreme Court of the United States has made that punishment unavailable to us") sentenced the murderer to 10,000 years in the penitentiary.

In this way such organizations as the Black Liberation Army were warned of the risks they increasingly ran. And there was evidence that by 1973-74 these black terrorists, although still sniping and killing, were in fact losing out even in New York, their main scene of action. In September 1973, the New York police estimated the strength of the Black Liberation Army in the metropolitan area at only 25 to 30 hardcore members, with some additional 75 sympathizers willing to work with them as auxiliaries. It was estimated that of the 25 or 30 activists, only 15 were then criminally involved in New York. A month earlier, District Attorney Eugene Gold in Brooklyn expressed his opinion that the number of the Black Liberationists was by that summer "much smaller than a lot of people like to believe," and that the Army was "in a period of descendancy." In mid-November the slaying of a BLA leader, Twymon Meyers, prompted the New York police commissioner to say that this "broke the back" of the terrorist Army. He recited the names of five other BLA leaders killed by the police in recent shootouts, and of 18 others of the BLA roster then in custody, either serving jail terms or awaiting trial in various cities.

25

The Weathermen

What the Panthers at their height meant to America's black rebels, the Weathermen were for the nation's white revolutionaries.[1]

Being white and middle-class, the Weathermen were from a more privileged background and were better educated than the usually lower-class blacks of the Panthers. And though the Weathermen exercised influence for a shorter period than did the Panthers, their roots reached deeper into an older organization—the Students for a Democratic Society.

In violence, the Weathermen caused few deaths and injuries. They usually gave—and even now, their few remaining members underground, still give—timely warnings before the detonation of bombs.

In their antecedents the Weathermen went the gradual route from protest to resistance to revolution. The Panthers, on the other hand, at their very inception, envisaged rebellion. But while many Panthers subsequently turned away from their methods of violence and their goal of revolution to work for peaceful, gradual reform, the Weathermen to this day have not renounced their revolutionary tactics and aims.

The Weathermen's parent organization, the Students for a Democratic Society, was founded as a liberal reform group in January 1960. Yet even this was not an entirely new formation, but rather a new name for what had been called the Student League for Industrial Democracy, which had billed itself as "a nonpartisan educational organization," seeking "to promote greater active participation on the part of American students in the resolution of present-day problems." This had a part-time central office in New York City and only three chapters: at Columbia, Yale, and the University of Michigan, all three groups barely noticed on their campuses.

The renaming meant the beginning of a divorce, not amicable, from the older, staid, and liberal leadership of the League for Industrial

Democracy, an organization of Socialist Party affiliations. The problems of the nation and its student youth were expected in the 1960s to be enormously challenging: hence the desire of these young men and women to strike out on their own, under a new name.

It took time for the Students for a Democratic Society to evolve. The reorganization, the acquiring of new muscle, took more than two years. And even then it did not emerge into a body advocating and implementing violence, though some development toward a more mercurial phase was achieved in June 1962, when 45 mildly idealistic youths assembled in Port Huron, Michigan, at an old camp belonging to the United Auto Workers, a labor union surely not disposed to producing or aiding political terroristic conspiracies. They met to discuss a 63-page program of action, written mostly by Tom Hayden, a University of Michigan student, then a liberal, not the radical he later became.

The document, rather than being a clarion call to decisive action, was a brilliant analysis of the ills of America and the world. While it did include a program for a New Left, it was primarily philosophical and abstract.

Though the "Port Huron Statement" was not a Communist text, the Old Left, which had sponsored these students, was upset by its slant, which was away from the Old Left's anti-Communist tradition. America, for instance, was heavily blamed in the document for everything unpleasant in the affairs of man, particularly for the Cold War, while the Soviet Union was only slightly chided. The Old Left perceived here an ominous drift. As the events of the next seven years proved, their premonition was well founded.

Still, the first few years of the SDS held no truly radical episodes. For the most part these students engaged in highly intellectual discussions based on thoroughly prepared position papers, written and distributed by its leadership and eagerly received on various campuses.

But organizationally and practically, the SDS was still groping for chapters, money, and even issues. It turned to the problems of poverty and unemployment, achieving in these areas some successes among both whites and blacks. It also occupied itself with the injustices of the campuses, gradually becoming a leader in the fight for what was soon known as "student power."

But violence was rising and spreading in the land. In November 1963, President Kennedy's assassination somehow served as an indication to many students that the peaceful liberalism for which he had stood was not enough. The disturbing shadow of the war in Vietnam darkened and lengthened through 1964. After February 1965 and the first direct large-scale involvement of American troops in Southeast

Asia, the SDS at last had its prime issue—its one cause for bellig-
erency, for war at home.

Draft protests, peace demonstrations, attacks on recruiters for the
armed forces and war industries, raids on induction centers, and confrontations with the police soon had the SDS, or at least its name, in
the forefront of the turbulence. Much of this new, violent activity was
only ascribed to the SDS, but much was initiated or backed by their
chapters, acting independently of their national office, as they rapidly
proliferated on campuses from coast to coast.

Many of the student leaders and members were at this time socialists, but the SDS as an organization remained nominally nonpartisan as
it became increasingly radical. However, with its anti-anti-Commu-
nism constantly growing stronger, the SDS began to attract and accept
as its members many applying Communists, representing both the pro-
Moscow and the pro-Peking factions. Some of these were first-generation radicals—young men and women from upper- and middle-class
families of conventional American traditions; but others were the so-
called "red-diaper babies"—sons and daughters of Communists (some
even Party functionaries) of the 1930s. Between the two extremes were
the offspring of well-off professionals and businessmen of the 1960s
who in their youth in the 1930s had been fellow travelers or sympathizers with sundry Red causes without having been card-holders in
either the Communist or Socialist parties.

When young pro-Moscow Communists joined the SDS, they did
not flaunt their Party membership nor did they try to subjugate the SDS
to Party rule. As for the Communist Party itself, in the America of the
1960s it was so hidebound and self-subdued that it probably did not
seriously consider taking over the SDS.

The pro-Peking Communists in the United States, however, were
different. These Maoists first formed their Progressive Labor Movement in New York in July 1962, the group's leaders coming from the
pro-Moscow Communist Party, which they, as ultraleftists, had quit
(or had been purged from) in 1961-62. In April 1964 they changed their
name by replacing the word *Movement* with *Party*. They tried to establish a student sector, but, being unsuccessful, what they were able to
organize was dissolved in February 1966. Thus, young Maoists of the
Progressive Labor Party began to join the SDS. Unlike the pro-Moscow Communists, they openly and often loudly proclaimed their PLP
membership. Soon they were both numerous and influential in the
Students for a Democratic Society.

As riots enveloped one campus after another, as antiwar marches
flooded the streets and grew in militancy, the media—particularly television—brought the student disorders into everyone's parlor, and the

SDS received its widest and most impressive publicity, causing thousands of applications for membership. The media elevated the SDS into one of the nation's best-known groups of radicals. It practically created the SDS as the celebrated and fearsome fact of American life in the decade's second half. In effect it helped the birth of scores of new SDS chapters, which at this time appeared even on the most conservative and hitherto stagnant campuses of the land.

In the spring of 1968, Columbia University was the scene of one of the largest and most dramatic of the student riots, with an SDS member, Mark Rudd, leading the rebel mass.[2] Not only the Nixon Administration, but many a liberal American was frightened by the widespread student disturbances and saw them as a foreshadowing of revolution— the takeover not only of this great university but of the White House itself. The concurrent near-revolution of French students in Paris reaffirmed the fear that Establishments all over the world were crashing, that the Red flag was everywhere ascendant.

Three years before the conflict at Columbia, in May 1965, Phillip Abbot Luce, a defector from the Progressive Labor Party, had contributed a frightening article to *The Saturday Evening Post* wherein he had attributed his defection from the revolutionary ranks to his disagreement with the PLP plans for terrorist activities. However, the PLP had no such plans. Moreover, this Party, through its members in the SDS, tried to halt America's students short of terror, attempted to stop them from carrying student violence from the campuses to the streets, for, the Party held, this would only alienate the workers from the revolution.

As a rule, the Progressive Labor Party stayed strictly within the law. When, in June 1969, a faction of the SDS, naming themselves Weathermen, resolved on a course of terror, they left the PLP contingent in charge of the nonterrorist part of the SDS. Ironically, these Maoists found themselves to be practically the only law-abiding citizens in the Students for a Democratic Society.

II

The break occurred at the ninth annual convention, held in mid-June 1969 in Chicago. A document signed by 11 members marked the division of the organization. The statement proclaimed the necessity to engage in immediate and drastic militancy. This paper's long title soon proved to be the source of the new group's name. It read: "You Don't Need a Weatherman to Know Which Way the Wind Blows."

This was taken from Bob Dylan's anti-Establishment song of 1965, "Subterranean Homesick Blues," a song highly popular among members of America's counterculture as a call to defy the authorities and to hew one's own path of independence. Dylan himself had once, in December 1963, addressed an SDS meeting in New York (at which, incidentally, Alger Hiss was also introduced and cheered). The statement was ornamented with pictures not only of Marx and Lenin but also of Mao, and throughout its six pages had silhouettes of charging armed guerrillas.

Later, particularly from 1970 on, in deference to the women's liberation movement, the word Weathermen was changed to Weatherpeople, Weatherforce, and finally Weather Underground, but the original version has survived and is the term still most commonly used.

As the SDS rose out of violence into prominence, America's ultrarightists muttered venomously about "so many Jews" in the country's radical movement. However, sober statistics show that in June 1969, at the point of the Weathermen's emergence, only five per cent of the 350,000 Jewish college and university students in America were in the New Left. It was estimated that in the SDS leadership at no time did the Jewish members occupy more than one-third of those positions. In June 1969, of the 11 national officers of the SDS, only two were Jewish, while one was half-Jewish.

Jews and non-Jews alike were, in many cases, talented and colorful, yet the two leaders who usually received the most attention were of Jewish origin. These were—and still are, somewhere in the underground—Bernardine Dohrn and Mark Rudd.

III

Bernardine Dohrn, born in 1942, was the daughter of Bernard Ohrnstein, a Hungarian Jew, and his Swedish-descended wife, who in her youth had been a secretary.[3] The father, a credit manager, had changed the name to Dohrn (the last letter of his first name added to the first four letters of his family name). In her radical years Bernardine would sneer at this bit of Americanization; still, she herself never went back to Ohrnstein.

When she was eight the father moved the family, including another daughter, from north of Chicago to a Milwaukee suburb, where Bernardine had a perfectly routine middle-class schooling and upbringing. She was at one time an enthusiastic member of Future Nurses, at another the editor of her high-school paper, and nearly always a winner of good grades.

For college she went first to Miami University at Oxford, Ohio, 1959-61, but then transferred to the University of Chicago to be closer to her family, who had by then moved to Chicago, and because of the rheumatic fever that troubled her in Ohio.

She was still far from a radical and only a tentative liberal. Her thoughts and work centered on her studies. After gaining a bachelor of arts degree in 1963, she began taking courses for a master's degree in history. But an awareness of social problems was increasingly affecting her, and in the autumn of 1964 she changed her studies to law. She would be a lawyer to help the downtrodden.

During her law-school years she worked in an antipoverty program in New York, then in Martin Luther King's integration program in the suburbs of Chicago and as a legal aide for ghetto rent-strikers. She also met and made friends with some SDS activists. Upon graduating from law school in June 1967, she decided against taking a bar examination and starting out on a lawyer's usual career. Instead, she plunged into radical work full time.

That fall she moved to New York to join the legal staff of the leftist National Lawyers Guild. No longer a mere liberal Democrat, she was busy with the defense of various radical organizations, including the Communist Party. Some SDS personalities came to her with requests for legal advice and help. Drawing ever closer to the SDS, by February 1968 she was not only a member, but a leader in the Students for a Democratic Society.

In the spring of that year, the draft resistance movement occupied her. In April the assassination of Martin Luther King, along with the immediate explosion of rioting blacks in a number of American cities, inflamed her rebelliousness. In May, in the second riot at Columbia University, she was at its barricades.

In his perceptive book *SDS*, Kirkpatrick Sale sums up the Bernardine Dohrn of this period as "a first-generation radical, campus-oriented, drawn more to the new-working-class analysis, sympathetic to the new youth culture, a supporter of the resistance strategies, and strongly behind the impulses to revolution as they expressed themselves during the spring." On June 14 she was elected Inter-Organizational Secretary of the SDS. At that election meeting, someone in the crowd below called out: "Do you consider yourself a Socialist?" She shot back from the stage: "I consider myself a revolutionary Communist."

That is, not formally a member of any Communist Party, either pro-Moscow or pro-Peking, but a fresh breed that would perhaps turn this SDS into a brand-new and much purer revolutionary force.

Soon she was the best known of all the SDS leaders; surely the most famous female in America's New Left. Young women longed to be like her. Young men were converted to, or strengthened in, their new revolutionary faith as they looked at and listened to this attractive, dynamic woman, this Joan of Arc of a history being made right before their eyes. As she stood or sat on those innumerable platforms, her shapely legs fascinated even the most monkish of the SDS males. "The most beautiful legs I have ever seen," one man after another observed. She had no lack of lovers to choose from, and choose she did. Later, in her terrorist phase, she would defeminize herself, her clothes becoming nondescript, and even her magnetic legs disappearing in dirty, worn, and sometimes torn jeans. It was she, more than anyone else in the ultraleft leadership, who carried a significant part of the SDS ranks into the new terrorist phenomenon called the Weathermen.

Mark Rudd, although superficially the more flamboyant of the two, in fact had less compelling charm and power.[4] He had first appeared on the scene as a gadfly in early 1967 when, as a Columbia sophomore and an ordinary SDS member, he had helped stage rallies and circulate antiadministration petitions. Yet, as a junior in the spring of 1968, he burst forth as the leader of the mass revolt at the venerable university.

His background was similar to that of Bernardine, except that both his parents were Jewish. The second son of a prosperous upper-middle-class real-estate dealer who was also a proud lieutenant colonel in the United States Army reserves, Mark had a conventional, happy childhood and a relatively uneventful adolescence in the suburbia of Maplewood, New Jersey. He made good grades in his classes, was a Boy Scout, and had many friends.

Entering Columbia University in the fall of 1965, he discovered the SDS with awe and delight, but it was not until the next year, as a sophomore, that he indulged his revolutionary tastes by becoming actively involved in radical politics. By the spring of 1968, he was the chairman of the SDS's Columbia chapter, with its agenda of violence. Suddenly, as the riots flared up and persisted, his name and photograph were on front pages and television screens across the country.

He was loud-mouthed, brazen, dramatic, threatening, and chillingly successful as he led the enraged and demanding student force into two prolonged episodes. It was then that the news came from France of a similar student uprising that nearly toppled President Charles de Gaulle and the entire ruling class of that nation. Although France did not collapse but reeled back from the brink, and the Columbia riots caused an ugly scar but no real end of America's System, the respite seemed but temporary. One more effort, and the Red triumph would be within sight. "One More Columbia" and "One More Columbia" was now an occasional slogan—an echo of Guevara's impassioned cry for one more Vietnam and yet another Vietnam.

For the rest of 1968 and much of 1969 Mark Rudd continued in the forefront of turbulence. Yet it was not he who initiated the June 1969 split and the Weathermen's emergence. He was there, at Chicago's Coliseum, loud and emotional but unclear; Bernardine Dohrn, though emotional, was very clear. She was the battering ram to terror. Rudd only followed her.

But from then on, as the Weathermen decided on their so-called National Action, on their go-for-broke try for terror and revolution, Rudd resumed his cross-country travels, this time with a new purpose. On countless stages he exhorted students and other young to be ready for this bloody National Action. He shouted and blasphemed as he orated. Between his obscenities he bragged that he was carrying a gun and recommended that everyone in his audiences should start this revolutionary pistol-toting. From New York to San Francisco he was the most visible of all the Weathermen.

He now dressed the proletarian—workshirt, Lenin-like cloth cap, leather jacket *à la* Cheka, and heavy boots.

Between their ceaseless trips, he and his fellow Weathermen and -women lived in apartments as collectives, in disorder as well as in constant excitement, their life style insisting on the avoidance of "man-woman hang-ups," the solution being in the everybody-sleep-with-everybody dictum, pretending high spirits as they forbade themselves to show jealousy or reluctance or depression. Drugs were used extensively. Infiltrators were feared, and the members of the collectives never stopped checking one another for loyalty. They had good reason: FBI agents were everywhere.

26

The Days of Rage and After

Dohrn, Rudd, and other Weathermen leaders decided that National Action would begin on October 8, 1969, in Chicago. They chose Chicago because of what had happened there the year before, during the Democratic Party's National Convention and the Grant Park rally, where thousands of antiwar, anti-System protestors had gathered and battled the Chicago police.

The Weathermen planned to put the Establishment "up against the wall." The Weathermen leaders had by then traveled to Cuba, where they had met a number of North Vietnamese. A few had journeyed to North Vietnam itself. In both places the North Vietnamese had told them that America had certainly lost the war in Southeast Asia and that there was to be a revolution in the United States. The Weathermen not only concurred but also were supremely certain that they, the Weathermen, would start this war at home—a civil war. Ché's One More Vietnam would be in America's own streets. It would result in the same Red victory now so patently clear in Vietnam.

They studied English translations of Red Chinese and Vietnamese guerrilla manuals, which taught that any nation's revolutionary guerrillas must have the overwhelming sympathy and support of the given country's masses, that the guerrillas must move among the masses as naturally as fish in the sea. The Weathermen were totally confident that the American masses formed such a friendly sea.

Weathermen organizers tirelessly spoke at colleges and on occasion even at high schools. Too, they thought they had successfully recruited young militant workers. From around the country, organizers boasted to the leaders that thousands upon thousands of young men and women were eager to come to Chicago in October for the decisive days of rage.

And this is what the Weathermen's National Action was now called: Days of Rage.[1]

II

The very first of the four Days of Rage was a disappointment to both the leaders and the rank-and-file members. Not the promised thousands, but only some 200 showed up, and not from all over the nation, as expected, but chiefly from Chicago itself, as well as from a nearby state or two, with but a slim representation from farther away.

So they gathered, in a queer assortment of ready-for-battle outfits, an especially strange sight being their protective headgear—which included borrowed hard hats, motorcycle helmets, and even a football helmet. This time they came not to Grant Park but to Lincoln Park, farther north in the city, adjacent to some of Chicago's affluent neighborhoods. Strong detachments of police waited nearby, poised for swift counteraction.

As dusk deepened, one member of the crowd remarked nervously: "This is an awful small group to start a revolution." At about nine o'clock that Wednesday evening, Bernardine Dohrn picked up a bullhorn for a pep talk.

So that these North American revolutionaries would be properly inspired, she reminded the ragtag rows and clusters of her young that this day was the second anniversary of Ché Guevara's death. But, as Kirkpatrick Sale aptly commented, "for those who remembered how Guevara had died, at the head of a tiny band without friends in a foreign territory he didn't know and surrounded by hostile police and soldiers, the evocation of his name was probably something less than cheering right then."

At 10:25, as no more reinforcements had arrived from anywhere, the long-delayed signal was given. The small mob charged out of Lincoln Park, yelling a wild range of slogans, some screaming Arab whoops they had learned from that much-admired film, *Battle of Algiers*. They were brandishing metal bars, blackjacks, lead pipes, sticks, cloth bags filled with pennies, cans of Mace, and other makeshift weapons. but apparently they had few, if any, guns.

Thus, what the first Day (Night, rather) of Rage amounted to was neither shooting nor barricade-building but plain counterculture trashing—smashing windows, damaging cars, and otherwise destroying property.

The waiting police, full of hate for the long-haired rebels, pent up with the wish of revenge for the previous year's Grant Park near-defeat, were nonetheless caught off guard. They had expected the Weathermen to go wild in Lincoln Park itself; the police had prepared themselves for a charge into the rebels. But here the revolutionaries were barging out of the park pell-mell, rampaging down the prosperous streets of the Gold Coast, breaking plate-glass windows, hitting at isolated cops. One military-like column amid the chaotic mob carried the Vietcong flag, and other clusters and bands in the crowd yelled and chanted:

"Ho! Ho! Ho Chi Minh! Dare to struggle, dare to win!"

"Bring the war home!"

"Revolution's begun! Off the pig! Time to pick up the gun! Off the pig!" (the Panther chant).

Windows of banks, hotels, restaurants, and apartments were crashing to the pavements under the impact of their stones and metal bars; car shields were smashed and splintered; innocent bystanders and people pulled from cars were pushed down to the sidewalks and roads and manhandled.

The police, recovering, struck back. They captured some 30 Weathermen, but the others—including the leaders—broke away, zigzagged along the streets, and split into two groups, each bellowing, trashing, wreaking damage.

Thus the battle went on till midnight, the wail of police sirens and the piercing screech of store burglar alarms adding to the shouts of the attackers, the cries of the hurt, and the crashing of smashed glass. When the Weathermen finally broke off into swirling groups, running in all directions, police counted 28 of their own injured, many Weathermen injured, six of them slightly, and 68 arrested, of whom 25 were women.

Bernardine Dohrn, although in the battle, escaped arrest. Mark Rudd avoided capture by not being in the fight at all. He stayed behind in Lincoln Park, not in any rough front-line clothes but in a conventional suit, and, at the first sign of restored calm, he softly disappeared into the night—as Sale put it, "a general who it seems had decided not to march with his troops."

Thursday and Friday, the ninth and tenth of October, though officially counted by the Weathermen as the second and third Days of Rage, were comparatively quiet. On Thursday there was in fact a procession of some 70 women, calling themselves "the militia." Although they shouted militant speeches and songs, at first they were not violent. Their leaders, however, began to scream and kick at the nearest policemen, but this, too, lasted only a few minutes. The police quickly herded them off to prison, and pushed the lesser offenders in the women's "militia" to a subway, where they looked quite sheepish and morose, their helmets in their shaking hands.

At various times during those two milder days there were a few other demonstrations. The SDS who were not Weathermen, with some Black Panthers and Young Lords assisting in a minor way, held three brief street rallies and a sizable march, but these were nonviolent. When the police recognized and arrested a few Weathermen among them, the rest did not intervene with any attempt at rescue. The Weathermen were truly on their own, fish out of any friendly sea.

The Weathermen leaders who were still at large held a marathon two-day discussion of their dilemma, and at last decreed one more battle for Saturday morning.

This fourth Day of Rage again mustered some 200 men and women—the arrested, injured, and disillusioned were replaced by new arrivals. This time they would plunge into the downtown shopping area, the Loop. The police were there, watching the Weathermen gather at their starting point. Suddenly they swooped down to arrest several leaders, among them Mark Rudd. Despite the dime-store fake mustache, he was easily recognized and apprehended.

The thousands of policemen were now backed up by 2,500 National Guardsmen, who, called to duty, were issued ammunition and kept ready for this battle—as it turned out, the last.

Now the Weathermen, even though bereft of some of their leaders taken by arrests, charged through the crowds of shoppers. Again they smashed store and restaurant windows and hit at parked and passing cars and taxis. They cut and wove their offensive through the Saturday traffic, striking at the police with fists, chains, bars, lead pipes, and other improvised weapons. The police fought into their midst, chased and captured and beat them, then hauled them to the waiting paddy wagons. The men of law and order were helped by sundry lay patriots, among them Chicago's Assistant Corporation Counsel Richard Elrod. In his fury he lunged headlong into a Weatherman, but instead hit a wall, breaking his neck. Elrod was paralyzed from his waist down.

Damages running into millions of dollars resulted; scores of policemen were injured, but none so seriously as Elrod the volunteer. No National Guardsmen were in that Saturday battle—they were not needed after all. The police were enough to do the job.

Of the Weathermen, many were injured and many arrested, including most of the leaders. Bail bonds of $2,200,000 were required, of which sum the immediate need was for $234,000. The Weathermen treasury was exhausted at once. Dismayed parents and stoic friends had to make up the difference.

Indictments were quick to come, but they were not followed by any significant trials and sentences, for the leaders, once on bail, fled. Within a few months they were all underground.

Most of the lesser Weathermen were let go after brief imprisonment; the longest time served in jail was 112 days by a man awaiting trial, which resulted in his release. Even the New York Weatherman

Brian Flanagan, age 22, accused of causing Elrod's paralysis, was in time acquitted.

III

As the Weathermen leaders prepared to go underground, they did not seem to realize the futility of their Days of Rage and of their terroristic program in general.

Certainly they failed to understand the reasons for their October fiasco. They still thought they had seen a mighty and ever-growing revolutionary mood involving ever-increasing numbers of activists and sympathizers, the revolutionary condition that Mao's and Ho's and Guevara's guerrilla warfare manuals had described as the prelude to terrorist success. By that time, in late 1969, several nationwide American campus polls indicated that about one million students considered themselves revolutionaries, and the Weathermen believed themselves to be the vanguard of this vast mass. But during the Days of Rage, where were the college and high school students, and those young workers both white and black on whom the Weathermen had counted? Why had they not followed the Weathermen?

One of the answers came in a press release on October 10 from the other part of the SDS, at its national headquarters in Boston, in the form of a denunciation of the Weathermen and their Days of Rage. Such appalling activity was sheer adventurism, the release declared. Worse: these Weathermen were "provocateurs" and "police agents" who had in that Chicago rampage attacked even some proletarian cab drivers. It said that no SDS chapter supported the Weathermen, these "hate-the-people lunatics," and that they had no right whatever to the use of the honored SDS name.

Another reaction was from the Black Panthers, who mocked the Weathermen as "a bunch of Custers," having undertaken as they did a pseudoheroic action with no thought of strategy or logistics.

The Weathermen were not as yet underground; they still postured publicly in their periodical, *New Left Notes*. In its very next issue they proclaimed their Days of Rage a resounding success, a turning of the corner, to be followed by more such onslaughts. "Pig Amerika—beware! "

That Christmas of 1969, at Flint, Michigan, the Weathermen held their last open meeting. It was a noisy, slaphappy gathering of their National Council—they called it the War Council. There they finally decided to forget the bail money, not to appear at trials, and to actually go underground.

They called their Flint sessions "wargasms." Between speeches they sang songs out of the Weathermen's songbook:

To the tune of "Nowhere Man" of the Beatles:

> He's a real Weatherman
> Ripping up the mother land,
> Making all his Weatherplans
> For everyone!
> Knows just what he's fighting for—
> Victory for people's war.
> Trashes, bombs, kills pigs and more:
> The Weatherman!

And in honor of the jolly season, to the tune of "White Christmas":

> I'm dreaming of a white riot
> Just like the one October Eighth,
> When the pigs took a beating
> And things started leading
> To armed war against the state.

> We're heading now toward armed struggle
> With ev'ry cadre line we write.*
> May you learn to struggle and fight
> Or the world will off you 'cause you're white.

Their speeches were filled with exuberance. Mark Rudd orated: "It's a wonderful feeling to hit a pig. It must be a really wonderful feeling to kill a pig or blow up a building." John Jacobs, of the original Columbia University rioters and erstwhile lover of Bernardine Dohrn, exclaimed: "We're against everything that's 'good and decent' in honky America. We will burn and loot and destroy. We are the incubation of your mother's nightmare."

And Bernardine capped the proceedings by extolling the recent Tate-La Bianca killings perpetrated by the drugged gang of Charles Manson and his girls in Los Angeles: "Dig it: first they killed those pigs, then they ate dinner in the same room with them, then they even shoved a fork into the victims' stomach. Wild!"

Kirkpatrick Sale, in his pages on the Flint meeting, adds: "In later months Dohrn would come to regret this adulation (her account of the facts, incidentally, is wrong), not the least because Charles Manson was obviously a cruel master of a virtual harem where women were

---

* The word "cadre" was originally used by Lenin and his entourage to denote Communist Party personnel. In time it came to mean anything that applied to the tried-and-true revolutionary.

treated as objects with less value than cow dung; but at the time Manson seemed the perfect symbol of American values stood on their head, and this is what the Weathermen were after."[2]

From then on, into the early and middle 1970s, the Weathermen did not stage new riots or engage in open confrontations. Instead, they concentrated on stealthy bombings from the underground.

A number of them had by then learned enough about dynamite and detonators to establish bomb-making shops in well-hidden basements. They grimly jested that, of all their college courses, chemistry was now proving the most relevant. As early as 1968 and all through 1969 teams of two or three and more of such young terrorists planted and exploded bombs against many targets, on campuses and at induction centers and other governmental buildings.

They had been careful not to injure people, either warning them by telephone messages or other communications in enough time for them to clear the endangered sites, or by making sure to time their explosions for night hours when no one was likely to be present.

Through the school year of 1969-70 there were hundreds of bombings on and off campuses all over the nation, many of them directly attributable to the Weathermen, but others only inspired or claimed by them. Most of the targets were military and other governmental buildings, but many were banks and corporate offices. Sometimes, however, they went after symbols: Two days before their Rage, they blew up the Chicago statue of a noble policeman that commemorated the Haymarket Riot of 1886.

The ghastliest and most sensational explosion occurred in March 1970, when three Weathermen—one woman and two men—were blown to death through error.

This happened in the late morning of the sixth of March, in the expensive and well-appointed four-story house at 18 West Eleventh Street in Greenwich Village, New York City. Its owner, James Platt Wilkerson, a wealthy radio-station owner, was away on a Caribbean vacation. In his absence, his 25-year-old daughter Cathlyn, a Swarthmore College graduate of 1966, had invited or allowed her fellow Weathermen to use the basement of the house for bomb-making.

That morning Cathlyn Wilkerson was in the front of the house, perhaps asleep. With her was Kathy Boudin, age 26, a Bryn Mawr graduate of 1965, the daughter of Leonard B. Boudin, a widely known New York lawyer for radical causes. Both survived the blast that ripped through the building. Both were last seen running away. To this writing, they are somewhere in the underground.

Three others were far less fortunate. Ted Gold, age 23, a Columbia graduate of 1969, known mainly for organizing Teachers for a Democratic Society, on this morning was either reading or puttering around in the luxurious Wilkerson study; and Terry Robbins and Diana Oughton were in the basement's workshop, busy making one more bomb. Terry, 21, was a Kenyon College dropout. Diana, 28, had been graduated from Bryn Mawr in 1963.

On the shelves and the floor all around Terry and Diana were sticks of dynamite, alarm clocks to be used for timing, batteries, wires, blasting caps, and completed bombs filled with roofing nails and explosives. A few minutes before the noon hour, either Terry or Diana or both must have connected a wrong wire to the bomb they were making. A tremendous roar was heard for blocks.

Much of the building collapsed instantly; everything was in smoke and dust. Two more blasts followed as the gas mains burst into flames. Window glass in many homes nearby shattered; people came running and shouting.

In the exploded house Diana Oughton and Terry Robbins perished at once. Diana's torso was found four days later, every bone in it broken, the flesh pierced by roofing nails meant for bombs, the head and hands missing. As for Terry, no sizable enough part of his body was ever identifiable, and his death was established only from the messages sent to the surface from the Weathermen's underground.

Late on the night of March 6 the body of Ted Gold was found, crushed and mangled under the old, heavy beams. The coroner's verdict was "asphyxia from compression."

IV

That spring of 1970 the wave of violence crested. The invasion of Cambodia by American troops set off new riots, demonstrations, marches, and bombings on the campuses and at large. On May 4, at Kent State University in Ohio, four white students were killed by the National Guard and nine wounded, including a youth who was paralyzed for life from the waist down. On May 14, at Jackson State College in Mississippi, police killed two black students and wounded 12. From their deep underground the Weathermen cheered the tumult and the blood as their prophecy coming true at last: This was really a nationwide revolution.

They would contribute to it; they would accelerate it. In June the Weathermen succeeded in bombing the New York City police headquarters, causing property damage but no human casualties. In August, in Madison, Wisconsin, a group of terrorists exploded the Army Mathematical Research Center, killing a graduate student who had stayed late that night to work on his thesis. The group called itself the New Year's Gang and said they were a cell of the Weathermen. The latter did not know of this group's existence until after the explosion, but gladly accepted these terrorists' allegiance. Karl (Karelton) Armstrong, one of the Gang's four bombers, was eventually captured, tried, and sentenced to 23 years in prison. His brother Dwight Armstrong and the Gang's two other members, David Fine and Leo Burt, remained at large. On January 7, 1976, Fine was recognized and arrested by the FBI in California.

A terrorist group, not definitely connected with the Weathermen but certainly sharing their program and methods, came into the headlines in late September 1970 in Boston. This formation consisted of two female college students and three men, former convicts who participated in campus programs specially set up for their rehabilitation (one said he wanted to become a lawyer). The five raided a National Guard armory for weapons, robbed a bank of $26,000, and machine-gunned a policeman to death.

In 1970, having jumped her bail, Jane Alpert, who was one of those responsible for the bombings by the Sam Melville terror group, found refuge in the Weather Underground.[3] That year, to improve security, the Weatherpeople disbanded their collectives. Instead, they would operate in small cells of a few terrorists each; only they would not use the word "cell," for it was a translation of the Soviet Communist *yacheika*. Now, in honor of Guevara, the Weathermen called each underground team by the Spanish word he had liked and used—*foco*. They also spoke of their units as "families" and "tribes."

On September 12, 1970, the Weathermen varied their activities by arranging Timothy Leary's escape from the San Luis Obispo minimum-security prison in California. He was taken up the Coast to Seattle, where Bernardine Dohrn, among other hiding leaders, greeted the ex-Harvard psychologist. Later they took him to Chicago, where, with a false passport, he boarded a plane and flew to Paris. From there he went on to Algiers to be with Cleaver.

In October, from their underground, the Weathermen announced a "fall offensive." Once more the police statue of Chicago's Haymarket Square fame was exploded. Courthouses in California and on Long Island were bombed, to show the Weathermen's concern for political prisoners in America—or so it was declared from the underground. A half-dozen other explosions across the country, with damage totaling a half-million dollars, were ascribed to or claimed by the Weathermen.

Sometime before that October, Mark Rudd was demoted from leadership in the central Weatherbureau underground. It was rumored that his lamentable male chauvinism and general arrogance had become for the *foco* "families" too much to bear. From December 1970 on, the Weathermen officially signed themselves as Weatherpeople.

There were, in 1971-72, also Weatherpeople-engineered explosions in San Francisco, Albany, and even at the Pentagon in Washington, which were proudly publicized as having been caused by the Weatherpeople. These acts and the stories about them kept up the myth and mystery of Dohrn and her group.

From time to time, it was reported, some of these terrorists surfaced momentarily, only to disappear. Mark Rudd was once seen at a public lecture, calm and almost defiant. Someone spotted Bernadine Dohrn in Boston in the spring of 1973, looking prim and neat, like any office secretary, which perhaps she then was.

In their infrequent communications to the aboveground, some Weatherpeople boasted that they were now living in residential neighborhoods, unsuspected by their new conventional friends, and that on occasion they would watch with these new neighbors and companions television newscasts about explosive activities that they, Weatherpeople, were responsible for.

Early in 1974, from their hiding places, the Weatherpeople relayed their admiring approval of the kidnapping of Patricia Hearst by the Symbionese Liberation Army. Two San Francisco newspapers received identical copies of a letter signed by Bernadine Dohrn, praising Patty Hearst's kidnapping as a telling blow at the System.

In late July 1974, a 158-page book was published by the Weather Underground entitled *Prairie Fire*. It was not for general sale, although on one day that summer, at least some copies of the book were briefly sold in front of a few bookstores in New York. The cover letter accompanying the book stated that it was being sent "clandestinely to thousands of people's organizations, collectives and projects." A few newspapers also received the book.

In *Prairie Fire*, the authors, while vowing to continue to carry the Red flag, nevertheless indulged in a bit of rare soul-searching and self-accusation: "We attacked those who could not come along the whole way. We did not learn from meaningful criticism from comrades. . . . Now the movement is disorganized, divided and defensive, unable to fulfill the whole potential to learn and to lead. In the movement the times are hard."

And yet marvelous possibilities still lay ahead: "The continuing social crises are accelerating the process of revolutionary consciousness.'' The book cited the activities of the Black Liberation Army and the Symbionese Liberation Army, with their brave and bloody exploits in "the development of the armed struggle and political consciousness"—this despite the undoubted fact that by July 1974 both Armies had suffered their defeats and were, like the Weatherpeople, only remnants in retreat and hiding.

In March 1975, the Weather Underground sent up to the surface a 32-page magazine called *Osawatomie*. The name was to honor the site of a battle in 1856 where John Brown and his 30 abolitionists (the editors explained), "using guerrilla tactics, beat back an armed attack by 250 slavery supporters." In *Osawatomie,* the Weather Underground claimed credit for some 25 terrorist bombings in the five years of its illegal existence. These included, among others, the bombing of the International Telephone and Telegraph offices in New York (September 1973) and of the State Department in Washington (January 1975).

In February 1975, the KPFA radio station in Berkeley received from the underground a tape with poems by Bernardine Dohrn, Kathy Boudin, and Cathy Wilkerson. In mid-April, *The New York Times* received through the mail, and featured on its prestigious Op-Ed page of the eighteenth, a long article by Bernardine Dohrn in which she glowed with happiness over the defeat of South Vietnam. Her outburst closed with what she laid down as "a law of revolution: The future will be what we the people struggle to make it."

In mid-November 1974, Jane Alpert repented and surrendered, and in January 1975 was sentenced to 27 months in prison. One of her codefendants in the 1969 bombing case, Patricia Swinton, was found and arrested in Vermont on March 12, 1975. Two weeks later, on a street in Philadelphia, Susan Saxe, a fugitive in the 1970 Boston terrorist holdup (in which a policeman was killed) was recognized and arrested. Miss Swinton's eventual trial ended in her acquittal, mainly on technicalities. Miss Saxe's trial was set for September 15, 1976.

But Bernardine Dohrn's name was still on the Ten-Most-Wanted-List of the FBI. Neither she nor any other Weather fugitive leader would repent and give up or could be found and caught. A documentary film *Underground*, shot in great secrecy in Los Angeles in early 1975 and first shown in New York in May 1976, contained interviews with five Weatherpeople, among them Bernardine Dohrn, Cathlyn Wilkerson, and Kathy Boudin. A curious bit of her own aberration was revealed by Bernardine as she contrasted her comfortable middle-class childhood and youth with her present armed underground existence: "I was more afraid growing up than I am now. Then it was paranoid; now it's real fear."

V

It is believed by some that, from 1966 on, the American people, in their growing opposition to the war in Vietnam, were encouraged by the violent campaigns of the Black Panthers, the Weathermen, and other terrorists. Yet, if anything, the bombs and other excesses in the latter 1960s and early 1970s proved to be counterproductive. By 1972 the reaction against terror and chaos manifested itself in the alarm of the population at large, of the so-called silent majority, which then went to the polls to vote overwhelmingly for Nixon's second term in the White House.[4]

The general American reaction in 1968-72 against our further involvement in Southeast Asia was fed not by the Black Panthers and the Weathermen, not so much by any moral outrage against the war aroused or fanned by violent rebels, but by the pragmatic realization that the war was hopeless, that we had lost, or were then losing the war, and that it would be best to cut our already tremendous losses by bowing out.

But one important political phenomenon did stem from all the violence on America's campuses and streets. It was not the radical result the black and white revolutionaries would have wished it to be, not the longed-for downfall of the System; but rather, it was Nixon's fright, his siege mentality. It panicked him into his—and his aides'—stumble into the Watergate morass, and finally, in August 1974, led to his resignation, the first such humiliating abdication in the nearly two centuries of the American Presidency.

A victory for the New Left? Not really. The terrorists had aimed not at this mere changing of the guard. Their aim had been to destroy the guard completely and pull down the entire edifice over which it stood watch. In that far larger design they had failed.

27

The Symbionese and
Patty Hearst

The Symbionese Liberation Army[1] may be seen as a direct heir to the Panther and the Weatherpeople. Chronologically its most sensational activities followed in their wake, when the militancy of the other organizations was on the wane. From November 6, 1973, when the Symbionese murdered Dr. Marcus A. Foster, the black educator in Oakland, to May 17, 1974, when their main contingent was annihilated in the Los Angeles shootout, the SLA filled the headlines that only a short while before had belonged to those earlier activists.

Yet there was one important difference that set the Symbionese apart: Whereas each of the two other groups comprised in the main either blacks or whites—the Panthers and Weathermen collaborating only occasionally and feuding quite often—the Symbionese appeared to be a rare case in which there was harmony between the two races.

The Symbionese Liberation Army took its name from *The Spook Who Sat by the Door*, a novel by Sam Greenlee, published in New York in 1959. The story is about a small terrorist group, the Cobras; the Symbionese made a sinister seven-headed cobra its symbol.

The world "symbiosis," a biological and psychological term used in the novel, pertains to organisms living together for comfort, advantage, or necessity. In its use by the Symbionese Liberation Army it connoted their goal of unity for the depressed and revolutionary minorities. In one of their clumsily phrased public statements the Symbionese themselves explained their "symbiosis" as "a body of dissimilar bodies and organisms living in deep and loving harmony and partnership in the best interest of all within the body," an Army "of the aged, youth and women and men of all races and people." The cobra's seven heads were meant to represent precisely these: the races black, brown, red, yellow, and white; the ages young and old. In actuality, these were far from completely or evenly represented. The SLA was predominantly white and female. There were no elderly or middle-aged in the Army's ranks. All the SLA were in their twenties.

The organization was founded during 1972-73 at Vacaville State Prison, 45 miles northeast of San Francisco, when a few white students at the University of California in Berkeley were being permitted by the prison authorities to visit the Vacaville inmates, ostensibly for the purpose of engaging in group therapy with the black convicts.

As conceived by Vacaville's staff, the prison's program for the inmates' psychological health was sound and, perhaps, effective. Its original link with Berkeley was through Colston Westbrook, a teaching assistant at the University of California, who helped the prison run the program. But the students and dropouts he eventually brought from Berkeley to participate in the activity were intent on teaching Maoism. Soon Westbrook lost control of the Vacaville therapy, and withdrew in disgust and fear.

The change to the left was wrought by three whites. Two were nonstudents: Joseph M. Remiro, 26, was an expert machinist, a former paratrooper, and a Vietnam veteran of two combat tours; Russell J. Little, 23, had been an engineering student in Florida and was now an instructor at Oakland's Peralto Junior College. William Wolfe, 21, was a student. (All three ages are given as of 1973.) Remiro had come to Oakland sometime after 1970, and had begun to organize a chapter of Vietnam Veterans Against the War. In a part of Oakland where it merges with Berkeley, he shared an apartment with Little and Wolfe.

Wolfe, the son of a prominent Pennsylvania physician, after graduating from an elite Eastern preparatory school, came to the University of California at Berkeley in the fall of 1971, enrolling in its Afro-American studies program. Within a short while he regarded himself as an ardent revolutionary. By his new friends Remiro and Little he was affectionately called Willie the Wolf.

All three were involved in the Black Cultural Association, which had units both inside and outside the Vacaville Prison. Its official purpose was to help the inmates in developing their educational skills and their ability, upon release, to cope with the outside world. In the summer of 1972, a spokesman for the Association addressed a black studies class at Berkeley. At the conclusion of his talk, he invited the students to visit the Vacaville Prison with the Association's representatives. It was then that Wolfe, showing intense interest, decided to join the Black Cultural Association. Subsequently he brought Remiro, Little, and other young whites into the group, which had been almost wholly black. It was through these visits and activities that they presently met Donald David DeFreeze, a black Vacaville inmate.

Most of the young whites who joined were ultraleft students and dropouts, members of a commune called Peking Man House, located a short distance from campus. Their living room was adorned with Red Chinese posters; its shelves held an imposing collection of Marxist-Leninist-Maoist books and brochures. The residents, many of them sporting Mao jackets and caps, would devote their evenings to guest lectures and seminars on violent revolutions, though the commune, as an organization, never practiced violence.

But in early 1973, one year after Wolfe's discovery of Peking Man House, he and some of his friends were ready to form a revolutionary group. He came to the House with rapturous tales of the wonderful opportunity at Vacaville. Immediately members of the commune and hangers-on, particularly girls, wanted to join him. Wolfe, Remiro, and Little took a bevy of them to visit Vacaville. Some of the young and shapely women wore mini-skirts: the inmates began to await eagerly the novel rap sessions.

In addition to the prison's methods of therapy, meant to reform the criminals, the clever guests from Berkeley and Oakland employed certain techniques designed to serve their own propaganda and organizational aims.

One of these techniques emerged from someone's suggestion at Peking Man House that what the black prisoners needed was intercourse with the white girl visitors. A number of the girls volunteered. Such service, they agreed, would assuage damage done to the blacks by capitalism and racism; for the girls felt they knew all about the uses and joys of the flesh. Some were lesbians, others bisexual, and still others were active heterosexuals. Of the two latter categories, some girls—before their philanthropic visits to Vacaville—had relished sex with black men keenly, often boasting of it to their friends, both female and male.

High on the list of the Vacaville recipients of the girls' favors was Donald David DeFreeze.

II

DeFreeze had an early preprison history of mental disturbance. Born in November 1943, the eldest of eight children, he grew up in the black ghetto of Cleveland, Ohio. Dropping out of school in the ninth grade, he ran away from home at 14; he already had a fascination for firearms, and this was noted in his childhood and youth records.

One dark evening he was stopped for riding a lightless bicycle, and held when a bomb was found in the bike's basket. In 1965, halting him on a freeway ramp, the police confiscated a .22-caliber rifle, a tear-gas bomb, an eight-inch knife, some gunpowder, blasting caps, wiring, and a security officer's badge. He explained that he needed this arsenal for protection from criminals. His arrests for bomb-possession and receiving stolen property were interlarded with periods of parole.

During the 1960s, DeFreeze, though a bully and a criminal, was thoroughly nonpolitical. In Watts and other parts of Los Angeles, between his stays in prison, he attacked and robbed fellow blacks. Once, after bedding a black prostitute, he refused to pay her fee; instead he beat the woman viciously and then took her money. Often, when caught by the police, he made deals of milder treatment for himself in return for turning in his black pals. But in 1969, convicted of armed robbery and assault, he was given a jail sentence of from five years to life.

At Vacaville, for some three years, from 1969 to 1972, DeFreeze spent much of the time as one of the subjects in the prison's psychiatric diagnosis and treatment program. In the fall of 1972, he was transferred to Soledad Prison. His behavior was apparently thought to be good, for there he was made a trusty. But on March 5, 1973, he escaped by simply walking away from a work detail. He was then 29 years old.

That March day he just kept on walking north, hitchiking the 110 miles to Oakland, where he contacted Little and Wolfe, who moved him to Berkeley and into the apartment and bed of Patricia Soltysik, a college dropout employed as a janitor in a public library. She was white, pretty, 23 years old, aflame with revolutionary zeal, and an ardent bisexual; her female lover was Camilla Hall.

As they and the others in the group clustered around DeFreeze, they praised him for his organizational ideas and for what they said was his amazing knowledge of texts by Marx and Lenin; and they taught him whatever of Maoism he had yet to master. Between these sessions, he prepared tasty (even if occasionally greasy) dishes for Patricia Soltysik and the others, for he liked to cook.

Through that spring and summer the group engaged in quasi-military exercises, Remiro's battle experience of his Vietnam years making him their much-respected instructor. He taught them endurance in the open in all kinds of weather. He trained them in tracking an unsuspecting man or woman on the city streets—the surveillance team was followed by an observer who later analyzed their mistakes or triumphs. He evolved what were for them ingenious techniques, which included the use of telephone booths as rendezvous points, and the ways a tape recorder could be used in communicating. On Sunday mornings, at Peking Man House, he held a class in weapons handling.

At first he worked with BB guns, but later on he brought MI carbines, shotguns, and revolvers. For shooting practice he took them to a commercial range, and was most patient with them as he molded them into excellent marksmen and markswomen. All told, there were ten of them.

III

It was in the summer of 1973 that the Symbionese organization was solemnly formed. DeFreeze was its black leader; Wolfe and the other eight members were white. On August 21 they prepared a 2,000-word statement of the Army's purposes. Entitled "The Symbionese Liberation Army of Revolutionary War and Symbionese Program," the document listed 16 goals and many slogans, such as, "To die a race and be born a nation is to become free." The writers vowed:

> Therefore, We of the Symbionese Federation and the S.L.A. DO NOT under the rights of human beings submit to the murder, oppression and exploitation of our children and people and do under the rights granted to the people under the Declaration of Independence of the United States, do now by the rights of our children and people and by Force of Arms and with every drop of our blood, Declare Revolutionary War against the Fascist Capitalist Class, and all their agents of murder, oppression and exploitation.

In late 1973 and early 1974, as the SLA burst into the world's headlines, a number of other leaders and prominent members, along with DeFreeze, Remiro, Little, and Wolfe, became known to the public.

William Taylor Harris, 29, fought in Vietnam, and at the Bloomington campus of Indiana University was one of the chief organizers of radical politics in the late 1960s. A friend said ironically that, in addition to his revolutionary itch, Bill Harris had "his need to attract a nice apolitical sort of dippy sorority girl."

Emily Montague Schwartz of Clarendon Hills, Illinois, was just such an Alpha Chi Omega sister, described as "generally a sweet, Chicago suburb kid," who at college met Bill Harris and succumbed to his charm. Marrying him, she embraced his revolutionary activism with no reservations. In the fall of 1972 she came with him to Berkeley, where they joined a revolutionary organization called Venceremos (not affiliated with those earlier Venceremos Brigades that went to Cuba). That summer they became members of the newly formed Symbionese Liberation Army. Later Emily was most assiduous about visiting Vacaville and other prisons to aid in organizational work. Unlike the other girls who went to bed with DeFreeze, she took her intercourse with him very seriously. To her father in Indiana she wrote: "I am in love with a beautiful black man who's conveyed to me the torture of being black in this country." She explained that her husband understood: "Bill and I have changed our relationship so it no longer confines us, and I am enjoying relationships with other men." At the group's end in 1974 she was 27.

Angela DeAngelis Atwood, 25 in 1974, and her husband Gary preceded the Harrises in the move from Bloomington to Berkeley, and Angela—but not Gary—followed them to the Symbionese. Gary left her in June 1973, when he returned to Bloomington to study law. Their marriage broke up and she slept with Joe Remiro, whose weapons class she had joined.

When Angela was 14, at home in neat North Haledon near Paterson, New Jersey, 20 miles from New York City, she became the center of strength in her family upon the death of her mother, who had been a zealous civic worker and an amateur athlete. Angel (the final "a" was usually dropped as they fondly talked of her) took care of her younger sister and brother and her widowed father, Lawrence DeAngelis, a minor official of the Teamsters' Union. While he was struggling to lift the brood from the lower middle class, she, as surrogate mother, held them together. At school Angel, with something of her late mother's energy and concerns, was the indefatigable joiner and leader: captain of the cheering squad, president of the Dramatic Club, a busy body in the Catholic Youth Organization, a delegate to the Girls' State of the American Legion, and a member of the Honor Society, the Student Council, and the American Field Service. At the end of her high-school years she was voted "the most school-spirited" of all the girl students.

Admired, sought out, fussed over, and ever on the triumphant move, in 1966 Angel went to Indiana University, where she wanted to continue to be popular and successful. But there she found that the activity of importance was radical politics. Only briefly was she a sorority sister like the fashion-conscious upper-level Emily Schwartz. Now Angel made her quick transition from middle-class platitudes to Red rhetoric, not only to be accepted but also to lead and be applauded.

Nancy Ling Perry, 27, from Santa Rosa, California, the daughter of a furniture dealer, was also a high-school cheerleader. During the 1964 presidential campaign, she was an energetic, vociferous supporter of Barry Goldwater. But her graduate studies at Berkeley veered her sharply to the left and to another way of life. After a brief marriage to a black pianist, she took a series of menial, though sometimes exotic jobs, including one as a topless blackjack dealer at a night club. On joining the Symbionese she gained a reputation as their spiritual and doctrinaire guide, even though the terror group at the height of its activity issued little more than turgid Maoist bombast. Among her many lovers was Russell Little.

Camilla Christine Hall, 29, was the daughter of the Reverend George F. Hall, pastor of St. John's Lutheran Church in Lincolnwood, near Chicago. After majoring in the humanities at the University of Minnesota and mourning the early deaths of her two younger brothers and a sister (from heart and kidney diseases), the big-boned, homely, unhappy girl toiled as a social worker in Duluth and as a counselor to unwed mothers in Minneapolis. A self-styled artist and poet, she lacked feminine traits and was an aggressive, defiant lesbian, proud of the verses she addressed to her women lovers, such as

> I will cradle you
> In my woman hips,
> Kiss you
> With my woman lips,
> Fold you to my heart
> And sing:
> Sister woman,
> You are a joy to me.

Patricia Soltysik, 24, came to Berkeley from a middle-class Catholic family in Goleta, California, a small town in the mountains near Santa Barbara. Her father, a druggist, had divorced her mother, who alone had to bear the burden of raising five daughters and two sons. Patricia, winning a scholarship and settling at Berkeley, was soon in the activist vortex. Eventually she abandoned her studies and became a radical feminist, taking Camilla Hall as her lover, despite Camilla's quiet yet intense resentment of Patricia's occasional male bedmates. In her poems and whispers Camilla tenderly called Patricia Soltysik "Ms. Moon," and Patricia adopted "Mizmoon" as her name. The Symbionese and others on the campus spoke of "Mizmoon" as a Maoist theoretician.

Because of the need of such Symbionese for bravado and play-acting rather than because of the requirements of their conspiratorial plans, they took picturesque code names. DeFreeze would soon be notorious as Cinque. It was DeFreeze's pseudonym that drew the world's sharpest notice. The name had been used before him, by other black radicals. The original Cinque was an African black who led a successful rebellion aboard a slave ship off Cuba's coast in 1839. But it was DeFreeze who gave the name its most recent and widest fame. It has been remarked, however, that DeFreeze (like other black rebels using the name before him) displayed little historical knowledge, for the Cinque of the mid-nineteenth century was not at all an inspiring example. Following his victory, the ex-slave kept the ship and took it to and from Africa to trade in captured brother blacks.

Remiro was called Bo, and Little was named Osceola. Wolfe was not only Willie the Wolf but also Cujo, and in her early June 1974 tape, Patty Hearst lovingly and sadly explained: "Cujo means 'unconquerable.' It is the perfect name for him. Cujo conquered life as well as death by facing them and fighting." She did not say from what language the word came. It sounds Spanish, but it is not to be found in any Spanish dictionary. Either Wolfe or she probably confused it with *cuyo*, the Spanish for a male lover, sweetheart, wooer, beau.

Bill Harris was Tico. His wife Emily was referred to as Yolanda; Angela Atwood, Gelina; Nancy Ling Perry, Fahizah; Camilla Hall, Gabi; and Patricia Soltysik added to her lesbian alias of Mizmoon the Russian revolutionary Zoya, most likely in honor and memory of Zoya Kosmodemyanskaya, the Soviet guerrilla girl who was hanged by her Nazi captors during the Second World War in occupied Russia.

Romanticism was not the only force moving those white intellectuals who made DeFreeze their violent leader and themselves into his dangerous band. There were other factors too. All these terrorists were young, talented, glib, witty and—with the exception of Camilla Hall—quite handsome. All of them could have made their mark in the Establishment, suburbia, exurbia, or at least in some reasonably comfortable stratum of academe. But they were suffering from their childhood and youth traumas, real or fancied; they wished the revenge of bringing the elders and the mighty to their knees; they were depersonalized and sought affirmation of their identities in bloody group action. By seeing and hearing their threats in the media, by watching their own old photos on the screens and the front pages, they felt that now they knew who they really were—the identity crisis was solved, their alienation from their elders' society was no longer a matter of guilt.

In reality, they never got over their sense of guilt. And so, to their finish, they were driven by a kind of desperate, shame-filled suicidal *Todesverlangen*, a yearning for death (to use a thought that can be found in Freud's works).

IV

By the mid-fall of 1973 the Symbionese were ready to kill. On the evening of November 6, election day, in a parking lot, they murdered Marcus A. Foster, black, age 50.

On the seventh and eighth, four letters reached a Berkeley radio station and two San Francisco and Oakland newspapers. All four texts announced that the Tuesday-night attack had been carried out by the undersigned—the Symbionese Liberation Army. They explained the shooting as punishment for the attempts by the late black educator to introduce into the Oakland schools measures combatting truancy and vandalism. Such steps were seen by the Symbionese as efforts to oppress blacks, as ways in which to bring the police into the Oakland schools. The Army's letters, each of which was accompanied by a picture of a deadly seven-headed cobra, threatened more such shooting and retribution in the near future.

To show that they were the murderers of Dr. Foster, the authors of the letters stated that the eight bullets they had pumped into him contained cyanide. This was proof enough. For no one except the murderers, the police, and the doctors who had performed the autopsy knew at the time that the bullets extracted from the man's body had been drilled and packed with cyanide.

Early on the morning of January 10, 1974, a policeman in Concord, near Oakland, during the course of a routine check, was fired on by one of two men in a van. The shot missed its target; other policemen converged on the scene.

The two men in the van were Joe Remiro and Russell Little, who, being overcautious, had driven around Concord aimlessly, to lose whatever police "tail" might have been following them. The erratic driving, however, caused the policeman to stop their van. Little was captured quickly, but Remiro broke away and was caught four hours later. A subsequent search of him produced a .38-caliber German-made automatic pistol. Soon a police ballistics test established that it had been used in the killing of Marcus Foster. In the van the police found Symbionese literature.

This first solid clue to the SLA was followed by more evidence. Later that day of the tenth, what looked like a bungled arson occurred in a three-bedroom house only two blocks from the site of Remiro's and Little's capture. A young white woman had been seen fleeing from the scene just before the fire, and as the police hunted for her in vain, her name became known: she was Nancy Ling Perry.

The police guessed that the singed house had served as Symbionese headquarters. Soon a five-page letter was received by *The San Francisco Chronicle*. Boldly signed by Nancy, the text declared that she had not meant to burn the building down completely: "The house was set on fire by me only to melt away any fingerprints that may have been overlooked. It was never intended that the fire would totally destroy the premises because there was nothing left that was of any consequence to us."

Nonetheless, the police announced that in the flame-licked trash they had found Symbionese notebooks that indicated the terrorists had engaged in surveillance of prominent businessmen in the Bay area, and had marked certain state prison officials and their wives for assassination with cyanide bullets. Among the documents was a map delineating the interior of the Oakland post office and pinpointing the location of a safe.

The police also ascertained that in the weeks prior to January 10, both Russell Little and Nancy Perry had repeatedly traveled to several California jails, where they had visited prisoners who could be defined as revolutionaries. And both Russell and Nancy were identified from photographs by the manager of an apartment building in Oakland as having been among a group who had in the previous fall rented a flat from him, Nancy Ling Perry signing the money order for the rent. The apartment was about a half-mile from the Board of Education parking lot where Dr. Foster was killed.

V

Now their main blow fell.

On Monday evening of February 4, 1974, at 9:20 P.M., a young white woman knocked on the sliding glass patio door of the Berkeley apartment shared by the newspaper heiress Patricia Campbell Hearst and her lover Steven Andrew Weed. Patty was two weeks short of her twentieth birthday; Steven was 26.

The pair lived quietly in their $250-a-month duplex. Though they apparently did not belong to any radical organizations, they did have a small number of avant-garde friends who were leftists without being activists. Patty, pretty and vivacious, was a sophomore majoring in art history at the University of California. Steven, having grown up in the Bay area, had gone to Princeton as a National Merit scholar, and was now working at Berkeley as a teaching assistant in logic at a salary of $400 per month, and attending classes as a graduate student of philosophy. He was tall and thin but not in any way striking of appearance; his mustache hung over his mouth somewhat lumpily, at times even comically.

Patty and Steven had first met when she was 15 and he 21, at an elite school for girls in Hillsborough, her parents' hometown, a suburb of San Francisco. Steven Weed was her mathematics teacher, his first job upon graduation from Princeton. At first she had a girlish crush on him, but this soon grew into what she believed was love. They went to bed. He was not her first man: at 14, with impatient curiosity, she had surrendered her virginity to another man who was then 26.

She liked older, experienced men; and Steven's sophisticated companionship was surely elevating: her grades, poor at the Hillsborough school, improved spectacularly when she came to Menlo College, where she soon stood first in her class. In the fall of 1972 she and Steven transferred to the University of California and moved into their five-room Berkeley duplex. She was then 18.

Her parents were at first shocked. Randolph Apperson Hearst and Catherine Campbell Hearst were not at all mollified by Steven Weed's upper-middle-class Bay background or his talent and perhaps brilliance. But, as with so many of the older generation, they had to accommodate to new mores.

Patty was virtually apolitical and only then beginning to upbraid her father for what she regarded as the stupidity of his newspapers, which, she said, were only for people older than 80. On occasion she would lecture her mother for her conservatism as a regent of the University of California. And yet, gradually, the Hearsts began to tolerate this singular union of their Patty with that "Toothbrush," as they called Steven behind his back—because of his mustache. Eventually Patty and Steven shared occasional dinners with her parents, and even spent weekends with them in their 22-room family mansion at Hillsborough or at the various Hearst ranches and other retreats. Relations were soon cordial rather than strained.

At Berkeley, the young pair's life was placid. They grew tomatoes and zucchini in their back yard, bought and nursed plants, listened to modern music, visited with friends, played touch football, and went to the movies. Much to her parents' relief, Patty and Steven finally decided to get married. Their formal engagement was announced in the press in December, 1973. Patty was already choosing china and silver patterns from Tiffany's. The knock on their door that Monday night in early February drastically changed their lives.

When the door was opened, the young woman visitor turned out to be a stranger. We now know she was Angela DeAngelis Atwood, a Symbionese. She told Patty and Steven that she needed a telephone because of trouble with her car. He declined the request, for she looked suspicious. But immediately behind her loomed two young men, armed. Both intruders appeared to be black, but only one was: Donald DeFreeze. The other, William Harris, had merely blackened his white face.

Steven tried to slam the door. The men pushed him back, barged into the apartment, and seized Patty Hearst.

Putting up a struggle, Steven was flung to the floor, where, face down, he was beaten on the head with a wine bottle.

Weed later said that he saw little of the actual kidnapping of Patty because, having picked himself up from the floor, he fled from the apartment to seek help, and it was then that the abductors dragged Patty down the stairs, in her panties and bathrobe, kicking and screaming, outside to a parked car. She was tied, gagged, and blindfolded. But the gag fell loose, hanging around her neck. She later said that to stop her resistance one of the kidnappers hit her on her left cheek with a rifle butt.

As she was pulled and pushed into the car trunk, she screamed, "Please let me go!" and "Not me!" Neighbors saw and heard the drama. To intimidate them, the abductors blasted their guns into walls, then drove off at a furious speed.

More than two days later, on Thursday morning, February 7, an envelope containing a letter and a Mobil Oil credit card reached the Berkeley radio station KPFA. The card bore the name of Randolph A. Hearst and was proof that the writers were Patty's abductors. It apparently was among the contents of the wallet taken from Weed during the Monday-night beating. The letter was arranged in the following form:

SYMBIONESE LIBERATION ARMY
Western Regional Adult Unit

Communique #3 February 4, 1974

Subject: Prisoner of War

Target: Patricia Campbell Hearst
       Daughter of Randolph Hearst
       corporate enemy of the people

Warrant Order: Arrest and protective custody; and if resistance, execution

Warrant Issued by: The Court of the People

On the above stated date, combat elements of the United Federated Forces of the Symbionese Liberation Army armed with cyanide loaded weapons served an arrest warrant upon Patricia Campbell Hearst. It is the order of this court that the subject be arrested by combat units and removed to a protective area of safety and only upon completion of this condition to notify Unit #4 to give communication of this action. It is the directive of this court that during this action ONLY, no civilian elements be harmed if possible, and that warning shots be given. However, if any citizens attempt to aid the authorities or interfere with the implementation of this order, they shall be executed immediately. The court hereby notifies the public and directs all combat units in the future to shoot to kill any civilian who attempts to witness or interfere with any operation conducted by the peoples forces against the fascist state. Should any attempt be made by authorities to rescue the prisoner, or to arrest or harm any SLA elements, the prisoner is to be executed. The prisoner is to be maintained in adequate physical and mental condition, and unharmed as long as these conditions are adhered to. Protective custody shall be composed of combat and medical units, to safeguard both the prisoner and her health. All communications from this court MUST be published in full, in all newspapers, and all other forms of the media. Failure to do so will endanger the safety of the prisoner. Further communications will follow.

S.L.A.

DEATH TO THE FASCIST INSECT

THAT PREYS UPON THE LIFE OF

THE PEOPLE

Mr. Hearst, advised by the radio station about the message, and having listened to its contents over the telephone, at once went to the broadcasting studio to get the letter. The same day, as directed by the kidnappers, it was made public—the first of the many obediences by the media to the will of the terrorists.

Further communications from the Symbionese, as promised, soon followed.

VI

Through tapes, incorporating Patty's piteous pleas to "Mom, Dad" to comply with her kidnappers, the Symbionese made known their demands. It was to be ransom of a special kind—in the Robin Hood manner, in modern times made famous by the Argentine revolutionaries: before the girl would be released, the Hearsts had to prove their good faith by distributing free food to the poor.

But while the essence of the proposed deal, as voiced by the terror chief DeFreeze, was feasible, its extent was not. DeFreeze's stipulation was that Mr. Hearst provide, in a period of four weeks beginning on February 19, high-quality meat, vegetables, and dairy products worth $70 per person to "all people with welfare cards, Social Security pension cards, food stamp cards, disabled veteran cards, medical cards, parole or probation papers, and jail or bail release slips." Presumably this was to be done in California alone, although other states might also be included then or later—DeFreeze was not clear on this score. For California alone, some statisticians quickly figured out that such a cornucopia would cost Mr. Hearst more than $250 million, while others said it was likely the figure would reach $400 or $500 million.

Mr. Hearst protested that this was beyond his fortune. He said he would spend two million dollars, of which a half million would come from his own funds and the rest from the Hearst Foundation.

A give-away food program was begun in several poor sections of the Bay area. By March 26, the two-million mark had been reached. The terrorists had by then demanded an additional four million dollars in food. The Hearst Corporation agreed to put this new sum in escrow—to be handed out in food once Patty was released. On April 2 the Symbionese declared that the girl would soon be freed; that the time and place of her release would be made known within 72 hours.

But the very next day, on the third, a tape from the Symbionese came to the Berkeley radio station KPFA. It contained two voices, those of Patty and DeFreeze. Now Patty informed the world that she had been converted to the Symbionese beliefs and was their latest and most dedicated member. DeFreeze said that "the prisoner had been freed" but that "she refused to go home."

In her lengthy speech, delivered in a monotone, Patricia Hearst asserted: "I have chosen to stay and fight for the freedom of oppressed people. . . . I have never been forced to say anything on any tape. Nor have I been brainwashed, drugged, tortured, hypnotized, or in any way confused." She then quoted the late George Jackson's words, so well cherished by America's New Left: "It's me, the way I want it, the way I see it."

She renounced and denounced her family and her lover, Steven Weed. "I have changed—grown. I've become conscious and can never go back to the life we left behind. . . . My love has expanded as a result of my experiences to embrace all people. It's grown into an unselfish love for my comrades here, in prison and on the streets." This love meant that "no one is free until we are all free." She did not expect Weed to become a comrade; therefore, good-by to him no less than to her old life.

DeFreeze added: "There is no further need to discuss the release of the prisoner, since she is now a comrade and has been accepted into the ranks of the people's army as a comrade and a fighter." She was no longer Patricia Campbell Hearst; her new revolutionary name was Tania, in honor of the Argentine-born German Communist girl who had joined Ché Guevara in the Bolivian jungle and was killed by soldiers shortly before his own capture and death.

The tape was delivered to Station KPFA with the supplement of a striking color photograph: Tania—née Patricia Hearst—not looking particularly buoyant, in the drab clothes of a fighting revolutionary, a submachine gun in her rather inert hands, the emblem of the Symbionese snake in the immediate background, and the muzzle of one more gun visible against the cobra symbol.

Mr. Hearst met briefly with reporters to express his complete disbelief: "We've had her twenty years. They've had her sixty days, and I don't believe she is going to change her philosophy that quickly and that permanently."

The nation and the world at large stood by in fascination, many aghast. But on some campuses and in numerous pads the girl was a heroine, her latest sensational photograph enlarged into posters, especially numerous at Berkeley, with the huge legend, "Tania, We Love You."

The government seemed powerless; its FBI alone had 125 agents on the case, this not counting the Bay-area police, none at any time even close to the solution of the mystery. In Cleveland the federal men searched the homes of DeFreeze's relatives, but found nothing.

VII

On April 15, Patricia Hearst reappeared in her new role; together with her new comrades, a sawed-off carbine in her hands, swearing profanely, she participated in a bank robbery in San Francisco. The raid was a success that provided the Symbionese with $10,600.

The Hibernia Bank holdup was staged because the Symbionese not only needed fresh funds but, apparently, also needed to prove that the Hearst girl was now a terrorist. It is likely DeFreeze and his group chose the particular bank because it had a surveillance camera that would take motion pictures of them. There was the documentary evidence: Patty in her SLA clothes, her gun at the ready, moving jerkily yet alertly.

On April 24 one more taped message was delivered, this time to San Francisco police headquarters. In this, her strongest statement since her alleged conversion, Patty—calling herself Tania—cursed her father as "pig" and "Adolph," used the same porcine epithet for Steven Weed, and assured everyone that she had been a willing participant in the bank robbery, and that no SLA guns had been trained on her that Monday morning.

As her family wrung their hands in despair, as press readers, television viewers, and radio listeners avidly waited for the next development of the unique show, the question everywhere was asked: Was hers a true conversion or a tragic coercion?

The answer by now is clear: In Patty Hearst's case sizable elements operated in a combination—brainwashing and violence both, skillfully done to a person physically frail and vulnerable, emotionally open to force and a new faith all at once.

We must reject the theory, at one time so prevalent, that Patricia Hearst and perhaps also Steven Weed had been cryptomembers of the Symbionese group, and that the kidnapping was a shrewdly enacted hoax. But there was surely a disposition on Patty's part to be influenced by the eerie theories and actions of her captors. She had in her early youth been rebellious, defying her parents and her school nuns; she had smoked pot even before she met Steven; she had gone against convention by living with him openly. And yet, despite what he and their avant-garde friends might have discussed in her presence, she had been apolitical to a curious extent. She had hardly read the newspapers for world news; it was later recalled of her that in those early 1970s she did not even know who Salvador Allende was.

So, in a sense, she was a blank slate on which her Symbionese captors could with ease write a new set of beliefs. It might have been better for her had she, before February 4, possessed some definite political ideas different from those of the Symbionese. Had she been that sophisticated, she could have possibly withstood their brainwashing.

One of the most important factors in their coercion-*cum*-conversion of her was undoubtedly her captors' knowledge and use of behavior-influencing techniques. They certainly had some mastery of them from their acquaintance with books on the subject, and, above all, from their leaders' Vacaville experience. As at Vacaville, sex was a significant element.

From early April on, after announcing her conversion, Patty spoke heatedly of a new love in her life—of the beautiful man she had met in the underground. He was William Wolfe.

From the beginning of their hold of her, the Symbionese knew that by then this young, healthy woman had been accustomed to sex, that in her captivity she missed her Steven, but that with the right behavioral control of her she would accept a substitute—would, indeed, need a substitute. So she accepted Willie the Wolf.

From literature and history and from some very recent cases, we know that women captives often—by degrees unnoticeable even to themselves—grow fond of their abductors, then fall in love with them and willingly surrender themselves to their enslavers. In recent times we have seen how stewardesses showed tender partiality for skyjackers even on short flights in their captivity. Later, once the hijackers were apprehended, such young women manifested extreme reluctance to testify against the daring, darling men. Something of this was doubtless operative in Patricia's instance.

How classically gradual was this transformation in Patty's case! Initially she was mortally frightened. Her early communications to her distraught parents appear to be sincerely desperate pleas to do everything to meet the Symbionese demands so as to set her free. It would have taken an accomplished professional actress (which she was not) to simulate the fears she showed in those initial tapes.

In her very first tape she said that she was tied and blindfolded but not uncomfortable, "not really terrified." In fact, she was forced to make that tape in a closet where she was kept prisoner the first few weeks of her experience with the Symbionese. But, once released from the closet, and under Wolfe's and others' skillful ministrations, also aided by drugs, her fright receded, she began to like her captors, and then to love at least one of them. In time on her tapes she proclaimed her physical passion, finally revealing it was Willie.

Many months later it was established that in their hideouts the Symbionese, like the Weathermen, also practiced group sex; that Patty witnessed it, was impressed by it as something genuinely altruistic and revolutionary—and soon participated in it. During her trial in San Francisco in early 1976 for her part in the bank robbery, she testified that, in addition to Wolfe, DeFreeze had intercourse with her. And although she claimed that in both cases it was rape, not consent, the jury concluded that she did love—or at least enjoyed—Wolfe.

VIII

In early May 1974, not feeling safe in the most recent of a series of shelters, the Symbionese decided on a drastic change of their base— away from San Francisco. They would move to Los Angeles, to its Watts and other black areas that DeFreeze had known so well in the 1960s. Surely they would find many fearless recruits there, and their new headquarters would be secure from the FBI and the police. But they omitted the precaution of sending Cinque with one or two fellow members on a preliminary scouting mission, to prepare the new turf in the southern ghetto.

They pulled out of San Francisco on May 8 or 9, in three vans that had been purchased by a black man paying $3,500 (probably from the proceeds of the Hibernia Bank robbery) and giving a name and address that later proved fictitious.

In the next week or so, they had in sequence three hideouts in Los Angeles, and these they obtained not through any reliable contacts but by two clumsy methods: scanning classified advertisements in the local newspapers, and haphazardly knocking on doors in black neighborhoods. Cinque seemed genuinely puzzled to find that Watts and the rest of his old black Los Angeles had changed in the five years since his arrest, with hardly any old acquaintances to be rediscovered and enlisted for his Army.

Having given up their first two hideouts in Los Angeles as inadequate or unsafe, the Symbionese finally came to the door at 1466 East 54th Street. Two black cousins, Christine Johnson and Minnie Lewis, lived there. Cinque offered them $100 to allow three people to stay for just one night. After a momentary hesitation, they agreed. When six people entered, Christine and Minnie protested; Cinque, however, quickly mollified them with more money. So the group moved in, for their last night on earth. This was on Thursday, May 16.

But Patty Hearst and the Harris couple were not in that doomed house on 54th Street. On the same day, they had gone on a shopping expedition. The trio had set out from the group's second hideout, a shack at 833 West 84th Street. Later, on learning from radio broadcasts that Patty and the Harrises had been recognized as Symbionese and were being hunted by the police, the other six realized that the 84th Street shack was no longer safe. This was how they came to Christine's and Minnie's place.

That Thursday, William and Emily Harris entered Mel's Sporting Goods Store in the Inglewood section of Los Angeles while Patty remained outside across the street, waiting for them at the wheel of a red and white Volkswagen van. The Harrises bought some heavy outdoor clothes (perhaps, as it was later surmised, in preparation for the group's flight to the rugged mountains of either California or Mexico). They paid the $31.50 bill, but as they were leaving, a clerk noticed that the male customer had shoplifted what looked like a 49-cent pair of extraheavy socks, stuffing it up his sleeve (later it proved to be not socks but a white-webbing bandoleer). The clerk hurried to the street to halt the pilferer. The two began to struggle, and other store personnel joined in. As he resisted, Harris dropped a .38-caliber pistol. (Soon, traced by the FBI as belonging to Emily Harris, it would become one more indication that the Symbionese were somewhere in Los Angeles.) At this moment, from the van across the street, Patty Hearst screeched, "Let them go, you motherfuckers, or you're all dead!", and sprayed the store front with her machine gun. The store people dived and crouched for safety. The three Symbionese made their getaway.

Speeding off, the Harrises and Patty drove around the city aimlessly, not daring to return to the group's second hideout in West 84th

Street and not knowing that the group now had its base in East 54th Street. The agreement between the three and the six was that, if separated, they were to rendezvous that night at a certain drive-in movie. But this was about 4:30 in the afternoon, several hours before the meeting time.

The trio left the van shortly after their escape from Mel's Store, and seizing and abandoning four more cars, one after another, drove on and on. The first car was a parked Pontiac, where a couple was sitting and conversing. Pulling up behind it, Harris climbed out of the van, pointed a gun at the car's surprised occupants, and announced: "We are the SLA. We need your car. I have to kill someone, and I don't want to kill you." The couple jumped out and ran off. Harris and the two girls took over the black-and-yellow Pontiac.

But the Pontiac stalled after a few blocks, and the trio at once spotted a blue Chevrolet station wagon, with two men standing beside it. The pair, father and son, were startled by the sight of the three young people leaping out of the Pontiac with guns aimed and one of them—Bill Harris again—yelling. "We're from the SLA. We need your car." The father, pale and speechless, gave up the car keys.

They drove the Chevy for an hour and a half, until they saw a "For Sale" sign in the window of a blue Ford van parked in front of a house. Emily rang the bell, was admitted into the house, and spoke to Thomas Matthews, 18 years old, a high school student, the van's owner. She asked for a test drive in the van. Around the corner Bill and Patty were waiting. Emily said to Tom that these were her friends who wanted to join the test ride. Tom agreed pleasantly; Bill and Emily came aboard. Then the trio brandished guns and Bill spoke to the youth: "Do you know who this is? This is Tania." Expertly, Patty-Tania snapped a clip into her automatic rifle.

Tying up and gagging Tom, placing him on the floor of the van, they rode for some 12 hours. At one point they stopped at a drive-in movie. Patty was wearing a wig for disguise—short, dark, Afro style. She grew talkative with Matthews, perhaps glad to find someone nearer her age than her comrades, and of the innocent, nonpolitical world she had once inhabited. She told Tom she had joined the Symbionese because her father did not do the right thing in the food give-away; that she had participated in the bank robbery because the SLA needed money; and that, yes, she was now a full-fledged terrorist.

The three Symbionese failed to meet the other six at that drive-in. Each group must have waited for the other at two different movie places; they did not know the intricate map of Los Angeles sufficiently well to agree on such a rendezvous clearly enough. The three (plus Tom) finally drove off, drowsy but determined not to be caught.

At last, at 6:40 Friday morning, somewhere in Hollywood Hills, the three released Tom unharmed, along with his van. Within a few minutes two girl hitchhikers hailed, and were gladly picked up by, another motorist—Frank Sutter, a building contractor. Once in his car, the girls leveled guns at the driver. William Harris then joined the women and their victim, whom they forced to lie in the car's rear. Some six hours later they let Sutter go in Griffith Park, unharmed, but minus $250 that Bill removed from his wallet, saying: "You can figure this as a loan, but you won't get it back."

They drove a short distance farther, then parked the car, and vanished. Patty and the Harrises never rejoined the six. The trio escaped death, and were on the run until captured in September 1975.

IX

On Friday evening, May 17, 1974, through one clue and another, the police and the FBI discovered the 54th Street hideout. The six refused to capitulate; the siege began. Bullets and tear gas must have hit cans of gasoline inside the house, for it erupted in flames. The Symbionese sought refuge in the basement, where they continued to shoot back, though it was almost impossible to aim through the air vents, which were the only openings. The two landlady-cousins had escaped before the shooting started.

The house was soon a torch; the fire was so intense that a 50-foot palm tree in the back yard was totally destroyed, and smoke from it and the house rose some 150 feet into the darkening sky.

For a time, however, the foot-thick concrete walls of the foundation, with its cool earth below and the remaining floorboards above, continued to protect the Symbionese. The gunfire kept up, but by seven o'clock all was silence. At exactly 7:00, after 70 minutes of fighting, a policeman radioed his headquarters: "Our mission is accomplished."

A sergeant managed to jerk open the back door of the house; before the flames and the heat drove him off he saw two female bodies on the floor, both apparently dead, their clothes afire, the corpses twitching as the bullets in their waist bandoleers exploded in the extreme heat.

The house fell in a heap of burning, smoldering debris four feet high. Firemen battled the flames and the smoke for more than an hour before a search of the ruins could be made.

At first, five bodies were found; later the sixth was discovered in the debris, along with an astonishingly sizable arsenal, a few charred pages of a handbook on terrorism, and a piece of paper inscribed, "We will never surrender."

Within the next few days Dr. Thomas Noguchi, Los Angeles county coroner, reconstructed the deaths of the six:

Camilla Hall was probably the first to die, a rifle bullet hitting the center of her forehead.

Nancy Perry was perhaps next to go, by bullets in her spine and lungs.

William Wolfe, Angela Atwood, and Patricia Mizmoon Soltysik were killed by massive burns and smoke inhalation. (Mizmoon turned 24 the day she died.)

Donald DeFreeze was probably the last to die—by his own hand, firing a .38-caliber pistol into his right temple. His body was found face down, powder burns deep in his final wound. He was 30 years of age, the oldest of the dead.

Concluded Dr. Noguchi: "They chose to stay under the floor as the fire burned. . . . In all my years as a coroner, I've never seen this kind of behavior in the face of live flames."

Their death in the inferno was much like the self-immolation of the Buddhist monks in Vietnam a few years before—fiery suicide in the name of what they believed was a reasoned idea. But in tragic actuality their death was brought about by the blind and insane force that Bakunin referred to when he stated that revolution was "instinct rather than thought."

X

Through 1974-75 the Symbionese continued to haunt headlines. Criminologists and psychologists wrote and spoke their analyses of those who perished in the pyre and the few survivors still at large. The FBI and the police all over the American map kept up their search for Patty and the Harrises, indictments waiting for all three. For the men of the law and the media, clues both definite and vague were one long frustration. There were indications that in the summer and fall of 1974 Patty and the Harrises were hiding out in Pennsylvania countryside but had moved on just before the FBI caught up with them. The SLA also reappeared in the media on June 27, 1975, when Little and Remiro were sentenced to life imprisonment for the murder of Dr. Foster.

At the summer's end came the big news: on September 18, in their two San Francisco hideouts, all three celebrated fugitives were captured: Patricia Hearst, and William and Emily Harris. Taken by surprise, they offered no resistance, although considerable armament was found in their two apartments.

By curious coincidence, that month of September in California was marked by other terror news: on September 5, on the state capitol grounds in Sacramento, a follower of Manson's "Helter Skelter" group, Lynette (Squeaky) Fromme, aged 27, was arrested on charges of attempting to assassinate President Ford on his way to address the state legislature; on September 22, in front of a hotel in San Francisco, Sara Jane Moore, 45 years old, was seized after a bystander struck her hand, thus deflecting the shot she had fired at the President. Among other facts of her unstable past, it was found that the Moore woman had been a volunteer bookkeeper in the food giveaway program wrested from Patty's father by the Symbionese. Both Fromme and Moore were sentenced to life imprisonment.

In the uproar around the arrests of Patricia, William, and Emily, while the Harrises maintained their revolutionary defiance, Patty soon abandoned her militant pose. With the aid of high-priced lawyers hired by her family, she filed an affidavit saying that she had become a most unwilling terrorist because of her extreme physical mistreatment in a closet, threats by her SLA captors against her life, and their use of drugs upon her. In its initial legal moves, Patty's defense quoted the supporting view of Dr. Louis J. West, a psychiatrist at the University of California in Los Angeles, that the young woman was "a prisoner of war for twenty months, who definitely has a traumatic neurosis and marked impairment of her previous mental condition."

Four separate studies by three psychiatrists and one psychologist were submitted to the court in San Francisco that would decide whether Patricia Hearst was mentally competent to stand trial. In early November, U. S. District Judge Oliver Carter announced that these psychological evaluations of Patty were "so complex and verbose" that he needed time to ponder them. Soon deciding that she was fit to face the court, the judge scheduled Patty's trial to begin on January 26, 1976.

On March 20, 1976, after a trial lasting 39 days and featuring 71 witnesses for both sides, the jury of 7 women and 5 men found Patricia guilty of her part in the April 1974 bank robbery. They did not believe her defense that she was not truly a revolutionary, not really a robber; that she had been forced by the Symbionese into the crime; that she was too terror-stricken and in fear for her life to try an escape back to her family and normal ways even after only the two Harrises remained as Symbionese survivors and so much of the time not even anywhere near her to stop her from returning to civilization. All through the trial her high-priced lawyers were most clever and articulate, while the prosecutor seemed dull and plodding. But the jury was swayed by facts, not fancy talk.

The jury was convinced by the films and witnesses of the bank robbery. These proved Patty a willing, noncoerced participant. The 1974 tapes wherein she proclaimed herself a wholehearted Symbionese did not appear to the jury as having been forced from her. Then there was a later tape, made unbeknownst to her by the authorities in prison right after Patty's capture in September 1975, wherein a conversation was recorded with a visitor, a girl friend of her childhood, during which chat Patty frankly declared her red-hot revolutionary convictions and how outraged she was by her arrest. So impressed was the jury with that recording that they had it played to them several times.

Her lie about the nature of her affair with Wolfe was exposed by the stone trinket he had given her. She kept it all her long months since the "rape," and it was found in her purse upon her capture, while another such monkey-face stone trinket was discovered beneath Wolfe's charred body in May 1974. Nor did the jury indulgently disregard the fact that during the trial Patricia Hearst refused to answer questions about the details of her many months in flight and hiding from the authorities, taking the protection of the Fifth Amendment to the Constitution against self-incrimination 42 times.

28

Canada's White Niggers

Coinciding in time with the Panthers and the Weathermen, but preceding the Symbionese, there flared up the terrorists of Canada.

They identified themselves not so much with their white brethren south of the border as with the blacks. In bitter pride they called themselves and those whom they imagined as their followers "the White Niggers of America," the phrase popularized in the latter 1960s by Pierre Vallières, one of their chief theorists and perhaps practitioners.[1]

Canada's white niggers, or sub-men (another expression used by Vallières), were the workers, farmers, and clerks, the country's oppressed masses from whom these terrorists said they sprang and whom they undertook to lead to the barricades and the bombings.

Two main aims were inscribed on these terrorists' banner. One was a complete separation of Quebec from Canada, into an independent nation with absolute sovereignty. The other, more important than a purely legal break-off, was a thorough socio-economic revolution, filled with fierce violence, meant to pull down and destroy not only the British and American capitalists exploiting Quebec's human and other natural resources, but also the native French Canadian bourgeoisie and clergy with their 350-year-long record of living on the muscle and blood of the *habitants*.

The political separation would involve a linguistic defiance. Some of these terrorist (and other radical) writers would not use the standard French of the province, laden though it was not only with borrowings from the English language but also with some singular French Canadian locutions. They insisted on the Joual, the truly native tongue of Quebec, they claimed, which had many holdovers from seventeenth-century French, even though it was also corrupted by loan words from English. (The name *Joual* came from the way some people of Quebec pronounced *cheval*.)

Ideologically, these terrorists were a curious amalgam of Trotskyites and Maoists. In the manner of modern Trotskyites all over the world, they made a point of deploring violence in principle while they practiced or supported it in fact. As Mao would have it, violence was distasteful but, nevertheless, Red violence had to be used. From his Montreal prison cell Vallières wrote in April 1968: "Even if violence is a phenomenon detestable in itself, it is nonetheless true that for exploited and colonized people like ourselves, freedom grows out of the barrel of a gun."

As Trotskyites and Maoists everywhere, so the French Canadian terrorists denounced the "neopharaoism" of the latter-day Soviet leaders, with their new brand of capitalism and imperialism, and called for a bloody rising of the masses not solely in the non-Soviet capitalist world but also inside the Soviet Union against the neo-Stalinist Establishment of the Brezhnevs and the Kosygins.

Yet, unlike Mao and many of his followers, Quebec's terrorists did not worship at the icon of Lenin. Vallières in particular blamed Lenin no less than Stalin for corrupting the revolution, for laying the foundations of the "Soviet and East European state capitalism" that "prevents humanity from coming out of its long prehistory."

With all the Canadian terrorists' fanaticism, they were not optimists. They were grim about their own chances of success with French Canada's masses, who, like Russians and their fellow East Europeans, were reluctant for a variety of reasons to progress out of their prehistory. The property owners, the bureaucrats, and the clergy were as entrenched in Canada as the Leninist and post-Leninist bureaucrats and lying propagandists were firmly rooted in the Soviet Union and the East European lands they had grabbed. Neither power really feared its befuddled subjects and slaves. Vallières urged his comrades to organize "the spontaneous violence" of Quebec's "white niggers," yet he admitted sadly that there was neither spontaneity nor violence in the mood of his countrymen. In despair he exclaimed: "What was one to do in this country whose inhabitants rejected all passion?"

II

Two terrorist groups emerged in French Canada in the 1960s. The more active and more widely known was *Le Front de Libération du Québec* (FLQ), or the Quebec Liberation Front. The other was the Popular Liberation Front (FLP). Here we will deal almost exclusively with the FLQ, for practically from its very foundation in 1961-62, it was the more adventurous and brutal.

Two friends came forth as theorists of the FLQ movement: Pierre Vallières and Charles Gagnon. Both, particularly Vallières, began as restless radicals but not terrorists. Vallières, the socialist son of a docile railroad-shop worker, in his youth was a bank clerk and later a reporter on *La Presse,* Quebec's largest daily. In 1963 he succeeded Pierre Elliot Trudeau as editor of the magazine *Cité Libre,* but in the spring of 1964 was forced out of this post because of his "separatist deviationism." In June 1965 he was also fired from *La Presse.* Embracing Marxism, Vallières, with his friend Gagnon, increasingly preached violence.

Not having been among the original founders of the FLQ, they were for quite some time only fervent sympathizers, later becoming the group's theorists without being actual members. But finally, in the mid-60s, they joined.

The degree of their physical involvement in the bombings of their time was never established by the Canadian authorities, yet, despite the pair's indignant and casuistic protests, the government was quite logical in arresting and trying them as clearly responsible for much of the era's terror in Canada. Both urged an immediate and bloody revolution. In 1969, Gagnon summed up the FLQ program: "There are not fifty strategies. There are only two: the electoral and the revolutionary." The Front and other such organizations "reject the electoral idea," having "opted for a revolutionary overthrow of the established order."

From about 1963 on, until the decade's end, there were many bombings of public buildings and banks, of offices inside factories on strike, of mail boxes, and other targets. From gasoline bombs the Front graduated to dynamiting, bank robberies, and armed raids, some with the intention of getting weapons or the money with which to buy them. In 1970 alone, the Front was believed to be responsible for the theft of some 9,000 sticks of dynamite. In early October of that year several cases of rifles vanished from a freighter tied up in the river at Montreal.

There were numerous injuries and a total of six deaths in those years up to October 1970, but apparently none caused deliberately. One such inadvertent victim was a 16-year-old activist of the Front, who was killed by his own bomb, which exploded as he was carrying it. Another was a female secretary who died in the bombing of a shoe factory in May 1966. The terrorists blamed her employers, who, they said, had disregarded the bombers' warning given ten minutes before the explosion and had failed to clear the premises.

But the authorities accused Vallières and Gagnon as the inspirers of terror and thus the cause of the secretary's death. The two friends went underground, and soon crossed into the United States where, on September 27, 1966, they demonstrated for their cause at the United Nations. They were arrested by the agents of the U. S. Department of

Immigration on charges of illegal entry into the country. Although the two cried out that their passports were in perfect order, they were kept for a few months in the Tombs in New York, and deported in mid-January 1967. There followed months and years of their Canadian incarceration punctuated by hunger strikes, a series of trials and retrials, verdicts of guilty and more jail sentences, releases, rearrests, and occasional demonstrations staged for them by their student sympathizers.

In and out of prison, both were voracious readers and prolific writers. The extent of their detailed but largely dry-as-dust knowledge of Marxist and other sacred texts was staggering. Their writings, long on rhetoric and hair-splitting, on underground backbiting and nit-picking, but short on hard facts, nearly equaled in bulk—though not in acridity—those of the Black Panthers, the Weatherpeople, and surely the Symbionese.

The rank-and-file FLQ members were lower middle class. While there were teachers and journalists among them, others were taxi drivers and a few had held various factory jobs. Dr. Gustave Morf, a psychiatrist and criminologist who interviewed captured FLQ members in jails, found that most of them were of more than average intelligence, but that only about one-half had had secondary education, and that many of these had dropped out of school at different levels, usually to go directly into terror.

The Front operated in groups or cells of five to seven members each. In October 1970, the Royal Canadian Mounted Police estimated the FLQ strength at 22 cells totaling 130 terrorists, concentrated mainly in Montreal, with some 2,000 less active sympathizers, who were a kind of auxiliary force, most of them students.

In the Nechayevist way of organizing and running such terror cells, the majority of them only knew members of their own units, but not those of other units. At one time the Canadian authorities even doubted the existence of any central guidance of all the cells. But the government was wrong: the Front was tightly interconnected and thoroughly managed from one principal underground directorate.

To penetrate the FLQ with informers turned out to be an exceptionally difficult job for the authorities, but finally it was done: on June 21, 1970, a secret agent betrayed a FLQ cell whose members were caught by the police outside a cottage in the Laurentian Mountains. This blow was particularly painful to the FLQ because its leaders did not even know whether the agent was an infiltrator or a real member turned traitor. Nor did they know or guess his identity, and so were at a loss to ferret him out before he could do further damage.

Toward the decade's end the terrorists were, however, much heart-ened by what seemed to be a swelling of a revolutionary tide in the country. In 1968-70, as in the United States and France, so in Canada there were outbursts by students seizing buildings and rioting—an ominous counterpoint to the continued bombings by the Front's cells.

And yet there was no evidence of any concurrent wider popular support for either the FLQ terrorists or the campus rioters. Dolefully, from behind bars, Vallières wrote of the sluggish French Canadian masses who did nothing besides working, eating, drinking (often to stuporous excess), and begetting children—who in time would doubtless be as submissive to the System as were their parents.

In reality, if there was any true indignation on the part of the general populace, it was aimed at the terrorists when, late in 1970, they mounted their most spectacular exploit marked by a deliberate murder.

III

On Monday morning, October 5, 1970, an FLQ cell kidnapped from his Montreal home, at gunpoint, James R. Cross, 49 years old, an Englishman who was the senior British trade commissioner in Quebec. Later the Front revealed that its original intention had been to abduct the United States consul, but the plan was changed to Cross, whose kidnapping, the Front leaders felt, would make a more telling impact upon the English Establishment in Canada.

There were four abductors, three of them armed with submachine guns. The operation had been planned with care and carried out smoothly. Cross was caught by complete surprise and put up no resistance. The kidnappers used a taxi, apparently stolen. Two days later it was spotted abandoned at Sorel, some 40 miles northeast of Montreal.

Soon a lengthy message from the kidnappers was left at the University of Quebec. As the price for the safe return of Cross, it demanded immediate release of 23 political prisoners, all of them evidently FLQ members; the identification, by name and photograph, of the informer responsible for the June arrests; payment of $500,000 in gold; and the arrangement of a plane flight for all those of the 23 who so wished, to political asylum in either Cuba or Algeria. The airborne contingent was to include wives and children, if so desired by any of the 23 prisoners. The message, with all its fulmination against capitalism and imperialism, was to be made public in all the Quebec media. A 48-hour deadline was set by the terrorists: 8:30 on Wednesday morning, the seventh of October.

The ransom document, eight pages and 1,400 words long, was entitled "*Communiqué–opération libération.*" It was a veritable manifesto. Its first page was adorned with a silhouette, over the outline of which the text was neatly typed. The picture was of a French Canadian "white nigger," a roughly dressed and shod habitant with the distinctive headgear of his class, which resembles a bedcap, a pipe in his mouth, and a gun in each of his decisive hands.

The government, obeying the terrorists, published and broadcast the text. Experts in such matters conceded that the manifesto was couched cleverly, in emotional yet simple phrases, easily understood by the average French Canadian, whose support the Front sought. Particularly effective was the manifesto's list of the principal recent labor-capital conflicts occurring in Canada, most of them ending unfavorably for the workers.

But the other demands were unacceptable to the authorities. Most emphatically, the 23 prisoners would not be released. They were serving either life sentences or a range of terms up to 25 years for armed robbery, homicide, bombing of public buildings, and a conspiracy to kidnap the United States consul. Nor would any money ransom be paid, or the informer's identity be revealed.

All decisions on what to do about the matter were made jointly by the federal and provincial governments. Both Premiers, Pierre Trudeau of Canada and Robert Bourassa of Quebec, now received from the terrorists indirect threats against their own lives as well. Both tried to play for time—by engaging the Front in negotiations while the Combined Antiterrorist Squad, specialists on Quebec's violent separatists, searched for the abductors' hideout.

The strategy seemed to work. The FLQ extended the deadline several times, repeating its terms in four messages in three days. The fourth message, delivered on the seventh to a Montreal radio station, included two letters written by Cross—dictated to him by the kidnappers—to prove that he was still alive. On the ninth, the FLQ declared in one more message:

> When we decided to kidnap the diplomat Cross, we calculated all the possibilities, including that of sacrificing our lives for a just cause. If the repressive police forces find us and try to intervene before the British diplomat Cross is freed, you can be certain that we will defend our lives dearly and that J. Cross will be liquidated on the spot.

The word "liquidated" was of interest as a direct linguistic debt to the Soviet secret police, who had begun using this term for execution from the very start of the Russian civil war in 1918.

The kidnappers soon dropped their demands for money and, surprisingly, even for the informer's identity. But they were adamant about the 23 prisoners. In response, the government offered only the kidnappers' safe passage to Cuba once James Cross was freed unharmed.

When the kidnappers demanded cessation of the police search, the authorities agreed to comply with this condition. Later, on being questioned about this in the Canadian Parliament, Premier Trudeau explained that the announcement of compliance had been a ploy.

Mitchell Sharp, Secretary of State for External Affairs (foreign minister), publicly remarked that the situation was most perplexing: "We don't know how to deal with it." But this puzzlement might have also been a camouflage. Actually, the authorities were not just sweating it out, but were taking a series of thorough measures, particularly those having to do with the continuous, ingenious search for the terrorists' hideout.

IV

But the FLQ would not be halted. On Saturday, October 10, another cell of the Front kidnapped from his home one more official—this time a Canadian, Quebec's Minister of Labor and Immigration, Pierre Laporte. While to the terrorists Cross meant Britain's exploitation of Canada's masses, Laporte symbolized the sins of the native French Canadian capitalists. More than three years before this second abduction, Vallières had listed Laporte in his best-known book (*White Niggers of America*) as an enemy of the people.

Only 15 minutes before Laporte's kidnapping, the authorities reiterated that the 23 would not be freed in exchange for Cross, and that the most the government would do would be to fly the Englishman's captors off to Cuba. Laporte's abduction came as the Front's response to this stubbornness. Cross later said that it appeared to be a complete surprise to his own FLQ guards when, on their radio, they first heard of Laporte's kidnapping. But soon the two separate cells were coordinated; they were presently issuing joint communiqués—rather, their top chiefs were issuing them from the Front's central headquarters somewhere in the Montreal underground. In their further negotiations with the government, the two cells had one and the same representative: Robert Lemieux, a radical lawyer.

Trudeau remained implacable: "We can't let a minority group impose their view on the majority by violence." The 23 will stay in jail because they "are not political prisoners, they are bandits," precisely the line used by Mexico's President with regard to his own country's terrorists.

The second kidnapping deepened the near-panic among certain strata of the population and heightened the sense of emergency in the

Establishment. Quebec's Premier Bourassa called for federal troops. On his own, Trudeau came to the same decision. Federal troops were sent to Ottawa on October 13 to aid the Royal Canadian Mounted Police in maintaining law and order, the first such use of the army in Canada's capital in time of peace. The police of Montreal were also aided by federals. The dispatch of army units was formalized by the War Measures Act, which Trudeau invoked on the sixteenth. When critics in Parliament and elsewhere cried out that this was a suspension of civil liberties, Trudeau the liberal replied: "The Society must take every means at its disposal to defend itself against the emergence of a parallel power which defies the elected power in this country."

Known and suspected members of the Front were rounded up. Both Vallières and Gagnon, free since early 1970, were rearrested. The Front's lawyer Lemieux was also taken into custody, on charges of obstructing justice, the search of his presence yielding compromising FLQ documents. The government's negotiations with him as the Front's spokesman were moved to the prison in which he was now lodged.

On the night of the seventeenth, one day after the War Measures Act's invocation, came the shock. In the trunk of a taxi abandoned in downtown Montreal was found the body of Pierre Laporte. The minister had been strangled by his kidnappers. From the cuts on his body it was ascertained that he had tried to escape through a window and had only succeeded in cutting himself badly before being murdered.

Twelve hours later a pathetic letter was received from Cross: he was begging the authorities to call off the search for him. This message made it clear that the Front still insisted on the freeing of the 23, to fly them to Cuba or Algeria.

But the government stood fast. After counsels with his cabinet, Trudeau repeated: no freedom and flight for the 23; such an opportunity will be given only to the kidnappers of Cross once he is released; the search for the hideout will go on; Laporte's killers will be brought to justice. What outrage for these men to call themselves Canadians: "They are members of a hard core devoted to a single purpose—to inspire within all of us fear and hatred, and in this atmosphere to destroy our nation." But they will not succeed; retribution will come; Laporte's murderers "will be found and will be dealt with in the calm and dispassionate atmosphere of Canadian courts. The FLQ has sown the seeds of its own destruction. It has revealed that it has no mandate but terror; no policies but violence and no solutions but murder."

So the search went on, and on November 6 there was a breakthrough; Bernard Lortie, a 19-year-old student, a suspect in the

Laporte case, was arrested in Montreal. He caved in, admitting his part in the minister's kidnapping, but not in the murder, for he named his three accomplices as the actual killers: Paul and Jacques Rose, brothers; and Francis Simard. All three were soon captured.

The search for Cross and his abductors intensified and narrowed. Weeks passed. At last, on December 2, the police located the northern suburban Montreal apartment, at 10945 Des Recolletts Street, in which an FLQ cell had held James Cross for nearly two months. It was learned that Cross was alive.

The place was tightly surrounded, but, rather than shoot it out, the two sides made a deal. As there were in the encircled apartment three of his four kidnappers (the fourth being away at the time the siege began), Cross was freed by them in exchange for these three, who, with four of their dependents, were allowed to fly to Havana. The kidnapping trio were identified as Marc Carbonneau, Jacques Lanctot, and Pierre Seguin.

On the morning of December 5, just before flying off to England for a reunion with his wife, the freed diplomat told the press: "My captivity gave me a sense of the importance of the ordinary things of life— living with one's family, talking to friends, and breathing fresh air. After weeks of captivity it's a wonderful relief to be back in the normal world."

All those 59 horrible days and nights Cross had been kept in a windowless room. All day long he was forced to sit with his head toward a wall, away from the door. He could talk to his guards but not see their faces. His bed was a mattress on the floor. There was great discomfort and fear, but no torture.

His captors talked to him of revolution, gave him many revolutionary books to read, and even allowed him to watch television. Cross recalled: "We discussed revolution a lot in the early days. They were fervent revolutionaries, that was clear, but after Mr. Laporte's death I didn't feel like discussing things with them."

His shock at Laporte's murder was aggravated when, on television and radio, the Canadian Broadcasting Corporation reported that he, Cross, was also dead. More than ever he now doubted his survival, and he was deeply distressed for his wife and her state upon hearing of his presumed death.

Then the morning dawned when his captors told him the searchers had finally been successful. "They told me the police had found us. I was roused out of bed and taken to an outside corridor where I was handcuffed to a doorknob. I remained in that position all night. It was most uncomfortable, and I had no idea how much time was passing."

The excruciating negotiations, in which the Cuban envoy to Canada participated, were at long last concluded. On December 4, after a fast automobile ride across Montreal, the exchange was accomplished at the Expo 67 fairgrounds, which were declared temporary Cuban territory.

Cross remained a hostage in the hands of the acting Cuban consul until word was received that the kidnappers and their dependents had landed in Havana. Now a completely free man, Cross remarked about his abductors: "I was always treated with courtesy. But I'm just glad they are now where they are, and I am where I am."

V

Throughout December 1970, as details of the Cross abduction gradually became known, it was apparent that although only four Front members did the actual kidnapping, many more had taken part in its preparation. The organization appeared to be powerful in numbers as well as in its determination, cleverness, and efficiency.

On December 5, in a tape sent to the media, the leaders boasted that, despite all the arrests, the Front continued to be strong and would yet undertake new action. True, the Front was surprised by Trudeau's unwillingness to give in. The 23 stayed in prison, and Laporte's four abductors were now jailed; no part of the $500,000 demand was paid to the Front, and the June informer remained a mystery. But the Front was nonetheless proud of all the sensation and commotion it had aroused, and even of Laporte's slaying. The tape stressed that the government had required two months and the services of 22,000 soldiers and policemen to flush out the abductors.

And yet the government, even though tragically losing Pierre Laporte's life, could and did point to its eventual triumph. In the period from October 16 (when the War Measures Act was invoked) to November 24, its police and troops carried out 3,068 raids and apprehended 453 suspects, more than one-half of whom (252) were in the 19-to-25-age bracket. The list of seized weapons included 159 firearms, 4,962 rounds of ammunition, 677 sticks of dynamite, and 912 detonators.

Most telling of all, the four abductors of Laporte awaited trial. Eventually, in March and May 1971 respectively, Paul Rose and Francis Simard were sentenced to life imprisonment; and in November 1971, Bernard Lortie to 20 years in prison.

At his own trial, Lortie misbehaved in court, throwing paper balls in the direction of the judge. He also announced that it was not important whether or not the jurors found him guilty; what was important was whether the jurors favored Quebec's separation. At the last of the four trials, that of Jacques Rose on kidnapping charges, Lortie refused to testify, apparently trying to win his comrades' forgiveness for his yielding to the police interrogators at the time of his November 1970 arrest. The result was that on December 9, 1972, Jacques Rose was acquitted, to the resounding cheers of the Front's sympathizers in the courtroom, while Lortie was given five more months for contempt of court, in addition to his 20-year sentence.

Paul Rose, Jacques's brother, was also defiant during his trial in late January 1971. This one-time teacher declined the services of a court-appointed lawyer, demanding instead that Robert Lemieux be brought from his prison cell to defend him. When the judge turned down his request, Paul Rose wheeled around to face the nearly 100 journalists filling the room and exclaimed: "The people of Quebec will judge us when the people of Quebec have taken over the government!"

But well into these middle 1970s the people of Quebec have failed Paul Rose's trust in them. These white niggers of Canada, these miserable habitants of the rich province, with their record of the most menial jobs at the lowest pay and the highest unemployment rate in the country, would not rise to join their would-be liberators. Nor has the Front itself been ablaze lately.

For a half-decade now, the terrorist Quebec Liberation Front has been dormant—if it exists at all.

29

Crimson in the Irish Green and Orange

A far more significant area in which the British Establishment has been combatted by non-English terrorists is Ireland.[1]

The current phase of the Irish conflict began in 1969, but its roots go back eight centuries. It was in the twelfth century that Pope Adrian IV gave overlordship of Ireland to King Henry II of England. In 1171, Henry's army sailed across the Irish Sea to stop the dissident barons from establishing their cantankerous rule on the Emerald Isle. Later, three intense revolts were crushed in the reign of Elizabeth I. Then, in 1641, a ten-year rebellion began. Some 600,000 Irish lives were lost, and in 1649 Oliver Cromwell, having executed Charles I, led cruel expeditions to put down the rebellion and to prevent Ireland from becoming a royalist shelter.

Cromwell continued the policy of settling more and more of the English in Ireland, particularly in her North. These new colonists were former officers of his army and militant Protestants. In time a majority of landlords in Catholic Ireland were Protestants. The religious difference turned into a socio-economic divide as well.

The discriminatory anti-Catholic laws solidified and strengthened Protestant rule in Ireland almost until 1800, when the island was placed completely under the command of the British Crown. The Protestant grip was now tight. Yet there were uprisings, one of which, occurring late in the eighteenth century, stemmed out of a short liberal respite of Britain's dominance and a hope inspired by the news of the French Revolution. Repression, however, set in once more, and, coupled with the devastating famine of the 1840s, only fed the smoldering fires of Irish nationalism and insurgence.

The next major revolt had to wait until Easter Day of 1916. And though the Irish lost the battle of 1916, they won the war in 1921, when the British finally agreed to the formation of the Irish Free State.

Yet for many Irish it was not a true victory: Ulster, comprising six Northern counties, with its Protestant majority, remained with Great Britain. Nevertheless, in 1949 the Free State became the Republic, seemingly reconciled to the loss in the North. But for the next 20 years a growing host of militants demanded the restoration of Ulster to the Republic. The Irish Republican Army, though outlawed by the Dublin government, was readying itself for action. In 1969 the conflict began.

II

In retrospect it now seems that had the Protestant majority of Ulster, in the middle and late 1960s, granted the Catholic minority at least a modicum of the rights they demanded, particularly in the sectors of government, job equality, and housing, the latest wave of terror—now swollen to a virtual civil war—would not have occurred or would have been much less bloody and otherwise not so costly. When in the 1970s some political concessions were at last offered to the Catholics, economic reform was still not extended, and by then it was too late in the crimson season.

The Catholic civil rights workers' movement, emerging in 1968, gave place to outright terror in 1969. This happened chiefly because the Protestant extremists responded to the civil rights demands with gang attacks and arson in Belfast's slums. It was then that members of the Catholic minority in Ulster asked the Irish Republican Army for help.

Although at the IRA convention in Dublin in late 1969, two-thirds of the delegates were for a peaceful political course—a near-Marxist one, in alliance with other leftist parties and groups—the other one-third felt that Ireland would be united only through terror, and they refused to abide by the "let's-wait" guidelines of their more cautious comrades.

Thus did the IRA in December 1969 split into two factions: the Officials, ostensibly for less militancy; and the Provisionals, or Provos for short, furiously charging into the battle with bombs and guns.

The terrorists were enthusiastically joined by those in the insurgence movement who for years had increasingly objected to the preoccupation of the latter-day IRA leadership with left-wing parties and trade unions, who seemed only to talk, not act. By June 1972, the total number of the Provos making and placing bombs and sniping at Protestants, at the army, and at the police in the six Ulster counties was estimated at 1,000.

The slaughter had begun in August 1969 when, during a riot, a Catholic named James Gallagher was killed by the Protestant reserve police. This first victim was followed by 12 more before the year's end. The toll was 25 deaths in 1970, 173 in 1971, 467 in 1972, and 250 in 1973. By the spring of 1974 the total since the opening of terror reached and passed the thousand mark. By that time the wounded numbered 14,000, and property damage and losses exceeded $200 million, many neighborhoods and whole towns lying in waste. Indiscriminate bombing and stray bullets killed and injured women and children. Both warring sides viewed such innocent bystanders as nonbeings.

British troops were introduced in 1969, and although they have tried to stop terrorists of both camps, the brunt of their intercession is still directed at the Catholics, who are the more active of the antagonists. Detention without trial of captured IRA members and other suspected terrorists was begun in August 1971. In the spring of 1973 some militant Protestants were also detained.

One of the aims of the IRA terror has been to compel the London government to withdraw from Ulster the British soldiers, who by the spring of 1974 totaled 15,750 officers and men. Yet, were these withdrawn or reduced in number, the British would claim their success as the reason. The British army, in late July 1972, had already said it was winning so decisively that the number of active Provos had been reduced from 1,000 to 300 or 400, and by late November to a mere 150 men. Even if not that catastrophic, the terrorist losses have to this day been high.

In Ulster, because of their losses, some Provo units began by 1972 to recruit adolescents, ever younger boys and girls, into their ranks. In November of that year, at least two companies of Provos, each consisting of 30 members, were said to be led by 16-year-old youths. By 1974 women began to rise in the central leadership of the IRA, and this also was caused by the continued loss of men.

The skillful use of informers by British intelligence has helped significantly. In mid-May 1974, because of infiltration of the main nerve centers of the Provos, the British security forces captured the so-called "doomsday battle plan." This scheme called first for inciting the Protestant majority to a bloodbath of the Catholic minority, then—using the massacre as the grand excuse—moving into Belfast as a protector of the Catholics. The Provos planned to take over the city by occupying the telephone, postal, and gas installations, the docks, newspaper offices, television and radio stations, and other such vital centers. During other raids, which occurred in the early morning of August 3, the British army arrested 28 suspected members of the Provos' command in Belfast, including two women. Again the army realized the fruit of informers' toil.

Dismayed, the Provo leaders who remained at large went to the extreme of offering amnesty to the informers, whoever they were, if only they would cross over, or recross, to the rebel side and confess. When no informers responded, the Provos reverted to their usual method: killing informers when they were caught; shooting suspected informers in their knees, thus crippling them for life. In 1974, by August, more than 80 persons suffered such bullet-shattered knee caps.

Other troubles within have plagued the rebels. That the much-claimed idealism is not the sole motive of some Irish terrorists may be seen from a report compiled by a leading Provo member held in the Maze Prison and meant for the higher Provisional command. It was intercepted by the British in April 1973 as it was being smuggled out of the prison. The report lamented that of the 17,000 pounds sterling ($42,000) taken by the Provos in robberies from Belfast banks over a period of 18 months, nearly one-third never reached the needs of terror, being embezzled by certain IRA officers for their own private use. We have seen that such personal enrichment is characteristic of the human frailty illustrated in the past by terrorists: from Robespierre's aides whose coffers gained in weight as they directed the guillotine; to Socialist Revolutionaries, such as the high-living Yevno Azef, who put money aside for his bourgeois-style comforts while directing executions in the Russia of the 1900s; to the many Nazi and Communist death-dealers in more recent times who grew rich as they tortured and killed millions of people.

III

In late January 1975, at the British army headquarters in Belfast, I asked a colonel in charge of information:

"Do the IRA men have many Soviet-made weapons? For instance, in the arms you capture from the Provos, do you find those famous Kalashnikov guns?"

The colonel picked up his telephone and soon produced the statistics: Only some ten such Russian guns were rounded up by the British in all the five and one-half years of Ulster warfare.

Up to 75 and even 85 per cent of the IRA's weapons come from the United States. Many and ingenious are the ways of transport. Even the Cunard liner *Queen Elizabeth II* has repeatedly been used to smuggle guns and explosives from New York to Southampton and, thence, to the battle zones in both England and Ulster.

Most of these arms are being paid for from donations made by Irish-Americans. Many of the donors do not know, or pretend not to know, that their money goes for bombs and guns. Naïvely, or hypocritically, they insist that their philanthropy is used to buy medical supplies for the Irish fighters and milk for the Catholic ghetto children of Ulster.[2]

There is, too, in both America and Europe, much ignorance about the political programs of the IRA's two factions. Typical was a friend in France, usually well versed in current international affairs, particularly pertaining to worldwide Communism, who was astonished to hear from me of the IRA's Communist premises and connections: "And I thought those Irish terrorists were merely nationalistic fanatics!" On the bloody stage itself, in Belfast, a Catholic laborer told me how horrified he was by the atrocities of Soviet Communism but argued with me heatedly when I mentioned that, after all, the IRA, too, had a Communist plan for Ireland. "Oh no," he cried out, "but you are mistaken, sir! All they want is a unified Ireland, that's all."

There is nevertheless a difference between the Officials and the Provos: the former are definitely Marxist, and their liaison with Moscow, though hidden, is a fact; the latter consider themselves left-Socialist, but not necessarily Marxist. Few of the Provos are clearly pro-Moscow; many say they are either Maoists or Trotskyites, or both. Often the Provos are vague and confusing in their leftism, but they do promise in the future unified Ireland abolition of capitalism, decentralization, and encouragement for people to live and work in autonomous communes or other such socialist or near-anarchist units.

The Official faction sometimes denounces the Provos as semi-fascist, but in Ulster as well as in England in early 1975 I heard voices of informed suspicion that secret contacts between the two camps of the IRA were kept up, that the Officials had their tabs and even controls on the Provisionals. Said one knowledgeable man to me: "The Officials stopped their own terror not due to any scruples but out of sheer practicality—when they saw that their bombs were killing simple people rather than the elite, and that this was counter to Marx and also hurt their public image. They were set back when their blasting at Aldershot killed a plain gardener and not the army officers they had aimed at. But they do not truly disapprove of the Provo terror. They stand ready to take over if it grows and becomes really effective. Such may be the line they get and obey from Moscow."

Another feature of Ulster's terrorism little known to the world at large is the children's involvement in that fratricide.[3] Yet we should always remember that indiscriminate bombs and stray bullets have struck down Protestant and Catholic children alike, among other passers-by and bystanders. Not at all accidentally, but deliberately, two small children were killed among the 12 victims of the IRA bomb that blew up a bus carrying British soldiers and their families in Yorkshire on February 4, 1974. Children were among the 42 injured in West-minster Hall in London when an IRA bomb was detonated in a crowd of sightseers on June 17 of the same year. Many of them were tourists from Germany and the Scandinavian countries.

In the spring of 1974 the IRA Provisionals accused the British Army of encouraging little children to accompany them on patrols so as to force the Catholic snipers to think twice before shooting at the soldiers. The army denied this, and countercharged that on March 14 a terrorist compelled some children to act as a shield for himself while he attacked a British patrol.

There is no denying by either side that many Catholic children, be they egged on by their elders or acting on their own juvenile initiative, have made a practice of pelting British tanks with stones and shouting obscenities at British soldiers, in an attempt—often successful—to arouse their tempers.

While some parents do protest against the terrorism of both sides, or at least try to control and safeguard their offspring, others fan the hatred in their neighborhoods and homes, thus infecting their young with their own bitter hostility. A North Irish physician remarked: "Every child I have spoken to in any part of Belfast has expressed hardened attitudes directed toward people of the other religion." From birth Ulster's children are separated by their two brands of Chris-tianity, and thus the enmity lives on into the next generation, intense and ugly. No visible effort is made to have the youngsters play or go to school together, Catholics with Protestants, so as to lessen the conflict in a meaningful, long-range way.

For too many of them this fratricide has become sheer, perverse enjoyment. Some treat the tragedy with black humor. When three Scottish soldiers were killed by an IRA gunman, the gleeful Catholic ghetto children wrote on walls, "Celtics 3, Rangers 0," in a triumphant allusion to the well-known Celtics (Catholic) and Rangers (Protestant) soccer rivalry. On the other side, Protestant children cheered when Catholic men were taken by the Army from their homes for intern-ment: boys and girls stood outside the homes of the arrested and sang derisive versions of "Where's Your Daddy Gone?"

One day in 1972, a London journalist visiting North Belfast streets watched Protestant boys and girls, some of them mere five-year-olds, as they marched past the scarred or smoldering barricades. The young-sters, wearing dark glasses and bush hats, chanted their calls and an-swers:

"Who are you fighting for?"

"For Ulster!"

"Who's your enemy?"

"The IRA!"[4]

Belligerent or not, North Irish youngsters do not escape the deep and widespread trauma called by physicians "the Belfast syndrome." Some, along with their parents, especially their mothers, bear marks of psyches damaged by the months and years of living in this hellish atmosphere. Many come to doctors and enter hospital wards as patients, very much disturbed, weeping and trembling uncontrollably. Some are victims of amnesia, not remembering their names or where they live.

Such patients comprise about 30 per cent of the cases in the ever-busy emergency section of Belfast's Royal Hospital. To them, the most unsettling feature of the North Irish terror is the sudden, blind-striking, arbitrary character of the explosions and the attacks by an enemy not easily identifiable. Among these patients the children are particularly numerous and pathetic. Said a Belfast physician:

"A number of four- to seven-year-olds are having anxiety reactions which, in my experience, have never existed before. In the last six months I've seen twenty-five such cases. Young children who won't look out of windows; any noise—and they run to their mothers."

And at the same time they feel that their mothers and fathers have failed them. The traditional parental control has told them to obey their elders; yet they see their fathers and even some mothers defy *their* superiors—challenge the authority of the land if this authority supports or merely tries to protect the opposing side. So the children of Ulster, at first frightened, grow up to be confused and rude, obsessed with fears and also with hatred—all this as part of the Belfast syndrome so grimly rising through these dragging years of incessant terror. They not only march with those anti-Catholic chants, or, if Catholics, taunt and stone the British soldiers—they disobey their own parents as they crack up together with their distraught and hatred-filled fathers and mothers.

Not a hopeful augury, this, for the future of Ulster and of mankind at large.

IV

Since we cannot give here a biographical dictionary of any inclusiveness, let us look at a Provo terrorist leader whose personality and activity are in many ways typical and revealing.

For a number of years the Provisionals were headed by their chief of staff, Sean MacStiofain.[5] Between the 1950s and 1969-70 he was a close friend and associate of Cathal Goulding, a Marxist leader of the Offical wing of the IRA, but in the split between the two factions the pair quarreled and separated. These days Goulding says that in Mac-Stiofain's character there is violence only, and no ideology: "He is not a person who thinks a lot. He is continually trying to prove that he is as much an Irishman as anyone else. He has no time for politics of any kind—and a revolutionary who has no time for politics is in my mind a madman."

But this is not the only trait that betrays MacStiofain as mentally unbalanced. His entire past is witness thereof. Born in London in February 1928 of scant Irish ancestry, if any, he was baptized a Protestant. His name was John Stephenson; and it was much later in life that he changed his name to its Irish version. He would be more Irish than the Irish. How true this was to the pattern of trying to be *plus royaliste que le roi*—the pattern of Napoleon the Corsican endeavoring to be not only a Frenchman, but first and foremost among all the French; the design of Adolf Schickelgruber, the Austrian outsider, becoming Hitler the Great German; the plan and success of Joseph Dzhugashvili turning into Russia's supreme ruler Stalin, who to his life's end spoke Russian with a heavy Georgian accent.

To look into another slice of Europe's history, John's childhood was much like those of the French and Italian anarchists of the 1880s-1900s. Bernard Weinraub describes it incisively: "Little John Stephenson trembled and cried with terror when his father stumbled into their London home and began beating his mother in an alcoholic rage." Frail, shy, insecure, he clung to his three half-sisters each morning as they left for work: "Please come back. You will come back, won't you?"

The perpetually drunken father, Edward George Stephenson, was an Englishman. His second wife, John's mother, Lilian Newland, was a native Londoner of remote Irish origin. Edward Stephenson's father sold beer in the East End, but Edward was a law clerk with pretensions to an aristocratic lineage—which was fictitious—who went to work in a black coat, striped trousers, a bowler hat on his head and a tightly rolled umbrella in hand. He returned in the evening drunk, to pummel his wife in the frightened presence of his three daughters (by a previous marriage) and little John.

In time the girls fled the horrible flat for good. They were followed by Lilian, who became a live-in maid, leaving the nine-year-old boy with his father. Edward placed John in a nearby parochial school, which instructed him in Catholicism. Thus began John's Irish phase. At school he met and admired boys who boasted of their Irish Republican forebears. He was 11 when his mother died of a brain hemorrhage. His father remarried, and John left him at 14.

By then he had run into some Irish insurgents in London who were

working underground for their island's reunification. Soon he was one
of the movement, though as a teen-ager he was lonely, sullen, quirky.
His new associates were impressed by his bitter and reticent quality.
At 22 he married a Cork-born girl and began his family, eventually of
three children.

In the 1950s he started his terrorist activism with his friend Goulding, a house painter-builder, and raided an Essex cadet armory to seize
weapons for the fight in Ulster. The two were caught and sentenced to
eight years in jail. It was at the Wormwood Scrubbs Prison that John
Stephenson made his name Irish, read guerrilla manuals, and learned
much from Greek Cypriote fellow inmates, who were anti-British terrorists of extensive experience.

While on release, Goulding and other leftists plotted nonbloody
political action and sang *The International;* MacStiofain and his non-
Marxist militants plotted a more explosive terrorism with *Faith of Our
Fathers* on their lips. By the late 1960s MacStiofain was an implacable
leader of dynamite-planters and bomb-flingers in Ulster. And yet he
rarely took any personal part in these exploits, directing the terror from
the safety south of the border. Notes Weinraub: "He has been ridiculed by women in Londonderry for urging violence while living outside Northern Ireland." Unwaveringly he insisted on blood-shed-
ding—by others. In 1971, to a visitor in his secluded house 30 miles
northwest of Dublin, he declared: "The civilians are casualties of war.
Killing is inevitable and is going to continue until the British withdraw
from Northern Ireland."

He was neither a drinker nor a smoker, and those who met him
spoke of an icy, stubborn man, filled with corrosive hatred for the
British and Ulster's Protestants. In his forties he was described as "a
chunky, gray-haired man who wears baggy suits, speaks stiffly and
somewhat inarticulately," his whole appearance and manner little suggesting a fearsome, efficient guerrilla chief.

But he trusted his luck too far. On November 19, 1972, he was
arrested by order of the Dublin government on charges of belonging to
an organization illegal in the Republic of Ireland. Tried and sentenced
to six months in prison, he announced a hunger strike. "I will be dead
in six days!" he shouted in the Dublin court.

He wasn't. Soon, though still refusing food, he did take water. A
rumor persisted that stealthily he was eating, too. Dubliners jested that
at the very least he was consuming "protein-enriched Hosts," and that
you could reach MacStiofain by telephoning the military hospital
where he was held and asking for "Extension Ate, Ate, Ate." On
release he was shunned by his Provo comrades. In April 1974 he was
known to say sadly: "I am no longer active in the Republican move-

ment. I would like to be, and it is not my fault that I am inactive, but I will remain a Republican revolutionary to my dying day.''

His successor as chief of the Provisionals' staff, Seamus Twomey, a native of Belfast, a paunchy, bespectacled man in his mid-fifties, has not been so well known. Twomey's principal assistant until the summer of 1973 was Gerry Adams, a self-declared Trotskyite, given to few words and much violence. On July 19, 1973, Adams and two other Provo officers were seized by a British army patrol in Belfast. Soon afterward, on September 1, Twomey himself was captured by the Irish police in a farmhouse some 15 miles south of the Ulster border. He gave up without resistance. Tried and sentenced to three years in jail, he was shortly free again—on the last day of October when he, with two other Provos, was sensationally airlifted out by a pair of their fellow terrorists, who landed a helicopter in the exercise yard of the Mountjoy Prison near the center of Dublin and swiftly took off again with the rescued trio after they had fought off the astonished guards.

V

In the Protestant camp of this most Christian fratricide of modern times, a widely publicized leader is the Reverend Ian Paisley, but he is not in actual charge of his side's terror campaign. He is an approver, a gifted oratorical inciter, rather than a practical organizer of the anti-Catholic outbursts in Ulster. A demagogue, he is often denounced by liberals and leftists as a neofascist. In Belfast in early 1975 a moderate Protestant journalist remarked to me: "Chills run down my spine when I see and hear Paisley at rallies. He reminds me of Hitler so.''

Mr. Paisley was among the founders of the Ulster Protestant Volunteers, but this organization has been eclipsed by the far more terrorist Ulster Defense Association, dominant since early 1972. In addition, by the summer of 1973, the increasing grumble in the UDA ranks that the leaders of the Association were not sufficiently aggressive led to the emergence of a new group, the Ulster Freedom Fighters.

Arguing that the Association was too much on the defensive, that it was devoting its time, men, and money to the protection of Protestant business firms and to an involvement in some rather peaceful politics, the Fighters set out to attack not only the Provo IRA and Catholics in general, but also those fellow Protestants who seemed too indecisive. Interlapping with the Freedom Fighters (if, sometimes, not actually the same group) is the left-wing Ulster Volunteer Force.

In 1972, Thomas Herron rose to prominence as one of the top leaders of the Ulster Defense Association. In his middle thirties, with a wife and five children, he was a former hotel porter who at times still lapsed into a kind of hesitance if not docility—or so charged his extremist critics. In June 1973, some young UDA militants captured Herron and demanded a stronger drive against Catholics. On his release Herron stepped up the UDA terror, but Protestant extremists agitated for yet more blood. On June 15 two gunmen burst into Herron's home and killed the bedridden Michael Wilson, Mrs. Herron's 18-year-old brother (he had been badly beaten up in a Catholic area of Belfast the week before). It was said that the gunmen were in fact looking for Herron and murdered his brother-in-law only because they did not find Herron. On September 14 Herron disappeared, and two days later his corpse was found on the outskirts of Belfast. He had been shot in the head, possibly by Catholic terrorists—or were his slayers those Protestant die-hards? Nor was it ever learned for certain who it was, Catholics or Protestants, that had killed his young brother-in-law three months earlier.

Yet, to their Catholic targets and to the British army, the Ulster Defense Association is militant enough, the charges by the die-hards against Herron-like "mildness" notwithstanding. By mid-June 1972, only a few months after its creation, the UDA was 25,000 men strong. Arms were easily and legitimately secured by UDA members, since many of them belonged to gun clubs, so numerous in Ulster, particularly in its countryside. Guns were also purchased abroad, both with UDA men's dues or donations and with those funds solicited in North America from Ulster Loyalist clubs, such as the strong and generous ones in Ontario and California.

In May 1974, the Ulster Defense Association was an important factor in the general strike that paralyzed industry, trade, and practically all other normal activities in the land. The strike was called by a newly formed organization, the Ulster Workers Council, a body of right-wing Protestant labor unionists, relying for its force primarily on the Ulster Defense Association and secondarily on the Ulster Volunteer Force.

The aim of the strike was to render stillborn the proposed Council of Ireland, which had been permitted to come into being by a vote on May 14 of the Northern Ireland Assembly. Its purpose was to satisfy Ulster's Catholics in their clamor for more rights. When many factory workers went to their jobs on May 15 as usual, gangs of toughs, wearing masks and combat jackets and brandishing clubs, forced them to return home. Other such gangs compelled recalcitrant businessmen to close their shops and offices. The enforcers were UDA members, helped by UVF youths.

On May 21, dissenting trade unionists tried to lead workers back to their jobs, but few responded. The intimidated majority stayed home. On the twenty-eighth the strikers won completely, the coalition government of Northern Ireland resigning and the plans of the Council of Ireland abandoned.

Terror by both sides went on, the civil war continued.

VI

In its special handbook on terrorism and counterterrorism issued to its brigade and group leaders, the UDA proclaimed: "We must learn to defeat our enemies by learning from their mistakes and by producing an equal or greater amount of terror among their followers than they can among ours." Those UDA members who had served in the British army were urged to forget most of what they had learned in its ranks, for the army's methods were too conventional and meant for operations against regular forces. Action against guerrillas, to be successful, had to be cardinally different. The UDA had to immerse itself not in Her Majesty's field-warfare manuals, but in those bold texts left behind by the Jewish terrorists of the Irgun and the Stern Gang of the 1930s and '40s, by the OAS of Algeria in the 1950s, and other such formations. The appropriate writings by Lenin, Trotsky, Castro, Guevara, and certain Irish rebel leaders were to be studied: "It would do well if all our officers had some knowledge of the above-mentioned names." And even if the British army was regarded by the UDA as an ally against the Catholics, there was always, it was to be remembered, a fundamental difference between them. "The British Army will always lack our determination, for they have principles to uphold, but we have something more lasting than principles, we have homes, family and a country to defend."

But the British army is not that conventional. The so-called "hooding," at one time practiced by it in Ulster, has been described by both prisoners and doctors as unusually cruel and as leaving lasting mental effects on its subjects. This method was applied during the interrogation of IRA suspects. A hood was put over the man's head and he was placed against a wall with his arms raised, while a continuous, monotonous roar was mechanically created and kept up around him. Some such subjects were, on release, examined by Professor Robert Day, a psychiatrist at the University of Cork, who reported finding in them "psychological disabilities" and "psychosomatic problems," with symptoms "of marked anxiety, fear and dread, as well as insomnia, nightmares and startle-responses," all being the result of these men's "traumatic experiences" resembling "wartime combat fatigue." In addition to hooding, there were such non-Geneva Convention methods as depriving the detainees of sleep and limiting them to bread and water for sustenance.

Whatever the truth about the army's ways, unmitigated brutality has marked the mutual Irish terror of the non-army varieties. Almost every murder and bomb blast since 1969 well into these days has been perpetrated with cold-blooded cruelty and total disregard for life and limb. While at the start Catholic and Protestant activists were prime targets of the opposing sides, increasingly—by the mid-1970s—there were random killings of Catholics by Protestants and of Protestants by Catholics. Noncombatants were not only torn by bombs and hit by stray bullets but deliberately drawn into battle. On June 29, 1974, in the town of Kilrea, 60 miles west of Belfast, gunmen—suspected to be IRA Provos—kidnapped a young girl in her teens and as the price of her life compelled her boy friend to plant a 200-pound bomb in a car. Fortunately, the explosion caused no casualties.

Both sides vie in the ingenuity of their methods. For the Catholic side, we have already noted the use of a helicopter in the prison break at Mountjoy on October 31, 1973. This technique most likely gave an idea to that colorful personality, Bridget Rose Dugdale, a millionaire's daughter and a doctor of philosophy in economics, who, on January 24, 1974, tried to bomb an Ulster police station by dropping from a helicopter two explosive-filled milk churns. Both missed the target; moreover, neither exploded.

And in late April 1974, the same imaginative Bridget Rose led a gang in stealing from the Irish mansion of another millionaire 19 paintings valued at more than $19 million. For their safe return she demanded the transfer of Irish prisoners from England to Ulster, where they would be closer to their homes. These terms were not met, but on May 4 the paintings were found and recovered and Bridget Rose was arrested in a vacation cottage at a fishing port 50 miles from Cork. On June 25, in Dublin's Special Criminal Court, after declaring herself "proudly and incorruptibly guilty," the 33-year-old terrorist was sentenced to nine years of prison.

In the same month of her arrest, this Catholic originality was matched on the Protestant side and rather more successfully by the scheme to free Samuel Tweed, a leader of the Ulster Defense Association, as he stood trial in the Belfast Magistrate's Court. On May 7, 1974, during the hearing of his case, some 50 Protestant youths rushed into the courtroom shouting, "Bomb! Bomb!" Naturally enough, all present stampeded out of the building. In the confusion, Tweed climbed over a five-foot partition, ran past the panicked policemen, and vanished in a delivery truck awaiting him.

At times the masterful inventiveness of one side is thwarted by the shrewd precaution of the other. One January day in 1975, a seemingly abandoned automobile was noticed on the Ulster side of the border by customs men and soldiers. Nearby lay a lifeless human form, its head hooded. A suspected spy murdered by the Provos? "We are not, as some people think, silly Britts," said an army officer to me. No one neared either the car or the figure. A long cable was hooked onto the car by a special army unit at a proper distance; as the cable was pulled, the car and the figure blew up, injuring no one. The car proved to have been stolen, the figure was a tailor's dummy. Both were filled with explosives.

VII

Farther and farther afield went the IRA Provos in an attempt to regain what they were losing in 1972-73 to the governments both in London and Dublin, as well as to the paramilitary contingents of Ulster's Protestants. On August 27, 1973, an exploding letter-bomb tore off the left hand of a woman secretary in the British embassy in Washington. Closer home, the spread of the IRA terror to London and other English cities rushed on swiftly. Bombs causing deaths, injuries, and much property damage were detonated in stores, on the streets, at railroad stations and public buildings, many of the destructive and panic-sowing blasts occurring in August, September, and at Christmastime of 1973, and again in the latter half of 1974.

In London, on June 17, 1974, a 20-pound bomb exploded in Westminster Hall, the 900-year-old part of the Houses of Parliament, leaving holes and rubble but neither death nor wounds. However, exactly one month later, on July 17, a powerful bomb went off in a cellar armory of the historic Tower of London, killing one person and injuring 42.

Some of the terrorists responsible for the bombs of 1973-74 were apprehended. These included two young Price sisters, eventually tried and sentenced to 20 years in prison for their part in a 1973 car-bombing in London, in which one man died and more than 200 were injured. In May 1974, the two girls—Dolours, 23, and Marion, 20—attracted world-wide attention by going on a hunger strike in Brixton Prison. They demanded their transfer to a jail in Ulster. On June 7, after three weeks of starvation, they won. But another IRA fighter, Michael Gaughan, sentenced for a bank robbery to get funds for the Provos, did not win the same demand: on June 3, after 65 days without food, he died in Parkhurst Prison on the Isle of Wight.

Bombings in England reached a frightful mark on the evening of November 21, 1974, when powerful explosions destroyed two crowded pubs in Birmingham, killing 21 persons and injuring 184, many of them teen-agers. A number of bodies were so dismembered that it was difficult to collect the parts and identify the dead. A high representative of the Provos denied that this was the work of his organization and promised to find out who did it. He declared, however, that the Provos approved of such bombings even when they did not know their exact authorship.

Horror seized the nation. The wave of indignation was so high throughout England that voices were heard for drastic measures to be taken against the IRA terrorists at once. Bills to outlaw the IRA and bring back the death penalty (abolished in Britain in 1969) were introduced in the House of Commons.

David O'Connell, chief of staff of the Provos, threatened retaliation if capital punishment came back: "We will hang two British soldiers for every IRA man hanged." A woman member of the House from Birmingham commented: "These are not ordinary killers and we cannot treat them as such. Prison sentences will not deter these men. To them, only fools and the vanquished use kid gloves."

Nonetheless, on the evening of December 11, after a long day of debate, the House rejected capital punishment by a vote of 369 to 217. But the IRA was at last outlawed in Britain (as it had been in the Republic of Ireland for some years), and wide powers were given to the police to hunt down and detain terrorists.

England and Ulster were not the only bloody theaters. As if to prove that two could play the deadly game as well as one, there were indiscriminate bombings in Dublin, apparently done by Protestant commandos from Northern Ireland. On May 17, 1974, 28 died and some 130 were injured, many of them permanently, when bombs exploded at the peak of the rush hour in three automobiles parked in the center of Dublin. Dozens of other cars nearby were demolished, and there was other widespread property damage. People were hurled through store and office windows with a tremendous force. Experts later estimated that each of the three bombs contained 200 to 300 pounds of gelignite. So perturbed was the government of the Republic of Ireland that the very next day it decided to bolster the country's defense by recalling 340 Irish soldiers serving in the United Nations troops in the Sinai.

A significant change in tactics of the Provos operating in England became apparent in August 1975: either their central command or an extremist faction defying the command resolved to shift the attack in London from the pubs and other lower- and middle-class points of congregation to the elite clubs, restaurants, and residences of the West

End and other upper-class neighborhoods. The aim was clear: Hit the decision-makers! It is they who must pull British troops out of Ulster!

In late August one explosive was detonated in London's Hilton Hotel, wreaking much damage; another blew up a car in front of a Parliament member's house where Caroline Kennedy, the late U. S. President's daughter, was a guest. She escaped by minutes, but a well-known British physician, a cancer specialist, was killed while walking his dog.

On November 9 a bomb was spotted and defused beneath a car parked outside the Belgravia home of Edward Heath, the former Conservative Prime Minister. At October's end, 28 people were injured when a bomb was set off near a fashionable Italian restaurant in Mayfair. On November 12, on the same street, at Scott's, one of London's best restaurants, an explosion killed one person and injured 15. On the eighteenth, a bomb thrown through the window of yet another restaurant—Walton's in the Chelsea district—killed two and wounded 17 people, five of them gravely.

Outraged, a citizen announced a private campaign of counterterrorism, with a personal contribution of $100,000 for a start. This was Ross McWhirter, publisher-editor of the world-famous *Guiness Book of Records*. The Provos responded by shooting him dead at his doorstep, on November 27.

By then wiring automobiles with explosives was deemed by the terrorists as not effective enough: some bombs failed to go off, leaving telltale fingerprints for the police. So the Provos intensified the flinging of bombs and firing of shots from fast-moving cars. On December 6 one such car was pursued by the police until its four gunmen abandoned the vehicle and holed up in an apartment in the heart of London, taking hostage its tenants, a middle-aged couple. Some 200 police besieged the flat, and the terrorists gave up after six days.

Still, the British would try conciliation along with their police and army measures. On December 5, 1975, in Ulster, they ended their detention of terrorist suspects without trial, a practice in effect since August 1971. The last 46 detainees were freed from the Maze Prison in Belfast in time for their Christmas shopping and family reunions. On December 11, the House of Commons once more defeated the motion to reinstitute the death penalty for acts of terrorism causing loss of life.

But British patience was wearing thin: the Parliament vote was 361 to 232, whereas a year earlier those voting for death numbered 217 and in 1965 only 104. A poll undertaken for *The Daily Express* showed that nearly nine out of every ten Britons favored restoration of the death penalty for terrorists.

Throughout Great Britain, wherever I went in 1975, people supported their government's resolve to keep troops in Ulster. "An all-out civil war will be the result if we pull our soldiers out," was the comment I generally heard. "And the Irish Republic would be drawn into it, too," came from one person after another. "Most Catholics no less than Protestants in Ulster want our army there." And: "The Dublin government, too, wants our troops to stay."

Officials in Belfast persisted in negotiations with the peaceful Catholic minority to mold a political settlement acceptable to both sides. Said one such hopeful leader in early January 1976: "We will keep up our talks until the Catholics who agree to the settlement finally gain more of a base among their own people than they have now."

VIII

Among melancholy effects of the Irish terror is the alarming rise of drug addiction in Ulster. From 480 known addicts in 1969 the number rose to 8,000 in 1973. Proclaiming their virtuous outrage, the terrorists of both sides murdered eight drug-pushers in those four years.

Others seek solution in a different kind of escape. The world at large does not generally realize how many peaceful people have by now fled from Ulster. In the summer of 1972, when the flight first assumed mass proportions, a Catholic woman refugee said to a journalist in Ireland: "We were pinned down by snipers for three days. They think we are Republicans but we are not—we are just ordinary Catholics. All this business is really the fault of the politicians. The ordinary people don't want it. My man wants work, not a united Ireland. We don't belong to any organization at all."

At Londonderry and other afflicted cities and towns, Catholic women tried to organize demonstrations for peace, collecting signatures to petitions and staging marches to the Official IRA headquarters (the Provo centers were too well hidden in the underground). In April 1973, from the signatures under a peace petition in the Creggan area of Londonderry, formerly dominated by the IRA, it was ascertained that fully 84 per cent of the residents wanted terror to stop. In the Anderstown area of Belfast many Catholic teachers actively supported the housewives' peace campaign. Almost everywhere in Ulster, Catholic priests increasingly encouraged and joined this movement.

By late 1974 the battle fatigue of the population was beyond doubt. Both Catholics and Protestants were now staging peace demonstrations instead of those earlier militant marches of force and hatred. The Provos were discovering, to their amazement, that no longer were they welcomed even in the worst ghettos of Belfast, Londonderry, and other such concentrations of perennial Catholic misery.

This ebbing of Catholic support, as well as the refusal of the British to be intimidated by the Provo bombings in England, gave the terrorists pause. They announced a cease-fire for Christmas, eventually prolonging it to the middle of January 1975.

Later that month, as bombings resumed but negotiations for a new cease-fire continued, I asked in Belfast, at the headquarters first of the army, then of the police: "Suppose there is indeed a new cease-fire. Will those Provo lads obey their leaders for long? Will they refrain from blasting and shooting beyond just a few weeks?"

The army colonel briefing me shrugged slightly: "If there is a cease-fire, the Provo rank-and-file will at first obey, as on the whole they did during the Christmas respite. But longer than a few weeks, no. They are not truly disciplined. Wild. Too full of hatred. Too used to their violent life-style. They know no other way. In time, can't say how soon, they'll burst out again, no matter what their leaders' cease-fire strategy may be."

The army men and the constabulary I talked to also mentioned the hatred churning in the extremists of the Protestant side. Some of the loyalists, it was predicted, would not honor the cease-fire. They would, on the contrary, step up their shooting of the Catholics to provoke the Provos into rejoining the carnage, which would allow the loyalists a chance to rally support for the smashing of the IRA. People on both sides were sick and tired of the slaughter, but the terrorists were not. The Provos would rise to meet the new loyalist challenge.

And so it happened: Soon after February 10, when the second cease-fire was announced, the Protestant extremists did attack, and the Provos responded in kind. There were also killings among the Catholics themselves, settlings of obscure scores between the Provos and the Officials. In a period of three days alone, in early April, 11 persons were killed and some 80 wounded in Belfast. From February 10 to April 6, despite the "truce," 35 persons were killed. By May 10, 1975, the total of those killed in Ulster since the start of the mutual slaughter (August 1969) was more than 1,200. By January 5, 1976, the tragic toll increased to 1,427. In just two days, January 4 and 5, in County Armagh alone, 15 men were murdered (five Catholics on the fourth, and ten Protestants on the fifth). On the sixth, the British government moved to send 600 additional soldiers to Ulster, bringing the army strength there to nearly 16,000.

Terror has a way of self-perpetuation. And history repeats itself, in Ireland no less than elsewhere. Wrote Paul Wilkinson in *Political Ter-*

rorism about the persistence of the earlier bloodshed after the establishment of the Republic of Ireland: "Many of those who fought for the IRA had known no other life since their demobilization from the First World War: many had been unemployed or came from the small-peasant class. There were few who felt impelled to return to the routine of ordinary civilian existence."[6]

The Protestant work ethic is said to make the opponents of the IRA inherently more law-abiding, but the behavior of the Ulster loyalists somewhat belies this thesis. Both extremes, Protestant and Catholic, are at each other's throats, making mockery of each successive cease-fire.

Nor is this an Irish condition solely. As in Robespierre's Great Terror, as in the Red and White civil war in Russia, as in a thousand other mutual massacres throughout history, so in Northern Ireland today the majority of people who want peace through compromise have no chance against the minority bent on destruction and death.

30

New Europe's Old Hatreds

On the continent of Europe, some of the busiest terrorists of modern times have been those of West Germany. They are on the far left, with a violent revolutionary program. The Bonn government and the world's media call them anarchists, but they define themselves as the truest Marxists-Leninists-Maoists to be found anywhere in creation. Known commonly as "the Baader-Meinhof Gang" (or "Band"), after the names of their most aggressive leaders, Andreas Baader and Ulrike Meinhof, the terrorists' official designation is *Rote Armee Fraktion*, or the Red Army Faction.

This group rose out of the student disorders of 1968 as a small but highly warlike organization of university dropouts and other restless intellectuals. Never larger than some 60 members, it declared as its goal a complete overthrow and destruction of the bourgeois Establishment and an introduction of "rule by the freed masses."

The Gang's first sensational exploit was setting fire to a Frankfurt department store in April 1968. Baader, then 27 years old, led the team of leftist incendiaries and later publicly lauded the virtue of their "torch against the capitalistic terror of consumerism." That spring came a counterpoint: a right-wing loner, a house painter-terrorist who crazily worshipped Hitler's portraits on the walls of his West Berlin room, tried to assassinate the well-known young revolutionary, Rudi Dutschke, wounding him seriously. At once, in West Berlin and elsewhere, street demonstrations and battles against the police by leftist students broke out in baleful abundance.

Meanwhile, Baader and his three fellow arsonists were arrested. During their trial in West Berlin in October 1968, they declared: "It's the rotten system of justice, not us, that is on trial." Found guilty, each of the four was sentenced to three years in prison.

At West Berlin's Tegel Prison, where Baader was confined, conditions were mild for privileged inmates. Since Baader, a former university student of sociology, wished for intellectual work, powerful friends in the government secured for him permission to research and write a book on juvenile delinquency. His collaborator was to be the well-known political columnist, Ulrike Meinhof, who had been a radical but had not been known as a terrorist, and who had once interviewed him. On May 14, 1970, she was waiting for Baader in the library of the German Central Institute for Social Problems, situated in Dahlem, a comfortable section of Berlin, when two Tegel guards brought the prisoner to meet her. Suddenly the collaboration in academe flared into quite a different kind of cooperation: several gunmen entered the Institute, shot and wounded one of its employees as well as one of the guards, and whisked both Baader and Meinhof away in a waiting silvery-gray Alfa Romeo coupe, which later was found to have been stolen.

Once they were successfully entrenched underground, Baader and Meinhof began a campaign of terror, Baader providing the Gang's technical skills, which included bomb-making and car-stealing, while Ulrike Meinhof supplied the Gang's ideology. She had diligently read the works of Herbert Marcuse and other revolutionary theorists.

As her fame spread, details of her background gradually came to light. Born in 1934 to two art historians, she was, reports tell us, an orphan brought up by leftist academics. In the mid-1960s she was the wife of Klaus Rainer Roehl, editor of *Konkret,* a Hamburg magazine of sex and leftist politics, described with reluctant admiration by the writer Melvin Lasky as a publication of superior quality that was prepared for "a wide following of agitators, students, anarchists, poets, terrorists, and assorted disenchanted spirits longing for a new Utopia."[1] Ulrike wrote radical columns for *Konkret* at profitable rates, and bore twin daughters for her husband-editor.

Both husband and wife were secret members of the Communist Party, and their magazine was financed by Communists in East Berlin who sent money via Prague, as Roehl, on his eventual disillusionment, would later divulge in a book. When Ulrike was working with Roehl, he and his friends would, in high spirits, play with firearms. At first their target practice frightened her into hysterics and utterly repelled her. Roehl would in time attribute her aversion to shooting not only to her early Christian pacifism (which had originally led her into mild leftist causes), but also to her ever-throbbing head pains—the consequence of a brain-tumor operation.

Some have speculated that the surgery, which left a metal clip implanted in her head, caused her to become a terrorist. But a specific influence was her association with Andreas Baader.

They had first met when she interviewed him in prison and had written a column on him for *Konkret,* full of frenetic admiration for his terrorism. This led to her break with Roehl and his group's relatively nonviolent radicalism, and marked the beginning of her affair with terrorists and terrorism. Although Andreas Baader had a girl friend, who had been arrested along with him, Ulrike, taking her daughters (then six years old), left her husband. No longer was Roehl the revolutionary enough for her. After his daughters' eventual return to him, he, dismayed by his wife's activities, became even less of a radical.

Yet for a while he wanted Ulrike back both as a wife and a columnist. He was humble; she was raging. In making her final gesture, she was assisted by her new friends. They raided her husband's comfortable home in a fashionable section of Hamburg. According to Lasky's description, "They sacked the premises, smashing the lamps, furniture, and stereo and painting a phallus on the front door. Before leaving, they collectively urinated on the double bed."[2]

Ulrike joined and soon headed the Red Army Faction as it stepped up its terrorism. Her first criminal act was the dramatic freeing of Baader from imprisonment. With that, she went underground.

In the early summer of 1970 the pair led their Gang on a visit to the Middle East for conferences and training with the Arab fedayeen. For a while they stayed in a guerrilla camp in Jordan, mixing their target-shooting and Jew-hating with drinking and sex. Their Arab mentors found these last two activities offensive. The Arabs expelled the entire German contingent.

The Gang returned to West Germany in August 1970, with novel ideas and new weapons. At one point they augmented their arsenal by a daring raid on a West German-NATO base. One member planted a bomb in a Berlin synagogue, to get rid of (as he explained) the last trace of his guilt sense over old Nazi atrocities. The group declared themselves Maoists as they launched a series of terror hits in various German cities. This campaign would last some two years, despite all the desperate police efforts to corner them.

Their activities crested in May 1972, when the Gang bombed the police headquarters at Augsburg and Munich; dynamited the Axel Springer Publishing House in Hamburg, with 17 persons injured, six of them gravely; set off an explosive at the headquarters of the United States Army Fifth Corps in Frankfurt, killing an American colonel; and blasted the car park of the United States military headquarters in Heidelberg, where three American servicemen died and eight were injured. In the winter of 1971-72, when the police were intensifying their effort to find and round up the terrorists, some left-wing intellectuals protested that the state was unduly frightened and harsh, that the whole problem could be solved amicably. The writer Heinrich Böll, in his liberalism, publicly suggested the authorities cease their hunt of the commandos and offer them free passage out of Germany.

But the state had no desire for any such negotiations, nor did the terrorists wish to leave Germany. Their bloody successes of May 1972 in particular seemed to prove that they, not the government, had the upper hand. From her hideout, Ulrike Meinhof issued a tape boasting of her Faction's accomplishments and promising new sensations.

She bragged too soon. The very next month the Faction's luck changed. On June 1, in Frankfurt, acting on a tip, the police besieged an apartment house in which Baader and three of his fellow terrorists were barricaded. After a 90-minute gun battle, all four were captured, Baader with a wound in his hip. On June 15, Ulrike Meinhof and a fellow Faction member, Gerhard Mueller, were located after a tip led the police to an apartment in a Hanover suburb. When the police rang the bell, Ulrike herself opened the door. After violent resistance, Meinhof and Mueller were captured.

Other arrests followed. Soon the police asserted that the Red Army Faction was reduced from its former strength of 60 members to 20 or less. From time to time there were uneasy reports, or guesses, that Arab terrorists would stage an airplane hijacking for the express purpose of demanding the release of imprisoned members of the Red Army Faction, especially the freeing of Baader and Meinhof. Such a demand did come in March 1973 from Khartoum, where Arab raiders had seized three Western diplomats; but the terms of exchange were not met, and the diplomats were murdered.

During 1973-74, the Gang's remnants tried to prove that, despite the arrests of their leaders and comrades, the group was still alive and fighting. On November 17 and 18, 1973, blasts ripped through the Nuremberg and West Berlin office buildings of a West German subsidiary of the International Telephone and Telegraph Corporation. The terrorists regarded the explosions as acts of retribution; the giant American corporation had meddled in the politics of Chile, and the Gang believed the company's interference had caused President Allende's downfall and death the previous September.

But arrests by the West German police also continued, a particularly effective series occurring in February 1974. Early that spring a West Berlin court tried six members of the Faction, who were charged with crimes of terror that had occurred between 1970-73. The five women and one man were in their twenties and thirties; they included a medical assistant, a lawyer, a mechanic, a former university student, and two others, dropouts or drifters. On July 2, 1974, after 133 days of hearings and deliberations, the court sentenced them to prison terms ranging from seven to 13 years.

The cases against the main contingent of the Gang—Ulrike Meinhof, Andreas Baader, and some two score of their closest followers—were being slowly prepared through 1972-74. The Gang's sympathizers at large were active and effective in enlisting support for the group. Soon it was a badge of radical chic to render them all manner of support. As many as 22 lawyers devoted themselves to Baader's case, while Meinhof had 16 attorneys.

Here and there Lutheran clergymen were recruited into support. In Berlin a young pastor was arrested. His record included providing terrorists with forged passports. The wife of another pastor was detained on similar charges. Another Lutheran clergyman sermonized from his West Berlin pulpit that the arrested pastor, in helping the terrorists, "behaved like a true disciple of Christ." Outraged parishioners began to leave the fold. In the late fall of 1974 it was estimated that some 700 believers a day were leaving, and that by Christmastime a total of 20,000 would defect.

The authorities seemed to bend backward in trying to prove to such persons that they, too, were brother-loving Christians: they made sure these terrorist prisoners had comfortable cells, with radio and television sets and an unlimited supply of books, with table tennis and frequent fresh-air exercise available, as well as the right to receive visiting kin and lawyers as often as they wished.

Nonetheless, the prisoners and their admirers complained bitterly, and on September 13 Meinhof and 39 of her fellow terrorists in the West German and Berlin jails went on a hunger strike. The design was plain: they would be transferred from the cells to the prison hospitals, from which escapes could be arranged.

Later it became known that the strikers cheated with the aid of their lawyers, who smuggled in food in their briefcases for the prisoners to eat stealthily at night. But one of the terrorists, Holger Meins, 33 years old, would be honest. He did not eat. Despite the intravenous feeding, he became weaker and weaker, and two months later, on November 9, 1974, he died.

The very next day, to avenge his death, a group of Meinhof-Baader terrorists murdered West Berlin's chief judge, Guenther von Drenkmann, a life-long Socialist who had had no involvement in the Gang's cases. He was picked as a victim at random. One of the terrorists telephoned the judge's house to say that flowers would be delivered from a friend to honor his sixty-fourth birthday. Half a dozen terrorists came; one of them rang the bell. Expecting the flowers, the judge's wife opened the door, one of the armed six rushed in, found the judge, and shot him dead.

In addition, several thousand leftists demonstrated in memory of

Holger Meins on the streets of West Berlin and Stuttgart. The government responded with a fresh roundup of 14 suspected terrorists. Among them, Wolf-Dieter Reinhard, a lawyer of Hamburg, was arrested on suspicion of membership in the Baader-Meinhof Gang's offshoot, the June 2nd Group, which was accused of killing in a Berlin park one of its activists, Ulrich Schmueckler, for talking to the police.

While searching the premises of those arrested, the police found 600 kilograms of bomb-making chemicals; quantities of explosive bullets; canisters of chloroform, apparently to be used on future kidnap victims; forged police-car license plates; a portable radio transmitter; floor plans of prisons holding the Baader-Meinhof Gang members; detailed schemes for bank robberies as well as for courtroom raids to free prisoners on trial; and maps of airdromes from which high Bonn officials usually took off. Too, there were photographs of the security guards accompanying the officials.

At last, on November 29, 1974, Ulrike Meinhof went on trial in West Berlin for her role in the May 1970 rescue of Baader. She was sentenced to eight years in prison, but both she and Baader were scheduled for trial that would be held in the late spring of 1975 for other acts of terrorism that had caused seven deaths.

Two attempts to free imprisoned Gang members occurred in early 1975. On February 27, three days before the local election, a terrorist team kidnapped Peter Lorenz, the Christian Democrat Party's candidate for Mayor of West Berlin. The commandos demanded the release of six of their comrades from Bonn's prisons, to be flown out of Germany, each of them to be supplied with $10,000 of state money. But Baader and Meinhof were not on this list; the commandos might have felt that such a stiff demand would be refused, and that they would fare better by naming lesser members. If so, they were right. The "moderate" terms were met. While one of the six declined to be freed because of involved revolutionary principle, the other five (two men and three women) agreed. With $50,000 in their pockets, they were flown to Communist South Yemen. Lorenz was set free after five and a half days of lying handcuffed and drugged in a West Berlin cellar.

Higher stakes were named by six German terrorists on April 24 when they shot their way into the West German embassy in Stockholm. Seizing hostages, including the Ambassador, they demanded freedom for 26 Baader-Meinhof Gang members, among them the two leaders. The Bonn government refused the demand. A shootout with Swedish police followed. The terrorists killed two hostages (the military and economic attachés), and tried to escape. All six were captured, one of them mortally wounded in a suicide attempt. The other five were extradited to West Germany for trial, but on May 4 one of these died of injuries in a Stuttgart hospital.

On the morning of May 9, 1976, Ulrike Meinhof was found hanged from toweling at the window rails of her maximum security cell in the Stuttgart prison, where she had awaited one more trial. It was clearly a suicide, but extremists shouted "Foul play" as they burst out in street riots in Frankfurt and elsewhere. On June 1, two time bombs were exploded at the Frankfurt headquarters of the United States Army's Fifth Corps, injuring 15 Americans (including several wives of soldiers) and one German civilian.

In all such battles, little sympathy for terrorists is evidenced by broad strata of West Germans. True, on occasion leftist students and dropouts demonstrate to protest a killing by the police, but they are not joined by any massive outpouring of workers. To the contrary, the general populace voices its disapproval of governmental weakness in such cases as the Lorenz abduction, and approves the firmness as shown in the Stockholm episode. In this era, so far distant from the reign of the Nazis, Germany rejects terror and any other tremor from whatever quarter. It yields to kidnappers only rarely and under extreme duress.

II

In Italy, that whilom partner of Hitlerite terror, the latest phase of political bloodshed is a crazy quilt of both extremes, left and right, seeming to meet in a common enterprise of violence and death.

At times it is difficult to sort out where the far left ends and the neofascist begins. The frustrated Italian police blame, for the same outrage, now the Maoists and anarchists, now the right-wing militants. Thus, on December 12, 1969, a blast in a Milan bank killed 16 persons and injured many others. The police arrested an anarchist, accusing him of having planted the bomb. He was still in prison in March 1972 when a neofascist was arrested on the same charge. Later, several other ultrarightists were listed as possible coconspirators in the case.

In the meanwhile came the Red Brigades, and the celebrated Feltrinelli episode.

The Red Brigades, active since 1970, is a terrorist group proclaiming Maoism its credo. Its flag bears the symbol of hammer and sickle with a novel variation: the two Leninist implements are crossed with a submachine gun. These men and women kidnap business executives, labor leaders, and government officials in Milan, Turin, and other cities, demanding either money or the release of political prisoners and sometimes both. Now and then they complain that in some instances the authorities only pretend to bow to these terms, for sometimes, after the Red Brigades free their kidnapped, the conditions of the exchange are not honored by the state.

Killings by the Red Brigades of their captives are frequent. In 1974, in Genoa, State Attorney Francesco Coco refused to negotiate with these terrorists their kidnapping of another local prosecutor, Mario Sossi. For years Coco kept up his investigation of the Red Brigades until June 8, 1976, when he was shot dead on a Genoa downtown street, along with his bodyguard and his chauffeur.

Giangiacomo Feltrinelli was said to have been closely connected with the Red Brigades, in Milan and elsewhere. The son of a vastly rich Lombardy family, who had also inherited much wealth in Austria from his German mother, a countess, the young man spent millions on a left-wing publishing house he owned and on other radical activities. Drawn by the first of his four wives into the Communist Party, he grew disillusioned by Moscow's policies and renounced his membership after Soviet tanks had crushed the Hungarian revolt of 1956. The next year, despite strong Kremlin displeasure, he was the first to publish Boris Pasternak's *Doctor Zhivago*, to great artistic and commercial success. This was followed by other publishing spectaculars.

In the early 1960s he became enamored with Latin American guerrillas, especially with Ché Guevara, and was soon fast personal friends with Fidel Castro. But his involvement in radical Italian militancy led to his being questioned by the police, and in December 1969 he vanished, possibly to one of his luxury apartments or villas in Austria.

Nevertheless he would from time to time stealthily revisit Italy, and on March 14, 1972, his mangled corpse was found at the base of a sabotaged power-grid pylon near Milan. The body bore tatters of military fatigues. He was 45 at the time of his death, and, in spite of all his expensive eccentricities, still a millionaire.

The police theory was that, in trying to blow up the pylon, he in his amateur way mishandled the explosive and so blasted himself fatally. Yet the leftists of Italy insisted that Feltrinelli must have been lured to the pylon by some neofascists who murdered him with that explosive, making his death appear as the result of his own terroristic clumsiness, all to discredit the nation's Maoists and other Communists and anarchists. The police seemed to be at a loss as to what to think and do. They arrested several leftists on suspicion of having been with Feltrinelli in the pylon misadventure, but the evidence was highly circumstantial, and so the suspects were soon released.

Thus perished postwar Italy's most picturesque terrorist or would-be terrorist. The well-known author Luigi Barzini, who at one time had been married to Feltrinelli's mother, wrote a perceptive obituary of his tragic stepson:[3]

> It is not important to know if Giangi died as the victim of a secret plot or because he made an error in charging electricity into the dynamite. The secret plot is always a fascinating explanation for the right-wing or the left-wing political fans. . . .
>
> He was that kind of man who is common in Italy and who is able to go from an extremist movement (Fascism) to the opposite (Communism) provided it be illiberal and mythological, without stopping at the stage of ideas (maybe boring and too serious because they don't promise any miracles but only toil) of the bourgeois revolution, of freedom laboriously conquered and defended every day, allowing problems to be faced and gradually solved, tolerating—or rather extracting and using—what is valid in dissident and heretical movements.

Barzini pondered the drive that had taken Feltrinelli in and out of the Communist Party:

> That he would have abandoned the Party as soon as he would have felt its discipline, its control, its constraints, and as soon as he would have noticed that it was not an organization of terrorists and dynamiters, spreading the corpses of foes in the streets at night, but a vast, cautious, and erudite movement treasuring fifty years of defeats in every country and determined to win while avoiding a catastrophic civil war (for Italy's and its own sake), was clear to anyone who knew him. . . .
>
> Giangi died because of his ideas and it is negligible now to see whether they were just, practical, or foolish. It is impossible not to feel respect for his sacrifice . . . his death with courage and levity, under the illusion he could provoke an immediate revolution that would never be stopped.

Neofascist terrorists have also been busy in Italy, bombing liberal and leftist publishing offices, gatherings, and individuals. Groups calling themselves New Order, Rose of the Winds, and Mussolini Action Squad have been suspect. In the industrial city of Brescia, a high-explosive time bomb, left in a plastic garbage bag, went off at an anti-fascist rally of May 28, 1974. Six persons were killed and 94 injured. In the early morning of August 4, 1974, a bomb exploded on a Munich-bound train, just as it emerged from a ten-mile tunnel between Florence and Bologna. Twelve persons were killed, and 48 were injured. The next day, in a note deposited in a Bologna telephone booth, Black Order, a rightist terror group, claimed responsiblity for the bombing, done—the note declared—to show "that we are capable of placing bombs where we want, at any time, in any place, when and where we please." Killings by both rightists and leftists reached their crescendo with a particular viciousness just before the national elections of June 1976.

The end is not in sight. Bogged down in economic troubles, which are exacerbated by the energy crisis, with leadership in part inept and in part corrupt, Italy appears to be among the first of West European countries destined for early chaos. In her woes the polarization of her classes grows deeper and sharper, and her new terror more threatening.

III

For a long time between the two World Wars, Red terror in France was carried on by non-French aganst other non-French. The most sensational episodes were kidnappings by Soviet secret agents, in broad daylight on the streets of Paris, of two prominent White émigré generals—Pavel Kutepov on January 26, 1930, and Yevgeny Miller on September 22, 1937. Both abductions were done with extreme skill; neither victim was ever again seen or heard from. Both, it is likely, were drugged and taken to Soviet freighters standing ready in French ports. They died either of an overdose of drugs aboard ships or were killed later in the Soviet Union.[4]

Terror in France went native after World War II. In the 1950s and early 1960s, French army officers initiated terror against the regime of President Charles de Gaulle over the Algerian problem and in the 1960s-70s the leftist nationalists of Brittany began their own terror.

At the start, the Breton movement, in addition to its secret activities, functioned in the open. The *Front de Libération de la Bretagne* was registered with the authorities; its president, Yann-Morvan Gefflot, was also director of the monthly journal *Bretagne Révolutionnaire*. The Front's surface program seemed innocent enough as it pledged to "promote, favor, support, and organize all initiatives toward a reform of the cultural, economic, and political structures of Britanny." Some members of the Front also belonged to the legitimate Breton Communist Party.

But this well-behaved aspect of the Front fell into abeyance as militants prevailed. Out of the peaceful groups grew two aggressive organizations: *Front de Libération de la Bretagne—Armée Révolutionnaire Bretonne* (FLB-ARB), and *Front de Libération de la Bretagne—Pour la Libération Nationale et le Socialisme* (FLB-LNS).

The first of these, FLB-ARB, soon declared itself a member-organization of the militant *Comité National de la Bretagne Libre*, run by its secondary general, Yann Goulet, a veteran activist. In the early 1970s it became known that Goulet was residing in the Republic of Ireland, where a small terrorist organization, *Saor Eire*, or Free Ireland, was his host. These Irish revolutionaries revealed in October 1972 that 16 members of the FLB-ARB had been trained in weapon-handling in the SE secret camps in Ireland and that arms and terrorists were busily exchanged between Brittany, Ireland, and Spain.

The Spanish contact was with the Basque terrorists, and here the *Front de Libération de la Bretagne* worked through its other creation: the group *Pour la Libération Nationale et le Socialisme*, or the FLB-LNS. This Breton formation issued on December 26, 1973, a joint communiqué with the Basque *Euzkadi Ta Azkatasuna*, the name meaning Basque Country and Freedom, the text reading: "By claiming the right to social, cultural, and political liberation, the Basque and Breton peoples are only demanding the recognition of their just rights, denied by the capitalist system."

The FLB-ARB made numerous bombing forays in France in the latter 1960s, until the authorities reacted by arresting 60 of its members in 1969. But in time they were amnestied, and some of them, together with new recruits, re-emerged with a series of explosions in 1971-72. This resulted in 11 arrests in 1972, but even more bombs were set off in various governmental installations the following year. Among other targets in Brittany, a monument to De Gaulle was blown up on October 11, 1973, the day before the scheduled visit by a Gaullist cabinet minister; an unfinished headquarters building of the gendarmerie was exploded on November 28; and two tax-collecting offices in two towns were bombed on December 8, all of these being "symbols of the exploitation of Brittany," in the solemn language of the terrorists.

In 1974, the FLB-ARB consisted of some 150 to 200 activists; the FLB-LNS membership was somewhat smaller. In late January of that year Raymond Marcellin, French minister of the interior, banned both FLB formations. Also outlawed were two other ethnic terrorist groups: the French Basque *Enbata* (a Basque name for a local wind), and the Corsican Liberation Front. As his reason for the ban, Marcellin gave not the quartet's open politics or even underground terrorism but their liaison with the pugnacious brethren in Spain and certain of the Italian bomb-throwers.

The non-Breton, non-Basque political terrorism in France has been sporadic and of several varieties and origins. In May 1968, during massive student riots, small groups of ultraleft terrorists acted in spontaneous and haphazard ways. They did not seem to have any definite program of assassination or other systematic violence; their leadership was mediocre. Daniel Cohn-Bendit, the student firebrand best known at the time, and rather feared by the Establishment, was not in fact a real organizer and true peril. As the French turmoil, so similar to other such student disorders in Western Europe and North America, gradually subsided, Cohn-Bendit was deported to his native West Germany and soon disappeared from the headlines.

In 1972, worried by the year's Breton explosions and by the Arab guerrilla attack on Israel's Olympic athletes in Munich in September, the French government ordered the organization of a specially trained Anti-Commando Brigade of 40 sharpshooters, set up in five teams of eight men each, the teams to rotate so that one of them was always on the alert. The Brigade was supplied with high-speed cars and helicopters, and with the latest arms able to wrench loose "madmen barricaded inside a house," as a police official put it.

Still, in 1973-74, the Brigade could not prevent the continuing series of Paris bombings by Breton and other occasional terrorists. On May 23, 1974, the dome of the Sacre Coeur basilica was blasted, huge blocks of its stone crashing to the street and damaging several parked cars but fortunately causing no deaths or injuries. Leftist telephone callers to the media took credit for this, saying it was their protest against the recent victory of Valéry Giscard d'Estaing as France's President over the left's candidate, François Mitterand, as well as their homage to the memory of the Paris Commune on the occasion of its hundred and third anniversary.

Political killings on the streets of Paris went on into 1975-76. On October 24, 1975, the Turkish Ambassador Ismail Erez was slain by foes unknown; on May 11, 1976, the Bolivian Ambassador Joaquin Zenteno was shot dead for his erstwhile role in hunting down Ché Guevara; and three days later, a lone anarchist killed Jacques Chaine, one of France's most prominent bankers, and then—on the same sidewalk—fired a bullet into his own temple, dying near his victim.

IV

In Spain, Generalissimo Francisco Franco, a miraculously long-lived relic of Europe's dictatorial era of the 1930s and '40s, was in the postwar years under an unremitting leftist terrorist threat.

As we have seen, the Basques have been in the forefront of terroristic pressure. Their three organizations, in order of strength, are: in Spain, *Euzkadi Ta Azkatasuna* (ETA), or Basque Country and Freedom; and in France, *Enbata* and *Anai Artea*, or Between Brothers— both principally politically oriented mutual-aid organizations. The two French Basque groups see their role not in any violence on French soil, which is indeed minimal or even nonexistent, as in active assistance to the Spanish Basque militants of the ETA with money, arms, and hideouts.

The Spanish Basque terrorists first asserted themselves in 1953, when they split from the *Partido Nacionalista Vasco* (PNV) or Basque Nationalist Party, which they scorned as handicapped by its aging and inactive leaders. But it was six years later, in 1959, that four impatient Basques organized the terrorist ETA. These were Julian Madariaga, Benito del Valle, Alvarez Emperanza, and Aguirre Bilbao.

As its grand aim, the ETA declared the unification and socialization of all the seven Basque departments in both Spain and France, the French Basque *Enbata*—headed by Simon Haran, a Spanish Basque— publicly joining in this goal. They not only conducted acts of terror in the name of their cause, but also became members of a community of terrorists. They arranged for young ETA recruits to be trained in arms at secret Irish Republican Army camps; and, alongside the Provos, they were involved with gun-running operations. At least one clandestine meeting of the Provos, the Basques, and the Bretons took place in Belgium. The ETA also claimed connections with the Arab fedayeen on the one hand, and with the Kurdish guerrillas fighting against the Iraqi Arabs on the other.

Franco's government was uneasy. In 1968 it declared a state of siege for all Spain. In December 1970, a group of 16 Basques, charged with the murder of a local police chief, were tried by a military court at Burgos. Six were sentenced to death, but later spared for life imprisonment; the other ten received long jail terms. Strikes and demonstrations followed, the Basques joined by anarchists and other leftists in their violence. In the same month of December the Basque militants kidnapped the West German consul general. He was released, with the help of the French Basques of the nonviolent *Anai Artea* acting as intermediaries.

The terror increased in 1972-73. Wealthy industrialists were kidnapped. Some would, however, later be released with no ransom paid but on the victims' promise to satisfy their workers' demand of wage raises and other benefits. But there were also bombings and battles with the police, in which some terrorists were captured or killed.

The attitude of certain leftists toward the Basque terrorists is of interest. The local Communists and Socialists, hurting because the police hit at them each time they could not snare the ETA activists and jealous of the latter's successes, kept saying that these Basques were all middle-class elitists with no real roots among the proletariat. And yet, in the northern Basque country, the police found it extraordinarily difficult to corner the ETA elements because, foremost, the populace—including the proletarians—was sympathetic to these militant nationalists and readily, despite risks, gave them food, shelter, and information. In addition, many of the local Roman Catholic clergy lent their support to the terrorists. Without explicitly approving their violence, these priests in public statements explained it as understandable—as a natural answer to the abject poverty of the people and the harsh ways of the Franco regime.

The year 1973 ended with an upsurge of Basque activities. On December 6, in a six-hour gun battle with the police at San Sebastian, an ETA member was shot dead, and December 7 blazed with eight explosive attacks, apparently timed by the ETA to mark the third anniversary of the Burgos trial.

The most spectacular attentat, on December 20, 1973, was a resounding triumph for the Basque terrorists of the ETA. This was their assassination in Madrid of 70-year-old Admiral Luis Carrero Blanco, Spain's Prime Minister, Dictator Franco's closest adviser and friend.

The method was this: The Basques blew up the Prime Minister by digging a tunnel from a basement apartment to the middle of the street upon which he habitually rode in a car each morning. In 1881, the Narodniki had abandoned their tunnel and their plan of exploding the Tsar's carriage from below; they came to the surface to murder him, thereby exposing themselves to the hands of the police immediately after their awful achievement. But the far-better-equipped Basques of 1973 remained in their basement to their successful end, safely hidden, and were able to escape undetected in the confusion following their underground blast.

The Basque ETA named it Operation *Ogro* (Ogre), and the victim himself thoughtfully helped his assassins accomplish their macabre plan. The Ogre—Prime Minister Admiral Carrero Blanco—paid the ultimate price of his own fixed routine: his faithful daily attendance, at exactly the same hour, of the morning mass in the Jesuit Church of San Francisco de Borja, a large red-brick structure a few blocks from his apartment house in the center of Madrid, quite close to the American embassy.

Four ETA members, intrepid men who learned digging and dynamiting, were detailed for the task. They found a vacant basement apartment in the Calle Claudio Coello, a street just behind the church, exactly the route punctually taken by the Premier's car after the mass. One of the terrorists rented the apartment, saying he was a sculptor, thus explaining to the building superintendent the constant noise of work in the basement as part of the "sculptor's" profession.

Just the same, there were close calls in the process of digging the tunnel. One time the ground seemed to collapse; fearing a cave-in and discovery, the terrorists had their guns on the ready for battle. Another crisis came on a night when the superintendent knocked on the door, trying to deliver a message. Were the plotters to admit him, he would have seen bags of earth taken out of the dig. Their situation was saved when a bed in the apartment crashed down, and one of the men pretended to curse for her clumsiness a woman who was not there. The superintendent grinned and went away.

Gas fumes wafted from the tunnel into the apartment, presenting grave danger. Yet the work proceeded. When carried to the middle of the street, the tunnel was 25 feet long, and from that point it was extended horizontally some 22 feet, forming a T. The terrorists brought in 165 pounds of TNT and other explosives, distributing them in three equal charges. They also installed a strong metal plate as the base for the explosives to guide the blast upward to the street.

For a more ample source of power, a wire had to be strung from the charges to the apartment and up to the street. Two of the terrorists undertook the delicate job, explaining to the superintendent that they had been sent by the electric power company to provide the "sculptor" with the extra voltage he needed for his art. And so they labored in the open, unsuspected and undisturbed.

The ETA first set the assassination for December 18 or 19. On the nineteenth, Dr. Henry Kissinger, the United States Secretary of State, was to visit Spain. In their naive ignorance of his Jewish faith, the terrorists hoped to kill him along with the Premier—for surely, they reasoned, he would accompany Carrero Blanco to the mass. They chuckled: How pleased the ETA's Arab friends would be!

But the Secretary's visit led to stepped-up precautions by Spain's security force. The ETA decided to let Kissinger escape—they would postpone the Premier's death by one day. Besides, the twentieth would have a special meaning: on that day a trial of ten leftists was to begin, and although these were not ETA members or allies, the symbolic value of the attentat would be enhanced.

Two nights before the twentieth, the plotters went to a film house to see *The Day of the Jackal*, which they enjoyed very much, except for the picture's end, where De Gaulle miraculously escapes his fate. Never mind, they assured one another, in *their* case there would be no such failure.

And there wasn't. But one final detail was in order: The plotters felt it necessary to double-park a car at a certain place on the street at the very last moment, both to mark the best possible spot for the detonation and to compel the Premier's chauffeur to drive precisely along the center of the street. And so the car was left at the designated point, casually, easily, that Thursday morning, the twentieth of December. At exactly 9:30 A.M., as the Premier's automobile was passing over the charged parts of the T, the explosives were set off.

The Premier's vehicle was hurled upward with tremendous force, over the roof of five stories, and landed on the terrace surrounding the inner patio of the church. The police, rushing to the fatal site in the street and seeing only a huge hole but no car in it, were at first puzzled. But in a trice the tragedy was clear. The Premier was dying in the wreckage; it was later said that he was still breathing when rushed to a hospital, but was soon dead. So were his chauffeur and a guard.

The four killers ran from the basement to the street, shouting, "Gas! Gas!" This gave the police their initial mistaken thought that gas had caused the blast—and provided the plotters with their getaway chance. A waiting car nearby picked them up; a few blocks farther on, they changed to another auto. Soon they were safe, having crossed overland into Portugal and then, by boat, to France.

That morning Dr. Kissinger was in Paris when he heard the tragic news. In Spain there was shock among Franco's officials and supporters and grim jubilation or at least satisfaction for many others. Black humor buzzed in the cafés, one joke noting that "Carrero rose toward heaven but didn't quite make it," another suggesting that the church that had proved to be the Premier's undoing should be renamed "Our Lady of the Ascension."

On the night of the twentieth, at Bordeaux in France, an underground Spanish Basque spokesman claimed the ETA's responsibility for the deed. Even more formally, on Friday night, December 28, again in Bordeaux, four hooded men held a secret news conference to declare that they were the Premier's successful and proud assassins.

In anger, Franco's government protested to the French government against this seeming asylum to the killers, but the Paris police asserted that the four could not be apprehended because they had slipped back into Spain right after their press conference. Still, to placate the Madrid regime, the Paris authorities did, on New Year's Day of 1974, round up six radical Spanish Basques and send them under police guard to northern France, away from the Spanish frontier. Most of the six indignantly denied any active part in the ETA.

In September 1974, two Spanish-language anti-Franco publishing houses in Paris issued a book that was an extended interview with the Premier's killers as taped by Julen Agirre, a Basque journalist, an émigré from Spain.[5] With his tape recorder he had been taken, blindfolded, to meet the Operation Ogre men in an ETA hideout in the French Basque country. The book was a detailed and boastful account of the Operation, particularly of how the now famous tunnel was dug.

Again the Franco government protested, and the French government reluctantly obliged by banning the book.

Still, that fall, the book in its entirety or in lengthy excerpts gained wide circulation in both France and Spain. The interest was heightened when on September 13 the ETA set off a bomb in the center of Madrid, at a restaurant frequented by the police. Eleven persons died and 82 were injured, including a girl whose legs were blown off.

A relatively minor role has been played by Spain's other, non-Basque, less-violent organizations of radicals, all of whom are underground. Experts count among these groups five different Communist parties, six Trotskyite groups, six other clusters that claim either Maoism or Marxism-Leninism or both, four anarchist formations, and a range of separatist movements not alone of the Basques but also of Catalonia, Galicia, and the Canary Islands. The police do not hesitate arresting and jailing random members of some of these organizations on charges of terrorism committed or plotted, be such accusations valid or not.

From late April 1974 on, as Portugal overthrew her totalitarian regime of 40 years, the Franco government tightened its security in the increased fear for its own continuance and safety. Border guards were drawn from the French frontier to the line facing Portugal. The severity of Spanish court sentences verged on the ridiculous. Thus in November 1974, at Burgos, three ETA Basque terrorists were sent to jail for 52, 53, and 78 years respectively. And the charges against them did not even include murder—only armed robberies, arson, and the destruction of a fascist monument to the civil war dead.

In August 1975 a stringent law against terrorism and those guerrillas who killed policemen, soldiers, or government officials was passed by Franco's government. In accordance with this law, five terrorists were executed in Spain on September 27. Three of them were Basques; the other two belonged to the newly active Revolutionary Anti-Fascist Patriotic Front. All at once, much of the world reacted with a furor of protest and boycott against Spain. Particularly in Western Europe, great multitudes angrily demonstrated in the streets and plazas. Not only Communists and sundry extreme leftists but even moderate Socialists in France, Italy, West Germany, and the Scandinavian lands joined in the massive marches on indignation—the very same moderates who were outraged by leftist terrorists in their own lands, and who knew—or should have known—that in the very first civil strife at home they would fall victim to such left-wing terror. The explanation was that they protested not so much the taking of those Basque and Spanish terrorists' lives by Franco's executioners as against his fascism—the abhorrent idea and repulsive regime of Franco, then (as soon turned out) in the last few months of his life.

After a long, lingering illness, Dictator Francisco Franco died on November 20, 1975. Prince Juan Carlos, hand-picked by Franco beforehand, took his oath as Spain's King. A slow, most cautious path to reform was the order of his new day. Yet the Basque and other terrorists kidnapped and killed, and were themselves hunted and captured or slain, well into 1976.

Until the revolution of April 25, 1974, the repressive right-wing Establishment of Portugal was seldom or seriously challenged by any opposition, violent or not. The only terror in the country was that by the government, to keep its subjects frightened and submissive. (This will be discussed in our subsequent chapter on White counterterror.)

VI

Later in the year 1974, another European right-wing dictatorship, that in Greece, came to its end. Here terror by leftists and rightists were so closely intertwined that it is difficult to untangle that nation's White atrocities from those of the Reds. The story is like a Greek tragedy, the chorus the antistrophe for the actors.[6]

In Greece the political terrorism of the immediate post-Second World War phase quickly developed into a large-scale civil war. In this, the two opposing forces of the natives were not only supported and guided but nearly taken over by the agents and military advisers of the great powers: on the right by those of Great Britan and, increasingly, the United States, and on the left by the Soviet Union and its Balkan satellites, which in the early days included Yugoslavia.

Unspeakable atrocities were committed by both warring sides of the Greeks, often literally of brother against brother. As Communists approached a given village, its men would flee to escape conscription into the guerrilla ranks, but women and children stayed, naïvely confident that they would not be drafted or harmed. But the guerrillas seized many women, dragging them on retreats into the mountains and shooting them when they were not able to keep up. Teen-age girls were pressed into the Red units, perishing in great numbers because of their insufficient training and scant physical strength, further sapped by malnutrition and illness. Children were taken from their families into Communist countries to be given Marxist schooling for future wars; in those latter 1940s many disappeared into the vast expanse of Stalin's Soviet Union without trace.

But then Tito had his historic quarrel with Stalin, and took Yugo-

slavia out of the Greek civil war. Also, the Western succor of the anti-
Communist Greeks, particularly reflected in the Truman doctrine of
resistance and aid, was proving too much for Stalin. Above all, many
Greek peasants were outraged by the deaths and misery wrought by the
Communists, and in time they turned against the Reds. As the rightists
triumphed, their counterterror was in many instances as horrible as
the guerrilla atrocities had been earlier.

Then came a pause: between the early 1950s and the mid-'60s,
Greek politics boiled on without too much bloodshed. But blood
flowed once more after April 1967, when the colonels seized power.
Hundreds of students, lawyers, journalists, and other intellectuals were
arrested, many beaten and tortured, and for months and years kept
prisoner on barren islands in the Aegean Sea. Dissidents and rebels
within the armed forces were added to the victim rolls. Those still at
large tried to strike back by bombings and attempts at assassination,
but they proved no match for the thorough terror of the military junta.

The courage of some of these would-be anti-junta terrorists was
truly awesome. There were, for instance, Anastassios P. Minis, a retired Greek air force lieutenant, and Stefanos Pandelakis, an Athens
pediatrician, both charged by the junta with belonging to an underground organization known as the AAA—the initials of the Greek
words for "Resistance, Liberation, Independence"—who planted
homemade bombs under parked cars in the Athens and Piraeus areas
as their protest against the neofascist regime. Both were tortured almost to death. Both endured staunchly. In February 1973, before
being sentenced to long imprisonment, Minis spoke up in court: "I
merely tried to overthrow the overthrowers of a lawful regime. . . . I am
prouder of what the indictment says about me than of any war record."
And that record included not only his fighting against the Nazis, but
also flying in 1949 in his Spitfire against the Communist guerrillas.

It would, however, be incorrect to assume, as was often done in
that period of 1967-74, that the neofascist junta had no popular support
in Greece whatever. The peasants remembered the Red terror of the
late 1940s only too vividly; they cheered on the colonels and generals,
particularly since so many of the junta members had originally hailed
from their rocky provincial soil.

But in the summer of 1974 the military usurpers brought about their
own downfall when they tried to extend their White terror to Cyprus,
the island so close to Turkish shores and whose Turkish minority was
about one-fifth of the population.

Not that terror was a novelty on that troubled isle. In the post-
World War II period the Greek terrorists of Cyprus had been persistent
in shooting and bombing the island's British masters. General George

Grivas, a bold adventurer but inept politician, began this guerrilla movement in 1950—and his massive warfare in 1955—when he took an underground force of Greek Cypriotes into the field to oust the British and achieve independence for the island. His few hundred warriors were called the EOKA, the Greek initials of its long and grandiloquent name. Eventually the British had to send 30,000 troops against this determined handful. For four and a half years the island's earth and streets shook with the violence of random killings and deliberate assassinations, of bomb blasts and arson fires and smoke. The toll was 600 killed and 1,300 wounded on both sides. The British set traps for Grivas and a high price on his head, but he proved elusive.

Next in command and cruelty was Nikos Glorgiades, better known by his alias of Sampson. From 1955 to 1959 he personally murdered 25 British soldiers and a number of British civilians. Once he killed a tourist while the man's wife and children looked on in horror. Later, in his newspaper *Mahi* (Combat) he described three of the murders he had committed. He was boastful of his reputation as the Al Capone of Cyprus. However, on one occasion in 1959, as he talked to a British correspondent, he attempted to shift the blame on others, saying: "Sometimes at night I lie awake and try to think about the families of those Englishmen I killed, and believe me, I really feel sorry for their loss. But it was something forced upon us by politicians." But, in truth, this killer was himself a politician as much as a terrorist.

At the height of the terror campaign he was captured, tried, and sentenced to death. In England and elsewhere liberals protested, and the sentence was commuted to a long imprisonment, of which Sampson served only three years. For by that time, in 1958-59, Great Britain had wearied not alone of the bloodletting but also of the economic burden Cyprus was becoming. She promised Cyprus its independence. And so the terror ceased in February 1959, and the island's independence was proclaimed in 1960.

Yet, Grivas and Sampson and their EOKA terrorists always wished for more. They wanted *enosis,* or union of Cyprus with Greece, and never mind the bitter objections of the island's Turkish minority. Grivas for a time retired from politics, being quite sure that his friend and the island's new President, Archbishop Makarios, would gain such enosis. But Makarios, now in power, grew cautious. He ceased scheming for that aim. Grivas re-emerged, again to lead his guerrillas, this time not against the British, but to join Cyprus to Greece. The Archibishop would not have this; in the renewed fighting of 1967, Makarios had Grivas expelled from Cyprus. Not content with his writing of memoirs, Grivas once more returned in 1971 to reorganize the guerrillas into his new EOKA-B force, now to battle the Archbishop.

Grivas had 800 armed activists and some 2,000 auxiliaries throughout the island when, on January 27, 1974, at the age of 75, at Limassol on the southern coast of Cyprus, he died of a heart attack.

The terror chieftancy devolved upon the stocky, boisterous Sampson, now 38 years old and still eager to spill anyone's blood. This time, he had equally determined bosses over him. They were the junta in Athens and its army officers sent to Cyprus, ostensibly for routine training of the island's Greek National Guard for the Archbishop's government, but actually to prepare a violent takeover from the clergyman.

The signal was given in mid-July 1974 from the mainland by the dictator, General Demetrios Ioannides. The principal battleground was Nicosia, the island's capital. On July 15, the government of Makarios was overthrown by the insurgents, and he himself barely escaped death or capture as the British flew him out of the sudden inferno to the safety of London.

Sampson formed the island's new government. But instant trouble came from the east: the outraged government of Ankara sent its invading Turkish force, and was soon the master of Cyprus—of 40 per cent of its territory with 70 per cent of its wealth. Hundreds died in the fighting, thousands were wounded, injured, raped; some 280,000 Cypriote Greeks were homeless refugees.

Caught between the grindstones of their own making, both Greek governments fell on July 23: the military junta in Athens, and the terrorist cabinet in Nicosia. With no help coming to them from anywhere, the freed but humiliated Greeks blamed the United States for not stopping the Turks. And the Greek Cypriote militants threatened to reopen their guerrilla warfare, now against the Turkish invaders.

Yet, when they killed groups of defenseless Turkish villagers on the island, all they achieved was murderous retaliation for Greek deaths and other losses. Two other victims of their rage were United States Ambassador Rodger P. Davies and his Cypriote secretary, killed as she rushed to aid him after Davies had been stricken by a terrorist bullet. These commandos of Sampson, despite their warlike appearance in those spruce military uniforms and neat green berets, proved helpless before the formidable Turkish might, but they were methodical and precise—just as Grivas and Sampson had taught them to be—when they gunned the American embassy to such deadly effect.

The next year, 1975, the very end of it, was marked by one more murder of an American official by Greek terrorists. This was Richard S. Welch, chief agent of the Central Intelligence Agency stationed in Greece. On December 23, while returning to his Athens home from a Christmas party, he was assassinated by gunmen unknown. Five days later a terrorist group, calling itself "Organization of 17 November," in a special communiqué, claimed the dubious honor of this murder. The group's name, it was explained, honored the date of the Greek student revolt in 1973 that was quelled by the former junta government, aided and abetted (the terrorists insisted) by the CIA.

On Cyprus, it was only in March 1976 that Nikos Sampson was arrested by the new government of the Greek part of the island, to be tried for his catastrophic coup of the summer of 1974.

31

Vietnam and
Other Jungles, Other Pyres

Through all such horrors in the two Americas and Europe the bloody specter of distant Vietnam loomed large.

The years of terror there are often cited as proving conclusively that small but dedicated groups of guerrillas and commandos could defeat mighty Establishments of the capitalist nations—if such groups are competently supported by powerful outside forces. Many revolutionaries have echoed Guevara's belief that one more Vietnam in Latin America, and yet another Vietnam in Africa or the Middle East, and many more elsewhere would in the end topple capitalism and usher in a global Socialist-Communist system for the entirety of mankind.

What such writers and orators choose to forget is that the terror and counterterror in both Vietnams have been something more than a result of a guerrilla war. In fact, some thoughtful experts decline to view it as a guerrilla contest at all. At the final collapse of South Vietnam, on May 1, 1975, Drew Middleton wrote in *The New York Times:* "In no respect was it a guerrilla war. The Vietcong participated occasionally in small local operations, but the main burden was carried by regular North Vietnamese divisions."

Moreover, without the active intervention of foreign powers, the Communist and anti-Communist terrors in the two Vietnams would have never reached their proportions. Here was a war between two sides and several nations—on one side, the Soviet Union and Red China aiding North Vietnam with their generous supplies of arms and economic aid as well as their skillful worldwide propaganda, and on the other side the United States sending her tremendous army, navy, and air force, not only to help South Vietnam, but practically to take over the latter's war.

Thus terror in Vietnam is a far cry from any other terror in mankind's recent annals. Despite Guevara's analysis and predictions, one more or several more Vietnams elsewhere on earth will not be decided by the brave actions of Vietcong-like rural guerrillas and urban commandos if these are not aided and guided by strong Communist governments from the outside.

One of the saddest results of the American involvement in Vietnam is the insistence of some critics on minimizing and even excusing the Communist terror, while denouncing the South Vietnamese terror and our share in it. In the words of James Jones, the novelist, "Applying our American Western-film morality, we decided that if we were the bad guys, then the other side must be the good guys."[1] But the larger truer picture of it is that both sides were equally guilty, since both engaged in terror, whatever its varying motives and extents.

It is not easy to ascertain the truth of what happened in either camp. The Communist Vietnamese, unlike the Red Chinese, have preferred not to boast or be frank about their own violence; their adversaries, the South Vietnamese, and particularly the Americans, would not define their actions as strictly terroristic. Only toward the conclusion of the active involvement of the United States would some Americans of the hawk category admit that the bombing and the napalming of Red areas and populations were terror in a way. When the militants of both sides conceded the incidents of terror, each said that its side's terror was good but that the other fellow's was bad, very bad.

Terror began in the North (not that the Southern terror was necessarily an outraged response to the Northern butchery) with the land reform of 1953-56, an effort to collectivize farms that used, as a matter of policy, wholesale terror on recalcitrant peasants. It was marked by the flight of multitudes of farmers from North to South Vietnam and even to neighboring Thailand. Many of these were Roman Catholics, since the land action happened to coincide with a Communist drive against religion.

In the South, the North Vietnamese-inspired terror burst out as Red Vietcong guerrillas raided villages to execute or kidnap local functionaries and attacked cities with satchel-bomb explosions. Together with the invading North Vietnamese troops, the Vietcong reached a grisly plateau of terror with the massacres at Hué during the Tet Offensive of early 1968. To quote James Jones:

> In 24 days of February 1968, the North Viets and VC systematically and deliberately shot to death, clubbed to death or buried

alive some 2,800 individuals of Hué—government personnel, administrative personnel, students, teachers, priests, rural-development personnel, policemen, foreign medical teams; anyone and everyone who had anything to do with training the young, running the city, or aiding the citizenry in any way.[2]

The terror on the South Vietnamese and American side took its most notorious form in Operation Phoenix, a program to weed out and kill Vietcong agents, to incarcerate in cruel "tiger cages" political suspects, to burn hamlets, and summarily to execute the enemy. As cruelties by Green Berets, a special American unit, were publicized, so too were rapes, mutilations, and even mass slayings by other American soldiers, the widest known of such episodes being the massacre at My Lai.

In March 1968 a company of American troops on a routine mission walked into the South Vietnamese village of Songmy, also known as My Lai, and shot dead hundreds of peaceful inhabitants, many of them women, children, and old men. The surviving peasants later said there were 567 dead; Frances FitzGerald, author of *Fire in the Lake,* gives the figure of 347 victims. It took time for conscience-stricken Americans to speak up and produce photographic evidence of the slaughter, but in late 1969 this particular horror rocked public opinion at home, by then tired and even ashamed of the war. Five officers and soldiers were charged with the My Lai massacre, but only one of them, Lieutenant William Calley, was found guilty (of murdering 22 civilians) and given a jail sentence. It was not a severe one, and, at that, protested by many self-proclaimed American patriots as too punitive. In 1974, Calley was freed.

This much must at all times be said for the anti-Communist side: Western liberties do make it possible for a public opinion, once aroused, to pressure the free world's governments into alleviating and ceasing atrocities, even though such remedial action may be reluctant and partial; but no such influence is discernible in a totalitarian society. The outcry in the United States finally moved the Saigon government to claim that its tiger cages were being made more humane, if they were not or could not be abolished entirely.

We know more about terror in the South than in the North. In the words of James Jones about the Hué massacre of 1968, "So far as is known, no VC soldier or North Viet vet has come forward with a formal protest to his government about the atrocity, or made a film about what it felt like [being a guard on that death march]. So far as is known, neither the VC's Provisional Revolutionary Government nor the Democratic Republic of North Vietnam has made a formal investigation of it, or sentenced any of the participants.''[3] The totalitarian regime of Hanoi is too efficient to allow any such protest by its own rebels (if any) or any detailed survey by outsiders. Little piecing-to-gether of the facts and figures brought out by defectors, refugees, and returned prisoners has been done to date, surely none of the most thorough kind done for the Soviet and the Red Chinese terrors.

For years the torture of American war prisoners in the North was concealed by the Hanoi government and pooh-poohed by its American sympathizers. When, finally, the surviving prisoners came back and the gruesome truth was out, Hanoi, and particularly its Western admirers, reiterated the now familiar argument that United States flyers and other servicemen had themselves been terrorists when they bombed the cities of North Vietnam or put to the torch the hamlets in the South, and so deserved fully the punishment meted out to them by their Communist captors, interrogators, and prison guards.

Although a comprehensive description of terror in both Vietnams has yet to be written, what happened there appears to be one of a number of outstanding examples of the continuing inhumanity of men struggling for power. The story awaits its Solzhenitsyn.

II

Now that South Vietnam, Cambodia, and Laos have succumbed to the Red might, the various guerrilla movements in the rest of East Asia become significant.

In Thailand[4] there are three locales of insurgency, whose units use a variety of high-flown and bewildering revolutionary names. The larg-est group, in the country's northeast, is said to have 3,000 fighters. It is also most strategically situated, being close to Vietnam. This is where the insurgency began in 1961, when the Thai Communist Party, or, rather, its leaders in Bangkok, decided to emulate the Maoist policy of rural guerrilla action. At first the insurgents were mainly Chinese, but in time native Thais returned from their training in China and Vietnam.

Another guerrilla contingent operates in the north, near the Lao-tian border. This consists mostly of the Meo and other hill tribesmen who have been fighting the Bangkok-sent soldiers and officials since 1967. The third and least effective insurgent group is in southern Thai-land, close to Malaysia. Here the guerrillas are tin miners and poor plantation workrs.

The most active group, the northeastern one, armed with modern Chinese and captured American rifles, emerge from their jungle bases to attack police stations, small military units, and road-building crews, from whom they capture dump trucks and other such equipment. At night they visit villages to press their propaganda sessions and gather recruits. As their raids increase and widen and the government detachments suffer casualties in dead, wounded, and missing, such units begin to abandon villages here and there, in effect handing them over to the guerrillas, who then intensify their indoctrination and taxation of the peasants.

Far more complicated is the insurgent situation in Burma.[5] Her several guerrilla forces are either connected only loosely with one another, or not at all in any liaison, or—at least in one case—represent an ideology and policy sharply opposed to both the Rangoon government and to the Chinese Communists. But taken altogether, the guerrillas of these various shades are a menace to the Rangoon rule: in toto they are said to control one-third of Burma's territory.

In the latest clashes at the end of March 1976, government troops with bayonets fixed attacked a rebel headquarters in eastern Burma near the Chinese border. In that battle, and in the pursuit of the fleeing guerrillas, 35 soldiers and 96 rebels were killed and a total of 212 were wounded on both sides. Elsewhere, in early April, rebels of the Karen tribe shelled a government position; in the ensuing fighting six guerrillas were slain.

Bordering on China and Laos as she does, Burma is vulnerable to the propaganda and arms flowing across these long frontiers. China alone has 1,200 miles of border with Burma. In Tokyo, in 1968, a Japanese political scientist said to me: "Why do you think the Red Chinese are so keen on supporting those rebel tribes in both Burma and India against the Rangoon and New Delhi governments? During the war I was a journalist with the Japanese army in precisely those mountains. I know those borderlands well. This is where your famous wartime Burma Road connected India with China for the Anglo-American military. Much of the Road is still quite viable; it was solidly built. And this is why the Peking government supports those Burmese and Nagaland rebel tribesmen: Peking wants the Burma Road."

III

In the immediate post-World War II period, a noteworthy example of mass-scale political terrorism was presented by the guerrilla movement in Malaysia.[6]

At that time the Red insurgents in the Malay jungles were so strong and growing so rapidly that it seemed as if the entire area, along with the rest of southeast Asia, would soon succumb to the Communists and become one great continuous mass-sphere of Red Chinese influence and even rule. But by 1960 the tide ebbed. A resurgence of the guerrillas did occur in the late 1960s and early 1970s, but with little of the success that had accompanied the movement in 1948-60. So far the resumption of Sino-Malaysian diplomatic relations since 1974 has not brought any marked decrease in the guerrillas' most recent abrasiveness. For the time being at least, the insurgents continue at their jungle bases, but do not really venture forth too aggressively.

In the latter 1940s the largest guerrilla group emerged in the north of the Malaysian states, near Thailand's border. It consisted mainly of Chinese living in Malaya (where they are now 34 per cent of the total population)*. Their skillful and intrepid leader was Chin Peng, a Chinese. During the war he and his followers had helped the British fight the Japanese; after the war, rewarded with honors, he took part in a victory parade in London. But from 1948 on, using the wartime organization and equipment provided by the British, he turned against them. He headed an armed Communist force bent on ousting the British and all Western capitalism from Malaya.

Mao's triumph in China in 1948-49 gave wings to Peng's crusade. Malaya, including the rich, strategic port of Singapore, was in disarray. Riots, strikes, arson, banditry, and seizure of district towns engulfed the entire peninsula. The British worried: What would happen to their across-the-world economy if Peng, and over him Mao, deprived them of Malayan tin and rubber?

The British acted cleverly and with dispatch. They were helped by the fact that the Chinese in Malaya, though numerous and energetic, were still a minority heartily disliked by the Malay majority. The conflict was soon clearly ethnic, with the British leading the law-abiding, even if somewhat indolent, Malays against the rebel Chinese. One British commander, Robert Thompson, became known for his cool resourcefulness in this new art and science of counterinsurgency.

Largely thanks to his ideas and planning, it was early decided that the guerrillas had to be stripped of popular support, particularly of the food and recruits given to them by the Chinese and others in north Malaya. Thus came the "strategic villages" into which these aid-given people, many of them squatters, were relocated from their farms and homes on the fringes of the jungle. This was actually the old concept of Lord Kitchener, put by him into effect in the Boer War of the early 1900s, when Boer families were forcibly segregated into this century's first concentration camps, to deprive their men of food and other supplies.

---

* Of Malaysia's nearly 12 million people in late 1974, the others were: Malays, 47 per cent; Indians, 9 per cent; tribals comprising the rest.

However, whereas the old South Africa camps afflicted those civilians with much illness and death, Malaya's "strategic villages" were built with far more efficiency and humanity. They were not exactly villages (despite their name) but semi-urbanized settlements with amenities not known to those settlers heretofore. In the 12 years of 1948-60 there was a total of 440 such settlements, holding some 500,000 people. A Home Guard, organized by the British and the Malays in each community, ably defended it against the sporadically attacking guerrillas.

Meanwhile, more British troops were sent to the peninsula, a state of emergency for the entire country was declared, and the Malayan Communist Party was banned. Outsmarted, outmaneuvered, low on supplies, constantly thwarted and defeated, the guerrillas were pushed deeper into the jungle and farther north. At last, in 1960, their ragged remnants fled into Thailand and calm and prosperity descended upon the land. The new state of Malay was formed in September 1963; Singapore, now equally quiet, withdrew from it in 1965 to be a city-state on its own. The British, officially no longer the masters, nonetheless remained in some of their military and naval bases and certainly as the economic beneficiary. Tin, rubber, and other riches of Malaya were not to be denied the white man after all.

While the practice of "strategic villages" was widely publicized (and for a time, rather unsuccessfully, emulated in South Vietnam), another British method of combatting Malayan guerrillas was less known. Professor Richard Clutterbuck, now in the Department of Politics at the University of Exeter, a retired major-general with Malayan jungle experience, recently told me:

"We also held out money rewards to the guerrillas to induce them to quit. We announced a carefully worked-out scale of such payments. And it worked. Oh, we heard some criticism at the time that we were rewarding sin. But this didn't bother us. We went on. The results were curious as well as satisfying. After that war, while researching my book on it, I met a well-known ex-terrorist chieftain who had, for a price, brought his whole unit over to us, their arms down. He invested his considerable reward in several business enterprises and was now most prosperous. We talked in the open, at a prominent Chinese restaurant in Kuala Lumpur. I asked him, 'Aren't you afraid being such an inviting target for those former comrades of yours who may consider you a traitor?' He laughed, 'Not at all. I am generally admired in Malaya, by Malays no less than local Chinese, for what I did. They see it as a smart financial transaction, not treason. No one will hurt me.'

"Later, at his rubber plantation, I talked to several of his industrious tree-tappers. They were his former guerrillas. He had not only delivered them to us—he, in time, gave them these jobs. They seemed to be grateful to him. Chatting with one of them I suddenly realized that once during that war I had spent twelve hours in a jungle ambush waiting for him and his pals to appear and be shot at by my men and me."

But other guerrillas would not give up. In June 1968 their leaders announced a new campaign, and soon moved some old fighters and young recruits from Thailand into five northern Malayan provinces. They reopened their grown-over trails in the jungle highlands; they established fresh bases, trained new volunteers, and collected supplies of arms and provender.

In mid-1969, from southern China, "the Voice of the Malayan Revolution" resumed its radio broadcasts into the peninsula. In April 1970, the ideological leadership of these guerrillas, sitting in Peking, celebrated the fortieth anniversary of the Malayan Communist Party with solemn promises of a new and glorious uprising.

By March 1972 the guerrilla force in north Malaya was estimated at between 1,200 and 2,000 fighters, divided into three regiments, one of these consisting of Malays rather than Chinese. This has remained its strength and structure to 1975-76. Its erstwhile primitive weapons have by now been replaced with the up-to-date American M-16 and Chinese AK-47 rifles, the American arms coming from the captured piles in Vietnam. These guerrillas also seem to have borrowed certain methods of action from the Red Vietnamese: like the Vietcong, the Malay insurgents in these mid-1970s tax the villagers in the areas they control, issuing receipts that are honored by other guerrilla units, who then refrain from taxing the peasants again; they conduct civic and medical programs of aid to the population.

It is not known whether Peng still leads the movement. He was last seen in public in late December 1955. In the two decades since then, a new chief may well have risen to take over, now perhaps a Malay rather than a Chinese.

In late May 1974, Malaysia's Prime Minister Abdul Razak journeyed to Peking to formalize the resumption of full diplomatic relations between his country and Red China. This was expected to lessen, but by no means to end, Peking's long-time encouragement of the Communist guerrillas in Malaysia. The broadcasts of "the Voice of the Malayan Revolution" continue to be beamed from China's Yunnan Province, and sizable units of Malaysia's soldiers and police are still tied up in the troubled jungles. On May 27, 1976, the government of Singapore announced that arrests of 50 suspects in that city-state revealed the existence of a terrorist control post in Kuala Lumpur, a training camp in southern Malaya, and of a network of cells of guerrilla sympathizers in Malaya, Thailand, and even among Singaporeans and Malayans living in Australia. A ballet teacher and several members of the Singapore and Malayan armed forces were among those detained.

IV

A far fiercer civil war with its attendant terror rages in these mid-1970s in the Philippines.[7] In fact, the conflict consists of two separate civil wars, although President Ferdinand E. Marcos brands his adversaries in both indiscriminately as Maoists.

But many of them are not Maoists or Communists of any kind. The largest force battling the troops of Marcos are Moslems on a part of the island of Mindanao and the isles of the Sulu Archipelago. Out of the 40 million Filipinos, two and a half million are Moslems. The Moslem rebels do not really care either for the Chinese or for Mao; they have revolted against the Christian Filipinos who in recent years encroached on these Moslem lands with the backing of the Manila regime.

In certain places the war is between the civilians, Moslems and Christians; in others, it is the Moslem insurgence against the government and the savage attack of the latter's troops with all their modern arms against the rebelling and resisting Moslems. If any weapons and other aid do come to these guerrillas from the outside, it is not Mao's help from Peking, but Arab assistance from West Asia and North Africa, particularly from that militant Moslem chief of the distant Libya, Colonel Muammar Qaddafi. In mid-1975 Marcos made strenuous efforts to pacify his Moslems. He craftily recognized their Moro National Liberation Front, then undercut its authority by making deals with individual rebel leaders: granting them amnesty and other compensations, he caused them to cease their insurgency. Precisely as in the earlier case of the Malay guerrillas and their British opponents, the rebellion of Moslem Filipinos first diminished, then died out when the bribed chieftains merely ordered their units to turn from terror to peaceful toil.

However, a few stubborn holdouts kept on fighting. In early April 1976 in northwest Mindanao 16 government soldiers were killed and 14 wounded in a Moslem ambush. On April 7 three Moslems hijacked a Philippine Airline jet and held 76 passengers and crewmen as hostages. Their demand for release of some political prisoners was refused; but a $300,000 ransom was paid and a larger jet was given to the skyjackers. They then freed most of their captives, while taking the last 12 with them as they forced the crew to fly them to Bangkok and other Asian airports and, finally, after a week, landing them in Benghazi, Libya. There the trio surrendered the plane and the last dozen captives, and even left the ransom money in the cabin, themselves receiving political asylum from their benefactor Qaddafi. The total flight was 8,800 miles, the longest distance on record for such crimes.

Less lucky for Moslem Filipino terrorists was their attempt of May 21, 1976 to seize another aircraft of the same line with more than 100 persons on board. Their demands were for $375,000 and a flight to Libya. Both were turned down by the Manila government. The next day the terrorists released five women and nine children. On the twenty-third they killed two women passengers, and the Philippine troops, surrounding the plane, attacked. Ten hostages died in the battle, three of the hijackers were killed, and the other three captured. Some 90 passengers and crewmen were rescued.

The other variety of guerrilla forces attempting to unseat the Establishment of President Marcos consists of Communists, mostly former Christians but now Marxist atheists, followers of Mao definitely, openly, and proudly.

Politically they are the heirs of the legendary Huks who, in their time adherents of Moscow, not Peking, are now no longer a force or even a fact. The Huks, like the Chinese rebels in north Malaya, were the result and the aftermath of pro-Allied and anti-Japanese guerrilla warfare. Their full name was Hukbalahap or the People's Army Against the Japanese, operating in the mountains and swamps of central Luzon but, after the victory of 1945, turning their weapons against the Americans and the new Philippine rulers.

The Huk rebellion reached its height in the early 1950s as a genuine popular protest against the country's postwar corruption, inflation, and general chaos. But from 1950 on, an energetic official, Ramon Magsaysay, initially as secretary of national defense and later as the republic's President, took vigorous steps against the Huks when he combined military action with a modicum of liberalization. By 1953 he severely weakened the Huks, especially by amnestying those dissidents who surrendered and by even giving them some land and other relief from the oppressing landlords. In 1957, Magsaysay died in an air crash. His successors in Manila were not nearly so wise and successful. Still, the Huks were on a decline, and in time deteriorated into sheer, nonideological extortionists, killers, and bandits.

In the late 1960s and early 1970s a few remnants of the Huks and, more importantly, new recruits were reorganized by young Communist leaders into a fresh formation, now of pro-Mao earmark. They called themselves the New People's Army. Bernabe Buscayono, alias "Commander Dante" of this Army, was accused by Marcos's government of killing a district captain in Tariac Province in 1967. Victor Corpuz, a lieutenant in the regular army, defected to the guerrillas to help them raid the armory of the Philippine Military Academy in December 1970. Still at large, he is now a military chief of the New People's Army.

The martial law proclaimed by Marcos in September 1972 and the mass arrests of liberals and radicals soon drove many students into the jungles and the rebel ranks. On joining the rebels, they were given special training, and are now the backbone of six teams organized for urban commando forays.

A former professor of political science at Manila University, a man in his mid-thirties, is the commander in chief of the New People's Army. He is José Maria Sison, described as tough, dour, and aloof, but with the qualities needed to be an effective leader. His past includes a spell of activity in Indonesia in the 1960s when the late Communist leader D.N. Aidit was his mentor, as well as several stays in China. But his group's Maoist program has recently been sorely tested by Red China's apparent *rapprochement* with the United States. Disagreements on the extent of the Filipino Marxist rebels' allegiance to Peking are said to be rife in the jungle bases of the New People's Army as well as among the several thousand detainees now being held by Marcos in his prisons.

And yet, despite ideological uncertainty and debate, Red guerrilla activity continues. On August 28, 1974, the Defense Department of the Marcos government announced the arrest of 57 Communist arms-smugglers and bomb-makers in the three previous months. This ostensibly aborted the plans of the New People's Army to extend its operations from the jungle to Manila's streets.

Significantly, the raid of September 10, 1974, in Tboli, South Cotabato, in which one government soldier was killed, was believed to have been staged by a combined force of Communist guerrillas and Moslem rebels. If there is such cooperation, the Communist terrorists may be sharing in the flow of weapons from Libya.

V

In India, there were no assassinations of outstanding political figures after the murder of Mahatma Gandhi by a psychopathic loner in January 1948 until the killing in January 1975 of Railway Minister Lalit Narayan Mishra by terrorists unknown. But the government of India is worried by the continuing Peking-assisted insurgency of the Naga and Mizo tribesmen in the northeastern mountains. This began in the late 1950s and has sharpened since 1966. Its latest outbursts were the slaying of 11 Indian policemen in the Nagaland (bordering on Burma) in July 1974 and of three high-rank officials in Mizoram (between Burma and Bangladesh) in January 1975. However, in mid-May 1976 the Indian authorities of the Nagaland state announced their release of all Naga political prisoners, including two top chiefs of the rebel Naga Nationalist Army, in accordance with a pledge by the Naga guerrillas to cease their 18-year-old rebellion. Whether the accord will hold is highly problematical.

In Calcutta and a few other cities are the Naxalites. These are self-proclaimed Maoists who specialize in the slaying of policemen on the now familiar theory that such drastic removals of the pillars of the capitalistic state are the surest way to the triumph of the revolution.[8]

Their name comes from the Naxalbari district of West Bengal, where they first appeared in 1967 trying to organize a revolt of landless peasants along Maoist lines. But the peasants were soon frightened by the Naxalites' terrorism, and, losing their support, the young rebels moved to Calcutta, West Bengal's capital, in 1970. In both the previous rural phase and their later urban-commando period, the Naxalites have been mainly students and unemployed intellectuals and semi-intellectuals in their mid-twenties. By 1974 the Naxalites established ties with various tribal rebels and other terrorist groups along the Bangladesh and Nepal borders. Their communication network is now quite sophisticated.

That their membership is fairly numerous may be seen from the claim by Indian journalists specializing in the study of the Naxalites that from 1967 to mid-1974 as many as 5,000 or 6,000 of these desperados were killed by the police in their antiterrorist campaign. The government's losses are not definitely known because of the tight censorship in India, but one private report in early August 1974 placed a recent three-month toll at 15 to 20 policemen killed. By early 1975 the Calcutta police announced that the Naxalite movement had been broken, but this may be too optimistic. In May 1975, after four years of a special internal security act introduced to combat the Naxalites, the number of detainees in the prisons of West Bengal and Bihar was officially stated as 5,000, but India's radicals and other oppositionists say the actual figure is much higher, and that the law against the Naxalites has been used to arrest not only these terrorists but also many other, milder dissidents.

Organized political warfare appeared in early 1973 in both India and Pakistan,[9] when a group of Pakistani terrorists struck at some Indian targets. These terrorists called themselves Black December, in imitation of the Arabs' Black September commandos, and swore to avenge the West Pakistan army's defeat by India in East Pakistan in December 1971. The Black December group claimed that it was three of its young members who were involved in a Pakistani terrorist attempt to storm the Indian mission in London, to take hostages, and to serve an ultimatum of a sort. The raid failed, two of the Pakistanis shot dead by the British police.

But the Pakistani themselves are a target of guerrilla violence. In Baluchistan, in western Pakistan, the two tribal areas Marri and Mengal are the scene of rebel action against the central government. The population of the two areas is some 100,000 out of Baluchistan's 2,400,000, but in October 1974 the guerrilla forces numbered only between two and four thousand. However, they are said to be aided by neighboring Afghanistan, which is blamed by Pakistan for arming these guerrillas with Soviet weapons. At issue is the attempt of the Pakistan government to break up the local feudal authority prevailing over the two tribes in an age-old manner. Here the guerrillas, unlike so many rebels the world over, resist the change.

Yet farther west in Asia, there was, until March 1975, the formidable guerrilla uprising of the Kurds against the Iraqi Arabs.[10] For a long time the insurgents were aided by Shah Mohammed Riza Pahlevi of Iran. Years earlier, the Kurdish chief, Mustafa al-Barzani, had been the Shah's foe. In 1947 the Shah expelled Barzani from northern Iran, where this Kurd cutthroat had tried to fan a revolt against the Teheran government. But in the early 1970s, Barzani, having broken with his Kremlin friends and having traveled from Moscow to the Iraqi Kurdistan and its rich oil fields, headed a sizable and stubborn insurgence against the Arabs of the Baghdad government.

These Kurds were hemmed into their mountains by Iraqi troops who were far better equipped with their latest Soviet arms and planes and mentored by their Soviet military advisers. But the Shah kept up the balance by sending weapons and other supplies to the Kurds. A curious sidelight of this war surfaced in time when it was revealed that much of this weaponry was also of Soviet origin: captured by the Israelis in their victory over the Arabs in 1967, it was sold by them as surplus armament and delivered to the Shah—and thus to the Kurds— through the obliging brokerage of the American CIA. In late 1974, Barzani achieved a notable success when his guerrillas shot down some Iraqi military planes with Iranian rockets, which in fact may have been Soviet rockets acquired by Israel in the Sinai sands and on the Golan Heights.

The end came with dramatic suddenness on March 6, 1975, when, at their meeting in Algiers, the Shah of Iran and Saddam Hussein— speaking for the Iraqi dictatorship—announced a deal: in exchange for important Iraqi concessions to Iran in their border waters of the Shatt al Arab, the Shah gave up his support of the Kurds. Their revolt collapsed forthwith. Barzani's frantic pleas to the United States State Department, which for so long had encouraged the Kurd rebellion, went completely unheeded.

Again, no Vietnam-like victory of any guerrillas is possible unless a strong foreign power goes all out in helping it with arms, food, diplomacy, and propaganda.

At home in Iran,[11] modern political terrorism dates back to the 1940s and '50s when the desperados of the Tudeh, an exceedingly aggressive Communist Party, struck with bombings and shooting. Their prime target was the Shah himself. At one point, in August 1953, these and other anti-Shah forces were so powerful that he left for Western Europe practically in flight, as the end of his reign seemed near. But America's help, some of it extended cleverly and successfully through the CIA, coupled with the efforts of those of his subjects remaining loyal to him and pro-Western in spirit, finally prevailed. The throne swayed but did not crash.

Even as the Tudeh was downed and destroyed, other bold radicals emerged, mostly (as in so many other countries) former university students and other eager recipients of Guevara's and Castro's appeals. Several attempts to kill the Shah were made but thwarted by his personal shrewdness and courage, by the precautions of his secret police, the Savak (an acronym drawn from its Iranian name), and sometimes by sheer luck.

American diplomats and officials in Iran were also among the terrorist targets. In November 1971, the U.S. Ambassador Douglas MacArthur (the renowned General's son) and his wife were returning home from a dinner party when a team of commandos stopped their car to kidnap the couple. A commando had already smashed one of the car's windows with an ax, but the chauffeur lost neither time nor his nerve as he stepped on the gas and roared the MacArthurs away to safety. Eventually, a number of terrorists captured by the Savak were charged with the miscarried attempt; on June 11, 1973, six of them were condemned to death while several others, including the wife of one of the doomed, were given long prison sentences. But early in the same month of June a terrorist killed Lieutenant Colonel Lewis Hawkins, an American military adviser in Teheran.

On May 21, 1975, two United States Air Force colonels, Paul R. Shaffer and Jack J. Turner, were ambushed and murdered in their car as they were driven to their offices in Teheran. Later that day anonymous telephone callers told Iranian journalists that the killers were members of the underground Iranian People's Fighters Organization, and that the slaying of the two Americans was in vengeance for the continuing execution of Iranian revolutionaries by the Shah's government. However, the efficient Savak agents apprehended these terrorists before the year's end. Eleven of them were tried in December 1975; they admitted killing Colonels Shaffer and Turner the previous May, as well as Colonel Hawkins in June 1973. Ten of them were sentenced to death by firing squad, and the eleventh to 15 years of solitary confinement.

In mid-May 1976, in a shootout in Teheran, 11 terrorists and three security agents were killed; and in police attacks on three hideouts northwest of the capital, ten more guerrillas and four passers-by were slain. The government declared that the machine guns, hand grenades, and sizable sums of American currency captured in the hideouts had come to the Iranian terrorists from Colonel Qaddafi of Libya and Dr. Habash of the Palestinian fedayeen. On May 28, in Geneva, the International Commission of Jurists issued a report detailing physical and psychological torture used by the Shah's police on terrorists and other political prisoners.

Others estimated that in the period from early 1970 until mid-summer of 1973 a total of 118 terrorists were executed by the Shah's firing squads and an equal number fell dead in shootouts with the police. By November 1974 the number of those executed was thought to have reached 200, and at the same time hundreds if not thousands were in jails. The Shah's critics claimed that in 1974 he kept in prison no fewer than 25,000 political offenders and perhaps as many as 45,000, and that the Savak consisted of 30,000 to 60,000 agents.

In his interviews with Western media, the Shah dismisses all such figures, saying the Savak numbers fewer than 3,000 operatives and that political prisoners are not so numerous either. He insists on branding as terrorists all the politicals in his jails, and it is a matter of peculiar pride for him to declare that among those executed there have never been those who attempted to kill him: "I have pardoned those who tried to kill me. Never has anybody who was in a plot to kill me been executed."

The Shah appears to be the master of the situation. In recent years his success is vastly facilitated by his tremendous oil wealth, with prices quadrupled and quintupled on his arrogant insistence, by the billions of dollars flowing into Iran's treasury incessantly, by his broad programs for the country's immense militarization, industrialization, and all-around modernization, making him and his state one of the newest and mightiest powers in the world.

He is aware of the dangers, of course. He knows that many of his restless intellectuals worship Marx and latterly Mao, not Mammon. Beneath the surface of his bustling empire, the plots against him and his system keep simmering. Many of the 40,000 Iranian students on Western campuses refuse to return home to serve him and grow rich, but stay away and participate in sporadic anti-Shah demonstrations on his triumphant journeys to the West.

Yet he continues at his pinnacle. Even the enormous deficits, which surprisingly showed up in Iran's budget by early 1976, do not seem to trouble the Shah too much. The recent mild winters in the West, the worldwide depression that caused oil consumers to reduce their purchases, and—above all—the Shah's excessive spending on his ambitious projects for Iran's modernization, all this has contributed to the sudden deficits. But, largely unperturbed, ever optimistic, the Shah keeps to his course of power and confidence as he quells the terrorists and other oppositionists at home and mocks the dissidents in the expatria.

32

Red Samurai
and Turkey's Nihilists

At Asia's opposite ends, two strikingly similar terrorist movements aimed at the native Establishments have come to the fore: those in Japan and Turkey.

The Japanese terrorists of the 1970s call themselves *Rengo Sekigun*, or United Red Army. Like many of the world's terrorist organizations, this group was originally a split-off from the Communist Party. Its nucleus, *Sekigun*, or Red Army, seceded from *Zengakuren*, or National Student Association, a campus affiliate of the official Japanese Communist Party. In January 1972, nine members of the Red Army joined with 20 members of *Keihin Ampo Kyoto*, or Opposition to the Security Treaty of Japan and the United States, to form *Rengo Sekigun*. Both before and after their fusion these militants were among the many angry student bands demonstrating and rioting against the Japanese-American pact and against the American presence in Japan.

Acting in small commando units, *Sekigun* members made headlines in 1970 by hijacking the *Yodo*, a 727 airliner, to North Korea, and by a series of robberies and kidnappings in Japan. During the same year they established close contact with the Arab guerrillas, particularly with Dr. George Habash's Popular Front for the Liberation of Palestine (PFLP). Some members traveled to the Middle East for discussions about cooperating with the Arab fedayeen and for commando training involving weapons and tactics. For a time a *Sekigun* unit was part of the PFLP forces. A Japanese guerrilla medical team, headed by Japanese doctors, worked within Palestinian refugee camps in the fedayeen's headquarters.

The ideology of these Japanese terrorists was reported as revolutionary Socialist-Communist, with strong nihilist tendencies. An echo of Nechayevism, with its murders in the inner circle, became apparent in February 1972, when the Japanese police, searching for the Red Army's winter hideouts in the mountains north of Tokyo, came upon 14 dead bodies. These turned out to be the corpses of terrorists charged by the group's leadership with dissidence and "bourgeois deviation"; they had been tortured and left naked in the snow to freeze to death or be strangled by their comrades to set an example of revolutionary discipline.

Most members, leaders, and aides of the Red Army and other terrorist groups are sons and daughters of Japan's upper- and middle-class families, either dropouts from, or currently registered students in, the nations's leading universities. They hold themselves to be the country's intellectual elite, and within their organization, in a traditional Japanese way, they insist on an elite above this elite. In 1970, on the eve of the hijacking of the *Yodo*, the structure of the Red Army was topped by some 50 self-styled "officers" constituting the group's Central Military Affairs Committee. At the time, they planned to declare themselves "officers" of the World Red Army, once they and their allies in the Middle East, Latin America, and elsewhere had formed the World Communist Party.

Takanari Shiomi, the first chairman of the Red Army, was among those arrested in 1970. His capture did not stop the carrying-out of the *Yodo* hijacking, which originally was part of a scheme to transport Shiomi to North Korea so he could "have talks with the Black Panthers and West German radical students." In 1971, in an interview with *Shukan Asahi*, a popular weekly of Tokyo, an anonymous leader elaborated:

> We could have chosen the destination from among China, Albania, North Korea, North Vietnam, and Cuba. China was eliminated from the list because we learned that some radical students of other sects had smuggled themselves into the Chinese mainland and have not been heard of since. . . . We were in touch with North Korea, although indirectly. In fact, we had obtained a guarantee in advance that North Korea would let Shiomi proceed to Cuba . . . for talks with American and West German revolutionaries. . . . Shiomi was to go to Cuba because his job was to help organize the World Communist Party.[1]

But the business of revolution was to go on, even if Shiomi was now in jail. Strictest secrecy veiled the planning of the hijacking. Said the anonymous leader: "Only a limited number of the leaders even within the *Sekigun* knew about it. Orders to raise funds were issued to all the members of the *Sekigun* without any explanation. I suspect that even a number of the hijacking group got aboard the plane without knowing what they were going to do." The leaders, no less than the rank-and-file members, were always under the most stringent of disciplines: "They have cut off all relations with their families, friends, and universities. They are preparing for our struggle, moving from one place to another every day."[2]

Indeed, it developed in 1972 that even the closest kin of the 24-year-old Kozo Okamoto and his two dead companions had not the faintest inklings of their activities until after the bloody drama of May 30 at the Lydda (Lod) airport was played out.

II

In 1971, Dr. Habash's Arab emissaries arranged for a secret office in Tokyo to widen and improve the recruiting of Japanese volunteers for training in, and operations from, Lebanon. In May 1972, three such Japanese commandos embarked on a suicidal mission to the Lydda airport in Israel. On May 30, arriving at Lydda from Rome, they took out from their unexamined baggage Czech assault rifles and hand grenades, and turned the passenger hall into a slaughterhouse. Some 28 men and women lay dead, including two of the Japanese attackers, killed by Israeli security guards or perhaps by their own crossfire, and 67 were wounded. Many of the victims were not Jews, but Puerto Rican and other Christian pilgrims to the Holy Land.

The trial of the lone Japanese survivor, Kozo Okamoto, is an illustration of the nature of his group's fanatacism. He could have claimed insanity but he declined to submit to a psychiatric examination, despite the urging by Max Kritzman, his Israeli court-appointed defense lawyer. On July 13, 1972, in his final statement in court, he declared that he was normal, and even superior in spirit to his Arab chiefs and allies: "The Arab world lacks in spiritual fervor, and, therefore, we felt that the Arab world could benefit from our cooperation."

He refused to say he had been misled or misguided. He stated that he and his companions had deliberately joined in the operation because Japan's terrorists stood in need of the world's attention: "We attacked the Tel Aviv airport [Lydda]; our action has been reported around the world. This cooperation with the Popular Front was one springboard for us to propel ourselves onto the world stage. This attack was proposed by them [the Arabs], and it afforded us unity of action. They approved of it. I am a soldier and I approved of it, so I joined the operation."

No remorse for the hideous deed, no sorrow for those murdered was voiced by him, but, on the contrary, a mystical joy on the victims' behalf: "Those people we killed are now stars in the firmament. The world revolution will continue, there will be more stars. When I think that their stars and our stars will one day shine in the same heaven, I am very happy." He explained the root of his belief: "When I was a child, I was told that a man became a star after his death. I was not convinced of this, but now I am prepared to be convinced." Perhaps he will yet join his two companions as stars after death, and be reunited with his victims.

However, the Israeli court would not grant Kozo Okamoto his death wish. He was sentenced to life imprisonment because, the prosecutor pointed out, "this country has a moral force" far above the brute force used by such murderers as Okamoto. Before the sentence was pronounced, Okamoto shouted his warning to "the whole world that the Red Army will slay anyone who stands on the side of the bourgeoisie." But as he heard the sentence, he not only scowled but seemed to fight back his tears, possibly tears of relief.[3]

In far-off Japan, his family felt regret and deep disgrace for the slaughter their son and his friends had caused. Kozo's father offered his and other kinsmen's profound apologies. And the Japanese government felt impelled, not only to join in similar apologies, but also to humbly present the victims' families with monetary compensation.

Kozo Okamoto almost regained his freedom nearly two years after the massacre when, on May 15, 1974, he was listed by the Arab terrorists at Maalot in Israel among the score or more of guerrilla prisoners in Israeli jails to be released as the price of sparing the Israeli children in the schoolhouse held by three fedayeen. But the negotiations between the Arab commandos and the Israel government broke down, the Maalot school was stormed by Israeli troops, and the terrorist trio murdered more than 20 children while themselves perishing. Kozo Okamoto, already on his way to the exchange with the children, was returned to his cell.

III

The year 1972 brought not only an increased public awareness in Japan of the existence and activities of the Red Army, but also a shock of revulsion. In this, both the February discovery of the 14 corpses—victims of the terrorists' mountain kangaroo court—and the May massacre at the Lydda airport played their role. A stepped-up counter-campaign by the Japanese police caused the terrorists to move their operations increasingly from their homeland to lands abroad. Their cooperation with the Arab fedayeen grew apace, taking them to far-away places.

A woman in her mid-twenties replaced Takanari Shiomi, jailed in 1970. She is in charge to this day. Her headquarters are in Beirut, her subordinates all over the world.

She is Fusako Shigenobu, also known under her Arab name as Samira, but with fondness and respect called "Auntie" by her terrorist crews. In the 1930s her father belonged to an ultrarightist group specializing in assassinations of Japan's moderate statesmen. She seems to have inherited his violence, if not his politics. As a high-school orator she dwelt on the topic of the importance of helping others, but in the 1960s she became a college campus radical and street rioter. She worked as a bar girl in Tokyo's Ginza district and was ready, she said, to be a prostitute to raise money for the Cause.*

But this was not necessary, for the Arabs soon came forth with plenty of oil money. She became the main link between the fedayeen and the Red Army; it was she who recruited for Dr. Habash his first 30 Japanese terrorists. She was the chief organizer of the Lydda airport slaughter, and had even married one of the three attackers, to get his name on one of her passports before coolly sending him to his death in Israel.

Her looks as well as daring have impressed some of the highest fedayeen personages, and reports indicate she has chosen her Arab lovers insouciantly, yet with a shrewd eye for the value they might bring to her position in the movement.

As she broadened the Red Army's adventures in both Asia and Europe, intelligence services of Western countries compiled dossiers on her, and the media sent eager interviewers to her Beirut lair. When a journalist remarked to her that the world regarded her Red Army as a plague, she responded with enthusiasm: "If that is so, we might infect the whole world. I am the germ of that plague."

Her later record of 1973-75 was frenetic. She detailed one of her terrorists to participate in the exploit of July 29, 1973, when five commandos skyjacked a Japan Air Lines jumbo jet over Holland, with 145 passengers and crew members, and forced the pilot to fly it to Dubai, a Persian Gulf sheikdom. There, for three days, they kept the plane's crew and hostages in cruel suspense, finally forcing the crew to fly the jet to a Libyan desert airport of Benghazi. There at last they

---

* In the early 1890s, Emma Goldman seriously considered selling herself to men on New York's 14th Street, a promenade of prostitution, so as to replenish the scant treasury of her anarchist organization.

released their captives and blew up the aircraft. The terrorists were at first described as an Arab, a Japanese, a Latin American, and a European, but this was later corrected to three Palestinians and one Japanese. The fifth, a woman of undetermined nationality, was killed during the hijacking inadvertently by her own grenade exploding in her clothing. The Israeli intelligence soon established that she was from the Habash organization, most likely an Arab.

There was also a bungled attempt on January 31, 1974, by four commandos, three of them Japanese and one Arab, to blow up an oil refinery at Singapore. More significant, the year 1974 was notable in the Red Army's annals by Auntie's vigorous effort to establish her group's headquarters in Paris, from there to launch an explosive campaign throughout Western Europe.

The French authorities stumbled upon her plan quite by accident when, in July 1974, they examined a Japanese man, Yutaka Furuya, as he landed at Orly airport near Paris, arriving from Beirut. The search of his person yielded three forged passports, coded letters, and $10,000 in counterfeit hundred-dollar American bills. The Japanese police were delighted to help the French to decipher the letters. This resulted in the detention and questioning of some 100 Japanese in Paris, eight of whom were presently deported from France as members or abettors of the Red Army. Among the eight were a professor of sociology, a film critic, and a saleswoman in a Japanese store in Paris.

When searched, the apartment of the Japanese saleswoman, Mariko Yamamato, produced a code book of addresses of 50 apartments in other European cities—hideouts of Red Army members preparing under Auntie's imaginative direction to attack, simultaneously, a French embassy in one place and offices of Japanese concerns in others.

As for Furuya, he, in a French jail since July 1974, was considered an important activist; he had been one of the Japanese-Arab team involved in the attempt to blow up the Singapore oil refinery the previous winter. At her Lebanese headquarters Auntie decided to rescue him. She prepared this plot carefully.

On September 13, 1974, three amply armed Japanese men seized part of the French embassy in The Hague, Holland, taking 11 hostages. They soon released two, but kept the other nine, among them Count Jacques Senard, the ambassador. The commandos threatened to kill their captives one by one unless Furuya was freed and flown from France to Holland to join them, whereupon all four Japanese were to have safe conduct on a plane from The Hague to an Arab country.

At the start, the French government refused to give in, insisting instead on a rescue mission. The very first night, eight French sharpshooters from the specially trained antiterrorist unit were sent to The Hague. But the Dutch government, wishing to avoid bloodshed, would not allow a battle. It argued that the three Japanese were well-armed and extremely desperate. Instead, it negotiated with the trio patiently, and, after a four-day siege of the embassy, came to an agreement with Auntie's dangerous nephews. The terrorists obtained Furuya's release, and $300,000 in ransom to boot.

However, Yutaka Furuya had certain misgivings about Auntie's solicitude and seemed reluctant to be exchanged for those nine hostages in The Hague. For he had talked to his French interrogators too loosely, and now feared Auntie's kangaroo court. But he was delivered to her men in the French embassy just the same, and all four were flown to Syria on a French jet manned by a volunteer Dutch crew. The plane landed at Damascus on the eighteenth, and the Japanese even returned the $300,000 ransom to its crew. After all, with so much Arab oil money at their disposal—not to mention Auntie's supply of counterfeit American dollars—this Dutch pittance was not really needed.

It is not known whether Auntie herself greeted the four terrorists at the Damascus airport, and just what fate befell the rescued Yutaka Furuya. But it was officially divulged by the Syrian government that all four terrorists were handed over to the protective auspices of Yasir Arafat's Palestine Liberation Organization, with passage guaranteed by Syria to any country that would accept these Japanese. Back in The Hague the French envoy and his eight fellow captives were grateful enough to be given their own lives and freedom.

The next Red Army exploit was played out clear across the Asian continent, in downtown Kuala Lumpur, Malaysia's capital, on the morning of August 4, 1975, when five Japanese terrorists burst into the consular section of the United States embassy. "This is holdup. Put your hands up!" they announced in English. But it was no mere holdup—it was a political action as the terrorists rounded up 53 hostages, including the American consul, the Swedish chargé d'affaires, and an assortment of other Americans, as well as Singaporeans, Japanese, and Malaysians—not only men, but women and children too. The demand was freedom of a number of Japanese terrorists from Japan's prisons. After 79 hours, on August 7, the Tokyo government yielded and provided the wanted prisoners with a plane that flew them—and the five activists at Kuala Lumpur—to asylum in Libya.

In the mid-1970s, in and around Japan, terrorist outbursts occurred involving newer and smaller groups, not necessarily under the Red Army's direction. On August 15, 1974, Mun Se Kwang, a Korean terrorist in his twenties, freshly arrived in Seoul from Japan, attempted to assassinate Korea's President Park Chung Hee at a gala meeting-concert. Instead, he murdered the President's wife. The killer had been brought up in Japan and did not even speak Korean. He was seized. In Japan, the police arrested a Japanese woman radical as an accomplice of the slayer.

A fortnight later, on August 30, unknown ultraleftists placed two powerful bombs on a Tokyo street in front of the main offices of the mammoth Mitsubishi Heavy Industries. One bomb failed to explode, but the other did detonate, killing eight persons and injuring some 330 others. The police searched for whatever activists of the Red Army might yet be astir in Japan, but they also looked for a new terrorist formation called the Black Helmets, which had a previous record of small-scale fire-bombing of the Mitsubishi factories.

The home office of the giant concern, Mitsui and Company, was bombed on October 14, and 16 persons were injured, two of them seriously. Telephone callers proudly claimed responsibility for the explosion on behalf of the Asian Continental Development Organization, a name heretofore not known to the police.

In mid-November 1974, on the eve of President Gerald R. Ford's visit in Japan, six members of the *Maruseido*, or the Marxist Youth League, hurled a dozen gasoline bombs into the compound and onto the roof of the United States embassy in Tokyo. They were soon arrested by the Japanese police. At the same time three other League members were captured after they had tossed fire bombs at the Soviet embassy—these students, being Maoists, hating the Soviet Union no less than the United States.

Terrorist acts were feared later in November during President Ford's visit, but none materialized. Security surrounding the visitor was extraordinary.

In 1975 it was ascertained that some of the most virulent bomb-throwers and kidnappers came from among the university students and dropouts of historic, charming, temple-and-garden-filled Kyoto. They wrote highly literate letters to the Tokyo newspapers after each new blast in a bank or an office, claiming explosive credit for the Red Army or for a new group calling itself the East Asia Anti-Japanese Armed Front, the latter divided into small action teams with such fanciful names as Wolf, Fang of the Earth, and Scorpion.

IV

What popular support may be discerned in Japan for these desperados of the Red Army and other terrorist groups?

Japan has a long tradition of political terror. In centuries bygone, dedicated and irrational samurai roamed the country on rampages in the service of their feudal lords. In the 1860s, after the opening of Japan to the Western world, samurai at loose ends with no masters to lead them tried to halt the reforms of the Meiji era by assassinations, often random. In the 1930s some army and navy officers and cadets, along with fanatical civilians, murdered statesmen who, they charged, were proforeign and antiwar.[4] All such assassins were widely admired, almost worshipped, by the populace at large as long as the murderers were clearly self-sacrificial. Closer to our era, during the Second World War, the *kamikaze* or suicide pilots were held in high esteem by their compatriots as the young flyers went to their flaming deaths by crashing their planes into American warships.

But there is hardly such applause by Japan's classes and masses for the suicidal terrorists of these 1970s. Perhaps the angry dropouts and students of the Red Army are too primitive for the Japan that has by now grown all too pragmatic and even sophisticated for such bloody antics. The very same bourgeois mood against which the terrorists launch their kidnappings and murders is too deep and strong to be dented, much less overwhelmed, by the new guerrillas. The largest leftist party in Japan's parliament, the Communists, claim only 300,000 members on their rolls; they have lately received only slightly more than ten per cent of the popular vote in the national elections. At that, the Communist Party has achieved even this ratio by trying hard to shed its former violent image, by going "respectable."

In the summer of 1973 a Gallup International poll showed that Japan's youth were more disillusioned and cynical than were their Western counterparts. When questioned about their views on man's essential nature, 33 per cent of the sample of Japanese in the age bracket between 18 and 24 years said they saw more evil than good—as against only 20 per cent of youths in the United States, Brazil, Britain, France, India, the Philippines, Sweden, Switzerland, West Germany, and Yugoslavia. These young Japanese had less interest in religion and fewer close friends, and felt less kindness toward their fellow humans, than did the youth in these other countries. Yet, we may add, very few of them would join the Red Army underground and its explosive revolt.

If anything, instead of turning against the Establishment, some of Japan's disaffected young have been warring upon one another, notably since the issues of the 1960s—the alliance with America, the outcry against the atomic bomb, the outrage over the war in Vietnam—seem to have receded or disappeared. So, with astonishing ferocity, young radicals of Japan have begun to feud among themselves. In May 1974, two groups of Tokyo's radicals, university students and recent dropouts, accused each other of being "counterrevolutionary" and in the pay of the capitalists. Armed with iron bars and bamboo poles, one group assaulted the other en masse, attacking the strongholds each gang had erected, complete with watchtowers and guards. At times the police had to sally forth to the combat areas to separate and disperse these bizarre warriors.

If terror there must be, this kind is by far preferable to the kidnappings and murders directed at society at large.

V

Just as Japan's Red Army terrorists have depended heavily upon their collaboration with the Arab guerrillas, so did the Turkish desperados at the height of their activity lean upon the arms and other aid from Damascus and Beirut. Significantly, when, on May 22, 1971, Turkish terrorists murdered Ephraim Elrom, the Israeli consul general in Istanbul, they explained their deed as "part payment" for the training they had received in the fedayeen camps of Syria and Lebanon.[5]

The consul's four kidnapper-slayers belonged to the Turkish People's Liberation Army, or TPLA, the most active of that country's three terrorist groups. The other two were the Turkish People's Liberation Front, or TPLF, and the Turkish People's Liberation Party, or TPLP.

All three had extremely radical programs, but the TPLA was particularly revolutionary, with tendencies often described as nihilist because its redprint called for total destruction and no new system whatever in the aftermath of the coming debacle. In the beginning it was a warpath wing of an organization called Revolutionary Youth, or in its Turkish acronym, *Dev Genc*, which in time was eclipsed by its TPLA offspring but was never completely phased out of its own aggressive existence.

In 1973, even after Turkish security forces had delivered telling blows against the TPLA, the latter's surviving membership deep in the underground was estimated at some 300, mainly university students, dropouts, drifters, and other irate intellectuals. By then its two principal founders and leaders, Mahir Cayan and Deniz Gezmis, were dead by the state's punitive hand. The identity of their replacement in the leadership is uncertain.

In addition to their ties with the Arabs, these Turkish commandos were in touch with the Red secret police and other such guiding offices in East Germany, Czechoslovakia, and North Korea. (From East Berlin, a Turkish-language station, *Bizim Radyo*, broadcast encouraging messages to these guerrillas.) Yet at certain junctures, dissatisfied with what they regarded as too cautious a line of the Moscow-oriented Communists, the Turkish terrorists spoke up against Soviet policy. Deniz Gezmis, for one, was known to have inveighed against "Soviet imperialism" in a definitely Maoist style. Turkish translations of Carlos Marighella's *Minimanual* on terrorism, a text not entirely approved by Brezhnev's Establishment, were diligently studied and used by Gezmis and his associates.

From the outset, the TPLA had carried out bank robberies to build up the group's treasury. Terrorist activities were stepped up in February 1971 when, on the outskirts of Ankara, three gunmen kidnapped James Finley, a United States airman stationed in Turkey. Presenting no demands, but merely making a typical radical anti-American gesture, the extremists released Finley, unharmed, after some 17 hours. A more serious incident occurred in March of that year, when five armed terrorists seized four U. S. Air Force servicemen. A ransom of $400,000 was demanded; the TPLA also called on the masses to revolt against the Turkish government and to take Turkey out of NATO. True to its policy, the American government would not pay ransom and suggested to the Turkish authorities that they refuse to negotiate with the kidnappers.

In Ankara the minister of labor agreed: "You don't bargain with bandits." Instead, some 30,000 soldiers and policemen were sent searching for the kidnappers and other terrorists. But on one Ankara campus, students rioted in protest against a dormitory search. In the ensuing gunfire, a student and a soldier were killed, and a dozen others on both sides were wounded or injured. Hundreds of suspects were arrested. Of these, 26 were found to be connected with the TPLA. The terrorist chiefs decided on a retreat: on March 8 the kidnapped Americans were freed by the mere expedient of being left unguarded in an apartment near the U. S. embassy in Ankara.

That March the Turkish army took over. Charging that Prime Minister Suleyman Demirel and his Justice Party, even though centrist in theory, were too soft and inefficient in combatting the terrorists, the generals and the colonels assumed practically all power in the nation. Forcing Demirel's resignation, and replacing him with Ferit Melen, a malleable politician, the military cracked down.

After some preliminary drastic steps, they declared martial law on April 25 in 11 of Turkey's provinces, including the cities of Ankara and Istanbul. That spring two trials of captured terrorists ended in severe punishment, including death sentences for some. Campuses and newspaper offices were combed, and scores of intellectuals rounded up. Many were beaten and horribly tortured by the interrogating gendarmes; of the means of torture, the bastinado method was the mildest. More than 3,000 young officers were expelled from the armed forces as possibly unreliable, and some of these were even brought to trial as coplotters with the civilian terrorists.

The TPLA struck back with resumed bank robberies, explosions in public buildings, and more kidnappings. On May 17 came the capture of Israel's Consul Elrom in Istanbul.

At first the kidnappers said they would release Elrom in exchange for all the jailed Turkish commandos. If not done by five o'clock in the afternoon of the twentieth, the Israeli hostage would be slain. Once more the Turkish government refused to negotiate with what it termed "a handful of adventurers." On May 18, a TPLA member, a student suspected of a part in the kidnapping, was apprehended. With this lead and a 15-hour curfew, a house-to-house dragnet was undertaken in Istanbul. Martial law throughout most of the nation resulted in hundreds of new arrests. Still, Elrom was neither found nor released. On the twenty-second, his body was discovered in an apartment only 500 yards from his consular office.

The search for his murderers narrowed down to a hunt in which two youths were cornered. Their new hostage was a 14-year-old girl. In the siege, her captors offered to free her in exchange for passports and safe conduct for them out of Turkey. This was declined, a battle flared up, and one of the commandos was killed while the other was wounded and captured. The girl was rescued.

The terrorist season of 1971-72 was one of wins and losses: In November, five TPLA members made successful jail breaks, but in the spring three convicted commandos awaited hanging. In March the TPLA, by then claiming a rebuilt strength of 500 members, staged a spectacular exploit: on the twenty-sixth, a group of 11 guerrillas, led by Ertugrul Kurkcu, kidnapped from a NATO base at Unye on the Black Sea coast three radar technicians—two Britons, aged 45 and 35, and one Canadian, 21. The terrorists demanded freedom for their three condemned comrades in exchange for the three Westerners.

Again the military and their government refused. Troops, police, and hundreds of outraged civilian volunteers combed the cities and the countryside. At last the kidnappers and their hostages were pinned down in a remote mountain village hideout. On March 30, a siege of the house began. To the call for surrender, the terrorists cursed the security force and yelled that they had come to these hills not to give up, but to die. They brought one of the three technicians to the window; he shouted to the besiegers: "You cannot make these people see sense. They are going to kill us."

And so they did. At the height of the battle, the terrorists murdered all three captives, shooting them through their heads, their hands tied behind their backs. In the hail of the incoming bullets and grenades, 10 of the 11 guerrillas were slain. The lone survivor was Kurkcu, the leader. He was captured while trying to hide in the hayloft of a barn near the house.

Also found, under a blood-stained pillow in the house, was the terrorist message on crumpled cardboard, addressed to "Traitors, pro-American dogs." It read: "These English agents are part of the NATO forces which occupy our country, and as the revolutionaries of an occupied country we consider it our basic right and a debt of honor to execute them."

Those at large would still keep up the cause of the fallen commandos. That very night of March 30 teams of activists of the Dev Genc organization bombed a large shop and some army stores in Istanbul. Through the rest of 1972 the terrorists kept up their desperate attempt to save their comrades from jails and gallows. In May and October, two Turkish airliners were skyjacked by commandos and landed in Sofia, the demand each time being liberty for political prisoners. Each time, the Turkish government refused to comply and the terrorists gave in, harming neither the planes nor the passengers and crews, accepting merely political asylum for themselves in Bulgaria. The Establishment was winning the battle of wills.

And sometimes, unexpectedly, even the hitherto sympathetic neighbors of the terrorists would turn against them. Thus, in July 1974, 14 fleeing guerrillas, while heading for shelter in Syria, were barred by the Damascus government that, playing power politics and for the nonce attempting to be friendly to Ankara, even notified the Turkish authorities of this expulsion, in effect facilitating these 14 terrorists' capture by the Turkish security officers.

Meantime, more arrests were sweeping Turkey. That fall of 1972 a TPLA member, Safa Asim Yildiz, who tried but failed to kidnap the commander in chief of the Turkish gendarmerie, was injured and caught. As the year 1972 closed with the hanging of three of his comrades, the year 1973 began with a trial and a death sentence for Yildiz and another university student.

Those dead in hangings and shootouts during 1972 included not only Mahir Cayan and Deniz Gezmis, the TPLA's top leaders, but also a number of their subordinates. By then the guerrillas knew they had little, if any, support of the masses. Popular sympathy was with the army and, to a lesser degree, with the police; the terrorist bombings, kidnappings, and killings repelled the man in the street. People agonized when the 14-year-old girl was seized and nearly slain. Some plain folk shed genuine tears over the murder of the three Western technicians. There was no cheering for the guerrillas.

But this began to change in early 1973 as the repressors in their turn went too far, arresting and sentencing not only those who were indeed terrorists but also hundreds of milder leftists, of liberals and moderates. Highly respected deans, professors, and writers were crowded into Turkey's jails on long terms and under rough treatment. Protests were heard in the parliament, which until then had been submissive. Yielding somewhat, the army-run government lifted its martial law in September 1973.

Still, in late 1973 and through much of 1974, military courts persisted in sending new batches of genuine terrorists to long imprisonment. In courtrooms the defendants chanted their defiant slogans and shouted at the judges: "Damn imperialism! "

But in the altering political contests of nonterrorist forces, liberals began to prevail. In the elections to the National Assembly of October 14, 1973, left-of-center groups—particularly the Republican People's Party of Social-Democratic tendencies—came out well, although not strong enough to take over the government—at least not yet. However, in February 1974, led by an agile politician Bulent Ecevit, the Republican People's Party did succeed in forming a cabinet in coalition with the smaller National Salvation Party of right-wing moderates and Moslem fundamentalists.

As Turkey's new Prime Minister, Ecevit pushed through a wide amnesty for moderates in prisons. By July 1974, of the 5,700 or more convicted in the three years of army rule, only a few hundred remained behind bars, and these were clearly terrorists. Executions ceased; even the severe tortures of politicals abated.

But from the terrorist viewpoint, the more things change, the less they change. Reforms never please the violent; if anything, these enrage them further. The respite granted by the new, more liberal government of Turkey did not at all inspire the surviving extremists to change their swords for plows, to embrace peaceful politics, to turn from bullet to ballot. For, now as always, revolutionaries dislike reform because it mollifies the masses, making the masses less prone to support terrorists.

But with so many fallen, new groups had to be formed and new members recruited. Some of the methods and bases would be different. In place of the practically demolished Turkish People's Liberation Army, one of the two other organizations—the Turkish People's Liberation Front—gathered the remnants into a new fist. The commando base was to be established not on Turkish soil, nor even in Lebanon and certainly not in Syria, but in what was thought to be the greater safety of France. The skilled assistance of the Arab fedayeen was, as ever, welcome.

French intelligence and police threw some of these plans into disarray when, on December 20, 1973, in and near Paris, they arrested ten Turks (including two women), two Palestinians, and an Algerian. A sizable and varied arsenal of weapons and explosives was uncovered and seized in the group's headquarters in a run-down villa in the countryside, some of the bombs secreted in hollowed-out books. The raiders found bomb-making equipment, as well as other tools and materials to produce false passports and identity cards.

The three Arabs were members of the Popular Front of Dr. Habash. They were there to train and aid the ten Turks in plotting murders of Turkish diplomats in several capitals of Europe and Asia. Eventually the Turks were to return to Turkey for the last decisive battle against the homeland's rulers.

In late October 1975, within two days, two Turkish ambassadors were assassinated: Danis Tulagil in Vienna on the twenty-second, and Ismail Erez in Paris on the twenty-fourth. In both cases the gunmen escaped. In the Vienna killing, responsibility was claimed by anonymous telephone callers to the Associated Press in New York saying they represented an "Armenian liberation organization" bent on avenging the mass murders of Armenians by Turks during the First World War. But after the second slaying, another anonymous phone caller to a West European radio station declared that both envoys were killed by Greek Cypriote terrorists.

The third possibility remains that both slayings were the handiwork of those native Turkish terrorists training in France.

In late 1975, some leftovers of the Turkish People's Liberation Army attempted a violent homecoming. During the next seven months, until early June 1976, the death toll—of both the terrorists and the police in Turkey—mounted to 54. On June 8, a raid of security men on a guerrilla hideout in the southeastern town of Gazienter led to a battle in which the terrorists used automatic weapons and hand grenades, and during which two policemen and three guerrillas were killed. The ensuing 24-hour siege of the hornets' nest ended in the capture of three more guerrillas.

VI

On my visit in Turkey in early 1975, I found little concern and hardly any talk about her terrorists. The general feeling was that they had been broken, the most dangerous of them safely dead or in prison. On the campuses, if any disorders flared up, they were not so much between the leftists and the police as they were clashes of the newly risen and strengthened right-wing students against their radical classmates.

As in Japan, so in Turkey in 1975, the general temper of the populace was restive, yet far from revolutionary. Problems of inflation and unemployment were to be dealt with in ways of reform, perhaps even drastic reform, but surely not by heeding the extremist calls to bombs and barricades. If violence was in the air, it was applauded by the man in the street mainly when it was visited upon the Greeks on the island of Cyprus.

The more distant violence of the Arab fedayeen was no longer deplored; their successes—as any successes of fellow Moslems anywhere—were in fact popularly appreciated. Even officially, there was an acceptance, however cautious, of Arafat's flirtation with the government of Ankara.

The oil might of the Arab states was increasingly respected—even deferred to—although diplomatic and trade relations with Israel were continued, and Turkish and Israeli airliners kept up their flights between the two countries.

33

Arafat and Other Sacrificers

Oil is the supreme source of power today. A tool of embargo economics and politics, it has of late been largely responsible for the world's bloodiest terror—the terror waged by Arabs (Palestinians and others) against the very existence of Israel. This terror is being openly financed by Arab oil money. And the constant threat of one more oil embargo intimidates most of mankind's governments and peoples into an extreme reluctance to come to the aid of the targets and victims of the Arab terrorists.

The modern world needs oil, and the Arab nations of the Middle East and North Africa hold 60 per cent of the earth's oil reserves. The quadrupling (and more) of oil prices by the producers is bankrupting the economies of the consumers. The embargo put into effect by the Arabs in 1973-74 showed their grip on the oil-consuming nations and the might of their help to the terrorists.[1]

These Arab terrorists object to being called terrorists. They insist on being honored as a liberation force. They are recognized and applauded as such in the United Nations, where the Arab, black African, Third World, and Communist states, all of them the terrorists' friends, form a majority. It is this majority that on November 13, 1974, hailed Yasir Arafat, head of the terrorist Palestine Liberation Organization, with homage usually rendered a chief of a legitimate and respected state. It is the bloc that one year later, on November 10, 1975, by a vote of 72 to 35, with 32 abstentions, maneuvered through the United Nations General Assembly a resolution branding Zionism as "a form of racism and racial discrimination." And the same array of forces saw to it that the UN Security Council invited the PLO to take part in the Council's debate, starting on January 12, 1976, on the Middle Eastern situation, thus granting Arafat's terror group the rights of a sovereign nation.

The names of Arafat, the Palestine Liberation Organization, Fatah,

Black September, and fedayeen are by this time almost household words, and not in the Middle East alone. This formidable guerrilla host may yet cause World War III, a holocaust that would engulf and perhaps destroy the entire earth.

It is not generally realized in the world at large that Fatah* and the Palestine Liberation Organization are practically one and the same body. Under Arafat's leadership Fatah had grown gradually through the years until, on the one hand, it took over the PLO, and, on the other, it became the PLO's main military force. At present, the PLO is an umbrella over some six guerrilla groups, not all of which, however, are always or entirely obedient to the PLO. Arafat's hold on them varies from strong to tenuous to nil.

Fatah is the Arabic word for "conquest." It is an acronym in reverse of the initial letters of *Harakat at-Tahrir al-Filistini,* or the Palestinian Liberation Movement. Fatah means just that: conquest— conquest of the Israeli state, a complete restoration of all its land to the Palestinian Arabs.

The guerrilla soldiers of Fatah (as of other Arab terrorist groups) are fedayeen, in the slight Westernization of this word. The correct native original is *fada'iyin,* from the Arabic verb *fada,* meaning "to redeem," "to sacrifice," particularly for a religious cause. The fedayeen are "men who are ready to sacrifice themselves." It would seem that, foremost of all, they are prepared and eager to sacrifice others.

The evil flowers of Fatah fanaticism did not blossom in the barren desert all of a sudden and all by themselves: these determined men learned much of their deadly trade in their youth from the activists and traditions of the Moslem Brotherhood that had fought against British rule and King Farouk. Some of the older fedayeen and especially their leaders had themselves been in the Moslem Brotherhood of those remote times.

But they also learned much of use from the methods of their enemies close to home—of the more aggressive of the Jews in Palestine in the 1930s and '40s, the able and cruel anti-Arab and anti-British terrorists of the Irgun organization and the Stern Group (or Gang, as it was often called). Of these two, the Irgun was by far the more important. Under its full name of *ha-Irgun ha-Zvai ha-Leumi be-Erez Israel,* or the National Military Organization in the Land of Israel, it was formed in 1935 as the military arm of the dissident and radical Zionist Revisionist Party. It battled the Arabs of Palestine in their revolt of

---

* The official name is Al Fatah, but throughout this narrative we simplify it to Fatah, particularly since this shorter form is most often used in the West.

1938; it opposed the British but joined with them against the Axis Powers in World War II; it turned against the British again, vehemently and bloodily, in the postwar period, and later claimed credit for ousting them from Palestine and paving the way for the new state of Israel. Yet the Irgun was too violent for Israel's government, which dissolved it in September 1948.

The Irgun's ways of plot and combat were audacious, innovative, and certainly instructive for a wide gamut of terrorists all over the world. These ways would in the years and decades to come be studied diligently in the hideouts and prison cells of Vietnam, Uruguay, French Canada, Ulster, Portuguese Guinea, and other flaming points of the globe. Fatah and other fedayeen also heeded the Irgun lessons.

At a later time the fedayeen were, in addition, excellent learners in the school of the Algerian Arabs as they successfully struggled against the French in the 1950s and early '60s. That victory at the other end of the Arab seas, formalized in 1962, gave Fatah new pride and courage. The film *The Battle of Algiers,* gaining worldwide attention in 1966, received enthusiastic applause from the Palestinians, while Latin America's guerrillas, North America's Weathermen and Black Panthers, and Ireland's Provos joined in with vigorous displays of approval.

The fedayeen began their terroristic forays against the Israelis in the mid-1940s. Together with the regular armies of several nearby Arab states, they were the losers in Palestine in the war of 1948-49. Fatah, formed as a fedayeen group by Arafat and other Palestinians in the Gaza Strip in 1956, gained influence among other guerrilla formations in the latter 1950s, particularly in Gaza, whence these commandos furtively sallied forth in their raids upon Israel.

Fatah eventually rose to the top because, among other factors, its leaders were a cohesive cluster, men who—by the time of their bid for power among the fedayeen—had plotted and fought together for a decade or more. These leaders were shrewd enough to eschew taking sides in the interstate jealousies and struggles of Arab monarchs, sheiks, presidents, and other strongmen. Thus money flowed into Fatah's treasury easily and constantly from all the warring Arab capitals. But another important reason for Fatah's early rise was its simple and forceful nationalism, which was understood and welcomed by militant Arabs everywhere. Though Fatah was later widely recognized as being Marxist, it, unlike other Arab terrorist groups, did not stress its Communist ideology.

Actually, Fatah did not emerge openly until the 1960s. When, in the fall of 1959, it began to publish its propaganda stating its views on warring upon Israel, the word Fatah still had not appeared. In January

1965, when Fatah launched its regular warfare, its many communiqués were being issued under the name of *Al-Asifah*, Fatah's military unit. Other than within the fedayeen milieu and with the oil-state chiefs, Fatah as yet did not enjoy too high a reputation. It did receive the money donations it needed, but many other influential Arabs were skeptical about its aims and efforts. As late as 1965, Arafat was making the rounds of Beirut's editorial offices to beg for newspaper space for his group. He and his friends were determined to succeed.

The overwhelming Arab defeat in the Six Day War of June 1967, while almost totally disheartening the Arab governments, seemed to have had just the opposite effect upon Fatah. Not only Egypt's Gamal Abdel Nasser and other state leaders but even a number of fedayeen chieftains were at a loss as to their future course, the most bitter of them wanting time in which to prepare for a renewed fight. But as early as August 1967, Fatah plunged into a fresh schedule of raids; its leaders would not temporize with any attempts at retrenchment and reorganization. As their example they cited the Algerian rebels, who never halted to retrain their soldiers but pushed on until the French were broken and out of North Africa.

Through 1968, proving itself a dynamic rallying center, Fatah grew in numbers of adherents and fighters. In February 1969, at a congress of Palestinian militants held in Cairo, Fatah formally assumed its control of the Palestine Liberation Organization.

The PLO had been founded in 1964, with Egypt's blessing and money, by Ahmed Shukairy, a hysterical Palestinian whose record included one-time service as Saudi Arabia's representative at the United Nations and the coining of "Drive Israel into the Sea" as the official PLO slogan. But his raucous, eccentric broadcasts on the eve of the Six Day War discredited him soon after even among Arabs, and he lost his post in the Palestine Liberation Organization. In 1968, Yasir Arafat replaced him. In February 1969, at the congress in Cairo, Arafat was elected chairman of the PLO executive committee, and became the movement's foremost leader.

II

Born in Jerusalem in 1928 (although some Arab sources cite the year as 1929 and even 1930), Yasir Arafat was the son of a textile merchant.[2] In 1947, Yasir's father and older brother were important members of a paramilitary anti-Israeli force called Holy Struggle. Through his mother he was related to the prominent Husayani clan, one of whose stalwarts was Haj Amin al-Husseini, the bitterly pro-Nazi Grand Mufti of Jerusalem, who, as a war criminal was exiled by the Allies to Cairo, where he eventually died. As a youth Arafat was a personal secretary to one of the Husayanis who took up arms to thwart the creation of the state of Israel in 1948.

He and his family fled Jerusalem to Gaza as refugees. By 1951 Yasir moved to Cairo to study engineering and participate in campus politics. By 1955 he had mastered the conspiratorial methods of the Moslem Brotherhood as he widened his contacts with militant Palestinians in Cairo and Gaza. In those mid-1950s he also found time to be trained at the Egyptian Military Academy, especially in the use of explosives. This was when he and his friends founded the political movement that later became known as Fatah.

The year 1956 was momentous for him. Elected that spring as chairman of the Palestinian Student Union in Cairo, he traveled later in the year to Prague as the Union's delegate to a Communist-sponsored international student conference. When, in October 1956, the British, French, and Israelis fought Egypt along the Suez Canal, Arafat saw action as a lieutenant in the Egyptian army.

After the war he moved to Kuwait, where he was employed in the Department of Public Works and ran a contracting firm of his own. But politics continued as the priority. The embryo Fatah was expanding; like-minded Arab intellectuals were streaming into its ranks. By 1959 Arafat and his friends were publishing a periodical, *Our Palestine*. Other militant nuclei took increasing notice of Arafat's group and held conferences with him and his men. And now money flowed in to found the first military unit of Fatah to be put into the field against the Israelis.

Arafat's personal involvement in battles came surprisingly late: it was on January 1, 1965, that he led five men out of a fedayeen camp in Syria in a raid into Israel to blow up a water-pumping station. Until then he had been an organizational and agitational leader behind the scenes. Following the Six Day defeat in 1967, he spent four months in the Arab underground in East Jerusalem, at considerable risk to himself. He also did some dangerous work on the West Bank under Israeli occupation. The legends of his bravery in the field include his admirers' boast of how once in Ramallah he had escaped through a back window while Israeli police were already breaking into the front of the house.

In the safety of the Arab states of Jordan, Syria, and Lebanon, he established new training camps for his guerrillas. Their headquarters were set up in refugee camps. As boys of the refugee families grew up, they were recruited into the fedayeen ranks. Arafat and other guerrilla leaders could be grateful to the Arab kings, presidents, and sheiks who, refusing to resettle the hundreds of thousands of refugees, kept them in those tents and huts for decades—and not even at the expense of their own state or personal treasuries, but paid for by the United Nations.

Traveling from camp to camp, visiting refugee families with a show of solicitude for them amid their squalor and misery, Arafat early tried to create the image of a wise and kind father no less than a fearless commander. On the whole, he has succeeded.

Short and pudgy, not at all handsome or otherwise attractive, this terrorist chief has been trying to compensate by cutting a romantic figure with a touch of mystery. He always wears dark glasses, but this is because his eyes are weak. He is never without his distinctive flowing black-and-white checkered headgear, the *kaffiyeah,* but this is because he is bald or balding. To show how busy he is, he goes without a shave for five or six days, so that his sharp face is usually fringed by a slightly graying, scraggly, untidy stubble. He disdains neat clothes, and is nearly always dressed in a short khaki bush jacket and over-sized, baggy military trousers.

He is unmarried, and neither drinks nor smokes. He eats on the run. He is surrounded by security guards, and is himself always armed. Nevertheless, he never sleeps in the same house for more than one night. Sometimes, in fact, he changes his sleeping place twice in one night. He practices a studied nonavailability to Western newsmen—only to call sudden wee-hour press conferences, to which journalists and television cameramen rush, interrupting their own sleep. Soon the image of Arafat is flashing triumphantly on screens and front pages and even on the covers of *Time* and other mass-circulation magazines. He speaks halting English; his voice is high-pitched; in his public orations in Arabic it is often staccato.

His policy is blunt, frank, and clear. It is stated in Article 19 of the PLO'S Covenant: "The establishment of Israel is fundamentally null and void." Although his Soviet mentors and other assorted friends on the international stage try to prevail upon him to be satisfied with the West Bank, East Jerusalem, and the Gaza Strip as his future Pales-tinian State, he wants more. He wants all of Israel, the Jews to be murdered or driven out, and only a few of them—old settlers, per-haps—to be tolerated as a depressed minority in his vision of "a secu-lar state of Moslems, Christians, and Jews."

The most he does concede is negotiating with the Israelis about their destruction. But even this pseudogradualism is not to the taste of certain other guerrilla groups, who want no negotiations at all. Only continued war.

III

For a time not Israel alone, but also King Hussein of Jordan was an opponent of Arafat's force.

But the enmity was not always there. For three years after the Six Day defeat of 1967, Arafat was tolerated—if not embraced—by Hussein. Beginning with that debacle, the main thrust of Arafat's guerrilla activity was across the Jordan River against the Israeli rule on the West Bank. But the clever Israeli policy of stick and carrot in the occupied territory hampered every effort of the terrorists to gain active supporters among the West Bank's population and establish a functioning foothold on that shore. In effect, the commandos were forced to retreat to their East Bank bases and make their forays from there.

In March 1968, the Israelis counterattacked by carrying this warfare into Jordan. Crossing the river, their tanks and troops attacked the guerrilla base in the town of Karameh. The Jordanian army joined the fedayeen resistance. This resulted not only in Arab losses but also in 26 Israeli dead and 70 wounded.

The Arabs hailed their fierce stand and the Israeli casualties as the first triumph of their side since the Six Day humiliation. Impressed, President Nasser included Arafat in the United Arab Republic's delegation sent to the Soviet Union in the summer of 1968.

As Fatah strengthened, its ranks swelled until, in the fall of 1970, they were estimated at some 10,000 armed men. To this hard core, Fatah added its claim to an unknown number of the so-called popular militia in Arab countries, notably in Jordan.

In that year, however, Fatah's success proved to be its undoing in Jordan. King Hussein stood by, first admiring, then helpless, and finally outraged and alarmed, as Fatah and other guerrilla groups used Jordan's territory, becoming a state within his state and at last imperiling Jordan's sovereignty and the King's own safety and very life. The climax came on September 6, 1970, when the guerrillas, capturing three American and West European airliners in non-Arab skies, brought two of them—a Trans World Airlines plane and a Swissair—to a Jordan airstrip, exploding them and holding their many passengers and crew members as hostages, minute after minute threatening to kill them. (The third aircraft, a Pan American liner, was taken to Cairo and blown up there.)

At long last King Hussein gave his battle order, and his troops—mostly Bedouins, hating the intruding Palestinian troublemakers—fought and massacred the guerrillas. The battle lasted for days, and its subsequent flare-ups for weeks, ending in the fedayeen's complete defeat. The survivors were either captured or sent fleeing for their lives into Syria. Some even crossed the Jordan River to seek safety on the Israeli-held West Bank. The well-populated parts of Jordan, including Amman, the capital, were free of the commandos, who, however, made their final stand in forests and fields. By the summer of 1971 the last holdouts were pinned down and finished by the King's men. The main activities of Fatah and other militants were from then on concentrated in Syria and Lebanon.

Meanwhile, the Israelis kept their own score. While suffering losses in the war of attrition on its newly acquired borders, as well as through terrorist action inside Israel, the Jerusalem government claimed at the end of 1970 more than 1,000 fedayeen killed by Israel's forces and some 2,500 terrorists in her prisons. It was estimated that more than one-half of these Arab losses came from the Fatah ranks, while the other guerrilla groups contributed casualties and captives within the other part in varying proportions—perhaps ten per cent for each of the other five groups.

In 1976 Arafat achieved one notable breakthrough—and suffered one grievous reverse.

The rather sudden advantage was in seeing the hitherto peaceful Arabs of the West Bank, particularly youths and girls, taking to the streets in violent demonstrations and riots against the Israeli occupiers, often with PLO banners and slogans. Israeli soldiers were stoned; their answering fire killed several Arabs over a period of weeks and months, and the victims' funerals served as occasions for more outbursts. While in part these disorders were the work of Arafat's agents, much of the movement was undoubtedly spontaneous.

The loss borne by Arafat, especially in the spring of 1976, was the Syrian military intervention in Lebanon's civil war which had been bloodying that country since April 1975—the strife of Arabs slaying Arabs as Arafat's fedayeen and other Moslem leftists fought the Phalangists and other Christian rightists, the mutual massacre that Arafat and his PLO were either unwilling or unable to stop. When, finally, Syria's President Hafez Assad sent his troops into Lebanon to pacify it and perhaps add it to his domains, Arafat protested—and for his pains was even barred at the border from revisiting Syria for one more round of negotiations with Assad, who by then had most definitely turned against Arafat, his whilom pet and protégé.

IV

Israeli intelligence estimates the entire fighting body of the Palestine Liberation Organization at still no more than 10,000 men. Western sources place it at 13,700, but say that only 3,650 of these are actual combat guerrillas, while the rest are second-line members and sundry auxiliaries. But there are, in addition, 17,000 full-time regular soldiers of the Palestine Liberation Army, supposedly under Arafat, but in fact serving in Egypt, Syria, Jordan, and Iraq. They are seldom used in guerrilla warfare, but reserved for such major conflicts as the October War of 1973 or the Syrian intervention in the Moslem-Christian battles in Lebanon in 1976.

In the guerrilla forces, Fatah continues to be the largest component. In November 1974, it was appraised at 6,700 members, of whom about 2,000 were trained guerrillas. The most active and the boldest part of Fatah is the Black September contingent.[3] First formed in July 1970 with no particular name to it, within a few months it called itself Black September—in vengeful memory of that fall's slaughter of the fedayeen by King Hussein's troops. Most of its personnel come from the Fatah ranks, but a minority volunteer from other guerrilla formations either permanently or for specific missions, such as killing King Hussein's right-hand man, Wasfi Tal, on a Cairo street in November 1971; massacring Israel's 11 Olympic athletes in Munich in September 1972; and slaughtering two American diplomats and one Belgian in Khartoum in March 1973.

The Black September roster is kept fairly fluid, new faces being added constantly to baffle Israeli intelligence officers. The group is loose and far flung in its operations, but its discipline is as thorough as its leaders' inventiveness is great, while the operatives' nerve is truly stupendous.

The total Black September strength was initially some 150 carefully chosen men, rising to 300 in mid-1974. In case of renewed large-scale hostilities against Israel, this elite force can easily be expanded into thousands. Its special treasury, separate from Fatah's other funds, was reported as 150 million dollars in December 1972. Following the October War of 1973, this sum was surely doubled. Most of it is Arab oil money; no secret of this was made when, in late October 1974, the heads of Arab governments meeting in Morocco announced a 200-million-dollar subsidy to Arafat's PLO and Arafat allotted much of it to Fatah and its Black September.

Almost all of Arafat's aides in command of Black September are bitter Palestinians with some education, mostly gained at Egyptian universities. One of the requirements is that each man highly placed speak at least one foreign language in addition to his native Arabic. The sincere or pretended Marxism in most of them is curiously alloyed with their stronger Arab nationalism and Moslem conviction. Some are graduates of Cairo's Al-Azhar University, a center of Islamic learning far more than an institution of modern secular subjects. A few, in their forties, are former members of that old but still fondly remembered radical-religious Moslem Brotherhood of Egypt. They intensely believe that their fight against Israel is *jihad*—holy war. One of these Black September chieftains, Khalil Wazir, a man from Gaza, chose Abu Jihad as his code name. *Abu* is the Arabic for "father"; the two words together mean something like "Father Holy War."

However, the courage of Fatah leaders is sometimes questioned. In Jerusalem, in February 1975, Professor Yehoshafat Harkabi, of the Department of International Relations and Middle Eastern Studies at the Hebrew University and former general and chief of Israeli Army Intelligence, spoke to me with icy disdain of the battle-shyness of most of the fedayeen leaders: "With very few and rare exceptions they do not participate in their men's raids. They prefer to stay deep in the rear."

These top-rank chiefs and aides live in apartments and houses in Beirut, Damascus, and other cities, moving often and in secrecy. Emulating Arafat, a Black September or other group chieftain may sometimes sleep in two different houses in one night. The lower-echelon commanders and their subordinates make their homes and bases in the United Nations-supported camps for Palestinian refugees, particularly in Lebanon. It was to get at their bases that the Israeli planes bombed certain targets within the camps when retaliating for the guerrilla raids into Israel.

Forged passports and other false documents, as well as money, flow into the guerrilla bases from practically every Arab country. Arms, on their last leg of delivery, arrive from Syria but particularly from Libya, the latter's dictator, Colonel Qaddafi, openly boasting of his role as the eager and efficient relayer. Some weapons are brought to the commandos not only in Lebanon and Syria but also, via diplomatic pouch, travel to various West European countries, where they are picked up by agents at conspiratorial points or, even more boldly, at the Arab embassies in those countries' capitals.

Following the October War, Arafat and other guerrilla leaders intensified their efforts to smuggle arms into Israel, to be used by terrorists on the West Bank and in Jerusalem, Tel Aviv, and other centers. On August 18, 1974, Israeli police arrested the 52-year-old Syrian-born Archbishop Hilarion Capucci, head of the Greek Catholic Church in Jerusalem, on charges of repeatedly smuggling across the Lebanon-Israel border, in his privileged automobile, arms and explosives from Fatah to its underground cells on the West Bank. After one such trip, large quantities of weapons and explosives were found in the Archbishop's Mercedes sedan. The Italian-sounding "Capucci" was the

Western version of Kapodji, his original Arab name. He had never hidden his sympathies for the Palestinian Arab cause, but he had also been known for his personally loose mode of living, which made him a vulnerable subject to Fatah blackmail, forcing him into being a carrier of guerrilla arms. On December 9, 1974, an Israeli court sentenced the archbishop to 12 years in prison.

The primary source of the guerrillas' arsenal is the Soviet government, which has never made a particular secret of selling—not donating!—both small arms and rockets and other advanced equipment to Fatah and other such formations, receiving Arab oil money in payment. Soviet armaments streaming to Arafat include the Kalashnikov rifle so beloved by the guerrillas, who tote it around as a status symbol; the AK-47, with its fame earned during the Vietnam War; as well as machine guns, mortars, and—the very latest—short-range anti-tank and surface-to-air missiles. For training in the proper use of the more sophisticated weapons, picked guerrilla officers are sent to the Soviet Union.

The Chinese flow of arms has never been sizable, but such deadly gadgets as "button" mines and booby-trapped pens used by Arab guerrillas are definitely of Peking origin.

The guerrilla chieftains who do not get along with Arafat obtain much of their arsenal from Libya's Qaddafi, and from private merchants of death. Said an American official at the United Nations to me in late 1973, with a grim sigh: "So many American weapons are floating around that free market in the Middle East."

V

What are those other guerrilla groups and chieftains in and out of the PLO tent?

Leading in its independence and often in defiance of Arafat and the PLO is the Marxist-oriented Popular Front for the Liberation of Palestine, headed by Dr. George Habash, an early practitioner of skyjacking, who first came to the world's notice by the capture and destruction of the airliners in September 1970 and subsequent battling against King Hussein's troops. At times during that bloody strife it was hard to say whether Habash or Arafat was the more prominent of the two, each, with his faithful force, trying to outdo the other.

Habash is a Christian Arab, born in 1926 at Lydda (*Lod* in Hebrew; *Ludd* in Arabic) in Palestine, who received his medical education at the American University in Beirut, Lebanon. His professional training as a supposedly compassionate healer of fellow humans has not prevented him from practicing violence.

As a Christian it might be presumed that he would be less uncompromising to his enemies than are Arafat and other Moslems believing in an all-out Holy War against the Israelis. The opposite is true, perhaps for the very reason that being born a Christian, he must prove he is even more militant than are Moslem Arabs, that there is no Jesus-inspired mercy in his heart as he directs his extremists in their depredations. But does he really consider himself a Christian? As a Marxist-Leninist-Maoist he is sworn to be a convinced atheist, with faith in no god but the class struggle and the revolution.

Blaming the Jews for the illness and death of his sister in the Arab panic of 1948, Habash was in radical politics from his youth on. By 1950 he was a leader in the Arab Nationalist Movement, which urged a united Arab effort to aid the Palestinians against Israel, but at first did not list socialism among its goals. In 1957 Jordan expelled Habash as a possible intelligence agent for Syria. In 1958-61 he was an ardent follower of Nasser, but stayed for the most part in Damascus, and when Syria broke with Egypt, Dr. Habash fled to Lebanon. He first organized his PFLP in 1967.

The Six Day War seeming to prove the bankruptcy of conservative Arab leadership, Habash and his friends veered to the left, embracing Marxism-Leninism as a more effective way of warring upon Israel. But in 1968, while Habash was in a Syrian jail (thanks to some obscure intra-Arab intrigues), some of his younger followers tried to take over his organization and radicalize it yet further leftward by proclaiming slogans of class warfare. When Habash, once more at large, struck back at the usurpers, he regained his Popular Front, but found that some of his best young subleaders and fighters were gone. Fuming and raging, he had to rebuild his Front from the ground up. To keep up with the competition on the left, he too had to become much more militant. By September 1970, with spectacular skyjackings and explosions of the airliners, Habash re-emerged as a power. Playing a significant role in the guerrilla challenge to King Hussein, he led the last resistance as the King's Bedouins encircled and crushed the fedayeen on Jordanian soil.

Eluding capture, Habash crossed over first to Syria and then to Lebanon, to fight another day. A pithy characteristic of Habash and his relationships was given me in Tel Aviv in February 1975 by Yaacov Caroz, commentator for the daily *Yediot Akhronot* on politics and defense and a man of much experience in Israeli intelligence:

"Habash used to be far more pro-Soviet than he is now, and until mid-1972 was favored by the Kremlin over Arafat. The Moscow shift toward Arafat occurred that summer, between the time of the Lydda airport massacre and the killing of the Olympic athletes in Munich.

This was the period of cooling between Anwar Sadat and the Soviets. Not that Habash was linked to Sadat. It was simply that both Sadat and Habash, each in his own way, appeared to Moscow as unmanageable. So, then, Moscow looked for a new Arab force to work with. Thus it began to prefer Arafat. True, in October 1972, it once more patched up things with Sadat, but the tilt toward Arafat continued.

"As Habash lost his standing with Moscow, as Russian weapons went to Arafat and not to him, Habash complained, but to no avail. So he became a Maoist. In fact, the enmity between him and Arafat is intensely personal rather than ideological. By the way, to Arafat and other Moslem leaders, Habash, as a Christian, is a *goy*." (Caroz smiled at his own jest.)

Now Habash, as a Maoist, began to get Chinese arms. On one occasion the Soviet government tried to pressure the Iraqi government into preventing a Chinese weapon shipment from being unloaded at the Persian Gulf port of Basra. But Chinese aid continued to reach Habash.[4] As this aid strengthened him, his group grew in numbers. In November 1974, his PFLP was estimated at some 3,500 guerrillas, or "P-Flippers," as Western diplomats in Beirut call them.

Now more than ever jealous of Arafat and his alliance with Moscow, Habash proclaims himself not only a staunch Maoist but generally a friend of the revolutionary Far East, with close ties with North Korea and North Vietnam and particular collaboration with the Japanese terrorists of the Red Army. His most spectacular and bloodiest mass murder was that of the 27 persons at the Lydda airport in May 1972, using the Japanese commandos as his tools. His PFLP is in and out of Arafat's PLO casbah, now quitting and then rejoining, sometimes expelled by Arafat and later readmitted. Habash is chief of the so-called rejectors of Arafat's pseudogradualism. With Habash, the leaders of Iraq and Libya make up this curious rejectors' club.

VI

Next in ferocity is the Popular Democratic Front for the Liberation of Palestine, headed by Nayef Hawatmeh, a Christian (Greek Orthodox) Bedouin from the Jordanian town of Salt. It was he who in 1968, taking advantage of Habash's imprisonment, tried to take the Popular Front for the Liberation of Palestine away from him. When Habash, on coming out of prison, recaptured his PFLP, Hawatmeh had to retreat. Branding Habash a "bourgeois," Hawatmeh and his ultraleftists split away, forming their PDFLP in February 1969.

Despite his extreme radicalism, Hawatmeh—unlike Habash—

snuggles up to Arafat and the PLO, and in late November 1974 even traveled to Moscow with him to confer with Brezhnev and Kosygin and lay a wreath at Lenin's tomb.

Nayef Hawatmeh has some 500 followers, all of whom claim to be convinced Marxists. Their goriest handiwork to date has been the killing, by three Hawatmeh terrorists, of more than 20 children and several adults and wounding some 70, in their seizure of the Maalot schoolhouse on May 15, 1974. The very next day, the sixteenth, at a specially called news conference in Beirut, Hawatmeh was happy and proud about his massacre of the innocents.

There is a singular similarity between Habash and Hawatmeh. Both in their forties, both born as Christians but converted to Marxism and atheism, they were medical students in their youth, except that Habash did become a physician while Hawatmeh dropped out of Cairo University's medical school after two years, moving to Beirut's Arab University to study philosophy and psychology—a great aid to him in his murderous vocation of so many subsequent years.

Still another split-away from the Habash nucleus is the Popular Front for the Liberation of Palestine—General Command, also with headquarters in Beirut. Consisting of between 150 and 400 terrorists, it is headed by Ahmed Jebreel, a former Syrian army captain and a demolition expert, 47 years old in 1976. He claims that it was his General Command that caused the explosion on an El Al (Israeli) airliner over Switzerland on February 21, 1970, 15 minutes after its takeoff from Zurich, when 38 passengers and nine crew members perished, 22 of them Israelis. He also brags about his men's attack on Colonel Yosef Alon, the Israeli military attaché in Washington, murdered in July 1973. And it was Jebreel's General Command that, on April 11, 1974, sent its three suicide raiders into the Israeli town of Qiryat Shemona to kill 18 men, women, and children in a peaceful apartment house. As he kept up his raids and rocket attacks across the Lebanese border into Israel, Jebreel sometimes supported Arafat and then again opposed him, demanding a wave of terror higher than Arafat would authorize, now that the Palestine Liberation Organization had been given respectability by the United Nations and the Soviet government.

There is, too, the Syrian-financed *As Saiqa* (the word means Thunderbolt), led by Zuheir Mohsen, also 47 years old in 1976. Militarily it is but a branch of the Syrian army; politically, it cheered Arafat as long as the Damascus government ordered Mohsen to do so. Founded in 1967, it was not too active until March 1975 when, in cooperation with Fatah, it sent specially trained naval commandos to raid the Hotel Savoy in Tel Aviv. Originally consisting of some 1,000 guerrillas and another 1,000 auxiliaries, As Saiqa, on instructions from its Syrian bosses, made a strenuous effort in 1975 to recruit new commandos—so as to compete with Iraq's latest influence in Lebanon. Thus, As Saiqa's strength rose to 3,000 and, by early 1976, 8,000 men. In the Syrian intervention in Lebanon, As Saiqa guerrillas were prominent as the invaders' aides and allies, although their foes claimed that many of these were neither Palestinians nor genuine fedayeen, but Syrian soldiers ordered to shed their uniforms and swell the As Saiqa ranks.

Iraq has its own Palestinian terrorist formation, the Arab Liberation Front of some 100 guerrillas, commanded by Abdel Wahab Kayyali, 39 years old in 1976. It is busy chiefly with inter-Arab politics, hard-lining for no palavers with the enemy and insisting on an immediate Final Solution for the Israelis, as well as opposing Syria's role in Lebanon.

As for Libya's Colonel Muammar el-Qaddafi, this most belligerent dictator backs the Arab National Youth Organization for the Liberation of Palestine. Since its inception in 1972 it has chalked up a number of terroristic acts in Asia and Europe. It claimed credit for the skyjacking of a Lufthansa plane over Turkey on October 29, 1972, which forced the Bonn government to free the three surviving Black September murderers of the Israeli Olympic Games athletes; for the attacks at the Nicosia airport and the residence of the Israeli ambassador on Cyprus of April 9, 1973; for the seizure of the Dutch KLM jumbo jet over Iraq on November 25, 1973; and for the hijacking of a British plane over Lebanon and its burning in Holland on March 3, 1974. Like several other Palestinian organizations financed by Qaddafi, this group fought bitterly in the Lebanese conflict of 1975-76, first against the Christian rightists, then against the Syrian intervention.

Throughout 1974, the aggressive ANYOLP issued statements against any gradualist settlement of the Palestine State problem such as Arafat and his PLO seemed to favor. Late that year, while Arafat increasingly confined guerrilla attacks to Israel's territory and people as targets, and practically forbade any new piracy in other nations' skies, the Arab National Youth Organization insisted on just that—continuing assaults on any "unfriendly" planes. On September 8, 1974, a TWA Boeing 707 carrying 88 persons out of Israel crashed into the Ionian Sea, everyone perishing. The Arab National Youth Organization took credit, declaring that its operatives had placed a bomb aboard during the plane's stopover at Athens.

As early as 1973 Arafat began to take measures against such dissidents. In September of that year an unruly guerrilla chieftain, known under his code name as Abou Mammoud (his real name is uncertain to this day), was mysteriously assassinated in Lebanon. Almost at once the ANYOLP detailed from its ranks a unit in his memory—the Martyr Abou Mammoud Squad.

It was this Squad that on November 22, 1974, defying Arafat, seized a British airliner with 47 persons aboard while it was on the ground in the Persian Gulf sheikdom of Dubai, and forced the crew to fly it to Tunis. Why these four Palestinian guerrillas of the Squad did not compel it to land in Libya, their patron's domain, remains a puzzle. From the Tunis airport the skyjackers demanded as their price the release of 13 guerrillas kept in Cairo and two held in Holland.

The Dutch complied. The Egyptian government sent over to Tunis the five Arab murderers of 32 persons at the Rome airport in December 1973 but not the eight assassins of three Western diplomats (two Americans and one Belgian) at Khartoum in March 1973. Enraged, the Squad placed one of the passengers, a 43-year-old West German banker, at the plane's door and shot him dead from the back within the horrified sight of hundreds of watchers at the airport. His body fell to the tarmac, and the door was closed.

On November 25, finally satisfied with the seven prisoners released and handed over to them by Holland and Egypt, and exacting from the Tunisian government a promise of immunity, the Squad released the last of their hostages and gave themselves up. Arafat immediately demanded that the four men be surrendered to him—for trial and punishment, he claimed.

Meanwhile, his PLO operatives seized 26 other insubordinate guerrillas in the streets of Beirut and other Arab capitals, solemnly vowing to make short shrift of them for membership in, or aid to, the Arab National Youth Organization.

Many guerrillas were upset by Arafat's new policy: for so long they had been enjoying this spectacular sport of snatching planes from the skies. Now their leader was taking their lovely toy away from them, even if temporarily. They were further incensed when, in early December 1974, yielding to Arafat's angry pressure, Tunisia's President Habib Bourguiba canceled his promise of immunity and surrendered to the PLO not only the four skyjackers but also the other seven fedayeen.

Libya and Iraq persisted in their support of unlimited skyjacking. In Baghdad a Palestinian extremist operating under the code name of Abou Nidal angered Arafat by acting as the Iraqi government liaison with the so-called rejectors among the guerrillas. Arafat blamed him for inciting the Dubai-Tunis episode, and issued a death warrant against him.

But the rejectors' defiance continued. In January 1975, twice within six days, two teams of Arab terrorists from Jebreel's organization tried unsuccessfully to blow up with rockets Israeli jumbo jets at Orly airport in Paris. A total of 18 persons were wounded; ten hostages, including women and children, were held at the airport by the second team for 18 hours. Release of the hostages and freedom for three terrorists were finally negotiated. A French plane flew the Arabs to Iraq. Ahmed Jebreel appeared on French television to vow that such attacks would be continued as his group's "suicide operations to disrupt a political settlement" planned by Arafat. His sharpest break with Arafat came in June-July 1975, when his General Command agreed to take over from another, smaller, and yet more radical guerrilla group (the Revolutionary Socialist Action Organization) the custody of Colonel Ernest R. Morgan of the United States Army, kidnapped in Beirut on June 29. For two weeks Jebreel refused Arafat's demands to free the American. He let his victim go only when the Syrian government, siding with Arafat, intervened.

A spectacularly violent sally by rejectors occurred at the year's end when, on December 21, 1975, six gun-toting terrorists—five men and one woman—burst into the Vienna headquarters of the Organization of Petroleum Exporting Countries (OPEC). They killed two of its Arab staffmen and an Austrian policeman, and captured some 80 men and women, including 11 oil ministers of the nations represented in OPEC (ten ministers, according to later reports). The terror sextet consisted of three Arabs and three Westerners. One of the latter, a German man, was wounded in the course of the raid. Another, a Latin American, seemed to be the group's leader; the victims thought this was the celebrated Moscow-trained Venezuelan, "Carlos."

Speaking Arabic, Spanish, German, and English, the captors read to the captives a lengthy statement proclaiming the rejectors' position of no negotiations with Israel, such as Egypt was carrying on through the United States, but an immediate all-out war upon Israel, and no support for Arafat and his "gradualism" with either Arab oil money or any other means. OPEC must stop dealing with the West but at once turn over the world's oil "for the benefit of the Arab people and other peoples of the Third World."

Demanding and getting a jetliner from Austria's Chancellor Bruno Kreisky, the terrorists ordered the crew to fly them and 50 of their prisoners, first to Algeria, thence to Libya, and back to Algeria. Gradually releasing all but the most important of the oil ministers, the terrorists were said to plan killing Saudi Arabia's Sheik Ahmed Zaki Yamani and Iran's Jamshid Amuzegar. At last they spared and freed even these. The bargain with Algeria's government was that, in return for their "mercy," the terrorists (including the gravely wounded German) would be allowed to go free and unpunished. On December 30 they departed for "a friendly Arab country," most likely Libya.

A leading Cairo newspaper wrote that the financing of the Vienna raid had come from Libya's Colonel Qaddafi. The terrorists themselves called their group "the Arab Armed Struggle Organization," and the Beirut press traced its link to Dr. Habash's Popular Front for the Liberation of Palestine.

VII

At the very beginning of the Arab air piracy and massive border raids, the Israelis, in their initial shock, had acceded to the guerrillas' demands. Thus in 1968 Israel did release from her prisons 16 Arabs in exchange for the seven crew members and five passengers of an El Al airliner skyjacked to Algeria. And much later in the terror season, in mid-May 1974, the Israeli government was ready to barter Okamoto and a score of Arab convicts for the lives of those children at Maalot. But otherwise the policy of the Israeli government has been unflinching. Early in the terror plague it began to take thorough measures of safeguarding its planes and airports, security guards and specially trained troops shooting it out with the skyjackers and other raiders. It refused to trade captured fedayeen for Israeli planes and hostages. Israeli military aircraft and gunboats attacked Beirut itself no less than guerrilla bases elsewhere in Lebanon, strafing and demolishing, capturing and punishing in a wide and persistent campaign of what amounts to determined counterterror.

One such action was truly breath-taking. On April 10, 1973, in a predawn raid upon Beirut and Saida on the Lebanese coast, well-armed Israeli commandos, landing from boats, their intelligence scouts preceding them, penetrated the main guerrilla offices not only in the refugee camps but in a Beirut residential sector as well. They hit and wrecked the headquarters of Fatah and of Hawatmeh's Popular Democratic Front. In the heart of Beirut, smashing apartment doors, they shot dead three prominent Fatah leaders: Kamal Adwan, Kamal Nasser, and Mohammed Yussef Najjar, together with Najjar's wife, who was hit by bullets when pathetically she tried to shield her husband. As the Israelis reboarded their boats, they carried not only their wounded with them, but also bags of captured documents. With the help of these, on the commandos' return to Israel, intelligence men made many arrests of secret guerrilla agents throughout the country.

For several months, beginning in April 1975, taking advantage of the large-sized street battles in Beirut between the fedayeen and other Moslem leftists on the one side and the right-wing Christian Arab Phalangists, in which thousands of these antagonists died, the Israeli command of Mossad (Jerusalem's counterterror organization) sent to Lebanon picked teams to kill particularly important members of various guerrilla units. The commandos, landing by helicopter and boat, and met and guided by Mossad's secret agents in and around Beirut, succeeded in killing eight and wounding 15 of those on their list before, just as stealthily as they had come, they returned to Israel. In the bloody chaos of the civil Lebanese strife of 1975, these 23 fedayeen were at first erroneously believed to have fallen to the Phalangists' bullets.

It is doubtful that the Mossad kept up such action for long. In late 1975 and early 1976 the Arab fratricide in Lebanon reached such proportions that there was no further point for the Israelis to mix in. In slightly more than one year of this civil war, by June 1976, the number of the Lebanese dead reached some 20,000, and many of these were the Palestinian fedayeen and other Israel-hating leftists. The Syrian tanks and troops rolling toward Beirut, although stubbornly resisted by the Moslem extremists and losing machines and men, did contribute to the fedayeen toll. In Tel Aviv, on May 12, 1976, Israel's Prime Minister Yitzhak Rabin aptly remarked: "In Lebanon, Syrian forces, or forces under Syrian command, have killed more guerrillas in the last week than Israel has killed in the last two years." For the nonce the Israeli counterterror operatives could turn their attention elsewhere.

At various times, for months and years on end, Israeli operatives found and killed Arab guerrillas on the streets of West European cities all the way from Italy to Norway. At home a comprehensive system of security checks was introduced and steadily expanded.

To be sure, there have been lapses of this Israeli alert, the most catastrophic of them on that Yom Kippur day of 1973, but also ones before and after—the slackness of the Israeli security guards at the Olympic Games in Munich in September 1972, at Qiryat Shemona in April 1974, and Maalot in May. But on the whole, the precautions against, and the answer to, Arab terrorists on Israel's part have been formidable.

Not the least of Israeli precaution and answer has been the strafing of guerrilla bases in southern Lebanon by Israel's military aircraft and gunboats; the bold organization of such enterprises as the firing of rockets from car roofs by time devices, as the one causing spectacular demoliton of the main PLO offices in Beirut on December 10, 1974; the incessant streams of artillery shells, tanks, and foot soldiers crossing the border to seek out and destroy the fedayeen hideouts that the feeble Beirut government cannot or will not uproot.

Yet the question arises: Has all this Israeli counterpressure been as truly productive as it would seem to be?

Before the October War of 1973 it did appear to many in the world at large that the Arab terrorists were losing. But such an evaluation may well have been a wishful error of the Israelis and their sympathizers. A careful observer could note even then certain signs of the Arab fedayeen's deadly march toward victory.

First, it was evident that in too many cases Arab skyjackers and kidnappers were winning when one team after another, in widely divergent parts of the world, were getting their ransoms in the release of their captured comrades as well as in large sums of money, and were succeeding in forcing Western governments to do their bidding. It was the audacity of these terrorists, no less than the determination of Egypt's President Anwar Sadat and Syria's President Hafez Assad, that finally moved King Faisal of Saudi Arabia to join the pack and lead in the oil embargo that really frightened the West into its near-abandonment of Israel.

Second, yet important, for years and months before October 1973, the Arab terrorists were winning in the long run by distracting the attention of Israeli leaders and intelligence experts from the ample manning of the Sinai and Golan lines to this job of hunting down the fedayeen in Lebanon and in various West European centers. Hence the near-fatal Yom Kippur slackness—precisely what the fedayeen and their chieftains strove for.

34

Fire in the African Bush

The Mideastern strife inevitably spills over into adjacent Africa, although here militant Arabs attack not Jews, but others whom they see as foes. Thus, in March 1975, in Mogadishu, capital of Communist Somalia, three guerrillas kidnapped the French ambassador. The commandos belonged to a movement seeking union with Somalia of the nearby French-ruled territory of Afars and Issas. Their terms were freedom for two of their comrades from a prison in France and a $100,000 ransom. The French bowed, and the ambassador was released.

French children, aged 6 to 12, were targets of a group of seven gunmen of the Front for the Liberation of the Somali Coast in early February 1976. This organization opposes a popular referendum on the future of the coast planned by France, demanding instead immediate independence for the territory. On February 4, the terrorists hijacked a school bus carrying 30 children of the French Air Force families in Djibouti, the major Red Sea port of this last African colony of France. The guerrillas tried to take the bus to Somalia, but were stopped by French soldiers 25 yards short of the border. In the shootout, six of the terrorists were killed. However, just before dying, one of them sent a burst of gunfire into the hostages. This killed a little girl and wounded four children, as well as the bus driver and a woman social worker who had gone aboard the bus to help the hostages. In the confusion, the Somalis gathered at the frontier kidnapped a 7-year-old boy. Specially trained antiterror sharpshooters were flown to the frontier from Paris. In a few days, the boy was returned. Throughout North Africa and the Middle East, the Arab press and governments voiced sympathy for the gunmen—not for the children.

But the most active Arab contribution to tumult in Africa is in the leadership and support of the Eritrean guerrilla campaign in Ethiopia, now raging, now ebbing on the Red Sea shores opposite Saudi Arabia and Yemen on the Asian side.[1]

Today's 1,200,000 Eritreans are of Ethiopian descent—a people part of Ethiopia until the sixteenth century, when the Ottoman Turks seized Eritrea. From the seventeenth century on, well into the nineteenth, Eritrea was a composite of local chieftaincies, but in 1890 it was appropriated by Italy, who ruled and exploited it until the Second World War. In April 1941, the British expelled the Italians. In 1949 the United Nations handed most of Eritrea over to Ethiopia.

As Emperor Haile Selassie tightened his hold on Eritrea, the guerrillas arose. Their aim was—and still is—complete independence for their land. The main rebel organization, the Eritrean Liberation Front (ELP), was formed by political exiles in Cairo in 1958. Groups of Eritrean émigrés, mainly Moslems, after serving as volunteers in the Sudanese army next door or living as students in Cairo and laborers in Yemen, recrossed into Eritrea to join the ELP's fighting ranks. Czech and Russian rifles, mortars, and mines were brought here, paid by Libyan and other oil-derived money, all easily delivered by boat to the Red Sea coast or by camel over the border from the Sudan. In the landscape of deserts, hills, and deep ravines, which provided the guerrillas with an ideal battleground, the Eritreans (like the Vietcong and other such guerrillas of modern times) would not leave their dead behind. To prevent the Ethiopian army from counting bodies, the dead were carried away and buried deep in unmarked graves elsewhere. A secondary guerrilla formation, often cooperating with the ELP, is the Marxist-oriented Popular Liberation Forces.

Although the guerrillas in Asmara, Eritrea's capital, and in the countryside are both Moslems and Christians, the former predominate. In early 1974, the ELP's General Command, also known as the Revolutionary Council, was headed by Idris Mohammed Adem, while its armed units (officially called Popular Forces) were led by Osman Saleh Sabbe. As arms and money came from the Arab lands, the ELP's main outside contact office was in Beirut.

The initial action of the Eritrean guerrillas largely followed the fedayeen model: hijackings and bombings of planes and other enemy property; kidnappings of selected victims; demands of money ransoms and the release of political prisoners. The target was the power and property of Ethiopia.

In March 1969, an Ethiopian Boeing 747 was exploded at the Frankfurt airport in Germany; in June, three Eritrean commandos attacked an Ethiopian airliner at Karachi in Pakistan; in September another plane was seized while flying from Addis Ababa to Djibuti and diverted to Aden; in December two guerrillas were killed while trying to capture an Ethiopian plane en route from Madrid to Athens. In March 1970, a time bomb was defused on an Ethiopian plane at Rome. In January 1971, the ELP succeeded in forcing an Ethiopian airliner to land in Libya, but in December 1972, Ethiopian security men killed six would-be skyjackers.

In early 1974, the ELP tactics diversified into kidnapping of Western oilmen and missionaries. The world's attention was roused when, on May 27, four armed guerrillas seized Mrs. Deborah Dortzbach, a 24-year-old Presbyterian medical missionary from New Jersey, then several months pregnant, and Anna Strikwerda, a Dutch medical nurse in her fifties. With sticks they began to prod both women on into the mountains. Twenty minutes later the men killed the Dutch nurse when she stopped to fix her shoes. Deborah, spared, was to recall:

"It was a grueling walk . . . difficult to walk on the rocky ground, and our captors made us separate. They forced me to walk ahead of Anna as she was stopping to put on her shoes. I heard a shot and when I turned around I saw her fall back. I felt a pang of fear, but I knew God had given her peace and was with me and I was not afraid."

Deborah Dortzbach was spared because the guerrillas needed medical help—cholera, among other diseases, was striking their ranks. She was freed four weeks later and soon returned to America, ready, however, to go back to Ethiopia someday, "if this is God's plan."

That the Eritrean guerrillas, like any other terrorists, are not converted to God as easily as Mrs. Dortzbach would wish them to be was proven by them three short weeks after her release. On June 12, the ELP gunmen killed Hamid Feraeg Hamid, a moderate Eritrean leader, as he knelt at prayer in a mosque. His sin, perhaps forgivable by Allah but not by the rebels, was his advocacy of a federal status for Eritrea instead of her complete independence.

The gradual loss of Emperor Haile Selassie's power, terminating in his dethronement on September 12, 1974, had its genesis in Asmara, where his soldiers—not guerrillas—began to voice their indignation over the corruption of Ethiopia's feudalistic masters. But the Eritrean guerrilla warfare had intensified the disaffection of Haile Selassie's own troops, reaching its historic climax in Addis Ababa, the capital.

On the eve of the Emperor's final overthrow by his military, the latter had 10,000 soldiers of the Second Division fighting the ELP's 2,000 rebels. One month after the dethronement, the ELP claimed an increase to 10,000 guerrillas. The Emperor's fall, however, did not solve Eritrea's problem. The new military bosses continued to fight the rebels, heavy battles occurring in mid-October 1974, when infantry, artillery, and air force jets were sent into the field against the emboldened guerrillas.

In late November, 60 members of Ethiopia's former elite were executed by the new military government. It became known that General Aman Michael Andom was among them, and that one of the reasons for his violent end was his refusal to send more troops against the Eritrean guerrillas. An Eritrean himself, he had hoped to reach a peaceful settlement with the insurgents.

After his death, additional forces were dispatched to Eritrea to try and quell the 16-year-old rebellion in one more all-out campaign. On December 1, the Eritreans responded by exploding bombs in Addis Ababa. The city hall and a downtown hotel were severely damaged, and 13 persons injured. As the military council ruling Ethiopia developed its program of arrests and death sentences dramatically, two terrors plagued the unhappy land—the warfare in Eritrea and the incessant atrocities of the central government.

In early February 1975, the rebellion in Eritrea spread and sharpened. The entire province, both the capital Asmara and the countryside, was aflame as the government threw into the battle ever new reinforcements and the guerrillas and their sympathizers put up a fierce fight. But it was a losing fight. For the new Addis Ababa government was not a democratic weakling; it was a ruthless totalitarian dictatorship with Communist ideas and practices. By mid-February the Eritrean guerrillas, defeated, retreated to their bases in the hills to lick their wounds and await another, better day.

A side activity of the guerrillas was kidnapping American technicians, both military and civilian, who in small numbers remained in Ethiopia to tend United States government installations and some business enterprises. In the spring of 1976, as new such victims were seized, some earlier captives were released—apparently with no ransom paid.

In May-June 1976 the central government hit upon a plan of mobilizing some 20,000 peasants against the guerrillas. A twofold inducement was held out: these Christians were to smash the militant Moslems once and for all; and upon victory, fertile lands in Eritrea were to be given to the loyal warrior-farmers. But the arms furnished to the advancing horde were too light and otherwise insufficient for any successful drive; the peasants were untrained and undisciplined. The Addis Ababa initiators of the scheme thought twice—and in early June halted the peasants at the border of Eritrea.

II

Elsewhere in Africa the outstanding post-World War II factor, lasting until the spring of 1974, was the guerrilla warfare in Portugal's

500-year-old overseas empire, or, rather, its few but rich remnants in Portuguese Guinea, Mozambique, and Angola. Here, by the early 1970s, the jungle-bred successes of the black rebels against their white masters at last resulted in the restiveness of the Portuguese armies. Their revolutionary Armed Forces Movement, finally rising on April 25, 1974, overthrew the half-century-old extreme right-wing dictatorship in Lisbon. Thus did the black insurgents in Africa win.[2]

They had called themselves guerrillas and patriots, but hardly ever terrorists, the name used for them by their white masters trying to stem or crush them. After the 1974 revolution, the liberal and leftist successors of the fallen Lisbon government banned the word "terrorist" and honored the black guerrillas with the name they themselves have always preferred—"the liberation forces."

Too, the prerevolution terror in Africa by the *Pide*, the Portuguese secret police, was now acknowledged by the new government—something the old authorities had always denied. And so the 1973 charges by Spanish, Dutch, and other missionaries concerning the atrocities committed in Mozambique were presently confirmed. These dated back to December 16, 1972, when, in the village of Wiriyamu, some 400 blacks were massacred by Pide operatives and regular Portuguese soldiers. The priests related that torture had preceded the slaughter; and that most of the victims were not even guerrillas, but peaceful villagers whose only fault lay in their suspected noncooperation with the colonialists.

Other mass murders of Mozambique blacks, both belligerents and nonbelligerents, were said to have occurred in February 1974 near other villages, whence the natives were taken in trucks to be executed in the jungle, bulldozers accompanying them to dig the pits for shooting and burial. In Angola, when eight blacks escaped from the San Nicolau detention camp and were soon recaptured, the Pide shot four of them at once and tied the other four to stakes in the camp's yard for later punishment—to be flogged by the guards, after which the Pide forced other prisoners to beat the unfortunate ones to death.

Prisoners died of malnutrition, thirst, or rotten fish fed to them by the Pide. One Pide guard enjoyed putting prisoners' eyes out with his saber. In Mozambique, captives were tortured with electric shock upon their genitals. Some children were among such victims. In one village, the headman was interrogated while hung by his feet from a tree.

In the spring of 1974, as the new Lisbon government ordered release of prisoners, 1,000 were freed in Mozambique, more than 1,200 in Angola, and still others in Guinea. Some of these had spent 13 years in captivity.

Nor, in those 13 long years of bush warfare, had the rebels been gentle with the Pide and other Portuguese when they captured them. Hatred and sadism in Africa have always had two faces.

After the revolution, at first many hated Pide men were gunned down by blacks, but the white authorities seemed hesitant about arresting or even dismissing the surviving ones. In fact, parts of the Pide apparatus were preserved, though placed under the army's supervision. But the roundup of Pide agents in Africa did not begin in earnest until early June, when in Mozambique some 200 were jailed, including its high-ranking commanders. That summer of 1974, with 1,700 informers in Mozambique and a hundred or so of the Pide's regular staffmen still at large, most of them began to flee to Rhodesia and South Africa, and some even to faraway Brazil.

III

Beginning in some cases in the late 1950s and in others in the early 1960s, and into these 1970s and their final triumph, the guerrillas of Portuguese Africa have been well organized.

In Portuguese Guinea on the Atlantic coast, the smallest of the three colonies, with its 660,000 blacks and some 20,000 whites, the rebels have called themselves the African Party for the Independence of Guinea and Cape Verde, or PAIGC, to use the initials of its name in Portuguese. Formed in 1956 and opening its warfare against the whites in 1959, it was headed by Amilcar Cabral, a remarkable personality.[3]

Cabral was born in 1925, in Guinea-Bissau, a mulatto of Cape Verdean and Guinea stock and a privileged member of the so-called *assimilados*, an elite group recognized by the Portuguese as full citizens. In the early 1950s, Cabral was graduated from the University of Lisbon as an agricultural engineer. While studying in Portugal he had met other black students from her colonies and had heatedly discussed with them the plight of their people. Within a few years after graduation Cabral was an ardent, active, nationalist revolutionary, once more proving how wrong were those European masters when they expected the gifted handful of blacks or browns or other colored, their education granted them by their masters, to serve these white overlords as faithful assistants in ruling the overseas empires. Appetite comes with food; ambition with education. The Cabrals would use their skill not to serve the whites, but to rebel and in time to rule.

Alas for Amilcar Cabral, he did not live to see and taste the triumph of his cause. On January 20, 1973, at Conakry, the capital of the Republic of Guinea, he was assassinated by a group of blacks, who were either dissidents within his own party or hirelings of the Portuguese or perhaps both. His younger brother Luiz assumed leadership.

By the time of the 1974 revolution there were in the guerrilla forces of Portuguese Guinea some 6,000 fully trained fighters and 4,000 less well-trained militiamen, while the Portuguese had 33,000 white soldiers and 17,000 black mercenaries. Despite this numerical disproportion, the rebels were increasingly successful, so that the whites seldom dared to venture out of the major towns and military bases. Here, as elsewhere in Portuguese Africa, the rebels followed the methods of the black Mau Mau terrorists of the Kikuyu tribe in British Kenya, who, in the period of 1952-55, ambushed, raided, and killed European settlers, making them flee the countryside. In Portuguese Guinea, by the early 1970s, the guerrillas held two-thirds of the entire colony, their song proclaiming: "We control the land; the Portuguese have only the sky."

But even the sky was in time no longer the Portuguese monopoly: In late 1972, a number of Soviet Russian SAM-7, the surface-to-air missiles, were supplied by Moscow through Conakry to the black rebels, who learned to use them adroitly against Portuguese planes and helicopters. The rebels' other Soviet and Chinese arms were AK-47 automatic rifles, B-40 bazookas with ample rockets, and machine guns and mortars. Foreign experts from Red lands served as advisers, and one of them, the 30-year-old Cuban army officer Pedro Rodriguez Pe-ra:ta, was captured by the Portuguese in a battle in November 1969. Brought to Lisbon, he was tried in June 1972 and sentenced to ten years' imprisonment, which, however, was cut short by the April 1974 revolution, when he was first transferred from his prison cell to a military hospital and then released to return to Cuba as a hero.

Through the years, as more and more of Portuguese Guinea-Bissau was taken over by the guerrillas, the conquered area was thoroughly organized, dotted with rebel offices, schools, propaganda centers, hospitals, and stores, thanks to the help from the neighboring independent Republic of Guinea and especially from the Soviet Union and its East European satellites. On September 24, 1973, at Conakry, the rebel leadership solemnly declared itself the government-in-exile of the Republic of Guinea-Bissau, with Luiz Cabral as its head. By April 1974, it was recognized as a sovereign government of an independent state by 81 nations.

After the April upheaval in Lisbon, Guinea-Bissau was the first of Portugal's African possessions to be handed over to the guerrillas, the 600,000 blacks of the former colony becoming its masters, and the

Portuguese troops and many of the 20,000 nonblack settlers beginning their evacuation. The final transfer of power took place on September 10, 1974. Soon the Republic of Guinea-Bissau was a member of the United Nations.

As the guerrillas with their Red insignia and Soviet arms came forth from the bush to watch the Portuguese leave, they conversed with the departing whites rather amicably, but refused ideological discussion. A number of them turned out to be Moslems who knew their Mohammed but not their Marx. Besides, they said, their job was to fight; it was up to their educated commanders and commissars to argue and agitate.

Mozambique, on the Indian Ocean shore, the second of the three Portuguese possessions in Africa in ascending order of importance, in April 1974 was a land of eight million blacks and 250,000 nonblacks. Of the latter, between 100,000 and 200,000 were whites, protected against insurgents by a Portuguese army of 60,000 to 65,000, of whom 40,000 were black mercenaries.

Here the struggle started in 1964, when several guerrilla groups merged into the Front for the Liberation of Mozambique, soon to be widely known as the *Frelimo,* an acronym, under the leadership of Dr. Eduardo Chivambo Mondlane. He was assassinated at Portuguese instigation by a letter-bomb in February 1969. His successor to this day is Samora Moises Machel, a peasant's son, a former medical assistant and a fervent Maoist (42 years old in 1976).

As the rebels of Portuguese Guinea had their bases across the borders, in the Republic of Guinea to the south and in Senegal to the north, so Mozambique's Frelimo depended on the aid of the neighboring Zambia and especially Tanzania. In the latter it not only had some of its most important bases but even camps for its Portuguese prisoners.

Highly organized and most effective, the Frelimo was a force of 10,000 fighters and 15,000 secondary auxiliaries. From their Tanzanian and Zambian bases they advanced into Mozambique as deeply as 300 miles. In early 1974 they even paralyzed the rail line from the Mozambique port of Beira to landlocked Rhodesia.

At all times the Frelimo leaders appeared to be skillful maneuverers between the world's two great Communist powers: while the chieftains' ideology is Maoist, their armaments come mostly from the Soviets. Their strategy was in the tradition of both the Chinese guerrillas and the Russian *partizany* as further developed by the Vietcong: to hit and run, to sap the strength and the morale of the Portuguese army and settlers and their black mercenaries and civilian adherents.

The toll was costlier to the rebels than to the whites: in the decade between 1964 and 1974, of the 25,000 persons killed in Mozambique, only 4,000 were Portuguese. The wounded on both sides were several times that many, but again more numerous among the blacks. Property loss and economic dislocations to both were tremendous, particularly when the Portuguese tried to combat the Frelimo in the manner tried out by the British in the Boer War early in the century and in the Malayan insurgency after the Second World War: To deprive the Frelimo of popular native support, the white commanders relocated about one million black men, women, and children from the countryside into well-guarded compounds. But this resettlement did not help.

While in battles the Portuguese had the initial advantage of their air force and napalm, the rebels struck back with an abundance of land mines. A shocking surprise for the whites was the Frelimo's use, even as late as the spring of 1974, of that sophisticated Soviet surface-to-air, heat-seeking missile against the colonialist aircraft. One Portuguese plane was hit but managed to land. The Portuguese command announced that these rocket-firing Frelimo soldiers had been trained in the Soviet Union.

When the revolution came in Lisbon, the triumphant Frelimo troops and commissars marched into Mozambique, gradually, in 1974, taking over from the Portuguese army and officials. It was clear to all that once the territory was handed over to the rebels completely, the white settlers' property and safety would certainly be jeopardized, nor would the future of all the other nonblacks—of East Indians, Pakistani, and mixed breeds—be secure. Stormy times were ahead for the nonblacks. After the 1974 revolution, even the lower classes of Mozambique's whites, such as artisans, chauffeurs, mechanics, and salespeople, were in a quandary. They knew they would not find the equivalent of their good livings either in Portugal or Rhodesia or South Africa. In Lourenco Marques, Mozambique's capital, they formed an organization *Fico,* meaning "We Stay," but prospects for their comfort or even survival under the new black regime of the Frelimo were dim.

So, in Mozambique's cities, clashes between whites and blacks began soon after that momentous month of April, accelerating toward the summer's end. There were numerous deaths and injuries, and panicky mass-flights of whites to Rhodesia, South Africa, Portugal, and Brazil. Full independence and black rule of Mozambique came on June 25, 1975. Under President Machel, the Frelimo took complete power, and a thoroughly Marxist regime was instituted. By early 1976 only some 50,000 Portuguese remained in their former colony, many in prison. On January 13, the revolutionary government of Portugal denounced this imprisonment, and in protest suspended all flights to Mozambique.

Hardest for the whites to give up to the rebels was Angola[4] on the Atlantic Coast, with its 481,000 square miles (14 times the size of Portugal) rich in diamonds, iron, offshore petroleum, coffee, tobacco, and sugar. In Portuguese hands since 1482, by 1974 it had 5,500,000 blacks and 150,000 people of mixed stock in addition to more than 500,000 whites, many of them Angolans for several generations, protected by a Portuguese army of 50,000.

The colony's armed strife with the guerrillas opened in March 1961, when Portuguese troops in the northern districts clashed with the formations of black rebels who within a year established the National Front for the Liberation of Angola, or the FNLA. In the spring of 1962, at Kinshasa in Zaire (formerly Leopoldville in the Belgian Congo), the FNLA established a government-in-exile. But, unlike the situation in Guinea and Mozambique, this was not Angola's sole guerrilla organization. The rebel movement here was not united; in fact, there were several such movements.

The FNLA claimed about 4,000 men, one-half of them armed, inside Angola, and 6,000 more in Zaire. Headed by Holden Alvaro Roberto, with headquarters at Kinshasa but foraying on a coffee-growing plateau in northern Angola, the FNLA was originally Chinese-oriented and Chinese-supported. Lately, it has also been appraised as pro-Western. In fact, it has always been a nationalistic, rather than a leftist, force. The FNLA had difficulty in recruiting Angolans, and so was replenishing its ranks with Zaire blacks more than with men of northern Angola's Bakongo tribe.

But there was also the Soviet-oriented Popular Movement for the Liberation of Angola, its contingents recruited in the colony's urban centers and its headquarters located in the safety of Brazzaville in the Republic of Congo (formerly French). While in 1974 it claimed 10,000 armed men and some 8,000 to 10,000 more in reserve or training, the Portuguese downgraded its total to 3,500. The MPLA, to use its Portuguese initials, occupied the lands in the east along the Zambian border, a well as the northwestern oil-rich enclave of Cabinda (separated from Angola by Zaire's narrow corridor to the Atlantic shore). Led by the able Agostinho Neto, the MPLA at first split into three factions, a result of tribal and personal enmity far more than of any ideological differences.

The three chieftains are colorful men: Agostinho Neto is a physician and a poet who manipulates his solid Soviet contacts well and often travels in style to Eastern Europe for more support; the Reverend Joaquim Pinto de Andrade is a Roman Catholic priest, also with pretensions to Marxism; and Daniel Chipenda, a former soccer star who tries to be a radical theoretician. In September 1974, at a meeting in Brazzaville, the trio finally came to a reluctant agreement, forming an umbrella organization of all three forces, with Neto named its president, the other two becoming vice-presidents.

One more guerrilla formation, the weakest of all, was a split from the FNLA, calling itself the National Union for the Total Independence of Angola. Led by Jonas Malheiro Savimbi, a former FNLA vice-president, it numbered anywhere between 500 and 5,000 rebel fighters, mostly tribesmen of Angola's eastern and southern regions, and it operated in the country's thinly populated east. Known also as UNITA, it was over the years the least active of all the Angola guerrilla groups, possibly because its locale was too close to the border where South Africa's security forces stood guard. Perhaps it was this Union's weakness that made it the first of all the rebel forces to agree to negotiations with the Portuguese. The others, for months after April 1974, stayed away or even continued on the warpath, each force quite separate, for they represented different tribes of traditional hostility to one another, even as they raided and ambushed their white masters.

By mid-October 1974, the FNLA was proving effective in its attacks upon the rich coffee plantations in the north. These rebels did not hesitate killing even blacks—those blacks who persisted in working for the white planters. The result was that thousands of frightened blacks forsook their jobs, fleeing the plantations and leaving the crops unattended.

But the greatest ferocity was reserved by Angola's various black guerrilla formations against one another. Widespread fighting burst out in and around Luanda, Angola's capital, in late April and early May 1975. Two organizations were pitted here against each other: the less leftist, West-oriented National Front for the Liberation of Angola (FNLA), and the more leftist, Soviet-oriented Popular Movement for the Liberation of Angola (MPLA). In five days some 500 dead were brought to the city morgue; by May 3, a total of at least 1,200 killed and wounded resulted from the carnage of blacks by blacks. Thousands more were killed through the rest of 1975.

Even before November 11, 1975, when the last Portuguese troops and administrators lowered their flag and departed, the civil war had crescendoed, with foreign intervention on all sides increasing. In October, by agreement between Brezhnev and Castro, whole regiments and brigades of Cuban troops appeared to bolster Dr. Neto's pro-Soviet MPLA. By the end of 1975 these Cuban soldiers numbered

16,000 and Castro in Havana boasted that, if need be, he stood ready to send more. Dr. Neto's own black forces had by then increased to 10 or 15 thousand combatants and, by some reports, even 30 thousand. These included numerous political émigrés from Zaire—those who had once unsuccessfully rebelled against its President Mobutu Sese Seko. The latest Soviet armaments were air- and sea-lifted to Neto's MPLA in quantity, among them rockets (Katyusha and others), recoilless guns, antiaircraft machine guns, submachine guns, tanks, grenade launchers, mortars, assault rifles, antivehicle and antipersonnel mines, amphibious armored cars, and armored personnel carriers. Some 200 Soviet military advisers were also with the MPLA.

Thus bolstered, the MPLA captured Luanda, and made it the capital of its government, claiming it to be the only legitimate one for all Angola. Although it controlled but one-fourth to one-third of the country, its backing by Soviet arms, diplomacy, and propaganda led to the MPLA's recognition as Angola's sole government by a growing number of Third World and Communist nations.

Yet the bulk of the country—and 80 per cent of its population—were claimed by the MPLA's rivals: the Chinese-encouraged and West-oriented FNLA, headed by Holden Roberto, and UNITA, led by Jonas M. Savimbi. In November 1975, these two finally composed their differences and formed an alliance, with their capital in Huambo, central Angola. North of Luanda, the aid from Zaire kept the FNLA in the field; to the south and east, the UNITA (with some FNLA units) was supported by South Africa, which even sent its white soldiers to help these blacks. Some Portuguese officers and noncoms stayed to assist in the training of the anti-MPLA blacks.

American arms and various supplies were channeled by the CIA to Roberto's and Savimbi's forces, mostly via Zaire and Zambia. At the year's end, alarmed by the presence of Cuban troops and massive Soviet weaponry in Angola, the Washington government protested to Moscow, stressing that this Kremlin expansionism in Africa would endanger the already fragile détente between the world's two super-powers. Moscow indignantly responded that its assistance to the radical black guerrillas in Africa was nothing new, that it had been a Soviet prerogative ever since 1961.

Meanwhile the United States Congress stepped in. Fearing another Vietnam-like involvement, it took steps toward cutting off further funds for arms to Angola's anti-Soviet forces. The Ford government now found itself chiding both Moscow and Congress at once.

In December and January, outgunned and outnumbered, the anti-MPLA alliance was losing battles and territory to the pro-Soviet black

contingents and the Cuban troops. By the spring of 1976 the victory of
the Red side was complete, and even the South African government
thought it wise to withdraw its rather successful units from Angolan
territory. On June 11, at Luanda, the Marxist government put on trial
before the Angola People's Revolutionary Court 13 Britons and Americans captured as mercenaries who had fought against the MPLA. The
trial was preceded by massive demonstrations of black citizens, organized by the government, demanding death for these white soldiers.
But at the same time the Luanda authorities admitted that the defeated
UNITA had started its own guerrilla warfare against the new Communist regime of Angola. Thousands of Jonas Savimbi's adherents were
still armed and were waging fresh resistance in the southern half of
Angolan jungles and fields.

IV

But in Africa there has been more than one black-versus-black
variety of terrorism. Briefly:

In Nigeria,[5] the postelection rioting of 1965 mushroomed into a civil
war in 1966 when the Hausas mounted their great slaughters and expul-
sions of the Ibos in the country's north and east. In May 1967, the Ibos
seceded, forming the Republic of Biafra, starting a fratricide that lasted
31 months. It ended in January 1970, with Biafra's defeat, in no small
degree due to Soviet aid in weapons to the suppressors. Hundreds of
thousands of Ibos were dead, great numbers suffered wounds and injuries, one million survivors were homeless and starving, and much of
Nigeria was completely devastated.

Only a few years later came the unspeakable holocaust in Burundi,
a Central African country once a possession of the Imperial Germans,
but from 1918 to 1962 governed by the Belgians. For centuries Burundi's Tutsi herdsman tribe of Hametic origin, tall, statuesque, and
graceful-moving, had, although a minority, enslaved the short, stocky
Hutu farmers of Bantu stock. From 1962 on, with Burundi's independence, the Tutsis were the government. When the Hutus became restive, the clashes that ensued were truly of an astonishing nature. The
short-statured Hutus, unable to strike higher, chopped off the Tutsis'
legs. The Tutsis cut off the Hutus' arms.

In the spring of 1972, outnumbering their tall masters six to one, the
Hutus flared up in a mass revolt. They failed. Panicked into savagery,
the Tutsis went mad in early May 1972, and for months afterward kept
up their frenzied extermination of the Hutus. They particularly sought
out educated Hutus, mowing them down ruthlessly. Later, any Hutu

man, woman, or child was their target. Bullets, axes, sledge hammers, bulldozers, and other weapons were used in the slaughter. In 1973 there were new mass murders, after groups of Hutu students had returned from Belgium to incite their fellow tribesmen in the refugee camps in Tanzania for incursions into Burundi. By early 1974 the total human toll was more than 200,000 Hutus dead and 100,000 driven out of the country. The Tutsis remained in power, now unchallenged, but living in fear and ready for more murders.

In Uganda, in a coup of January 25, 1971, an army officer named Idi Amin overthrew President Milton Obote's government and made himself dictator of that country's nearly ten million inhabitants. In 1972 he gained worldwide notoriety by terrorizing, robbing, and expelling more than 30,000 Indian and Pakistani settlers, although most of the dispossessed had lived in Uganda for generations, contributing considerably to her economy. Less known is the steady killing by Amin not only of his cabinet ministers and army officers, but also of considerable numbers of Uganda's tribesmen, particularly Christians. Himself a member of the small Kakwa tribe, he ordered the slaying of many of the Acholi and Lango tribesmen whom he considered unfriendly, and then widened the blood bath by including the Lugbaras, his former allies, among his victims.

Early in 1974, the total of General Amin's three years of atrocities was estimated at 90,000 dead. If he had any chance beyond Uganda, this dictator would with great relish, by his own boast, happily exceed the record of Hitler, Lenin, Stalin, and all the other mass murderers of history. A Moslem (the Mohammedan minority in Uganda numbers less than ten per cent of the population), Amin shrilly cheered the Arab terrorists in their warfare against the Israelis, urging the Arabs to land their paratroopers in the center of Israel. On one occasion he telegraphed Kurt Waldheim, Secretary General of the United Nations, that Hitler had not killed enough Jews. His favorite saying is reported to be, "No one can run faster than a rifle bullet." He would gladly prove this any time, on anyone. But Amin was much humbled on July 3-4, 1976, when a daring Israeli air raid upon his Entebbe airport rescued more than 100 hostages, killing in the battle seven of his Arab and German hijacker-friends and some 20 Ugandan soldiers.

Even in Kenya, which, since the days of the Mau Maus had seemed so peaceful, terror burst out on March 2, 1975, when assassins unknown murdered Josiah Kariuki, a leading politician who had dared to criticize corruption in the country's government and elite. In the republic of Chad, formerly part of French Equatorial Africa, for 15 long years its black dictator François Tombalbaye tortured and put to death many of his subjects as suspected plotters, but finally, on April 13, 1975, was overthrown and killed by his own military, who promptly launched a blood bath of their own.

In one African country after another, the years 1973-76 were marked by wholesale persecution, torture, rape, robbery, expulsion, and murder by blacks of fellow blacks—even of those blacks whose only transgression was their staunch faith as Jehovah's Witnesses.

The most horrendous accounts of blacks slaying blacks come from the former Spanish colony of Equatorial Guinea in western Africa. Here is one account of how its native dictator Francisco Maücias ordered a mass execution:

> One day, prisoners were taken out of jails to an old slaughterhouse on the edge of a swamp. They were forced to dig a very deep ditch and fill it with mud from the swamp. Then the guards threw the prisoners into the ditch. It was a public execution, so there were hundreds of people watching—lots of women and children. Then the popular militia took the shovels and the picks and some clubs and they beat the drowning prisoners on their heads. Every time the prisoners tried to take a breath or to grab hold of the firm ground at the side of the ditch, they were beaten down. When the prisoners stopped moving or sank into the mud, the torturers stopped. But if one of them surfaced, they hit him again until all of them were dead.

The black dictator and his aides had "invited the people in order to create an atmosphere of terror, and they succeeded. Some people were sick. Others cheered. Many looked away."[6]

V

When the question is asked, What next on the turbulent agenda in Africa? the inevitable answer is: Rhodesia and South Africa.

Of the two, Rhodesia is already in the moderately active phase. Insurgent organizations have by now established their bases in the northeast of Zimbabwe, their ardently nationalistic name for Rhodesia, as well as in Mozambique and Zambia. The guerrilla attacks on isolated white-owned Rhodesian farms were stopped by the security forces and armed farmers in 1966, but other sporadic forays occurred until 1970. Then, for nearly three years, until late 1972, there was a lull. The antiguerrilla campaign directed from Salisbury, Rhodesia's capital, appeared to succeed. South African security men sent here did help. But starting with late 1972, the guerrillas re-emerged. Murderous attacks on whites in the Mau Mau manner were again reported. The black raiders' newest Soviet and Chinese automatic rifles, mortars, grenades, and rockets were impressive; the raiders' skill in their use increased; their recruiting efforts among the country's young blacks gave them fresh soldiers.

All through the latter 1960s and early '70s many blacks of Rhodesia were waiting for "when the day comes." A Rhodesian lady whom I met on a South African trip in early 1971 recounted: "Back home I have a black houseboy who not so long ago said to me, 'Mrs. Townsend, you've been so good to me. When our time comes I won't kill you.' I was surprised and touched, and exclaimed, 'Why, John, how nice of you!' And he went on: 'No, I won't kill you, Mrs. Townsend. I'll kill the lady next door, and her boy will kill you.' So there!"

As the guerrillas stepped up their warfare, the security forces lost 13 dead in the period from the fall of 1972 to the spring of 1973, when six whites were also killed and eight wounded in raids upon outlying farms. The Salisbury government strengthened its measures. Mass resettlements of tribesmen included, by late July 1974, the moving of an entire community of 60,000 people of 21 "protected" villages. This was to save them from "the harassment by terrorists within the area," as the official statement put it, but even more, it was to deprive the guerrillas of the tribesmen's food and other support—the Malayan and South Vietnam method repeated in Rhodesia.

In addition, in 1972-74, other ways of collective punishment or precaution—arrest of the insurgents' suspected sympathizers; closings of suspects' stores, grain-grinding mills, schools, and beer halls; confiscation of cattle—did empty and at times quiet the countryside.

Armed rebels, when caught, were judged harshly. Several were condemned for bringing into Rhodesia what was described as a whole arsenal, with a battle plan for killing not only whites but also those blacks who were too submissive. One of the doomed said: "We were told we were going to fight for the redemption of the people." On May 21, 1973, three of them were hanged; on June 22 three more were strung up in the Salisbury prison.

The guerrillas retaliated on the night of July 5 with a raid on a Roman Catholic mission in the northeast, near the Mozambique border, carrying away 282 children, teachers, and nurses, most of them black. This was very much in the pattern of the Greek Communist guerrillas who, in their fight after the Second World War, took many children from their parents, across the border into Bulgaria and farther on, into the Soviet Union, to be brought up as future Marxists, lost to their families forever.

In the Rhodesia of 1973 the outcome was different. The security forces gave chase, at least one guerrilla was killed while the others vanished, but most of the children were reclaimed.

Until December 1973, Rhodesian law threatened a 20-year jail sentence for harboring guerrillas or failing to report their appearance. That month the penalty was raised to life imprisonment or death.

After the Portuguese revolution of April 1974, both Rhodesia and South Africa tightened their alert. Greater cooperation between the two governments was the order of the uneasy day; more South African security men were sent into Rhodesia to help the Salisbury regime hold its imperiled ramparts. But not for long, as it turned out. By 1976, the Pretoria government, while tightening its own country's defense, was prepared to leave Rhodesia to her bleak fate.

In South Africa itself, so thorough is the government's watch for any sign of black insurgency and so efficient is its frontier guard that little—if any—guerrilla movement exists there. The state's well-known and much-dreaded Terrorism Act is applied stringently not so much against any actual and active black rebels but to arrest, try, and punish whatever white or black opposition to apartheid dares to raise its voice too loudly and persistently.

The ruthless suppression of the riots in Soweto and other black ghettos in South Africa in mid-June 1976 showed clearly how that country's whites, in particular its ruling Afrikaans, will—much unlike their Portuguese neighbors to the north and east—fight for every inch of the land and their supremacy.

This white minority in South Africa would like to avoid a holocaust if possible. Of late, its government seems to think that the whites may be able to avoid a bloody showdown and still keep their power—through clever negotiation and a minimum of concessions to the blacks.

In the fall of 1974 the government at Pretoria chose Rhodesia as a testing field of this new policy. In September, South African Prime Minister John Vorster contacted the Ivory Coast's President Félix Houphouët-Boigny and Senegal's President Léopold Senghor, the least militant of Africa's black rulers. Together they approached Zambia's President Kenneth Kaunda, who then suggested to the Rhodesian guerrilla chieftains that they agree to negotiate with Rhodesia's white minority Prime Minister Ian Smith.

Smith, on his part, had no choice but to agree with Vorster's strategy. Now that Portugal's former colonies on his frontiers were fast becoming black-governed domains, his only route to the sea and sole friend in the outside world was South Africa. So, in late November 1974, Smith released several black nationalist leaders whom he had kept imprisoned for more than a decade and flew them to Zambia for talks with Rhodesian delegates. Representatives of Zambia, Tanzania, and Botswana were also participants.

The Vorster-Smith plan was not a surrender to the majority, but a détente. These whites would yield not universal suffrage for Rhodesia's blacks, but only for the blacks who had had at least one year in a secondary school. And since they were so few, the white voters would prevail at the polls and the blacks would have a small share in the government without taking it over.

Some of Africa's moderate blacks advised the Rhodesian insurgents to accept this as better than nothing—as a transition phase to full power in the future. But militant African rulers opposed such acceptance violently. In early December, Smith thought that his (rather, Vorster's) scheme had been accepted by the Rhodesian insurgents. From his office at Salisbury, Smith triumphantly announced a cessation of guerrilla warfare in Rhodesia. South Africa began to withdraw her 2,000 security troops. But the black nationalists felt otherwise: Smith presumed too much, too early. The war was not over. The worst and the bloodiest was yet to come.

Nor were there for South Africa's white government sound enough grounds to feel optimistic. In the fall of 1975 the civil war and Soviet intervention in Angola drew Pretoria's nervous attention and, soon enough, active military participation. Dr. Neto's pro-Soviet MPLA gleefully exhibited several white South African prisoners, first at news conferences in Luanda, then—in January 1976—at the meeting of the Organization of African Unity in Addis Ababa.

And there was also ominous fighting in South-West Africa, the former Imperial German colony taken over by South Africa, which has refused to release her grip on it despite all the protests in the United Nations. In South-West Africa (Namibia, as the United Nations and others call this land), black guerrillas try to shake off the Pretoria rule. These guerrillas are members of the Namibia People's Liberation Army, the military force of the South-West Africa People's Organization. In December 1975 scores of them were killed by Pretoria's white troops in numerous clashes, mainly along the Angolan border and within Angola itself, whither the battle had spread. Some South African soldiers were also slain then and later. In mid-May 1976 a group of guerrillas penetrated into South-West Africa from Angola, seized a village, and staged a public execution of a 70-year-old black man. On May 19 the government of South Africa announced its plan to establish a 1,000-mile-long no man's land between Angola and South-West Africa to thwart such raids.

The fire rages on.

35

Right-wing Terror

Red is not the only color terrorism wears. Sometimes it wears white.

This White or right-wing terror is of two kinds. One is a preventive repression to derail and overturn a real or imagined radical threat to the Establishment; the other is a counterterror on the heels of a defeated Red regime.

White terror is sometimes a spontaneous rage on the part of anti-Red individuals and groups, often encouraged by rightist governments. More often it is a deliberate campaign of arrests, tortures, and killings by a rightist government.

We have had glimpses of this in the French history of the eighteenth and nineteenth centuries. We have watched the horror of Hitler's Germany. We have touched upon White terror of yet later times all the long way from Argentina and Uruguay to Greece and Rhodesia. Now we look at other manifestations of the phenomenon.

II

Like Red terror, White terror has a myriad of ugly faces. One of the ugliest was seen in Indonesia in 1965 when, in just the last three months of that year, between a half-million and one million people were killed.[1]

What rare contrast between the hate-filled passion with which most of these men, women, and children were shot, knifed, and chopped to death and the gentle tradition of the Indonesian people living on those 3,000 beautiful islands of lovely climate and bountiful nature!

Signs that a tragedy was approaching were plain in mid-1965 as Indonesia was completing her first two decades of independence from Dutch colonial rule. Her flamboyant, autocratic President Sukarno, still widely acclaimed by Indonesians as the father of his country, the leader of the now fabled anti-Dutch revolution of 1945, was a Marxist growing increasingly, stridently anti-West and pro-Communist. In 1964-65 he encouraged his young followers to attack and set on fire the British embassy in Djakarta, the capital, and several United States Information Service offices in various cities. He sent his army to battle the British and Malayans in the north. He removed Indonesia from the United Nations. And, although his state was heavily in debt to the Soviet Union for military and economic aid, Sukarno turned his back on Moscow and his smile upon Peking. He spoke of establishing a Peking-Djakarta axis, with himself as the head of a new worldwide alignment of developing and anticolonialist nations.

Although Sukarno had a political party of his own, he opened all paths to Indonesia's Communist Party, which was now the third largest in the world (after those of Red China and the Soviet Union) and surely the largest in the non-Communist countries. Under D. N. Aidit, a forest worker's son and a skilled and ambitious leader, the Communist Party of Indonesia grew from 8,000 members in 1952 to three million in 1965. In addition, there were large youth and women's organizations of the Party, destined to play their singularly disastrous roles in the coming conflict, as well as pro-Communist peasant formations, labor unions, and other front organizations, a grand total of 16 million out of the nation's population of 105 million.

The Communist Party was particularly influential on the overcrowded islands of Java and Bali, where peasants were promised land by Aidit and his propagandists. As a compromise with the strict Marxist atheism of the Party, wide tolerance for the people's Moslem religion was stressed. In Bali, however, the Hindu beliefs and festivals of the islanders were openly mocked by the Communists. Yet the Communists had many followers even there.

As traditional Moslem parties warned their faithful not to trust the Red side, their organizations were banned by Sukarno and their politicians were attacked and persecuted. Finally, in September 1965, three elements joined in an all-out attempt at a coup that would place Indonesia firmly in the world's Red camp by removing the last obstacle, the stubbornly non-Communist and even anti-Communist leadership of the nation's armed forces.

The first of the three elements was Sukarno himself, who cautiously, without explicitly involving his own person, permitted the coup to be readied. He did this because more and more he resented the intransigent army generals, many of whom, similar to his own past record, had come to power through that oldtime guerrilla war against the Dutch. With these military crushed, Sukarno would of necessity acquiesce in the Communists' increased control, but he hoped to dominate even them as he would take Indonesia yet closer to Mao.

The second ingredient was Aidit, with his millions of Communists and fellow travelers, a mighty host encouraged and aided by Peking. Once the generals were destroyed, the Communists would purge all other opponents, particularly the mullahs and other Moslem politicians, and in time would subjugate Sukarno himself, who, in his vain strutting and his mad expenditures on giant monuments and other unproductive projects, was damaging his country's prestige and economy. To end this reckless profligacy, this corruption and inflation, the Communists would bring in their own drastic measures. But they felt they had to hurry: there were at the time rumors, which proved to be premature but which were being reinforced by acupuncturists sent from Peking to treat Sukarno's kidney trouble and other ills, that he was very sick and on the verge of death—the Communists must take power before the generals had a chance to proclaim themselves his heirs.

The third element was a small but foxy group of dissident military, mostly captains and colonels, but also two radicalized generals, one of them the commander of the Indonesian air force. Some of them were either Communists or pro-Communists; most were personally ambitious and hungry for power, which they thought they would share with the Communists.

The plotters struck on the night of September 30—October 1. With them were some troops, including elite palace guards of Sukarno's as well as eager units of armed Communist youths and women. But the coup miscarried. They did kill six of the most prominent generals on their proscription list, and in the process Communist girls and women tortured several of the victims by plunging razors into the victims' bodies before these men were shot dead. But the seventh and most important general on the list, Abdul Haris Nasution, escaped, even though his five-year-old daughter was mortally wounded in the raid on his home.

The conspirators' most serious error was overlooking a general named Suharto, who was not included on the assassination list and thus survived the butchery of his colleagues. That night and the following morning, seizing the center of the capital, he swiftly appraised the situation as not entirely hopeless for the anti-Communists. Within hours Suharto regained the loyalty of some of the rebel troops, recaptured the pivotal radio station, and checkmated the rest of the attackers, first putting them on the defensive and then defeating them. The plotters missed their vital opportunity when somehow they failed to use the air force planes they had on their side.

The Communist youths and women, though willing to fight for their Party and soon for their very lives, were ineptly led and soon scattered or surrendered. Those peasants who were pro-Communist never had enough modern arms, for at the time of the coup Sukarno and Aidit were still negotiating with Peking for 100,000 small weapons for such a rural "people's force" that just was not there for their impatient rebellion.

Seeing the debacle, Sukarno, the supreme actor, pretended he had nothing to do with the attempted coup, but took care not to denounce it. The other main conspirators, among them Aidit, fled from Djakarta to the provinces.

Now the army struck in all its fury. Inflaming the soldiers and officers with photographs of the tortured bodies of their slain generals, Suharto and his men launched a mammoth drive of terror. But they found they could not touch Sukarno. He was still the nation's ruler, even if only nominally; his complicity in the attempted coup was unproven; and the worship of "the father of his country" was as yet too strong on all the islands for the army to topple him. He even tried to protect the Communists, but, as it turned out, completely in vain.

Thousands upon thousands of Communists, as well as members of their front organizations and those suspected of being members or sympathizers were taken out of their homes or hunted down in their hiding places and killed. On Java the troops had the enthusiastic cooperation of many pious Moslems, and on other islands the energetic help of Christians, in addition to individuals of these and sundry faiths who had personal grudges, feuds, and debts to settle.

Any and all informers were believed. But, as their main source, the army had the seized Communist Party membership rolls, and the arrests and executions of men and women were methodically checked off against these lists. The people of Java, when lagging in their adherence to White terror, were urged by the troops to betray and slay their Red neighbors. But on Bali the army had to restrain the populace in their frenzied, cathartic, near-mystical mass killings, the troops soon taking over the guidance of the grisly enterprise.

Throughout Indonesia whole villages were assigned or themselves volunteered to massacre other, pro-Communist villages. Many a village delivered to the troops its own Communists and suspects or murdered them itself. Anti-Communist members of families would bring to the army the names or the living bodies of their Communist brothers, sisters, and other kin; they themselves, with nicety of feeling, would be excused from the actual killing of their relatives. Many victims were genuinely puzzled as they were led to their execution and graves: they really did not know anything about this thing called Communism—they had only signed up for that hammer-and-sickle party, whatever *that* was, which had promised them farmland and respite from heavy taxes and high interest rates on loans.

But others felt they knew and were guilty—now, with their own deaths, they had to atone and purge the nation back into lost righteousness. Many died mutely, even putting on their white burial robes before being marched to the shootings and the beheadings. Some obediently dug their own graves, as ordered. Others responded to the axmen's requests to lift their heads a little to help the executioners wield their tools more handily. On Sumatra a line of condemned Communists, with no guards or other restraints, meekly shuffled along to the middle of a bridge, where a perspiring executioner chopped off their heads in turn, pushing both the severed heads and the bodies into the rushing river below.

To facilitate the choppers' labors, they used ingenuity—in one place the local anti-Communists fashioned a smoothly operating guillotine.

There was mockery of the dead as soldiers occasionally played soccer with the heads of the executed.

As the anti-Communists went on with their gigantic hunt and kill, hysterical anger was the prevailing mood. But on occasion the executioners were more polite than angry, some even delivering short speeches of apology to the victims about merely doing their anti-Red duty.

Corpses choked the streams. For a long time survivors would not eat fish for fear of finding human fingers inside the food. Prisons were filled beyond capacity, and schools and other public buildings were used to hold the unfortunate. When this writer visited Djakarta and Bali in the summer of 1968, tens of thousands were as yet behind bars.*

To the anti-Red drive, a vast anti-Chinese campaign was added in 1965-66. Of the two to three million Chinese living in Indonesia, many held Red China passports. These were robbed of their property (many were prosperous merchants, particularly in small towns), beaten, and deported to China en masse, some anti-Reds among the Chinese gleefully helping the Indonesians in this activity.

Resistance to the anti-Communist terror was in spurts and ineffective, especially when the few Communist leaders still at large tried to rally Indonesian peasants to their cause. Aidit himself attempted to organize a counterstrike in Central Java, but soon lost out. On November 22, 1965, he was captured in his hideout. He was executed, and first

* The number of political prisoners in Indonesia was still 50,000 in November 1975.

buried but later burned in total secrecy. The army did not want to create a martyr by publicizing his end: no furtive pilgrimages to any sites, if the army could help it.

And it could. In 1965-66 the army of Indonesia left no stone unturned, no man or woman unpunished, in its massive onslaught against the Communists. Well did Suharto remember that the Communist Party had risen in its revolts before—in 1926 in Batavia (now Djakarta) against the Dutch rulers, and in 1948 at Madium in East Java against the new Indonesian state. Each time it had failed but had recovered and even grown mighty. Now the army would make sure that never again would the Communists, be they pro-Peking or pro-Moscow, rise from these ashes.

But against Sukarno the army had to proceed as cautiously as ever. Time and again from his splendid palatial isolation, he endeavored to stage a return to power, to take over from the army. All for naught.

At last, students helped the army by rebelling in the Djakarta streets against Sukarno and the few politicians still clinging to him. Thus came his downfall. On March 12, 1967, Sukarno was stripped of his rank, honors, and all authority, and sent to seclusion in his palace in the Western Java mountain town of Bogor as "Doctor Engineer Sukarno." Suharto, Indonesia's acting President until Sukarno's final demotion, was made President in 1968. Sukarno died in June 1970, having just celebrated his sixty-ninth birthday.

Calm and Suharto reigned in the torn land, with inflation still rampaging and new corruption replacing old. And even then no definite statistics of the great fratricide of 1965-66 were made known. They may never be known. Estimates have varied from as low as 60,000 to as high as over one million. The figure rather generally accepted by Western experts is 500,000 dead, as a conservatively reliable number.

John Hughes of *The Christian Science Monitor,* who was on the scene in Indonesia through much of this terror, rightly observes in his book *Indonesian Upheaval:* "In one sense, however, it is tragically academic whether 100,000 or 200,000 or 500,000 people lost their lives in the bloodbath. For whichever of these figures is most nearly accurate, any one of them makes the Indonesian massacre one of the ghastliest and most concentrated bloodlettings of current times."[2] And he wonders what prospects of mass-scale revenge may yet be in store for Indonesia when the children of the massacred grow to adulthood with their traumatic memories and with a desire to placate their parents' grieving spirits.

A curious by-product of Indonesia's recent history was a minor, yet significant, outburst by right-wing East Asian terrorists in Holland in

December 1975. On the second of that mouth, six East Asian commandos halted a local train in the bleak northern Netherlands countryside, killing its engineer and a passenger, and declaring 54 others in the
cars as their hostages. Later they killed one more passenger, in full
view of Dutch police and troops by then surrounding the train. On the
fourth, seven other East Asian terrorists seized the Indonesian consulate in Amsterdam, taking 30 hostages, including 16 children. One of
the hostages, trying to escape, died in jumping from a high window.

The two groups of desperados were young South Moluccans, most
of whom had never seen their native Spice Islands, off Indonesian
shores. They were born in Holland, sons of émigrés—of the South
Moluccans who on becoming Christians (Lutherans, mostly) grew up
in piety, as well as in loyalty to their Dutch masters. In the war for
Indonesia's independence, many South Moluccans served in the Netherlands army, fighting the rebels. When the rebels won, the Dutch
promised the Moluccans an independence from Indonesia. The promise was not kept simply because the ousted Dutch were powerless to
honor it. Some 35,000 Moluccans were, however, brought to Holland
and settled in its towns and villages.

It was their restless sons who in these December days seized the
train and the consulate, demanding a belated sovereignty for their far-
distant isles. Both groups finally surrendered, those on the train after
12 days of siege, the ones in the consulate after 16 days. In March 1976,
the train group was sentenced to 14 years in jail; in April, the consulate
seizers drew 6-year terms.

III

White terror can be waged by one part of the conservative Establishment upon another. Such was the case of those French army officers who, in the late 1950s and early '60s, tried to halt the tide of
anticolonialism by turning against their own beloved leader Charles de
Gaulle—because he used his power to do the inevitable, to write finis
to Imperial France. To recall the origin of this struggle:

The warfare of the *Front de Libération Nationale,* formed by Algeria's Arabs against their French colonial masters, spread to the European continent in the latter 1950s. The Front's operatives chose their
targets not alone in Africa but also in France, while the French die-
hards, political police, and troops carried their action to wherever the
Arab insurgents or their agents were—and this included metropolitan
France.

The *Organisation Armée Secrète* (OAS) was a large fighting force, composed not so much of the French settlers in Algeria as of French army officers and former staffmen of the French Bureau of Psychological Warfare. It used the vast intelligence gathered by the government services, and it had seemingly unlimited supplies of explosives, particularly of the new dynamite derivative known as *plastique*.

During and after President De Gaulle's stormy but successful efforts to take France out of Algeria, the OAS, in its fierce despair, burst out against him and his government (traitors to France, in their view) with a series of explosions on the mainland. It was then that plastic bombs received their first wide use and terrible notoriety in Paris and elsewhere.

Yet the tide was ebbing for the colonialists. On July 3, 1962, France transferred her sovereignty over Algeria to the Arab rebels. The Secret Army Organization was now underground, and to kill De Gaulle was its prime goal. One of its attempts on his life was highly dramatized in the novel, and later the film, *The Day of the Jackal*. Altogether, there were in succession 31 serious plots to murder De Gaulle, by the OAS and other of his enemies.[3] He escaped them all, and not through luck alone. It took a great deal of careful counterplanning by his security men. Finally gaining the upper hand, his intelligence ferreted out, one by one, most of his terrorist foes. They were captured, jailed, and some executed. By the mid-1960s De Gaulle was safe.

In their convictions, such French army officers were close to postwar Europe's neofascists—even though during the war, as French nationalists, many of them had fought against the Nazis either in the underground resistance or in the open field as the Free French warriors of De Gaulle. Ten years after the plotting and bombing by the OAS, the right-wing terror of their successors in the France of the 1970s was of definite neofascist cast.

In 1974, on the Sunday afternoon of September 15, in Paris, two persons were killed and 26 wounded, one little girl losing an arm, when someone dropped a powerful bomb from a dining balcony onto the crowded main floor of the celebrated Le Drugstore on the Boulevard St. Germain. Because the business belonged to a Jew, Arabs and French neofascists were suspected, especially since another of the owner's enterprises had been burned to the ground on the Champs Elysées two years earlier.

Indeed, on September 18, an extreme right-wing group sent a message to the media, declaring its authorship of the Le Drugstore bombing. It announced its neofascist program, decrying the volume and enthusiasm of the 1974 celebrations in France of the twentieth anniversary of French liberation from Nazi occupation. The message said that this terrorist organization was "sick of all the guff on television, radio, and in the newspapers about the Resistance, the concentration camps, German and Fascist war criminals." Expressing the group's anti-Semitism, the message cursed Le Drugstore's Jewish proprietor.

These French guerrillas, like their Croat Ustashi fellows and their Italian neofascist friends, hankered after the long-dead but not forgotten glory of Der Fuehrer and Il Duce.

IV

In Old Europe, between the two World Wars, besides the Soviet and Nazi mass terror, there were sporadic commando and guerrilla outbursts of Slavs versus Slavs—of Ukrainians against Poles, of Croats against Serbs, with the inevitable Polish and Serbian counterblows. Hardly any of these can be classed as Red terror. They were nationalistic campaigns of rightists against rightists, varieties of White terror all.

But after World War II, one of these Slav guerrilla movements became clearly a White fight against the Reds. We speak of Yugoslavia where, in the 1950s, Croat terrorists resurfaced, now to challenge not the Serb monarchists or anybody's democracy but the new Communist rule of their fellow Croat, Marshal Josip Broz Tito.

Before World War II, their most prominent victim had been Yugoslavia's King Alexander, murdered by Croat assassins during his visit in Marseilles on October 9, 1934 (with him the French Minister of Foreign Affairs, Louis Barthou, also perished). All during the Second World War these violent Croats were with the Nazis and ran Croatia and other Yugoslav areas as a suzerainty formally granted to them by Hitler on April 10, 1941. Blatantly fascist, they fought against the Allies. Militantly nationalist, ardently Roman Catholic, they hated the Serbs, who were Orthodox Christians, and who were accused by the Croats of unduly dominating all the other peoples of Yugoslavia in the period between the two World Wars.

For decades these Croat terrorists called themselves *Ustashi*, the word literally meaning "insurgents." Their leader before and during the Second World War was Ante Pavelić, secretly backed by Mussolini before Hitler openly sponsored his cause. During the war, given a free hand by the Nazi command, the Ustashi ran prisons and concentration camps of their own and staged wholesale massacres of Serbs, Jews, Gypsies, and those Croats whom they suspected of allegiance to Tito. The total of their victims is estimated at 800,000 men, women, and children shot, hanged, or tortured to death. After Hitler's defeat, Pavelić vanished either into Spain or Argentina. His surviving followers, those who managed to escape the Tito and Allied retribution, scattered all over the world, their most active groups re-emerging in Latin America and later in Australia.

With funds brought from their wartime looting of Yugoslavia, and with money accumulated thanks to their industry and prosperity as businessmen, professionals, artisans, and farmers in their emigration across the seas, the Ustashi established new training camps in Australia and elsewhere for those of their young who craved action.

Proudly, they used for their organization the old name, *Hrvatsko Revolucionarno Bratstvo* (HRB), or the Croatian Revolutionary Brotherhood—more commonly, the Ustashi. They proclaimed April 10 as their annual holiday, again to underline the Hitlerite memory in their movement. From the war's end on, well into these 1970s, their main hostility has been aimed not only at Tito and his Communist reign, but also at the Serbs as a people, be they pious Orthodox Christians or the new brand of atheist Marxists. Their stubborn program is to retake Croatia somehow, anyhow; to split it away from Yugoslavia, be she Titoist or post-Tito; and mold their old land into a neofascist state.

The most recent phase of their activities began in late March 1971, when they detonated a bomb in the Yugoslavia consulate in Milan. This was followed in mid-April by their murder of Vladimir Rolović, the Yugoslav ambassador in Stockholm. Seven Croats—two of them the actual assassins, and five accomplices—were captured by the Swedish police and sentenced by the Swedish court to long prison terms.

The Ustashi continued their campaign in January 1972 by planting a bomb on a Yugoslav airliner before it took off from Stockholm for Belgrade. The terrorists thought, mistakenly, that a Yugoslav statesman was aboard. The plane exploded over Czechoslovakia, killing 27 out of 28 passengers and crew. The lone survivor was a stewardess, found gravely injured in the wreckage after a 30,000-foot fall.

On September 15, 1972, three Ustashi gunmen hijacked a Scandinavian Airlines plane with 90 persons aboard on its way from Goeteborg to Stockholm. The terrorists demanded, in addition to a large money payment, freedom for the seven Croat prisoners in Swedish jails. The Swedish government gave in, paying $100,000 in ransom and delivering six of the seven prisoners to their bold comrades (the seventh, being cautious, refused to come along). The three skyjackers and their six mates were flown to Spain. There the nine Croats were held by the Spanish authorities, and the plane was returned to Sweden—because Franco, although having no diplomatic relations with Tito, was on good terms with the Swedish government. On December 5, 1974, a Spanish court sentenced the three skyjackers to 12 years in prison.

The most spectacular exploit by the Ustashi came in the period between the two plane episodes. This was their attempt to invade Yugoslavia itself.

In June 1972, starting out from their Australian and other training camps, with money and weapons supplied by militant Croat groups in a number of Western cities—including (it was said) a clandestine organization in Cleveland, Ohio—19 young Ustashi terrorists moved first to West Germany, then to Austria, and on June 20 crossed the frontier into Tito's land.

In launching this raid, the émigré Ustashi leadership was apparently motivated by the news of nationalist demonstrations and other unrest that had occurred in Zagreb and other Croat cities in late 1971. If so, this hope was quickly dashed. The populace did not rise to support the invaders, but Tito's troops were ready to greet them with lead.

Once on Yugoslav territory, the raiders captured a truck with its terrified driver on one road and six astonished hunters on another. Later they released the truck driver but kept the hunters, lecturing them for hours on the Ustashi aims. At last they let the hunters go, with a parting gift of propaganda leaflets to be distributed to villagers. The hunters at once reported to the police, as did the truck driver at another station.

Security soldiers and local paramilitary units (militia organized by Tito throughout Yugoslavia following the Soviet suppression of Czechoslovakia in 1968) sprang into action at once. They tracked down and cornered the Ustashi raiders in the craggy mountains of Bosnia-Herzegovina, northwest of historic Sarajevo.

The raiders fought desperately. With them they had modern long-range rifles with telescopic sights and silencers, and they used them efficiently. But evidently they did not have either the time or skill or both to assemble the radio equipment they had brought along for a powerful sender with an 800-mile radius, and so failed to broadcast for help from any sympathizers who could have been stirred up. The small band made its last stand alone. In the battle, 13 of Tito's soldiers and militiamen were killed, and 15 raiders fell dead.

The four captured survivors were tried by a military court at Sarajevo in December 1972. Three of them, naturalized Australian citizens, were sentenced to death. In April 1973, on losing appeals, they were executed. The fourth, a Yugoslav citizen, having turned state's evidence, was spared to 20 years in jail. The evidence, according to the court's statement, included the detail that the 19 raiders had carried not only arms, leaflets, and radio equipment, but also poison with which to contaminate Yugoslavia's water and food.

In the summer of 1972, soon after the raid, Tito's government protested to the Australian government against its negligence in allowing the Ustashi terrorists to train on its territory. In the spring of 1973, as if in response, Australia's Prime Minister Gough Whitlam complained to Tito indignantly that Belgrade had three Australians executed without first notifying Canberra. The Prime Minister had first learned of the trial and executions from a radio report.

However, various stringent police measures against the Ustashi in Australia, be they naturalized or not, were ordered. On April 1, 1973, the police searched some 80 Croat homes in the Sydney area. Arms, explosives, and incriminating documents were seized; 12 men and one woman were arrested on charges of possessing weapons and assaulting the police.

Tito protested not only to the Canberra government for its sloppy permissiveness but also to the governments of West Germany, Austria, and Sweden for not controlling the Ustashi in those countries tightly enough. But these European authorities pleaded that they were often quite helpless in the face of the thousands upon thousands of Yugoslavs and other so-called "guest workers" living in ghettos of their own, and thus difficult for the police to handle.

The Belgrade regime has in fact created some of this danger by allowing so many of its subjects to work outside Yugoslavia in their—and its own—eagerness to earn desirable hard Western currency. In a speech of December 8, 1972, Tito himself admitted that 300,000 Yugoslav men of military age were then abroad, "enough for three big armies." Ustashi propagandists and recruiters have been busy among the many Croats found in this human mass. Some do become converted, and return home to spread extreme rightist dissidence. In November 1972, a 28-year-old Croat was arrested on his return home after a three-year stay in West Germany. The charge was that he had become a member of the Ustashi while there. The sentence was three years in jail. In the same month of November, trials were announced in Zagreb of two groups of students and other youths accused of planning Ustashi-inspired terrorism.

On Christmas Day in 1975, Miljenko Hrkač, 28, an Ustashi terrorist, was sentenced to death for a bombing of a Belgrade court dating back to 1968. At the same time it was stated by the head of the police that some 200 members of 13 different underground groups, mostly right-wing, had been arrested in Yugoslavia during 1975. Foreign intelligence services are sometimes blamed in Belgrade and Zagreb as guilty of aiding and even inciting the Ustashi. Wherefrom, the question is semiofficially asked, would those latest-made arms and radio equipment of the June 1972 invaders have come if not from the CIA? But other, equally near-official sources in Yugoslavia hint that the Soviet secret police are in fact responsible.

That this may be true can be seen from the well-established fact that the recently deceased Dr. Branko Jelić, a Croat émigré leader who had for many years made his headquarters in West Berlin and held West German citizenship, was not only a former aide of the Ustashi chief Pavelić, but was also, in the postwar era, in busy touch with Soviet secret agents. It is common knowledge that the Ustashi are no exception to the penetration by Soviet intelligence-gatherers and provocateurs of practically every Croat organization of students and guest-workers outside Yugoslavia.

Still, many nonterrorist Croats in the West doubt the possibility of any success of this and other attempts to fish in the muddy, bloody waters of Yugoslav politics. The nonterrorist Croats also insist that the Ustashi and their supporters number no more than one per cent of the total Croat community in the free world.

But Tito's secret police take no chances. Some of the recent mysterious murders of Croat activists in West Germany and Italy can be traced to the Marshal's far-reaching punitive or prophylactic hand. Though well into his eighties, this dictator is alert and ingenious. The terrorist tricks of the extreme right-wingers are an open book, a familiar story, to this old revolutionary of the left. He hits back at the Ustashi, as at all other milder oppositionists, quickly, effectively, cruelly.

V

The organization of right-wing secret police in charge of White terror can be as efficient as any comparable Red network, even if generally not as well known or global. The Gestapo of the Hitler-Himmler era is still remembered, but not many can identify the *Siguranza* as the dreaded secret police of right-wing Rumania between the two World Wars; or the *Piragues* (meaning "people with hairy feet") of Paraguay, where these secret policemen have been safeguarding the long-time iron rule of Dictator Alfredo Stroessner well into our own time, with some of his prisoners languishing as many as 15 or even 20 years; or the Shah's *Savak*, an acronym drawn from the Iranian name of his ferocious secret police. Americans, if not Europeans, have been familiar with the name *Tontons Macoutes*, a Creole equivalent of "bogeymen," who have for years gunned down or tortured and then killed opponents of the Duvalier dictatorship in Haiti. Europeans, better than Americans, know the word *Pide* as the symbol of the decades of right-wing rule in Portugal that finally fell in April 1974.

The example of the Pide is instructive. Its history goes back to the time when Portugal's dictatorship of the extreme right was established by Antonio de Oliveira Salazar, a doctor of philosophy and professor of economics, who was appointed finance minister and rose to be Portugal's Premier in 1932. The next year, 1933, he devised a constitution of what he called the New State, a fascist structure, and in 1934 he was finally in the saddle as the nation's unlimited autocrat.

Until 1934 his secret service was known as the Information Police. From its very start it used torture; one political prisoner was reported to have cut off his own tongue to keep himself from talking under brutal interrogation. In 1934 Salazar had his police reorganized with the expert aid of a Gestapo agent gladly sent by Himmler. The new name was the Police for State Defense, commonly shortened to Pide, the acronym of the full title. The very word "Pide" threw most Portuguese into a cold sweat. For four decades the Pide men, from their sinister headquarters on a narrow street in Lisbon's old section, ruled Portugal relentlessly—for Salazar, until 1968 when he suffered a stroke and lapsed into a coma, dying in 1970; and for his successor, Dr. Marcello Caetano, until the revolution of April 25, 1974.

Once the wife of the Brazilian ambassador, from her window overlooking the Pide building, saw a prisoner being tossed out of its third floor to land on electric wires below, which killed him. The ambassador dared to protest, and was recalled to Brazil.

The Pide operatives beat and starved their captives. They kept them sleepless and on their feet for days and nights until they keeled over in dead faint; this the Pide called "making a statue." In the fearful whispers of the population these torturers were known as "the nail parers" for their way of tearing off the victims' fingernails. Wide use was made of the bastinado, the medieval Spanish way of beating prisoners, of both sexes and all ages, with heavy and painful sticks upon their buttocks or on the soles of their feet or both. In these and other methods the Pide ogres offered little variation from either the centuries-old Mid- and South-European interrogating ingenuities or the modern Nazi, Soviet, Red Chinese, and Chilean junta techniques.

In 1936 a concentration camp was set up by the Pide in the Cape Verde Islands, with punishment cells so small that prisoners could only stand up to bake under the African sun (much like the "Tiger Cages" in South Vietnam in the 1960-'70s). Of the murders by the Pide, most prominent was the case of General Humberto Delgado, a leading oppositionist who had fled from Portugal but who, in February 1965, was either tricked or kidnapped by Salazar's agents near the Spanish border, to be slain in Spanish woods, his secretary and mistress, Arajarira Campos, sharing his fate.

In his short reign Dr. Caetano attempted to camouflage the Pide's horrors by renaming it the General Directorate of Security, but both its staff and the populace at large continued to refer to it as the Pide. On the eve of the 1974 revolution the Pide numbered 3,000 regular officers and many more thousands of secret informers reporting on citizens from all walks of life. The regular staffmen were readily recognizable, if only because of their peculiarly uniform gray suits and pointed shoes. They knew they were hated, and almost revelled in this, keeping to a minimal social relationship with anyone outside their jobs. The Pide's after-hours visiting was within those 3,000 men and their families. They went for their vacations in groups to the same select resorts. They married within their own milieu, an obscure caste of highly elevated untouchables, repeating the pattern of many another secret police complex in many another country and period.

And then, like a thunderbolt, came the revolution. Among other breath-taking steps, the old secret police were stricken down. In late April and early May 1974, about 1,000 of the 3,000 Pide regulars were caught by the insurgent military and the vengeful populace. The hunt for the other 2,000 and for secret informers continued into the rest of that year, although many had managed to escape into Spain. On July 31, seven Pide officers among those arrested were charged with the murder of Delgado and his woman friend, but the actual slayer and his two on-the-scene accomplices were still at large.

As the hunt for the thousands of killers and torturers went on, it recalled November 1956 in Budapest, when the Freedom Fighters searched for the hated secret police in the Soviet Russian service— except that in Budapest the captured ones were at once shot dead or hung from lampposts while in Lisbon the secret policemen were jailed after beating.

In the prison cells over which these police and executioners had reigned in the old days of the Pide mastery, they were in the fall of 1974 increasingly joined by those conservative Portuguese whom the newly risen leftists considered a dire threat to the revolution. In April 1975, one year after the revolution, more than 1,500 prisoners were awaiting trial on charges of opposing the new regime. Many of the alleged "counterrevolutionaries" and "economic saboteurs" were taken to the very same Caxias jail outside Lisbon, made notorious by Pide atrocities of the old regime. Many of these freshly arrested men were neither reactionaries nor conservatives but clearly moderates who, in history's crises, are usually the most common victims of terror, be it White or Red. In November 1975, after the failure of a coup d'etat attempted by extreme leftists, hundreds of radicals were added to Portugal's prison population. In 1976, as the country tilted rightward, many moderates and conservatives were freed. Reports have it that even some Pide agents were let go.

VI

Currently two instances of White terror are among the most publicized and protested the world over. Both pertain to Latin America. The attention of the London-based Amnesty International and other human-rights organizations in the West is concentrated on the rightwing repressions in Brazil and Chile.

In June 1974, Brazil's lawyers handling political cases estimated the number of such prisoners at some 1,000 as the very least. For a while there seemed to be a respite. In mid-August 1974, the Brazilian Bar Association acknowledged that under General Ernesto Geisel, who on becoming President in March had promised a modicum of relaxation, the regime was somewhat milder. There was less violence in Brazil in 1974 than in the previous two or three years, both because the opposition—especially on the campuses—had lessened its extremism and the military and the police had diminished their counterterror.

But by late August and early September 1974 this respite was cancelled by a new wave of arrests. In the first three months of 1975, in São Paulo alone, more than 100 new political arrests occurred. Men and women continued to disappear in police stations and jails, their families in vain trying for months to find out their whereabouts and sentences or whether they were still alive. In Rio de Janeiro, São Paulo, and elsewhere the authorities reported a much smaller number of political prisoners by the simple expedient of classing, and treating, them as plain criminals, thus paralleling the practice of the Mexican government.

Torture of prisoners is kept up in Brazil to this day, and the infamous *Operacao Bandeirantes*, a kind of advanced torture school for all military and police branches, still exists. As in the '60s and early '70s, so now, too, the school's experts may yet be visiting other dictatorial capitals in Latin America as instructors.

In Chile, thousands of leftists were killed in 1973 and after, not only in the heat of the overthrow of President Allende's radical government by the military junta, but in the long months afterward. Of the many arrested, those surviving and finally released tell in frightened whispers blood-chilling particulars of tortures to which they were subjected by the junta's army and police. Delegates from abroad, representing humanitarian organizations, appeal to the government to temper its harshness and to the country's Roman Catholic Church to influence the junta into easing the terror. Much of this pressure is for naught. So much censorship conceals the true state of affairs that even the scale of Chile's White terror is unknown. While leftists outside Chile speak of scores of thousands of victims, churchmen in Chile cite 5,000 prisoners as of the spring of 1975 but the junta admits only 3,000. In November 1975, the regime's opponents charged that since September 1973 some 10 to 15 thousand people had been killed or simply vanished in the dungeons of Chile's five secret police forces, particularly of *Dina*, the most ferocious of them. In late 1974, in the United Nations, the main answer of the Chilean delegate to all accusations was of the look-who's-talking brand: he charged the Soviet bloc with leading this campaign against his government, an "unjust and hypocritical" vituperation by the Moscow rulers, themselves guilty of basing themselves on terror. During 1976, mainly under pressure from the United States government, particularly Secretary of State Kissinger, the junta of Chile freed several hundred prisoners, allowing them to go abroad. But thousands of others are still in their cells.

Whence comes the support for such White terror waves as those in Brazil and Chile? The classical Marxist explanation blames big capital, the superrich, the traditional exploiters of the masses. But, a paradox of modern times, it is precisely the powerful industrialists and the mighty bankers of the West who brush aside the humanitarians' pleas and protests regarding suppression of civil rights and liberties behind the Iron Curtain, who are too eager for their profits from trading with the totalitarian Red governments to decry Red terror and urge White terror.

Contrary to Marxist predictions, it is the middle class rather than the plutocrats of the West that fears Red terror and often generates White terror. Only a small portion of the middle class, its intellectuals, cheer for Lenin and Mao, for Guevara and Ho Chi-Minh. In Chile, in the crucial summer of 1973, middle-class sympathy was not with Allende and even less so with the MIR farther left, but with the right-wing Fatherland and Liberty organization, thus described by Marvine Howe in her dispatch to *The New York Times* of August 10: "A typical Fatherland and Liberty militant is the 21-year-old son of a businessman who owns a shoe factory and some land. The youth, who goes to the Catholic University, is afraid that the Socialist regime will take away his privileges and inheritance." In its leaflets his organization urged an immediate overthrow of the Allende government, a "direct punishment of leftists," and sabotage of those state enterprises through which the Allende regime was then taking over private industry and trade.

Listing eight ways to effect such sabotage and overthrow, the Father-land and Liberty leaflet appealed: "Stop being a little slave of Commu-nism. Be a man, be a patriot, sacrifice yourselves, rebel!" On the levels immediately below the small-factory owners and petty landowners there were in Chile such modest entrepeneurs and fierce anti-Reds as independent truckers.

Allende was surely no Lenin, and Allende's Chile was a far cry from Lenin's Russia, not alone in time and distance. In the Russia of 1917 there was relatively little of that sizable and stubborn middle class that would have—could have—resisted the Bolsheviks successfully. But Chile in 1973 did have precisely such a class, whose hardy and well-organized spearhead proved to be those 45,000 truckers. Among other points these men—and their energetic, vociferous women—showed how wrong Karl Marx had been a century earlier when he so confidently predicted a total disappearance of the middle class between the two grindstones of the capitalists and proletariat. Marx did not foresee the rise of the complex technology that since his time has produced new ways of society giving birth to entirely novel service industries, manned and even owned by unprecedented types of the middle class. It was Allende's ill luck that by the decisive year 1973 Chile turned out to be one of the few Latin American countries to have developed a middle class of strategic importance along with a middle-class psychology of much tenacity, a class that, to boot, had enough daring and intelligence to use aid from abroad, particularly from the CIA, as smartly as it did.

President Allende and his Popular Unity politicians were blind and deaf in their discounting of the armed forces as a threat to the Socialist-Communist regime. They relied too much on the overrated tradition of the army's and navy's neutrality. They compounded this error by trying to draw a few high military figures into their government. They should have known, but did not, that Guevara was right, that revolu-tionaries bent on a radical blow to a current state-society cannot and must not trust a regular armed force, that such a well-established insti-tution must be disbanded and eventually destroyed or thoroughly radi-calized, so that a brand-new, leftist military strength is created to serve the revolution.

They did not read history closely enough. In 1917-20 Lenin suc-ceeded largely because the nation's old army no longer existed—the Imperial Germany had done the job for Lenin in the three years since August 1914 by killing, maiming, or capturing the millions of Tsarist soldiers and their officers. The replacements were reservists, draftees, and civilian volunteers whom, in the winter of 1917-18, Lenin and Trotsky either sent home or molded into their newly loyal Red Army and Cheka execution units. In addition, at decisive junctures of the ensuing civil war, many adventurous foreigners volunteered to serve the Bolsheviks, to make their determined stand against the Whites, to man the countless firing squads—and thus to turn the tide.

In Allende's Chile of 1973, there were numerous foreign leftists, waiting and eager for a civil war. Thousands of Bolivian, Uruguayan, Brazilian, and other Latin American exiles had flocked to Chile to make up here for their failure as guerrillas at home. Cuban and even North Vietnamese instructors were rumored to be in charge of the burgeoning training camps.

But in late summer of 1973 the right-wing military struck first, using among their pretexts the threat of this very foreign revolutionary presence. Soon after September 11 and Allende's violent death, the triumphant junta indignantly exhibited a "Plan Zeta," which, according to the new rulers, was a well-prepared leftist scheme to smash Chile's capitalists completely by seizing all their property, by depriving them of the last of their dwindling rights, and executing some 20,000 persons of the upper and middle classes on the carefully drawn-up proscription lists.

How much more farsighted were the leftists of Portugal, penetrating and taking over the regular military forces. There, throughout the late 1960s and early 1970s, leftist students did not resist the draft but made a point of being trained as officers, of being promoted to captains and majors. When the revolution of April 1974 came, these radicals in uniform seized leadership in the Armed Forces Movement. Although a numerical minority among the officers, it is these leftists who by their determination, cleverness, and ruthlessness have recently tried to lead Portugal to a Red totalitarianism.

One final word on White terror as compared to Red terror. Such humanitarian organizations as Amnesty International are doing a yeoman job in decrying both kinds. They have done much in recent years to redress the balance—to counter the hypocrisy of so many other defenders of mankind's liberties who protest when a reactionary government hits hard with its terror but are profoundly silent when revolutionaries on the left kidnap and kill.

How far more forceful and effective would our indignation at rightist atrocities be, were we consistently to couple it with our outrage over leftist terror. A plague on both terrorist houses—Red and White—should be mankind's devout wish.

PART IV

Terror with a Difference

"Another Jew who can't stand our
beautiful Soviet Union anymore."

(Horst in *Nebelspalter*,
Rorschach, reprinted in
Atlas, March 1971)

36

Genghis Khan with
the Telephone

What new element is there in today's terror as compared with its yesteryears?

At first glance it may appear that the aims and the cruel ingenuity of the terrorists have been basically the same through the ages. Indeed, some very clever ways of hitting at the System, which seem so novel, turn out to be leaves from old books. In December 1973, Premier Luis Carrero Blanco of Franco's Spain was killed by the ETA Basque terrorists in a manner ostensibly highly original but in historical reality first tried in March 1881 against Tsar Alexander II by the Narodniki plotters.

And yet nothing is ever the same in this world. Certainly, modern technology—the complex machinery and extraordinary speed of our jet and electronics age—makes the latest terror against the Establishment and by the Establishment far more intense, inventive, and widespread than it could possibly have been before.

A profound departure from the old script is in the scientific paraphernalia of modern terror. Resourcefulness was always there, to be sure. Recall the scarf-wrapped hand of Leon Czolgosz concealing the revolver with which he shot President William McKinley in 1901, or the 1905 conspiracy (unsuccessful) to kill Tsar Nicholas II by using live cannon shells while saluting him.

But the technology of our era gives terrorists an unprecedented potential for destruction. Since the invention of the airplane, terrorists have pondered its use. In 1908, on an assignment from the Socialist Revolutionary Terrorist Brigade, a certain engineer Bukhalo (no first name is available) holed up in Munich to draft and build an aircraft, from which his fellow terrorists planned to swoop down upon Nicholas II and kill him. When Azef, the double agent, on his exposure that year fled his comrades' wrath, he took the blueprint with him, apparently hoping someday to make a commercial success of it. The blueprint was confiscated by the Kaiser's police when, in June 1915, they arrested Azef and searched his Berlin apartment. The plane's blueprint may still repose somewhere in the German state archives. But it has taken mankind several more decades of progress in the air to bring us to today's political jet-plane hijackings and kidnappings. Political skyjacking is in truth an innovation—a latter-day version of the nonpolitical captures of likely prospects, for money ransom, by sea pirates, medieval highway robbers, and twentieth-century gangsters.

Nor did the intellectual socialists and anarchists of the nineteenth and twentieth centuries take political hostages. The only faint hint of such practice was in Nechayev's unfulfilled plan, shortly before his death as the Tsar's prisoner in 1883. He intended to use his guards (whom he had by then managed to propagandize) to seize Tsar Alexander III and his family on one of their customary visits to pray in the cathedral of the fortress in which Nechayev was incarcerated.

Hostages were taken—but as arrested, not kidnapped, men and women—in Lenin's time by both sides in the civil war of 1917-21, and summarily executed, more by the Reds than by the Whites. The latter usually shot or hanged their captives without bothering to declare them hostages.

Today's kidnappings of plane passengers and crews is done with an ease unknown in the days of swashbuckling brigands.

First, it is nearly impossible to combat a hijacker once he has initiated the hijacking. The limited crowded space within the plane allows a single skyjacker to command many people, while it renders most forms of defensive action, expecially the shooting of guns, impractical.

Second, when an aircraft is disabled in flight, all human life on it may be doomed. This is why pilots have orders from their superiors on the ground, and usually obey them, to submit to the skyjackers and take the planes to whatever destinations the commandos decree. There are, however, some who are prepared to take the risk of resisting. The most successful airline carrying security guards who do not hesitate to fight it out with the skyjackers is El Al of Israel. This is why, after the few initial attacks on El Al planes in 1968-70, hardly any further attempts to seize Israeli liners have been made. Instead, the plotters have tried to place explosives aboard them surreptitiously—yet also unsuccessfully, for the Israeli precautions against this have also been thorough.

Third, the quick availability of Cuban and Arab airports as recipients of the hijacked planes had no parallel in the old days of highway snatchers and sea pirates. The long-ago routes of those outlaws to their own borders or ports were slow and difficult. Their adversaries had time to intercept the criminals. A chase after the brigands was possible, catching up with them was frequent, and so was the pursuers' victory, the victims' triumphant release, and the wrongdoers' punishment. But in our 1970s, even though Cuban asylum for hijackers has been at last discontinued thanks to an arrangement between Fidel Castro and the Washington government, some Arab governments still give shelter to the terrorists as they force planes to their territory.

Fourth, the success of today's hijackings and kidnappings is assured by a whole range of other boons of modern man's inventiveness, particularly by the speedy electronic means of communication used between the terrorists and their allies on the one hand and their targets on the other. Threats and ultimatums are carried by radio, telephone, tape recordings, and other new methods and channels swiftly and terrifyingly. Electronics put a safe distance between the kidnappers and the police, yet keep the two sides in close touch—to the advantage of the terrorists, who remain in their lairs far away and yet so tantalizingly near.

II

Military and civilian craft in the air and on the ground are being used not only by governments trying to suppress terrorists, but in their turn by terrorists striking at governments.

Thus helicopters have been used not only to strafe such besieged desperados as the black ex-sailor Mark James Essex, who held out on a New Orleans hotel roof for many hours in January 1973, but have also been employed by terrorists—expecially by the Irish Republican Army. In October 1973, a helicopter was used to effect the escape of three captured IRA leaders. Suddenly it landed in the middle of the Mountjoy jail yard in Ireland. The anxiously expectant prisoners were carried up and away before the astonished guards could thwart the daring exploit. In January 1974, members of the IRA used a helicopter in an attempted bombing (unsuccessful) of a police station in Ulster.

Automobiles filled with explosives and wired to blow up have been a common terrorist weapon in Ulster, Israel, Argentina, and many other points on earth. Occasionally motorboats also figure in such roles. Death and destruction are the appalling results.

On November 27, 1973, the IRA guerrillas stole many cars and trucks and placed them across 90 auto roads, railroads, and bridges, tying up traffic in all six counties of Ulster. On January 30, 1974, the stunt was repeated south of the border when 15 determined Provos seized a number of buses and trucks all over Dublin, then abandoned them across bridges and busy avenues to tie up traffic—all this as a pressure tactic in the campaign of forcing the Irish government to influence the British to transfer the two Price sisters, the bomb-planters sentenced for life, from an English prison to one in Ulster. And seizures and burnings of automobiles, trucks, buses, and even entire railroad trains by a wide variety of urban guerrillas occur the world over.

The latter-day terrorist takes skilled advantage of the very latest weapons as they come out of mankind's laboratories and armament plants: plastic bombs, letter-bombs, booby-trapped books and candy, and—last but not least—hand-operated rockets.

On September 5, 1973, the Italian police in Rome arrested five Arabs on suspicion that they were plotting to use heat-seeking Soviet-made rockets, effective at a five-mile distance, to shoot down an El Al airliner on its takeoff from the Rome airport. These ground-to-air missiles were complete with their light-weight portable launchers, and the infrared homing devices were ready for action. The arrested Arabs were found to be members of Black September. They must have received these supermodern weapons either directly from their Soviet suppliers or by way of the Egyptian and Syrian armies that, in exactly one month, in the October War, would hurl these rockets against Israeli tanks and fighter-bombers with telling force. Because by early September only a few such advanced rockets had reached the West, the Cairo newspaper *Al Ahram* on the ninth of that month chided the Black Septembrists for presenting the North Atlantic Treaty Organization with this little-anticipated gift. Since that time, as NATO strategists and tacticians could no longer be kept from a close knowledge of these Soviet rockets, a quantity of them were supplied by Communist munitions sources to the guerrillas of Portuguese Africa as well. By now there can be no doubt that terrorists in other parts of the world have been, or soon will be, provided with these deadly heat-seeking missiles.

The shrewd use of modern inventions by terrorists today is exemplified, among others, by the mind-boggling scheme of a group of Iranian commandos to kill or kidnap Shah Mohammed Riza Pahlevi, together with his Empress Farah and their 12-year-old son, Crown Prince Riza, in October 1973. This was planned for the day of a royal ceremony to present prizes for the best films for children. But the plot was discovered in time, and 12 terrorists were arrested, among them a movie-maker chosen to receive one of the prizes and a cameraman who was to film the presentation: his camera lens disguised a deadly gun muzzle (a method once tried by French terrorists hunting De Gaulle).[1]

Brilliant up-to-date ingenuity of terrorists was illustrated in Uruguay on May 25, 1972, when a major Tupamaro base was discovered and captured by soldiers and policemen on a provincial estate amid a forest of eucalyptus trees. Of truly large proportions, the hideout had been dug under the ground and solidly lined with reinforced concrete. An enormous boulder shielded the entrance. It could be rolled aside by a skillfully hidden mechanism. A sizable arsenal was uncovered: numerous machine guns, several hundred rifles and automatic weapons, cases of cartridges and grenades, many radio transmitters, and an enormous wardrobe of military and police uniforms, with a fascinating array of masks and wigs. At the base were also a library, a target-practice tier, and an ample electro-mechanical shop with welding units, among other machines and equipment. To cap the inclusive character of the base, a medical and surgical section excelled in instruments and drugs. Of the nine Tupamaros captured here, two turned out to be physicians, one of them a surgeon. A mile or so away from the base, an underground "people's prison" was found. To this was attached a depot of explosives in large quantities and of great variety.[2]

III

Modern arms, modern vehicles, and the very latest ingenuity in electronics lend today's terrorists their ability to challenge the Establishment on equal terms or at times even with superior means—an advantage surely denied the terrorists and other revolutionaries of previous eras.

Not that the Establishment does not possess enough modern means to fight the terrorists. But when a government is not totalitarian or otherwise autocratic and adheres to democratic precepts and practices, it often lacks the will to use such weapons in time and in sufficiency.

To the contrary, authoritarian governments, such as the Nazis and other fascists and neofascists, or the Soviet and other Communist apparatuses, not only battle the rebels whenever those attempt to rise— as a rule they initiate the fight, the massive repression, not allowing the insurgents to have their very first barricade or bomb. As they do so, they introduce the very latest electric, electronic, and psychological methods to vary and immeasurably sharpen the torture of their prisoners.

Earlier, I have spoken of some of the ancient methods of inhumanity of man to man. Let me here remind the reader, in a slightly expanded list of those ways, that in ancient Greece and Rome the rack was widely used; that at Sparta a despot had an enclosure constructed in the form of a woman (actually, an approximate representation of his wife!) in which to torture and kill his victims; that the Roman Code included, in addition to the rack, leaden balls, barbed hooks, hot plates, and arm-compressing cords. There were also crucifixion, mutilation, and throwing of humans to the lions and other wild beasts in the arena. In medieval Germany there was the Iron Maid and in England the Scavenger's Daughter to compress the body in that old Spartan despot's manner, breaking bones and causing hemorrhages and ruptures until death. The more common rack, on the other hand, stretched the body rather than compressing it, until the bones were pulled from their sockets. And everywhere in medieval and Renaissance Europe were the techniques of thumbscrews, iron gauntlets to squeeze men's and women's hands, quantities of water forced down the victim's throat, deprivation of his sleep and food, of feeding him rotten food, or not giving him anything to drink after having him eat too much salted fish, or the methods of the strappado and the bastinado.

Study this list closely—and then consult the reminiscences of survivors of modern torture chambers: how many of these methods are used by today's sadists in power—but with the addition of the latest advances in electricity, electronics, gas, hypnosis, and brainwashing.

The oldtime strappado, where the victim, his hands tied behind his back and heavy iron bars hung from his legs, was hoisted off the floor by a pulley, has acquired the refinement of automatic, clock-regulated, and far more continuous lifting and lowering of the body with the aid of electricity. In Brazil, in the torture techniques of the right-wing state's police of today, the device is varied and known as "the parrot's perch": a naked prisoner is beaten and given electric shocks while suspended by his legs and arms from a metal bar, his head hanging down toward the floor. The traditional bastinado by sticks hitting the victim's limbs, buttocks, and genitals has now been accentuated in a number of authoritarian states by the application of electricity to the same parts of the body.

Electricity is used in Brazil's police instrument called "the pianola"—a keyboard sending electric current through the victim's body. A similar device was evolved by the South Vietnamese police torturers. In several totalitarian regimes there is "the electric microphone," activating such shock treatment by magnifying enormously the sounds around the prisoner, including his own screaming. The more he screams, the more current is shot into his body by this machine.

Intense light from unshaded 500-watt electric bulbs nearly blinds a prisoner. "The refrigerator"—a small cubicle, operated by electricity or gas, where the victim is kept in freezing temperatures for hours—is truly a chilling experience. Some men and women die under this and other such treatment; many come out total physical and psychic wrecks.

Many of these triumphs of science and technology were first introduced or improved upon by the Soviet and Nazi masters of sadism. According to Solzhenitsyn, a Soviet secret police unit in the Northern Caucasus in the 1930s furthered the age-old torture of nail-pulling by inventing and utilizing a special mechanical gadget to squeeze and tear off the prisoners' fingernails one by one, a modern twist, so to say, yet in essence only bringing the medieval iron gauntlet up to date. The ancient custom of killing captives punitively or festively, as sacrifices in religious rites, was vastly expanded and mechanized by Hitler's gas chambers and full-blasting crematoria for the millions.

Pseudomedical experiments were cruelly performed by Nazi doctors on hundreds and thousands of concentration-camp inmates. Certain results were achieved by psychological pressures as devised and practiced by men in white on many of Stalin's prisoners. Some of the most recent anti-Establishment terrorists in the West have also proved that it is possible to convert a kidnapped victim to a fellow terrorist, as was evidently done in 1974 to Patty Hearst with the aid of techniques learned from books in the Berkeley pads and from therapy sessions at Vacaville.

Sophisticated manuals on bomb-making, skyjacking, kidnapping, and other ways of terror are written and printed by and for guerrillas. Films of torture techniques are produced by secret policemen of totalitarian states for instruction of novices. Both the manuals and the films are but the latest superstructure upon the primitive foundation of the Roman Code, the Inquisition directives, the expertise of the guillotine-operating masters handed down to their eager apprentices, as well as Emperors' decrees and Tsars' ukases to their henchmen. The more all this torture changes, the less it changes—in spirit, if not in technology.

The frightful growth in the cruelty of the latter-day suppressors, thanks to their power's enhancement by modern discoveries and inventions, was foreseen by Lev Tolstoy when he spoke of tomorrow's autocratic ruler as "a Genghis Khan with the telephone." Now this clairvoyance is made more acute by the inclusion of the terrorist, side by side with the ruler.

37

The New Robin Hoods,
the Media, and the Police

Another new dimension in modern terror is the variety of uses its practitioners have developed in public relations. How to win friends and influence people while kidnapping and killing fellow men is the name of this bloody game.

As in the realm of technology, so in public relations, too, even if some old methods are being employed, certain startling improvements have been added. One of the most significant and successful innovations is a change rung on the venerable Robin Hood theme.

This is the kidnapping or the threat of kidnapping—and sometimes murder—of executives of Ford, Fiat, Exxon, and other large international corporations in Latin America, as well as of domestic concerns in Spain, to compel such firms to rehire and compensate discharged workers, but particularly to deliver huge amounts of ransom in supplies, not only for the terrorists themselves, but for the poor at large, through the provision of hospitals and children's homes with hefty quantities of medicine, milk, and other necessities.

The technique was borrowed and brought to North America in February and March 1974 by the Symbionese Liberation Army when its terrorists kidnapped Patricia Hearst and demanded—and got—from her father a distribution of two million dollars' worth of food to the slum dwellers of San Francisco and its environs.

This variation has indeed resulted in a gain in sympathy for the guerrillas on the part of some of the lower classes and intellectuals. More often, however, this kind of propaganda or welfare work can be directly counterproductive.

In Tsarist Russia, as we have seen, the Narodniki in their preterror-ist phase had tried peaceful propaganda and good works among the peasants, but for their idealistic pains they were often seized, cursed, beaten up, and delivered to the police by the very muzhiks who were genuinely outraged that these young men and women of the gentry would dare to talk against the throne and the Church. The Narodniki, as we know, finally gave up their pure-hearted and futile agitation, changing to outright terror precisely because they despaired of ever winning the peasantry and the rest of the nation by talk or philanthropy alone.

Nor did their many assassinations, finally of the Tsar himself, win over the masses to their banner and bombs. Contrary to the naïve hope of these intellectuals, their murder of Alexander II was not taken by the peasants as a signal to rise against the Establishment. And in the cities, the scant proletariat, which was only beginning to form, and other members of the lower class were stunned by the event rather than aroused to cheers for the bloodshed. In fact, from then on and well into the twentieth century, whenever the Tsarist police felt they needed help, they could count on a city mob to run wild in the streets against the university students who were suspected of radicalism and the Jews who were so easy to pogrom and rob.

In America, the inflammatory teachings of Johann Most and the hanging of the Haymarket Riot defendants did not cause the nation's masses to rally behind the anarchists and applaud programs of terror. In Western Europe the several decades of anarchist violence up to the outbreak of the First World War were not marked by any wide popular support or sympathy for these bomb-throwers.

In our own times, the lack of any such support has been the well-known rule. How wrong were the Weatherpeople and the Black Panthers and certainly the Black Liberation Army in their sanguine expectations!

At the height of their activism the Weatherpeople were confident that America's working classes, basically discontented, would follow their lead. This soon proved a silly, sorry illusion. Nor can it be said that Black Panthers had a strong base among this country's blacks, though, to be sure, blacks had more sympathy for them than the whites had had for the Narodniki or for the West European anarchists or (among Russia's lower classes in the long term) for the terror of Lenin, Trotsky, and Stalin. Yet, in general, American blacks who had become or were about to become members of the middle class feared the disturbing Panthers and Black Liberationists. They wanted further enhancement of their status through successful honest work, not through guns and bombs and arson.

But in a few cases support for terrorists is increasing and may yet become massive—perhaps decisive. Significantly, successful terrorist propaganda has been the result of two different approaches: First, when the guerrillas pick North American and other foreign business-men as their targets; here, the xenophobian nerve of the Latin American masses is skillfully touched; second, when the ransom demanded and soon delivered is in the Robin Hood category—the milk, the medi-cines, and other necessities exacted from the corporations for the good of the poor.

In North America, in the Hearst episode, at first there were signs of anti-Symbionese feeling even among the poor. Some slum-dwelling whites and poor blacks spoke up in revulsion and indignation: they would not accept meat and other groceries at the price of the sufferings of Patty Hearst and her family, they said.

But as the actual distribution of food began, other poor—and some of the initial indignant ones, too—came to claim the handouts. The Symbionese were especially clever in the conditions they imposed on Randolph A. Hearst and his staff: charitable organizations of the Estab-lishment were not to be in charge; radical lower-class committees were specifically designated by the kidnappers; police and television cam-eras were to keep their discreet distance from the distribution centers; no identity cards, nor any proof of poverty and need were to be demanded of those in lines; no forms of any kind were to be filled out and signed by any beneficiary. (Many who were not needy did profit.)

Most important was the order that the food not be of the dull quality usually handed out by the Salvation Army and other such philanthropic organizations; it was to be good-grade pork, ham, roast beef, and chicken. These instructions were carried out after only a brief delay and precisely. To drive the lesson home to Hearst, a radical commu-nity group in charge of food distribution in San Francisco sent back a shipment of hamburger meat for being low grade.

These were the tactics that influenced even many of those poor who at first had seemed upset by Patty's brutal kidnapping and who had vowed they would not accept morally tainted bounty. They were also impressed by the spectacle of the mighty Hearst, and the Estab-lishment he represented, so distraught and meek before the peremp-tory orders of the terrorists. Here was Hearst eating crow while the poor ate his high-grade chicken.

The imperious lingo of the Symbionese Liberation Army, pretend-ing to the grandeur of a military power, what with the titles of "Field Marshal Cinque" and the like, even claiming to be a government in the underground with the right to take prisoners and execute its victims, now no longer appeared as so much foolish claptrap—not to these urban poor of California. The Symbionese were a real power. At the same time, the kidnappers were running a deadly risk to their own liberty and lives. So there were soon very few moralists to refuse this food. An official at a distribution center in the black ghetto of Hunter's Point in San Francisco said to a newspaperman, with awe and fervent sincerity: "The brothers put their lives on the line so people can get food. People understand that. It's that simple."

To strengthen their case for accepting the fine groceries, the poor and their radical advocates seized upon any clumsy move or statement from the Establishment. When Governor Ronald Reagan publicly wished the accepters of this food to be stricken with botulism, the Symbionese cause appeared to shine effulgently in comparison. Even nonradicals of America joined in the feeling of outrage caused by the Governor's sally, and he had to backtrack, explaining his utterance as only a jest. But many of the bounty's recipients had neither fears nor qualms. A volunteer at a center observed: "Everyone on line is for the food and they don't care where it comes from."

But such acceptance of terror because of its sudden beneficence to the poor is usually short-range. Let us recall that when terror was first introduced by Lenin in Russia in 1917-18, it was initially popular among large sections of the people because of his early teaching that urged the poor—and even the lower-middle class strata—to "rob from the rich that which has been robbed from you." But this popularity waned and disappeared as Lenin's terror, continued and expanded by Stalin, hit frightfully at so many of those who had in the beginning of the revolution profited from it at the expense of the terror's early victims.

II

These Robin Hood exploits and other public-relations efforts are greatly aided by the streamlined technology of today's media. The swift press coverage, the instant television and radio broadcasts, and such films as *The Battle of Algiers* and *State of Siege* do arouse sympathy and support for the terrorist, while they often inhibit identification with the victim. There is a definite parallel between the spectators' sympathy felt for the Tupamaros in *State of Siege* and the sympathy felt for the gangsters in *The Godfather*.

But there are exceptions. Argentinians feel keen sorrow for the bereaved families of men murdered on the streets of Buenos Aires and Córdoba—because when such slaughter becomes too frequent, too indiscriminate, even people innocent of politicking begin to fear for their lives and the future of their families. This is where the Robin Hood technique and the aid of the media (witting or not) cease to benefit terrorists.

Another exception is where terrorists, notably the Arab fedayeen, kill women and children. No matter how much the guerrilla image may be romanticized by the media, it suffers immeasurably when there is a massacre in a schoolhouse.

Yet, on balance, the broad scope and the swiftness of modern communications have helped the terrorists recruit a wider following. Terrorism is still a bastard child of weakness. Yet, thanks to the changes noted here, it is gaining in popular acceptance.

In former times, in fact until quite recently, among those who were not terrorists, there were very few, usually alienated upper-middle class intellectuals, who would applaud terrorism. But during the early 1970s, in large part because of the media, sympathy and support for terrorists widened and began to spread downward, percolating into the middle and lower classes. An episode that typifies the media's role in this development occurred in 1970-71. Headlines and photographs, which appeared throughout the world, created the impression that Leila Khaled was glamorous and adventuresome. In sober reality, this gun-toting Arab moll had attempted to hijack an Israeli airliner. She was responsible not only for a criminal act that had endangered many lives, but also for the failure of her mission—her companion had been killed and she herself had been captured. After the British released Khaled, her freedom being the result of Arab threats, eager interviewers and photographers, while relaying a romantic image of her, almost ignored the sober truth of her fiasco. The heroic Israeli security guards, who had killed her comrade, seemed dull compared to Leila.

Sometimes media coverage of modern terror is not given willingly. As part of the price for the release of hostages, terrorists demand that the Establishment print and broadcast unexpurgated statements. Governments and media in Latin America have complied. In the United States, the Symbionese forced Mr. Hearst to make public their communiqués, while he, in response to the situation, did not dare publish what his daughter's captors might have found displeasing.

In West Germany in early 1975, terrorists promised to release their hostage, Peter Lorenz, if five of their comrades in prison were flown out of the country to freedom. The kidnappers demanded that the process of the release be televised. Melvin J. Lasky notes pertinently that the state's television network "was hijacked, in effect, to serve the kidnappers' master plan." He quotes one TV editor: "For seventy-two hours we just lost control of the medium. We shifted shows to meet their timetable. Our cameras had to be in position to record each of the prisoners as they boarded the plane, and our news coverage had to include prepared statements at their dictation. . . . It was the gangsters who wrote the script and programmed the mass media."[1]

But, without coercion, there still is the media's eagerness to serve the public with sensational stories, in the spirit of journalistic competitiveness.

III

One more difference in today's terror: In olden times, revolutionaries did not make a policy of stalking and killing individual lower-rank guardians of law and order as deliberately and systematically as they do now.

To be sure, oldtime Marxists and anarchists saw no redeeming traits in the capitalist police. Such police stood for a system of rule alien from, and hostile to, the people. Those revolutionaries accepted no other definition. The past prophets of revolution drew no distinction between a policed society and a police state: any police were a bad phenomenon. But those prophets, while condemning the police, did not call for their preliminary extermination. The police had to be destroyed, but not necessarily prior to the revolution, and surely not by assassination of rank-and-file officers one by one. We have seen that, prior to 1917, Lenin came out for drastic action against the Tsar's lower echelon police only in one short period, from late 1905 through 1906, when he thought the revolution was at last winning. It was then that he briefly not only praised the revolutionary execution of spies helping the police, but even urged raiding police stations and taking guns (so needed for the insurgents' arsenal) from lone policemen or Cossacks surprised at their posts.

Combat against the capitalist police, as both Marxist and non-Marxist revolutionaries envisaged and practiced it, was waged (or was to be waged) in three ways:

1. A series of terroristic acts against a number of carefully selected chiefs and other top-bracket officers of the police and the gendarmerie.

2. The takeover of the entire police network, as part of a sudden, successful revolution.

3. Gradual infiltration of a police system, demoralization of its rank and file, and the final takeover of the system.

The first method was used by the Narodniki (1870s–'80s) and the Socialist Revolutionaries (early 1900s) in Tsarist Russia, and by Italian, Spanish, and other West European anarchists (1880-1914). The result was that the police were at times undermined but never collapsed.

The second method is best illustrated by what happened in the

Bolshevik coup of 1917: in the process of that coup, Lenin acquired his instruments of coercion. This was exactly what Marx had predicted, as Sorel commented in his *Reflections on Violence*: "Marx compared the passage from one historical era to another to a civil inheritance; the new age inherits prior acquisitions."[2] Among such inheritances, we can include the police: Lenin inherited this institution from the Tsarist and Kerensky eras; he purged the police drastically; their Red personnel and much of their violence were new; but the institution itself was old. To the rest of the world, Lenin's (and his heirs') apparatus was a police state, but in Communist eyes it was a laudable and righteous policed society.

The third method, of more recent origin, is favored by those Communist parties that hope to capture and immobilize the police via coalition governments, where they usually try for a few strategic cabinet posts, among them the Ministry of the Interior controlling the country's police. If, as in Eastern and East-Central Europe after World War II, the Communists do succeed in transforming such coalitions into their total government, the taken-over police apparatus is quickly and quietly purged, the surviving policemen are jailed or shot, and the new pure-Red police are installed. Thus, under the third method (as in the second) the old-line police are removed through wholesale terror *after*, not before, the inheritance of which Marx and Sorel spoke.

In contrast, modern terror against the police *before*—not after—the projected revolution has been waged by militants considerably to the left of Moscow's Communists: by the Black Liberation Army in the United States; by the Tupamaros and other such guerrillas of Latin America; by the commandos in Japan, India, Turkey, Mexico, West Germany, and elsewhere. Although many of these terrorists call themselves Marxists, they are rather heirs to Mikhail Bakunin, Marx's anarchist foe, and to such oldtime non-Marxists as the Narodniki, the Socialist Revolutionaries, and the Italian and Spanish bomb-throwers.

These modern terrorists also differ from their anarchist or semianarchist forerunners in the level of the police they attack and kill. The oldtime militants fired their guns or hurled their bombs at the generals and colonels of the gendarmerie. Lower ranks were usually spared. Simple servitors—of any kind—of a capitalist state were not to be harmed. In 1884, Hermann Lopatin, a prominent Narodnik, passionately protested to his comrades when a Tsarist postman was killed by their revolutionary team in the course of a mail robbery. In 1907, Russian revolutionaries were outraged when the Bolshevik hold-up of a Tsarist treasury coach in a Tiflis square, masterminded by Stalin and secretly blessed by Lenin himself, had cost the lives of three members of the coach convoy. To most revolutionaries no murders, deliberate or accidental, of low-rank servants of the Tsarist state were accept-able—not until the last, all-out, decisive battle of the revolution was to be fought.

The only notable exception to this overall rule was the custom of the Polish Socialists in the late nineteenth and early twentieth centuries (with Josef Pilsudski as their outstanding leader) to gun down, not alone Russian governors and generals, but also simple Russian *goro-dovyie*—the Tsar's police on the street corners of Warsaw and other Polish cities. The late David Shub, historian of that period, once explained to me: "The Polish terrorists thought that they would thus drive the Russian rule out of Poland—by striking at the very pillars of the Tsarist structure."

But what was a rare exception then is a wide and growing phenomenon now: the extremists of the 1970s mean to bring the Establishment down by killing off, or at least panicking and immobilizing, the general run of the police, these most basic and indispensable defenders of the System.

This is a brand-new development in the Western world, and possibly a weighty augury for the future. When applied on a large enough scale, it has a logic that bears fruit: if you terrorize the base of the Establishment, you deliver a telling blow at the System's main body perhaps more surely and swiftly than if you concentrate on its top reaches. For a time, in both Americas, for instance, some policemen were in fact becoming intimidated or at least uncertain.

In some countries the terrorist onslaught proves at times to be so massive and ingenious that the police, no matter how efficient in most other situations, prove feeble before the guerrillas and soon retreat. The army then is asked to intervene and take over, and it usually does, sometimes quite effectively. At least initially the army is warmly approved by sizable sectors of the population tired of terror. In any case this support is stronger than the popular help extended to the police. Such were the developments, in the early 1970s, in North Ireland, Turkey, Uruguay, and Argentina.

But terrorists, as they confront the army, still reserve their deepest venom for the police rather than for the soldiers. They view soldiers as more naïve and ignorant than policemen. Most soldiers are drafted, they don't realize the evil of their deeds. But policemen are volunteers and thus fully accountable. Even more important, soldiers can be propagandized into coming to the side of the revolution, as events proved in Russia in 1917 and in Portugal in 1974. There is no such hope for policemen. The intensity of terrorist hatred for the police was illustrated in mid-March 1975 in Tucumán, a city in northwestern Argentina, when a guerrilla approached a policeman, fired a submachine gun at him, and then, looking down at the dead man at his feet, calmly reloaded the gun and emptied it into the policeman's corpse once more. The mutual hostility of terrorists and policemen has of late been at its highest in Spain. The execution of five police-slaying guerrillas by the Madrid government in September 1975 triggered off not only mass demonstrations of protest outside Spain but also renewed killings of more policemen within that country. The police, bitter and ferocious, struck back by their stepped-up hunt and shooting of terrorists.

The police almost everywhere know there is no retreat for them or any possibility for lasting survival even if the terrorists, once triumphant and becoming the Establishment themselves, accept them for service under the new Red banner.

As already noted, the police often refuse to regard terrorists as a truly political formation. At Belfast, in January 1975, an official at police headquarters said to me: "We in the constabulary have never called the Irish Republican Army by the name they want to be known as—terrorists. To us they have always been criminals, nothing more, nothing else. Politics has always been an excuse or, at best, a secondary matter with them. They often kill out of habit, they rob for money, not for the Cause. And for excitement. They love being outlaws too much. They have no other skills or interests, no other ways to spend their days and nights. It's their life style."

The governments and the police of Mexico and Brazil have also often rejected the labels "terrorist" and "political" for the urban commandos and rural guerrillas of their countries, preferring the terms "criminal" and "bandit" for them. In such cases it is not so much that the Establishment is searching for a sound and precise definition as it is trying for a propaganda dividend—to deprive the terrorists of glamor, of their claim to noble aims, to idealism. This makes it easier for the System to use repression rather than reform in combatting terror, not to concede defeat if the terrorists do not succumb and fade away. It is simpler to admit the continued existence of criminals. For, after all, criminals—like the poor—are always with us.

38

Terrorists Then and Now

In the changing course of history there have been weighty differences as well as certain constants among terrorists—in their social origins, in individual and group motivation, and the action stemming from such origin and motivation.

All the long way from Robespierre to Arafat there is one significant constant: The prevailing origin of terror's leadership is in the middle class, particularly the upper middle class—numerically a small proportion of it, but a proportion strong socio-economically and eccentric psychologically. Taine and Engels had early noted the responsibility of the middle-class irrationalism in the Great Terror of 1793 (as did Engels also in the Paris Commune of 1871). Taine was among the first to observe the presence of lawyers at the Great Terror's top.

Not only Robespierre but Lenin, too, was a lawyer. In our own times some young radical lawyers become so concerned with terrorists as their courtroom clients that they themselves become active terrorists. This has been the recent case in Canada and West Germany, among other countries. Somehow, with what they claim as sudden or gradual clarity of vision, they come to despise and fight the very law they have studied and occasionally practiced.

Of other middle-class professionals, physicians can be found among terrorists. We begin with Dr. Guillotin who, though not himself a terrorist, surely helped the Great Terror by his improvement of the head-cutting machine. The line leads directly to Dr. Guevara and Dr. Habash, who gave up their humane profession to become killers and leaders of killers; and to Dr. Fanon, who moved from treating the illnesses of fellow humans to becoming a foremost theorist of terror, a glorifier of mass bloodshed. And we must of course include the German physicians experimenting in the Nazi concentration camps no less than those Soviet medical men who today torture Russia's political dissidents in mental asylums.

Among the functionaries of the Great Terror could be found teachers sending their fellow humans to the ax, as they were to be found among the Socialist Revolutionaries of Russia and the anarchists of France and Italy who tossed their bombs. In our times Mexico's Cabañas, the guerrilla chief, had been a teacher; and in the Philippines, Sison, a former professor of political science, left the classroom to lead his jungle band.

This is not to say there is not an admixture of the less educated too, and of those who spring from the slums and other lower depths. In his time, in the mid-nineteenth century, Bakunin expected his students and other intellectuals to be desperate because they were poor. And in those times, indeed, by far not all the Narodniki or Bakuninite anarchists were noblemen or other affluent young. Some were, but many were not. In that era's Russia they were *raznochintsy,* which meant people of sundry middle or lower origins and stations, sons and daughters of petty officials and minor-rank priests, of struggling clerks, of a variety of the dispossessed, and soon enough of peasants. Kropotkin was a prince, Bakunin was a high-caste nobleman, but Nechayev came from a serf's family. Perovskaya was a gentlewoman, a governor's daughter brought up in luxury, but her lover and terrorist chief Zhelyabov was the son of a peasant serf. Later, factory workers listened to such students and, in a trickle, joined them. The Socialist Revolutionary terrorists rising in the wake of Bakunin and the Narodniki counted in their ranks some noblemen who, however, were not necessarily of rich or famous stock. *Raznochintsy* were numerous among them, as they had been among their predecessors.

West European anarchists and North American dynamiters 70 and 100 years ago were also principally of humble socio-economic strata. These included some university graduates, but most of them were self-educated rather than products of lecture halls.

This has not been quite the case in our times—with the Weathermen, the Tupamaros, the Japanese and Arab terrorists, and especially with their leaders: many of them came from well-to-do homes where advanced degrees were a routine. If young scions of the privileged have always been conspicuous among terrorists, their predominance in numbers has become more pronounced in recent decades.

At one point in the latter 1960s the Weathermen joked among themselves that the only new members accepted were those whose fathers made not less than $30,000 a year. In 1970, in his *Future Shock,* Alvin Toffler remarked: "Affluence makes it possible, for the first time in history, for large numbers of people to make their withdrawal [from their society] a full-time proposition."[1] One form of the withdrawal made possible by this unprecedented affluence was suicidal terror.

This withdrawal was simultaneously an identification of the privileged young with the poor and the oppressed. But in 1970 this was not a completely new phenomenon, nor is it now. From time to time in past history, members of the middle and upper classes, picturing themselves as selfless and self-sacrificing idealists, came forth as allies of the masses—whether or not the masses wanted them as such or were at all aware of their would-be heroism, even when they actually exploded proudly and bloodily in terrorism. But in this modern era, withdrawal-identification has acquired a novel face.

More than ever before, this ultraradical activism of the elite youth is an attempt to find meaning in their otherwise untested lives, to discover an "identity"—or merely to fight their way out of their own sheer boredom.

Born and reared in comfort and even luxury, these young men and women renounce their privileges as they join what they consider to be the righteous cause of the exploited and suppressed. In great part, modern technology is responsible for the way they feel and act. Modern technology—the complexity, speed, and overstimulation it so often brings in our jet age—makes this elite's participation in terrorism far more intense and widespread than it was formerly, lending new and awful depths and dimensions to the phenomenon. Terror as these young radicals' main occupation, in Toffler's words, is one kind of person's "total surrender before the strain of decision-making in conditions of uncertainty and overchoice."[2] To these extremists, terror appears to be the simple answer to problems that burden them; what they do not understand is that this violence is an explosion of frustration rather than a corrective force.

Toffler shows today's revolutionary as "the Super-Simplifier." To such a short-cutter violence comes naturally. "For those . . . who cannot cope with the novelties and complexities of blinding change, terrorism substitutes for thought. Terrorism may not topple regimes, but it removes doubts."[3]

Among the doubts that today's revolutionary tries to remove by his participation in terrorism is his sense of guilt. He, or she, feels guilty of being born to, and reared in, wealth and privilege, luxury, or at least comfort. Compared with olden times, this sense of guilt is today tremendously heightened, both individually and collectively. And while this guilt feeling results in the radical and even terroristic behavior of the prosperous youth, it also leads to hesitation among the elders (the perhaps-we-the-parents-are-wrong-after-all kind)—and to laxity and permissiveness in the modern nontotalitarian state and society, making terrorism that much more possible in the lands of democracy.

As with so many other socio-political phenomena, this guilt development is not wholly new. It was first observed in Russia and Western Europe more than one hundred years ago. "The repentant nobleman," a semipraise and a semimockery, was the old Russian phrase for those sons and daughters of well-off parents who were ashamed of their privileged status. But today's terrorists with this sense of guilt are far more numerous, and their violence results in much more bloodshed and debacle.

II

There is also this feature of modern terrorism: Most of these violent men and women "lack an intelligent, comprehensive program" for the day after the destruction of society, says Toffler.

Indeed, most of today's bomb-tossers do not have any blueprints for the aftermath. This is something new compared with former times. The old Narodniki and the Socialist Revolutionaries did have programs of peaceful life for the survivors of the holocaust they planned. Even Nechayev, at his trial in 1873, pretended to have some sort of harmonious plan for the "after" phase. And the Western anarchists of the turn of the century had surprisingly orderly visions of a future stateless society.

Not so most of today's terrorists. They have no program beyond the vague "power to the people" or the more specific and ominous "all power to the good shooters," as expressed in May 1970 at Yale University by the New Haven Black Panther chief, Doug Miranda. And Ambassador Geoffrey Jackson recalled this about his Tupamaro captors and guards of 1971: "Ideologically, though aiming in theory at a transformation of society, they never seemed to look beyond the apocalypse of its violent upheaval."

Some of the most erudite among the prophets and preachers of revolution today do not really have a clear vision for the steps after the overthrow. In my travels I was told of this bit of dialogue between a student and Professor Herbert Marcuse:

Student: But, Dr. Marcuse, what system of life will there be after this System is destroyed?

Marcuse (*with some surprise*): You know, I've never given thought to this. I just want to see what the damned thing looks like when it is destroyed.

Could it be that he said this in jest? Yet, when we examine Marcuse's writings in detail, we establish that the learned apostle of cataclysm really does not have anything constructive for his Red dawn.

When hard-pressed for a serious answer (as he once was in a discussion with Raymond Aron, the French sociologist), Professor Marcuse unreels something suspiciously like a new variety of Soviet regime "but with justice"—a patent contradiction in terms.

Perhaps the plans for the future in the days of Marx and Bakunin, Lenin and Trotsky, stemmed from the nature of the times. Though miserable and confused enough, they were not as swift and tense as ours. The revolutionaries of, say, 1848 to 1917 had more leisure and desire to study. Theirs was not an era of drugs, excessive sex, and constant and chaotic confrontations. And, often, so mild was the police regime that some of their best reading and writing was done in their prison cells.

Another new factor is the ignorance of so many modern violent Marxists-Leninists-Maoists on the very sources of their inspiration. They get their classics of revolutionary literature secondhand from Guevara's interpretation and other such texts. When they do read the originals, the effect is slight. Cleaver admits that he went through Lenin "with very little understanding."*

It is astonishing to find so many modern left-wingers dismally unversed about Dostoyevsky's *The Possessed,* based as it is on the Nechayev case and full of unique and penetrating insights into the passions and pitfalls of professional revolutionaries. Nor do the young terrorists of our times know of Raskolnikov of *Crime and Punishment* and the bitter fruit of his self-elevation above morality. The great truths of "The Grand Inquisitor" section of *The Brothers Karamazov,* with its discourse on the nature and meaning of human freedom, have not touched them.

Many of today's young extremists have read parts of Albert Camus's *The Rebel* out of context, particularly such of his declarations as, "Real rebellion is a creator of values." From his pages they have idealized the Narodniki and other oldtime terrorists far more than did Camus himself. They fail to draw from the book the all-important lesson that the Russian terrorists, by the success of the Tsar's murder in 1881, only delayed reforms in Russia by several decades, and by their bombs of the early 1900s merely paved the way for the institutionalized violence of the Soviet state.

Because the oldtime revolutionaries had education in addition to emotionalism, and because no drug-and-sex culture stopped them from

* In the summer of 1975, on a Stockholm street corner, a tall, blond-maned Swede enthusiastically peddling to-the-left-of-Communism magazines, conceded to me that, although he had heard of Kropotkin, the name Bakunin was totally unknown to him.

reflecting on the theories and facts they had learned, some of them lived to sober up—to leave terror. But the new pseudo-Narodniki and would-be anarchists, the Black Liberationists and the Irish Provos, the Arab physicians and ex-teachers leading their murderous commandos, and all other guerrillas of today have no such knowledge or potential.

H. G. Wells defined human history as a race between education and catastrophe. In fact, the kind of half-baked schooling modern terrorists have is one of the chief causes that could take the planet to its extinction.

III

The affluence, the permissiveness, the elitism into which these modern young terrorists were born have led them to feel (rather than to think) that, having resolved their earlier guilt sense and other doubts, they now possess an exclusive pipeline to eternal truth. The oldtime terrorists had something of this feeling too, but to their fanaticism was added an element of idealism, however distorted. For his Republic of Virtue, Robespierre invented that high-minded, spectacular festival for the Supreme Being. In 1904-05, Ivan Kaliayev's exaltation of "pure" spirit was typical of that period's terrorists, who killed driven by remorse and went to the gallows almost happily. No such near-religious idealism, even if perverted, can be seen in the majority of today's terrorists.

True, in the 1870s-'80s many Narodniki were atheists. When the regicides of March 1881 were waiting their turn for the gallows, Sofiya Perovskaya and her lover Andrei Zhelyabov refused to see a priest, while Nikolai Kibalchich received the priest only to argue with him. But two other doomed men made their confessions. Earlier, in his speech at the trial, Zhelyabov did declare himself "a follower of Christ," and another Narodnik plotter on the eve of his own execution had written in a farewell letter that he was thinking of Jesus. In 1887, before he was hanged. Lenin's brother kissed the cross offered by a priest, and so did three of his fellow condemned. Only one of the five abruptly pushed away the priest's hand. And there is an eyewitness account of a terrorist stopping before an icon en route to his assignment and crossing himself with one hand while holding his bomb with the other.

At present there are only traces of any belief in God among most of today's terrorists. There are the Arab fedayeen who, while labeling themselves Marxists, are overwhelmingly and old-fashionedly Moslems, carrying on their Holy War against Israel as a command from Allah and Mohammed. And there are a few Roman Catholic priests and ex-priests who somehow combine Christ's teachings of brotherhood and love with a bloodthirsty devotion to terror.*

In his book, Geoffrey Jackson tells us how, as a captive of the Tupamaros of Uruguay for more than eight months in 1971, he observed among his guards a young man who admitted to him that he was a practicing Roman Catholic, and whom the prisoner guessed as being possibly an ex-priest and almost certainly a former seminarist. "He would not admit to being simultaneously a Marxist-Leninist, though he considered this a perfectly reasonable Third World Catholic position," Sir Geoffrey wrote. "Most of his comrades in the 'Movimiento' were straightforward Marxist-Leninist atheists."[4]

Most terrorists of our era have been atheists to a man and a woman. There is neither trust in the Supreme Being nor any love for a fellow human. One cannot imagine a soulful discussion, full of mutual forgiveness, between an Argentinian or Symbionese killer and his victim's widow, such as was held in 1905 between Kaliayev and Grand Duchess Elizabeth when she visited her husband's assassin in his death cell. Nowadays it is a snarl, a sneer—not a melancholy chest-beating.

A truly remarkable and baffling exception to the terrorists' utter rejection of God and organized religion today is, then, the phenomenon of the few Roman Catholics, particularly of some young priests and nuns, who by their advocacy of, and even participation in revolutionary violence, have in recent times garnered sensational headlines.

In Guatemala in 1954, Ernesto Guevara argued with Hilda Gadea "that it was not possible to count on militant Catholics to make a revolution, but that it was possible to count on those Catholics who abandoned the faith through a process of reasoning." On her part, to the contrary, Hilda "was confident that within the Catholic Church a revolution would take place and that part of the Church would join the true proletarian revolution."[5] Within a decade, in the very same Latin America and later in North America as well, some servitors of the Church undertook to prove that Guevara was wrong and his first wife was right. By now we have several instances of priests who, even after they went into the slums and the jungles to fight with weapons in their hands alongside the guerrillas, still viewed themselves as pious Christians and effective clergymen—in fact, as better ones than those of their brethren of the cloth who sermonized against terrorism.

---

* There is also the already mentioned case of the Christian Arab, Archbishop Hilarion Capucci, head of the Greek Catholic Church in Jerusalem, sentenced by the Israeli court in December 1974 to 12 years in prison for having smuggled weapons for Arafat's terrorists, but we will not discuss it here because, all his pious protestations notwithstanding, he had carried arms from Lebanon into Israel not out of any Christian motivation but because he was either paid or blackmailed (or both) into it by his fedayeen friends.

In June 1965 a Roman Catholic padre, Camilo Torres Restrepo of Bogotá, angered his superiors by preaching revolution.[6] The young, handsome, perpetually nervous priest was from a socially prominent family. He had been trained, among other campuses, at the University of Minnesota and the University of Louvain. In Bogotá his last post was that of a professor of sociology and a chaplain at the National University. Father Camilo, or simply Camilo, as he was known to thousands of adoring students and slum-dwellers, announced on one occasion:

"I consider the work of a priest is to take a person to God, to work toward the love of one's brother. I consider there are circumstances that do not permit a man to offer himself to God. A priest must fight those circumstances, and for me they are political. The grave problem is political, because the fundamental decisions have to be political decisions. And these decisions are now produced by the minorities and not the majorities. Because of this, the majority must produce political pressure groups; it must take political power."

To stir up and lead the majority, Father Camilo formed a political organization, the United Front. He toured Colombian cities, drawing large crowds whom he urged to overthrow the System. But Luis Cardinal Concha Córdoba of Bogotá declared: "The Church cannot involve itself in socio-economic measures that may fail, for the truth of the Church is forever." He had Father Camilo defrocked, saying that "Father Torres's advocacy of violent revolution" separated him "from the consciousness of the Church."

In his continuing tours of the country the ex-priest was denied transportation by commercial airlines, but radical labor unions chartered a plane for him. On the night of August 12, 1965, rioting broke out in the industrial city of Medellín as the police tried to prevent him from speaking in the main square to which a sizable crowd accompanied him. His supporters pelted the police with stones. Three policemen were injured, one of them seriously. One hundred rioters and Camilo himself were arrested. Restraining the crowd, he nevertheless promised: "This is the first act toward the revolution."

Soon he disappeared. In early January 1966 it became known that the ex-priest had become a Marxist and joined a guerrilla movement in the mountains of Colombia. To his admirers in Bogotá he sent a photo that showed him standing in a uniform, holding a rifle. He also sent copies of a leaflet wherein he proclaimed his intention to fight the ruling class at the head of "the Army of National Liberation." He called upon the masses to enroll in it. Below this text, the words "Liberation or Death" followed his signature.

Fate decreed the second choice. On a night in February, at San

Vincente de Chucuri, near the oil fields and refineries of Barrancaber-
meja, where Communist labor unions were traditionally strong, a band
of 25 guerrillas ambushed an army patrol. The soldiers fired back.
Four of them were killed, but the attackers lost five. One of the bodies
was identified as that of the ex-priest. Camilo lay dead, clutching a rifle
stolen in a guerrilla assault the year before. The army buried him
secretly, to thwart pilgrimages to his grave.

In Bogotá, on hearing of his death, students marched and rioted,
their placards reading, *Camilo, We Will Not Mourn You, We Will
Avenge You*. The next winter's conferences of the Christian Democrat
Youth in Venezuela held a moment of silence in his memory. In May
1974 his name was painted on many Bogotá walls; his portraits adorned
newsstands side by side with Guevara's; mothers named their baby
sons after Camilo. A film *Camilo, the Guerrilla Priest* was shown to
full, worshipful houses—yet arousing much controversy, too, for many
disputed the propriety of a man of God as a terrorist. Camilo was
indeed to be remembered and venerated on campuses and in slums, if
not in villas and peasant huts.

One more priest came into the news as a guerrilla gunman. This was
Father Domingo Lain Sanz, a Spaniard in his mid-thirties, expelled
from Colombia in 1969 for his radical activities, but returning to the
country clandestinely in 1970 to join the National Liberation Army.
But when, in February 1974, he was killed in a guerrilla clash with
government troops, hardly any excitement resulted. For he was little
known, and besides, by that time, the mood of the Colombian masses,
although still resentful, was less radical. In fact, the violence of the
National Liberation Army had by then angered many more peasants
than before; and when, in November 1973, a leader second in command of that Castroite organization was captured, it appeared that his
arrest was largely due to the help given to the security forces by peasants.

In the summer of 1974 Colombia's left-wing priests spoke of Camilo's memory with deep reverence, but then, even in their most extreme preaching and activism, they always stopped short of violence.
The most militant action was that of the Reverend Saturnino Sepuvelda, who joined the homeless as they defied the law by occupying
vacant land on which to build their cardboard shacks. In 1972-73 an
American nun in Bolivia left her Maryknoll Order to work with the
guerrillas, but not necessarily to fight, rifle in hand, as had Camilo and
Father Domingo. For her exalted pains, Mary Harding was eventually
jailed and deported to the United States. But still the involvement of
priests in active terror was not over. It manifested itself once again in
the renewed guerrilla fighting of the summer of 1975, when an ambush

by a peasant insurgent force upon an army patrol was grandiloquently called by the attackers "Operation Domingo Lain" in memory of the priest-terrorist killed in February 1974, and Colombia's minister of defense divulged that this guerrilla force was led by one more Spanish priest, Father Miguel Garcia.

In the early 1970s in Brazil a number of Catholic priests were arrested on charges of aiding and abetting the terrorists of Rio de Janeiro and São Paulo. In the late 1960s as high a Brazilian Church personage as Helder Camara, the Archbishop of Olinda y Recife, publicly voiced his admiration for Guevara. In 1968 he organized a social-conscience movement called *Acao, Justicia y Paz* (AJP), or Action, Justice, and Peace, whose aims, he explained, were not more reform but a deep-reaching, structural transformation of society. He and his movement would not, he vowed, be violent, yet would "respect those who, in all conscience, opt for armed violence."

Thus would the archbishop bless the terrorists in the name of God and Jesus.

IV

In North America, for all their flamboyance, the two Berrigan brothers, Philip and Daniel, Jesuit priests, came close to uniting Christ with bomb-hurlers, yet did not cross the fateful line of human bloodshed as had Fathers Camilo, Domingo, and Miguel in Colombia.

And there are still other priests in North America who, while neither initiating nor participating in terrorism, find its bloody manifestations truly Christlike. On May 25, 1974, in New Jersey, during the funeral services for one of the six Symbionese, a youthful Catholic pastor, the Reverend Frank Citro, likened the mission of the late-departed guerrilla woman to that of Jesus Christ. Angela DeAngelis Atwood, who had grown up in this New Jersey area only a few blocks from the priest's childhood home and died in that Los Angeles shootout together with her five Symbionese fellow terrorists, was "a dear, honest, sincere girl," her death an act of martyrdom, Father Frank preached. "Christ died for what he believed in. So did Angela."

The next day, in a press interview, he tried to tone down his eulogy and analogy: "I was certainly not seeking to justify the means she used. The whole point I was trying to make was that when peaceful change is impossible, violent change becomes inevitable." But, while not trying to justify little Angela's bloody terrorism, he was doing just that. This Angela DeAngelis Atwood, once upon a time a pious church-goer, had left the fold for revolution and atheism and was now dead, but Father Frank would gladly take her back as a martyr and practically a saint. The blood and fire amid which she died with such noble intentions made her holy.

In the turbulent America of the late 1960s and early '70s at least a part of the rebellious youths elected not terror but peaceful communal living in the name of Jesus or of assorted gurus. Most of those who strummed religious hymns on their guitars did not at the same time make and plant bombs, nor did the young explosive-experts double as Jesus freaks or other kinds of God-seekers. There was little, if any, traffic or interchange between the two kinds of withdrawal from the System.

While atheism is almost a rule among today's terrorist intellectuals, or, shall we say, terrorism itself is a religion, a few of the less educated of their brethren in revolutionary arms do tend to have at least a vague belief in God, but it is their special category of God—a vengeful deity invoked against the System.

And when a terrorist, sometimes after his apprehension and a period of brooding in his prison cell, does adopt a formal religion, his may be a rather unexpected faith. In March 1974, Robert Hayes, a reputed member of the Black Liberation Army, was found guilty of murdering a New York policeman the previous June. It was then revealed that while in jail awaiting trial he had embraced the Jewish faith, taking the fanciful name of Seth Ben Ysaak Ben Ysrael.

But since the Jews nowadays, certainly those in Israel, are the target rather than the inflictors of terror, it would be more logical for terrorists suddenly finding God to become Black Muslims—out of sympathy for the Arab fedayeen, most of whom are more Moslem than Marxist. Some terrorists do become Black Muslims, and, conversely, some Black Muslims have turned toward terrorism, at times practicing it not against Whitey but against one another, in their intercamp religious and political-financial jealousies and squabbles.

Others become known as Black Muslims only after death. Most spectacularly, the Symbionese chief Donald DeFreeze was buried in Cleveland in May 1974 with an Islamic service by that city's Sunni Orthodox Moslem sect.

But, as in Mrs. Atwood's case, DeFreeze's revolutionary atheism might very well have been preserved by him to the very last bullet fired into his own brain. The sect was asked to conduct the Moslem funeral rites not by his last will and testament but by his grieving family. That May the Reverend Frank Citro was not alone in claiming the atheistic terrorists for God, as the Lord's own and special saints.

In sum, from the partial atheism of the Narodniki and the complete lack of belief in God among the Western anarchists of the 1880s-1900s as well as among the Weathermen of the 1960s and the Symbionese of the 1970s, we come to an entirely novel appearance of a few guerrilla priests in Latin America in the very same 1960s-'70s and the concurrent curious attempt in both Americas on the part of some clergy to nearly canonize the modern terrorists—even when these terrorists themselves so vigorously deny God's existence. This is, verily, terrorism with a difference.

39

The New International

In 1973, in an essay entitled "The Ecology of Terror," two professors in Israel wrote that in these times "an operation can be planned in Germany by a Palestine Arab, executed in Israel by terrorists recruited in Japan, with weapons acquired in Italy but manufactured in Russia, supplied by an Algerian diplomat financed with Libyan money."[1] What needs to be added is the origin of the Libyan and other Arab money making such wild-flung guerrilla blows possible: American dollars, British pounds sterling, French francs, and other Western currency paying for North African and Mideastern oil. Let us remember, too, that, in addition to the Soviet weapons, a small portion of the terrorists' arms comes from China.

Again, the essence of this is not new. Even in older times some of the terror in Europe and America was of international character. Near the nineteenth century's end, the Italian, Spanish, and French bomb-throwing anarchists were inspired by those Russian masters Bakunin and Kravchinsky, as well as by Kropotkin in his earlier, violent phase. In 1894, in Lyons, it was an Italian who knifed President Sadi Carnot of France to death. In 1898, in Geneva, it was another Italian who fatally stabbed Empress Elizabeth of Austria. In the early 1900s some of the arms of Russia's Socialist Revolutionary terrorists were purchased in, and smuggled from, Western Europe. Part of the money for this importation was solicited from American sympathizers by special emissaries sent across the ocean by the Russian underground. In 1906 Maxim Gorky came to New York to obtain not alone good will but also financial aid for his country's revolutionary forces, and this money was to be, among other needs, for the Bolshevik arsenal.

In America, immigrant German anarchists were prominent in the Haymarket affair, a few breathing their last on the gallows that Black Friday of November 11, 1887. Preaching the total destruction of America's mighty, even if not participating in any actual bombings, was

Johann Most, that remarkable arrival from Germany. The younger anarchists in the American cities of the 1890s, Alexander Berkman and Emma Goldman, were of Russian Jewish origin. The assassin of President McKinley in 1901 was a son of Polish immigrants.

But all this pales compared with the intensive internationalization of terror today. In 1970, at an international revolutionary congress held in Pyongyang, North Korea, the Arab fedayeen leader Habash harangued its 400 delegates: "At this time of people's revolution against the worldwide imperialistic system there can be neither geographic and political borders nor any moral prohibitions against the terrorist enterprises of the people's camp." In September 1972, in Munich, the Olympic Games were the target of the Arab guerrillas because, among other reasons, the Games were mankind's foremost symbol of international peace and brotherhood—a symbol the world's terrorists rejected, trampling it into mud and blood and replacing it with international strife and murder.

The more countries they involve in one single action, the better for their cause, the terrorists feel. Consider the route of the three Japanese terrorists who perpetrated for their Arab friends the mass murders at the Lydda airport in May 1972: From Japan they first flew to the United States and Canada, thence to France, and then, most important, to Lebanon, where they were given a commando course at a fedayeen camp. From there they returned to Paris and journeyed to Rome and Frankfurt for false passports. It was in Rome that their Italian aides supplied them with grenades and automatic guns of Czech make, and a German businessman-sympathizer sheltered this arsenal in his apartment. And it was from Rome that they took their final flight to Tel Aviv and their horrible crime.

The demands by the Palestinian guerrillas, who seized the Saudi embassy in Khartoum and killed three Western diplomats in early March 1973, comprised a veritable international agenda: For West Germany—freeing of the Baader-Meinhof terrorists. For the United States—release of Sirhan Sirhan, Senator Robert Kennedy's assassin of 1968. For Israel—freeing all the Arab guerrillas in that country's jails. For Jordan—freedom for 17 of the Fatah men captured by King Hussein's soldiers. (Of all these demands, Jordan alone eventually gave in, months later, in a general amnesty of the fedayeen as part of Hussein's change of policy, in preparation for his support of the Egypt-Syria attack on Israel in October 1973.)

Several nations were involved by the three Japanese terrorists who on September 13, 1974, seized part of the French embassy in The Hague, holding the French ambassador among their other hostages: Japan, whence the commandos came; France, of whose government they demanded the release of a comrade jailed in that country; Holland, where the daring exploit occurred and whose authorities induced the Paris authorities to comply; and Syria, to whose Damascus airport the French jet with its Dutch crew delivered the three Japanese terrorists with their freed comrade making up the triumphant quartet.

On one occasion the police in Switzerland found a large cache of arms that was soon traced as a source of weaponry for the Tupamaros of Uruguay. While most of the money and the guns of the Irish Republican Army come from their sympathizers in the United States and Canada, it was recently revealed that two-thirds of the ingredients used by the IRA for its explosives in Ulster are smuggled in from France, where the chemical firm, Pechiney Ugine Kuhlmann, produces and sells to mysterious clients in Dublin sizable quantities of sodium chlorate. (This chemical, ordinarily used as a weed killer, becomes a powerful explosive when mixed with household sugar. For incendiary action, diesel oil or nitrobenzine is an effective admixture.) And, of course, Soviet and Czech guns and even rockets also somehow reach the Provos. The Irish terrorist connection with the Spanish and French Basque commandos has been notable. While the Basques provide the Irish with some of their weapons, the Irish return the compliment by giving training to the Basques in secret commando camps on Irish soil.

A remarkable instance of the new international at work came to light on June 27, 1975, when a Venezuelan terrorist killed a Lebanese informer and two French intelligence officers who came to question the man in his Latin Quarter apartment in Paris, then calmly walked out and disappeared. The slayer, Ilyich Ramírez Sánchez, was born in Caracas 25 years before, the son of a rich lawyer and his charming wife, who was a great success in diplomatic salons. A fervent Communist, the lawyer named their elder son Ilyich (Lenin's patronymic), and sent him (and a younger son named Lenin) to Moscow for their secondary schooling. Ilyich stayed in the Soviet capital to attend Lumumba University, and in 1969 he came to London, where he lived with his mother and escorted her to incessant diplomatic parties.

But from 1973 on, Ilyich Ramírez Sánchez varied his activities with travels all over Europe and the Middle East. His several languages included fluent Arabic. He established links with the Baader-Meinhof Gang, the Japanese Red Army, the Basque separatists, the Turkish activists, and the Arab fedayeen. They all knew him by his underground name of Carlos but, increasingly, also as the Jackal—in memory of the legendary terrorist who had once tried to kill De Gaulle. The organization of exploits in Holland and explosions in France was among the ventures traced to him. That he must also have had a Castro connection may be seen from the fact that the French authorities, in the course of investigating the June 1975 murders, expelled two Cuban diplomats from France.

By the time of the Latin Quarter murders, this calm, pudgy terrorist was sought by the police in 12 countries. By mid-July several of his accomplices (including two or three of his women friends of sundry nationalities) were picked up in Paris and London, as were some of the passports he had used. At least six false passports, two of them American, were found in his effects left behind in his various hurried flights. In late December 1975 the daring raid on the OPEC headquarters in Vienna, with its murder of three persons and kidnapping of the near-dozen oil ministers, was thought to have been commanded by Carlos, but there is still no definite proof of this.

It is definitely known, however, that the deadly network he ran from Paris was called the International Terrorist Collective.

II

It is the Arab tie and, particularly, the guerrilla combat schooling provided by the fedayeen in their Lebanese and Syrian camps that figure outstandingly in the terrorist activities of many other nationals from all over the world who come to the Middle East for this purpose.

In the early 1970s the Arab training camps largely took over the role formerly performed by Castro's hospitable installations: those apt Japanese students came for their lessons not to Cuba but to Lebanon and Syria; the Turkish terrorists learned well in the fedayeen camps, in time gratefully paid their tuition fee by murdering the Israeli consul in Istanbul, and yet later had more Arab teachers as they tried to establish their new base in a French province; the Irish Provos had the close collaboration of Arab guerrillas sent to London, where the IRA struck rather at random while their fedayeen allies concentrated their attacks on Jewish businessmen known for their Zionist sympathies.

Black Panthers and other Americans came to the fedayeen strongholds in the Middle East for conferences and instruction. In early September 1970, the commando teammate of Leila Khaled in the bungled seizure of an Israeli airliner near London was an American from San Francisco, of Irish stock and some Latin American background—Patrick Arguello, a member of a Nicaraguan terrorist organization. While Leila survived, Patrick was killed by an Israeli security guard aboard the plane. A little later, in the miniature war in Jordan between the fedayeen and King Hussein's troops, a Frenchman was slain, his training and fighting by the side of his Arab guerrilla friends cut quite short.

From West Germany not only Meinhof, Baader, and other Communists and anarchists traveled to the fedayeen's Mideastern headquarters and training camps, but some neo-Nazis also made the pilgrimage and were apparently accepted. In 1970-71 this advertisement appeared in the ultrarightist *Deutsche National Zeitung:* "Courageous and audacious young Germans are wanted to study the liberation war of displaced Palestinians. . . . Financial considerations should stop no one from participating. . . . If you are attracted by the proposed venture, contact us immediately."

In addition, some training camps for such and other volunteers have been established and maintained in Libya by its dictator, Colonel Muammar Qaddafi. Far more important, however, is the ready landing and enthusiastic welcome he provides for the Arab hijackers of Western airplanes. A yet more significant contribution by Qaddafi to modern terror consists of money and arms. In September 1972, he presented five million dollars to Arafat as an expression of gratitude for the Fatah-Black September murder of the 11 Israeli athletes at the Olympic Games in Munich. This was, of course, over and above the many steady subsidies and donations paid to the fedayeen out of Libya's ample oil profits. That summer of 1972, Qaddafi openly boasted that he was also supplying arms to the IRA desperados in Ulster and to the Moslem insurgents in the Philippines, and would gladly send weapons to blacks "unfurling in the United States the banner of struggle against American racism." In April 1973, in an interview with *Le Figaro* of Paris, he repeated his resolve to support the Irish commandos in Ulster as well as "many other" terrorist groups the world over. In May 1976 the Shah accused him of sending arms and money to Iranian terrorists.

With much less fanfare but quite concretely, some training of terrorists on an international scale is done in Communist countries. At one time in the latter 1960s Mexican guerrillas received their special combat schooling in North Korea, and some others in North Vietnam. In the early 1970s, instruction of African insurgents against the Portuguese in the handling of such sophisticated weapons as the heat-seeking ground-to-air missiles was successfully carried out by Soviet officers at bases within the Soviet Union. Somewhat less fruitful was an earlier Soviet program to teach terror techniques to certain specially chosen African, Asian, and Latin American students brought to Moscow's Lumumba University. A number of these eventually rebelled and demanded repatriation. They staged demonstrations in their countries' embassies in Moscow, and some sit-ins at Soviet railroad stations, before the Soviet authorities finally yielded, sending the rebels home. One such African student told me:

"Originally I went to Soviet Russia to Lumumba University to become a physician. But instead of medical studies I was surprised to find myself being trained in making explosives and how to plant them at various strategic points of my homeland. That was why I, together with others in similar situations, mounted those strikes in Moscow and Baku to be returned home at once as peaceful citizens, not terrorists. We won. But some others did remain, to continue and complete such training."

Young Arab fedayeen, selected to go to Moscow for special instruction and liaison work, show no such reluctance. They are too handpicked to be anything but enthusiastic. By their Soviet allies and mentors they are increasingly given encouragement and freedom of action to the point of assisting their hosts in cracking down on those Russian dissidents who dare to protest against the Kremlin's policy in the Middle East.

An outstanding example is the case of Andrei D. Sakharov. On October 12, 1973, Academician Sakharov, one of the inventors of the Soviet hydrogen bomb but now a leading opponent of the Soviet regime, declared in an interview with a foreign correspondent his sympathy for Israel, saying that the Israelis were fighting for their survival while the Arabs were the aggressors, and that the West should match with its aid to Israel whatever the Soviets were doing to help the Arabs. Soon two Arabs, one apparently armed, came to the Sakharov apartment, cut off the telephone, and forbade the family to answer the doorbell. For over an hour the pair shouted at the scientist and threatened his family, castigating him for his support of Israel:

"The organization of Black September will not permit that. The organization of Black September is everywhere—in Moscow, in New York—everywhere. We can do worse things than kill you. We do not stop at anything. If you were a political figure, we would give no warning. But since you are a scientist, we are warning you. We will not give you a second warning."

They had spoken German when they first entered, then changed to fluent Russian. In fact, one of the two spoke very good Russian, explaining that some years earlier he had been graduated from Moscow's Lumumba University, that school for the ambitious young men and women of the Third World.

Exactly one year later the pair's threat of reaching New York proved to be prophecy—in October 1974, when the United Nations Assembly, perverting its noble purpose of peace-keeping, invited Arafat to address it. On November 13 he came as a conquering hero and was given the Assembly's tumultuous welcome. A few days later, in the Vatican, the Pope himself received a member of the terrorist Palestine Liberation Organization in solemn audience.

The triumph of the new international of murderers was nearly complete. All that remains is a Hitler-like Final Solution to be administered to Israel, and the victory will be crowned.

III

Several factors, absent or in mere embryo in pre-1914 times, are responsible for this internationalization—and, concurrently, legitimatization—of terror.

There is the modern technology in the service of the terrorists. There is the swiftness and the power of modern communications employed by them to help their action and further their propaganda.

Terror is used or abetted by certain governments against other governments, and while such aggressors or abettors steadily grow stronger, the victim governments and their peoples become ever weaker. Foremost among such agents and abettors of terror, ever since Lenin's era, is the Soviet government. It has vastly expanded the Tsarist brand of Russian nationalism by adding the ideology and appeal of Marxism.

Even when nationalistic expansionism is absent or muted, as in Mao's China or in Latin America's revolutionary movements, terror is glorified and employed in the name of Marx. Terror everywhere is facilitated and by some even justified and applauded thanks to the worldwide impact of Marxism, which has by now approached the dimensions of a religion neither to be argued against nor to be resisted— only to be feared, if not admired and followed.

The latest factor on the international scene is the energy crisis, which in recent years has enormously helped both the terrorists and the governments supporting them. We know how greatly have the fedayeen been strengthened by the urgent and ever-growing need for oil on the part of the United States, Western Europe, Japan, and other industrial areas of the world. The influx of American and other money into the Arab treasuries in payment for oil, and the use of the oil embargo against the industrialized countries in 1973-74, have been among the significant changes on the international stage that reinforced Arab diplomacy in support of the Arab terrorists.

It has been said that in the non-Communist and non-Arab nations the Establishment has lost its will to dominate; hence its current retreat in the face of Marxism and oil shortage and before the rampaging spread of terror. If this be so, the loss of the will is due, on the one hand, to the sheer physical difficulty of combatting supertechnological terror delivering its blows and eluding punishment by the magic swiftness of today's planes and communications, and, on the other, to the numbing omnipresent might of the nineteenth-century ideologue, Karl Marx, come to its fruition one hundred years after his time, the power now singularly enhanced by the concentration of fuel for this machine age in that one spot on earth—the Middle East.

But perhaps we should go back to square one—to the basic state of the world today. To too many clamorers and doubters neither capitalism nor Socialism-Communism seem to offer a better life. Food, fuel, and other resources diminish dramatically as consumers and their appetites multiply. Malthus may have been right after all.

Rising expectations are counterpoint to intensifying fears of shortages and other perils. And there are expectations of a better life—even ultimatums for a better life—throughout the Third World, in the wide range of ghettos, in all those groups and whole nations that are oppressed and deprived or consider themselves oppressed and deprived.

No matter how draconian or appeasing the measures of the Establishment may be, such groups keep on articulating their grievances. Terror, sometimes mutual terror, is the result. Here and there students burst out. Women are in a rage against male domination. Blacks rise against whites, and after winning the fight proceed to exterminate one another, as in Burundi and Uganda, Nigeria and Chad.

With all this, improvements in mass communication and mass education in modern democracies are factors in the diminishing respect for the Establishment and its fumbling ways of mass control. The instantly televised or headlined accounts of governmental repression or corruption or retreat before the terrorists and their Soviet and Arab mentors and inciters, the people's increasing awareness of their government's ebbing strength, cannot but lead to a feeling of cynicism or resignation or, soon enough, to panic, to a sentiment of support for those who criticize and oppose this failing Establishment—and sometimes even a modicum of sympathy for these very same rebel terrorists who are out to pull down the System.

And this is how and why the new international of terror is winning.

40

Five Minutes to Midnight

What of the future? Is there a future?

Much of the answer to this has already been given or implied—it has presented a bleak view of our prospects. But if we are to exert any influence on our future, we must continue to attempt to know the truth of our past and present.

Terror is on our very doorstep, often wrought by hands unknown, as was that powerful bomb detonated in New York's LaGuardia Airport on the evening of December 29, 1975, taking its toll of 11 innocent lives and many injuries, for which no guerrilla group would even claim its sinister credit. It is disturbingly evident that in recent times terror has widened and intensified, in great part because of the increasing vulnerability of technological and highly centralized societies. Taking advantage of scientific and technical advances, terrorists acting either as outlaw groups or as legitimized governments may soon challenge and blackmail the rest of the world by getting hold of, and threatening mankind with, some other new compact and cataclysmic weapon.

The atomic bomb is a foremost instance. In their book *Nuclear Theft: Risks and Safeguards*, Mason Willrich and Theodore B. Taylor[1] state that a determined group of five to ten terrorists, using the latest firearms and ultrasophisticated equipment, can attack an atomic installation, such as a reprocessing plant or a fuel fabrication unit, or even ambush a truck or convoy carrying atomic materials between two such plants, and whisk off fissionable matter with a minimum of danger to themselves. With this loot and some needed high explosives in their hands, the terrorists can then easily obtain other materials necessary to make an atomic bomb from commercial suppliers of scientific high-school equipment or even from hardware stores. A mere five-kilogram quantity of plutonium, hijacked or otherwise stolen from available stocks, is enough for such a do-it-yourself A-bomb. Just one "crude, low-yield fission explosive," the authors declare, can "kill tens of thousands of people and cause hundreds of millions of dollars of property damage.''

As to the actual technique of building an atomic device, this has by now been spelled out in many books, both scholarly and popular. A bright group with evil intents or even a desperate or deranged loner can manufacture such a bomb. In fact, two or more manuals on the subject are known to have been written and circulated in the radical undergound in America and England. These are mimeographed rather than printed, but all the diagrams are clearly reproduced.

With the energy crisis compelling industrial nations to turn to nuclear power as a substitute for oil, plutonium- and uranium-processing plants and laboratories are proliferating and so are trucks hauling enormously lethal atomic-material shipments. These developments increase the ease with which fissionable material can be stolen. Dr. Taylor, a physicist who from 1949 to 1956 designed nuclear weapons at Los Alamos in New Mexico, and Mr. Willrich, a lawyer specializing in legal aspects of atomic energy and weapons, urge a vastly strengthened system of safeguards and controls to prevent the raiding and stealing of the crucial material by terrorists. Some experts even suggest military convoys to accompany trucks carrying plutonium between laboratories and plants.

In America, the authorities in charge of atomic energy have been taking measures to protect its installations against raids or thefts. In 1970, rules were issued requiring any quantity of fissionable material heavier than 11 pounds to be stored in a locked building equipped with an alarm that can summon security men quickly. There were also regulations banning transport of atomic shipments by passenger airliners vulnerable to hijacking.

The concern of these officials increased markedly after the attack by the Arab terrorists who killed 11 Israeli athletes at the Olympic Games: the murderous outburst was so well planned, organized, and enacted that it created intense fears about how daring and efficiency could be applied in a successful raid on an atomic installation. Security measures were widened and tightened at all atomic energy units after that September 1972. One year later, in October 1973, guards were instructed to shoot to kill anyone found tampering with atomic military weapons, and within a short time protective steps were introduced at civilian plants, to prevent sabotage and to safeguard such plutonium and uranium as were used for peaceful purposes but could be of bomb-making potential in the hands of knowledgeable thieves. ''We believe the problems are manageable,'' Commissioner E. Kriegman of the Atomic Energy Commission asserted in the fall of 1973. ''Not so,'' Willrich and Taylor protested in their book in the spring of 1974, finding all the existing measures inadequate and calling for far stricter and more comprehensive controls.

But what controls can there be over the possible atom-bomb ambitions of Yasir Arafat? In late October 1974, at the Arab summit meeting in Rabat, Morocco, it was decided not only to recognize Arafat and his terrorist organization as a legitimate entity on the world's stage but to bolster it with an annual subsidy of $50 million for a four-year period. What with the many other millions of dollars previously accumulated by Arafat, now fattened by this new cornucopia, and the honors showered on him by the United Nations Assembly in 1974 and on his organization by the UN Security Council in 1975-76, the terrorist chief may yet decide to use this wealth and prestige to buy or hire or hijack whatever is needed to make him an atomic-bomb possessor and threat. Indeed, in his press interviews in the fall of 1974, Arafat said that atomic bombs would most likely be used if the fifth Arab-Israeli war broke out, and it was fairly clear that he himself meant to be among the users.

There is also oil-rich Libya, led by the eccentric and hateful strongman, Colonel Muammar Qaddafi ("that crazy fellow," as the Shah of Iran has called him). With billions of dollars flowing into his coffers from his deserts' superabundant oil wells, with his shrilly reiterated policy of providing terrorists almost everywhere with both money and weapons, Qaddafi may finally turn to the manufacture and use of nuclear weapons.

Before the October War and the success of the Arab oil embargo of 1973-74, even the Soviet government, whose weapons have so readily reached both Arafat and Qaddafi, seemed at times to have second thoughts about the Pandora box it was helping to unlock. It chose to rebuke Jamil M. Baroody of Saudi Arabia when, on November 9, 1972, in the United Nations Legal Committee, he extolled terrorists as modern versions of Robin Hood. Replying to Baroody on November 17, the Soviet delegate Dmitry N. Kolesnik, a legal expert of Moscow's Ministry of Foreign Affairs, pointed out: "This comparison is not accurate, especially with regard to the scale of the danger that can be created by the modern terrorists."

The Moscow delegate asked his fellow conferees to recall that Robin Hood's weapons were bows and arrows, but that terrorists today were armed with greatly more dangerous guns and bombs and that, moreover, they may in the near future use "stolen atomic bombs" and "death-carrying germs."

As to this last menace: In one American city on a recent occasion young terrorists threatened to poison or infect that city's water supply.

They claimed that the poison or germ they would use was so powerful that even a small dose of it would be deadly.

In London, on June 7, 1972, in the House of Lords, a warning was sounded that terrorists might resort to the use of chemical weapons. Lord Chalfont, who had served as minister of disarmament in Harold Wilson's previous Labor government, reminded his peers that war chemicals "had been called the poor man's weapon of mass destruction." He spoke of small states that could employ chemical weapons to blackmail great powers, then added:

"But there is another and more serious implication—the possibility that these weapons might spread out of the hands of governments and into the hands of private people. One has only to think of the appalling incident at the Lydda airport to realize that international terrorists will stop at virtually nothing."

He noted that chemical weapons were easily made, that they were quite portable, and really safe for their users when these knew how to handle them, and that most assuredly the terrorists had such knowledge and capability. Lord Chalfont urged precautions by the British and other governments to prevent terrorists from either stealing chemical arms or acquiring them from existing military stocks for their awesome ends "of indiscriminate destruction."[2]

II

To prevent all such unspeakable future catastrophe, to combat political terrorism that in its more conventional forms is already engulfing or endangering so many countries, concerted and intelligent international action must be devised and taken.

One of the earliest moves in this direction dates back to 1898, when an international conference of governmental delegates from a number of nations met in Rome to consider a plan of a united drive against anarchists, then so turbulent and effective in Western Europe and America. The conferees proposed that the anarchists' offenses should, by international agreement, no longer be viewed as political, thus tending to be glorified and immune, but as rank common-law crimes, their perpetrators subject to extradition. Another far-reaching suggestion was that of suppressing the revolutionary press by international action. Police of all the countries were to cooperate in this denial of political asylum and in press suppression. But nothing came of the speeches and various drafts of proposals. The conference closed with no binding pacts whatever.

From then on, for three-quarters of a century, no similar attempt at coordinated international measures against terrorism was made. The next effort along these lines took place in the United Nations in 1972-73. It died stillborn. Moreover, in October and November 1974, this august body put itself definitely on the side of terrorism when it hailed the armed head of the Arab murderers as a noble hero. In late 1975 its Security Council invited the Palestine Liberation Organization to participate in the Council's debate as if the terrorist PLO were a sovereign and respected state.

Initially, in 1972, the prospects for some international steps against terrorism seemed good. Through the first nine months of that year a worldwide revulsion against terror was built up by the guerrilla excesses in Latin America, Ulster, West Germany, and elsewhere: by the continuous airplane hijackings all over the world; and, most of all, by such mass atrocities as the slaughter by the Japanese terrorists of 26 persons at the Lydda airport in May 1972 and the massacre by the Arab commandos of 11 Israeli athletes at the Olympic Games the following September. Even Soviet representatives at various capitals and in the United Nations said—privately rather than publicly—that they were sickened and outraged by all such massacres, and perhaps they really were.

It was immediately after the Munich slayings that Kurt Waldheim, Secretary General of the United Nations, placed the problem of terrorism on the agenda of the 27th General Assembly of the UN. Three resolutions were introduced. One, authored by the United States, called for an international conference on terrorism, to be convened in early 1973 to draw up a pact against acts of terrorism. Another, signed by Britain, Canada, Italy, and Austria, among other nations, proposed that the UN International Law Commission write a convention condemning terrorism, the document to be considered by an international conference as early as possible. But the third resolution was meant to defeat the first two.

Sponsored by Afghanistan, Algeria, India, Kenya, Yugoslavia, and Zambia, among other supposedly nonaligned nations, but actually inspired by the Arab bloc, this third resolution did not condemn terrorism. Instead, it denounced "alien regimes" that it held guilty of denying to peoples "their legitimate right to self-determination." It mentioned terrorism only to say that the United Nations should investigate its causes. Not terrorism was to be combatted, but the Establishment that allegedly caused it.

In 1972, the Arab delegates felt, rightly, that the whole issue, as placed on the UN agenda, was directed against their countries as the most active allies and harborers of terrorists. At first they even tried to

keep the issue from being placed on the UN agenda at all. Not succeeding in this, they quickly mustered votes for their side in the Legal
Committee and the General Assembly.

It was easy for them to rally the African bloc to their camp, with the
argument that an international drive against terrorism would also inevitably mean the white man's attempt to still the guerrilla movements in
the Portuguese colonies, Rhodesia, and South Africa.

China and the Soviet bloc were naturally on the Arab side. Their
stand on the matter, for once similar despite all their other differences,
followed the well-known Leninist dictum of damning terror when generated by their foes but not by themselves or by their friends.

Speaking in the General Assembly on October 3, 1972, China's
Deputy Foreign Minister Chiao Kuan-hua stated that his government
"has always opposed assassination and hijacking of individuals as a
means of waging political struggle." Faithful to its Leninism, the Peking regime "is also opposed to terrorist acts by individuals or a handful of people divorced from the masses, because they are harmful to
the development of the cause of national liberation and people's revolution." But Peking was nonetheless filled with admiration for the Arab
struggle "against Israel's armed aggression," particularly for the cause
of "the injured Palestinian people" who are no more than "regaining
their national rights."

As for the Moscow government, with its continued record of post-
Stalinist terror at home and its flow of arms to the fedayeen and other
guerrillas abroad, its words in the world forum of the United Nations in
the fall of 1972 followed an all-too-familiar scenario. In his speech in
the General Assembly on September 26, Soviet Foreign Minister Andrei A. Gromyko was moralistic and pragmatic at one and the same
time. He declared, in effect, that his government was against sin because sin was not truly in these sinners' interest. (Echo of Robespierre's peculiar argument!) Somewhat regretfully Gromyko spoke of
"the recent tragic events in Munich." Without really condemning or
even shaming Moscow's clients, the fedayeen, he pronounced that it
was "certainly impossible to condone the acts of terrorism committed
by certain elements . . . in the Palestinian movement." Practically
speaking, Arab terrorism would only boomerang against Arab aspirations: "these [Arab] acts are used by the Israeli criminals in order to
cover up their policy of banditry against the Arab peoples."

So then, who is in fact responsible in the first place and the long
run? Those Israeli victims of the Arab terrorists, naturally. And Israel's American sympathizers and suppliers, of course.

Joining the debate in the Assembly's Legal Committee on November 14, 1972, the Cuban delegate Alvarez Tabio singled out the United

States as the cause of terrorism. The American air attacks upon the cities of Vietnam were "terrorism within the full meaning of the term" of the unjust category. As for the just terror by guerrillas and other revolutionaries, "to deny the people the right to struggle for their liberation is to deny history," said Comrade Tabio as he praised the violence of the French and Russian revolutions and of "Cuba's hundred years of revolution."

The Arab delegates were delighted. As one of them was soon to proclaim, "one man's terrorism is another man's patriotism." Never mind the so-called "negative" effects of the hijackings and the murders—what was more important and must come first for the United Nations was a thorough exploration of terrorism's causes.

Upon which, on November 13, the American delegate W. Tapley Bennett protested that this was the same as "to say that no treatment can be given the cancer patient until we know the causes of cancer." He asked: "Is there one among us here who, when faced with a diagnosis of malignancy in a member of his family, would say to the attending physician: 'No, I am not ready for you to undertake treatment. We can only consider treatment after I have determined the cause of the cancer.'?"

And so, on December 11, 1972, the General Assembly's Legal Committee swept the first two of the three resolutions aside. They approved by an ample majority vote the third document, so glaringly proterror. On the eighteenth of that month, by a vote of 76 to 35, with 17 abstentions, the General Assembly adopted it.

As if to provide one more refrain to the tragic chorus, at this time— on December 20—the Soviet government declined the official British request to help trace the origin of the rockets being used by the Provo terrorists in Ulster. It was quite plain to everyone—from the make and markings of these deadly weapons—that they were manufactured in the Soviet Union. The London request was to ascertain the route and agents that had brought them to Northern Ireland. No, Moscow replied, we cannot honor your request.

At the United Nations, the Soviet-Arab-African blocs dominating the General Assembly seemed to relent somewhat when, on September 21, 1973, the Assembly did include in its future provisional agenda a consideration of a convention "on the prevention and punishment of crimes against diplomatic agents and other internationally protected persons." It allocated the document's preparation to the Assembly's Sixth Committee. On December 1, 1973, the Committee, by a vote of 85 to 0, with four abstentions, adopted what appeared to be a final text of the agreement for the protection of diplomats, to be submitted to the Assembly. Both West and East supported the text; only Burma, Cuba,

Libya, and Sudan abstained. But more than a year later, only one government had signed the pact. This was the United States. The world is still waiting for all the other states to adhere.

As for the general problem of terrorism, this in 1973 was relegated to a committee of the Assembly. On July 16 of that year the committee met for its four-week sessions. Some of its 35 participating nations had singular views on the duty of the United Nations in this area. Syria, for example, asserted that "the international community is under legal and moral obligation to promote the struggle for liberation and to resist any attempt to depict this struggle as synonymous with terrorism and illegitimate violence." On July 24, the committee members representing Great Britain and the United States nevertheless called for urgent and decisive measures against terrorism. In vain. For the rest of 1973 there was no such action or any prospect of it. On December 7 the General Assembly postponed its debate on terrorism until 1974, but in fact indefinitely.[3] That year witnessed the first apotheosis of Arafat and his terrorists by the United Nations.

It was a different body from the United Nations of its founding years. Its expanded membership contained states risen from the blood and ashes of guerrilla warfare. Arafat was factually correct when, in his speech at the General Assembly on November 13, 1974, he joyously proclaimed: "I know well that many of you present here today once stood in exactly the same adversary position I now occupy and from which I must fight."

And so they cheered him uproariously as he promised the waiting world more bloodshed, the ominous holster on his hip as he gestured violently in the house of peace.

III

In a less general way there have also been attempts to achieve international agreement on combatting one particularly heinous form of terror: hijacking of airplanes.

The United States was especially eager to bring about worldwide cooperation by governments on this, since at the height of such crimes 90 per cent of the victimized aircraft were American. Pilots' associations throughout the world were quite naturally in the forefront of indignant demands for concerted, energetic action by all governments.

Even the Soviet government, faced with skyjacking attempts by its dissenters and defectors, did not object when, on June 20, 1972, the UN Security Council issued a strong statement against skyjackings, calling upon the world's nations "to take appropriate measures within their jurisdiction to deter and prevent such acts and to take effective

measures to deal with those who commit such acts,'' so as to terminate
"the threat to the lives of passengers and crews arising from the hijacking of aircraft and other unlawful interference with international civil
aviation.'' This "consensus agreement" of the Security Council was in
fact a stinging rebuke to those governments that gave asylum and even
honors to the hijackers. Yet, sadly, the statement stopped short of
urging sanctions against the guilty governments.

Nonetheless, over recent years there have been some good examples of limited intergovernmental accords aimed at thwarting aerial
piracy. Some such pacts, emphatically supported by the world's pilots,
have actually been signed and adhered to in practice. Yet, the anti-
hijacking actions specified in the documents did not go far enough, and,
most deficiently, the agreements were not signed by all the governments involved in the problem. A number of them, whose signatures
would have been crucial, refused to join.

There remained a possiblity of one-to-one agreement, formal or
informal, even between otherwise hostile governments, and here some
success has actually been accomplished. Fidel Castro in 1973 finally
consented to cease giving asylum to the skyjackers from the United
States on the reciprocal American promise not to encourage escapes of
dissidents from Cuba. The government of Algeria, eager for trade with
America, in time turned cool to the Black Panthers, curtailing or sometimes withdrawing the lavish aid formerly given to these and other non-
Arab revolutionaries flocking to North Africa. No longer the old
welcome to any newly arriving hijackers, kidnappers, and other terrorists from the West, and the most belligerent of such activists were
asked to leave Algeria.

But the largest gap of all—the asylum extended to Arab skyjackers
in Algeria, Libya, Syria, Lebanon, Uganda, and the Gulf emirates—has
remained to this day. The worst that has happened to some Arab
pirates of the air was Kuwait's and Tunisia's turning over of several
such terrorists to their own fedayeen organizations in other Arab
countries for "trial" on charges of breaking their own commando discipline, *and* the Israeli air raiders' killing of the hijackers in Uganda.

It is possible and necessary to point to one main factor for the
absence or failure of any concerted international action against our
era's political terrorism. It is the Soviet government.

There is no doubt as to the Soviet Union's grave responsibility for
the terrorism of the 1960s and '70s. There were and are Kalashnikov
guns, Moscow-made rockets, and other Soviet weapons in the murderous hands of the Arab guerrillas and even turning up in the Provo
arsenal in Ulster. Perhaps more than any eager Arab head of state, it is

Leonid Brezhnev who launched Arafat on his route to political stardom.

True, until about the time of the October 1973 war in the Middle East, Soviet delegates in the United Nations joined in some anti-terrorist statements, even if cautiously and ambiguously. The official Communist Party line in America, as publicized by such a prominent spokeswoman as Angela Davis in early 1974, with the blessing from Moscow, was to deplore the Symbionese terror. In Latin America, the pro-Kremlin Communists disapprove of the Maoist or neo-Trotskyite kidnappers and killers. But what in actuality the Moscow line amounts to is a fostering of a kind of "moderate" terror—of Arafat more than of Habash, of the pro-Soviet MPLA of Angolan blacks, of the continuation of the fratricide in Ulster, but not necessarily any aid to the terrorists in, say, North America or West Germany so long as détente brings the grain and machinery so badly needed by the Soviet Union.

In the world's most perilous area, the Soviet government resists any true pacification short of Israel's defeat. This does not mean that Moscow shares with Arafat and Habash, as well as Egypt's Sadat and Syria's Assad, their intense desire to destroy the Israeli state completely. Rather, it plans to reduce Israel to a very small space under the sun, eventually making it a satellite like enslaved Czechoslovakia or a semisatellite on the order of timid Finland, but preserving it as a potential irritant to the triumphant Arabs, whom Moscow does not wish to be completely victorious and wholly independent of the Soviet master.

Cleverly, persistently, the Soviet government forges on with its policy of suppressing even nonterrorist opposition at home while encouraging and aiding certain varieties of guerrillas and urban commandos in particular situations abroad. It picks its path and chooses its targets with a singular alloy of boldness and caution, with telling results on the international arena.

IV

The antiterrorist struggle in the United Nations is lost irretrievably, no meaningful international cooperation against terror seems possible, and so each embattled government or people has to go it alone, hoping against hope that some aid or at least expression of sympathy may yet come from the world at large.

In Ulster, the British Army battles on against the terrorists; in Argentina, the government tries to crush the murderous commandos of the left; the state of Israel fights on, refusing to negotiate its own destruction, and answers each blow with blow by crossing the border into Lebanon and raiding the guerrilla bases in that country by sea and air as well as over land, halting such operations only when Arabs in that country (as in 1975-76) keep on killing one another and thus have less time to raid Israel.

In their steadfast stand against terrorists, the Israelis do not succumb to the hostage-holding fedayeen, do not release from Israel's prisons any Arab captives in exchange for hostages, but adamantly shoot it out even at the cost of the lives of the hostages. A remarkable example was the daring Israeli air raid against Amin's terrorist-friends in Uganda resulting in the rescue of more than 100 skyjacked Jews and French crewmen in July 1976.

Among Western governments, the United States is among the few to exercise something akin to the Israeli policy of no concessions to terrorists. This hard course has resulted in some American deaths, most notably those of the two diplomats trapped and killed by the Arab commandos in the Saudi Arabian embassy in Khartoum in March 1973. But in nongovernmental American cases—at home more often than abroad—the response of affected citizens and corporations has been much more submissive. Within the country, relatives of victims usually ask the FBI to stay away as they negotiate with the kidnappers and pay ransom. The FBI complies. It moves in later, to hunt down and capture the perpetrators, and the outcome is frequently successful, the victim being released, the criminals captured, and even the ransom money, or most of it, recovered.

In certain other countries the line of the governments changes from case to case. The British are fighting it out with the IRA, returning gunfire for gunfire, and handing out tough prison terms to dynamiters both in Ulster and in England, but they have, under Arab pressure, released a fedayeen, as they did in September 1970 when they let Leila Khaled go. The West German authorities shot it out with the Black Septembrists at the Munich airport in September 1972, but subsequently, under the threat of fresh Arab depredations, they sent back to their homes the surviving murderers of the Israeli athletes caught at the Olympic Games. In February-March 1975, the Bonn government bowed to the demands of the kidnappers of Peter Lorenz in West Berlin, but in early May of that year it was adamant in its refusal to meet the terms of the German terrorists seizing the German embassy in Stockholm when lives were lost but the terrorists were defeated.

At the end of October 1974, the Dutch authorities succeeded in effectively dealing with four convicts, including a Palestinian terrorist, who seized 22 hostages in a prison chapel. Pretending to be ready to submit to the criminals' demands of freedom for them and for one more Palestinian then in a prison hospital, the Dutch dragged out their negotiations, exhausting the convicts until, 105 hours later, they sent a yelling, shooting marine unit into the chapel in a surprise early-morning attack. All the hostages were released safe and sound, and the four criminals captured. The Dutch took the risk, departing from the cautiousness they demonstrated in an earlier episode involving Japanese terrorists. The four convicts in the chapel were poorly armed, not so desperate as the Japanese, and, above all, they had been skillfully fatigued by the procrastinating negotiations.

Long drawn-out negotiations sometimes exhaust kidnappers, sapping them of their revolutionary rage—this is the advice given by those who disagree with the Israelis' shooting ways. Occasionally such a method does work, as the Dutch experience of October 1974 shows. Nor is Holland alone in proving that this can be done. Earlier that very same month, in Santo Domingo, President Joaquin Balageur of the Dominican Republic tried the same waiting game with the seven guerrillas who held seven captives, including an American woman diplomat, in the Venezuelan consulate—and won after nearly 13 days of a nonshooting siege. The terrorists demanded freedom for 36 leftist Dominican prisoners and one million U. S. dollars in ransom, but got neither. They did, however, receive safe conduct and a flight to Panama for themselves.

The method known as "patient siege" came into particular prominence in late 1975, with good results. In November, two Irish kidnappers released a Dutch industrialist, Dr. Tiede Herrema, after a 19-day siege laid by the Dublin police who would neither shoot nor storm into the building but talked to the terrorists calmly and, as the climax showed, persuasively. The good doctor himself, being a trained psychologist, helped by his judicious conversation with his captors all through those long days and nights in their nervous hands. In December, London's police, by playing-for-time tactics, likewise brought about the surrender of four Provos and freedom for the middle-aged couple they had held in the latter's apartment for 138 hours. Also in December, Holland's police and troops waited out the murderous South Moluccans holding numerous hostages in a train and a consulate for 12 and 16 days respectively.

In New York, Washington, and other American cities similar nonbloody sieges and sessions of persuasion have been successful, ending in the kidnappers' surrender. In New York particularly, the so-called Hostage Unit of the city police has had a positive record. It was formed in the wake of the Munich tragedy of September 1972, to train specially selected policemen to persuade rather than kill terrorists and other kidnappers. Chief among the unit's instructors was a detective with a degree of doctor of philosophy in psychology (earned while he was a traffic patrolman). Since its establishment it has tired out and convinced a number of half-crazed kidnappers to release their hostages.

But, say the many doubters, what may be effective in New York or Dublin or Santo Domingo does not work with the Symbionese, the Meinhof-Baader Gang, and the Arabs. With these there is no choice but a shootout.

Some nonbelievers in persuasion or concessions suggest not only a battle to the end, but even this drastic counterultimatum in reply to a kidnapper's demand: "We give you until noon tomorrow to release your victims unharmed. If not, promptly at noon tomorrow one of your comrades will be taken out of the prison where we hold him and will be shot by a firing squad. If you don't then release your victims within one more set period of time, we will execute another, and so on, until you surrender or are dead." In West Germany in early 1975 many people spoke up in anger when terrorists went on a rampage in West Berlin and Stockholm; the immediate answer to the commando demands, they said, should be taking all the Baader-Meinhof prisoners out of their prison cells and executing them.

Arguments against such and other toughness are several. One is: "Easy for you to threaten the kidnapper, but suppose it is you who are his victim or the victim's close relative. Would you still insist on this stubborn refusal to give in to the kidnapper's terms and even threaten countermeasures of executing the desperado's captive comrades?" And, says another school of opposition, democracies should not fight terror with terror: "Human values, for which democracies stand, suffer and vanish when you combat atrocities with atrocities; democracy then ceases being democracy."

Nonyielding, tough policies of the state against terrorism may prove counterproductive, some argue. The counterterror will create martyrs, will increase the sympathies of certain sectors of the people at home and abroad for the terrorists, will surely enhance the terrorists' ability to justify their violence.

But, thus far, has resistance to terrorists and other criminals been in truth counterproductive? Has public opinion in all its fluctuations of recent times ever shifted sweepingly in favor of anti-Establishment violence? The available evidence is to the contrary. Clearly there is a growing common feeling of many people in many lands, in the United States especially, that terror and crime, at least in part, have owed their rise to society's permissiveness. A movement for the restoration of the death penalty for certain crimes has been under way in a number of American states. Typically, two categories of crimes are on the list of what is now again punishable by death: slaying of policemen and other law enforcement officers, and murder of kidnapped victims. Quite understandably, in Israel the popular demand for the death penalty for the Arab terrorists has been strong. Yet more recently, great pressure for the reintroduction of capital punishment for the Provos has been witnessed in England. When, in December 1974, the House of Commons defeated the bill to hang terrorists, Home Secretary Roy Jenkins commented that this rejection was "probably at variance with public opinion and dangerously so."

Israel is a particular illustration of both popular pressure and governmental resistance. Death for captured terrorists has been increasingly demanded in public speeches and street demonstrations, as well as in letters to editors and in mass petitions. One such petition, begun right after the Munich massacre of September 1972, reached a total of 100,000 signatures following the Maalot slaughter of children in May 1974. But the government dismisses this clamor. It adheres to its abolition of capital punishment ruled in 1954, when the sole exception was for Nazi criminals. The only prisoner executed in Israel since then was Adolf Eichmann, the Gestapo mass murderer, abducted from his hideout in Argentina by Israeli secret-service operatives in 1960, and brought to Israel where he was tried and hanged. After Maalot in 1974 the Israeli government explained its continued refusal to execute captured fedayeen. First, when cornered without hostages, the Arab terrorists tend to surrender, knowing they will not be executed; thus further loss of Israeli lives is avoided. Second, the death penalty would not deter the Arabs from abducting people outside Israel, for such a penalty would threaten them in Israel but not elsewhere. Third, the halo of martyrdom would be enhanced for the fedayeen if they were executed. Fourth, the customary Israeli counterblows by raiding the guerrillas' Lebanese bases are sufficient as Israel's revenge and possible deterrent.

Prevention rather than punishment is often recommended by critics of counterterror. In the Western world many rich or otherwise prominent persons, in their fear of kidnapping, hire special 24-hour security guards for themselves and their families. Police dogs are suddenly in high demand. Quietly, kidnapping insurance has been on the rise, and the insurance companies see to it that the insured surround themselves with guards and various other precautionary measures. Rulers and political leaders live in virtual prisons of their own making. De Gaulle survived those 30-odd attempts on his life thanks to his legions of bodyguards and such superfast, bullet-proof cars as the Citroen specially made for him after the assassination try of August 1962. When Tito visited Copenhagen in October 1974, sharpshooters were stationed on the airport's roofs to protect the Yugoslav dictator, 3,000 other guards were mustered, and newfangled bullet-proof limousines were imported from West Germany for the occasion. In November of that year, during his stay in Tokyo, the United States President Ford was protected against the Japanese terrorists by a mobilization of 160,000 policemen—the equivalent of ten infantry divisions. But there can be too much of such caution. As Senator Edward Kennedy, the brother of two victims of assassins, has remarked about his own disinclination to take precautions: "If you are obsessed with security, you become completely ineffective."

Nevertheless, certain measures of prevention, especially when introduced for the many rather than for the few, can be of value.[4] Checking of threatened stadiums, theaters, and various public buildings, though bothersome, is by now being done quickly and efficiently. That governments and airlines can successfully screen plane passengers and baggage has been proven in the United States, West Germany, and other countries, while providing imperiled aircraft with security guards or sky-marshals has also been shown to be a potent method of thwarting terrorist attacks.

Prevention of terrorism can be accomplished by wise use of intelligence, by agent penetration of the ultraleft and the ultraright bent on violence. The Israeli intelligence has been effective. The British secret service in Ulster has been remarkably agile in finding or planting informers in Irish terrorist ranks.

This brings up the question of morality—is it permissible for a democratic government to use such underhanded methods to immobilize or at least hamper the terrorists by such means as the use of spies and double agents? Or for the CIA to plot Castro's assassination? Do not corrupt means inevitably result in corrupt ends?

So ask the purists. Quite often they forget the context of the time in which various underhanded methods were used or earnestly recommended against totalitarians and terrorists. In the early 1960s most Americans would not have considered immoral the idea and scheme of doing away with that "bad guy" Fidel Castro—as two decades earlier most Americans (and many others) had held their breath in hopes that somebody would finally kill Hitler. Purists usually forget also the dangers that mankind faces in post-Hitler times from imitators of Hitler (or Stalin). They ascribe a modicum of their own purity to men of sheer evil.

Purists also invoke the general idea of anyone's personal rights. They have even protested the precautionary searching of airplane passengers as a violation of privacy. And yet, while philosophically understandable, this concern for the supposed offense against rights must not halt the screening that saves lives. If mankind has for centuries accepted as legal and necessary the border guards' and customs men's inspection of travelers and their luggage at national frontiers, the new era's security searches at airports to safeguard our peace and very survival should also be taken for granted—a boon, not an offense.

Should a democracy risk some of its freedoms by adopting draconian measures against terrorists? In October 1970 it took courage for the libertarian Trudeau government in Canada to use the War Measures Act as a drastic way of combatting the Quebec terror group. But perhaps Trudeau's victory was achieved because these particular terrorists had bragged and threatened far beyond their real strength, while the nation's democracy was deep-rooted and truly strong. The record of suppressing left-wing terror in some other countries has not been as happy. Supposedly temporary suspension of democratic processes becomes long-term; suppression of terrorists is extended to nonterrorist liberals. Left-wing terror is replaced with ultrarightist atrocities. Such has been the recent experience in Brazil, Uruguay, Chile, and, for a time, in Turkey.

The right-wing totalitarians point out that violent revolutionaries are usually so expert in their bloody trade that one has to be a thousand times cleverer, more ingenious and resourceful, and at least as brutal as those masters of conspiracy and firearms; that the only thorough way to root them out is to arrest and shoot any and all of their liberal sympathizers and defenders. Hence the horrors of rightist terror in the wake of leftist guerrillas; hence the awful, increasing polarization the world over, bringing all of us to the brink of catastrophe and chaos.

But if a democracy cannot strike back at anti-Establishment terrorists, what other ways of resistance can there be? Some well-meaning citizens recommend a policy of compromise, of part-way concessions. Yet, in sad practice, no halfway concessions will mollify terrorists, who are outraged by compromises that could cause what supporters they have to turn away from them, and who always demand complete surrender. The cases of the Arab fedayeen, the IRA killers, and the Argentine commandos are proof enough.

A capitulation, a precipitate withdrawal from the contested area, is surely possible. Today families of foreign businessmen and diplomats are being evacuated to their home countries whenever guerrilla warfare and kidnappings increase alarmingly. Corporations whose executives in Argentina have been gravely endangered by threats, blasts, and abductions are solving the problem by liquidating or even abandoning their properties and getting out of the country.

The French quit Algeria in the 1960s and the British left Kenya in the 1950s rather than fight it out to mutual near-extinction with the native guerrillas. The Portuguese have fled from their former African colonies. But the Arab rebels in Algeria were not fighting to oust the French from France; the Mau Maus of Kenya were not invading the British Isles; and the guerrillas of Mozambique and Angola were not about to wipe out the Portuguese in Portugal herself. Yet the Provos do mean to exterminate most, if not all, the Protestants in Ulster, and the fedayeen clearly aim to destroy the state of Israel in Hitler-like Final Solution. So, quite often, there is no place left for any compromise or agreement with the killers of children.

Fortunately, or at least hopefully, intelligent and fearless voices have of late been raised among us not to submit nor to panic. Ambassador Daniel P. Moynihan courageously inveighed against the menace and obscenity of the virtual control of the United Nations by Arab terrorists and their allies. He spoke not alone for the United States but for all mankind, surely for that major part of it that abhors murder—as witness the thousands of approving letters he received from everywhere.

There are signs that some measures taken by opponents of terror do work, all the long way from the thorough screening of air passengers for arms and the "patient sieges" of the kidnappers by the police and troops to bloody shootouts with terrorists when no other solution is possible. There is a ray of hope in the inner quarrels of the enemy camp, such as between the Arab terrorist factions of the pseudogradualists and the rejectors, or the mutual carnage of the leftists and the Phalangists in Beirut, or the sporadic differences between Egypt and her Soviet weapon supplier. As Talleyrand once remarked, our best way out is "when Jacobins begin to strangle Jacobins."

And yet, we cannot be overoptimistic. If err we must, it is better to err on the side of precaution and caution. Too many individuals, if not nations, react to terrorism in total passivity and submission. In the late 1930s I knew a few highly moralistic Americans and Europeans who, in their deep religious pacifism, advocated turning the other cheek to Hitler. Confronted by this Christian meekness, terror of the Nazi kind would inevitably disappear, "even if it takes three hundred years," as one such pious person said to me.

When a terrorist wave subsides in a given area or country, as it did in North America in the early 1970s, hope is expressed that this has been but a passing phenomenon and may not, will not, return. Some terrorists indeed perish, or, if they survive, grow older and calmer, and rejoin the society they had tried to undo by violence. A few of these even begin to serve the institutions, the classes, and the very persons they once attempted to destroy. Historically, there is the example of Lev Tikhomirov, a People's Will leader involved in the assassination of Tsar Alexander II, who later, in his repentance, faithfully served Alexander III, the son of the murdered sovereign. He has been followed by many others—down to our own years when Sam Melville, in his disillusionment, wrote to his former wife Ruth, just before he was killed at Attica, of his doubts about the usefulness of terrorist bombing: "Mostly, now I feel whatever I may have hoped to accomplish simply was a waste. . . . ''

But there are not enough disenchantments to assure us of a true passing of the raging storm, of a better, more peaceful tomorrow. The terroristic conquests of Russia and China, among other places, continue to fill the dreams of incipient violent revolutionaries. They wear mustaches like Guevara's, hats like Lenin's, as they march in a narrow, seemingly endless column, their souls warped by a vast array of aberrations, their minds obsessed with the false justice of the terror they believe necessary.

Hope at this particular juncture of history is minimal. The world is in a vise of a malaise caused by the sharp contrast between wealth and poverty, by frustrated expectations, and by knowledge without understanding. Within this environment, terrorists, supported by the Soviet Union, China, and certain Arab countries, have been, even if reluctantly, accomodated; they have been provided with the physical and mental capability of bringing to mankind the ultimate evil in the name of the ultimate good.

APPENDIX

The Lethal Record

Let us, for the record, cite in chronological order the most murderous or otherwise spectacular skyjackings, kidnappings, and other ravages by Arab terrorists in recent years (some of which have already been referred to).

The campaign of sky piracy opened on July 23, 1968, when three guerrillas—two Palestinians and one Syrian—seized an El Al airliner en route from Rome to the Lydda airport in Israel, forcing the pilot to fly it to Algeria. The Popular Front for the Liberation of Palestine claimed responsibility for the exploit. But further management of the ensuing international crisis was taken over from Dr. Habash by Algeria's President-dictator Houari Boumedienne, who allowed the non-Israeli captives their freedom but detained 21 Israeli passengers and crewmen, demanding as the ransom price Israel's release of certain Arab prisoners. Reluctantly, the Israel government eventually complied.

At the end of 1968, on December 26, Habash and his Front took credit for a gunfire attack on an El Al plane on the ground at the Athens airport. Two Israelis—a passenger and a stewardess—were wounded, but the assault miscarried, and two Palestinian guerrillas were captured, tried by a Greek court, and sentenced to 17 and 14 years in jail. They were, however, freed when, on July 22, 1970, six other Palestinians hijacked an Olympic Airways (Greek) plane, forcing it to land in Beirut. Nor was any one of these six ever punished.

In 1969, the year's very first blow was aimed at an El Al plane again, but this time the Israelis were ready. On February 18, at the Zurich airport, five Arab terrorists (including one woman) opened fire at the Israeli aircraft bound for Tel Aviv. They killed the copilot and wounded the pilot and several others, but a high Israeli government official aboard remained unharmed. The onslaught was thwarted when an Israeli security guard counterattacked, slaying one of the Arabs, while the rest of the team were captured by the Swiss airport personnel. A Swiss court sent them to prison for varying terms, but these raiders were also later freed, under pressure of more fedayeen skyjackings.

After half a year's lull, Habash sent two of his boldest operatives on a new mission: on August 29, 1969, the 25-year-old Leila Khaled and a male companion, both Palestinians, seized a TWA jet with 113 persons aboard, which had started out from Los Angeles and, at the time of its skyjacking, was over Italy bound for Athens and Tel Aviv. The information given by Habash to Leila and her subordinate had Yitzhak Rabin, the Israeli leader, aboard the plane. This turned out to be in error; Rabin must have changed his travel plans at the last moment. The woman guerrilla commander ordered the TWA pilot to circle the Lydda airport as her gesture of defiance. Two Israeli Mirage fighter planes went up. Not wishing to endanger the plane and those aboard, they did not shoot, but stayed close to the hijacked plane until it crossed the Lebanese-Syrian border. Leila ordered the captain to land at the Damascus airport. After everyone rushed through the plane's exits to the ground, the two terrorists tried to blow up the craft, but succeeded only in damaging it.

This was followed by two Arab grenade attacks on the El Al offices, in Brussels on September 8 and in Athens on November 27, 1969. No deaths were caused at Brussels, where one of the two Arab boys who hurled their grenades escaped by taking refuge in the Iraqi embassy, while the other was captured but never prosecuted. At Athens a Greek child was killed and 13 persons were wounded. Two Jordanian terrorists were captured, but had hardly begun their 11- and 8-year jail sentences when the Greek plane's hijacking, on July 22, 1970, compelled the government of Greece to release them, along with the two Palestinian raiders of December 1968.

The skyjackings for the year 1969 ended on December 21 with a successful attempt by two Lebanese commandos to capture a TWA plane at Athens. Arrested, they, too, were later freed by a successful July 1970 hijacking of an Olympic Airways liner.

Several major hits at planes by Arab terrorists marked the year 1970. On February 10 a guerrilla team attacked an El Al plane at the Munich airport, killing one passenger and wounding eight. One Egyptian and two Jordanians were apprehended and imprisoned, but were released by West German authorities after the three skyjackings and plane explosions of September 6. As already mentioned, on July 22 an Olympic Airways plane was seized by another Arab squad, forcing the Greek government to free its accumulation of fedayeen prisoners. Earlier, on February 21, 1970, there was the tragic loss of 47 lives on the Swissair liner exploded on its flight to Israel 15 minutes after leaving Zurich, about which achievement Ahmed Jebreel's General Command in Beirut crowed proudly.

On September 6, the triple hijacking and an attempt (which failed) to seize a fourth plane broke all records for one day. Millions of newspaper readers, radio listeners, and television viewers held their breath as they followed the course of the four events. In the skies of Europe, three terrorist teams captured three planes—a Pan American, a TWA, and a Swissair—bound for New York, diverting the Pan American to Cairo, and the other two to a Jordan desert airstrip. All three were emptied of their passengers and crews; all three were exploded. While the passengers and crew of the Pan American 747 were set free in Cairo, those of the TWA and Swissair planes found themselves hostages in Jordan and soon were caught in the crossfire between the fedayeen and King Hussein's attacking Bedouins. Days and nights of suspense followed before all were free, unharmed.

The fourth skyjacking of that singular day ended in a fiasco for the Arabs—for Leila Khaled, no less. Once more she was in charge when she and a subordinate—a non-Arab man—seized an El Al 707 plane bound from London for New York. But before the Israeli pilot would heed her orders to turn to the Middle East, he banked sharply, throwing everything into confusion. The Israeli security guards aboard the plane took quick advantage of the moment, shooting Leila's companion dead and wounding the woman terrorist. A steward was wounded, but recovered. The pilot took the plane back to London, with Leila a prisoner. But the British, after keeping her under arrest for a time, released and sent her home to Lebanon. The official reason for her release was that she had committed her crime of terrorism outside British jurisdiction; the real motive was the desire of the London government to ensure the safety and freedom of the victims still held by the Arab guerrillas. In vain did the Israelis ask for Leila's surrender to them, since it was, after all, an El Al airliner she had tried to hijack. Leila returned to Beirut in triumph, to be feted by excited throngs, among others by the entire Arab student body of the American University, once famous for its enlightenment and liberalism, but now seething with hatred for the Israelis and all those Westerners who dared to sympathize with them.

In the next year, 1971, there were two attempts—both failures—to blow up El Al planes, and one murder by the fedayeen of a prominent Jordanian Arab whom the guerrillas blamed for the Black September massacre of thousands of their comrades.

The two failures occurred on July 28 and September 20, when two Western women were given by their Arab men friends booby-trapped luggage to be carried aboard the Israeli planes, bound for Lydda, in the first instance from Rome, in the second from London. But the Israeli security men knew their business, and the two plots were foiled.

The fedayeen's one success that year came on November 28, when four Black September terrorists assassinated Jordan's Prime Minister and King Hussein's right-hand man, Wasfi Tal, in front of the Sheraton Hotel in Cairo where he was on a state visit to President Anwar Sadat of Egypt. As all four gunmen were arrested by the Egyptian police, one of them halted over the dead statesman long enough to lick his blood in sickly ecstasy over the vengeance finally done. Within a few months, in February 1972, all four were freed by the Egyptian authorities on a low bail of $2,300 each—and were never brought to justice. Soon they were back in Beirut to plot more of their deadly forays against both Hussein and the Israelis.

The Black September group, with assistance of the Habash and Hawatmeh operatives, dominated the headlines of 1972. On February 22 a Lufthansa 747 jumbo jet on a flight from New Delhi to Beirut, with 100 passengers, including a son of the late Senator Robert F. Kennedy, was seized and diverted to Aden in Southern Yemen. The plane with all its passengers and crew was released after the West German government paid a ransom of five million dollars, which went into Dr. George Habash's treasury. On May 8, at Vienna, an Arab squad of two men and two women hijacked a Belgian Sabena plane with 91 passengers and a crew of ten, brought it to the Lydda airport, and demanded that the Israeli government free Arab guerrillas from its prisons. The Israeli security force, commanded by War Minister Moshe Dayan, encircled the plane and opened fire, killing the two male guerrillas (as well as, unfortunately, a passenger) and capturing both females. Tried by an Israeli court, both women fedayeen are now serving life sentences in prison.

The world was stunned when, on May 30, 1972, a three-man Japanese assassin team organized by Habash and Auntie landed from Rome at the Lydda airport, and, taking from their unscreened luggage Czech assault rifles and grenades, transformed the arrival hall into an inferno. The Israeli guards, recovering from their surprise, counterattacked. All told 28 men and women sprawled dead and 67 were wounded, many of them Jews but many others Puerto Rican and other Christian pilgrims to the holy sites. Two of the three attackers were killed, either by security men or by their own cross fire. The third Japanese, Kozo

Okamoto, was captured alive, tried by an Israeli court, and is now imprisoned for life.

Willing allies were not the only non-Arabs used by the fedayeen. On occasion there were also unwitting, duped accomplices who, in doing the guerrillas' work for them, could have become their victims. Thus, on August 16, 1972, a booby-trapped tape recorder exploded in the luggage hold of an El Al plane bound from Rome to Lydda. Only slight damage and no casualties resulted—because the Israelis had foresightedly reinforced the baggage hold against just such sabotage. An investigation showed that the booby-trapped tape recorder had been given by two Arab men in Rome as their parting present to their two British women friends. None of the saved passengers was shaken as much as these two foolish girls: to think that their two charming Arabs would try to kill them just to get even with the Jews! Both Arabs were arrested by the Italian police but soon freed, since the Rome government was by then—similarly to most other West European governments—thoroughly intimidated by the fedayeen power.

A shocking apogee of Arab terror was reached on September 5, 1972, at the Olympic Games in Munich, when eight Black September commandos penetrated the living quarters of the Israeli athletes, killed two of them, and captured nine more, carrying them in helicopters forced from the German police to the airport. There, in a final shootout with the police, all nine Israelis were slain, together with five of the Arab terrorists and a German policeman. Thus a total of 11 athletes were murdered. The three surviving Arabs were captured, but subsequently—in late October of that year—the trio were released and repatriated to the Middle East under the blackmailing pressure of their terrorist brethren in Lebanon and Syria.

On September 19, 1972, in the Israeli embassy in London, a letter-bomb sent by the Arabs killed Dr. Ami Shachori, the counselor for agricultural affairs who was about to return to his homeland and was in fact opening some of his last mail before the end of his tour of duty. On October 29, two Palestinians hijacked a Lufthansa plane over Turkey, thus forcing the Bonn government to free the three surviving Black September terrorists of the Olympic Games massacre. The Palestinian pair compelled the German pilot to fly the plane first to Zagreb in Yugoslavia, then to Tripoli in Libya. When Germany's Arab prisoners were released, the plane and its 20 passengers and crewmen were let go. The two hijackers, far from being tried or extradited, were greeted in Libya as heroes.

In the following year the United States and Belgium found themselves the fedayeen's target when, on March 1, 1973, in Khartoum,

Sudan, eight Black Septembrists, armed with pistols and submachine guns, invaded a farewell party at the Saudi Arabian embassy honoring George C. Moore, the outgoing American chargé d'affaires. The next day, when their demands for release of Arab fedayeen and other assassins and of West German terrorists (presented to a total of four governments—two in the West, and two in the Middle East) had not been met, the commandos beat and killed three of their Western captives: Mr. Moore; the newly arrived U. S. Ambassador Cleo A. Noel, Jr.; and Guy Eid, a Belgian diplomat. One of the refused demands was freedom for Sirhan Sirhan, the Palestinian Arab who assassinated Senator Robert F. Kennedy in Los Angeles in June 1968 and was serving a life sentence in a California prison. The eight terrorists, after a 60-hour siege in the embassy, surrendered to the Sudanese police. President-dictator of the Sudan, General Gaafar al-Numeiry, promised a speedy trial and severe punishment. But it was not until June 1974 that the eight were at last brought to court, which sentenced them to life imprisonment, a sentence promptly commuted by Numeiry to seven years—to be served under the custody of Arafat's Palestine Liberation Organization! Thus were these sharks thrown back into the bloody seas to rejoin the other sharks. In vain did the United States Government formally protest to General Numeiry—the murderers were already safely in Cairo, to be held there under loose house arrest by President Sadat in trust for Arafat.

The tumultuous rollcall of 1973 continued on April 4, when two Arabs failed in their attack on passengers of an El Al plane at the Rome airport (both were arrested but later released and packed off to Lebanon); on April 9, when a fedayeen team struck at an El Al plane at the Nicosia airport in Cyprus (eight Arabs were arrested and sentenced to seven years in jail but were soon freed by Archbishop Makarios, President of the island republic); and on April 27, when a Palestinian Arab killed an Italian employee in the Rome office of El Al (arrested, the killer was sent to an Italian psychiatric institution, which meant he would never be tried).

On the American side of the Atlantic, early in the morning of July 1, 1973, the Israeli military attaché in Washington, Colonel Yosef Alon, was shot to death after parking his car and while he was about to enter his suburban Chevy Chase home. His murderers were never found or identified, but in time in Beirut the Arab General Command under Ahmed Jebreel bragged that it was responsible for the death of the Israeli, the first diplomat to be killed in the American capital in recent memory. It was of little consolation to Colonel Alon's bereaved family when, five days later, on July 5, in Tel Aviv, Major General Aharon Yariv, in charge of countering terrorism, stated that in the last 15 months more than 70 per cent of Arab overseas plots either miscarried or were thwarted, of the 67 terror acts planned, 48 failing.

One such fiasco occurred on July 19, 1973, at Athens, where a Palestinian armed with a submachine gun tried to invade the local El Al office but was barred in time by a keen-eyed Israeli security guard who triggered an automatic lock on an inner glass door. The terrorist then retreated to a hotel, where he seized 40 hostages, holding 17 of them until the ambassadors of Egypt, Iraq, and Libya helped the Greek authorities negotiate freedom for all 17 and escorted the hapless fedayeen to the airport for a flight to Kuwait.

Other terrorists had hardly better success the next day, July 20, when five of them—four males (three Palestinians and one Japanese) and one woman (of unknown nationality)—seized a Japan Air Lines jumbo jet over Holland. They forced it with its 145 passengers and crew members on a grueling three-day flight, first to the Persian Gulf sheikdom of Dubai, and finally to Benghazi in Libya, where, not gaining the demanded freedom for the Japanese prisoner in the Israeli jail, and after releasing their own captives, they blew up the plane. There were now only four of them, since their woman companion had been killed early in the skyjacking by her own grenade, inadvertently touched off in her clothes. During the stop at Dubai they had ordered a coffin for her, put the body into it, and placed it inside the plane's first-class compartment. When the plane was exploded and the flames shot up, the plane's captain said: "I could not help thinking that this was her funeral pyre." Later it was established by Israeli intelligence that she was a member of the Habash organization, quite possibly an Arab. And, needless to add, the four surviving terrorists were never brought to justice either in Libya or elsewhere.

On August 5, at the Athens airport, two Black Septembrists—a Palestinian and a Jordanian, both in their early twenties—arriving from Beirut by air, threw three grenades at a waiting line of Trans World Airlines passengers bound for New York. Five persons were killed and 55 wounded, many of them Americans. The terrorists then seized 35 hostages but soon released them and gave themselves up to the Greek police, explaining they had mistaken the line for that of Israelis and others waiting to fly to Tel Aviv. In a one-day trial on January 24, 1974, a Greek court sentenced both to death, yet, under continuing Arab blackmail pressure, both were spared—to return to Beirut and Damascus for new terrorist missions.

In early September, exactly one month before the Yom Kippur War, the guerrillas tried to free their mates in Jordan: on the fifth a group of Palestinian gunmen took over the Saudi Arabian embassy in Paris, and the next day left on a Syrian airliner for Cairo and Kuwait, carrying with them four Saudi Arabian diplomats bound hand and foot, and demanding that Jordan's King release his fedayeen prisoners. From Kuwait they took their captives on a flight to Riyadh, Saudi Arabia's capital, threatening to throw them off the plane unless King Faisal exerted his influence upon King Hussein. Meeting with no response, they returned to Kuwait and freed their Saudi Arabian prisoners.

What they did not know was that, in preparation for the Yom Kippur War, King Hussein was making secret arrangements to aid the Egyptian and Syrian armies by sending some of his best troops to participate in the invasion of the Golan Heights—and by releasing all the Arab guerrillas from his jails. On September 18, Hussein announced the amnesty, and during the next two days personally supervised the release of 754 fedayeen. As they departed to be ready for the combined Arab blow against Israel on the day of Yom Kippur, they were joined—in October, after the war had begun—by the five young guerrillas of the recent Paris escapade, who, having surrendered in Kuwait their Saudi diplomat captives, also departed for the battlefront.

One more daring exploit was tried, and succeeded, on the very eve of the Yom Kippur surprise. On September 28, a week before that blow, two Arab terrorists boarded a train with Jewish emigrants from the Soviet Union bound for Austria, whence they were to be airlifted to Israel. The train was still on Czechoslovak territory but approaching the Austrian border when the Arabs pulled out their weapons, fired them into the air, and seized four hostages. These were three Jewish emigrants and an Austrian customs official. At the end of 15 hours of their captivity on the train, Austria's Chancellor Bruno Kreisky, himself of Jewish origin, bowed to the terrorists' ultimatum that his country's transit facilities for Israel-bound Jews be closed. The hostages were then released, and the terrorists were flown to Libya in triumph. Of importance, the preoccupation of the Israeli government during those days with the sudden Austrian-transit problem, brought on by the guerrillas' seizure of the train, contributed to the distraction of Israeli leaders away from the threat then facing them on the Suez Canal and the Golan Heights.

In mid-October, when the Israeli forces, having recovered from their initial shock and fall-back, turned around to hit at the Egyptian and Syrian armies successfully, particularly in the brilliant breakthrough to the Canal's western side, and before Brezhnev, Nixon, and Kissinger rescued (by arranging a cease-fire) the Arab armies from their imminent defeat, a squad of guerrillas in Beirut tried to help their side by a strange escapade. On October 18, five armed commandos calling themselves the Marxist-Leninist Socialist Revolutionary Movement stormed into the Bank of America in Beirut's center. Seizing 39 hostages, they made two demands: the bank was to contribute ten million dollars to the Arab war chest, and the Lebanese government was to free all guerrillas then in its jails. As the police and troops besieged the bank, grenades were thrown and bullets flew. During the 25-hour battle, three of the five guerrillas were killed and one was wounded, and finally the fifth surrendered, but not before a policeman and an American hostage were killed.

The October War of 1973 ended with Israel badly hurt but not crushed. The guerrilla organizations felt impelled to resume their campaign of attrition. In late November, letter-bombs were mailed from Geneva to various Tel Aviv addresses, but none blew up, being intercepted in time by the Swiss and Israeli authorities. On November 25 commandos from the Arab National Youth for the Liberation of Palestine seized a Dutch KLM 747 jumbo jet over Iraq, after its take-off from Beirut to Tokyo. The 247 passenger hostages included 174 Japanese. They were gradually freed as the skyjackers took the plane to Damascus, Nicosia, Tripoli, Malta, and thence to Dubai, where finally— on the twenty-eighth—they released the last 11 of the captives and gave up the jet. The price exacted by the skyjackers was a solemn promise by the Dutch government not to permit passage through its territory of emigrants and arms to Israel.

A particularly gruesome massacre was perpetrated at the year's end, on December 17, 1973, by five Palestinian guerrillas. These began at the Rome airport, where they shot up a passenger lounge and attacked a Pan American airliner on the ground, killing a total of 31 persons, including their own Arab brethren—four high Moroccan officials en route to the Middle East on a mission for King Hassan II. Then the attackers commandeered a Lufthansa Boeing 737, forcing it to fly to Athens, where they murdered their thirty-second victim, an Italian hostage. They demanded the release of two Arab guerrillas jailed by the Greek government, but they did not persist, instead compelling the German pilot to lift off first for Damascus and thence for Kuwait where, at last, they released their 12 hostages and surrendered the plane and themselves. The Kuwait government said it would have nothing to do with them, but Arafat declared he would take over the five guerrillas, his Palestine Liberation Organization to try them—if necessary! To their chiefs their only crime was apparently their inadvertent murder of the four Moroccan Arabs in Rome—never mind the other 28 non-Arabs, some of them women and girls. Whether or not any of the five slayers was ever punished by their own Establishment remains unclear to this day. Even the exact identity of their guerrilla organization is not known; all that was ascertained at the time was that they had first reached Rome from Tripoli in Libya via Madrid. The Egyptian government held them in custody for Arafat until late November 1974 when, on demand of the hijackers of a British airliner, these five were sent from Cairo to Tunis to join the plane's snatchers, who were members of the Libya-backed Arab National Youth Organization. In early December 1974 they were handed over to Arafat.

As the year 1973 waned and 1974 dawned, the Arab commandos went yet farther afield. On December 30 a prominent British chain-store executive and active Zionist, Joseph Edward Sieff, was shot in the mouth at close range in his London home (but survived), and Dr. Habash in his Beirut stronghold proudly announced that the gunman was one of his Popular Front guerrillas. In early January a tight ring of troops and police was thrown around London's Heathrow Airport, and similar precautions were taken at the airports in Germany, France, Spain, Greece, as well as in Israel. Rumors of new impending attacks by guerrillas were rife.

At the globe's other end, in Singapore, on January 31, four Arab and Japanese guerrillas tried to blow up a Shell Oil refinery but failed, then hijacked a ferryboat with five hostages. On February 2, three gunmen seized a Greek freighter at Karachi, holding two hostages until the Greek junta government commuted the death sentences of the two Arabs in its jails. These hijackers revealed they belonged to the Moslem International Guerrillas, active in the Philippines and Indonesia with money and arms from the Arab states and insurgents. No one was either hurt or punished in these two episodes of sea piracy, the Singapore gunmen releasing their hostages and being flown to Kuwait after five of their comrades, on February 6, had seized the Japanese ambassador in Kuwait and several of his staff, thus compelling the exchange, and the Karachi episode terminating similarly in appeasement and safety for its guerrillas. There was but one reservation on the part of the Kuwait government: it would give asylum neither to the four Singapore commandos nor to the five who had seized the Japanese diplomats in Kuwait. All nine were flown to Aden, where senior officials of South Yemen's Marxist government came to the airport to welcome them.

Britain and Holland were targets once again when, on March 3, two Palestinians hijacked a British Airways VC-10 plane, forced it to land at Amsterdam's Schilpol airport where, upon freeing the 102 hostages, they set it afire, completely destroying it. The plane had been seized shortly after leaving Beirut, the headquarters of the skyjackers' Arab National Youth for the Liberation of Palestine, an organization comparatively new in guerrilla warfare but already with a record of several assaults, among them the hijacking of the Dutch jumbo jet over Iraq the previous November. Arrested on March 3 by the Dutch police, the two Palestinians were tried and sentenced in June 1974 to five-year terms in jail. In late October, one of the pair participated with three other prisoners in a raid, with the help of smuggled-in arms, on a chapel in their penitentiary near The Hague. They took 22 hostages, including a priest, members of a visiting choir, and relatives of the singers, some of them children, women, and old men. The captors held out for 105 hours, gradually releasing seven of the hostages, but keeping the other 15 to the end. They demanded a plane to take them out of Holland to an unspecified asylum, apparently an Arab country, and to add to them the other of the two guerrillas who was then in a prison hospital. But the other fedayeen was afraid, and refused to join. Finally, in a surprise predawn attack on October 31, Dutch marines and police stormed the chapel, seized and disarmed the four criminals, and rescued their 15 captives.

The anticlimax came only a few weeks later when, in late November, the guerrillas of the Martyr Abou Mammoud Squad (of the Arab National Youth Organization) hijacked a British airliner at Dubai on the Persian Gulf, forcing it to fly to Tunis, where they killed one of the passengers while demanding freedom for 15 captive comrades. Seven were surrendered, among them the two Arabs held in Holland. Handcuffed, they were flown to Tunis and handed over to the triumphant Squad. In early December all 11 fedayeen—the four of the Squad and the seven others—were surrendered by the Tunisian government to Arafat.

But the most appalling atrocities during 1974 were reserved by the fedayeen for actions closer to home. On April 11 three Arab guerrillas of Ahmed Jebreel's General Command—a Palestinian, a Syrian, and an Iraqi—crept from Lebanon into Israel, evading Israeli patrols, and entered the border town of Qiryat Shemona. Here they killed 18 people, including five women and eight children, one of the latter a 2½-year-old. Their method was that of trying one apartment door after another, in one place surprising and slaying an entire family at their breakfast table, before they themselves were blown up with the dynamite they were carrying.

Nayef Hawatmeh and his Popular Democratic Front took boastful responsibility for the next slaughter, that of Maalot on May 15, when three of his guerrillas crossed the border from Lebanon to seize a schoolhouse and some 90 teen-age hostages. Their demand was release of the guerrilla prisoners from Israel's jails. Ordinarily the Israelis firmly refuse to bend in such situations, but the youthfulness of so many captives in guerrilla hands compelled the Israel government to agree. Prisoners, among them that lone Japanese survivor, Kozo Oka-moto, had already been taken out of their cells to be exchanged for the children when the negotiations went awry and the Israeli troops opened fire in their desperate attempt to free the hostages. The guer-rillas then began to shoot the youngsters. Altogether scores were wounded and 26 perished, most of them killed by the fedayeen on the spot while the rest died later of wounds. Among the dead was an Israeli soldier and several others who were not students but had been killed by the guerrillas en route to the schoolhouse. Most of the dead and wounded were the unfortunate youngsters. All three murderers died in the troops' onslaught. In Beirut, eloquent demonstrations honoring these fallen fedayeen as noble martyrs of the cause were ordered by Hawatmeh.

On June 13, Ahmed Jebreel and his General Command again came into the news when their four commandos attacked Shamir, a pros-perous kibutz settlement in northern Israel, and killed three women, one of them a young girl-volunteer from New Zealand. Surrounded by the armed kibutzniks, the Arab raiders blew themselves up with gre-nades. Near their mangled bodies lay leaflets demanding that 100 of Israel's Arab captives be freed within six hours.

Twelve days later, on the twenty-fifth, Arafat's own Fatah bragged that it was its squad of avengers who on the previous night murdered an Israeli woman, two children, and an Israeli soldier, at the north coastal town of Nahariya. Under cover of darkness they had made their way from the Lebanese waters in boats. All three Arab raiders were slain by the counterattacking Israeli troops.

Not to be outdone, Hawatmeh went into action next, on November 19 sending three of his guerrillas to infiltrate into Israel from Jordan (whither they had apparently come from Syria). Crossing the Jordan River, the commandos staged a predawn attack on an apartment house at Beit Shean, killing four Israelis before they themselves were slain by Israeli soldiers. In the battle, 19 others were injured, some of them children whom their parents tried to save by dropping them out the windows. The enraged settlers, Jews of North African origin, stormed up the stairs to vent their fury upon the dead Arabs. They battered the corpses savagely, then threw them out the windows and burned them in a bonfire. In their rage they did not realize that, in an error, along with the Arab bodies they also tossed out and burned a dead Israeli, a victim of the guerrillas. In the safety of his Beirut headquarters, Hawat-meh rejoiced.

But Hawatmeh had little cause for joy when on November 30 his intelligence service revealed its gross ineptness. It sent two guerrillas across the Lebanese border into the Upper Galilee's village of Rihaniya, mistaking it for a settlement of the Israelis, whereas it was well known to everyone else in the area as one of the two villages in Israel populated by Moslem Circassians, descendants of migrants from Tsarist Russia. These Arabs killed a Circassian man and wounded his wife, then spoke to their nine-year-old daughter in Hebrew. They were astonished when she answered in Arabic, saying that she spoke no Hebrew, and explaining that the family and all their fellow villagers were Circassian Moslems. The dismayed guerrillas (one of them accidentally wounded by his clumsy mate) apologized to the girl for murdering her father and injuring her mother. And so unnerved were they by their mistake that, very much unlike the fedayeen's usual way, they did not fight the oncoming Israeli soldiers, meekly surrendering to them instead.

On the night of March 5-6, 1975, eight Saiqa-Fatah guerrillas landed in the heart of Tel Aviv, sneaking in by sea from Lebanon. They attacked passers-by, then dashed into a small hotel near the shore, rounding up a number of hostages. Israeli soldiers besieged the hotel; in the gunfire and the final bomb explosion set off by the terrorists, six Israelis, three of them military and three civilians (including two women and one Dutch-Jewish youth), were killed. Of the eight raiders, seven perished and one was captured alive.

On the morning of July 4, 1975, a dynamite-charged refrigerator left by unknown Arabs on the sidewalk of Jerusalem's main square exploded, killing 15 and injuring 70. Among the wounded were two young American women tourists. In Beirut, central guerrilla offices attributed the blow to the operatives of the Martyr Farid Al Boubaly Brigade (a Fatah unit named in memory of fedayeen killed earlier in the year in an unsuccessful attack on an Israeli patrol).

On December 21, 1975, a team of Arab and Western terrorists, in their daring raid upon the Vienna headquarters of the Organization of Petroleum Producing Countries, demanded of the near-dozen OPEC oil ministers they captured that the world's oil resources be denied to the West, and that war be declared against Israel immediately. However, no Jews were found in those Vienna offices to be killed. Two Arab staffmen of OPEC and an Austrian policeman were murdered instead. The hostages, most of them Moslems, were flown to Algeria and Libya and soon released, but so were the terrorist slayers as well—after a brief detention by the Algerian authorities.

While in 1976 the attention of Arafat, Habash, and other Arab terrorist leaders was somewhat diverted by the fraternal war and the Syrian invasion in Lebanon, some terrorist attacks continued on Israel's soil, possibly by local Arabs, as well as one by a Western agent of a fedayeen organization. On May 3, a high-explosive bomb, left on a busy street in Jerusalem atop a parked motor scooter, injured 28 persons, including two Dutch tourists and the Greek consul general and his wife. On May 25, a man arriving at the Lydda airport from Vienna was asked by a woman guard to open his suspicious-looking suitcase. As he opened it, the small red case blew up, killing the guard and the terrorist. He was later identified as a 25-year-old West German with a prison record. In Beirut, Dr. Habash's PFLP jubilantly claimed credit for the attack in the name "of the uprising in the occupied lands of Palestine." The West German terrorist was a member of the Arab guerrilla Front.

On Sunday, June 27, 1976, three men and one woman hijacked a giant Air France plane over Greece on its Tel Aviv-Paris flight, with 244 passengers and a 12-member crew. The four terrorists had boarded the plane at its stop in Athens with their weapons undetected, thanks to lax Greek security. Two of the men were Arabs; the third, Wilfried Boese, was a West German from the Baader-Meinhof Gang and the team's chief; the woman was a Turk. Announcing they were part of Dr. Habash's PFLP, they forced the plane to land at Uganda's Entebbe airport, where the hijackers were warmly greeted by Dictator Idi Amin and joined by four more Arab terrorists. Ugandan troops helped the eight guard the hostages. The demand: release of 53 guerrillas from the jails of Israel, Kenya, and Europe. Of these, 40, including Kozo Okamoto and Archbishop Capucci, were in Israeli cells. At midweek the hijackers freed 47 hostages, and later another 101, but kept more than 100 Jews under the threat of execution. Reluctantly, the Israeli government agreed to negotiate. In secret, it prepared a raid of rescue. Late on Saturday, July 3, Israeli planes with specially trained troops, including doctors and nurses, flew the 2,620 miles to Uganda. Near midnight they swooped down on Entebbe, killed seven hijackers (among them Boese and the woman) and some 20 Ugandan soldiers, and rescued 103 hostages and the entire crew, flying them to Kenya and Israel. Only three hostages and one Israeli officer fell dead during the battle in this boldest and most successful rescue mission of modern times—this sensational defeat of terrorists. Soon after, enraged Ugandan toughs murdered an elderly British-Jewish woman, a hostage who had been moved from the airport to a hospital before the rescue raid.

Bibliography

Below is a selected list of general works on guerrilla warfare and, particularly, recent urban terrorism. Other titles appear in the notes arranged by chapters, dealing with specific movements, areas, and periods.

Yonah Alexander, ed., *International Terrorism* (New York: Praeger, 1976).

Amnesty International, *Report on Torture* (London: Duckworth, 1973).

Hannah Arendt, *On Violence* (paperback, New York: Harcourt, Brace & World, Inc., 1970).

Raymond Aron, *History and the Dialectic of Violence*, transl. by Barry Cooper (Oxford: Blackwell, 1975).

Robert Asprey, *War in the Shadows: The Guerrilla in History*, two volumes (New York: Doubleday & Company, 1976).

Carol Edler Baumann, *The Diplomatic Kidnappings: A Revolutionary Tactic of Urban Terrorism* (The Hague: Martinus Nijhoff, 1973).

J. Bowyer Bell, *The Myth of the Guerrilla: Revolutionary Theory and Malpractice* (New York: Alfred A. Knopf, 1971).

J. Bowyer Bell, *Transnational Terror* (Washington: American Enterprise Institute, 1976).

James Burnham, "The Protracted Conflict," *National Review*, March 1, 15, and 29, 1974; contents: "Entering the Terrorist Age?", "Roots of Terrorism," and "Anti-terror Problems."

Anthony Burton, *Urban Terrorism* (London: Leo Cooper Ltd., 1976).

Richard Clutterbuck, *Protest and the Urban Guerrilla* (New York: Abelard-Schuman, 1974).

Richard Clutterbuck, *Living With Terrorism* (London: Faber & Faber, 1975).

T. A. Critchley, *The Conquest of Violence: Order and Liberty in Britain* (London: Constable, 1970).

Brian Crozier, *The Rebels: A Study of Post-War Insurrections* (London: Chatto & Windus, 1960).

Régis Debray, *Revolution in the Revolution?* (New York: Grove Press, Inc., 1967; Harmondsworth: Penguin Books, 1968).

Terrence Des Pres, *The Survivor* (New York: Oxford University Press, 1976).

Harry Eckstein, ed., *Internal War: Problems and Approaches* (New York: Free Press, Macmillan, 1964).

John Ellis, *A Short History of Guerrilla Warfare* (New York: St. Martin's Press, 1976).

Geoffrey Fairbairn, *Revolutionary Guerrilla Warfare: The Countryside Version* (Harmondsworth: Penguin, 1974).

Lewis H. Gann, *Guerrillas in History* (Stanford: Hoover Institution Press, 1971).

Roland Gaucher, *The Terrorists: From Tsarist Russia to the O.A.S.,* translated from the French by Paula Spurlin (London: Secker and Warburg, 1968).

General Vo Nguyen Giap, *People's War People's Army* (Hanoi: Foreign Languages Publishing House, 1961).

Lt. Colonel T. N. Greene, *The Guerrilla—and How to Fight Him* (New York: Praeger, 1963).

Samuel B. Griffith, *Mao Tse-tung: On Guerrilla Warfare* (New York: Praeger, 1961).

Ché Guevara, *Guerrilla Warfare* (New York: Monthly Review Press, 1961; Harmondsworth: Penguin, 1969).

J. B. S. Hardman, "Terrorism," *Encyclopedia of the Social Sciences,* Vol. 14 (New York: Macmillan, 1937), pp. 575-79.

Eric J. Hobsbawm, *Revolutionaries: Contemporary Essays* (New York: Pantheon Books, 1973).

Donald C. Hodges, ed. and transl., *Philosophy of the Urban Guerrilla: The Revolutionary Writings of Abraham Guillén* (New York: William Morrow & Company, 1973).

Edward Hyams, *Terrorists and Terrorism* (New York: St. Martin's Press, 1974).

Brian Jenkins, *International Terrorism: A New Mode of Conflict* (Los Angeles: Crescent Publications, 1976).

Frank Kitson, *Low Intensity Operations: Subversion, Insurgency and Peacekeeping* (London: Faber & Faber, 1971).

H. T. Lambrick, ed. and transl., *The Terrorist* (London: Ernest Benn, 1972).

Carl Leiden and Karl M. Schmitt, *The Politics of Violence* (Englewood, New Jersey: Prentice-Hall, Inc., 1968).

Jay Mallin, ed., *Terror and Urban Guerrillas: A Study of Tactics* (Coral Gables, Florida: University of Miami Press, 1971).

Carlos Marighella, *Minimanual of the Urban Guerrilla* (Havana: Tricontinental, 1970).

Lt. Colonel John J. McCuen, *The Art of Counter-Revolutionary War: The Strategy of Counter-Insurgency* (Harrisburg, Pennsylvania: Stackpole Books, 1966).

Edward McWhinney, *Hijacking of Aircraft and International Law* (Hague Recueil, The Hague Academy of International Law, 1973).

Maurice Merleau-Ponty, *Humanism and Terror,* transl. and annotated by J. O'Neill (Boston: Beacon Press, 1969).

Robert Moss, *Urban Guerrillas: The New Face of Political Violence* (London: Temple Smith, 1972).

H. L. Nieburg, *Political Violence: The Behavioral Process* (paperback, New York: St. Martin's, 1969).

Johan Niezing, ed., *Urban Guerrilla: Studies in the Theory, Strategy and Practice of Political Violence in Modern Societies* (Rotterdam University Press, 1975). Papers read at a conference organized by the Polemological Center of the Free University of Brussels in 1974.

Franklin Mark Osanka, ed., *Modern Guerrilla Warfare* (New York: Free Press, 1962).

Leslie Paul, *The Age of Terror* (Boston: The Beacon Press, 1951).

Lucian W. Pye, *Aspects of Political Development* (Boston: Little, Brown & Co., 1966), Chapter VII, "Insurgency and the Suppression of Rebellions," pp. 126-52.

Sam C. Sarkesian, ed., *Revolutionary Guerrilla Warfare* (Chicago: Precedent Publishing, 1975).

D. V. Segre and J. H. Adler, "The Ecology of Terrorism," *Encounter*, London, Vol. 40, Number 2 (February 1973), pp. 17-24.

Terrorism. Special issue of *Skeptic, the Forum for Contemporary History*, Santa Barbara, Calif., No. 11, January/February 1976. Contributions by Irving Rowe, Walter Laqueur, and staff members of the London Institute for the Study of Conflict.

Sir Robert Thompson, *Revolutionary War in World Strategy, 1945-1969* (London: Secker and Warburg, 1970).

H. Hessell Tiltman, *The Terror in Europe* (New York: Frederick A. Stokes Company, 1932).

Eugene V. Walter, "Violence and the Process of Terror," *American Sociological Review*, Vol. 29, Number 2 (Spring 1964), pp. 248-57.

Paul Wilkinson, *Political Terrorism* (paperback, London: The Macmillan Press Ltd., 1974).

Renee Winegarten, "Literary Terrorism," *Commentary*, New York, Vol. 57, No. 3 (March 1974), pp. 58-65.

To the above must be added the periodic *Conflict Studies* and special reports being issued by the Institute for the Study of Conflict, London. I am particularly grateful to Brian Crozier (editor) and Peter Janke for their courtesies during my visit at the Institute (early 1975) in acquainting me with its work, library, and files.

(Vadillo in *Siempre!*, Mexico City, Rothco)

Notes

Introduction

1 Cf. Bakunin's phrase: ". . . until now every forward step in history has been achieved only after it has been baptized in blood," in G. P. Maximoff, ed., *The Political Philosophy of Bakunin: Scientific Anarchism*, preface by Bert F. Hoselitz, introduction by Rudolph Rocker, biogr. sketch of Bakunin by Max Nettlau (Glencoe, Illinois: Free Press, 1953), Part IV, Ch. 4, "Revolution and Revolutionary Violence," pp. 372-79.

Chapter 1
Violence: Genesis of Terror

1 Antoine de Gramont, "Relation de mon voyage en Pologne," *La Revue de Paris*, April 15, 1922, p. 732.
2 A. G. Man'kov, *Zapiski inostrantsev o vosstanii Stepana Razina* [Foreigners' accounts of Stepan Razin's rising] (Leningrad: Nauka Publishing House, auspices of the Leningrad Branch of the Institute of History of the Academy of Sciences, 1951), p. 96. The text is in Russian, German, and English.
3 Hannah Arendt, *On Violence* (New York: Harcourt, Brace & World, Inc., paperback), p. 8.
4 Carl Gustav Jung, *Psychology and Religion* (New Haven: Yale University Press, 1938), pp. 15-16.
5 Erich Fromm, *The Anatomy of Human Destructiveness* (New York: Holt, Rinehart and Winston, 1973), on "Malignant Aggression"—pp. 218-324. Also see his "Why Do We Crave Calamity?", *The New York Times*, June 9, 1974.

6 Konrad Lorenz, *On Aggression*, transl. by Marjorie Kerr Wilson (New York: Harcourt, Brace & World, Inc., 1966), chapters 3 and 4, "What Aggression is Good For" and "The Spontaneity of Aggression."
7 L[ev] Trotsky, *Kak vooruzhalas' revolyutsiya* [How the revolution armed itself], Volume II, Book 1 (Moscow: Supreme Military Editorial Council, 1924), pp. 143-48.

Chapter 2
Terror: An Overall View

1 A useful translation of *The Catechism* into English is in Robert Payne, *The Terrorists: The Story of the Forerunners of Stalin* (New York: Funk & Wagnalls Company, 1957), pp. 21-27. In his "Bibliography" (p. 351) Mr. Payne states that this translation is based on the authoritative text of *The Catechism* published by order of the Tsarist government in the St. Petersburg *Pravitel'stvennyi viestnik* [Government Herald] for July 11, 1871. The argument that *The Catechism of a Revolutionary* was authored by neither Nechayev nor Bakunin but by an obscure Nechayevist is developed by the noted French radical scholar Boris Souvarine in his letter to the editor of *Russkaya Mysl'* [Russian Thought], Paris, November 11, 1971, and again in his letter to the editor of *Novyi Zhurnal* [New Review], New York, Book 121 (December 1975), pp. 281-83.
2 V. I. Lenin, "Zadachi soyuzov molodezhi" [Tasks of leagues of youth], *Polnoye sobraniye sochineniy* [Complete

works], fifth edition, 1958-1970 (Moscow: Political Literature Publishing House), Vol. 41, p. 313.

3 David Shub, *Lenin* (New York: Doubleday, 1948), p. 105.

4 Hilda Gadea, *Ernesto: A Memoir of Ché Guevara,* transl. from the Spanish by Carmen Molina and Walter I. Bradbury (Garden City, New York: Doubleday, 1972), p. 12.

5 Lucinda Franks and Thomas Powers, "The Story of Diana: the Making of a Terrorist," as serialized in five parts in *The Cleveland Press* starting September 14, 1970, especially Part 2 on Diana's two years among the Indians in Guatemala. In book form this was published as Thomas Powers, *Diana: The Making of a Terrorist* (Boston: Houghton, Mifflin, 1971). See also Melvin J. Lasky, "Lady on the Barricades," *Encounter,* Vol. 39, No. 1 (July 1972), pp. 19-22.

6 Crane Brinton, *A Decade of Revolution, 1789-1799,* in the series *The Rise of Modern Europe,* William L. Langer, ed. (New York: Harper & Brothers, 1934), p. 162.

7 *Ibid.,* pp. 160-161.

8 *Ibid.,* p. 159.

9 *Ibid.,* p. 123.

Chapter 3
Terror as Aberration

1 "Russia: In the Dark Ages of Psychiatry," *The Economist,* London, July 8, 1972, pp. 34 and 41.

2 However, in 1964, toward the end of Nikita Khrushchev's reign, laudatory biographies of Menzhinsky appeared. One such was a book by Colonel M. A. Smirnov. An article praising Menzhinsky's secret police work was published in Moscow *Izvestiya* [News] on September 1, 1964, to commemorate the 90th anniversary of his birth.

3 Lawrence Z. Freedman, "Terrorism: Policy, Pathology, Politics—Problems of the Polistaraxic," *The University of Chicago Magazine,* Summer 1974, pp. 7-10. An excellent psychiatric study of terrorists is David G. Hubbard, M. D., *The Skyjacker: His Flights of Fantasy* (New York: Macmillan, 1971), but the cases of aberrant behavior Dr. Hubbard studied were mostly those of non-political terrorists. Political terrorists

are the subject of Gerald McKnight, *The Mind of the Terrorist* (London: Michael Joseph, 1974), but the author is a journalist, not a trained psychiatrist or psychologist.

4 "Patty's Twisted Journey," statement by Dr. Robert Harrington, *Time,* September 29, 1975, p. 21.

5 Max Nomad, *Apostles of Revolution* (paperback, New York: Collier Books, 1961), chapter on "The Preacher: Johann Most, Terrorist of the World," pp. 257-99.

6 John Kifner, "Cinque: A Dropout Who Has Been in Constant Trouble," *The New York Times,* May 17, 1974.

7 "Patty's Twisted Journey," statement by Dr. Lewis Yablonsky, *Time,* September 29, 1975, p. 21.

8 See Bernard Lewis, *The Assassins: A Radical Sect in Islam* (London: Weidenfeld and Nicolson, 1967).

9 David Wechsler, *The Measurement and Appraisal of Adult Intelligence,* fourth edition (Baltimore: The Williams & Wilkins Company, 1958), pp. 176-77.

10 Russel V. Lee, "The Menace of Madness in High Places," *The Pharos of Alpha Omega Alpha* (Alpha Omega Alpha Honor Medical Society), January 1974, Vol. 37, No. 1, pp. 2-4. Dr. Lee informed me in his letter of January 9, 1975: "I am writing a book for Harper and Row on this subject."

11 K. Takhtarev. "V. I. Lenin i sotsialdemokraticheskoye dvizheniye (Is lichnykh vospominaniy)" [V. I. Lenin and the Social-Democratic movement (From personal recollections)], *Byloye* [The Past], Leningrad, No. 24, 1924, p. 27; same author's essay in the anthology *Ob Ilyiche* [About Ilyich], Leningrad, 1924, quoted by Mikhail Koryakov, "Listki iz bloknota" [Leaves from a notebook], *Novoye Russkoye Slovo,* [New Russian Word], New York, April 19, 1970.

12 Summary by the Munich Institute for the Study of the USSR, "Lenin: kul't i deistvitel'nost' " [Lenin: the cult and the reality], *Novoye Russkoye Slovo,* July 27, 1969.

13 Franco Venturi, *Roots of Revolution: A History of the Populist and Socialist Movements in Nineteenth Century Russia,* transl. from the Italian by Francis

Haskell, with an introduction by Isaiah Berlin; first published in Italy in 1952 as *Il Populismo Russo* (English paperback, New York: The University Library, Grosset & Dunlap, by arrangement with Alfred A. Knopf, Inc., 1966), p. 428.

14 See Vincent Bugliosi, with Curt Gentry, *Helter Skelter: the True Story of the Manson Murders* (New York: W. W. Norton & Company, Inc., 1974). Bugliosi was the prosecutor in the Manson case.

Chapter 4
Robespierre's Bloody Virtue

1 Norman Cohn, *Pursuit of the Millenium* (Fairlawn, New Jersey: Essential Books, Inc., 1957), p. 267.

2 Literature—and variety of interpretation—on the French Revolution and its Great Terror are enormous, as I found out in my student days in the inspiring classes of my late friend and teacher, Professor Louis R. Gottschalk, at the University of Chicago. Sources for my Chapters 4 and 5 may be found in the following titles:

Lord Acton (John Emerich Edward Dalberg-Acton), *Lectures on the French Revolution* (London: Macmillan, 1910).

Alphonse Aulard, *The French Revolution: A Political History, 1789-1804*, transl. by Bernard Miall, four volumes (New York: Russell & Russell, 1965).

Louis Barthou, *Le neuf thermidor* ([Paris], Hachette, [1926]).

Hilaire Belloc, *Robespierre: A Study* (New York: G. P. Putnam's Sons, 1928).

P. Bessand-Massenet, *Robespierre et l'Idée* (Paris: Librairie Plon, 1961).

Richard Bienvenu, ed., *The Ninth of Thermidor: The Fall of Robespierre* (New York: Oxford University Press, 1968).

Crane Brinton, *A Decade of Revolution, 1789-1799*, in the series *The Rise of Modern Europe*, William L. Langer, ed. (New York: Harper & Brothers, 1934).

Edmund Burke, *Reflections on the Revolution in France*, edited, with an introduction, by Thomas H. D. Mahoney; with an analysis by Oskar Piest (Indianapolis: The Bobbs-Merrill Co., Inc., 1955).

Thomas Carlyle, *The French Revolution; A History*, three volumes (New York: AMS Press, [1974]).

John Laurence Carr, *Robespierre: The Force of Circumstance* (London: Constable, and New York: St. Martin's, 1972).

Guglielmo Ferrero, *The Two French Revolutions, 1789-1796*, ed. by Luc Monnier, transl. from the French by Samuel J. Hurwitz, with a foreword by Crane Brinton (New York: Basic Books, 1968).

Max Gallo, *Robespierre the Incorruptible: A Psycho-Biography*, transl. by Raymond Rudorff ([New York:] Herder and Herder, [1971]).

Leo Gershoy, *The French Revolution and Napoleon* (New York: Appleton-Century-Crofts, Inc., 1933).

V. Gerye, "Terror (la terreur)," *Brokgaus-Yefron Entsiklopedicheskiy Slovar'*, St. Petersburg, Russia, Vol. 33 (1901), pp. 69-81.

James L. Godfrey, *Revolutionary Justice: A Study of the Organization, Personnel and Procedure of the Revolutionary Tribunal* (Chapel Hill: University of North Carolina Press, 1951).

Louis R. Gottschalk, *The Era of the French Revolution* (Boston: Houghton, Mifflin, 1929).

Donald Greer, *The Incidence of Terror During the French Revolution* (Cambridge, Mass.: Harvard University Press, 1935).

Earl L. Higgins, ed. and transl., *The French Revolution as Told by Contemporaries* (Boston: Houghton Mifflin, [1938]).

Ralph Korngold, *Robespierre, First Modern Dictator* (London: Macmillan, 1937).

Peter Kropotkin, *The Great French Revolution, 1789-1793*, transl. from the French by N. F. Dryhurst, two volumes (London: W. Heinemann, and New York: Putnam, 1909; New York: Vanguard Press, 1927; New York: Schocken Books, [1971]).

Georges Lefebvre, *The French Revolution from Its Origins to 1793* (London: Routledge and Kegan Paul, 1965).

Georges Lefebvre, *The Great Fear of 1789: Rural Panic in Revolutionary*

France, transl. by Joan White (New York: Pantheon Books, [1973]).

Georges Lefebvre, *The Thermidorians and the Directory: Two Phases of the French Revolution* (New York: Random House, [1964]).

Gwynne Lewis, *Life in Revolutionary France* (London: Batsford, 1972).

Stanley Loomis, *Paris in the Terror, June 1793—July 1794* (Phildelphia: J. B. Lippincott Co., 1964).

Colin Lucas, *The Structure of Terror: The Example of Javogues and the Loire* (London: Oxford University Press, 1973).

Louis Madelin, *The French Revolution* (London: W. Heinemann, 1922).

Albert Mathiez, *The French Revolution,* transl. from the French by Catherine Alison Phillips (New York: Russell & Russell, 1962).

Jean Matrat, *Robespierre, or, The Tyranny of the Majority,* transl. by Alan Kendall (New York: Charles Scribner's Sons, [1975]).

Louis Mortimer-Ternaux, *Histoire de la Terreur, 1792-1794,* eight volumes (Paris: M. Lévy, 1868-81).

Robert R. Palmer, *Twelve Who Ruled the Committee of Public Safety During the Terror* (Princeton, N. J.: Princeton University Press, [1941]).

Robert R. Palmer, *The World of the French Revolution* (New York: Harper & Row, 1971).

Edgar Quinet, *La révolution* (Paris and Brussels: A. Lacroix and Verboeckhoven, 1865). Includes discussion of theory of terror.

George Rudé, *Robespierre: Portrait of a Revolutionary Democrat* (New York: Viking Press, 1976).

Gaetano Salvemini, *The French Revolution, 1788-1792.* transl. by I. M. Rawson (London: Cape, [1954]).

Friedrich Sieburg, *Robespierre, the Incorruptible* (New York: Robert McBride and Co., [1938]).

John B. Sirich, *The Revolutionary Committees in the Departments of France, 1793-94* (Cambridge, Mass.: Harvard University Press, 1943).

Hippolyte Adolphe Taine, *The French Revolution,* transl. by John Durand, second revised edition (New York: Henry Holt and Co., 1878-85).

Jan Ten Brink, *Robespierre and the Red Terror,* transl. from the Dutch by J. Hedeman (London: Hutcheson & Co., 1899).

Adolphe Thiers, *History of the French Revolution,* transl. by Frederick Shoberl, four volumes (New York: Appleton, 1897).

James M. Thompson, *Robespierre and the French Revolution* (London: The English Universities Press, [1952], and New York: Macmillan, 1953).

Henri A. Wallon, *La Terreur, études critiques sur l'histoire de la Révolution française* (Paris: Hachette, 1873).

Michael Walzer, ed., *Regicide and Revolution: Speeches at the Trial of Louis XVI,* transl. by Marian Rothstein (London: Cambridge University Press, 1974).

Reginald Somerset Ward, *Maximilien Robespierre: A Study in Deterioration* (London: Macmillan, 1934).

3 Singularly, no less an admirer of the French Revolution than Friedrich Engels held that at least the final month of the Great Terror was unnecessary because victories on the war fronts had already been achieved. See Karl Marx and Frederick Engels, *Selected Correspondence* (Moscow, Foreign Languages Publishing House, [1953]), pp. 488-89, Engels to Victor Adler, December 4, 1889: Terror "was rendered entirely superfluous by the victory of Fleurus on June 24, 1794, which not only freed the frontiers but delivered Belgium and indirectly the left bank of the Rhine into the hands of France." And yet "the terror was intensified to a pitch of insanity" only "to keep Robespierre in power." Also, p. 483, Engels to Karl Kautsky, February 20, 1889: In time Robespierre lost the real revolutionary reason for terror, since "*now terror became in his hands a means of self-preservation* [italics in the original] and thus absurd . . . untenable."

Chapter 5
The Guillotine Athirst

1 M[ark] A. Aldanov, *Devyatoye Termidora*; third, revised edition (Berlin: Slovo Publishing House, 1928), pp. 215-16. In English, *The Ninth Thermi-*

dor, translated from the Russian by A. E. Chamot (New York: Alfred A. Knopf, 1926), p. 204. I used my own translation of the passage quoted by me. Aldanov's novel, based on meticulous research in the French archives by this well-known Russian émigré writer, is one of the most profound studies of Robespierre's Grand Terror.

Chapter 6
In the Name of Marx

1 Freedman, "Terrorism: Policy, Pathology, Politics" (previously cited), p. 8.
2 Arendt, *On Violence* (previously cited), p. 11.
3 Letter from Oscar J. Hammen to Albert Parry, November 3, 1973. Prof. Hammen, of the Department of History, University of Montana, is the author of *The Red '48ers: Karl Marx and Friedrich Engels* (New York: Charles Scribner's Sons, 1970). I am greatly indebted to Dr. Hammen for his generous assistance in tracing Marx's attitude toward terror through Marx's references to it in the *Neue Rheinische Zeitung* of 1848-49.
4 These two quotations come from Bertram D. Wolfe, *Marxism: One Hundred Years in the Life of a Doctrine* (New York: The Dial Press, 1965), p. 152. I am grateful to Mr. Wolfe for the points on the Marx-Engels attitude toward terror he made during our conversation in September 1974.
5 Hammen to Parry, letter of November 3, 1973.
6 *Ibid.*
7 Wolfe, *op. cit.*, pp. 165-66.
8 *Ibid.*, p. 166.
9 *Perepiska K. Marksa i F. Engel'sa s russkimi politicheskimi deyatelyami* [Correspondence of K. Marx and F. Engels with Russian political activists] (Moscow: State Publishing House of Political Literature, second edition, 1951), pp. 308-11, letter to Engels from Vera I. Zasulich, Geneva, February 14, 1885, and reply to her from Engels, London, April 23, 1885.

This celebrated prophecy by Engels, being quite uncomfortable for Soviet propagandists, is hardly ever quoted in Soviet literature. However, the daring nonconformist Andrei D. Sakharov referred to it approvingly in his samizdat (underground) memorandum *Razmyshleniya o progresse, mirnom sosushchestvovanii i intellectual'noi svobode* (Moscow, 1968), translated into English as *Progress, Coexistence, and Intellectual Freedom*, with introduction, afterword, and notes by Harrison E. Salisbury (New York: Norton, 1968), wherein Sakharov wrote of the Hegelian-Engelsian "irony of history" which "took the form of Stalinism in our country" (p. 75 of the English translation; see also p. 144 of the same translation for Salisbury's able discussion of this prophecy by Engels).

The late David Shub, author of *Lenin*, in exchanging with me his views on this passage in Engels' writings, asked me to remember that Engels forecast such miscarriage "not for all revolutions, certainly not for truly spontaneous and popular revolutions, but only for those deliberately programmed, artificial ones, such as the one led by Lenin."

10 Georges Sorel, *Reflections on Violence*, authorized translation by T. E. Hulme (New York: Peter Smith, 1941), p. 99.
11 *Ibid.*, this and following quotations are from pp. 108-10, 121-22, 125, and 297-98.
12 There is another book by Georges Sorel, *The Illusions of Progress*, translated by John and Charlotte Stanley, with a foreword by Robert A. Nisbet, and an introduction by John Stanley (Berkeley and Los Angeles: University of California Press, 1969), with brief references to terror on pp. 61, 90, 96, and 125.

Chapter 7
Anarchists: Philosophers with Bombs

1 Eldridge Cleaver, *Soul on Ice*, with an introduction by Maxwell Geismar (New York: McGraw-Hill Book Company, 1968), p. 12.
2 Michael Prawdin [pseudonym of Michael Charol], *The Unmentionable Nechaev: A Key to Bolshevism* (New York: Roy Publishers Inc., 1961); René Cannac, *Aux sources de la Révolution russe: Netchaiev, du nihilisme au terrorism*, pref. d'André Mazon (Paris: Payot, 1961); Max

Nomad, "The Fanatic," *Apostles of Revolution*.

3 The Soviet edition of *The Possessed* in my library is Volume Seven of Dostoyevsky's *Sobraniye sochineniy* [Collected works]. This volume was issued in Moscow, by the State Publishing House of Artistic Literature, in 1957, the height of Khrushchevian relaxation (the year after Khrushchev's anti-Stalin speech at the 20th Congress of the Communist Party). The availability of the book in the Soviet Union has lessened in the post-Khrushchev years. A good English translation is by Constance Garnett (New York: Random House, The Modern Library, Inc., 1936). A later but less satisfactory translation is by Andrew R. MacAndrew (Signet Classics, a paperback, New York: The New American Library of World Literature, Inc., 1962).

4 Albert L. Weeks, *The First Bolshevik: A Political Biography of Peter Tkachev* (New York: New York University Press, 1968); Michael Karpovich, "A Forerunner of Lenin: P. N. Tkachev," *The Review of Politics*, University of Notre Dame, South Bend, Indiana, Vol. 6, No. 3 (July 1944), pp. 336-50.

5 E. H. Carr, *Michael Bakunin* (London: Macmillan, 1937); Max Nomad, "The Heretic," *Apostles of Revolution*; Arthur Lehning, comp., *Michel Bakounine et ses relations avec Sergei Nečaev, 1870-1872. Écris et matériaux* (Leiden: Brill, 1971); Michael Confino, *Bakunin & Nechayev: An Upublished Letter*, transl. from the Russian by Lydia Bott, *Encounter*, Vol. 39, No. 1 (July 1972) and Vol. 39, No. 2 (August 1972). G. P. Maximoff, ed., *The Political Philosophy of Bakunin: Scientific Anarchism* (Glencoe, Illinois: Free Press, 1953); E. H. Carr, *The Romantic Exiles: A Nineteenth-Century Portrait Gallery* (first published in 1933; paperback, Harmondsworth: Penguin, 1949).

6 Michael T. Florinsky, *Russia: A Short History* (New York: Macmillan, 1964), p. 278.

7 While on the scaffold, just before the reprieve, one of the fellow-condemned pointed out to Dostoyevsky "a cart covered with a mat which hid, so he thought, their coffins." Avrahm

Yarmolinsky, *Dostoevsky: A Life* (New York: Harcourt, Brace and Company, [1934]), p. 87. Tsar Nicholas I had apparently decided to reprieve the group even before the condemned were taken to the scaffold. All the preparations for the execution were carried out, the prisoners and possibly most of the officials remaining ignorant of the prearranged reprieve. The preparations must have indeed included those coffins.

8 Paul Avrich, "The Legacy of Bakunin," *The Russian Review* (Stanford, Calif. : The Hoover Institution on War, Revolution and Peace), Vol. 29, No. 2 (April 1970), p. 132.

9 Typical is the article by B. Stolpovsky, "Gerbert Markuze, postavshchik TsRU" [Herbert Marcuse, supplier to the CIA], *Trud* [Toil], Moscow, August 8, 1969.

10 Max Nomad, *A Skeptic's Political Dictionary and Handbook for the Disenchanted* (New York: Bookman Associates, 1953), p. 4.

11 The best study of the subject is James Joll, *The Anarchists* (London: Eyre & Spottiswoode, 1964). See also James Joll, "Anarchism, a Living Tradition," in J. Joll and D. Apter, eds., *Anarchism Today* (London: Macmillan, 1971); David Stafford, *Anarchism and Reformism* (London: Weidenfeld & Nicolson, 1972); George Woodcock, *Anarchism: A History of Libertarian Ideas and Movements* (Cleveland: Meridian Books, World Publishing Company, 1962); Paul Avrich, *The Russian Anarchists* (Princeton: Princeton University Press, 1967).

12 Peter Kropotkin, *Memoirs of a Revolutionist* (Boston: Houghton Mifflin, 1899 and 1930; Garden City: Doubleday, 1962); George Woodcock and Ivan Avakumovic, *The Anarchist Prince: A Biographical Study of Peter Kropotkin* (London: T. V. Boardman & Co., [1950]; New York: Schocken Books, [1971]); Natalya Pirumova, *Pyotr Alekseyevich Kropotkin* (Moscow: Nauka, 1972); Herbert Read, ed., *Kropotkin: Selections from His Writings* (London: Freedom Press, [1942]); Emile Capouya and Keitha Tompkins, eds., *The Essential Kropotkin* (New York: Liveright, [1975]).

Chapter 8
America's Pie

1 Louis Adamic, *Dynamite, The Story of Class Violence in America* (New York: The Viking Press, 1931).

   Lillian Symes and Travers Clement, *Rebel America: The Story of Social Revolt in the United States* (New York: Da Capo Press, 1972; reprint of the 1934 edition).

   Richard Hofstadter and Michael Wallace, eds., *American Violence: A Documentary History,* (paperback, New York: Vintage Books, A Division of Random House, 1971).

   Hugh Davis Graham and Ted Robert Gurr, eds., *Violence in America: Historical and Comparative Perspectives, A Report to the National Commission on the Causes and Prevention of Violence, June 1969* (paperback, New York: Signet Books, The New American Library, 1969).

2 Symes and Clement, *op. cit.,* pp. 143, 151-52, 154-59, 180, and 195; Nomad, *Apostles of Revolution,* pp. 257-99.

3 Symes and Clement, pp. 152, 172-77, and 180; M. B. Schnapper, *American Labor: A Pictorial Social History* (Washington, D. C. : Public Affairs Press, 1975), pp. 150-60.

4 Emma Goldman, *Living My Life,* two volumes (New York: Alfred A. Knopf, 1931); Emma Goldman, *My Disillusionment in Russia* (Garden City: Doubleday, Page & Co., 1923); Emma Goldman, *Anarchism and Other Essays,* with biographic sketch by Hippolyte Havel (New York: Mother Earth Publishing Association, 1910); Alix Kates Shulman, ed., *Red Emma Speaks: Selected Writings and Speeches* (New York: Random House, 1972); Richard Drinnon, *Rebel in Paradise: A Biography of Emma Goldman* (Chicago: The University of Chicago Press, [1961]); Alexander Berkman, *Prison Memories of an Anarchist,* intr. by Hutchens Hapgood, new intr. by Paul Goodman (New York: Schocken Books, [1970]).

5 Margaret Leech, *In The Days Of McKinley* (New York: Harper & Brothers, 1959), pp. 592-603.

Chapter 9
Hunting the Tsar

1 On the Narodniki, in addition to the already cited Robert Payne, *The Terrorists* and Franco Venturi, *Roots of Revolution,* see relevant chapters in: Philip Pomper, *The Russian Revolutionary Intelligentsia,* in "Europe Since 1500: A Paperbound Series" (New York: Thomas Y. Crowell Company, 1970); Avrahm Yarmolinsky, *Road to Revolution, A Century of Russian Radicalism* (New York: Macmillan, 1959; paperback, New York: Collier Books, 1962).

   A sound biography of the main terrorist of the People's Will is:

   David Footman, *The Alexander Conspiracy: A Life of A. I. Zhelyabov,* introduction by Leonard Schapiro (LaSalle, Illinois: Open Court Publishing Company, 1974). This is a streamlined, illustrated edition of the original British edition of 1944, reprinted in England in 1968 and in the United States in 1969. The author is a British Foreign Service officer and a novelist.

   For a wider background of the Russian locale and period in which these terrorists operated, see M. A. Aldanov's novel *Istoki* [Sources] (Paris: YMCA Press, 1950); in English, *Before the Deluge,* transl. by Catherine Routsky (New York: Scribner's, 1947).

Chapter 10
Azef: Terror Chief as Double Agent

1 In my childhood and youth in Rostov on the Don, from which city Azef also came, I heard many recollections of Azef by my fellow townsmen who had known that unusual man both before and during his terrorist years.

   Main printed sources on the Terror Brigade and Azef's treachery are:

   B[oris] Nikolayevsky, *Konets Azefa* [Azef's End] (Berlin: Petropolis Publishing House, 1931).

   B[oris] Nikolayevsky, *Istoriya odnogo predatelya* [A Traitor's History] (Berlin: Petropolis Publishing House, 1932). Transl. into English as: Boris I. Nicolayevsky, *Azev, the Spy, the Russian Terrorist and Police Stool* (Garden City: Doubleday, 1934).

   Boris Savinkov, *Memoirs of a Terrorist,* translated by Joseph Shaplen

(New York: Albert & Charles Boni, 1931).

Added to these must be the novel by Roman Goul [Gul'], *General Bo* [General Terrorist Brigade] two volumes (Berlin: Petropolis, 1929); in English, *Azef*, transl. by Mirra Ginzburg (Garden City: Doubleday, 1962). Although fiction, it is good history.

2 On the Russian revolution of 1905, see:

David Floyd, *Russia in Revolt— 1905: The First Crack in Tsarist Power* (New York: American Heritage, 1969).

Sidney Harcave, *First Blood: The Russian Revolution of 1905* (New York: Macmillan, 1964; reprinted as a Collier-Macmillan paperback under the title, *The Russian Revolution of 1905*).

3 Paul Avrich, *The Russian Anarchists* (paperback, Princeton University Press, 1971), Part I: 1905, pp. 9-119.

4 Savinkov, *op. cit.*, p. 317.

5 Peter Durnovo, "Memorandum to Nicholas II," in Thomas Riha, ed., *Readings in Russian Civilization*, second edition (Chicago: The University of Chicago Press, 1969), Vol, II, pp. 465-78. An excellent commentary is by Mark Aldanov, "P. N. Durnovo— Prophet of War and Revolution," in Dimitri von Mohrenschildt, ed., *The Russian Revolution of 1917: Contemporary Accounts* (New York: Oxford University Press, 1971), pp. 62-74.

Chapter 11
Lenin: High Priest of Terror

1 Certain parts of my three chapters on Lenin in this book are adapted from my essay, "A Look Back at Lenin as His Centenary Celebrations Begin— 'Power Was Lying in the Street; We Picked It Up, ' " *The New York Times Magazine*, September 28, 1969, pp. 30-31 and 124-32.

There is no work, in English or any other language, solely devoted to Lenin as the supreme terrorist of modern times, but this role of Lenin is among the main features of Alexander Solzhenitsyn's great work on the Soviet slave system.

In Russian: A. Solzhenitsyn, *Arkhipelag GULag, 1918-1956, opyt khudozhestvennogo issledovaniya* (Paris: YMCA-Press, Vol. I, Parts I-II, 1973;

Vol. II, Parts III-IV, 1974; Vol. III, 1976).

In English: Aleksandr I. Solzhenitsyn, *The Gulag Archipelago, 1918-1956; an experiment in literary investigation,* transl. by Thomas P. Whitney (New York: Harper & Row, vol. 1, parts I-II, 1974; vol. 2, parts III-IV, 1975).

The three outstanding biographies of Lenin, in English, in the order of their excellence, are:

David Shub, *Lenin* (New York: Doubleday & Company, Inc., 1948).

Louis Fischer, *The Life of Lenin* (New York: Harper and Row, 1964). In Russian, *Zhizn' Lenina* (London: Overseas Publications Interchange, Ltd. 1970).

Stefan T. Possony, *Lenin: The Compulsive Revolutionary* (Chicago: Henry Regnery Company, The Hoover Institution Series, 1964).

To these must be added the part on Lenin in Bertram D. Wolfe, *Three Who Made a Revolution, A Biographical History* (paperback, A Delta Book; New York: Dell Publishing Co., Inc., 1964).

Of personal reminiscences of Lenin, particularly valuable is Nikolay Valentinov (N. V. Volsky), *Encounters With Lenin,* transl. by Paul Rosta and Brian Pearce, foreword by Leonard Schapiro (London: Oxford University Press, 1968).

A concise summary of Lenin's statements on terror, with precise references to where in his works they can be found, is the article by Panas V. Fedenko, "Lenin i gumannost' " [Lenin and humaneness], *Russkaya Mysl'*, Paris, September 3, 1970. The author of the article was a researcher on the staff of the Munich Institute for the Study of the USSR.

For other works on Lenin, see my notes below, also my review article, "On Lenin: Recent Contributions in the West," *The Russian Review*, Stanford, Calif., Vol. 29, No. 4 (October 1970), pp. 457-63.

My quotations of Lenin's own texts come from V. I. Lenin, *Polnoye sobraniye sochineniy* [Complete Works], fifth edition, 1958-1970 (Moscow: Political Literature Publishing House), unless—in a few cases—otherwise specified.

2 Shub, *op. cit.,* p. 23, cites the reminiscences of Lenin's sister Anna on this point, but elsewhere I have encountered suspicion that she might have invented this episode.

3 An especially detailed and convincing discussion of this influence is in Nikolai Valentinov (N. V. Volski), *The Early Years of Lenin,* translated and edited by Rolf H. W. Theen, introduction by Bertram D. Wolfe (Ann Arbor: The University of Michigan Press, 1969), Part II, pp. 109-282.

4 N. Valentinov, *Vstrechi s Leninym* [Encounters with Lenin] (New York: The Chekhov Publishing House, 1953), p. 117. The 1968 English translation of this book by Rosta and Pearce, p. 75, gives a somewhat different rendition of this passage.

Lenin reaffirmed his belief in a violent dictatorship in November 1918, one year after seizing power in Russia, saying that this was the only true Marxist interpretation: "Dictatorship is rule based directly upon force and unrestricted by any laws. The revolutionary dictatorship of the proletariat is rule won and maintained by the use of violence by the proletariat against the bourgeoisie." See "Proletarskaya revolyutsiya i renegat Kautsky" in V. I. Lenin, *Polnoye sobraniye sochineniy,* Vol. 37, p. 245; transl. as "Proletarian Revolution and Renegade Kautsky" in V. I. Lenin, *Collected Works* (Moscow; Progress Publishers), Vol. 28, 1965, p. 236.

5 In his "Chto delat'?" [What is to be done?] 1902, Lenin, *Polnoye sobraniye sochineniy,* Vol. 6, p. 127; in English, a slightly different translation than given by me, *Collected Works* (Moscow: Foreign Languages Publishing House), Vol. 5, 1961, p. 467.

6 Somewhat paraphrased by Merle Fainsod, "Soviet Communism," *International Encyclopedia of the Social Sciences,* Vol. 3, p. 106, on the basis of Trotsky's *Nashi politicheskiya zadachi* [Our political tasks] (Geneva: Published by the Russian Social-Democratic Party, 1904), p. 54.

7 Vladimir Bonch-Bruyevich, "Lenin o khudozhestvennoi literature" [Lenin

on fine fiction], *Tridtsat' dnei* [Thirty days], Moscow, January 1934, p. 18.

8 D. Shub, "Lenin, Bakunin, Tkachev," *Novoye Russkoye Slovo,* June 22, 1962; also D. Shub, *Politicheskiye deyateli Rossii (1850ykh-1920ykh gg.)* [Russia's political activists (the 1850s-the 1920s)] (New York: Published by *Novy Zhurnal,* 1969), Chapter II, pp. 54-100.

9 Lenin, *Polnoye sobraniye sochineniy,* Vol. 4, p. 223.

10 *Ibid.,* article "S chego nachat'?" [Where to begin?], Vol. 5, pp. 7-8. This is my translation. *Cf.* translation by J. Fineberg in *Collected Works of V. I. Lenin,* edited by Alexander Trachtenberg, Vol. IV, *The Iskra Period, 1900-1902,* Book I (New York: International Publishers, 1929), pp. 110–11.

11 *Ibid.*

12 *Ibid.*

13 For references to terror in "Chto delat'?" in Vol. 6 of Lenin's *Polnoye sobraniye sochineniy,* see in particular pp. 121, 173-75, and 180-81.

14 For this and other references by Lenin to terror in 1902, see *ibid.* Vol. 6, pp. 371, 375-76, 378, 380-84, 386-87, and 406; and Vol. 7, pp. 58-63, 251, and 359-62.

15 *Ibid.,* Vol. 7, p. 251.

16 *Ibid.,* Vol. 9, article "Samoderzhaviye i proletariat" [Autocracy and proletariat], pp. 129-30; originally published in *Vperyod* [Forward] Jan 4, 1905.

17 *Ibid.,* Vol. 10, pp. 137-38.

18 *Ibid.,* Vol. 11, p. 47.

19 *Ibid.,* Vol. 11, article "Ot oborony k napadeniyu" [From defense to attack], pp. 268-71; originally published in *Proletariy,* September 26, 1905.

20 *Ibid.,* Vol. 11, pp. 339-43; the Russian title of the instructions is "Zadachi otryadov revolyutsionnoi armii."

21 *Ibid.,* Vol. 13, p. 375; article "Uroki moskovskogo vosstahiya" [Lessons of the Moscow uprising], written in August 1906.

22 Valentinov, *Vstrechi s Leninym,* p. 75. Here I used my own translation. *Cf.* a somewhat different rendition in *Encounters With Lenin,* p. 42.

23 Shub, *Lenin,* p. 105.

24 Lenin, *op. cit.,* Vol. 16, pp. 438-42.

25 *Ibid.,* Vol. 22, p. 286.

26 *Ibid.,* Vol. 24, pp. 60-61.

27 Lenin's letter to Alexander G.
Shlyapnikov, in *Polnoye sobraniye
sochineiy*, Vol. 49, pp. 12-15.
28 In "Polozheniye i zadachi Sotsialisti-
cheskogo Internatsionala" in *Polnoye
sobraniye sochineniy*, Vol. 26, p. 41. In
English (in a somewhat different translation than used by me) see "The Position and Tasks of the Socialist International," *Collected Works*, Vol. 21,
1964, pp. 39-40.
29 In "Krakh II Internatsionala," *Polnoye sobraniye sochineniy*, Vol. 26, p.
212. In English (in a different translation than used by me) see "The Collapse of the Second International,"
Collected Works, Vol. 21, p. 208.

That the revolution of 1917 did not
make Lenin a pacifist, that until his
death in 1924 he continued to expect
and favor wars, but only those of his
own making or for his own purposes, is
clear from his writings of this latter period as well. A useful compendium of
such final-phase warlike statements is
V. Volgin, "V. Lenin o voine" [Lenin
on war], *Russkaya Mysl'*, June 17,
1971.

Chapter 12
Now Is the Time

1 Possony, *op. cit.*, pp. 173-84, based on
original Imperial German documents.
2 " 'We did stupid things in July,' Lenin
said later, in private conversations as
well as, so far as I remember, in a conference with German delegates about
the March events in Germany 1921."
Leon Trotsky, *Lenin* (New York: Min-
ton, Balch & Company, 1925), p. 89.
3 Robert Payne, *The Life and Death of
Lenin* (New York: Simon and Schuster, 1964), p. 336; also quoted as
"Aren't they getting ready to shoot
all of us?" in Leon Trotsky, *The History of the Russian Revolution* (New
York: Simon and Schuster, 1936), Volume Two, p. 93.
4 Shub, *Lenin*, p. 211.
5 Lenin, "O vragakh naroda" [About
the enemies of the people], *Pravda*
[Truth], Moscow, June 20, 1917.
6 *Polynoye sobraniye sochineniy*, Vol.
49, p. 444.
7 *Ibid.*, Vol. 34, pp. 20, 27-28, and
44–46, containing Lenin's writings of
August 1917.

8 *Ibid.*, Vol. 34, pp. 67, 94-97, and 174,
containing Lenin's writings of September 1917.
9 John Reed, *Ten Days That Shook the
World*, with a foreword by V. I. Lenin
and an introduction by Granville Hicks
(New York: The Modern Library,
1935), p. 125.
10 *Polnoye sobraniye sochineniy*, Vol. 35,
p. 125.
11 A. D. Naglovsky, "Lenin," in *Lenin:
vospominaniya i dokumenty* [Lenin:
reminiscences and documents] (London, Ontario, Canada: [Zarya Publishing House], 1969), p. 17. Naglovsky
knew Lenin, and worked with him,
since the underground days. His description of Dzerzhinsky is from his
first-hand acquaintance with the terror
chief as a fellow Soviet leader after
1917. Appointed the Soviets' first trade
envoy to Italy, Naglovsky broke with
the Communist government soon after
arriving in the West, where he remained for good. Moscow declared
him "the enemy of the people."
12 "Plekhanov o terrore" is reproduced
in *Polnoye sobraniye sochineniy*, Vol.
35, pp. 184-86.
13 *Ibid.*, Vol. 35, pp. 195-205. The Russian title is "Kak organizovat' sorev-
novaniye?" The instructions were
written by Lenin on January 6-9, 1918,
but remained top-secret for 11 years.
They were first published in *Pravda* of
January 20, 1929.
14 Quoted by Yu. Srechinsky in his article "*Leninskkiye normy*" [Lenin's
norms], *Novoye Russkoye Slovo*, July
15, 1972. Srechinsky notes that the
Latsis article was reprinted in *Pravda*
of December 25, 1918, and "to get into
Pravda such an article had to have approval of the [Party's] Central Committee headed by Lenin and on direct
orders" from the Committee and Lenin
"as a program declaration of the Party
and the government."
15 M. I. Latsis, *Chrezvychainyie komissii
po bor'be s kontr-revolyutsiei* [Extraor-
dinary commissions to fight counter-
revolution], (Moscow, 1921), quoted in
Roy A. Medvedev, *Let History Judge:
The Origins and Consequences of Stalinism* (New York: Alfred A. Knopf,
1971), p. 389.
16 G[eorgy] A. Solomon, *Lenin i yego*

semiya [Lenin and his family] (Paris: Imprimerie des Travailleurs Intellectuels, 1931), pp. 88-90.

17 W. S. Woytinsky, *Stormy Passage: A Personal History Through Two Russian Revolutions to Democracy and Freedom: 1905-1960* (New York: Vanguard Press, 1961), pp. 119-20.

18 In his "Vnimaniyu rabochikh" [Attention of workers], first printed in Gorky's newspaper *Novaya zhizn'* [New life], Petrograd, November 23, 1917; reproduced in Maxim Gorky, *Nesvoyevremennyie mysli, Stat'i 1917-1918 gg.* [Untimely thoughts, articles of 1917-1918], compilation, introduction, and notes by G. [Herman] Yermolayev (Paris: Editions de la Seine, 1971), pp. 111-13. Translations different from mine appear in the English version of that book, Herman Ermolaev, ed., *Untimely Thoughts; Essays on Revolution, Culture and the Bolsheviks 1917-1918* (New York: Paul S. Eriksson, Inc., 1968), pp. 87-88; also in Payne, *op. cit.*, pp. 408-09. The second sentence is actually longer than I present it in my text. In the translation by Ermolaev (Yermolayev) it reads: "Lenin is a 'leader' *and* a Russian nobleman, not without certain psychological traits of this extinct class, and therefore he considers himself justified in performing with the Russian people a cruel experiment which is doomed to failure beforehand."

19 Naglovsky, *op. cit.*, p. 18.

20 "Ocherednyie zadachi sovetskoi vlasti" [Next tasks of the Soviet government], in *Polnoye sobraniye sochineniy*, Vol. 36, pp. 195-96.

21 *Ibid.*, Vol. 36, pp. 214-15.

22 *Ibid.*, Vol. 36, p. 369.

23 *Ibid.*, Vol. 50, p. 106.

24 *Ibid.*, Vol. 36, p. 482.

25 *Ibid.*, Vol. 36, p. 503.

26 *Ibid.*

27 For Lenin's statements and telegrams in August 1918, see *ibid.*, Vol. 37, pp. 39-40 and Vol. 50, pp. 142-45. The first official decree of the Council of People's Commissars establishing concentration camps was dated September 5, 1918 (see *Dekrety sovetskoi vlasti* [Decrees of the Soviet government], Moscow, 1964, Volume 3, p. 291).

28 "Pis'mo k amerikanskim rabochim,"

in *Polnoye sobraniye sochineniy*, Vol. 37, pp. 59-60.

29 *Ibid.*

30 Fischer, *op. cit.*, p. 283, quoting Angelica Balabanova on Krupskaya's tears over Dora Kaplan's fate, and Kaplan's executioner on when (September 3, 1918) and how he had shot the woman.

31 *Polnoye sobraniye sochineniy*, Vol. 50, p. 178.

32 *Ibid.*, Vol. 37, pp. 254-55.

33 *Ibid.*, Vol. 37, pp. 173-74.

34 *Ibid.*, Vol. 37, p. 194.

Chapter 13
Thought Waves of Hatred

1 Occasionally Lenin hoped that all the major nations of the West would stage an immediate revolution to help the Soviets. As early as January 1918 he said that his Russian Communists had to carry on a mere holding operation until "the German, the Frenchman and the Englishman will complete it—and socialism will triumph." See Lenin's report on the work of the Council of People's Commissars delivered January 24, 1918, at the Third Congress of the Soviets, in *Polnoye sobraniye sochineniy*, Vol. 35, p. 279; in English (in a somewhat different translation than used by me), *Collected Works*, Vol. 26, 1964, p. 472.

2 *Polnoye sobraniye sochineniy*, Vol. 37, p. 434.

3 *Ibid.*, p. 497.

4 *Ibid.*, Vol. 38, p. 388.

5 *Ibid.*, Vol. 39, pp. 113-14.

6 *Ibid.*, pp. 136-37.

7 *Ibid.*, pp. 177-80.

8 *Ibid.*, pp. 183-84.

9 *Ibid.*, pp. 417-18.

10 *Ibid.*, p. 404.

11 *Ibid.*, Vol. 40, p. 57.

12 *Ibid.*, pp. 100-01.

13 *Ibid.*, Vol. 44, pp. 88-89.

14 Mark Weinbaum, "Otkrytoye pis'mo general'nomu sekretaryu Ob' edinennykh Natsiy gospodinu U Tanu" [An open letter to the Secretary General of the United Nations, Mr. U Thant], *Novoye Russkoye Slovo*, April 15, 1970.

15 Some biographers still doubt that Inessa Armand was Lenin's mistress, but Bertram D. Wolfe, "Lenin and Inessa Armand," *Slavic Review*, New

York, Vol. 22, No. 1 (March 1963), pp. 96-114, convincingly proves the historical fact of the Lenin-Armand intimacy. See also P. Berlin, "Inessa Armand," *Novoye Russkoye Slovo,* September 17, 1954; and P. Margushin, "Inessa—lyubovnitsa Lenina" [Inessa—Lenin's mistress], *ibid.,* June 28, 1970.

16 H. G. Wells, *Russia In the Shadows* (New York: George H. Doran Company, 1921), p. 155. Other editions of this book, also certain newspaper articles and interviews by Wells preceding the book, give slightly different versions of his statements on Lenin.

17 Clare Sheridan, *Naked Truth* (New York: Blue Ribbon Books, originally published by Harper & Brothers, 1928), Part Six, "Russia," pp. 149-223.

18 *Polnoye sobraniye sochineniy,* Vol. 45, p. 86; in English (in a translation somewhat different from mine) see *Collected Works,* Vol. 33, 1966, p. 279.

19 Maxim Gorky, *Days With Lenin* (New York: International Publishers, [1932]), p. 52. Soviet propagandists have for a long time endeavored to present Lenin's violent reaction to music as a particularly noble evidence of his "humanism." Typical is An. Tarasenkov, "Svet gumanizma" [The light of humanism], *Literaturnaya gazeta,* Moscow, February 15, 1955.

20 *Polnoye sobraniye sochineniy,* Vol. 43, p. 234.

21 Quoted by Leonid Gendlin (a recent émigré from the Soviet Union), "O zazhivo pogrebennykh, unizhennykh i oskorblennykh" [About those buried alive, humiliated, and insulted], *Novoye Russkoye Slovo,* August 13, 1972.

22 *Polnoye sobraniye sochineniy,* Vol. 45, p. 9.

23 *Ibid.,* pp. 190-91.

24 Angelica Balabanoff, *Impressions of Lenin,* translated by Isotta Cesari (Ann Arbor: The University of Michigan Press, 1964), Chapter XII, "Ethics and Communism," pp. 143 ff.

25 Here I took the liberty of slightly paraphrasing Charles Malamuth's translation of Trotsky's phrase. In Malamuth's rendition it reads: "And it was not he who created the machine, but the machine that created him." In my opinion Trotsky meant *apparat* rather than *mashina;* quite possibly, in Trotsky's original Russian manuscript, the word *apparat* was used instead of *mashina.* See Leon Trotsky, *Stalin, An Appraisal of the Man and His Influence,* edited and translated by Charles Malamuth (New York: Harper & Brothers, 1946), "Introduction," p. xv.

Chapter 14
Trotsky: Target of Boomerang

1 Outstanding among the biographies of Trotsky, is the scholarly (although somewhat too partial to the man) trilogy by Isaac Deutscher (New York and London: Oxford University Press):

The Prophet Armed, Trotsky: 1879-1921, published in 1954.

The Prophet Unarmed, Trotsky: 1921-1929, published in 1959.

The Prophet Outcast, Trotsky: 1929-1940, published in 1963.

My main sources on Trotsky's attitude to, and activities in, terror were:

L[ev] Trotsky, *Kak vooruzhalas' revolyutsiya* [How the revolution armed itself] (Moscow: Supreme Military Editorial Council; Vol. I, 1923; Vol. II, books 1 and 2, 1924; Vol. III, book 1, 1924, book 2, 1925).

Leon Trotsky, *Terrorism and Communism: A Reply to Karl Kautsky,* with foreword by Max Shachtman and introduction to the second English edition by Leon Trotsky (The University of Michigan Press: Ann Arbor Paperbacks for the Study of Communism and Marxism, 1961).

John Dewey, chairman of the Preliminary Commission of Inquiry, *The Case of Leon Trotsky: Report of Hearings on the Charges Made Against Him in the Moscow Trials* (New York and London: Harper & Brothers, 1937). The hearings were held April 10 to 17, 1937, at Coyoacan, Mexico. References to this book in my text are given as *The Case of Leon Trotsky.*

Jan M. Meijer, editor and annotator, *The Trotsky Papers, 1917-1922,* Vol. I, 1917-1919 (The Hague: Mouton & Co., 1964); Vol. II, 1920-1922 (The Hague: Mouton, 1971).

I have also examined certain folders of the Trotsky Archives at Harvard University.

For the man who on Stalin's orders killed Trotsky, see Isaac Don Levine, *The Mind of an Assassin* (New York: Farrar, Straus and Cudahy, 1959).

2 *The Case of Leon Trotsky,* p. 15.
3 *Ibid.,* p. 489.
4 *Ibid.*
5 *Ibid.,* p. 490.
6 Leon Trotsky, *1905,* transl. by Anya Bostock (New York: Vintage Books, a Division of Random House, 1972), Chapter 31, "My Speech Before the Court," pp. 384-400.
7 *The Case of Leon Trotsky,* p. 490.
8 *Ibid.,* p. 491.
9 *Ibid.,* p. 492.
10 *Kak vooruzhalas' revolyutsiya,* Vol. I, p. 8.
11 *Ibid.,* p. 15.
12 *Ibid.,* pp. 61 and 63-64.
13 *Ibid.,* p. 70.
14 *Ibid.,* pp. 232-33 and 151.
15 *Ibid.,* p. 158.
16 *Ibid.,* pp. 158-59.
17 *Ibid.,* p. 206.
18 *Ibid.,* Vol. II, book 1, p. 253.
19 *Ibid.,* Vol. II, book 2, p. 7.
20 *Ibid.,* Vol. I, p. 235.
21 *Ibid.,* pp. 325-26.
22 *Ibid.,* p. 336.
23 *Ibid.,* p. 356.
24 *Ibid.,* p. 358.
25 *Ibid.,* Vol. II, book 1, pp. 135 ff.
26 *Ibid.,* Vol. II, book 2, p. 292.
27 *Ibid.,* p. 142.
28 *The Case of Leon Trotsky,* p. 492.
29 *Kak vooruzhalas' revolyutsiya,* Vol. I, pp. 295-96.
30 Trotsky, *Terrorism and Communism,* pp. 48-59 and *passim.*
31 *Ibid.,* p. 58.
32 *Kak vooruzhalas' revolyutsiya,* Vol. III, book 2, p. 78.
33 *Ibid.,* Vol. III, book 1, p. 87.
34 *The Case of Leon Trotsky,* pp. 492-93.

Chapter 15
Stalin's Archipelago

1 On the Stalinist period in Soviet terror, in addition to the pertinent parts of the already cited Solzhenitsyn's *The Gulag Archipelago,* see:

Roy A. Medvedev, *Let History Judge: The Origins and Consequences of Stalinism,* transl. by Colleen Taylor and edited by David Joravsky and Georges Haupt (New York: Alfred A. Knopf, 1971). Unfortunately, while blaming Stalin for terror, the author tends to exonerate Lenin.

Robert Conquest, *The Great Terror: Stalin's Purge of the Thirties,* revised edition (New York: The Macmillan Company, 1973). One of the best accounts and analyses of the Stalinist terror.

An earlier, thorough, and well-documented study is David J. Dallin and Boris I. Nicolaevsky, *Forced Labor in Soviet Russia* (New Haven: Yale University Press, 1947). More embracive geographically is Alexander Dallin and George W. Breslauer, *Political Terror in Communist Systems* (Stanford University Press, 1970).

Among the innumerable individual memoirs by survivors of the Stalinist terror, three of the latest and most impressive are:

Alexander Vardy, *Das Eisloch* [The Icehole], transl. from the Russian by Josef Hahn (Stuttgart: Henry Goverts Verlag, 1966).

Joseph Berger, *Nothing But the Truth* (New York: The John Day Company, 1971).

Alexander Dolgun with Patrick Watson, *Alexander Dolgun's Story: An American in the Gulag* (New York: Knopf, 1975).

Much of my knowledge and understanding of the Stalinist terror came from my acquaintance and long talks, over the years, with numerous survivors of the Soviet concentration camps. Among others, I am indebted to Alexander Vardy for the recollections he so readily and fully shared with me during our many get-togethers in his Munich home.

2 N. Otradin, "Po ostrovam 'Arkhipelaga' " [On the islands of the 'Archipelago'], *Novoye Russkoye Slovo,* March 3, 1974.

3 For biographies of Stalin, besides the already cited Trotsky, *Stalin,* and the relevant parts of Wolfe, *Three Who Made a Revolution,* see:

Boris Souvarine, *Stalin: A Critical Survey of Bolshevism,* translated by C. L. R. James (New York: Alliance

Book Corporation, Longmans, Green & Co., 1939).

Adam B. Ulam, *Stalin: The Man and His Era* (New York: The Viking Press, 1973).

Robert C. Tucker, *Stalin As Revolutionary, 1879-1929: A Study in History and Personality* (paperback, New York: Norton 1974).

4 A. Sharagin (pseudonym of Georgi A. Ozerov, one of the victims), *Tupolevskaya sharaga* [Tupolev's secret camp-laboratory], (Frankfurt, West Germany: Published by the Posey House, [1971]), *passim.*

5 John Barron, *KGB* (paperback, New York: Bantam Books, 1974).

6 Despite the historical importance of Beria's life and activity, there is not a single comprehensive biography of him in any language. The book by Thaddeus Wittlin, *Commissar: The Life and Death of Lavrenty Pavlovich Beria* (New York: Macmillan, 1972), notwithstanding its size—566 pages— is a complete failure.

7 How close in those March days of 1953 Beria came to seize all power in the Soviet Union, may be seen from Harrison E. Salisbury, *American in Russia* (New York: Harper & Brothers, 1955), Chapter X, "The Seventy-five Hours," particularly pp. 170-72.

8 George F. Kennan, *Memoirs: 1925-1950* (Boston: Little, Brown, 1967), pp. 503-04.

9 The fullest story of the slaves' uprising at Vorkuta is Joseph Scholmer, *Vorkuta,* translated from the German by Robert Kee (London: Weidenfeld and Nicolson, 1954).

10 *The New York Times,* July 5, 1974, the Op-Ed Page, accompanied by Arthur Miller's short essay, "Sakharov, Détente and Liberty." For the role of Soviet courts as instruments of terror in the current Brezhnev period, see Telford Taylor, *Courts of Terror: Soviet Criminal Justice and Jewish Emigration* (New York: Knopf, 1976).

Chapter 16,
Hitler's Holocaust

1 Of the vast literature on Hitler and his terror, I select the following titles (others are given in the course of the notes):

Hannah Arendt, *The Origins of Totalitarianism* (New York: Harcourt, Brace & World, Inc., 1966). The last one-third of this book is particularly valuable.

Lucy S. Dawidowicz, *The War Against the Jews, 1933-1945* (New York: Holt, Rinehart & Winston, 1975).

Raul Hilberg, *The Destruction of the European Jews* (Chicago: Quadrangle Books, 1961).

Gerald Reitlinger, *The Final Solution: The Attempt to Exterminate the Jews of Europe, 1939-1945,* second revised and augmented edition (South Brunswick, New Jersey: Thomas Yoseloff, 1968).

Gitta Sereny, *Into That Darkness: From Mercy Killing to Mass Murder* (New York: McGraw-Hill, 1974).

My many conversations with survivors of the Nazi concentration camps were also of help.

2 Bella Fromm, *Blood and Banquets: A Berlin Social Diary* (New York: Harper & Brothers, 1942), p. 31. *Cf.* William E. Dodd. Jr, and Martha Dodd, eds., *Ambassador Dodd's Diary, 1933-1938,* with an introduction by Charles E. Beard (New York: Harcourt, Brace, 1941), *passim.*

3 Hans Peter Bleuel, *Sex and Society in Nazi Germany,* edited and with a preface by Heinrich Fraenkel, translated from the German by J. Maxwell Brownjohn (paperback, New York: Bantam Books, 1974), pp. 217-24 and 271-79.

4 Fromm, *op. cit.,* p. 187.

5 Roger Manvell and Heinrich Fraenkel, *Dr. Goebbels: His Life and Death* (paperback, New York: Pyramid Books, 1961), pp. 121-22.

6 Rita Thalmann and Emmanuel Feinermann, *Crystal Night: November 9 and 10, 1938* (New York: Coward, McCann & Geoghegan, 1974).

Chapter 17
The Final Solution

1 Joachim C. Fest, *Hitler,* translated from the German by Richard and Clara Winston (New York: Harcourt Brace Jovanovich, 1973). p. 680.

2 For one family's experience in the Nazi camps, see Alexander Donat, *The Holocaust Kingdom: A Memoir* (New

York: Holt, Rinehart and Winston, 1965). I am also indebted to William Donat, the son, who was a student in my classes at Colgate University 1956-60, for his verbal reminiscences of his family's experiences.

3 A. Anatoli (Kuznetsov), *Babi Yar: A Document in the Form of a Novel,* translated by David Floyd (New York: Farrar, Straus and Giroux, 1970), p. 97.

4 For a horrifying example, see Curzio Malaparte, *Kaputt,* translated from the Italian by Cesare Foligno (New York: E. P. Dutton & Co., Inc., 1946), Chapter XIV, "The Soroca Girls," pp. 288-300.

5 Isaiah Trunk, *Judenrat: The Jewish Councils in Eastern Europe Under Nazi Occupation* (New York: Macmillan, 1972).

6 Joseph Wechsberg, "The Outsider," *The New Yorker,* January 14, 1974, p. 50.

Chapter 18
Mao's Muzzle

1 For the preparation of my two chapters on Mao's terror I depended, among my other sources, on my many interviews in 1968 with refugees and other knowledgeable persons in Istanbul, New Delhi, Katmandu, Colombo, Singapore, Phnom Penh, Hong Kong, Taipei, Seoul, Tokyo, and other eastern cities.

For official Chinese Communist statements on terror, I used *Chinese Communist World Outlook: A Handbook of Chinese Communist Statements, the Public Record of a Militant Ideology,* U. S. State Department, Bureau of Intelligence and Research, June 1962 (Washington: U. S. Government Printing Office, Department of State Publication 7379, Far Eastern Series 112, released September 1962).

For facts and views on the Red Chinese terror of the earlier phase by Western specialists, see Suzanne Labin, *The Anthill: The Human Condition in Communist China,* translated from the French by Edward Fitzgerald (New York: Praeger, 1960); and of the later phase (Cultural Revolution), Robert S. Elegant, *Mao's Great Revolution* (New York and Cleveland: The World

Publishing Company, 1971); and of both phases, the files of *The New York Times, The Washington Post, The Christian Science Monitor, Time, Newsweek, The Manchester Guardian,* and other major publications.

On Mao's theory of terror as warfare in the countryside, see Samuel B. Griffith, *Mao Tse-tung: On Guerrilla Warfare* (New York: Praeger, 1961).

Of paramount importance is James L. Walker, *The Human Cost of Communism in China* (Washington, D. C.: U. S. Government Printing Office, 1971).

2 Karl A. Wittfogel, "Social Revolution in China," *The Alternative,* Bloomington, Indiana, December 1973, p. 16 and *passim.*

3 "On the People's Democratic Dictatorship," as quoted in *Chinese Communist World Outlook,* p. 4.

4 "Report of an Investigation into the Peasant Movement in Hunan," *ibid.*

5 "On the Correct Handling of Contradictions Among the People," *ibid.,* p. 76.

6 "A Basic Summary of the Victorious Experience of the Chinese People's Revolution," *ibid.,* p. 11.

7 Henry R. Lieberman, "Mao's China-Wide Purge Claiming Many Victims: Thousands of Arrests and Executions Are Reported in Reign of Terror," *The New York Times,* March 18, 1951; Robert Guillain, "Revolution in China: Terror As a Policy," *The Manchester Guardian Weekly,* December 13, 1951.

8 "China: High Tide of Terror," *Time,* March 5, 1956, p. 27.

9 *Ibid.,* pp. 28-29.

10 *Chinese Communist World Outlook,* p. 75.

11 Chou En-lai, report to National People's Congress, June 26, 1957, *ibid.,* p. 76.

12 Fred Hampson, "2 Chinese, Denouncing Reds, Leap to Deaths," Associated Press dispatch from Hong Kong, April 21, 1952.

13 "Communist China Campaign Against Suicide Revealed," Associated Press dispatch from Hong Kong, July 22, 1954.

Chapter 19
Three Innovations

1 For old China's sense of the family, see Dennis Bloodworth, *The Chinese Looking Glass* (New York: Farrar, Straus and Giroux, 1967), Chapter 10, "The Tribal Custom," pp. 101-11. I am indebted to Mr. Bloodworth for the time and insights he gave me during our meeting in Singapore in the summer of 1968.

2 *Cf.* Bloodworth, *ibid.*, p. 106: "For a child to testify against a parent was a criminal offense in Confucian China."

3 Henry R. Lieberman, "Canton Radio Airs Death Trial of 23," dispatch from Hong Kong, *The New York Times,* April 26, 1951; "China: 'Kill Nice!' ", *Time,* May 21, 1951; Graham Peck, "China: Lynchings for a Purpose," *The Reporter,* New York, September 4, 1951; Peggy Durdin, "They're Ruling China by Mass Murder," *The Saturday Evening Post,* October 13, 1951; Robert Guillain, "Revolution in China: Public 'Confessions' and Executions," *The Manchester Guardian Weekly,* November 29, 1951; "10,000 See Red China Execute 2," Reuters dispatch from Peking, *The Washington Post,* April 6, 1960; Richard Hughes, "Mao Makes the Trials Run on Time," *The New York Times Magazine,* August 23, 1970.

4 "China: The First Million," *Time,* June 11, 1951; R. H. Shackford, "2 Million Slain: Peiping Brags About Mass Executions," dispatch from London, *New York World-Telegram & Sun,* November 1, 1952; "Red China's Press Shows Millions Slain," dispatch from the United Nations, New York, *Denver Post,* June 11,1957. Other sources on the Red Chinese self-revelations are given in the text of this chapter.

5 Walker, *The Human Cost of Communism in China* (previously cited), pp. 14-15 and Table, "Casualties to Communism in China," on p. 16; also *passim.*

Chapter 20
Wanton Romantics:
Guevara, Debray, Marighella

1 Biographies and evaluations of, and reminiscences about, Guevara are:

Daniel James, *Ché Guevera: A Biography* (New York: Stein and Day, [1969]).

Hilda Gadea, *Ernesto: A Memoir of Ché Guevara,* transl. from the Spanish by Carmen Molina and Walter I. Bradbury (Garden City: Doubleday, 1972).

Ricardo Rojo, *My Friend Ché,* transl. from the Spanish by Julian Casart (New York: Dial Press, 1968).

Martin Ebon, *Ché: The Making of a Legend* (New York: New American Library, [1969]).

Léo Savage, *Ché Guevara: The Failure of a Revolutionary,* transl. from the French by Raoul Frémont (Englewood Cliffs, N. J.: Prentice-Hall, [1973]).

Michael Lowy, *The Marxism of Ché Guevara: Philosophy, Economics, and Revolutionary Warfare,* transl. by Brian Pearce (New York: Monthly Review Press, [1973]).

Guevara's writings:

Guerrilla Warfare (New York: Monthly Review Press, 1961, and Harmondsworth: Penguin, 1969).

"Guerrilla Warfare: A Method," in John Gerassi, ed., *Venceremos!* (New York: Simon and Schuster, 1968).

"Message to the Tricontinental," in Irving Louis Horowitz, Josué Castro, and John Gerassi, eds., *Latin American Radicalism* (New York: Random House, [1969]).

Daniel James, comp., *The Complete Bolivian Diaries of Ché Guevara and Other Captured Documents* (New York: Stein and Day, [1968], and London: Allen & Unwin, 1968).

Bolivian Diary [of] Ernesto Ché Guevara, introduction by Fidel Castro, transl. by Carlos P. Hansen and Andrew Sinclair (London: Cape; Lorrimer Publishing, 1968).

Ernesto Guevara, *Episodes of the Revolutionary War* (New York: International Publishers, [1968]).

Ernesto Guevara, *Reminiscences of the Cuban Revolutionary War,* transl. by Victoria Ortiz (New York: Monthly Review Press, [1968]).

Jay Mallin, ed., *Ché Guevara on Revolution; a Documentary Overview* (Coral Gables, Florida: University of Miami Press, [1969]).

2 James, *op. cit.,* p. 160.

3 A sound analysis of the Guevara-

Nechayev affinity is in James, *op. cit.*, pp. 308 and 314-16.

4 *Ibid.*, p. 89.

5 The parallel between Trotsky and Guevara is ably drawn by James, pp. 311-12.

6 Marta Rojas and Mirta Rodríguez Calderon, ed., *Tania: The Unforgettable Guerrilla* (New York: Random House, 1971). Originally published in Spanish (Havana: Instituto del Libro, 1970).

7 Leo Huberman and Paul M. Sweezy, eds., *Régis Debray and the Latin American Revolution* (New York: Monthly Review Press, 1968); Régis Debray, *Revolution in the Revolution?* (New York: Grove Press, Inc., 1967); Régis Debray, *Strategy for Revolution*, edited by Robin Blackburn (New York: Monthly Review Press, 1970); Régis Debray, *Prison Writings*, transl. from the French by Rosemary Sheed (New York: Random House, 1973; London: Allen Lane, 1973); Jean Paul Sartre, preface, *Le Procès Régis Debray* [Paris: F. Maspero, 1968]; John L. Hess, "New Left's Philosopher-Hero: Régis Debray," *The New York Times*, December 25,1970.

8 James, *op. cit.*, p. 254.

9 Debray, *Strategy for Revolution*, p. 7.

10 J. Camara Ferreira, *Carlos Marighella* (Havana: Tricontinental, 1970); Carlos Marighella, *Minimanual of the Urban Guerrilla* (Havana: Tricontinental, 1970); Carlos Marighella, *For the Liberation of Brazil*, transl. by John Butt and Rosemary Sheed (Harmondsworth: Penguin, 1971); Baumann, *op. cit.*, pp. 6, 20-28, 75, 77 and 80; Robert Moss, "Marighella: Letter from South America," *Encounter*, Vol. 39, No. 1 (July 1972), pp. 40-43; Robert Derval Evans, "Brazil: the Road Back from Terrorism," *Conflict Studies*, No. 47, July 1974.

11 Lionel Rotcage, "Going for a Ride with Brazil's Guerrilleros: The War in Rio," translated and reprinted from *Le Nouvel Observateur*, Paris, by *Atlas*, New York, August 1970, p. 51.

Chapter 21
The Morbid Tango

1 Kenneth F. Johnson, *Argentina's Mosaic of Discord, 1966-1968*, in collaboration with Maria Mercedes Fuentes and Philip L. Paris (Washington, D.C.: Institute for the Comparative Study of Political Systems, [1969]); Jeane J. Kirkpatrick, *Leader and Vanguard in Mass Society: A Study of Peronist Argentina* (Cambridge, Mass.: Massachusetts Institute of Technology Press, [1971]); Kenneth F. Johnson, "Peronism: The Final Gamble," *Conflict Studies*, No. 42, January 1974; same author, "Guerrilla Politics in Argentina," *Conflict Studies*, No. 63, October 1975.

For this chapter I talked to a number of well-informed Argentinians visiting the United States and Europe, but also depended on the most enlightening "Pis'ma iz Argentiny" [Letters from Argentina] by Irina Astrau of Buenos Aires, periodically published in the New York *Novoye Russkoye Slovo* throughout the turbulent 1970s. Excellent coverage of terrorism in Argentina has been given by *The New York Times* and other major publications in North America. Chapters on Argentinian terrorism can be found in almost every recent book on political violence cited by me in the notes so far.

For general discussion of Latin American guerrillas, see in particular:

Carol Edler Baumann, *The Diplomatic Kidnappings* (The Hague: Martinus Nijhoff, 1973), Chapter VI, "Latin American Kidnappings: Assassinations and Terrorism," pp. 94-110.

Georgie Anne Geyer, "Latin America: The Rise of a New Non-Communist Left," *The Saturday Review*, New York, July 22, 1967.

Alexander Craig, "Urban Guerrilla in Latin America," *Survey*, London, Vol. 17, no. 3 (80) (Summer 1971), pp. 112-28.

Robert Moss, "Urban Guerrillas in Latin America," *Conflict Studies*, No. 8, October 1970.

2 On an early phase of Peronista terrorism, see a report translated and reprinted from Cuba's official periodical, *Granma*, in the New York *Atlas* for March 1971, pp. 33-35, under the title "Long Live Cuba, Long Live Perón."

Chapter 22
Heirs to Tupac-Amaru

1 Published in the United States as *Surviving the Long Night* (New York: Vanguard Press, 1974). See also Carlos Nunez, *The Tupamaros: Urban Guerrillas of Uruguay* (New York: Times Change Press, 1970), and Robert Moss, "Uruguay: Terrorism Versus Democracy," *Conflict Studies*, No. 14, August 1971.

2 Robert J. Alexander, *The Bolivian National Revolution* (New Brunswick, New Jersey: Rutgers University Press, 1958); Inti Peredo, *Guerrilla Warfare in Bolivia Is Not Dead: It Has Just Begun* [Havana, 1968]; Edgar Millares Reyes, *Las Guerrillas: Teoría y práctica* (Sacre, Bolivia: [Impr. Universitaria], 1968); Yuri A. Fadeyev, *Revolyutisiya i kontrrevolyutsiya v Bolivii* (Moscow: Nauka, 1969). Press reports in the 1970s.

3 Robert Moss, "The Santiago Model—1, Revolution Within Democracy?", and "The Santiago Model—2, Polarisation of Politics," *Conflict Studies*, Nos. 31 and 32, January 1973. James F. Petras and Morris H. Morley, *How Allende Fell: A Study in U.S.-Chilean Relations* (Nottingham, England: Spokesman Books, 1974); Armando Uribe Arce, *The Black Book of American Intervention in Chile,* transl. from the Spanish by Jonathan Casart (Boston: Beacon Press, [1975]). Press reports, 1973-76.

Chapter 23
Siempre la Violencia!

1 Kenneth F. Johnson, "Guatemala: From Terrorism to Terror," *Conflict Studies*, No. 23, May 1972.

2 Pablo González Casanova, *Democracy in Mexico*, transl. by Danielle Salti (New York: Oxford University Press, 1970); Kenneth F. Johnson, *Mexican Democracy: A Critical View* (Boston: Allyn and Bacon, [1971]); Martin C. Needler, *Politics and Society in Mexico* (Albuquerque: University of New Mexico Press, [1971]). Press reports of the early and middle 1970s.

3 Luigi R. Einaudi, *Revolution from Within? Military Rule in Peru Since 1968* (Santa Monica, Calif.: Rand Corporation, 1971); Ricardo Pumaruna-Letts, *Pérou: révolution socialiste ou caricature de révolution?* transl. from the Spanish by Jacques-Francois Bonaldi (Paris: F. Maspero, 1971); David Scott Palmer, *"Revolution from Above": Military Government and Popular Participation in Peru, 1968-1972* (Ithaca, New York: Cornell University Press, 1973). Press reports of the 1960s-70s.

4 U. S. Department of Defense, "Soldiers, Guerrillas and Politics in Colombia," Report R-630-ARPA, December 1971; Walter J. Broderick, *Camilo Torres: A Biography of the Priest-Guerrillero* (New York: Doubleday, 1975).

5 Leo B. Lott, *Venezuela and Paraguay: Political Modernity and Tradition in Conflict* (New York: Holt, Rinehart and Winston, [1971]); José A. Silva Michelena, *The Illusion of Democracy in Dependent Nations* (Cambridge, Mass.: M.I.T. Press, [1971]).

6 Manuel Cordero Reyes, *Nicaragua under Somoza: To the Governments and People of America* (San Salvador: [Imprenta Funes], 1944); R. E. Leshchiner, *Nikaragua* (Moscow: Mysl', 1965), in Russian. Press reports of the 1960s and '70s.

7 Leslie F. Manigat, *Haiti of the Sixties, Object of International Concern; a Tentative Global Analysis of the Potentially Explosive Situation of a Crisis Country in the Caribbean* (Washington, D. C.: Washington Center of Foreign Policy Research, [1964]). Press reports of the 1970s.

8 Dan Kurzman, *Santo Domingo: Revolt of the Damned* (New York: Putnam, [1965]); Juan Bosch, *The Unfinished Experiment: Democracy in the Dominican Republic* (London: Pall Mall Press, 1966); Carlos Maria Guitiérrez, *The Dominican Republic: Rebellion and Repression* (New York: Monthly Review Press, [1972]).

9 Robert W. Anderson, *Party Politics in Puerto Rico* (Stanford University Press, 1965); Henry Wells, *The Modernization of Puerto Rico: A Political Study of Changing Values and Institutions* (Cambridge, Mass.: Harvard University Press, 1969); press reports of the 1970s; Brian Crozier, "Soviet Pres-

sures in the Caribbean,'' *Conflict Studies,* No. 35, May 1973.

Chapter 24
Fanon and the Black Panthers

1 David Caute, *Fanon* (London: Fontana, Collins, 1970).

Peter Geismar, *Fanon* (New York: Dial Press, 1971).

Irene L. Gendzier, *Frantz Fanon: A Critical Study* (New York: Pantheon Books, a Division of Random House, 1973).

B. Marie Perinbam, ''Fanon and the Revolutionary Peasantry—the Algerian Case,'' *The Journal of Modern African Studies,* 1973, pp. 427-45.

2 The American editions of Fanon's four books were published in New York by Grove Press, the first one in 1967, the second and the fourth in 1968, and the third in 1969.

3 Of the vast literature on the Black Panthers, the following is a selected list (other titles are given in this chapter's subsequent notes):

Earl Anthony, *Picking Up the Gun: A Report on the Black Panthers* (New York: Dial Press, 1970).

Michael J. Arlen, *An American Verdict* (Garden City: Doubleday, 1973).

Sara Blackburn, ed., *White Justice: Black Experience Today in America's Courtrooms* (New York: Harper & Row, 1971).

Paul Chevigny, *Cops and Rebels: A Study of Provocation* (New York: Pantheon Books, 1972).

The Collective Autobiography of the New York 21 (New York: Random House, 1971).

Erik H. Erikson, *In Search of Common Ground: Conversations with Erik H. Erikson and Huey P. Newton,* introduced by Kai T. Erikson (New York: Norton, [1973]).

Philip S. Foner, ed. *The Black Panthers Speak* (Philadelphia and New York: J. B. Lippincott Company, 1970). Includes the manifesto of the Party and an extensive record of the Panthers' program.

Donald Freed, *Agony in New Haven: the Trial of Bobby Seale, Ericka Higgins and the Black Panther Party* (New York: Simon and Schuster, 1973).

James McEvoy and Abraham Miller, eds., *Black Power and Student Rebellion,* paperback (Belmont, Calif.: Wadsworth Publishing Company, Inc., 1969).

Chuck Moore (as told to), *I Was a Black Panther,* (paperback, Garden City: Doubleday, 1970).

Gilbert Moore, *A Special Rage* (New York: Harper & Row, 1971).

Don A. Schanche, *The Panther Paradox: A Liberal's Dilemma* (New York: David McKay Company, Inc., 1970).

Bobby Seale, *Seize the Time: The Story of the Black Panther Party and Huey P. Newton* (New York: Random House, 1970).

Gail Sheehy, *Panthermania: The Clash of Black Against Black in One American City* (New York: Harper & Row, 1971).

Roy Wilkins and Ramsay Clark, chairmen, *Search and Destroy, a Report by the Commission of Inquiry into the Black Panthers and the Police* (New York: Metropolitan Applied Research Center, 1973).

4 Huey P. Newton's best-known works are:

To Die for the People, introduction by Franz Schurmann (New York: Random House, 1972).

Revolutionary Suicide, with the assistance of J. Herman Blake (New York: Harcourt Brace Jovanovich, 1973).

5 Eldridge Cleaver's most important works are:

Soul on Ice, with an introduction by Maxwell Geismar (New York: McGraw-Hill Book Company, 1968).

Post-Prison Writings and Speeches, edited by Robert Scheer (New York: Random House, 1969).

6 Edward Jay Epstein, ''A Reporter At Large; The Panthers and the Police: A Pattern of Genocide?'', *The New Yorker,* February 13, 1971, p. 45 ff.; ''Department of Amplification,'' exchange between Edward Kosner and E. J. Epstein, *ibid.,* May 8, 1971, p. 125.

7 *New Left Notes,* Chicago, April 4, 1969, p. 3.

8 Kirkpatrick, *SDS* (New York: Random House, 1973). p. 590.

9 Bart Mills, "A Show-Biz Saint Grows Up, or, Whatever Happened to Jean Seberg?", *The New York Times,* June 16, 1974, Art and Leisure Section, pp. 17 and 34.
10 Merrill Panitt, "America Out of Focus," *TV Guide,* February 5, 1972, p. 29.
11 Lee Lockwood, *Conversations with Eldridge Cleaver, Algiers* (New York: McGraw-Hill, 1970).
12 Eldridge Cleaver, "Why I Left the U.S. And Why I Am Returning," *The New York Times,* November 18, 1975, Op-Ed Page.
13 Tom Buckley, "Black Political Leaders Taking Closer Look at Power," *The New York Times,* February 5, 1974, p. 39.
14 Andrew H. Malcolm, "Kansas Hometown Baffled by Violent End to Life of Marx Essex," and Everett R. Holles, "Navy Co-Workers Recall Marked Change in Essex," *The New York Times,* January 11, 1973; John Kifner, "Details of New Orleans Shootout Emerge, but Two Crucial Questions Remain," *ibid.,* January 15, 1973.

Chapter 25
The Weathermen

1 For this chapter, as well as the next one, my main source was the definitive work on the Students for a Democratic Society and the Weathermen by Kirkpatrick Sale, *SDS* (New York: Random House, 1973).

Other sources were: Harold Jacobs, comp., *Weatherman* [Berkeley: Ramparts Press, 1971]; Susan Stern, *With the Weathermen: The Personal Journal of a Revolutionary Woman* (New York: Doubleday, 1975); U. S. Senate, 94th Congress, 1st Session, *The Weather Underground: Report of the Subcommittee to Investigate the Administration of the Internal Security Act* (Washington: U. S. Government Printing Office, 1975).
2 Daniel Bell, "Columbia and the New Left," in McEvoy and Miller, *Black Power and Student Rebellion* (previously cited), pp. 31-74.
3 In addition to Kirkpatrick Sale, *passim,* see Saul Friedman, "Bernardine, Revolutionary on the Run," *The Cleveland Press,* October 17, 1970.

4 Sale, *op. cit., passim;* Bell, *op. cit., passim.*

Chapter 26
The Days of
Rage and After

1 An excellent summary of the Days of Rage is in Sale, *op. cit.,* pp. 602-613.
2 Sale, p. 628.
3 Edward Grossman, "Jane & Sam: A Requiem for Two Bombers," *Midstream, a Monthly Jewish Review,* New York, Vol. XX, No. 3 (March 1974), p. 26.
4 How immediate the danger of a nationwide revolution appeared to be in Middle America, may be seen from Garry Wills, *The Second Civil War: Arming for Armageddon* (New York: The New American Library, 1968).

Chapter 27
The Symbionese
and Patty Hearst

1 As yet, there are very few books on the Symbionese and Patricia Hearst that present thoughtful enough inquiries into the subject. The few available include:

Steven Weed, with Scott Swanton, *My Search for Patty Hearst* (New York: Crown Publishers, 1976).

David Boulton, *The Making of Tania Hearst* (London: New English Library, 1975).

Marilyn Baker and Sally Brompton, *Exclusive! The Inside Story of Patricia Hearst and the SLA* (New York: Macmillan, 1974).

Other, briefer accounts are:

Hank Messick & Burt Goldblatt, *Kidnapping: The Illustrated History* (New York: Dial Press, 1974), pp. 154-200.

Michael Wolff, "Cheerleader for a Revolution," *The New York Times Magazine,* July 21, 1974, pp. 11 ff.

Bill & Emily Harris, as told to Susan Lyne and Robert Scheer, "Twenty Months With Patty/Tania," *New Times,* New York, March 5, 1976.

Bill and Emily Harris, Russell Little and Joseph Remiro, as told to Susan Lyne and Robert Scheer, "The Story of the SLA," *ibid.,* April 16, 1976.

Howard Kohn and David Weir, "The Lost Year of the SLA," *Rolling*

Stone, San Francisco, April 22, 1976.
News accounts and photographs in *Time* and *Newsweek* for February 25, April 15 and 29, May 27, and June 3, 1974, and September 29, 1975. *The New York Times, The Washington Post,* and other newspapers for the same periods.

Chapter 28
Canada's White Niggers
1 For the background and theory of the movement, see

Anonymous ("by a Canadian correspondent"), "Quebec: The Challenge from Within," *Conflict Studies,* No. 20, February 1972.

Pierre Vallières, *White Niggers of America: The Precocious Autobiography of a Quebec "Terrorist,"* translated by Joan Pinkham (New York and London: Monthly Review Press, 1971).

For a factual account of the two kidnappings—

Baumann, *The Diplomatic Kidnappings* (previously cited), Chapter VII, "North American Counterparts: The Canadian Cases," pp. 110-128, based on reports in *The New York Times, The Milwaukee Journal,* and *The Globe and Mail* (Toronto).

For other material on the subject—

Patricia Welbourn, "A Talk With Two Would-Be Assassins," *The Vancouver Sun,* reprinted in *Atlas,* New York, November 1970; and Fernand Beauregard, "Who Inspired the FLQ Terrorists?", translated and reprinted from *La Presse* (Montreal) and *The Montreal Star* in *Atlas,* December 1970. Quotations from the terrorists' ultimatums and the government's statements are taken from Baumann and from *The New York Times* and other newspapers of 1970-72.

Chapter 29
Crimson in the
Irish Green and Orange
1 In addition to my personal visits and researches in Ulster and England, the following sources were of help (a selected list):

Boris Bannov, *The Ulster Tragedy* (Moscow: Novosti Press Agency Pub-

lishing House, 1973). The Soviet view, in English.

Tom Barry, *Guerrilla Days in Ireland* (Tralee: Anvil Books, 1968).

David Barzilay, *The British Army in Ulster* (Belfast: Century Services Ltd., 1973).

J. C. Beckett (and others), *The Ulster Debate: Report of a Study Group of the Institute for the Study of Conflict* (London: Bodley Head, 1972).

J. Bowyer Bell, *The Secret Army: A History of the IRA, 1915-1970* (London: Sphere, 1972).

Conor Brady, *Guardians of the Peace* (Dublin: Gill and Macmillan, 1974).

Richard Howard Brown, *I Am of Ireland* (New York: Harper & Row, [1974]).

Tim Pat Coogan, *The I.R.A.* (New York: Praeger, [1970]; London: Pall Mall Press, [1970]).

Freedom Struggle, by the Provisional IRA (London: Red Books, 1973).

Lord Gardiner, chairman, *Report of a Committee to consider, in the Context of Civil Liberties and Human Rights, Measures to Deal with Terrorism in Northern Ireland,* presented to Parliament January 1975 (London: Her Majesty's Stationery Office, 1975).

John F. Harbinson, *The Ulster Unionist Party, 1882-1973: Its Development and Organization* (Belfast: Blackstaff Press, 1973).

"Ireland: The Tactics of Terror," *Time,* January 10, 1972 (cover story).

Tom Mangold, "The Case of Dr. Rose Dugdale," *Encounter,* Vol. 44, No. 2 (February 1975), pp. 18-27.

Alf McCreary, "The Taste of Freedom: An Ex-Detainee Talks," *Belfast Telegram,* January 16, 1975.

Maria McGuire, *To Take Arms: A Year with the Provisional IRA* (London: Macmillan, 1973).

P. Michael O'Sullivan, *Patriot Graves* (Chicago: Follett, [1972]).

Richard Rose, *Governing Without Consensus: an Irish Perspective* (Boston: Beacon Press, [1971]).

A. T. Stewart, *The Ulster Crisis* (London: Faber, 1967).

Loudon Wainwright, "A People

Lost in Hate," *Life*, August 20, 1971. In *Conflict Studies:* Iain Hamilton, "The Irish Tangle," No. 6, August 1970. Iain Hamilton and Robert Moss, "The Spreading Irish Conflict," No. 17, November 1971. ISC, "Ulster: Politics and Terrorism," No. 36, June 1973. Peter Janke and D. L. Price, "Ulster: Consensus and Coercion" No. 50, October 1974.

2 Jim Landers, "Running Guns to Ulster," *The Washington Post*, September 8, 1974; Christopher Dobson, "How I.R.A. Gets Guns and Cash: American 'Relief Funds' Used to Buy Arms; Taxpayers' Money Aids Provo Bombers," *The Sunday Telegraph*, January 26, 1975; Derek Brown, Tim Allman, and Peter Niesewand, "Arms Across the Sea," *The Guardian*, January 29, 1975; Bernard Weinraub, "Bronx I. R. A. Aid Unit Linked to Arms Flow," *The New York Times*, December 16, 1975.

3 Gloria Emerson, "In Belfast, Children Fight a War, Too," *The New York Times*, April 26, 1972; Unsigned, "Belfast Syndrome—Irish Violence Damages Psyches," *Science Digest*, New York, September 1973; Morris Fraser, *Children in Conflict* (London: Secker and Warburg. 1973).

4 Denis Herbstein, "UDA: Learn About Lenin," *The Sunday Times*, London, June 18, 1972.

5 Bernard Weinraub, "I.R.A. Leader and Would-Be Martyr: Sean MacStiofain" *The New York Times*, November 28, 1972. *Cf.* Sean MacStiofain, *Revolutionary in Ireland* ([London:] G. Cremonesi, [1975]).

6 P. 88.

Chapter 30
New Europe's Old Hatreds

1 Melvin J. Lasky, "Ulrike & Andreas," *The New York Times Magazine*, May 11, 1975, pp. 14 and 73 ff.

2 *Ibid.* See also Lasky, "Ulrike Meinhof & the Baader-Meinhof Gang," *Encounter*, Vol. 44, No. 6 (June 1975), pp. 9-23; and Hans Josef Horchem, "West Germany's Red Army Anarchists," *Conflict Studies*, No. 46, June 1974.

3 Barzini quoted by C. L. Sulzberger, "Sadness in the Family," *The New York Times*, May 3, 1972, Op-Ed Page. See also Luigi Barzini, "Feltrinelli," *Encounter*, Vol. 39, No. 1 (July 1972), pp. 35-40; and John Earle, "Report on Italy," *Conflict Studies*, No. 19, January 1972.

4 Ronald Seth, *The Executioners: The Story of Smersh* (New York: Hawthorn Books, 1967), Chapter Six, "The Disappearing Generals," pp. 40-54.

5 Julen Agirre, *Operation Ogro: The Execution of Admiral Luis Carrero Blanco*, translated from the Spanish, adapted and with an introduction by Barbara Probst Solomon (New York: Quadrangle/The New York Times Book Co., 1975).

6 Col. J. C. Murray, "The Anti-Bandit War" (on the Greek civil war), in T. N. Greene, *op. cit.* See also: Unsigned, "A Political Incompetent" (on General George Grivas), *The Guardian*, London, February 2, 1974; and Kenneth Mackenzie, "Cyprus: The Ideological Crucible," *Conflict Studies*, No. 26, September 1972.

Chapter 31
Vietnam and
Other Jungles, Other Pyres

1 James Jones, *Viet Journal* (New York: Delacorte Press, 1974), p. 93.

2 *Ibid.*, p. 91.

3 *Ibid.*, p. 94.

4 Alan Bennett, "Thailand: The Ambiguous Domino," *Conflict Studies*, No. 1, December 1969; Arnold Abrams, "Rebel Resurgence in Northern Thailand: Revisiting the Hill Tribesmen," *The New Leader*, New York, November 1, 1971, pp. 8-9. ISC, "Thailand: The Dual Threat to Stability," *Conflict Studies*, No. 44, May 1974.

5 Burma, Department of Information and Broadcasting, *Insurgent Atrocities in Burma* [Rangoon: Ministry of Information, 1952?]; Lucian W. Pye, *Politics, Personality, and Nation Building: Burma's Search for Identity* (New Haven: Yale University Press, 1962); a study from the Center for International Studies, Massachusetts Center for International Studies; Till-

man Durdin, dispatch from Hong Kong, "Peking Broadens Attack on Burma, Voices Approval of Armed Struggle by Reds There," *The New York Times,* July 1, 1967. Other press reports in the 1960s-'70s.

6 Lucian W. Pye, *Guerrilla Communism in Malaya—Its Social and Political Meaning* (Princeton: Princeton University Press, 1956), interviews with many former terrorists; Sir Robert Thompson, *Defeating Communist Insurgency: Experiences from Malaya and Vietnam* (London: Chatto & Windus, 1966); Richard L. Clutterbuck, *The Long, Long War: The Emergency in Malaya, 1948-1960,* with a foreword by Sir Robert Thompson (London: Cassell, 1967); Richard L. Clutterbuck, *Riot and Revolution in Singapore and Malaya* (London: Faber, 1973); R. W. Komer, *The Malayan Emergency in Retrospect: Organization of a Counterinsurgency* (Santa Monica, Calif.: Rand Corporation, February 1972).

7 Robert Trumbull, "The Huks Bring Terror to the Philippines," *The New York Times Magazine,* March 14, 1965; Unsigned, *Why Lt. Victor Corpus Left the AFP to Join the New People's Army* (Manila: Gintong Silahis Publications, 1971); Harvey Averch and John Koehler, *Explaining Dissident Success: the Huks in Central Luzon* (Santa Monica, Calif.: Rand Corporation, January 1972); Beth Day, *The Philippines: Shattered Showcase of Democracy in Asia* (New York: M. Evans, [1974]).

8 Mohan Ram, *Maoism in India* (Delhi: Vika Publications, [1971]). J. C. Johari, *Naxalite Politics in India* (Delhi: Research [Publications, 1972]).

9 Press reports from India in the 1970s.

10 Edgar O'Ballance, *The Kurdish Revolt, 1961-1970* (London: Faber, [1973]). Daily press reports in 1974-75.

11 Isaac Don Levine, *Eyewitness to History: Memoirs and Reflections of a Foreign Correspondent for Half a Century* (New York: Hawthorn Books, 1973), Chapter 11, "The Shah by a Hairbreadth," pp. 251-71; James Alban Bill, *The Politics of Iran: Groups, Classes and Modernization*

(Columbus, Ohio: Merrill Political Science Series, [1972]).

Chapter 32
Red Samurai
and Turkey's Nihilists

1 "Hijackers of the World, Unite: Japan's 'Red Army' on Air Piracy and Communism," interview with a terrorist leader translated from the Tokyo *Shukan Asahi* and printed in *Atlas,* New York, July 1970, p. 30.

2 *Ibid.*

3 Unsigned, dispatch from Jerusalem, "Terrorist Gives Israelis His Political Testament," *The New York Times,* July 14, 1972; Peter Grose, "Terrorist Is Given Life Term in Israel," *ibid.,* July 18, 1972. See also Thomas Ross, "Die drei Terroristen aus Japan," *Frankfurter Algemeine Zeitung,* June 3, 1972; and Martin Collick and Richard Storry, "The New Tensions in Japan," *Conflict Studies,* No. 48, August 1974.

4 Hugh Byas, *Government by Assassination* (New York: Alfred A. Knopf, 1942.)

5 Baumann, *The Diplomatic Kidnappings* (previously cited), pp. 89-91 and 172-74; Kenneth Mackenzie, "Turkey: After the Storm," *Conflict Studies,* No. 43, April 1974.

Chapter 33
Arafat and Other Sacrificers

1 In addition to my interviews during my three visits in Israel, the following printed sources were of use (other titles appear in this chapter's subsequent notes):

J. Bowyer Bell, *The Long War: Israel and the Arabs Since 1946* (Englewood, N. J.: Prentice-Hall, [1969]).

Gerard Chaliand, *The Palestinian Resistance,* transl. by Michael Perl (Harmondsworth: Penguin, [1972]).

"Chaos in the Sky: Palestinian Guerrillas Strike Savagely at the Big Jets and Their Helpless Passengers," *Life,* September 18, 1970.

Joseph Churba, *Fedayeen and the Middle East Crisis,* ([Maxwell Air Force Base, Alabama]: Documentary Research Division, Aerospace Studies Institute, 1969).

John K. Cooley, *Green March, Black*

September: The Story of the Palestinian Arabs (London: Cass, 1973).

Ezzeldin Foda, *Israeli Belligerent Occupation and Palestinian Armed Resistance in International Law* (Beirut: P. L. O. Research Center, 1970).

The Futility of Terror: A Summing Up of Palestinian Terrorist Activity (Tel Aviv: Israelis Reply, [1971]).

Paul Y. Hammond and Sidney S. Alexander, eds., *Political Dynamics in the Middle East* (New York: American Elsevier Publishing Company, [1972]).

Y. Harkabi, *Palestinians and Israel* (Jerusalem: Israel Universities Press, and New York: John Wiley & Sons, 1974).

"Horror and Death at the Olympics," *Time*, September 18, 1972, cover story.

Leila S. Kadi, transl. and comp., *Basic Political Documents of the Armed Palestinian Resistance Movement* (Beirut: P. L. O. Research Center, 1969).

John Laffin, *Fedayeen: The Arab-Israel Dilemma* (New York: Free Press, [1973]).

Edgar O'Ballance, *Arab Guerrilla Power, 1967-1972* (London: Faber, [1974]).

Bard O'Neill, *Revolutionary Warfare in the Middle East: The Israelis vs. the Fedayeen*, foreword by S. L. A. Marshall [Boulder, Colorado: Paladin Press, 1974].

"The Palestinians Become a Power," *Time*, November 11, 1974, cover story.

David Pryce-Jones, *The Face of Defeat: Palestinian Refugees and Guerrillas* (London: Weidenfeld and Nicolson, 1972).

William B. Quandt, *Palestinian Nationalism: Its Political and Military Dimensions* (Santa Monica: Rand Corporation, November 1971).

William B. Quandt, Fuad Jabber, and Ann Mosely Lesch, *The Politics of Palestinian Nationalism* (Berkeley: University of California Press, [1973]).

Zeev Schiff and Raphael Rothstein, *Fedayeen: Guerrillas Against Israel* (New York: McKay, [1972]).

Hisham Sharabi, *Palestine Guer-*

rillas: Their Credibility and Effectiveness ([Washington, D.C.]: Georgetown University, [1970]).

Edward R. F. Sheehan, "Colonel Qadhafi—Libya's Mystical Revolutionary," *The New York Times Magazine*, February 6, 1972.

Gideon Weigert, *Whoso Killeth a Believer* [Jerusalem: Israel Communications, 1971 or 1972].

Dan Yahalom, *File on Arab Terrorism* (Jerusalem: Carta, [1973]).

In *Conflict Studies:*

Tom Little, "The New Arab Extremists: A View from the Arab World," No. 4, May 1970.

J. Kimche, "Can Israel Contain the Palestine Revolution?" No. 13, June 1971.

ISC, "Since Jordan: The Palestinian Fedayeen," No. 38, September 1973.

2 Edward R. F. Sheehan, "Why Sadat and Faisal Chose Arafat," *The New York Times Magazine*, December 8, 1974; David Holden, "Which Arafat?", *ibid.*, March 23, 1975.

3 Eric Pace, "The Black September Guerrillas: Elusive Trail in Seven Countries," *"The New York Times,* October 12, 1972; Christopher Dobson, *Black September: Its Short, Violent History* (New York: Macmillan, [1974]).

4 W. A. C. Adie, "China, Israel and the Arabs," *Conflict Studies*, No. 12, May 1971; Ching-lang Tsai, *Chinese Communists' Support to Palestinian Guerrilla Organizations* ([Taipei]: World Anti-Communist League, China Chapter, 1973); Moshe Ma'oz, *Soviet and Chinese Relations With the Palestinian Guerrilla Organizations* (Jerusalem: The Hebrew University, Jerusalem Papers on Peace Problems, March 1974).

Chapter 34
Fire in the African Bush

1 Estelle Sylvia Pankhurst, *Ethiopia and Eritrea: The Last Phase of the Reunion Struggle, 1914-1952* (Woodford Green, Essex: Lalibela House, [1953]); Godfrey Morrison, *The Southern Sudan and Eritrea: Aspects of Wider African Problems* (London: Minority Rights Group, 1971). Press reports in the 1970s.

2 Helio Felgas, *The Terrorist Movements of Angola, Portuguese Guinea, Mozambique: Foreign Influence*, transl. from *Revista Militar*, Lisbon, 1966 (Washington, D. C.: U. S. Department of Commerce, Joint Publications Research Service, 1966). A collection of articles from the world's press: "Portugal: Last of the Old-Fashioned Empires," *Atlas*, January 1971; Neil Bruce, "Portugal's African Wars," *Conflict Studies*, No. 34, March 1973.

Thomas A. Johnson, dispatch from a jungle camp, Portuguese Guinea, "Blacks Building Nation While Battling Portugal," *The New York Times*, April 29, 1974. Press reports from Lisbon and Africa since the revolution of April 1974.
3 Gérard Chaliand, "The Legacy of Amilcar Cabral," *Ramparts*, April 1973, pp. 17-20.
4 Douglas L. Wheeler and René Pélissier, *Angola* (New York: Praeger, 1971); Joaquim Dos Santos, "Tragediya Angoly" [Angola's tragedy], *Pravda*, June 8, 1959.
5 Frederick Forsyth, *The Biafra Story* (Harmondsworth: Penguin, 1969); Arthur A. Nwankwo and Samuel U. Ifejika, *Biafra: The Making of a Nation* (New York: Praeger, [1969 and 1970]); Peter Schwab, ed., *Biafra* (New York: Facts on File, [1971]).
6 Unsigned, "Equatorial Guinea: Tales of Terror," *To the Point International*, Antwerp, January 25, 1975, pp. 31-32.

Chapter 35
Right-wing Terror

1 John Hughes, *Indonesian Upheaval* (New York: David McKay, 1967); Horace Sutton, "Indonesia's Night of Terror: Exclusive Report from Jakarta on the Red Purge," *Saturday Review*, New York, February 4, 1967, pp. 25-31 and 75-81; Arnold C. Brackman, "Indonesia: The Critical Years 1976-1978," *Conflict Studies*, No. 49, September 1974. For a typical Soviet view, see editorial (unsigned), "Protiv razgula reaktsii v Indonezii" [Against the excesses of reaction in Indonesia], *Pravda*, Moscow, December 26, 1965. How close D. N. Aidit, the Communist leader, came to seizing power in Indonesia in 1965 may be seen from Neil Sheehan, "A Simple Man in Pursuit of Power," *The New York Times Magazine*, August 15, 1965. My own research on the subject was done during a visit in Djakarta and Bali in the summer of 1968.
2 Hughes, *op. cit.*, p. 189.
3 Pierre Démaret and Christian Plume, *Target—De Gaulle: The True Story of the 31 attempts on the life of the French President*, transl. from the French by Richard Barry (New York: Dial, 1975); Ted Morgan, "The Real Jackal: His Only Regret—Not to Have Killed De Gaulle," *The New York Times Magazine*, September 2, 1973.

Chapter 36
Genghis Khan
with the Telephone

1 For other spectacular attempts by Iranian terrorists to kill the Shah, see Isaac Don Levine, *Eyewitness to History*, Chapter 11, "The Shah by a Hairbreadth."
2 M. Karateyev, "Reportazh iz Uruguaya" [Reporting from Uruguay], *Novoye Russkoye Slovo*, June 29, 1972.

Chapter 37
The New Robin Hoods,
the Media, and the Police

1 Lasky, "Ulrike & Andreas," p. 74.
2 Sorel, *Reflections on Violence*, p. 92.

Chapter 38
Terrorists Then and Now

1 Alvin Toffler, *Future Shock* (New York: Random House, 1970), p. 323.
2 *Ibid.* Toffler also explains the terrorism of some modern young as a kind of nostalgia: "Turn-of-the-century terrorism and quaint Black Flag anarchy are suddenly back in vogue. The Rousseauian cult of the noble savage flourishes anew. Antique Marxist ideas, applicable at best to yesterday's industrialism, are hauled out as knee-jerk answers for the problems of tomorrow's super-industrialism. Reversionism masquerades as revolution." (pp. 320-21).
3 *Ibid.*, pp. 321-22.
4 Jackson, *Surviving the Long Night* (previously cited), p. 68.

5 Gadea, *Ernesto: A Memoir of Ché Guevara* (previously cited), pp. 51-52.

6 Walter J. Broderick, *Camilo Torres: A Biography of the Priest-Guerrillero* (New York: Doubleday, 1975). See also Eugene C. Bianchi, *The Religious Experience of Revolutionaries* (Garden City: Doubleday, 1972).

Chapter 39
The New International

1 D. V. Segre and J. H. Adler, "The Ecology of Terrorism," *Encounter,* Vol. 40, No. 2 (February 1973), pp. 17-24.

Chapter 40
Five Minutes to Midnight

1 Mason Willrich and Theodore B. Taylor, *Nuclear Theft: Risks and Safeguards* (Cambridge, Mass.: Ballinger Publishing Company, [1974]). See also David Burnham, "Nuclear Agency Is Reported Ready to Oppose Special Force to Combat Terrorist Attacks at Facilities," *The New York Times,* January 12, 1976.

2 Our Parliamentary Staff, "House of Lords: Chalfont Warning on Terrorists Acquiring Chemical Weapons," *The Daily Telegraph,* London, June 8, 1972.

3 "U. S. Action to Combat Terrorism," News Release, Bureau of Public Affairs, Department of State, 1972 (documents for the period Sept. 25—Oct. 2, 1972); "The Role of International Law in Combating Terrorism," pamphlet issued by Bureau of Public Affairs, Department of State, January 1973; United Nations General Assembly, "Draft Convention on the Prevention and Punishment of Crimes Against Diplomatic Agents and Other Internationally Protected Persons," Report of the Sixth Committee, released December 10, 1973.

4 Clutterbuck, *Living With Terrorism.*

Index

Acholi tribe, 482
Adams, Gerry, 385
Addis Ababa, Ethiopia, 470, 471-72, 486
Adem, Idris Mohammed, 470
Aden, South Yemen, 470, 566, 572
Adler, Friedrich, 175, 180
Adrian IV, Pope, 376
Adwan, Kamal, 466
Afars and Issas, 469
Afghanistan, 315, 429, 549
Africa, 39, 248, 302, 469, 550-51; black, 449; blacks against blacks in, 478-83, 484, 544; blacks against whites in, 473-79, 483-87, 512, 541, 544, 550; China in, 475, 476, 478, 480, 484; Communism in, 470, 476, 477, 480-81; and Soviet Union, 470, 475-81 passim, 484, 486; UN bloc, 550-51; see also individual countries
Agirre, Julen, 410-11
Aidit, D. N., 427, 489, 490-91, 492
Air France, 576
Al Ahram, 512
Alarm, 98
Al-Azhar University, 457-58
Albania, 15
Albany, New York, 339
Albizu Campos, Pedro, 299
Aldanov, Mark, 60
Alegria de Pio, Cuba, 247
Alexander, King of Yugoslavia, 209, 496
Alexander II, Tsar of Russia, 81, 85, 107-09; assassination of, 86, 90, 95, 107, 109-16, 408, 509, 517, 561-62
Alexander III, Tsar of Russia, 116, 117, 118, 120, 121, 131, 249, 510, 562
Alexander Obrenovich, King of Serbia, 91 n.
Alexandrovsk, Russia, 112
Alexis, Tsar of Russia, 7
Algeria, 369, 372, 465, 466, 553, 563, 575; Cleaver in, 303, 311, 313-15, 553; FLN of, 301, 313; independence from France, x-xi, 253, 301, 404, 451, 452, 494-95, 560-61; OAS in, 301, 387, 494-95; torture in, 34, 302; UN resolution on terrorism and, 549
Algiers, Algeria, 313, 338, 429
Allende Gossens, Salvador, 256, 271, 283-84, 357, 398, 503, 504-06
Alon, Colonel Yosef, 462, 568
Alpert, Jane, 24, 338, 340
Altgeld, John Peter, 99
Alton, Illinois, 93
American Federation of Labor, 241

American Revolution, 92 and n., 157
American University, Beirut, 459, 565
Amin, General Idi, 482, 555, 576
Amman, Jordan, 67, 456
Amnesty International, 200, 281, 503, 506
Amsterdam, Holland, 572
Amuzegar, Jamshid, 465
Anabaptists, 40
anarchists, 3, 66, 84-89, 98-99, 510, 521, 528, 535; among artists and writers, 88-89; black flag of, 87, 96, 123; in France, 87-89, 90, 383, 526, 537; as inspiration to terrorists, 78, 87, 101; in Italy, 80, 81, 83-85, 88, 90, 383, 401, 402, 521, 522, 526, 537; mental disturbance of, 83, 89, 101-02; peaceful philosophy of, 97, 101, 123; and police, 88, 98-99, 103; and proletariat and peasants, 81-82, 83-84, 85, 121, 122, 517; in Russia, 123, 168, 174, 180-81, 521, 526; in Spain, 80, 83, 88, 90, 407, 411, 521, 522, 537; in United States, 83, 86, 89, 90, 94, 96-106, 517, 526, 537-38, 548; in Western Europe, 79-80, 517, 521, 526, 548; see also assassinations; individual anarchists
Anaya Rosique, Raúl, 290
Andom, General Aman Michael, 472
Andropov, Yury, 193
Angola, 478-81, 486-87; civil war in, 479-81, 486; Cuban troops in, 289, 479-81; FNLA of, 478-80; foreign intervention in, 478, 479-81, 486; independence for, 289, 473, 479, 561; MPLA of, 478, 479-81, 486, 554; Pide in, 473; UNITA of, 479, 480-81
Ankara, Turkey, 252, 443
Anne, Princess, of the United Kingdom, 33
Arab fedayeen, 15, 29, 92 n., 244, 314, 449-68, 526, 530, 539, 557, 560-61, 562; arms for, 458-59, 461, 512, 531 n., 537, 547; and Basques, 407; and China, 459, 461, 537, 550; and Communism, 451, 455, 457, 460, 462, 530; financed by oil, 437, 439, 449, 457, 459, 543; inspirations of, 16, 67, 131, 251, 451, 460, 461, 462; and Israel, terror against, 67, 244, 406, 435-36, 437, 442, 448-68 passim, 482, 511, 512, 520, 530, 535, 538, 540, 541, 546, 548, 549, 550, 555, 558, 561, 563-76; and Israeli counterterror, 455, 456, 458, 466-68, 482, 553, 554-55, 558, 563-64, 566, 574, 576; and Japanese terrorists, 433, 437-39, 442, 538, 540; Jordan's attack on, 67-68, 455-56, 457, 459, 460, 538, 540, 565, 570; and October War, 289, 457, 458, 467, 468, 512, 538, 554, 570-71; Red terror of, 448, 450, 463-66, 520, 540, 541, 552-53, 555, 566, 567-68,

Arab fedayeen (*continued*)
571-73; and Six Day War, 429, 452, 453, 455, 460; and Soviet Union, 454, 455, 459, 460-61, 462, 512, 542, 547, 550, 553-54; training camps of, 397, 398, 433, 442, 540-41; and Turkish terrorists, 442, 447, 540; and West German terrorists, 397, 398, 541; *see also* individual organizations
Arab Liberation Front, 463
Arab Nationalist Movement, 460
Arab National Youth Organization for the Liberation of Palestine (ANYOLP), 463-64, 571, 572-73
Arabs, 469, 470, 511; UN bloc, 239, 449, 549-51, 561; *see also* Arab fedayeen; individual groups and leaders
Arab University, 462
Arafat, Yasir, 47, 67, 168, 314, 439, 448, 450-62 *passim*, 531 *n.*, 541, 547, 554, 568, 571-72, 573, 574, 575; gradualism of, 454, 461, 463-65, 561; at UN, 23, 92 *n.*, 131, 157 *n.*, 449, 462, 542, 547, 549, 552; *see also* Palestine Liberation Organization
Arana Osorio, Carlos, 287
Araya Peters, Captain Arturo, 283
Arbenz Guzmán, Jacobo, 246 and *n.*, 250, 286
Arendt, Hannah, 7, 69, 216, 219; *On Violence*, 8
Argentina, 218, 246, 251, 261-73, 497, 558; Anti-Communist Alliance of, 270-72; ERP of, 171, 261-74 *passim*, 285, 354, 531, 560; ERP-*Augosto 22* of, 262-63; ERP-*Fracción Roja* of, 171, 262; labor unions of, 261, 267-72 *passim;* Montoneros of, 263-73 *passim;* PRT of, 171, 262, 263; Red terror in, 172, 260-73, 511, 519, 554, 560; White terror in, 262-64, 270-72, 488, 523, 554
Arguello, Patrick, 540
Armand, Inessa, 165, 166
Armenia, 219, 447
Armstrong, Karl and Dwight, 338
Aron, Raymond, 529
Arras, France, 44, 59
arson, 395, 414, 419, 420
Asmara, Eritrea, 470, 471, 472
Assad, Hafez, 456, 468, 554
As Saiqa, 462-63, 575
assassinations, 24, 69, 82, 89 and *n.*, 91 *n.*, 142, 259; in Africa, 475, 476, 482; by Arabs, 67, 244, 398, 406, 436, 457, 461-69 *passim*, 538, 541, 546, 548, 549, 555, 565-76 *passim;* in Argentina, 262-72 *passim;* in Austria, 180, 209, 447, 465, 540, 575; by Basques, 111; in Brazil, 257; of businessmen, 123, 266, 267, 270, 272-73, 296, 406, 516; in Canada, 372; in Chile, 283; in Colombia, 296; in Cyprus, 413-14, 415; in England, 391; in Eritrea, 471; in France, 90, 252-53, 281, 406, 495, 537; in Geneva, 90, 537; in Germany, 207, 218; in Greece, 413, 415-16; in Guatemala, 286, 287; in Holland, 494; in India, 427; in Indonesia, 490; in Iran, 430-41; by Israelis, 466-67; in Italy, 86, 90, 102, 203, 402; by Japanese, 435-36, 437, 441, 461, 538, 548, 549; in Khartoum, 398, 457, 464, 538, 555, 567-68; mental illness in, 29-30, 34-35, 101, 104; in Mexico, 292; in Nicaragua, 298; in Poland, 523; in Portugal, 90, 144, 501-02; prevention of, 558-59; in Puerto Rico, 299; for revenge, 252-53, 257, 281, 286, 399, 406, 415, 447; in Russia, 78, 85, 86, 90-91, 95, 107, 109-17, 120, 121-22, 123, 124, 129, 139, 140, 155, 509-10, 517, 521, 522-23; in Sarajevo, 91; in S. Korea, 440; in Spain, 90, 111, 408-10, 509; in Turkey, 442-47 *passim*, 540; in Uganda, 576; in Ulster, 388; in United States,

90, 94, 102-03, 104, 117, 300, 316-21, 323, 324, 349-51, 509, 538; in Uruguay, 274, 277, 278; by Ustashi, 209, 496, 497; of Ustashi, 500; in West Germany, 399, 400; *see also* anarchists
Astrakhan, Russia, 6
Athens, Greece, 413, 415, 463, 471, 563, 564, 569, 571, 576
Atlanta, Georgia, 316
Attila, 22
Atwood, Angela DeAngelis (Gelina), 347, 349, 352, 362, 534-35
Atwood, Gary, 347
Auckland, New Zealand, 310
Augsburg, Germany, 397
Auschwitz, 213
Austin, Texas, 308
Australia, 425; Ustashi in, 497-99
Austria, 42, 46, 49, 70, 81, 95, 129, 402, 498, 499; Nazis of, 208, 209; Social Democratic Party of, 175, 180; terrorism in, 40, 180, 209, 447, 465, 540, 566, 570, 575; and UN resolution of terrorism, 549
Austro-Hungary, 91, 157 *n.*
Avrich, Paul, 82
Azef, Yevgeny (Yevno), 379, 510; as double agent, 124-28, 129, 175
Azul, Argentina, 270

Baader, Andreas, 395-400
Babeuf, François Noël ("Gracchus"), 13
Baghdad, Iraq, 464
Baku, USSR, 189, 542
Bakunin, Mikhail, xiii, 3, 13, 15, 16, 17, 66, 78-84 *passim*, 91, 95, 136, 362, 522, 529 and *n.*, 537; *Confession* of, 81; disciples of, 80, 82, 83, 85, 86, 89, 95, 101, 123, 526; mental disturbance of, 27
Balabanova, Angelica, 169
Balaguer, Joaquin, 299, 556
Bali, 489, 491, 492; *see also* Indonesia
Balkans, 129, 412
Ball, Peter Sydney, 33-34
Balmashov, Stepan, 139
Baluchistan, W. Pakistan, 429
Bangkok, Thailand, 420, 425
Bangladesh, 428
Banzer Suarez, General Hugo, 282
Barère, Bertrand, 47, 51, 60-61, 64
Baroody, Jamil M., 547
Barras, Paul, 61-62, 63
Barthou, Louis, 209, 496
Barzana, Mustafa al-, 429-30
Barzini, Luigi, 402-03
Basque terrorists, 408, 539; and Arabs, 407; Between Brothers of, 406, 407; and Bretons, 405, 407; ETA of, 171, 405, 406-11, 509; French, 405, 406-07, 539; PNV of, 407; Red terror of, 111, 407-11, 412; Spanish, 111, 171, 405, 406-11, 412, 539; trained by IRA, 407, 539
Basra, Iraq, 461
Batista, Fulgencio, 246, 247-48, 250, 252
Batlle y Ordoñez, José, 275
Baton Rouge, Louisiana, 103
Battle of Algiers (film), 331, 451, 519
Bavaria, 204, 206
Beauharnais, Alexandre de, 62
Beauharnais, Josephine de, 62, 63
Beethoven, Ludwig van, 166
Beira, Mozambique, 476
Beirut, Lebanon, 67, 244, 437, 442, 452, 458-67 *passim*, 470, 563-76 *passim*
Beit Shean, Israel, 574
Belfast, N. Ireland, 377, 378, 380, 385, 392, 524
Belgium, 407, 481-82, 567-68

Belgrade, Yugoslavia, 91 n., 497, 499
Bellarmine, St. Robert, 19
Belorussia, 211-12
Belsen, 213
Benghazi, Libya, 425, 437, 569
Bennett, W. Tapley, 551
Beria, Lavrenty, 25-26, 195-96, 197, 198, 199, 228
Berisso, Admiral Emilio, 264
Berkeley, California, 78, 309, 349, 515
Berkman, Alexander, 100-01, 105 and n., 538
Berlin, Germany, 127, 161, 179, 204, 216, 510; East, 396, 442; West, 395, 397, 398, 400, 557
Bernstein, Mr. and Mrs. Leonard, 309
Berrigan, Philip and Daniel, 534
Biafra, 481
Bihar, India, 428
Bilbao, Aguirre, 407
Billaud-Varenne, Jean Nicolas, 47, 51, 58, 61, 62, 64
Billings, Warren, 105
Birmingham, England, 390
Black Cultural Association, 343
Black Flag (Chyornoye Znamya), 123
Black International, 96-97
Black Liberation Army, 14, 18, 316-21, 340, 517, 522, 530, 535
Black Muslims, 319, 535
Black Panthers, 15, 68, 78, 302-13, 315, 319-20, 322, 332, 334, 342, 365, 368, 434, 451, 517, 528; in Algeria, 313-15, 553; in Europe and Middle East, 309-10, 314, 540; as gradualists, 312, 322; violence of, 303, 304-09, 341
blacks, 4, 92, 308, 311, 327; civil rights movement of, 303, 304, 327; militant, 302, 303, 311, 315-16; and violence, 14, 307-08; see also Africa; United States; individual groups
Black September, see Fatah
Blanco, Major Jesus Sosa, 250
Blank, Dr. Alexander, 132
Blum, Léon, 106 n.
Boeckeler, John (John of Leyden), 40
Boer War, 157 n., 422-23, 477
Boese, Wilfried, 576
Bogdanov, Dr. Alexander, 31
Bogotá, Colombia, 296, 532-33
Bogrov, Dmitry, 129
Bolívar, Simón, 251
Bolivar, Colombia, 295
Bolivia, 256, 272, 274, 282-83, 506; CIA in, 249, 252; Communist Party of, 249, 251; ELNB of, 282; Guevara in, 244-55 passim, 282; peasants of, 251; Red terror in, 261, 533; torture in, 282-83; White terror in, 274, 282-83
Böll, Heinrich, 397-98
Bologna, Italy, 81, 403
Bolsheviks, 31, 135, 139-40, 142-43, 146-48, 152, 155, 159, 167, 176, 189, 537; see also Communists, Soviet Union
Bombay, India, 310
bombings, 12, 24, 562; of airliners, 460, 462, 463, 470-71, 497, 510, 565, 567; by Arabs, 460, 462, 463, 464, 564-71 passim, 576; in Argentina, 269, 270; in Brazil, 257, 258; in Canada, 367, 369; in Cyprus, 413-14; in England, 381, 389-91, 393; by Eritreans, 470-71, 472; in France, 87, 405, 406, 495; in Greece, 413; in Haiti, 298; innocent victims of, 68, 98-99, 104-05, 115, 300, 338, 378, 380, 381, 388, 389-91, 397, 401, 403, 410, 411, 414, 418, 420, 440, 462, 463, 464, 472, 495, 497, 545, 564, 567, 569, 576; in Iran, 430; in Ireland, 390; in Italy, 84-85, 401, 403-04, 405; in Japan, 440; prevention of, 559; in Puerto Rico, 299-300; in Rus-

sia, 115-16, 123, 142; in Spain, 407, 408-10, 411; in Turkey, 444, 445; in Ulster, 377-78, 380, 388; in United States, 68, 98-99, 104-05, 299-300, 322, 336, 337-39, 340, 341, 389, 545; in Uruguay, 279; by Ustashi, 497, 499; in Vietnam, 418, 420; in West Germany, 397, 398, 401; see also anarchists
bombs, 259; booby-trapped books and candy, 512; car, 389, 390-91, 511; construction of, 86, 96, 336-37, 396, 400, 447, 515, 539, 545-46; grenades, 564, 569; letter-, 389, 476, 512, 567, 571; napalm, 418, 477; nuclear, 9, 441, 545-46; plastic, 495, 512; time, 401, 403; tunnel, 111, 114-15, 408-10
Bonch-Bruyevich, Vladimir, 136
Booth, John Wilkes, 93
Bordaberry, Juan Maria, 278-81
Bordeaux, France, 64, 410
Bormann, Martin Ludwig, 204
Born, Jorge and Juan, 269
Bosnia-Herzegovina, 84, 498
Boston, Massachusetts, 106, 334, 338
Botswana, 486
Boudin, Kathy, 336, 340
Boudin, Leonard B., 336
Boumedienne, Houari, 313-14, 563
Bourassa, Robert, 370, 372
bourgeoisie, 41, 58, 71, 76-77, 158, 161, 162, 163, 164, 181; in Russia, 140, 143-44, 148, 152, 155, 157, 159-60, 176, 178, 182-83, 183; see also middle classes
Bourguiba, Habib, 464
Braintree, Massachusetts, 106
Brandt, Willy, 216-17
Brazil, 275, 295, 441, 474, 477, 501, 506; ALN of, 257-58; Communist Party of, 257; Red terror in, 257-60, 524, 534; torture in, 260, 503, 514; VRP of, 257-58; White terror in, 260, 503, 504, 560
Brazzaville, Congo, 478, 479
Bremer, Arthur Herman, 34
Brescia, Italy, 403
Breton terrorists, 404-06; and Basques, 405, 407; and Communism, 404; FLB-ARB of, 404-05; FLB-LNS of, 404, 405; trained in Ireland, 405
Breuss, Eric, 267
Brewster, Kingman, Jr., 309
Brezhnev, Leonid, 172, 188, 193, 201, 202, 284, 289, 366, 443, 462, 479, 554, 570
Bridge and Structural Iron Workers' Union, 105
Brimcombe, Francis Victor, 266
Brinton, Crane, 55, 65; Decade of Revolution, A, 18-19
British Airways, 572, 573
British American Tobacco Company, 266
Brittany, 405; see also Breton terrorists
Brixton Prison, 389
Brown, Elaine, 315
Brown, H. Rap, 92, 303
Brown, Henry S. (Sha Sha), 317-18
Brown, John, 340
Brussels, Belgium, 64, 172, 564
Bucharest, Rumania, 240
Buchenwald, 213
Bucher, Giovanni Enrico, 258
Budapest, Hungary, 502
Buenos Aires, Argentina, 252, 261, 265, 266, 267, 270, 271, 274, 282, 284, 519
Buffalo, New York, 90, 101-02
Bukhalo (engineer), 509
Bulgaria, 445, 485
Bunge & Born, 269-70
Burgos, Spain, 407, 408, 411
Burma, 421, 551

Burt, Lee, 338
Burtsev, Vladimir, 125-27
Burundi, xi-xii, 481-82, 544
Buscayono, Bernabe, 426
Buttini, Federico, 297

Cabañas, Lucio, 291-92, 526
Cabinda, 478
Cabral, Amilcar, 474-75
Cabral, Luiz, 475
Caetano, Dr. Marcello, 501-02
Cafiero, Carlo, 32-33, 83-85
Cairo, Egypt, 452, 453, 455, 457, 464, 470, 565, 566, 568, 569, 572
Calais, France, 58
Calcutta, India, 428
Cali, Colombia, 296
California, 94, 315, 363, 386
Calley, Lieutenant William, 419
Camara, Helder, 534
Cambodia, 337, 420
Camilo, Father (Camilo Torres Restrepo), 296, 532-33, 534
Camilo, the Guerrilla Priest (film), 533
Campóra, Dr. Hector J., 263, 264-65, 269
Campos, Arajarira, 502
Camus, Albert: Rebel, The, 79, 529
Canada, 92, 525, 538, 539; FLQ of, 366-75; Red terror in, 68, 131, 365, 366-67, 369-75, 560; rejected demands of terrorists, 370-74; students in, 368, 369; and UN resolution on terrorism, 549; War Measures Act invoked in, 372, 374, 560; "White Niggers" of, 365-66, 369-70, 375; see also Quebec
Canadian Broadcasting Corporation, 373
Canary Islands, 411
Canovas del Castillo, Antonio, 90
Canton, China, 233, 235, 237
Cape Verde Islands, 501
capitalism, 13-14, 16, 31, 68, 83, 85, 172, 175, 182, 183, 249, 273, 365, 366, 371, 395, 417, 544; and Lenin, 131, 138, 147, 148, 154, 161-62, 163, 166
capital punishment: in Israel, 557-58; rejected in Britain, 390, 391, 558; in Soviet Union, 147, 148, 149, 151, 155-56, 162, 164, 200; in United States, 320, 557-58
Capucci, Hilarion, 458-59, 531 n., 576
Caracas, Venezuela, 296
Carbonneau, Marc, 373
"Carlos," (Ilyich Ramírez Sánchez), 297, 465, 539-40
Carlos I, King of Portugal, 90
Carlyle, Thomas, 53
Carmichael, Stokeley, 303, 311
Carnegie, Andrew, 100
Carnegie Steel strike, 100
Carnot, Lazare, 46, 51, 52, 62, 64, 65, 90
Carnot, Sadi, 90, 537
Caroz, Yaacov, 460-61
Carrero Blanco, Luis, 111, 408-10, 509
Carrier, Jean Baptiste, 57
Carter, Oliver, 363
Carter, Ronald, 317
Carthage, Illinois, 93
Castanedo Paiz, Olivero, 287
Castrejohn, Dr. Jaime, 290
Castro, Fidel, 171, 253, 402, 479-80, 511, 539-40, 553; and CIA, 559; and Cuban revolution, 17, 244, 246, 247-48, 254; encouraged export of revolution, 248, 288, 289; and Guevara, 17, 244, 246, 247-49, 251; as inspiration to terrorists, 171, 262, 387, 430, 540; and Soviet Union,

248-49, 262, 289; terror of, 47, 74, 168, 240, 250, 289 n.
Castro, Raúl, 171, 244, 247-48, 250, 253
Catalonia, Spain, 411
Catamarca Province, Argentina, 266
Catechism of a Revolutionary, The, 15, 78, 136, 244-45, 305
Catherine II, Empress of Russia, 7
Catherine Dolgorukaya, Princess, 114, 115
Catholics, 4-5, 262, 376, 408, 418, 496, 504, 543; and Nazism, 208, 215; riots against in United States, 93; as terrorists, 531-34, 536; of Ulster, 377-78, 385-87, 388, 392-94
Caucasus, 515
Cavaignac, General Louis Eugène, 71
Caxias jail, 502
Cayan, Mahir, 442, 445
Céline, Louis-Ferdinand, 215
Central Intelligence Agency (CIA), 293, 301 n., 500; in Angola, 480; in Bolivia, 249, 252; and Castro, 559; in Chile, 283, 284, 505; in Greece, 415-16; in Guatemala, 246 and n.; in Iran, 429, 430
Cermak, Anton J., 103
Chad, 483, 544
Chaine, Jacques, 406
Chalfont, Lord, 548
Chandler, Captain Charles, 257
Charles I, King of England, 376
Chaval, Nadine, 292
Cheka, 150, 152, 159-60, 162-63, 167, 168, 188, 193-94, 199, 203, 506
Chelmno, 213
Chernov, Viktor, 167, 168
Chernyshevsky, Nikolai, 107; What Is To Be Done?, 133-34, 135
Chesimard, Joanne Deborah, 317, 318
Chiang Kai-shek, 226, 228
Chiao Kuan-hua, 550
Chicago, Illinois, 310; Red terror in, 96-99, 101, 102, 103, 305-06, 307, 330-34
Chihuahua, Mexico, 291 n.
Chile, 246, 256, 264, 271, 274, 283-85, 295, 398, 506; CIA in, 283, 284, 505; Fatherland and Liberty of, 283, 504-05; MIR of, 283-85, 504; Red terror in, 261, 283; torture in, 285, 501, 503-04; truckers in, 283, 505; White terror in, 13, 250, 256, 274, 283-85, 503-06, 560
China, Communist, xiii, 15, 32, 223-27, 242-43, 251, 313, 427, 434, 543; and Africa, 475, 476, 478, 480, 484; and Arabs, 459, 461, 537, 550; arms supplied by, 459, 461, 475, 484, 537; citizen informants in, 229; civil wars in, 236, 242; collectivization in, 227, 230, 242; Communist Party of, 225, 228, 230, 235, 236, 241, 289, 489; concentration camps of, 230, 231-32; Cultural Revolution in, 230, 236, 242; dissenters in, 225-31 passim, 237-39, 242; forced labor in, 229, 230, 231-32, 242; and India, 421, 427; masses in, 225-26, 227-28, 230, 235-40; public trials and executions in, 225-28, 235-40; secret police of, 228-29, 241; shattered reverence for family, 234-35, 239; and Southeast Asia, 420-24; suicides in, 232-33; terror in, 224-43, 303, 418, 420, 562; torture in, 229, 501; and UN resolution on terrorism, 550; and United States, 241-42, 289, 427; victims in, 226-28, 230, 232, 236-43; and Vietnam War, 417; youth of, 230, 234-39 passim; see also Mao
China, Nationalist, 144, 226
Chipenda, Daniel, 479
Chou En-lai, 171, 231, 241, 242, 289
Christians, 533; and anti-Semitism, 204, 215-16; in Eritrea, 470, 472; in Indonesia, 491; in Leba-

non, 456, 457, 463, 466; in Philippines, 425; in Uganda, 482; *see also* Catholics
Churchill, Winston, 165
Cinque, 348-49
Cité Libre, 367
Citro, Frank, 534-35
Clark, Mark, 306, 307
Cleaver, Eldridge, 78, 302, 304 *n.*, 305, 307, 311, 319-20, 529; in Algeria, 303, 311, 313-15, 316, 338; *Post-Prison Writings and Speeches,* 313; *Soul on Ice,* 15, 78, 305, 313
Cleaver, Mrs. Eldridge, 313, 315
Cleveland, Grover, 99
Cleveland, Ohio, 102, 103, 344, 356, 498, 535
Clutterbuck, Richard, 423
Cochabamba, Bolivia, 282
Coco, Francesco, 420
Cohn-Bendit, Daniel, 406
Collot d'Herbois, Jean Marie, 51, 61, 64
Colombia, 246, 295-96; Communist labor unions in, 532-33; ELN of, 295, 533; FARC of, 295, 296; peasants of, 295, 533, 534; Red terror in, 295-96, 532-34; United Front of, 532
Columbia University, 322, 325, 327, 328
Communism, 13, 223, 403, 544; in Africa, 470, 476, 477, 480-81; and Arabs, 451, 455, 457, 460, 462, 530; and Hitler, 153, 204; Internationals, 79, 171-72, 181; and IRA, 380; and morality, 14-16, 74, 132, 143; and peasants, 149, 153, 156, 160, 177, 185, 418, 489, 491-92; worldwide, 136, 163, 165, 184, 248, 380, 434, 489; *see also* individual countries
Communists, 69, 72, 379, 411, 522; at UN, 23, 449; *see also* individual countries
Conakry, Guinea, 474, 475
concentration camps, 157 *n.*, 422; *see also* individual countries
Concord, California, 350
Condorcet, Marie Jean, Marquis de, xi
Congo, the, 4, 249, 251, 478
Conquest, Robert, 187; *Great Terror, The,* 26, 196-97
Cooper Union, New York, 96, 100
Copenhagen, Denmark, 558-59
Corday, Charlotte, 50
Córdoba, Luis Cardinal Concha, 532
Córdoba, Argentina, 267, 269, 270, 519
Cornell University, 305
Corpuz, Victor, 426-27
Cossacks, 6-7, 129, 149, 157 *n.*, 521
Costa-Gavras, Constantin, 274
Costa Rica, 246
Coston, James F. (Zayd Malik Shakur), 319-20
Courbet, Gustave, 88
Couthon, Georges, 51, 62
Crimea, 107, 165
Cristi, General Esteban, 280
Croatia, 496, 497, 500; *see also* Ustashi
Croce, Benedetto, 69
Cromwell, Oliver, 71, 73, 376
Crónica, 265
Cross, James R., 369-74
Cuba, 157 *n.*, 252, 258, 330, 369, 371, 372, 373-74, 434, 511, 540; aided Latin American guerrillas, 257, 276, 288, 298, 506; Communist Party of, 247-48; exiles of, 247, 256; public trials in, 240, 250; revolution in, 17, 244-54 *passim,* 551; terror in, 240, 289 *n.*; troops of, in Angola, 289, 479-81; troops of, in Syria, 289; and UN resolution on terrorism, 550-51
Cyprus: and British, 413-14; EOKA of, 414; and Greece, 384, 413-16, 447, 448; Red terror in, 412-15, 463; and Turkey, 413, 414, 415, 448; White terror in, 413

Czechoslovakia, 199-200, 442, 470, 497, 498, 539, 554, 566, 570
Czolgosz, Leon, 101-03, 509

Dachau, 213, 219
Dallas, Texas, 103
Damascus, Syria, 439, 442, 458, 460, 539, 564, 569, 571
Danton, Georges Jacques, 42, 46-47, 51, 58, 61
Darrow, Clarence, 104-05
Davie, Carlos Frick, 280
Davies, Rodger P., 415
Davis, Angela, 14, 554
Davydov, G. S., 192
Day, Robert, 387
Dayan, Moshe, 566
Day of the Jackal (film), 409, 495
DeAngelis, Lawrence, 347
Debray, Jules Régis, 253-56; *Revolution in the Revolution?* 253, 255
DeFreeze, Donald David (Cinque), 18, 27-28, 47, 168, 344-62 *passim,* 535
De Gaulle, Charles, 256, 328, 404, 405, 409, 494-95, 513, 539, 558
Degayev, Sergei (Alexander Pell), 117-18
Delgado, General Humberto, 501-02
Delta Airlines, 314
Del Valle, Benito, 407
Demirel, Suleyman, 443
Denikin, General Anton, 164, 182
Denmark, 216
Desmoulins, Camille, 41, 44, 46, 53, 58, 61
Detroit, Michigan, 101, 103
Deutsche National Zeitung, 541
Diels, Rolf, 206
Djakarta, Indonesia, 489-93 *passim*
Djibouti, French Somalia, 469, 470
Dobrolyubov, Nikolai, 107
Dodd, William E., 204
Dohrn, Bernardine, 33, 326-40 *passim*
Dollfuss, Engelbert, 209
Domingo Lain Sanz, Father, 533
Dominican Republic, 556; *Movimiento Popular Dominicano* of, 299
Dortzbach, Deborah, 471
Dostoyevsky, Fyodor, 117, 118-19; *Brothers Karamazov, The,* 529; *Crime and Punishment,* 529; *Gambler, The,* 8, 80-81; *Possessed, The,* 79, 118, 136, 529
Draga, Queen of Serbia, 91 *n.*
Drenkmann, Guenther von, 399
Dresden, Germany, 81
Dubai, 437, 464, 569, 571, 573
Dublin, Ireland, 377, 385, 389, 390, 512, 539, 556
Dugdale, Bridget Rose, 388
Dühring, Eugen Karl, 16, 74
Duluth, Minnesota, 348
Dunkerque, France, 58
Duplay, Eléonore, 45
Duplay, Maurice, 45
Durnovo, Pyotr, 129
Dutschke, Rudi, 395
Duval, Clement, 89
Duvalier, François "Papa Doc," 298, 500
Duvalier, Jean-Claude, 298
Dylan, Bob, 325-26
Dzerzhinsky, Feliks, 150, 152, 153, 154, 164, 193-94, 228
Dzhugashvili, Colonel Yakov, 212

East Germany, 200, 442
East Indians: in Mozambique, 477
Eastland, James O., 243
Ecevit, Bulent, 446

Echavarria, Octavio, 296
Echeverria Alvarez, Luis, 290, 292-93, 371
Egan, John Patrick, 267
Egypt, 452, 453, 457, 460, 464, 465, 468, 512, 538, 561, 564, 566, 569, 570, 572
Egyptian Military Academy, 453
Eichmann, Adolf, 208, 218, 558
Eid, Guy, 568
Eisner, Kurt, 204
El Al, 462, 466, 510, 512, 563-69 *passim*
Elbrick, Charles Burke, 258
Elizabeth, Empress of Austria and Queen of Hungary, 90, 537
Elizabeth I, Queen of England, 33, 376
Elrod, Richard, 333-34
Elrom, Ephraim, 442, 444
Emperanza, Alvarez, 407
Engels, Friedrich, 24, 39, 68, 69, 72-75, 76, 77, 121, 134, 181, 191, 224, 525; *Anti-Dühring, The,* 15-16, 74
England, xiii, 49, 70, 92, 107, 157 *n.,* 158, 182, 208, 215, 301 *n.,* 365, 371, 414, 514, 546; IRA terror in, 381, 389-91, 393, 555, 556; *see also* Great Britain
Entebbe airport raid, *see* Uganda
Epstein, Edward Jay, 306
Equitorial Guinea, 483
Erez, Ismail, 406, 447
Eritrea, 469-72; ELP of, 470-72; terror in, 260, 470-72
Erzberger, Mathias, 204
Essex, Mark James, 316-17, 511
Establishment, *see* state, the
Estonia, 162, 213
Ethiopia, 469-72
Europe, 73, 83, 91, 95, 185, 514, 522, 576; Eastern, 100, 366, 475, 478, 522
Europe, Western, 3, 39, 40, 41, 68, 70, 73, 80, 81, 107, 121, 144, 158, 164, 181, 183, 223-24, 411, 458, 467, 468, 524, 528, 537, 543; Black Panthers in, 309-10; Red terror in, 67, 79-80, 83-91, 94-95, 406, 517, 521, 526, 548
Exxon, 267, 516

Faisal, King of Saudi Arabia, 468, 570
Fanon, Frantz, x-xi, 29, 301 and *n.,* 302-03, 305, 311, 313, 314, 525; writings of, 302
Farah, Empress of Iran, 512
Farouk I, King of Egypt, 450
Fascism, 167, 203, 403, 411-12, 496, 501, 513; neofascism, 401, 402, 403, 413, 495-96, 497, 513; *see also* individual countries
Fatah, 290, 314, 449-50 and *n.,* 451-59 *passim,* 462, 466, 538, 574, 575; Black September, 67, 428, 457-58, 463, 512, 541, 542, 555, 565-69 *passim;* and Palestinian refugees, 450, 453-54, 458; *see also* Arab fedayeen; Palestine Liberation Organization
Federal Bureau of Investigation, 35, 306 and *n.,* 307, 313, 315, 320, 329, 340, 356, 358, 359, 362, 555
Feltrinelli, Giangiacomo, 32, 402-03
Ferreira, Joaquim Camara, 257, 260
Fest, Joachim C., 211
Fiat-Concord, 266, 516
Figaro, Le, 541
Figueroa, Ruben, 291
Fine, David Sylvan, 68, 338
Finland, 143, 146, 148, 155, 160, 189, 554
Finley, James, 443
Firestone-Argentina, 266
Firmenich, Mario, 269
FitzGerald, Frances: *Fire in the Lake,* 419
Flanagan, Brian, 334

Flint, Michigan, 334-35
Florence, Italy, 84-85
Foerster, Werner, 318, 320
Fonseca Amador, Carlos, 298
Ford, Gerald R., 28, 34, 201, 363, 440, 480, 559
Ford Motor Company, 267, 516
Foster, Dr. Marcus, 342, 349-51, 362
Fouché, Joseph, 60-61, 63, 65
Fouquier-Tinville, Antoine, 53, 62, 64
Fourier, Charles, 80
France, 40, 41, 44, 56, 58, 63, 64, 65, 66, 70, 76, 79, 106 *n.,* 107, 144, 163, 176, 215, 301 *n.,* 410-11, 441, 447, 453, 538-40, 572; Algerian independence from, x, 34, 253, 301, 302, 404, 451, 452, 494-95, 560-61; Dreyfus Affair, 159; OAS in, 404, 494-95; Red terror in, 73-74, 82, 87-89, 90, 210, 404-06, 526, 537; student rioting in, 325, 238, 369, 405-06; White terror in, 40, 63-66, 70, 71, 72, 82, 159, 404, 406, 488, 494-96, 513; *see also* Basque terrorists; Breton terrorists; French Revolution; Paris; Terror, Reign of
Francis, Bishop, 40
Francis I, Emperor of Austria, 42, 43
Franco, Francisco, 293, 406, 407-08, 410-12, 497
Frankfurt, Germany, 207, 395, 397, 398, 401, 470, 538
Franz Ferdinand, Archduke, 91
Franz Joseph II, Emperor of Austria-Hungary, 90, 91
Fraunces Tavern, N.Y., 300
Frederick William II, King of Prussia, 42
Freedman, Dr. Lawrence, 26-30, 68, 74
Freiheit, 95, 96, 100
French Revolution, 39-66, 70, 76, 158, 376, 551; Commune of Paris, 41, 42, 58, 62; Constitution of 1791, 42; Cordeliers, 42, 46, 53, 58, 59; émigrés of, 42, 55-56, 60, 65; Girondins of, 42-53 *passim,* 58, 59; Jacobins, 18-19, 42-49 *passim,* 52, 53, 55, 60, 61, 64, 135, 147, 183, 561; National Convention of, 42-51 *passim,* 55-56, 60, 61, 62, 64; storming of Bastille, 41, 43; Thermidorians, 63-64; Wars of, 42, 43, 46, 49, 50; *see also* Terror, Reign of
Freud, Dr. Sigmund, 8, 10, 27, 349
Frick, Henry Clay, 100
Fromm, Erich, 10: *Anatomy of Human Destructiveness, The,* 8-9, 190-91
Fromme, Lynette (Squeaky), 27, 28, 363
Frondizi, Arturo and Silvio, 270
Fuentes Mohr, Alberto, 287
Fukien, China, 238
Furnier, Vincent ("Alice Cooper"), 54
Furuya, Yutaka, 438-39

Gadea, Hilda, 17, 246-47, 531
Gagnon, Charles, 366-68, 372
Galicia, Spain, 411
Gallagher, James, 378
Gallo, Charles, 87
Gandhi, Mahatma, 427
Garfield, James, 90, 94, 117
Garry, Charles, R., 306
Gaughan, Michael, 389
Gaza Strip, 451, 453, 454
Gazienter, Turkey, 447
Gefflot, Yann-Morvan, 404
Geisel, General Ernesto, 503
Geneva, Switzerland, 90, 431, 537, 571
Geneva Convention, 212, 387
Genghis Khan, 5-6, 509, 515
Genoa, Italy, 402
George, Henry, 99
Germany, 40, 68, 69, 70-71, 73, 74, 87, 91, 95,

163, 204, 287, 514; Communists of, 95, 161, 204, 205, 208; Social Democratic Party of, 95, 159, 162, 164, 167, 205, 206, 208; Weimar Republic of, xi, 203, 205, 206; White terror in, 162, 167, 179-80, 203-04; and World War I, 86, 146, 157 n., 204, 505; *see also* East and West Germany; Nazi Germany

Gestapo, *see* Nazi Germany

Gezmis, Deniz, 442-43, 445

Giap, General Vo Nguyen, 251

Giscard d'Estaing, Valéry, 406

Goebbels, Dr. Josef, 208-09, 218

Goering, Hermann, 206, 218

Goethe, Johann, 169

Golan Heights, 289, 468, 570

Gold, Eugene, 320

Gold, Ted, 337

Goldenberg, Grigory, 111

Goldman, Emma, 100-01, 102, 103, 105, 106 n., 437 n., 538

Goldshtein-Volodarsky, Moisei, 155

Goldwater, Barry, 347

Goleta, California, 348

Gorbanveskaya, Nataliya, 200

Gorky, Maxim, 153, 166, 195, 537

Goulding, Cathal, 382-83, 384

Goulet, Yann, 405

Gray Panthers, 310

Great Britain, 441, 450, 453, 463, 464, 489, 548, 560-61, 565, 572; capital punishment rejected in, 390, 391, 558; and Cyprus, 413-14; and Greece, 412; and Ireland, 167, 376-79, 381, 382, 386-94 *passim*, 512, 523, 554, 555, 559; and Israel, 215, 451; and Malaya, 422-23, 425, 477; and UN resolution on terrorism, 549, 551-52; *see also* England

Greece, 572, 576; AAA of, 413; CIA in, 415-16; civil war in, 412-13; Communists of, 412-13, 484-85; and Cyprus, 384, 413-16, 447, 448; military junta of, 413, 415; peasants of, 412-13; Red terror in, 412-13, 415-16, 563, 564, 569; and Soviet Union 412-13, 485; torture in, 413; and the West, 412-13, 415; White terror in, 412-13, 488

Greece, ancient, 3, 514

Greenlee, Sam: *Spook Who Sat by the Door, The*, 342

Grinevetsky, Ignaty, 116

Grivas, General George, 413-15

Gromyko, Andrei A., 550

Grynszpan, Herschel, 210

Guadalajara, Mexico, 290, 292

Guatemala, 17, 246, 286-88, 531; CIA in, 246 and n.; FAR of, 287; overthrow of Arbenz, 246-47, 250, 286; Red terror in, 286-88; torture in, 287; White terror in, 286-88

Guatemala City, Guatemala, 286

Guerrero, Mexico, 291 and n.

guerrillas, 3, 69, 70, 83, 223, 253-60, 387, 417-18, 430, 470, 515, 549; inspirations of, 39, 67-68, 75, 78, 131, 172, 244, 257, 476; and peasants (masses), 251, 260, 294, 295, 298, 330, 412, 420-21, 424, 428, 472, 533-34; urban, 57, 83, 223, 251, 257, 258-60, 276, 427, 428, 512, 554; *see also* Guevara, Dr. Ernesto Ché; individual groups

Guevara, Dr. Ernesto Ché, 244-53, 331, 355, 402, 525; in Bolivia, 244-55 *passim*, 282; and Castro, 17, 244, 246, 247-49, 251; in Congo, 249, 251; death of avenged, 252-53, 257, 406; and destruction of armed forces, 247, 250, 505; in Guatemala, 246 and n., 250, 531; guerrilla methods of, 245, 249-57 *passim*; as inspiration to terrorists, 96, 244, 245, 251, 252, 264, 338,

387, 430, 529, 533, 534; manuals of, 245, 250-51, 334; and Maoism, 248, 251; and Old Guard Communists, 247-48, 257, 276; rejection of gradualism, 17, 248, 249; on revolution, 245, 261, 272, 328, 330, 417, 418; and terrorism, 47, 247-50, 504

Guillotin, Dr. Joseph, 53-54, 525

Guinea, Republic of, 475, 476

Guinea-Bissau, 475-76

Guiteau, Charles J., 117

Gumilyov, Nikolai, 153

Gurevich, Mikhail, 192

Gypsies, 211, 213, 496

Habash, Dr. George, 16, 67, 431, 433, 435, 437, 447, 459-61, 462, 466, 525, 538, 554, 563, 564, 566, 569, 572, 575-76

Hague, The, Holland, 438-39, 538-39, 573

Haile Selassie, 470, 471

Haiti: Red terror in, 298-99; *Tontons Macoutes* of, 298, 500

Hall, Camilla (Gabi), 345, 348, 349, 362

Hall, George F., 348

Halle, Germany, 167

Hamburg, Germany, 252, 397

Hamid, Hamid Feraeg, 471

Hammen, Oscar J., 69, 72

Hampton, Fred, 305, 307

Hanover, Germany, 398

Hanrahan, Edward V., 307

Haran, Simon, 407

Harbin, China, 230, 238

Harding, Mary, 533

Harkabi, Yehoshafat, 458; *Palestinians and Israel*, 29

Harrington, Dr. Robert, 27

Harris, Emily (Yolanda), 346-47, 349, 359-61, 362

Harris, Frank: *Bomb, The*, 99

Harris, William (Tico), 346-47, 349, 352, 359-61, 362

Hassan II, King of Morocco, 571

Hausas, 481

Havana, Cuba, 240, 247-48, 251, 257, 281, 290, 296, 312 n., 373, 374, 480

Hawatmeh, Nayef, 67, 131, 461-62, 466, 566, 573-74

Hawkins, Colonel Lewis, 430-31

Hayden, Tom, 323

Hayes, Robert (Seth Ben Ysaak Ben Ysrael), 317, 318-19, 535

Haymarket Square Riot, 97-99, 100, 101, 336, 338, 517, 537

Haywood, William D., 104

Hearst, Patricia (Tania), 351-52, 357; kidnapping of, 267, 339, 351, 352-53, 516, 518-19, 520; transformation of, 14, 27, 28, 349, 355-61, 362, 515; trial of, 24 n., 358, 363-64

Hearst, Randolph A., 34, 352-56, 358, 360, 363, 516, 518, 520

Hearst, Mrs. Randolph A., 352, 358

Heath, Edward, 391

Hébert, Jacques René, 58

Heidelberg, Germany, 397

Heilungkiang, China, 238

Henry, Emile, 87-88, 89

Henry II, King of England, 376

Herrema, Dr. Tiede, 556

Herron, Thomas, 385-86

Herzen, Alexander, 81, 82, 108

Heydrich, Reinhard, 207-08, 209, 218, 228

Hilberg, Raul, 213

Hilliard, David, 308, 309

Hillsborough, California, 351-52

Hilton, Fred, 318

Himmler, Heinrich, 171, 190-91, 206-07, 208, 212, 216, 217, 218, 228, 500, 501
Hindenburg, Paul von, 205
Hirschfield Almado, Julio, 290
Hirt, Dr. Norman, 25
Hiss, Alger, 326
Hitler, Adolf, 153, 171, 204-05, 207, 218, 262, 383, 385, 395, 496-97, 559; and Jews, 202-20 *passim*, 482; *Mein Kampf*, 204; mental disturbance of, 31, 190-91; terror of, x, xi, 3, 22, 47, 57, 132, 168, 202-19 *passim*, 223, 228, 230, 231, 235, 240, 241-42, 488, 500, 515, 561; *see also* Nazi Germany
Hobbes, Thomas: *Leviathan, The,* 3
Ho Chi Minh, 47, 251, 334, 504
Hoedel, Max, 87
Hoffman, Julius, 312
Holland, 215, 437, 463, 464, 488, 489, 493, 539, 555-56, 569, 571, 572-73; East Asian terrorists in, 493-94, 556
Hollenben, Ehrenfried von, 258
Holly, Sean, 287
Homestead, Pennsylvania, 100
Honan, China, 238
Hong Kong, 229, 232, 233, 238
Horsley, Albert E. (Harry Orchard), 104
hostages, 510, 520; of Arabs, 455, 464-65, 469, 482, 540, 555, 565, 569-76 *passim;* in England, 391, 556; in Holland, 494, 555-56; of Japanese, 438-39, 538-39; in Nicaragua, 298; and patient siege, 555-57; in Philippines, 425-26; in Soviet Union, 183; in Sweden, 400; in Turkey, 444, 446; *see also* kidnappings; skyjackings
Hotel Savoy, Tel Aviv, 462
Houphouët-Boigny, Félix, 485
Howe, Marvine, 504
Howells, William Dean, 99
Hrkač, Miljenko, 499
Huambo, Angola, 480
Hué, S. Vietnam, 418-19
Huggins, Erika, 309
Hughes, John: *Indonesian Upheaval,* 493
Humbert I, King of Italy, 84, 86, 90, 102
Humphrey, Hubert H., 34
Hungary, 16, 73, 161, 167, 212, 215; revolt in, 199, 402, 520
Hung Ch'I (Red Flag), 225
Huns, 5
Hunt, E. Howard, Jr., 246 *n.*
Huss, John, 4
Hussain, Saddam, 429
Hussein, Ibn Talal, King of Jordan, 457, 566, 570; and war against Arab guerrillas, 67, 455-56, 457, 459, 460, 538, 540, 565, 570
Husseini, Haj Amin al-, 452-53
Hutchison, Barbara A., 299
Hutton, Bobby, 307
Hutus, ix-x, 481-82

Ibos, 481
India, 144, 175, 310, 427-29, 441; and China, 421, 427; Communists in, 427-28; Red terror in, 427-28, 522; settlers of, in Uganda, 482; and UN resolution on terrorism, 549; White terror in, 428
Indians: American, 92; Latin American, 4
Indonesia, 427, 488-93, 494, 572; Communists of, 488-93; military of, 489-93; Moslems of, 489, 490, 491; peasants of, 489, 491-92; Red terror in, 490; White terror in, 250, 488, 491-93
Industrial Workers of the World, 104
Ingersoll, Robert, 99
Inner Mongolia, China, 238
Innocent IV, Pope, 3

Inquisition, 3-4, 515
intellectuals, 121, 155-56, 167, 178, 309, 397-98; sympathy with terrorists, 21-22, 23, 140-41, 274, 504, 516, 520; terror against, 153, 182, 197, 201, 228, 443; as terrorists, 132, 175, 260, 453, 526
International Business Machines, 273
International Commission of Jurists, 431
International Telephone and Telegraph Corporation, 340, 398
International Terrorist Collective, 540
Ioannides, General Demetrios, 415
Iran, 429-32, 465, 569; Red terror in, 430-32, 541; Savak of, 430-41, 500; torture in, 431; White terror in, 430-32
Iran, Mohammed Riza Pahlevi, Shah of, 429-32, 512, 541, 547
Iraq, 457, 461, 462, 464, 465, 564, 569, 571, 573; Kurdish uprising in, 407, 429-30
Irbid, Jordan, 68
Ireland, 159, 172, 376, 390, 405; detention without trial in, 378, 391; and Great Britain, 167, 376-79, 381, 382, 386-94 *passim,* 512; SE of, 405; *see also* IRA; Ulster
Irgun, *see* Israel
Irish Republican Army (IRA), 17, 251, 377-80, 384-89 *passim,* 407, 511-12, 539, 541, 555, 558-61 *passim;* Officials of, 377, 380, 393; outlawed, 390, 524; Provos of, 131, 171, 377-93 *passim,* 407, 451, 512, 530, 540, 551, 553; terror of, 377-84 *passim,* 388-94, 540, 551, 556
Iskra, 134, 137, 142, 173
Israel, 310, 451, 453, 543, 554; Arab arms smuggling in, 458-59, 531 *n.;* Arab fedayeen terror against, 67, 244, 406, 435-36, 437, 442, 448-68 *passim,* 482, 511, 512, 520, 530, 535, 538, 540, 541, 546, 548, 549, 550, 555, 558, 561, 563-76; counterterror of, 455, 456, 458, 466-68, 482, 553, 554-55, 558, 563-64, 566, 574, 576; and Eichmann, 218, 519; Intelligence of, 456, 460, 466-68, 558, 559, 569; Irgun of, 215, 387, 450-51; Mossad of, 466-67; October War, 289, 457, 458, 467, 468, 512, 538, 554, 570-71; precautions against terror in, 510, 540, 565, 566, 567, 569; rejected demands of terrorists, 293, 466, 538, 555, 556; Six Day War, 429, 452, 453, 455, 460; Stern Group of, 387, 450; and the West, 215, 451, 542, 550, 565; West Bank, 453, 454, 455, 456, 458
Istanbul, Turkey, 442, 443, 445, 540
Italy, 70, 203, 401-03, 411, 467, 470, 500, 564, 567, 568; Carbonari rebels in, 70; Communist Party of, 402-03; Fascism in, 167, 403, 403; neofascism in, 401, 402, 403, 496; Red terror in, 70, 80-90 *passim,* 102, 203, 401-03, 404, 405, 521, 522, 526, 537; rejected demands of terrorists, 402; and UN resolution on terrorism, 549; White terror in, 401, 402, 403-04
Ivanov, Ivan, 78
Ivory Coast, 485

Jackson, Geoffrey: *People's Prison (Surviving the Long Night),* 274, 528, 531
Jackson, George, 14, 304, 355
Jackson State College, 308, 337
Jacobins, *see* French Revolution
Jacobs, John, 335
James, Daniel, 244, 255
Japan, 122, 128, 142, 242-43, 448, 543, 572; Communist Party in, 432, 441; Red terror in, 433-35, 437, 439-42, 522; and World War II, 421, 422, 426, 441
Japan Air Lines, 437, 569
Japanese terrorists, 526, 538-39, 556, 559, 569;

and Arabs, 433, 437-39, 442, 538, 540; and Communism, 432, 440; discipline of, 434, 435, 436, 439; inspirations of, 68, 131, 252, 440; and Lydda airport massacre, 67, 435-36, 437, 461, 538, 548, 549, 566-67; and PFLP, 433, 435, 437; Red Army (*Sekigun*), 433-42 *passim,* 461, 539; and students, 433, 434, 440, 441-42
Jaurès, Jean, 76
Java, 489-93 *passim; see also* Indonesia
Jebreel, Ahmed, 67, 462, 464-65, 565, 568, 573, 574
Jehovah's Witnesses, 213, 483
Jelić, Dr. Branko, 500
Jenkins, Roy, 558
Jerusalem, 310, 454, 458, 575, 576
Jews, 100-01, 125, 326, 387, 538; and anti-Semitism, 203, 204, 211, 215, 495-96; in Nazi Germany, 202, 204-05, 208-17, 220, 397, 482; as refugees, 215, 230; submissiveness of, 216, 219
Joan of Arc, 4
Johnson, Andrew, 93
Johnson, Christine, 359, 361
Joll, James, 86
Jones, James, 418-19
Jordan, 67, 397, 453, 457, 460, 564, 565, 566, 569, 574; war against Arab guerrillas, 66-67, 455-56, 457, 459, 460, 538, 540, 565, 570
Juan Carlos, King of Spain, 412
Juarez, Mexico, 290
Juarez, Spain, 88
Jung, Carl, 8, 27, 30
Junta of Revolutionary Coordination, 261, 274, 282, 283, 284
Jura Anarchist Federation, 88, 95

Kaliayev, Ivan, 530, 531
Kaltenbrunner, Ernst, 208, 218
Kamenev, Lev Borisovich, 194
Kampf, Der, 175
Kaplan, Abraham, 28-29
Kaplan, Dora, 158-59, 166, 168
Karachi, Pakistan, 470, 572
Karaganda, USSR, 198, 220
Karakozov, Dmitry, 110, 112
Karameh, Jordan, 455
Kariuki, Josiah, 482
Karlsruhe, Germany, 124
Kaunda, Kenneth, 485
Kautsky, Karl, 159, 181-83; *Dictatorship of the Proletariat, The,* 181; *Terrorism and Communism,* 164, 181
Kayyali, Abdel Wahab, 463
Kazakhs, 230
Kazakov, A. N., 192
Kazan, USSR, 159, 179
Kennan, George F., 197
Kennedy, Caroline, 391
Kennedy, Edward, 559
Kennedy, John F., 34, 103, 323
Kennedy, Robert F., 103, 538, 566, 568
Kent State University, 308, 337
Kenya, 475, 482, 549, 560-61, 576
Kerensky, Alexander, xiii, 129-30, 147, 148, 149, 151, 155, 161, 167, 176, 182, 522
KGB (MGB), 25, 193, 194 *n.,* 199-201, 252, 288
Khaled, Leila, 520, 540, 555, 564, 565
Khalturin, Stepan, 112-13, 117
Kharkov, Russia, 124
Khartoum, Sudan, 398, 457, 464, 538, 555, 567-68
Khrushchev, Nikita, 25, 188, 189, 190, 196, 199, 200
Kibalchich, Nikolai, 112, 115, 116-17, 530

kidnappings, 12, 18, 24, 510-11, 515; Arab, 468, 469; in Argentina, 264-72 *passim;* in Brazil, 257, 258; of businessmen, 266-73 *passim,* 296, 401, 407, 516, 518, 560; in Canada, 369-75; in Colombia, 296; counterterror for, 557-58; in Dominican Republic, 299; in Eritrea, 470, 471, 472; in France, 404; in Guatemala, 287; in Haiti, 298; Hearst, 267, 339, 351, 352-53, 515, 518-19, 520; in Ireland, 556; in Italy, 401-02; by Japanese, 433; in Mexico, 290, 291, 292-93; patient siege in, 556-57, 561; prevention of, 273, 558; in Rhodesia, 484-85; in Spain, 407; in Turkey, 443, 444; in Ulster, 388; in United States, 555, 556-57; in Uruguay, 274-80 *passim;* in Venezuela, 297; in West Germany, 400, 401, 520-21, 555; *see also* hostages
Kiev, Ukraine, 91, 129, 213-14
Kilrea, N. Ireland, 388
King, Martin Luther, 103-04, 307, 327
Kinshasa, Zaire, 478
Kirov, Sergei, 184-85
Kissinger, Dr. Henry, 201, 409, 410, 504, 570
Kitchener, Lord Horatio, 157 *n.,* 422
KLM, 463, 571
Knights of Labor, 97
Knox, Clinton, 298
Koestler, Arthur: *Darkness at Noon,* 194
Kolchak, Admiral Alexander, 162, 182
Kolesnik, Dmitry N., 547
Kollontai, Alexandra, 165
Kolokol (The Bell), 108
Konkret, 396-97
Korean War, 236, 242, 275
Kornilov, General Lavr, 151
Korolyov, Sergei, 192
Kosmodemyanskaya, Zoya, 349
Kosygin, Aleksei, 202, 289, 366, 462
KPFA radio station, Berkeley, 340, 353-54, 355
Krasnov, General Pyotr, 155-56, 161
Kravchinsky-Stepniak, Sergei, 84-85, 111, 537
Kreisky, Bruno, 465, 570
Kriegman, E., 546
Kritzman, Max, 435
Kropotkin, Prince Dmitry, 111
Kropotkin, Prince Pyotr, 85-86, 88, 90, 95, 101, 111, 123, 126, 526, 529 *n.,* 537; *Conquest of Bread, The,* 88
Krupp, Gustav von Bohlen, 164, 205
Krupskaya, Nadezhda (Lenin's wife), 31, 134, 158, 165
Kuala Lumpur, Malaysia, 423, 424, 439
Ku Klux Klan, 93
Kurkcu, Ertugrul, 444-45
Kursky, Dmitry, 168
Kutepov, General Pavel, 404
Kuwait, 453, 553, 569-70, 571, 572
Kuznetsov, Anatoly, 214
Kwangsi, China, 238
Kwantung, China, 238
Kyoto, Japan, 440

labor, 94, 97, 98, 104-05, 261, 267-72 *passim,* 532-33; violence in, 75-77, 94-100 *passim*
Labourbe, Jeanne, 163
Lacombe, Lucien (film), 34
LaGuardia Airport bombing, 545
Lamarca, Carlos, 257, 260
Lamballe, Marie, Princess de, 43
Lanctot, Jacques, 373
Lango tribe, 482
Laos, 420
La Paz, Bolivia, 251, 254, 282
La Plata, Argentina, 272
Laporte, Pierre, 371-74

Lasky, Melvin J., 396-97, 520
Latin America, 17, 39, 99, 248, 251, 261, 274, 282, 283, 284, 286, 451, 497, 506, 518, 531-34, 536, 543; Maoists in, 257, 265, 289, 554; terror in, 4, 12-13, 17-18, 68, 131, 275, 286, 289, 503, 516, 520, 522, 549, 554; Trotskyites in, 248, 253, 262, 289, 554; see also individual countries
Latsis, Marty, 152
Laun, Alfred, 3rd, 267
Laurel, Maryland, 34, 103
Lavoisier, Antoine Laurent, 59, 153
Leary, Timothy, 315, 338
Lebanon, 21, 435, 442, 453, 456, 458, 460, 462, 466, 467, 468, 531 n., 538, 540, 553, 554-55, 558, 564-75 passim; civil war in, 456, 457, 462, 466-67, 555, 561, 575; Syrian intervention in, 456, 457, 462, 467, 575
Lee, Dr. Russel V., 31
left-wing terror, see Red terror
Leipzig, Germany, 134
Lemieux, Robert, 371, 372, 375
Lenin, Vladimir Ilyich, 13, 17, 39, 47, 66, 67, 69, 71, 110, 120, 121, 128 n., 129-30, 131-70, 176, 179, 184, 185, 187, 189, 194, 272, 292, 304 n., 335 n., 345, 366, 505, 525, 529; as inspiration to terrorists, 16, 39, 67-68, 132, 224, 244-45, 289, 297, 326, 387; mental disturbance of, 31-32; rejection of morality by, 14-15, 16, 74, 132, 143; and Social Revolutionaries, 136-40, 143-45, 149, 154, 155, 158, 162, 168, 250, 278; terror of, xii, xiii, 3, 4, 13, 16, 57, 59, 74, 75, 76, 130-70 passim, 172, 176, 186-98 passim, 202, 203, 205, 210, 219-20, 223-28 passim, 231, 240, 482, 504, 510, 517, 519, 521, 522; and Trotsky, 135, 171, 173, 176, 189; writings of, 134, 135, 138, 148, 181
Leninism, 131-32, 148, 169, 171, 254, 366, 401, 550
Lentino, Italy, 84
Leonhardy, Terrance G., 290, 292-93
Lewis, Minnie, 359, 361
Lhasa, Tibet, 230
liberals, 71, 85, 120, 121, 129-30, 143-44, 146-47, 151, 155, 162, 168, 176, 185, 204, 208, 303, 309, 325; and the Left, 243, 260, 277, 398, 414, 560; Lenin's hatred of, 17, 71
Libya, 425, 426, 427, 439, 458-65 passim, 470, 471, 541, 547, 552, 553, 567, 569, 570, 575
Lidice, Czechoslovakia, 208
Liebknecht, Karl, 161, 164, 180, 203-04
Lima, Peru, 275, 294
Limassol, Cyprus, 415
Lincoln, Abraham, 93, 94, 182
Lingg, Louis, 99
Lin Piao, 32, 230
Linz, Austria, 208
Lipari Islands, 203
Lisbon, Portugal, 475, 477, 501, 502
Little, Russell J. (Osceola), 343-51 passim, 362
Liu (Chinese farmer), 227-28
Liuchiatsun, China, 227
Liu Shao-ch'i, 230, 238
Liuvras, Jorge Manera, 279
Lodz, Poland, 216
Lo Jui-ch'ing, 225, 226, 228-29
London, England, 71, 72, 85, 86, 88, 95, 108, 139, 141, 150, 173, 383, 415, 422, 429, 539, 540, 565, 566, 567, 572; IRA terror in, 381, 389, 390-91, 540, 556
London Daily Express, 391
Londonderry, N. Ireland, 392-93
Long, Huey P., 103, 303
Lopatin, Hermann, 522

Lopez, Atilio, 270
Lopez Michelson, Alfonso, 295
Lopukhin, Aleksei, 126-28
Lorenz, Konrad, 9
Lorenz, Peter, 400-01, 520, 555
Lortie, Bernard, 372-73, 374-75
Los Angeles, California, 340, 342, 358-59, 568
Los Angeles Times, 104
Louis XVI, King of France, 41, 42-43, 45, 46, 50, 57, 60, 61, 64
Louis XVIII, King of France, 65
Lourenco Marques, Mozambique, 477
Lovejoy, Elijah P., 93
lower classes, 41, 516-17, 520, 526
Luanda, Angola, 479-81, 486
Luce, Phillip Abbot, 325
Ludendorff, General Erich, 204
Lufthansa, 463, 566, 567, 571
Lugbaras, 482
Luis Filipe, Prince of Portugal, 90
Lumumba, Patrice, 301
Lumumba University, 288, 539, 541-42
Luxemburg, Rosa, 161, 164, 180, 203-04
Lydda airport, 563, 564, 566, 576; massacre, 67, 435-36, 437, 461, 538, 548, 549, 566-67
Lyons, France, 56, 61, 63, 81, 90, 537

Maalot massacre, 67, 244, 436, 462, 466, 467, 558, 573-74
MacArthur, Douglas, 430
MacDermot, Niall, 281
Machel, Samora Moises, 476, 477
Machiavelli, Niccolò, 15
MacStiofain, Sean, 382-85
Madariaga, Julian, 407
Madelin, Louis, 62
Madrid, Spain, 88, 408, 411, 471, 572
Magsaysay, Ramon, 426
Magyars, 73
Majdanek, 213
Makarios, Archbishop, 414-15, 568
Malatesta, Enrico, 83-85, 86, 88
Malaya, 421-26, 484, 489; and Britain, 422-23, 425, 477; and China, 421-22, 424
Malaysia, 421, 422 n., 424
Malcolm X, 316
Malle, Louis, 34
Malraux, André, 256
Malta, 571
Malthus, Thomas, 544
Mammoud, Abou, 463
man: lack of humanity in, 215, 217, 420; and violence, 7-11, 22, 30, 34, 56-57, 75
Managua, Nicaragua, 298
Manchester Guardian, The, 240
Manson, Charles, 27, 28, 33, 335-36, 363
Maoism, 14, 82, 172, 223-24, 248, 251, 257, 265, 289, 310, 317, 324, 325, 343, 344, 345, 348, 365-66, 380, 395, 397, 401, 402, 411, 420, 425, 426-27, 428, 431, 440, 443, 460, 461, 476, 489-91, 529, 554
Mao Tse-tung, 15, 32, 171, 191, 223, 226, 228, 229, 289, 422, 425, 489, 543; boasts of terror, 224-25, 240-43; as inspiration to terrorists, 78, 96, 223-24, 244, 326; terror of, xii, 47, 57, 74, 168, 172, 223-43, 366, 504; writings of, 223, 224, 238, 251, 334; see also China, Communist
Marat, Jean Paul, 42, 50, 57; L'Ami du peuple, 43
Marcellin, Raymond, 405
Marcha (Progress), 281
Marcos, Ferdinand E., 425, 426, 427
Marcuse, Herbert, 14, 82, 396, 528-29

Marie Antoinette, Queen of France, 42, 43, 53, 57
Marighella, Carlos, 256-60; *Minimanual of the Urban Guerrilla*, 96, 258-60, 443
Marseilles, France, 65, 209, 496
Martinique, 301, 302
Martov, Yuly, 138, 139, 162, 167, 168, 177
Marx, Karl, 13-14, 16, 17, 39, 66, 67-77, 79, 81-83, 121, 141, 159, 180, 181, 191, 220, 345, 380, 505, 522, 529; as inspiration to terrorists, 16, 39, 67-68, 75, 121, 132, 224, 244, 289, 326, 522; and terror, 3, 11, 68-75, 76, 77, 130, 134; writings of, 68, 69, 71, 134
Marxism, 10, 15, 75, 82, 95, 121, 155-56, 178, 223-24, 246, 256, 268, 269, 303, 367, 368, 380, 431, 440, 462, 470, 477, 480-81, 521, 530, 543-44; and proletariat, 121, 122, 134, 135, 139, 140, 151, 155, 158, 174-75, 177, 178, 181-82
Marxism-Leninism, 16, 39, 57, 67-68, 75, 78, 223-24, 344, 395, 411, 460, 529, 531
masses, 13, 137, 139, 144, 148, 153, 154, 187, 220, 225-28, 230, 235-40, 286, 302, 331, 365-66, 369-70, 375, 395, 446, 517, 518, 527; passive acceptance and submission in, 21-22, 216-18, 219-20, 232, 357-58; *see also* peasants
Matos, Huber, 256
Matteoti, Giacomo, 203
Matthews, Thomas, 360
Maùcias, Francisco, 483
Mau Mau terrorists, 475, 482, 561
Mauriac, François, 256
Mauthausen, 213
Maze Prison, 379, 391
Mazzini, Giuseppe, 90 *n*.
McCormick Harvester plant, 98
McKinley, William, 90, 101-02, 509, 538
McNamara, John J. and James, 104-05
McWhirter, Ross, 391
Medellín, Colombia, 532
media: terrorists' use of, 18, 21, 324-25, 349, 354, 369-70, 374, 454, 519-21
Medvedev, Roy, 187
Mein, John Gordon, 286
Meinhof, Ulrike, 395, 396-401
Meins, Holger, 399-400
Melen, Ferit, 443
Melville, Samuel, 24, 338, 562
Memphis, Tennessee, 103, 307
Mendoza, Argentina, 271
Mensheviks, 31, 135, 139-40, 143, 144, 149, 155, 157, 162, 168, 173, 177, 180, 189
mental illness, 21-35, 56-57, 83, 89, 101-02, 104, 190-91, 200, 220, 383; Belfast syndrome, 382; in secret police, 25-26, 152, 217; Soviets' use of asylums as punishment, 24-25, 166-67, 199, 200, 202, 525
Menzhinsky, Vyacheslav, 25, 194
Mercader, Caridad, 196
Meslier, Jean: *Testament*, 40
Mexico, 173, 184-85, 247, 288-91 and *n*., 292-93, 503; Communism in, 288-89, 541; FRAP of, 290, 292-93, MAR of, 288; Red terror in, 288, 289-93, 371, 522, 524, 526; rejected demands of terrorists, 293; student riots in, 288; White terror in, 288, 293; and Zionism resolution, 293
Mexico City, Mexico, 256, 258, 288, 292, 298
Meyers, Twymon, 321
Mezentsev, General Nikolai, 111
MGB, 196, 199
Miami, Florida, 103, 310
middle classes, 13, 41, 59, 97, 99, 132, 276, 322, 520; blacks in, 311, 517; and Red terror, 504,

525-27; and White terror, 283, 504-06; *see also* bourgeoisie
Middle East, 82, 223-24, 252, 260, 289, 293, 309, 314, 540, 544; *see also* individual countries
Middleton, Drew, 417
Miguel Garcia, Father, 534
Milan, Italy, 401, 402, 497
military installation raids, 257, 259, 265-66, 270, 271, 276, 291 *n*., 292, 338, 384, 397, 427
Miller, General Yevgeny, 404
Milwaukee, Wisconsin, 103
Mindanao, Philippines, 425
Minis, Anastassios P., 413
Minsk, Russia, 134, 151
Mirabeau, Count Honoré Gabriel, 44
Miranda, Doug, 528
Mishra, Lalit Narayan, 427
Misiones, Argentina, 265
Mitrione, Daniel, 274, 276-77
Mitsui and Company, 440
Mitterand, François, 406
Mizoram, India, 427-28
Mobutu Sese Seko, 480
Mogadishu, Somalia, 469
Mohsen, Zuheir, 462
Molly Maguires, 94
Mondlane, Dr. Eduardo Chivambo, 476
Mongols, 4-5, 7
Montevideo, Uruguay, 252, 275-76, 277, 279
Montreal, Canada, 366-74 *passim*
Mooney, Thomas J., 105
Moore, George C., 568
Moore, Sara Jane, 34-35, 363
Morales Bermúdez, Francisco, 294-95
morality: of communism, 14-16, 74, 132, 143; of prevention of terror, 559-60; of terror, 14-16, 19, 132
Morf, Dr. Gustave, 368
Morgan, Colonel Ernest R., 465
Morgan, J. P., 105
Morocco, 459, 571
Morozov, Pavlik, 234
Moscow, USSR, 70, 109, 112, 122, 123, 142, 156, 165, 177, 182, 185, 192, 193, 201, 462, 542
Moslem Brotherhood, 450, 453, 458
Moslem International Guerrillas, 572
Moslems, 457-58, 460, 530, 535, 575; in Africa, 476, 482; in Eritrea, 470, 472; in Indonesia, 489, 490, 491; in Lebanon, 456, 457, 466-67; in Philippines, 425-26, 427, 541; in Turkey, 446, 448
Most, Johann, 27, 95-97, 100-01, 103, 223, 517, 538
Moumié, Felix, 301
Mountjoy Prison, 385, 388, 511
Moynihan, Daniel P., 561
Mozambique, 473-74, 476-78, 483, 561; *Frelimo* of, 476-77
Mueller, Gerhard, 398
Muenster, Westphalia, 40
Muenzer, Thomas, 40
Mukden, China, 239
Mundo, El, 270
Munich, Germany, 204, 206, 219, 397, 509, 564; *see also* Olympic Games
Mun Se Kwang, 439-40
murders, 92-93, 539-40; *see also* assassinations
Mussolini, Benito, 47, 75, 168, 203, 215, 262, 496
MVD, 196, 199
My Lai massacre, 419

Nagaland, India, 427-28
Nagel, Kurt, 297
Nahariya, Israel, 574

618   Index

Najjar, Mohammed Yussef, 466
Namibia (South-West Africa), 486-87
Nanking, China, 239
Nantes, France, 50, 57
Naples, Italy, 84
Napoleon I, 22, 40, 52, 56, 62, 63, 64, 65, 70, 153, 383
Napoleon III, 65, 89 *n.*
Narodniki, 57, 69, 107-18, 121, 123, 136, 202, 516-17, 521, 526, 530, 535; assassination of Alexander II, 86, 90, 109-16, 408, 509; as inspiration to other terrorists, 107, 522, 529-30; Land and Liberty, 109, 111; People's Will, 109-18, 120, 173, 561; program of, 109, 528
Nasser, Gamal Abdel, 452, 455, 460
Nasser, Kamal, 466
Nasution, Abdul Haris, 490
Nazi Germany, 203-04; concentration camps in, 203, 208, 212-13, 215, 216-17, 219, 220; Gestapo of, 4, 203, 205-12 *passim,* 218, 500, 501; terror in, 205-19, 228, 231, 234, 239, 379, 397, 488, 496, 513, 515, 525; torture in, 4, 203, 204, 208, 213, 501, 515
Nechayev, Sergei, 15, 17, 78-79, 108, 110, 135-36, 510, 526, 528, 529
Necker, Jacques, 41
Neebe, Oscar W., 99
Nepal, 230, 428
Neto, Dr. Agostinho, 478-80, 486
Neue Rheinische Zeitung, 71
New Haven, Connecticut, 309
New Left, 79, 223-24, 253, 308, 323, 326, 327, 341, 355
New Orleans, Louisiana, 94, 316-17, 511
Newton, Huey P., 302, 303, 309, 312 and *n.,* 316
New Year's Gang, 338
New York City, New York, 310, 316-22 *passim,* 327, 336-37, 339, 340, 368, 537, 556-57; terror in, 89, 94, 96, 100, 101, 103, 105, 299-300, 310, 337
New Yorker, The, 306
New York Times, The, 243, 286, 340, 417, 504
New Zealand, 310, 574
Ney, Marshal Michel, 65
Nicaragua, 297-98, 540
Nicholas I, Tsar of Russia, 80, 81, 107
Nicholas II, Tsar of Russia, 91, 118, 121, 122-23, 127, 128, 129, 137, 140, 141, 146, 156, 509-10
Nicosia, Cyprus, 415, 463, 568, 571
Nidal Abou (code name), 464
Nigeria, 481, 544
Nihilists, 107-09, 434, 442
Nikolayev, Russia, 111
Nimes, France, 65
Niquero, Cuba, 247
Nixon, Richard M., 34, 201, 309, 325, 341, 570
Nizhni Novgorod, USSR, 156, 179
NKGB, 194 *n.*
NKVD, 194 and *n.,* 195-96, 199
Nobel, Alfred, 98
Nobel Peace Prize, 201
Noble, John H., 197
Noel, Cleo A., Jr., 568
Noguchi, Dr. Thomas, 362
Nomad, Max, 83; *Dreamers, Dynamiters, and Demagogues,* 105 *n.*
North America, 39, 163, 250, 258, 297, 406, 516, 531, 554, 561; *see also* individual countries
North Atlantic Treaty Organization (NATO), 397, 443, 445, 512
North Korea, 288, 313, 433, 434, 442, 461, 541
North Vietnam, 251, 288, 313, 330, 417, 420, 461, 506, 541; American sympathizers of, 418, 420; Red terror of, 417-20; torture in, 420

Norway, 467
nuclear power: in terror, 545-47; in warfare, 9, 250, 441
Nuclear Theft: Risks and Safeguards (Willrich and Taylor), 545-46
Numeiry, General Gaafar al-, 568
Nuremberg, Germany, 209, 398
Nuremberg Trials, 218

Oakland, California, 303, 305, 306, 311, 312 and *n.,* 315, 342, 343, 345, 350-51
Obote, Milton, 482
O'Connell, David, 390
Odessa, Russia, 112, 117, 122, 163
Ogaryov, Nikolai, 108
Oglesby, Richard J., 99
OGPU, 194, 199
oil, 429, 431-32, 448, 449, 465; embargo, 449, 468, 543, 547; energy crisis, 543, 546; financing terror, 437, 439, 449, 457, 459, 470, 537, 541
Okamoto, Kozo, 435-36, 466, 567, 574, 576
Olympic Airways, 563, 564
Olympic Games, 288; Munich massacre, 67, 406, 457, 463, 467, 538, 541, 546, 549, 550, 555, 556, 558, 567
Omsk, USSR, 192
O'Neal, William, 307
Ontario, Canada, 386
Organization of African Unity, 486
Organization of Petroleum Exporting Countries (OPEC), 465, 540, 575
Orly airport, 464
Orsini, Felice, 89 *n.*
Orwell, George: *Animal Farm,* 304 *n.*
Oswald, Lee Harvey, 34
Otis, Harrison Gray, 104
Otis Elevator, 273
Otradin, Nikolai, 187-88
Ottawa, Canada, 372
Oughton, Diana, 17, 337
Ovando Candia, Alfredo, 256

Paisley, Ian, 385
Pakistan, 428-29, 477, 482
Palestine, 215, 433, 450-51, 453-54, 458, 460, 463, 538, 550, 563, 564, 567, 568, 569, 573
Palestine Liberation Army, 457
Palestine Liberation Organization (PLO), 439, 449-64 *passim,* 467, 543, 547, 549, 552, 568, 571; *see also* Arab fedayeen; Arafat; Fatah
Palmer, A. Mitchell, 105
Panama, 246, 266, 297, 299, 556
Pan American, 455, 565, 571
Pandelakis, Stefanos, 413
Paraguay, 295; *Piragues* of, 500
Paris, France, 210, 281, 315, 410, 438, 469, 538, 540; student rioting in, 325, 328, 369, 405-06; terror in, 40, 41, 42, 43, 46, 52, 53, 55, 57, 58, 61, 62, 63-65, 68-76 *passim,* 82, 87-89, 183, 252-53, 281, 404, 406, 447, 464, 495, 525, 539-40, 569
Park Chung Hee, 440
Parkhurst Prison, 389
Parry, Albert, 22
Parsons, Albert R., 96-99
Pasternak, Boris: *Doctor Zhivago,* 402
Paul VI, Pope, 256, 543
Pavelić, Ante, 496-97, 500
peasants: and anarchists, 81-85, 121, 122, 517; and Communism, 149, 153, 156, 160, 177, 185, 418, 489, 491-92; and guerrillas, 251, 260, 294, 295, 298, 412, 420-21, 424, 428, 472, 533-34; Marx's contempt for, 81-82, 121; *see also* masses; individual countries

Peasants' War of 1524-26, 40
Pechiney Ugine Kuhlmann (firm), 539
Peking, China, 238, 240-41, 424
Peng, Chin, 422, 424
Penkovsky, Colonel Oleg V., 200
Pentagon, the, 339
Penza, USSR, 157
People's Daily, 225, 240-41
People's Will, *see* Narodniki
Peralta, Pedro Rodriguez, 475
Peredo, Coco, Inti, and Chato, 282
Perez Zukovic, Edmundo, 283
Perón, Evita, 261-62
Perón, Isabel, 262, 265, 267-72
Perón, Juan, 171, 261-65, 267-68, 270
Perovskaya, Sofiya, 112, 115, 116-17, 526, 530
Perry, Nancy Ling (Fahizah), 347-38, 349, 350-51, 362
Peru, 246, 274, 293-95
Peter and Paul Fortress, 78, 81, 110, 136, 173
Petrashevsky, Mikhail: Circle of, 80-81
Petrograd, USSR, 129, 146, 147, 148, 151, 155, 176, 189; *see also* St. Petersburg
Philippine Airlines, 425-26
Philippines, 425-27, 441, 572; Communists in, 425, 426-27; Moslems in, 425-26, 427, 541; Red terror in, 425-27, 526; rejected demands of terrorists, 426; White terror in, 427
Pilsudski, Josef, 523
Pinto de Andrade, Joaquim, 479
Piraeus, Greece, 413
Pisa, Italy, 85
Pisarev, Dmitry, 107
Pissarro, Camille, 88
Pita, Colonel Juan, 272
Plautus, Titus Maccius: *Asinaria*, 3
Plehve, Vyacheslav von, 122, 124, 140
Plekhanov, Georgy, 134-35, 139, 150-51
Pobedonostsev, Konstantin, 117
Poland, 73, 81, 200, 203, 210-16 *passim*, 496, 523
police, 94, 98-99, 103, 105, 411, 521-24; and anarchists, 88, 521; and Black Liberation Army, 14, 316-21; and Black Panthers, 304 and *n.*, 305-07, 309, 312; terror against, 142, 279, 331-33, 407-08, 427, 428, 521-24, 557-58
Polyarnaya Zvezda (The Polar Star), 108
Popular Democratic Front for the Liberation of Palestine (PDFLP), 67, 461-62, 466, 573-74
Popular Front for the Liberation of Palestine (PFLP), 16, 67, 433, 435, 437, 447, 459, 460-61, 466, 563, 569, 572, 576
Popular Front for the Liberation of Palestine—General Command, 67, 462, 464-65, 565, 568, 573, 574
Port Arthur: fall of, 122
Port-au-Prince, Haiti, 298
Port Huron, Michigan, 323
Portugal, 410; African empire of, 289, 472-81, 486, 512, 541, 550, 561; leftist military regime in, 295, 506; Pide of, 473-74, 501-03; Red terror in, 90, 144, 502; revolution in, 411, 477, 485, 502, 506, 523; White terror in, 412, 501-02
Portuguese Guinea, 451, 473, 474-76, 487; PAIGC of, 474
Posse, General Hugh Chiapee, 280
Potresov, Alexander, 142
Pound, Ezra, 215
Po Yi-po, 240
Prague, Czechoslovakia, 81, 208, 218, 396, 453
Prats Gonzales, General Carlos, 270-71
Pravda, 147, 148, 150, 151, 189
Presse, La, 367
Pretoria, S. Africa, 485
Price, Dolours and Marion, 389, 512

Progressive Labor Party, 324, 325
proletariat, 13, 14, 71, 72, 132; and anarchists, 81-82, 83, 85, 517; anti-Bolshevik, 153, 185; *see also* Marxism
propaganda, 136-39, 145, 160, 176, 179, 227, 258, 267, 366, 451, 489, 524; of terrorists, 421, 480, 498, 499, 516-18, 523, 543
Protestants, 376; of Ulster, 376-78, 384-94 *passim*, 561; *see also* Christians
Proudhon, Pierre Joseph, 13, 88
Prozorovsky, Prince Ivan, 6
Prussia, 42, 49
Puerto Rico: FALN of, 300; *Furia* of, 299; Red terror in, 299-300; terrorists of, in United States, 103-04, 299-300; Young Lords, 310, 332
Pugachev, Yemelian, 7, 108, 109, 129
Pullman works strike, 99
Pushkin, Alexander: *Captain's Daughter, The*, 7
Pyongyang, N. Korea, 538

Qaddafi, Colonel Muammar el-, 425, 426, 431, 458, 459, 463, 466, 541, 547
Qiryat Shemona, Israel, 67, 462, 467, 573
Quebec, 365-66, 371; separatists in, 68, 131, 365, 367, 374, 451, 560
Queen Elizabeth II, 379
Quijada, Admiral Hermes, 264

Rabat, Morocco, 547
Rabin, Yitzhak, 467, 564
Rackley, Alex, 306
radio stations: raids on, 257, 258, 490
Ramallah, Israel, 453
Rathenau, Walter, 204
Ravachol, François-Claudius, 89
Ravensbrueck, 213
Razak, Abdul, 424
Razin, Stenka (Stephen), 6-7, 108, 109
Razuvayev, G. A., 192
Reagan, Ronald, 519
Red Army, 176-79, 181, 189, 197, 250, 505
Red terror, 366, 488, 502, 504, 506, 560; as counterterror, 68, 71, 73, 131, 151, 163-64, 181, 262, 365, 389, 406, 473-79 *passim*, 483-87, 502, 523; *see also* Terror, Reign of; terrorism; individual countries
Reed, John: *Ten Days That Shook the World*, 148-49
Rega, José López, 268
Reinhard, Wolf-Dieter, 400
Remiro, Joseph M. (Bo), 343, 346-47, 349, 350, 362
Reverbel, Ulysses Pereyra, 280
Révolté, Le, 86
revolution, 19, 58, 136, 137, 253-54, 521-34; destruction of armed forces in, 247, 250, 505; dislike of reform in, 17, 109, 278, 297, 446, 560; Guevara on, 245, 261, 272, 328, 330, 417, 418; and war, 47, 72, 145, 154, 183-84; *see also* terrorism, in revolution; violence, in revolution
Rhodesia (Zimbabwe), 474, 476, 477, 483-86, 488, 550; and S. Africa, 484, 485-86
right-wing terror, *see* White terror
Rihaniya, Israel, 474-75
Rincon Quinones, General Ramon, 296
Rio Blanco, Nicaragua, 298
Rio de Janeiro, Brazil, 503, 534
Riyadh, Saudi Arabia, 570
Riza, Prince of Iran, 512
robberies: in Brazil, 257, 258; in Canada, 367; in Ireland, 379, 388, 389; in Japan, 433; in Mexico, 288, 292; in Russia, 123, 142, 189; in Tur-

robberies (*continued*)
    key, 443, 444; in United States, 316, 356, 359-60; in Uruguay, 276-77
Robbins, Terry, 337
Roberto, Holden Alvaro, 478, 480
Robespierre, Augustin, 62
Robespierre, Maximilien, 43, 44-45, 47-48, 58-62, 64, 65, 172, 184, 550; and Reign of Terror, xii, 3, 18-19, 22, 23, 39, 44, 46-60, 66, 67, 69, 70, 73, 76, 130, 132, 135, 153, 168, 187, 210, 223, 234, 379, 394, 525; religious fanaticism of, 18-19, 48, 51, 204, 530
rockets, 467, 475, 477, 480, 484, 512, 539, 541, 551, 553
Rodriguez, Victor, 287, 288
Roehl, Klaus Rainer, 396-97
Roehm, Captain Ernst, 209, 230
Rolović, Vladimir, 497
Rome, Italy, 464, 471, 512, 538, 548, 566, 567, 568, 571, 572
Rome, ancient, 3, 235, 514, 515
Roosevelt, Franklin D., 103
Roosevelt, Theodore, 99, 103
Rosario, Argentina, 245, 266
Rose, Jacques, 373, 375
Rose, Paul, 373, 374-75
Rostov, Russia, 124, 138, 164
Rousseau, Jean Jacques, 42, 44-45, 48
Royal Canadian Mounted Police, 368, 372
Rucci, José Ignaci, 268
Rudd, Mark, 16, 325-35 *passim*, 339
Rumania, 122, 212, 215; *Siguranza* of, 500
Russia, 6, 39, 73, 85, 91, 111, 125, 137, 522, 523, 528; émigrés from, 81, 117-18, 120, 134, 143, 144, 146, 173, 174, 230, 404; liberals in, 120, 121, 129-30, 143-44, 146-47, 151, 155, 162, 168, 176, 185; peasants of, 6-7, 80, 85, 107, 108-09, 121, 122, 128-29; Red terror in, 78, 85, 86, 90-91, 95, 107, 109-17, 120, 121-22, 123, 124, 129, 139, 140, 155, 168, 174, 180-81, 509-10, 517, 521, 522-23, 526, 529; reforms in, 107, 108-09, 120, 122-23, 128-29, 529; repression in, 80-81, 110, 116, 117, 120, 121, 128, 140, 174-75, 529; revolution of 1905, 86, 122-23, 140, 142, 143, 174-75; revolution of 1917, 129-30, 146-47; uprisings in, 6-7, 13, 80, 85, 121, 122, 138, 144; *see also* Soviet Union
Russian revolution (Bolshevik), xii, 22, 75, 129-30, 147-49, 152-53, 176, 178, 181, 182-83, 189, 202, 272, 505-06, 522, 523, 551
Russo-Japanese War, 122, 128, 142
Russo-Turkish War, 111
Rysakov, Nikolai, 115, 116-17

SA (storm troopers), 204, 205, 209
Sabbe, Osman Saleh, 470
Sabena, 566
Sacco, Nicola, 106
Sachsenhausen, 213, 216
Sacramento, California, 305
Sacre Coeur basilica, Paris, 406
Sadat, Anwar, 461, 468, 554, 566, 568
Sade, Donatien Alphonse, Count de, 57
Saida, Lebanon, 466
Saint Bartholomew's Night and Day Massacre, 40
Saint Just, Louis de, 51, 62
St. Louis, Missouri, 316, 317
St. Petersburg, Russia, 78, 109-12 *passim*, 122, 123, 133, 134, 139, 141, 148, 174; *see also* Petrograd
Saint-Simon, Claude Henri, Count de, 80
Sakharov, Andrei D., 201, 542
Salazar, Antonio de Oliveira, 501

Sale, Kirkpatrick: SDS, 327, 331, 332, 335
Salisbury, Rhodesia, 484, 486
Sallustro, Oberdan, 266
Sampson (Nikos Glorgiades), 414-16
Samuelson, Victor E., 267
San Antonio, Texas, 320
Sanchez, General Juan Carlos, 266
San Diego, California, 306
Sandino, Augusto Oscar, 297
San Francisco, California, 105, 316, 339, 350, 358, 362, 516, 519
San Francisco Chronicle, The, 350
San Juan, Puerto Rico, 299
San Lupo, Italy, 84
San Martin, General José de, 264
San Sebastian, Spain, 408
Santa Agueda, Spain, 90
Santiago, Chile, 256, 284
Santo Domingo, Dominican Republic, 556
Santucho Juarez, Mario, 263-64, 268
San Vincente de Chucuri, Colombia, 533
São Paulo, Brazil, 257, 258, 503, 534
Sarajevo, Yugoslavia, 91, 498
Saratov, USSR, 157
Sardinia, 107
Sartre, Jean-Paul, 253, 254, 256
Saturday Evening Post, The, 325
Saudi Arabia, 452, 465, 468, 538, 568, 569-70
Savelyev, S. A., 192
Savimbi, Jonas Malheiro, 479, 480-81
Savinkov, Boris, 126-28 and *n.*, 149
Saxe, Susan, 340
Saxony, 81
Scali, John A., 92 *n.*
Scandinavia, 411
Scandinavian Airlines, 497
Schafer, Peter: *Political Criminal, The,* 16, 23
Schleicher, General Kurt von, 209
Schmueckler, Ulrich, 400
Schnaubelt, Rudolph, 99
Schneider, General René, 283
Scythians, 4
Seale, Bobby G., 302, 304, 308, 309, 311-12, 316
Seberg, Jean, 309-10
Seguin, Pierre, 373
Senard, Count Jacques, 438
Sendic, Raúl, 277-79, 281
Senegal, 476, 485
Senghor, Léopold, 485
Seoul, S. Korea, 439-40
Sepuvelda, Father Saturnino, 533
Serbs, 84, 91 and *n.*, 496, 497
Serbsky Insane Asylum, USSR, 200
Sergei, Grand Duke, 122, 124, 140
Severo, Richard, 286, 290-91
Shachori, Dr. Ami, 567
Shaffer, Colonel Paul R., 430-31
Shamir, Israel, 574
Shanghai, China, 229, 230, 232, 236, 237, 238, 239
Sharp, Mitchell, 371
Shaw, George Bernard, 99
Shell Oil, 572
Sheridan, Clare, 165-66
Shigenobu, Fusako ("Auntie"), 437-39, 566
Shiomi, Takanari, 434, 437
Shub, David, 147, 523
Shukairy, Ahmed, 452
Shukan Asahi, 434
Siberia, 81, 110, 111, 118, 120, 128, 132 *n.*, 134, 162, 168, 173, 189
Sieff, Joseph Edward, 572
Simard, Francis, 373, 374
Simbas (US), 306

Sinai, 390, 468
Singapore, 422-25, 438, 572
Sinkiang, China, 230, 238
Sino-Japanese War, 242-43
Sipyagin, Dmitry, 122, 139, 140
Sirhan, Sirhan, 538, 568
Sison, José Maria, 427, 526
Skinner, B. F., 9-10
skyjackings, 12, 24, 67, 510-11, 515, 546, 549, 552-53; by Arabs, 455, 459, 460, 463-66, 468, 482, 520, 540, 541, 553, 555, 563-76 *passim;* in Argentina, 264; in Brazil, 258; in Colombia, 296; by Eritreans, 470-71; in Japan, 433, 434-35, 437-38; in Philippines, 425-26; preventing, 559-60, 561, 566; resisting, 510, 563-64, 565, 566; in Turkey, 445; and United States, 67, 313-14, 455, 463, 552, 553, 559, 564, 565, 571; by Ustashi, 497; in Venezuela, 297; *see also* hostages
slaves, 4, 5-6, 92, 93, 198, 348-49; for labor, 4, 57, 167, 168, 188, 191-98 *passim,* 212, 217, 229-32, 242
Slavs, 73, 84, 211, 496
Smith, Ian, 485-86
Smith, Joseph and Hiram, 93
Snow, Edgar, 226
Sobibor, 213
Soca, Uruguay, 281
Social Democratic Party, 121, 123, 134-45, 147, 150, 154, 172, 189; split in, 31, 135, 139-40, 143, 173, 189
Socialists, 161, 223, 510, 523, 544; in Soviet Union, 79, 80, 83, 121, 133, 144, 147-55 *passim,* 161-62, 167, 168, 172, 174, 180; in United States, 94, 95-96, 97, 100, 102, 104, 323-24; in Western Europe, 76, 144, 181, 183, 205, 208, 407, 411
Social Revolutionaries (Ess-Ers), 69, 90-91, 120-21, 123-28, 129, 180, 379, 521, 522, 526, 528, 537; and Lenin, 136-40, 143-44, 145, 149, 154, 155, 158, 162, 168, 250, 278; Terror Brigade of, 120-25 *passim,* 128 and *n.,* 143, 155, 173, 174, 175, 202, 509
Sofia, Bulgaria, 445
Soledad Prison, 14, 345
Solingen, Germany, 208
Solis Juarez, Hector, 288
Solovyov, Alexander, 111, 112
Soltysik, Patricia (Zoya), 345, 348, 349, 362
Solzhenitsyn, Alexander, 151, 187, 188, 197, 201, 515; *First Circle, The,* 193; *Gulag Archipelago, The,* 131, 194 *n.,* 202, 219-20
Somalia, 469
Somoza, Anastasio, 297-98
Sophie, consort of Archduke Franz Ferdinand, 91
Sorel, Georges, 75-77; *Reflections on Violence,* 75, 522
Sorel, Canada, 369
Sossi, Mario, 402
South Africa, 157 *n.,* 474, 477, 479, 480-81, 483, 485-87, 550; and Rhodesia, 484, 485-86
South Korea, 440
South Moluccans, 493-94, 556
South Vietnam, 340, 417-20, 423, 484; White terror in, 417-20, 501, 514
South-West Africa (Namibia), 486-87
South Yemen, 400, 572
Soweto, S. Africa, 485
Soviet Union, 79, 80, 83, 104, 121, 133, 140, 143-44, 146-202, 224, 248-49, 262, 288-89, 323, 366, 402, 412-13, 417, 443, 454, 455, 460-61, 462, 475-81 *passim,* 484, 485, 486, 498, 502, 522, 529, 542, 543, 549, 553-54, 570; arms supplied by, 429, 459, 461, 470, 475-76, 480, 481, 512, 537, 539, 541, 547, 550, 551, 553, 561; civil war in, 149-50, 153, 154, 155-57 and *n.,* 159-68 *passim,* 176-84 *passim,* 187, 188, 189, 193-94, 370, 394, 506, 510; Communist Party of, 82, 128, *n.,* 130, 167, 171-72, 181, 184, 189, 193, 289, 489; concentration camps in, 157 and *n.,* 166, 177, 188, 194, 197, 199, 200, 202, 203, 220; and détente, 201, 289, 480, 554; dissenters in, 24-25, 151-52, 167, 182, 199-202, 525, 542, 554; intellectuals in, 121, 140-41, 153, 155-56, 167, 175, 182, 197, 201; mitigation of terror in, 198-99, 201; and Nazis, 211-12, 213; abuse of psychiatry in, 24-25, 166-67, 199, 200, 202, 525; Red terror in, xii, 13, 22, 59, 105, 130-32, 149-70, 172, 176-202, 210, 219-20, 228, 234, 239, 303, 420, 496, 504, 510, 513, 517, 519, 521, 550, 562; secret police of, 4, 24-26, 74, 128 *n.,* 131, 150, 152, 159-60, 162, 167, 168, 185, 188, 191-201, 217, 228-29, 252, 288, 370, 404, 500, 502, 506, 515; slave labor in, 4, 167, 168, 188, 191-98 *passim,* 231; submissiveness in, 219-20, 234; torture in, 4, 194, 197-98, 200, 203, 217, 501, 515, 525; training terrorists in, 288, 541-42; trials in, 185, 191, 193, 194, 195, 199, 200; and UN resolution on terrorism, 550-52; White terror in, 22, 151, 155-56, 162, 167, 176, 179, 181-82, 193, 226, 510; *see also* Red Army; Russia; individual leaders
Spain, 70, 157 *n.,* 262, 497-98, 502, 516, 572; Communists in, 407, 411; Red terror in, 80, 83, 88, 90, 111, 172, 406-12, 509, 521, 522, 537; White terror in, 293, 407-08, 411-12, 524; world reaction against, 411, 524; *see also* Basque terrorists
Spandau, 217
Sparta, 514
Spies, August, 96, 98-99
Spreti, Count Karl von, 287
Squire, Clark E., 14, 317, 318, 319
SS elite guards, 205, 206, 207, 217
Stalin, Joseph, 135, 157 *n.,* 188-90, 200, 212, 224, 366, 383, 412-13, 515, 559; mental disturbance of, 31, 190; terror of, xii, 3, 4, 22, 57, 59, 131, 163, 168, 169-70, 185-202 *passim,* 203, 205, 219-20, 223, 228, 231, 234, 235, 240, 241, 482, 517, 519, 522; and Trotsky, 184, 196, 230
Stalingrad (Volgograd), 189
Stalinism, 172, 184
state, the, 85, 174; democracy, 419, 543-44, 560; terrorism against, 12-14, 16, 17, 83, 132, 509, 513, 523; terrorism as authorized system in, xi, 24, 39, 40, 47, 51-52, 65, 135, 168, 205, 224-28, 509, 524, 529; totalitarian, 4, 91, 223-24, 419-20, 504, 513, 514, 515; violence of, 4, 12-14, 16, 31, 79
State of Siege (film), 274, 519
Stephenson, Mr. and Mrs. Edward G., 383
Stern Group, *see* Israel
Steunenberg, Frank, 104
Stevens, Thaddeus, 93
Stockholm, Sweden, 400, 497, 529 *n.,* 555, 557
Stolypin, Pyotr, 90-91, 128-29
Strasser, Gregor, 206, 209
Strikwerda, Anna, 471
Stroessner, Alfredo, 500
Student Nonviolent (National) Coordinating Committee, 303, 311
Students for a Democratic Society (SDS), 308-09, 322-26, 327-28, 332, 334; *see also* Weathermen
student terrorists, 14, 260, 434, 544; anti-Vietnam War demonstrations, 308, 323-24, 327; *see also* Weathermen; individual countries

Stuergkh, Count Karl, 180
Stuttgart, Germany, 400, 401
Sudan, 552, 568
Sudeikin, Colonel Georgy, 117
Suez Canal, 453, 570
Suharto, 490-91, 493
Sukarno, 488-91, 493
Sulu Archipelago, Philippines, 425
Sumatra, 492; see also Indonesia
Sutter, Frank, 361
Sweden, 146, 216, 310, 441, 497-98, 499
Swint, John, 267
Swinton, Patricia, 340
Swissair, 455, 565
Switzerland, 79, 86, 143, 146, 163, 189, 315, 441, 462, 539, 563-64
Symbionese Liberation Army, 21, 23, 27, 28, 34, 68, 267, 342-49, 361-62, 365, 368, 516, 518-19, 531, 534, 536, 557; sex in, 344, 345, 347, 348, 357-58; terror of, 14, 18, 131, 256, 316, 339, 340, 342, 346, 349-64, 520, 554
Syndicalists, 75-77
Syria, 29, 289, 439, 442, 445, 453, 456, 457, 458, 460, 462, 465, 468, 512, 538, 539, 540, 552, 553, 563, 567, 569, 570, 573, 574; intervention in Lebanon of, 456, 457, 462, 467, 575
Szechwan, China, 239

Tabio, Alvarez, 550-51
Tailhade, Laurent, 87
Taine, Hippolyte, 55, 56, 525; Révolution, La, 76
Takhtarev, Dr. Konstantin, 31
Tal, Wasfi, 457, 566
Talleyrand, Charles de, 561
Tamerlane, 5, 240
Tania (guerrilla), 252, 254, 355
Tanzania, 476, 482, 486
Tatars, 5-6, 7
Taylor, Dr. Theodore B., 545-46
Tboli, South Cotabato, 427
technology, 505, 509-13, 527, 543-45; in communication, 511, 519-21, 543-44; in torture, 4, 513, 514-15
Tegel Prison, 395
Teheran, Iran, 430-31
Tel Aviv, Israel, 310, 435, 458, 460, 467, 538, 571, 575
Terror, Reign of, xii, 23, 39, 42-67, 69, 71, 73-74, 76, 141, 144, 168, 177, 182, 183, 234, 394, 515, 525-26; Committee of General Security, 20, 49, 50, 51, 61; Committee of Public Safety, 18-19, 20, 46, 49, 50, 51, 52, 55, 60; in provinces, 46, 49-58 passim, 64; religious fanaticism of, 18-20, 48; Vendéean revolt against, 50, 59-60; White terror in, 63-65; see also French Revolution
terrorism, 7, 12, 17-18, 21-35, 39, 51, 56-57, 75, 83, 89, 101, 107, 117, 123, 324, 336-37, 343, 346, 434, 451, 509-22, 526-30, 543-45, 561-62; asylum in, 258, 272, 290, 292, 296-99, 313, 369, 371-74, 400, 425-26, 444, 445, 511, 539, 541, 553, 555, 556, 569, 570, 572; double agents in, 117, 120-21, 124-29, 368, 369-70, 374, 378-79, 559; fear of, 21, 24, 51, 53, 61, 69-70, 73-74, 76, 163, 190, 198-99, 234; to free prisoners, 258, 266, 277, 287, 290, 292-93, 298, 299, 300, 369-72, 374, 398, 400, 401, 425, 436, 438-39, 444-45, 463, 464, 466, 468, 469, 470, 497, 520-21, 538-39, 563-76 passim; individual, 135-45 passim, 173, 175, 176, 180, 184, 250, 521, 523-24, 550; international, 297, 537-62; lack of program in, 528-30; leadership in, 136, 137, 525-26, 530; manuals on, 27, 84, 96, 97, 223, 245, 250-51, 258-60, 330, 334, 384, 387, 443, 515, 546; minorities' use of, 12, 22, 23, 25, 55, 392-94, 517, 532; mistaken idealism of, 23, 32, 48, 524, 530, 562; morality in, 14-16, 19, 132, 559-60; personal enrichment in, 56, 124-25, 290, 379; premature, 131, 137-41, 174; prevention of, 273, 558-59, 561, 566; ransom in, 266-67, 269-70, 273, 276-77, 287, 290, 292, 298, 313-14, 400, 468, 469, 470, 497, 510, 516, 518, 566; rationalization of, 9, 12-14, 18-19, 74, 557; in revolution, 11, 16, 69, 71, 74-75, 135-44, 149-58, 162, 172, 183, 224-25, 249-50, 253-54, 256, 428; Robin Hood approach to, 267, 277, 354, 516, 518-20, 547; sympathy with, 21-23, 140-41, 157 n., 274, 303, 308-09, 397-99, 401, 408, 449, 504, 516-20, 534, 536, 537, 539, 542-43, 544, 547, 549, 552, 557, 560; theological element in, 18-20, 56-57, 204, 530-36; training for, 288, 397, 398, 433, 442, 540-42; see also media; Red terrorism; state, the; violence; White terrorism; individual countries, forms of terrorism, men
Thailand, 418-25
Thiers, Adolphe, 71-72
Third World, 14, 23, 480, 449, 544
Thompson, John R., 266
Thompson, Robert, 422
Thoreau, Henry D., 97
Thyssen, Fritz, 205
Tia Juana, Mexico, 290
Tibet, 230
Tientsin, China, 230, 238
Tiflis, USSR, 189, 522
Tikhomirov, Lev, 561-62; Why I Have Ceased to be a Revolutionary, 118
Tilicheyev, M. D., 192
Time, 241, 454
Tito, 412-13, 496-500, 558-59
Tkachev, Pyotr, 32-33, 79, 135-36, 138
Toffler, Alvin: Future Shock, 526-28
Tokyo, Japan, 435, 437, 440, 559
Tolstoy, Lev, 515
Tombalbaye, François, 483
Toropov, F. A., 192
Torquemada, Tomás de, 4, 22
Torres Gonzales, Juan José, 256, 272
torture, 3-7, 387-88, 501; psychological, 4, 513-15; and sadism, 4, 195, 210, 474, 514-15; and technology, 4, 513, 514-15; see also individual countries
Toulon, France, 61
Trabal, Colonel Ramon, 281
Trans World Airlines, 455, 463, 564, 565, 569
Treblinka, 213
Tripoli, Libya, 567, 571, 572
Trotsky, Lev, 122, 147, 169, 272, 529; assassination of, 172, 173, 184-85, 196; as inspiration to terrorists, 78, 171-72, 244, 249, 387; and Lenin, 135, 171, 173, 176, 189; as Red Army head, 176-79, 181, 250, 505; and Stalin, 184, 196, 230; terror of, xii, 3, 4, 10, 47, 159, 167, 172-87, 190-91, 196, 197, 198, 203, 205, 219-20, 223, 517; Terrorism and Communism, 181
Trotsky family, 185
Trotskyites, 171-72, 223, 248, 253, 262, 289, 365-66, 380, 385, 411, 554
Trudeau, Pierre E., 367, 370-74, 560
Truman, Harry S, 103, 299; doctrine of, 413
Tsaritsyn (Stalingrad), USSR, 189
Tsyurupa, Alexander, 157
Tucker, Benjamin, 97
Tucumán, Argentina, 271, 523-24
Tulagil, Danis, 447
Tunis, Tunisia, 464, 572, 573

Tunisia, 464, 553
Tupac-Amaru, 274-75
Tupamaros, *see* Uruguay
Tupolev, Andrei, 192
Turgenev, Ivan, 107
Turin, Italy, 401
Turkey, 84, 107, 111, 211, 219, 443-48, 463, 523; and Cyprus, 413-15, 448; Red terror in, 442-47, 522; rejected demands of terrorists, 443-45; torture in, 443-44, 446; White terror in, 442-47, 560
Turkish terrorists, 443-46, 539; and Arabs, 442, 447, 540; and Communism, 442-43; inspirations of, 68, 131, 443; TPLA of, 442-47
Turner, Colonel Jack J., 430-31
Turner, Nat, 93
Tutsis, xi-xii, 481-82
Tweed, Samuel, 388
Twomey, Seamus, 385

Uganda, 482, 544; Entebbe airport raid, 482, 553, 555, 576
Uigurs, 230
Ukraine, 155, 211-12, 496
Ulster, 159, 377, 451, 559; Catholics of, 377-78, 385-87, 388, 392-94; British army in, 377-82 *passim*, 386-93 *passim*, 523, 554; children of, 380-82; peace desired in, 392-94; Protestants of, 376-78, 384-94 *passim*, 561; terror in, 21, 68, 260, 377-93 *passim*, 511-12, 539, 541, 549-55 *passim*; UDA of, 385-88; UVF of, 385-86; White terror in, 159, 167
Ulyanov, Alexander, 120, 131, 133, 135, 137, 249, 530
Ulyanov, Anna, 133, 143
Ulyanov, Ilya, 133
Underground (film), 340
United Arab Republic, 455
United Auto Workers, 323
United Nations, xiii, 281, 293, 367, 390, 449, 454, 458, 459, 470, 476, 486, 489, 504, 561; Arafat at, 23, 92 n., 131, 157 n., 449, 462, 542, 547, 549, 552; efforts against terror in, 549-53, 554; Zionism resolution of, 293, 449
United States, 4, 92, 93, 157-58, 182, 241-42, 246 n., 277, 289, 379-80, 386, 412-13, 415, 427, 430, 433, 440, 441, 465, 480, 489, 539, 546-47, 550; blacks in, 78, 92, 93, 159, 302-03, 307-08, 311, 315-16, 517, 541; communes in, 535; Communist Party in, 324, 327, 554; and détente, 201, 289, 480, 584; ethnic groups in, 93-94, 100, 101, 310; labor violence in, 94-100 *passim*, 104-05; in Latin America, 257, 266, 277, 286, 504; military of, terror against, 397, 401, 430-31, 443, 465; New Left in, 79, 223-24, 253, 308, 323, 326, 327, 341, 355; reaction against terror in, 341, 555-58; and Red terror, 67, 68, 83, 86, 89, 90, 94, 95-106, 117, 299-300, 305-07, 313-14, 316-22, 323, 329-42, 346, 349-64, 389, 398, 455, 457, 463, 464, 509, 516, 517, 522, 526, 537-38, 547-48, 552, 553, 555, 559, 564-68 *passim*, 571; rejection of demands of terrorists, 277, 293, 299, 443, 538, 555; rioting in, 93-99 *passim*, 307-08, 311, 324-25, 327, 330-34, 337, 369; Socialists in, 94-97, 100, 102, 104, 323-24; students in, 14, 308, 324-25, 334, 337; and UN resolution on terrorism, 549-52; and Vietnam War, 252, 308, 311, 323-24, 330, 341, 417-20, 551; White terror in, 92-94, 97, 99, 103, 105, 159, 167, 303, 308, 541; *see also* Central Intelligence Agency; Federal Bureau of Investigation; individual groups of terrorists
University of California: at Berkeley, 343, 346, 347, 348, 351-52, 356; at Los Angeles, 14, 306

University of Michigan, 322
University of Wisconsin, 68, 338
upper classes, 13, 27, 59, 97, 99, 132, 520; terrorists from, 27, 324, 336-37, 343, 434, 526-28, 530
Uruguay, 272, 274-81, 451, 506, 523; Communist Party of, 276, 278, 279, 280; Red terror in, 131, 261, 274, 276-78, 280; torture in, 279-81; Tupamaros of, 68, 131, 267, 274-81, 285, 513, 519, 522, 526, 528, 531, 539; White terror in, 274, 278-81, 488, 560
Ustashi, 209, 496-99
Uvarov, Count Sergei, 80

Vacaville State Prison, 343-47 *passim*, 357, 515
Vaillant, Auguste, 87
Vallières, Pierre, 365, 366-68, 369, 372; *White Niggers of America*, 371
Valparaiso, Chile, 283
Vandals, 5
Vandor, Auguste, 262
Vanzetti, Bartolomeo, 106
Varennes, France, 42
Velasco Alvarado, General Juan, 294
Vendée, France, 50, 59
Venezuela, 246, 296-97, 533, 539; Communist Party of, 296-97; FALN of, 296; students in, 296; terror in, 297; Zero Point of, 297
Venturi, Franco: *Roots of Revolution*, 33
Victor Emmanuel II, King of Italy, 84
Victoria, Queen of the United Kingdom, 90 n.
Videla, General Jorge Rafael, 272
Vienna, Austria, 180, 209, 447, 465, 540, 566, 575
Vietcong, 417-19, 424, 470, 476
Vietnam War, 252, 308, 311, 323-24, 327, 330, 340, 341, 362, 417-20, 424, 441, 451, 459, 551; *see also* North Vietnam; South Vietnam
violence, 3-11; in man, 7-11, 22, 30, 34, 56-57, 75; nonpolitical, 33-35; political terror as, 3, 24, 26, 35, 527; in revolution, xii-xiii, 16, 70, 74, 79, 97-98, 131, 148, 224, 239, 245, 259, 302-03, 366, 367; *see also* terrorism; torture
Vladimir, Grand Duke, 122
Voinov, Ivan, 148
Volgograd (Stalingrad), USSR, 189
Vologda, USSR, 157
Voltaire, 40
Vorkuta, USSR, 198, 220
Vorster, John, 485-86

Waldheim, Kurt, 482, 549
Walker, General Edwin A., 34
Walker, Dr. James L., 241-43
Wallace, George C., 34, 103
war, 145; and revolution, 47, 72, 145, 154, 183-84
Warren, Josiah, 97
Warsaw, Poland, 523; Ghetto, 211, 214-15, 216
Washington, George, 92 n., 300
Washington, D.C., 103, 556
Washington Post, The, 243
Wasseige, Eric de, 282
Watts, California, 345, 358-59; riot in, 311
Wazir, Khalil, 458
weapons, 141-42, 259, 367, 459, 461, 470, 475-76, 477, 480, 481, 484, 512, 537-41 *passim*, 547, 550, 551, 553; chemical, 547-48; nuclear, 545-47; *see also* bombs; rockets
Weathermen, 16, 17, 33, 68, 107, 308, 322-41, 342, 358, 365, 368, 517, 526, 536; bomb-making of, 336-37; inspirations of, 326, 330, 338, 451; National Action of, 329-34; underground, 311, 333-40
Wechsler, Dr. David: *Measurement and Appraisal of Adult Intelligence, The*, 30-31
Weed, Steven Andrew, 351-53, 355, 357

Weinraub, Bernard, 383, 384
Welch, Richard S., 415-16
Wells, H. G., 165, 530
West, Dr. Louis J., 363
West, the, 163, 164, 183, 412-13, 468, 478, 479, 480, 504, 523, 528, 542, 565; see also individual countries
West Bengal, India, 428
Westbrook, Colston, 343
Western Airlines, 314
Western Federation of Miners, 104
West German terrorists (Red Army Faction, Baader-Meinhof Gang), 395-401, 434, 482, 520-21, 538, 539, 554, 555, 557, 568, 576; inspirations of, 68, 395, 397; students, 295, 401; trained by Arabs, 397, 398, 541
West Germany, 397, 406, 411, 441, 463, 498, 499, 500, 522, 525, 559, 566, 567, 572; Red terror in, 67, 397, 401, 406, 457, 463, 467, 538, 541, 546, 549, 550, 557, 558, 564, 567; rejection of demands of terrorists, 400-01, 538, 555
White Panthers, 310
White terror, 283, 488, 494, 496, 500, 502, 504-06; as counterterror, 63-66, 70, 250, 260, 270, 274, 278-82, 286-88, 293, 297, 407-08, 413, 425, 442, 443, 472, 488, 491, 503, 523-24, 554, 557-58; as repression, 40, 163-64, 181-82, 298, 303, 411-12, 427, 428, 430-32, 473, 477, 484, 488, 503, 513, 560; see also terrorism; individual countries
Whitlam, Gough, 499
Wilde, Oscar, 99
Wilhelm I, Kaiser, 87, 95
Wilhelm II, Kaiser, 127, 146
Wilkerson, Cathlyn, 336, 340
Wilkerson, James Platt, 336
Wilkinson, Paul: Political Terrorism, 393-94
Willrich, Mason, 545-46
Wilson, Harold, 548
Wilson, Michael, 386
Wilson, Woodrow, 105
Wiriyamu, Mozambique, 473
Without Authority (Beznachaliye), 123
Witte, Sergei, 122, 128

Wittfogel, Dr. Karl A., 223, 240
Wolfe, William (Cujo), 343-46, 349, 357-58, 362, 364
World Confederation of Labor, 287
World War I, 86, 91, 101, 104, 127, 129, 144-45, 146, 155, 157 n., 158, 161, 176, 204, 219, 275, 447
World War II, 203, 210-19, 275, 301, 349, 421, 422, 426, 441, 451, 452-53, 470, 495-96
Woytinsky, Vladimir, 153
Wrangel, Baron Pyotr, 165
Wuhan, China, 238

Yablonsky, Dr. Lewis, 28
Yagoda, Genrikh, 194-95
Yakubova, Appolinaria, 132 n.
Yale University, 322, 528
Yalta, USSR, 201
Yamamato, Mariko, 438
Yamani, Ahmed Zaki, 465
Yariv, General Aharon, 568
Yaroslavl, USSR, 178
Yediot Akhronot, 460
Yekaterinburg (Sverdlovsk), USSR, 156
Yemen, 470
Yennan, China, 226
Yezhenedel'nik Ch. K., 152
Yezhov, Nilolai, 25, 195-96
Yildiz, Safa Asim, 445
Yugoslavia, 441, 499; and Greece, 412-13; and UN resolution on terrorism, 549; and Ustashi, 496-500

Zagreb, Yugoslavia, 498, 499, 567
Zaire, 478, 480
Zambia, 476, 480, 483, 485-86, 549
Zasulich, Vera, 75, 138
Zenteno Anaya, Colonel Joaquin, 252-53, 406
Zhelyabov, Andrei, 112-13, 114-15, 117, 526, 530
Zinovyev, Grigory, 155, 167, 194
Zuno, Vincente, 293
Zuno Hernández, J. Guadalupe, 292-93
Zurich, Switzerland, 462, 563, 565